Principles of Educational Measurement and Evaluation

Gilbert Sax

University of Washington

Wadsworth Publishing Company, Inc.
Belmont, California

ISBN 0–534–00338–9

L. C. Cat. Card No. 73–93789

Printed in the United States of America

2 3 4 5 6 7 8 9 10——78 77 76 75

To
Lois, my wife, friend, and partner;
to our children,
Laurie, Kathy, Karen, Debbie, and Jenny;
and to our parents
and friends

Preface

Educational testing has a long past but a short history. Measurement has probably always played an important role in man's life, but the formal study of educational and psychological testing is primarily a twentieth century enterprise. It developed out of practical needs in the classroom, in the psychology clinic, in industry, and in the military; and testing applications abound in our culture from consumer studies and polling to experimentation and research.

Because of the professional and academic status achieved by teachers, they must become proficient in the use and interpretation of the basic tools of education. Most colleges and universities offer introductory courses in tests and measurements that typically cover such topics as test construction, elementary statistical concepts, reliability and validity, and various types of standardized tests. This text is no exception in this regard, but it also attempts to accomplish additional objectives that I believe are too often slighted or disregarded in introductory texts:

1. The assumptions, implications, and effects of testing on minority members, on the right to privacy, and on public policy are discussed not only in a separate chapter but also in chapters on the use of standardized tests (particularly tests of intelligence, personality, and attitude). Current problems and issues of concern to students in education are also discussed.

2. Principles and concepts related to the purposes of testing are also examined. A principle that is useful in one situation may not be relevant in another. Each chapter discusses how the principles in it relate to such uses of measurement as selection, placement, diagnosis and remediation, mastery, and program evaluation.

3. No attempt is made to force students to memorize the names and details of the many educational and psychological tests available. Rather, certain standardized tests are described as prototypes to demonstrate the variety of available tests. A separate chapter on selecting and evaluating standardized tests provides criteria, principles, and sources of information needed to select the best test for the student's purpose.

4. The text presumes no mathematical sophistication. Conceptual formulas are presented in the text, and an appendix contains more convenient computational routines. All formulas are accompanied by verbal descriptions and numerical examples. The text emphasizes the use of these formulas. Assumptions for all formulas are also included, but mathematical derivations have been omitted. References to sources that include these derivations are provided as supplementary readings at the ends of chapters.

5. The concepts of reliability and validity are discussed in detail in two separate chapters and again in those chapters on specific types of standardized tests. Reliability and validity, except for content validity, are stressed as characteristics of *measurements* (observations or data) rather than as characteristics of *tests* (tasks). Methods of improving reliability and validity are included throughout the text and of course in the chapters on those topics. The repetition of principles and concepts in different circumstances and contexts is deliberate.

6. Principles of measurement are not divorced from other educational and psychological principles, concepts, and theories. Thus in the chapter on intelligence, various theories of intelligence are considered along with questions frequently raised by students regarding the heredity-environment controversy, the classroom correlates of intelligence, and their relationship to socioeconomic level, ethnic background (including an analysis of the Jensen controversy), and sex.

7. The function of history is to provide the student with the background needed to appreciate current principles and controversies. The typical chapter on "historical backgrounds of measurement" often has little meaning to students when topics are presented in chronological order without regard to the individual and societal forces that led to the development of trends and innovations. Thus historical information is presented within the context of relevant chapters rather than treated separately in this textbook.

8. In addition to detailed chapter summaries and annotated reading lists, a separate student workbook accompanies the text to help students improve their understanding of tests and principles of measurement by applying what they have read to realistic classroom problems. A teacher's manual containing test items on each chapter is also available.

9. An attempt has been made to make principles of educational testing interesting to students by including examples, anecdotes, and cartoons. Rather than detracting from the seriousness and importance of these principles, humor can be an important ally in motivating students to appreciate and see the relevance of these principles.

I want to thank the many individuals who have helped with the development of this book. Dr. Dorothy Adkins, Dr. Joan Michael, Dr. D. Cecil Clark, Dr. Alan Klockars, and Dr. Enoch Sawin read the manuscript and offered numerous suggestions for improvement; any deficiencies that may still be present are, of course, entirely my own. Many persons typed and retyped the manuscript, and I owe them gratitude and appreciation. In particular, Wilma Boyd, Leona Castile, Nancy Mickelberry, and Jeanne Shelton translated my poor typing and impossible penmanship into a finished manuscript. Many students and colleagues too numerous to mention also read portions of the manuscript, took the practice exercises, and provided much useful information. Mary Johnson read some of the mathematical sections of the text and helped point out passages that required reworking.

Two other persons devoted long hours in helping produce this text, and I owe both of them more than I can ever hope to repay. Dick Greenberg, my editor and friend, gave me his help, encouragement, and suggestions throughout the writing and publication. His patience and understanding advice were available whenever they were needed.

I have no words that can express my appreciation for the many hours my wife, Lois, spent with me on this manuscript. She read and critiqued each draft, spent hundreds of hours in the library, checked all references for accuracy, and resolved many details and problems. It is to her especially that I dedicate this text.

Contents

5 Principles of Test Construction: Completion and Essay Tests 112

6 Summarizing and Interpreting Measurements 134

7 The Reliability of Measurement 172

8 The Validity of Measurements 205

The Role of Measurement, Testing, and Evaluation in Education

1

Man used principles of measurement to build shelters and tools, to select a mate, to kill prey, and to fashion clothing long before the advent of educational or psychological tests. The ancient Egyptians devised sophisticated, complex measurements to construct pyramids. By 2700 B.C. they had mastered geometrical concepts and were able to use measurements in three dimensions.

The Bible also attests to the early use of measurement. Noah was commanded to build an ark three hundred cubits long, fifty cubits wide, and thirty cubits high (Genesis 6:15). A cubit, like most physical measurements, was based on the length of familiar and readily available standards of comparison—in this instance, the length of the forearm to the tip of the middle finger, or roughly 18 to 21 inches. A foot was approximately the size of a man's foot; an inch was a twelfth of a foot, or approximately the distance from the joint of the thumb to its tip. Although convenient, these measurements were too arbitrary and unstable for business and scientific purposes; thus less variable standards such as the length of the king's forearm (a ruler) evolved. However, as international trade expanded, stable measures capable of surviving a specific monarch became necessary.

Measurement requires a standard by which quantities can be compared. The meter, for example, was originally intended to be one-ten-millionth of the distance between the equator and one of the poles measured along one meridian. Actually this measure was so laboriously obtained and so inaccurate that it was redefined (from 1889 to 1960) as the distance between two lines on a platinum-iridium bar located at the International Bureau of Weights and Measures near Paris. This definition also proved to be too inaccurate for scientific purposes, and the meter is now defined as 1,650,763.73 wavelengths of the orange-red radiation of krypton 86 under specified conditions.

In contrast to measurement in the natural sciences, educational and psychological measurement has had a relatively brief history. Tests of strength appeared early in recorded situations (Ramul 1963),* and the Bible also refers to the use of tests. The test "constructed" by the Gileadites to detect escaped Ephraimites (Judges 12:5–6) yielded rather dramatic consequences:

> And the Gileadites took the fords of the Jordan against the Ephraimites. And when any of the fugitives from Ephraim said, "Let me go over," the men of Gilead said to him, "Are you an Ephraimite?" When he said, "No," they said to him, "Then say Shibboleth," and he said "sibboleth," for he could not pronounce it right; then they seized him and slew him at the fords of the Jordan. And there fell at that time forty-two thousand of the Ephraimites.

This was an examination with vengeance. Fortunately not all educational or psychological tests have such dramatic repercussions, although many students look upon them with a degree of fear and distrust. To these persons, tests—like death and taxes—are an inevitable and inescapable part of life, to be feared, disliked, or tolerated, but rarely desired or appreciated. Often teachers too face their task of constructing tests with the same enthusiasm as a Christian entering the lions' den.

Yet tests can be helpful, and the consequences of testing are not necessarily aversive. As a result of testing, for example, J. M. Rice (1897) found negligible differences in spelling achievement between students who studied an hour and those who devoted only 10 minutes a day to spelling. As a result of this and other investigations, spelling became more practical, less time-consuming, and less painful an endeavor for many students.

Measurement, Testing, and Evaluation

Measurement

Measurement involves the assigning of numbers to attributes or characteristics of persons, objects, or events according to explicit formulations or "rules." In measuring physical characteristics such as height or weight, the quantification rules have been agreed upon and "standardized" to the point where everyone understands the procedures to be followed. More complex physical measure-

---

* Complete references are given in the bibliography in the back of the book.

ments (e.g., hearing, vision, and so forth), however, require explicit and detailed formulations of rules or procedures to be followed if all observations of the same characteristic are to be quantified the same way.

Educational measurement also requires the quantification of attributes according to specified rules. What is measured are the attributes or characteristics of students, objects, or events, not the students, events, or objects themselves. Teachers can measure attributes such as the heights of fifth-grade children, the interests of tenth-graders, the intelligence of special-class students, or the achievement of pupils in different curricula. These examples are characteristics of students that are being measured. No one would try to measure a "table"; rather, its length, height, or hardness (i.e., its attributes) may be measured.

Tests

A *test* may be defined as a task or series of tasks used to obtain systematic observations presumed to be representative of educational or psychological traits or attributes. Typically tests require examinees to respond to items or questions from which the examiner infers something about the attribute being measured. Nothing in the definition implies that tests can only measure cognitive or intellectual attributes or that the examinee is necessarily aware that he is being tested. What is important is that tests involve *tasks* and that these tasks be arranged so as to yield systematic observations of a trait.

Most individuals think of tests as being limited to true-false, multiple-choice, or essay questions used to measure knowledge in arithmetic, reading, or other school subjects. This narrow definition of a test fails to include many kinds of tasks that can be devised to observe how a student might behave in a situation that appears uncontrived to him. The purpose might be to observe frustration, anger, protectiveness, or the ability to solve problems without help.

Some measurements are obtained without subjecting the individual to any task. Teachers often keep records of student behavior as it occurs in the classroom or on the playground. Since no tasks were devised to elicit behavior, there could be no test. Nonetheless, the teacher's observations can still be used to measure or to describe attributes of the child.

Evaluation

Evaluation is a process through which a value judgment or decision is made from a variety of observations and from the background and training of the evaluator. Tests should accurately measure specified attributes. But no matter how good tests may be, someone must interpret test results and decide upon the course of action that can best help the student. Before any far-reaching decision is made, as much relevant information as possible about the student should be gathered.

An example from the field of medicine may clarify the relationships among the terms *measurement, test,* and *evaluation.* Suppose that a patient complains of such symptoms as a running nose, sneezing, watery eyes, and a cough. These symptoms can reflect a variety of causes, each of which can require different treatment. Proper diagnosis requires the physician to prescribe various laboratory and clinical tests. These tests in turn "assign" numbers to different attributes of the patient's symptoms according to clearly specified procedures. One test might tell the physician that the patient has a fever of $102°$; another could indicate a white blood count of 10,000 per cubic millimeter. The physician must evaluate what these measurements mean and decide on the most effective treatment. He must also consider carefully the risk inherent in all decisions.

Essentially the same process is followed in education. A child who experiences reading difficulties often displays a host of symptoms (such as refusing to read voluntarily, making numerous errors in oral reading, holding the book too far from or too close to his eyes) that are cues to the teacher that something is wrong. The teacher may recommend some or all of the following tests: vision and hearing to rule out physical causes, an orally administered intelligence test to measure the child's general level of scholastic ability, a diagnostic reading test to pinpoint possible areas for remediation. From such data, or *measurements* (20/20 vision, 30-decibel loss of hearing, IQ of 115, two years behind his age level in phonetic analysis), the teacher needs to evaluate or decide upon the nature and extent of the child's problem and determine which steps would most effectively help him.

Each person constantly receives and evaluates stimuli from the environment. As an object with headlights speeds toward the individual, he quickly translates these sensory impressions to form the concept *danger,* and he tries to act accordingly. Should he see a stranger resembling someone he has met in the past, he has to decide whether the stranger is a friend or a foe. Of course, everyone has made errors in forming these judgments, but fortunately many decisions made on faulty data do not prove to be very serious. However, when professionals make decisions, and when those decisions can seriously affect the lives of youngsters in schools, the most dependable knowledge available and the skills to use that knowledge most effectively are needed.

The assignment of numbers to attributes is an important phase of measurement. Teachers often want to know the degree to which students differ on some attribute and not only that they are different. Some *qualitative* scales simply describe attributes but do not *quantify* differences. Examples of qualitative scales are male-female, Democrat-Republican, and mother-father. The most sophisticated measurements are those that yield absolute zeros and equal intervals (called *ratio scales*). When attributes are measured by ratio scales, differences between successive intervals are equal, and zero means that the attribute is entirely lacking. Measuring length by a ruler is an example of using a ratio scale, but measuring achievement is not. A zero on a test of achievement does not mean that the attribute is nonexistent for that person; it could simply mean the test was too hard. Chapter 6 discusses four types of measurement scales: *nominal, ordinal, interval,* and *ratio.*

Another element of measurement involves the formulation of "rules" or procedures used to measure some attribute. As used here, a rule is neither a moral imperative nor a prescription to be followed blindly. Indeed, each person can establish his own rules which others are free to follow or not. This does not mean that all rules are equally good. The rules established by one teacher for measuring creativity may turn out to be of little empirical value. Other rules, such as allowing students exactly ten minutes to complete a test, will have to be followed if the teacher wants to know how her pupils performed in comparison with those who were all given that time limit.

Reasons for Using Tests

Tests are administered with the expectation that measurements derived from them will be helpful in making decisions with a minimum of risk. Although a test may be useful in one situation, it may not be suitable in another. Knowing what kind of test to construct or recommend for a given purpose increases the likelihood that better decisions can be reached.

The extent to which tests minimize risk and increase the probability of effective decisions is a function of the amount of dependable knowledge the test provides beyond the teacher's current information. Using a test implies that there is a relationship between measurements and the ability to make effective decisions. Having students take a spelling test presumes a relationship between students' scores (measurements) and the decision, for example, to recommend remedial work or additional exercises or perhaps to repeat an assignment or an entire course. The use of tests and measurements to aid in making better decisions presumes that these measurements can predict a more effective course of action than would be possible without them.

Using Tests for Selection Decisions

Tests may be used to help decide who will be accepted or rejected by an institution. Selection decisions demand of tests the ability to predict success and failure with minimum risks both to the institution and to the individuals involved. The risks can be of two types: admitting individuals who later are not successful or failing to admit those who would have been successful if admitted. The "ideal" selection test would admit only those persons who subsequently proved to be successful while rejecting all applicants who would prove to be unsuccessful.

Unfortunately, tests are fallible predictors of success, and all selection decisions involve the risks described.

Selection decisions are greatly improved when a close correspondence exists between the testing tasks and those skills, abilities, and attitudes required for success in the institution. Often much empirical testing is required to develop tests capable of selecting competent individuals and rejecting those who would prove to be unsuccessful. Although selection tests are widely used by industry and by colleges and universities, they are not ordinarily used by the public schools except when counseling with high school students. Criteria for admission to kindergarten or the first grade differ from state to state, but most states require only some minimal chronological age. This practice is not entirely satisfactory since it denies admission to those pupils who might benefit from attending school earlier if criteria other than age—such as emotional maturity or scholastic aptitude—were used instead. To be sure, these criteria also have limitations and involve risks and additional costs that should be studied and evaluated.

Using Tests for Placement Decisions

Once an individual has been selected, he must be placed in a program where he is likely to be the most "successful." In the public schools placement decisions determine what curriculum a student will pursue, what reading group he will be assigned to, and which special classes (remedial or advanced) he will take. The placement decision involves both prediction—success—and the risk that predictions will lead to incorrect placements.

A test may be useful for selection but not for placement. A test of general academic aptitude, for example, may be able to predict who will probably succeed in college but may not necessarily help place the student in an optimal program. The teacher, counselor, or admissions officer usually has many more options for placement than for selection.

The "ideal" placement test predicts success in one program and discourages or rejects placement in another. Again, as with any decision, risk is involved. The risk becomes greater as placement tests assign individuals incorrectly or as individuals with varying degrees of success in a given program all attain the same test score.

Using Tests for Diagnostic and Remedial Decisions

A test that is used to determine a person's strengths and weaknesses in order to improve performance serves a diagnostic function. Before teachers and counselors can recommend remedial help, they must know in what specific areas an individual is having difficulty. The type of decision made on the basis of test results differs for diagnosis, selection, and placement. In diagnostic testing the individual usually has already been *selected* into a school or industrial setting. What type of program will be recommended to him is a matter of *placement*. In neither selection nor placement does the school necessarily provide remedial services.

However, the uses of tests for placement and for remedial decisions overlap to some degree. As a result of diagnostic testing, for example, the teacher may recommend that the child be *placed* in an easier or more advanced reading group. Although diagnostic testing can lead the teacher to recommend differential *placement,* some diagnoses suggest continuing a current program of remediation or proposing some other treatment not involving placement, such as hiring a tutor or using a simpler textbook.

In medicine the ability to diagnose a patient's problem is a prerequisite of its treatment. Diagnosis serves no end in itself, but it is needed if reasonable treatment decisions are to be made. In education too the teacher will be better able to recommend specific types of remediation if he knows in what areas the student is deficient.

Diagnostic tests can be used in different ways. First, they can help identify which students have problems. Since there are numerous problems students can have, tests can usually contain only a very limited number of items designed to measure each potential source of difficulty. For example, the Sequential Tests of Educational Progress (STEP) consists of six separate subtests: reading comprehension, writing, mathematics, science, social studies, and listening comprehension. Students with low scores on any of these subtests can be identified as "having a problem," but the specific nature of that problem is not likely to be discovered without further diagnostic testing.

Suppose the teacher has been able to identify a student as being weak in mathematics. He might next administer the Stanford Diagnostic Arithmetic Test (Level II), which measures concepts (number systems and operations), computation (addition, subtraction, multiplication, and division), common fractions (understanding and computation), decimal fractions and percent; and number facts (addition, subtraction, multiplication, division, and carrying). The publishers recommend seven testing periods from fifteen to fifty-three minutes, making it impractical to administer this test to all students without first identifying those who need this amount of testing.

Ideally, diagnostic tests should contain a relatively large number of items measuring very specific objectives. Since no test is capable of measuring all aspects of arithmetic, spelling, or reading, the tester has to be satisfied with a *sample* or limited number of items presumed to represent the *population* or *universe* (totality) of all possible items that could be constructed and administered.

In constructing diagnostic tests, the first criterion is specifying what the items are to measure. Some items could be designed to measure the addition of single-digit whole numbers without carrying; others could attempt to measure the addition of two-digit whole numbers with carrying, and so forth.

Suppose a teacher constructs an item such as $\frac{1}{8} + \frac{1}{4}$, and this item is to be representative—a sample—of all items (the universe) that measure the addition of proper fractions with unlike denominators. If the student looks at the item and responds "$\frac{1}{12}$," how sure can the teacher be that the child will miss other similar items? No doubt the teacher would feel more comfortable about his diagnosis if he gave the student a larger number of items to sample. This implies the second criterion for diagnostic tests: as many items should be administered as is possible within practical time limits and considering the maturity of the child tested.

Almost all the commercially available diagnostic tests are in arithmetic and reading, probably because it is easier to agree upon and analyze the objectives in those areas than in others. In other areas of the curriculum teachers may have to construct diagnostic tests that measure their own specific objectives.

Using Tests to Provide Feedback or Knowledge of Results: Norm-Referenced and Criterion-Referenced Tests

A good amount of evidence argues that knowledge of results increases student learning and decreases the error rate. Generally the more specific the feedback is, the greater will be the learning. Sometimes, of course, the student is able to provide his own feedback and correct his own errors, but more often the novice needs direct guidance from the teacher. This is the function of feedback—to guide the student to the most effective means of improving his performance.

Tests can be constructed to provide two kinds of feedback: the individual's progress may be compared with the performance of some specified reference group (other members of his class or a sample of third-graders throughout the United States) or in comparison with criteria specified by the teacher. When tests are used to compare individuals with others, they are called *norm-referenced tests;* when pupil progress is compared to criteria established by the teacher (e.g., a minimum typing rate of forty words per minute or at least ten words correctly spelled per week), the test is referred to as a *criterion-referenced test*.

Norm-referenced tests demonstrate that a student has more or less knowledge, interest, or ability than do other members of the reference group. If a test is so simple that almost everyone attains a perfect score or is so difficult that no one answers more than a few items correctly, it will not be very helpful; a norm-referenced test should maximize the differences among individuals.

In contrast, criterion-referenced tests compare the individual not in relationship to others but in relationship to the level of performance he will be expected to achieve. For example, instead of saying that a student is "average" (a normative judgment), he can be required to attain at least some minimal level of *mastery* (such as 90 percent or 100 percent) before he is allowed to proceed to the next higher or more complex instructional level. A student's failure to reach criterion standards may suggest diagnostic testing to discover reasons for the lack of achievement, but it is often assumed that all students will eventually reach criterion but perhaps at different rates. Thus before allowing students to add numbers, a teacher may require them to first learn to write the numerals from 1 to 100 without error (a criterion-referenced judgment). On the other hand, a student who is given a D mark in comparison to the perform-ance of others in his class is usually allowed to continue his learning (or lack of it) without having demonstrated the skills requisite to more advanced in-struction.

As stated earlier, norm-referenced tests try to maximize individual differ-ences. *Maximizing individual differences* means that (1) different scores among individuals reflect actual differences in ability, and (2) differences among scores are as large as possible. Thus on a 100-item examination, more meaningful decisions can be made if one person receives a score of 100 and another receives a score of 0. In practice, of course, this ideal is only approximated.

Criterion-referenced tests are particularly useful in the following situations:

1. In subject areas that are cumulative and progressively more complex, students might have to reach some level of proficiency on preceding tasks before being advanced to a higher level. In courses such as mathematics, foreign languages, and reading there is a progression in the sequencing through which the student must pass. A student who has not learned the meaning of whole numbers should probably not be taught to work with fractions; the child who is about to learn the principle that a period is placed at the end of a sentence must know what a sentence is. In these examples criterion-referenced measure-ments provide feedback about whether or not these minimal levels of competence have been reached.

2. In subject areas that demand competence, criterion-referenced tests should be used. Performing surgery, for example, requires a degree of proficiency that probably should not be entrusted to those who do not meet minimum standards. Licensing examinations for automobile drivers, airline pilots, dentists, lawyers, and accountants invariably require some stated minimal level of proficiency before individuals are allowed to practice. Here again, the interest is not in comparing one person against another but in being sure that those who are certified or licensed are capable of performing at a high level.

3. In diagnostic work criterion-referenced feedback is more important than norm-referenced feedback. That is, it is probably more important to know that a student is experiencing difficulty (i.e., has not become proficient) in a specific area of the curriculum than it is to know that he is an average student in the class. A C grade in naming the letters of the alphabet is not as useful in helping the child as is knowing that he could name the letters from *A* to *G* only.

On the other hand, norm-referenced tests have their greatest use under the following circumstances:

1. Sometimes the subject matter is not cumulative, and the student does not need to reach some specified level of competency. The social studies curriculum, for example, is usually not highly sequenced, and it is possible to skip some courses altogether and still do well in a more "advanced" class. In such courses feedback regarding student performance may be norm-referenced since no minimal degree of competence need be specified.

2. For selection purposes norm-referenced tests are useful if an institution is forced to accept only the highest-performing individuals. A college admissions officer, for example, might be able to accept only the highest-scoring 5 percent of the students from a given high school. In this case the comparison is with all other graduates from that school. On the other hand, a criterion-referenced test would be preferred if the admissions officer were required to take all qualified individuals. Instead of comparing individuals with each other, the comparison would be with a stated level of excellence.

3. When tests are used to predict degrees of success, they should be norm-referenced. Because individuals can be expected to differ on whatever criterion is used to predict success, the tests must be capable of distinguishing among students. Thus predicting success in graduate school requires the use of tests that measure individual differences. Otherwise, all students might attain the same score on the predictor test and there would be no way to determine which persons were likely to succeed or fail.

One of the most exciting trends in education is the move away from teacher-made tests that emphasize *grading* to tests for *mastery*. Mastery implies relating test outcomes to instructional criteria or objectives rather than for the purpose of assigning marks. If mastery consists of learning the multiplication facts from 1 to 10 without error, both teacher and student have a definable task, and the criterion for mastery is clear. The teacher's responsibility is to provide the student with strategies and materials to meet this objective and to construct examinations that allow him to determine whether or not the criterion has been met. If the student fails to reach criterion using one instructional method, the teacher should be able to recommend others.

Mastery also implies the need to modify traditional classroom procedures. First, it means that teachers must be capable of specifying objectives explicitly and unambiguously (see chapter 3) and that they can determine minimum levels of proficiency either for the class as a whole or for each individual child. How much progress can reasonably be expected of a child depends on a number of factors: the extent to which he has mastered prerequisite skills, the availability of pretested teaching materials and methods, administrative flexibility that allows teachers to work with pupils on a one-to-one basis when necessary, and perhaps the lack of emotional blocks to learning.

Second, using tests for mastery implies that teachers are more concerned that students meet objectives and are less concerned with constructing tests to assign letter or percentage grades. Students should be told what is expected of them and how proficient they must become to satisfy at least minimal course requirements. The notion that students work "for the grade" and not for the sake of knowledge may be deplored, but students work for grades because heavy emphasis is placed on them by both teachers and parents. As teachers increasingly emphasize mastery in courses where it is relevant, students may concern themselves more with the attainment of useful skills and less with the attainment of grades (Block 1971).

Tests as a Source of Motivation

Tests can be used to motivate students to learn, and because pupils study for the type of examination they expect to take, it is the teacher's responsibility to construct examinations that measure important course objectives. If items are trivial in content, students may well be motivated to study trivia.

Sometimes teachers ask meaningless and trivial questions on examinations in an effort to determine whether students have "read the book." It is not uncommon to find such questions on examinations as "Who is the author of the textbook?" and "In what year did Columbus die?" And if such items appear frequently on tests, students will assume that teachers consider such items important, and they will devote inordinate amounts of time studying trivia.

© 1968 United Feature Syndicate, Inc.

Figure 1.1

The announcement that there is soon to be an examination can affect students either positively or negatively. Students can perceive tests as threats or punishment and can become fearful, distrustful, and unhappy. By using tests for diagnostic work and mastery, the teacher can help students overcome their fear of taking tests and help prevent the needless anxiety illustrated in figure 1.1.

A number of conditions are related to student motivation. For example, the directions that students are given apparently can affect test performance. In one study (Yamamoto and Dizney 1965, pp. 89–90) three different sets of directions for an intelligence test were randomly distributed (to reduce any initial differences among groups) to a total of 557 students in grades 4, 7, 10, and 12. The directions were as follows: ,

Set I: *Intelligence*. The test you are going to take today is a test of *intelligence* and a very good one, too. As you know, a test of *intelligence* will give us your *IQ*, which tells us how *smart* you are, how *clever* you are, and how *capable* you are. Your *IQ* also tells us how *bright* you are compared to other students (pupils) like yourself. A *high* IQ is necessary to make good grades in school, to learn things quickly and well, to go to college, and to hold a good job. A *bright, able* student (pupil) makes a high score on this test. Listen carefully to the directions I am going to give you and do your best to get a *high IQ*, O.K.?

Set II: *Achievement*. The test you are going to take today is a test of *achievement* and a very good one, too. As you know, a test of *achievement* will tell us how *well* you have *learned* your lessons, how much you *know* about many things, and how *skillfully* you can *use* what you know. Your *achievement* also tells us how *much* you have *learned* compared to other students (pupils) like yourself. A *good*, hard-working student (pupil) makes a *high score* on this test. Listen carefully to the directions I am going to give you and do your best to get a *high achievement score*, O.K.?

Set III: *Routine*. This is just a routine test on how well you understand words, their meanings and uses, and how well you can answer questions and do work with numbers and figures. Listen carefully to the directions I am going to give you and do your best to get a high score, O.K.?

The investigators found that the average IQ for students who had the first set of very ego-involving directions was significantly higher (116.3) than those given sets II and III (112.1 and 109.1, respectively). The average IQ for all girls in the study was 114.4; for all boys it was 111.7. Evidently the directions were able to motivate students—especially girls—to respond differently to the same test items.

Sometimes students intentionally do poorly on tests if they believe they will be penalized for attaining high scores by being given additional or more difficult assignments. Or students may do badly if they believe their peers will look upon them with disfavor if they do well. To be part of the ingroup is a strong motive, and the teacher who disregards this factor does so at the expense of creating discipline problems in the classroom.

With some children it may be advisable to avoid written examinations entirely (perhaps in favor of individual conferences) until they learn that examinations can be beneficial. Students may be more willing to take examinations if they see advantages that such tests can have to them.

Using Tests to Improve Programs and Curricula

Tests can be of value in making decisions about programs and curricula. Programs can involve innovative projects instituted either by a school or district or by an individual teacher who wants to evaluate the effectiveness of her or his teaching methods. In these instances tests may help decide whether or not the innovation or method is effective and therefore worth keeping.

Curriculum evaluation depends not only on student achievement but also on the attitudes and values of the community. Even though a particular program has been shown to produce high levels of achievement, a school administrator may also want to know about the attitudes of students and their parents before recommending adoption of the program. Also, he might want to know if the gains in one area of the curriculum were accompanied by losses in others.

The use of tests to improve programs often presumes some form of cost/benefit ratio. Costs include not only the expenditures of funds for books, salaries, buildings, and materials but also the amount of time required for students to reach some objective. Benefits can be measured by student performance on tests, public support in the form of money voted for the operation of schools, or the extent to which a school is capable of reducing dropout rates. The most effective program is the one that involves the lowest cost per unit of benefit to the individual student.

All programs involve both cost and benefits (or losses). The teacher who insists on working individually with students will incur higher costs than will the teacher who lectures to a class of fifty students. The assumption—although rarely investigated—is that the benefits outweigh the costs. The teacher who recommends new textbooks is increasing the cost per pupil, but he may not be able to demonstrate that the benefits (student achievement and enjoyment) are worth these additional expenses. If there has been no formal program evaluation, costs may be incurred with little benefit to the students.

Formative evaluation   *Formative evaluation* of a program is designed to help the teacher or administrator make effective decisions throughout the project's duration. This type of evaluation provides continuous information that can be used to modify the program to improve its effectiveness and efficiency. Short unit tests, measures of interest and attitude, and interviews or conferences with students and their parents *during* the program can provide important clues as to how it can best be redirected to meet long-term goals.

Formative evaluation is closely related to the feedback and diagnostic functions of testing. When students complete each unit or phase of instruction, tests can inform them of their knowledge, whether or not they are pacing themselves adequately to meet course objectives, and in what areas they need to improve. With the teacher's help, new remedial materials or methods can be used to facilitate learning.

Summative evaluation   *Summative evaluation* occurs at the end of a program or course and is used to determine its overall effectiveness. The term *summative* means the summing up of all available information regarding a program at its terminal point. This information can be a valuable way of assessing the effectiveness of the whole program and often implies corrections if the program is to be continued.

The purpose of summative evaluation is not so much to help individual students currently participating in the program as to make a decision about whether the project has been successful and should be continued or modified or whether it was unsuccessful and should be dropped.

Teachers need not decide between using tests exclusively for either formative or summative evaluation. Both are needed in any well-developed program evaluation. The improvement of the curriculum depends on having knowledge about each phase of an instructional sequence (formative evaluation) as well as whether or not the whole program has met its objectives efficiently and with as low costs as possible (summative evaluation).

Using Tests for Theory Development

In addition to the many practical uses of tests, tests have also furthered the development of educational and psychological theory. For example, the understanding of child growth and development has been increased as a result of testing children's intelligence, achievement, attitudes, interests, and personalities at different phases of their development. Similarly, studies investigating how children learn concepts and principles could not have been conducted without tests that measure these higher mental abilities.

Sometimes educational and psychological theories have been developed from carefully observing children solve unfamiliar problems. The Swiss psychologist Jean Piaget, for example, observed the behavior of children as they tried to solve "conservation" problems (Flavell 1963). In a typical conservation problem, the child is given a tall, thin beaker of water. This water is then transferred into a much larger container and the child is asked whether the amount of water increased, decreased, or remained the same—that is, if the amount was "conserved." Preschool and primary grade children typically will say there is less water in the second container than in the first. Studies such as this led Piaget to develop a theory concerning the growth of intelligence in children.

Another way that testing contributes to theory is in developing the science of measurement itself, sometimes called *psychometry,* or *psychometrics.* Some test specialists construct new and useful educational and psychological tests; others develop mathematical formulas that lead to better understanding of assumptions and interrelationships among different factors and variables. Still others seek new theories of personality, attitudes, or intelligence by studying how different groups of people respond to tests of different types. Thus in addition to having a practical bent, the study of measurement creates its own body of knowledge.

Types of Tests

Tests may be classified by administrative conditions (individual and group tests), scoring criteria (objective and subjective), response limitations (power and speed), content (verbal and nonverbal), response mode (performance and pencil-and-paper tests), purposes (sample and sign), and extent of standardization (teacher-made and standardized tests).

Individual and Group Tests

Tests designed to be administered to one person at a time are called *individual tests;* those that can be given to many persons at a time are called *group tests.* Most individually administered tests are given orally and require the constant attention of the examiner, someone who is as interested in how the examinee responds as he is in the score the subject attains. Administering individual tests generally requires that the examiner have much training and experience, whereas group tests require little training to administer. However, both types of test can require a great deal of skill and knowledge to interpret.

Individual tests are often administered by school psychologists and counselors to motivate young children and to observe *how* the student responds. The examiner often looks for responses or signs suggesting some psychological disorder. The student can be given as much freedom in responding to a given task as the examiner desires, and the examiner often records and evaluates the pupil's degree of nervousness, confusion, and other idiosyncratic behavior.

Typically the school counselor or psychologist decides which individual tests will be administered. Because these tests are time-consuming to give and require the services of trained, experienced examiners, they are generally used only when a crucial decision is necessary, such as when considering a child's transfer into a special class for the mentally retarded. In the typical classroom situation, group tests are adequate for measuring cognitive skills to survey pupil achievement, strengths, and weaknesses.

Objective and Subjective Tests

The objectivity of a test refers to the method of scoring and not necessarily to its item format. Tests are *objectively scored* to the extent that competent observers can agree on how responses should be scored. When scoring criteria are unambiguous and agreed upon, subjective judgments and opinions can be minimized and the test is said to be *objective.* Scoring procedures on some objective tests have been so carefully planned that scoring can be accomplished by a computer.

Objectivity in scoring is necessary if measurements are to be useful. The teacher who constructs a long, vague essay question will find it difficult to score papers objectively. Inept expression might be disregarded for some students, but could penalize others.

Multiple-choice, true-false, and matching items are often called objective tests because they can be scored routinely according to a predetermined key, minimizing the judgments of the scorers. Extended-answer essay tests allow greater "freedom" in scoring and therefore are often not scored objectively. However, some instructors have devised careful scoring keys for essay examinations that rival some multiple-choice tests for objectivity. And conversely, items that may at first appear to be objective may turn out to be highly subjective. Take, for example, the item $10 \div 5 = ?$ Superficially it appears to yield either a right or a wrong response. But suppose a student responds as follows:

$$\begin{array}{r} 2 \\ 5\overline{)10} \\ 9 \\ \hline 0 \end{array}$$

How many points would you give this answer? If some scorers give full credit while others give half or no credit, the item is *subjectively scored*. The item can be scored more objectively if criteria for full and partial credit are established.

Power and Speed Tests

Another way of classifying tests is by whether they emphasize power or speed. A *power test* has generous time limits so that most students will be able to attempt every item. Items tend to be difficult on power tests, or they may vary in difficulty. In contrast, *speed tests* have severe time limits, but the items are so easy that few students are expected to make errors. On speed tests only the most exceptional students will be able to complete the examination within the time restrictions.

Power tests demonstrate how much knowledge or information a person has. Speed tests reveal how rapidly he can respond within a restricted time limit to rather simple items. Many clerical aptitude tests, for example, place heavy emphasis on how rapidly workers can perform routine tasks such as alphabetizing or sorting.

Whether a test is a power test or a speed test depends in part on the nature of the students for whom it was designed. An arithmetic test for sixth-graders could emphasize speed if it contained items that were easy for that group, but the same test could be a power test for younger or less well prepared students. Should difficult items be given under restricted time limits, the test may be thought of as *partially speeded*. Thus pure power and speed tests are extremes of a continuum on which time restrictions vary from ample (power) to limited (speed) and on which difficulty varies from relatively hard (power) to relatively easy (speed). These relations are summarized in figure 1.2.

Figure 1.2. Relationship Between Power and Speed Tests

Verbal, Nonverbal, and Nonlanguage Tests

A *verbal test* emphasizes reading, writing, or oral expression as the primary form of communication. Verbal examinations are used in most areas of the curriculum, including English, social studies, and science. *Nonverbal tests* deemphasize (but do not eliminate) the role of language by using pictures, figures, or other symbolic materials. For instance, the student might be asked to choose one of several figures that is identical to an example or to compute answers to addition problems. Nonverbal tests are commonly used with young children and illiterates to measure nonverbal aspects of intelligence such as spatial perception. The potential ambiguity between an *oral verbal test* and an "oral examination" is shown in Fig. 1.3.

Nonverbal tests do not avoid the use of language entirely because the directions are read either orally by the teacher or by the student if he is capable of reading. In contrast, *nonlanguage tests* do not depend on any form of written,

Figure 1.3

spoken, or reading communication. Rather, the examiner gives instructions through gestures and pantomime, and the student responds by pointing at or manipulating objects such as blocks, puzzles, or pictures. These tests are administered to deaf children or to those who cannot communicate in any form of ordinary language.

Performance and Pencil-and-Paper Tests

Performance tests are nonverbal examinations that require examinees to perform a task rather than answer questions. They are usually administered individually so that the examiner can count the number of errors committed by the student and can measure how long it takes him to complete each task. Many individually administered intelligence tests, for example, yield a verbal score (usually oral) as well as a performance score. This allows the examiner to compare these two scores and to determine whether the student has a language defect. Performance items are also used on aptitude tests to measure hand-eye coordination.

Many different kinds of performance tests are available. On some the subject is asked to place pegs in a board as rapidly as he can; on others he might be asked to assemble a puzzle, place pictures in a correct sequence, point to missing parts of a picture, or write an essay to demonstrate writing style. The common feature of all performance tests is their emphasis on the subject's ability to perform a task rather than answer questions.

Pencil-and-paper tests are almost always given in a group situation in which the subject is asked to write his answers on paper. Thus they can be administered to large numbers of persons at a time. Pencil-and-paper tests may be either verbal or nonverbal, depending on the degree of reading, writing, or oral expression required.

Sample and Sign Tests

If a teacher wishes to assess student knowledge, he must be content to measure only a partial aspect or *sample* of the student's total behavior. No test is capable of measuring all the knowledge a student has in any given subject. Thus it is necessary to work with selected aspects of behavior and to infer from these samples how the individual would probably perform if he were to answer all possible items on that topic. For example, a test to measure how well students can add fractions obviously cannot ask the student to respond to all possible fraction combinations. A general impression of the student's knowledge will have to be inferred from his performance on this limited sample of behavior.

At times, however, a test can act as a *sign* that distinguishes one group of individuals from another. The inability of a student to repeat three digits in correct sequence, for example, might empirically distinguish retardates from "normal" children. Or the failure of a student to assemble colored cubes into a simple pattern might be a sign of possible brain damage. In these examples, the examiner is not concerned about estimating how well these students can repeat digits or assemble colored cubes; rather, he uses these tests as diagnostic signs to suggest that some form of remediation is needed. Most teacher-constructed tests are samples, but many psychological tests are used as signs.

Teacher-Made and Standardized Tests

Teacher-made tests are constructed by teachers for use within their own classrooms. Their effectiveness depends on the skill of the teacher and his or her knowledge of test construction. *Standardized tests* are constructed by test specialists working with curriculum experts and teachers. They are standardized in that they have been administered and scored under standard and uniform testing so that results from different classes and different schools may be compared.

Teachers use the results of both their own examinations and those provided by standardized tests. When carefully constructed, their own tests can be used to assess performance or knowledge among the students within a given class. Thus on norm-referenced tests the teacher can state that one student performed better than another, or on a criterion-referenced test he can say that some percentage of students met course objectives.

Sometimes teachers are concerned not only with comparisons among students in their own classes but also with student performance in relation to some external representative group of students, called a *norm group*. Although Billy may have obtained the highest score in his class, this says nothing about his performance in comparison with, let us say, sixth-graders in general. To determine how Billy stands nationally, nationally obtained *normative data* are needed.

Table 1.1. Characteristics of Teacher-Made and Standardized Tests

	Teacher-Made Tests	**Standardized Tests**
Specificity of objectives	Objectives are specific to the needs of students in a given classroom.	Objectives are general to the needs of students in most classrooms.
Content	Content may come from any area of the curriculum. Items may be added, eliminated, or modified as desired.	Items are fixed and are not modifiable; only the most common areas of the curriculum are surveyed.
Rules for administration and scoring	Determined by the teacher. They should be uniform *within* the class and can be adapted to the particular needs of students.	Determined by test publishers; they must be followed exactly as provided in test manual.
Norms	No norms are provided, but they may be developed by the teacher for his own class.	Norms are provided by the publisher to all teachers to compare class performance to different age and grade groups.
Evaluation of tests	Determined by the teacher.	Data on the quality of examination are provided by the publisher.

These data usually appear as tables indicating the typical performance of a specified group such as sixth-graders.

Differences between teacher-made and standardized tests are summarized in table 1.1.

In general, then, teacher-made examinations have flexibility for use within a given classroom but provide little data for comparing students with other groups. In contrast, standardized tests have their greatest advantage when it is desirable to compare students' performance across different classrooms or schools.

Summary

1. Measurement has always played an important role in helping man cope with his environment. The history of measurement is one of developing, refining, and improving upon the accuracy of observations.

2. The terms *test, measurement,* and *evaluation* are defined as:

   a. A *test* is a task or series of tasks used to obtain systematic observations presumed to be representative of educational or psychological traits. Tests consist of items or tasks that are *samples* or elements of a *population* or *universe* of all possible items or tasks.

   b. *Measurement* is the assigning of numbers to attributes of persons, objects, or events according to explicit formulations or rules.

   c. *Evaluation* is a process through which a value judgment or decision is made from a variety of different measurements and from the background and training of the evaluator.

3. The purpose of testing is to obtain the accurate and relevant data necessary to make important decisions with the least amount of error. Tests can be used to make decisions related to:

   a. *Selection.* Tests may be used to select individuals into an institution or organization. Tests are useful if they can distinguish applicants who would and would not be successful. Selection decisions presume that there is a relationship between measurements and eventual success in the organization.

   b. *Placement.* Once selected, individuals must be placed in appropriate positions within the institution. Tests used for selection are not necessarily useful for placement since placement requires more than an "accept" or "reject" decision.

c. *Remediation.* When tests are used to determine strengths and weaknesses, they serve a diagnostic or remedial function. Diagnostic tests can identify which persons are experiencing educational or psychological problems, and they can help identify the specific type of problem the individual may have. Diagnostic tests should contain a relatively large number of items that measure the same specific objectives.

d. *Feedback.* Tests serve an important function when they inform students about their progress. Feedback may be either *norm-referenced,* which informs the individual on his progress in comparison with others, or *criterion-referenced,* which indicates what tasks the individual can perform.

e. *Motivation.* Because tests motivate students to study course content, examinations should be constructed to measure important course objectives. Students appreciate tests that are used to help them, but tests used punitively will produce fear and dislike. How students take tests is related, at least in part, to their motivation. For example, the more ego-involved students are, the better they tend to do, and sometimes students do poorly on tests because of peer pressures to be a part of the ingroup.

f. *Program improvement.* Some tests are given to help evaluate the effectiveness of curriculum innovations, new textbooks, and other program changes. Evaluation must consider costs along with measures of improvement, proficiency, and attitude. Two types of program evaluation, both of which may require testing, are formative and summative. *Formative evaluation* of programs is designed to help the teacher or administrator make effective decisions throughout the duration of the project. *Summative evaluation* occurs at the end of a program or course and is used to determine its overall effectiveness.

g. *Theory development.* Tests help educators and psychologists develop comprehensive theories about human behavior. Specially designed tasks can confirm or fail to support the expectations of a theoretical position. *Psychometry* (or *psychometrics*) is the science of educational and psychological measurement, and like other sciences, it has practitioners and theoreticians who differ in degree and type of training.

4. Many types of tests exist:

a. *Individual and group tests.* Individual tests must be administered to one person at a time, whereas group tests may be administered to two or more persons simultaneously. Individual tests are given to motivate young children and to observe how the subject responds; they tend to be time-consuming and expensive. Group tests provide a relatively inexpensive method of obtaining measurements but do not allow the examiner to directly observe how the subject attacks problems or answers questions.

b. *Objective and subjective tests.* Objectivity is the extent to which two or more persons agree on the number of points to be accorded a given response or observation; if two or more persons cannot agree, the test item is subjective. Objectivity in scoring is necessary if measurements are to have utility.

c. *Power and speed tests.* Power tests have generous time allowances which make it possible for most students to attempt every item; speed tests, in contrast, have so many items that no one is expected to complete the test within the allotted time limits. Because items are relatively difficult on power tests, the individual's score is the number of correct responses on all items. The score on a *pure speed test* will equal the number of items attempted since it is expected that no one will miss any attempted items. In practice, tests may be *partially speeded* if items are difficult and time limits restricted.

d. *Verbal, nonverbal, and nonlanguage.* A verbal test emphasizes reading, writing, or speaking as the primary form of communication; nonverbal tests deemphasize these modes of communication by using drawings or numerals. Nonlanguage tests are administered in pantomime to those persons who are deaf or unable to communicate with ordinary language symbols.

e. *Performance and pencil-and-paper tests.* Performance tests require that the examinee perform some task (rather than answer questions) in response to instructions from the examiner. Most are administered individually so that the examiner can observe how each task is approached. The examinee may be asked to assemble a puzzle, place pictures in correct sequence, or point to a missing part of a picture. Pencil-and-paper tests are usually administered to groups. Subjects are asked either to write their answers to questions or to select one or more choices.

f. *Sample and sign tests.* Sample tests attempt to measure some specified aspect of a person's ability, knowledge, aptitude, or interest by selecting a sample of tasks from the individual's total repertoire of responses (called a universe or population). While concern is always with the universe, almost all tests are samples of tasks that only approximate the universe. Sign tests, in contrast, empirically differentiate between groups and do not derive their importance from being samples of some item universe. Having adults repeat digits in sequence from memory might indicate (be a sign of) possible brain dysfunction rather than be a sample of memory for digits. Most teacher-made tests are sample tests.

g. *Teacher-made and standardized tests.* Teacher-made tests are prepared by teachers for use in their own classrooms to meet their own specific objectives. They are often used to compare individuals within the group. Standardized tests facilitate intergroup comparisons. They are standardized in the sense that the directions and scoring systems are uniform for all persons. They also provide *norms,* or tables indicating how individuals compare with some specific group (such as a sample of sixth-graders).

Suggested Readings

Bloom, Benjamin S. "Recent Developments in Mastery Learning." *Educational Psychologist,* 10, no. 2, (Spring 1973), pp. 53–57. A highly readable article on the author's experiences with Mastery Learning.

Glaser, Robert, and Nitko, Anthony J. "Measurement in Learning and Instruction." In Robert L. Thorndike, ed., *Educational Measurements,* 2d ed., pp. 625–70. Washington, D. C.: American Council on Education, 1971. A detailed treatment of how tests can be used in education. A summary of Glaser's approach can be found in chapter 18 of this text.

Hills, John R. "Use of Measurement in Selection and Placement." In Thorndike, ed., *Educational Measurements,* 2d ed., pp. 680–732. Although most of the examples relate to selection and placement in colleges and universities, the implications for elementary and secondary schools are evident. Some portions of this chapter assume a rather sophisticated background, but most of the chapter is highly readable.

Jones, Lyle V. "The Nature of Measurement." In Thorndike, ed., *Educational Measurements,* 2d ed., pp. 335–55. This chapter contains both a simplified and a more complex discussion of the nature of educational measurements. It also contains an interesting section comparing physical and educational measurements.

Schutz, Richard E. "The Role of Measurement in Education: Servant, Soulmate, Stoolpigeon, Statesman, Scapegoat, All of the Above, and/or None of the Above." *Journal of Educational Measurement* 8, no. 3 (Fall 1971): 141–46. A humorous but instructive description of how tests can be used within lessons, at the end of lessons, at the end of units, and at the end of programs.

Thorndike, Robert L. "Educational Measurement for the Seventies." In Thorndike, ed., *Educational Measurements,* 2d ed., pp. 3–14. An excellent summary of recent developments and trends in educational measurement. The chapter is divided into four sections: "The Impact of Technological Development," "Conceptual Developments," "Social and Political Issues," and a brief summary, "Continuity in Spite of Change."

Instructional Image Corporation, 25 Broadway, Pleasant, New York 10570. "iic Responsive Answer Sheets." The student uses a special pen to mark his responses on preprinted or custom-printed answer sheet. When the pen touches the answer sheet, a "latent image" appears. The teacher can prepare a message to the student of any length from "Right" to a detailed description of how the student can improve.

Van Valkenburgh, Nooger & Neville, Inc., 15 Maiden Lane, New York, N. Y. 10038. "Trainer-Tester." The student receives immediate feedback by erasing blocks of chemically treated responses. If the answer is correct, an R (or other symbol) will appear; if incorrect, the response will be blank, or show a different symbol.

Research Media, Inc., 4 Midland Avenue, Hicksville, New York, 11801. "Rapid-Rater©." Provides immediate feedback to students. An advantage is that students must answer an item correctly before they can proceed to the next item. The disadvantage is the relatively high initial cost per unit.

Social and Ethical
Implications of Testing

QUALM 23

The prof is my quizmaster;
I shall not flunk.
He maketh me to enter the
*   examination room;*
He leadeth me to the alternate seat.
He restoreth my fears;
He leadeth me into a deep problem
*   for the grade's sake.*
Yes, though I know not the answers
*   to the questions,*
The class average comforts me.
I prepareth before me in
*   the presence of my proctors;*
I anointeth my blue book with figures;
My time runneth out.
Surely grades and blue books will
*   follow me all the days of my life;*
And I shall dwell in this class forever.

(*Found on a campus bulletin board*)

2 Rapid growth in the number, variety, and uses of educational and psychological tests and the fact that educational decisions are increasingly based on their results have brought tests into public view. Although the advantages of careful appraisal in decision making are considerable, some serious allegations against the use of tests warrant further consideration.

This chapter considers a number of criticisms leveled at tests and testing practices and examines some of the ethical and moral issues involved.

Criticisms of Testing

Tests Represent an Invasion of Privacy

In June 1959 the Houston Independent School District voted to burn some 5,000 answer sheets because of protests by parents against the alleged personal nature of questions asked ninth-graders during a national survey (Nettler 1959). Students were asked to agree or disagree with the following types of statements:

> A girl who gets in trouble on a date has no one to blame but herself.
> Sometimes I tell dirty jokes when I would rather not.
> I enjoy soaking in the bathtub.
> If you don't drink in our gang, they make you feel like a sissy.
> Dad always seems too busy to pal around with me.

Six years later the American Psychological Association (APA) was picketed by a dozen citizens carrying leaflets and banners stating "Don't be brainwashed by some Ph.D. See your clergyman or doctor" and "Write your Senator or Representative and ask him to support legislation to stop the use of sex-ridden psychological tests in schools, Civil Service, and private industry" (APA 1965).

Whether tests represent an invasion of privacy or not depends in part on how they are used. Certainly there is no invasion of privacy when subjects are told how test results will be used and then the subjects volunteer. The code of ethics of the American Psychological Association (APA 1963) states:

> The psychologist who asks that an individual reveal personal information in the course of interviewing, testing, or evaluation, or who allows such information to be divulged to him, does so only after making certain that the responsible person is fully aware of the purposes of the interview, testing, or evaluation and the ways in which the information may be used.

When children are involved, invasion of privacy is somewhat more complex. Legally the schools function *in loco parentis,* as parent substitutes, while the child is at school. Therefore, teachers can require students to take tests specifically designed to meet stated and agreed-on school objectives. Ethically, however, educators have the responsibility of selecting and using tests prudently. The decision to require that students take examinations—especially those measuring personality or attitudes—might best be made by a panel of concerned citizens with the help of professionals who are knowledgeable about testing. The panel should consider such aspects as: (1) the ability of the test to measure precisely those objectives the school or district intends to measure, (2) the possibility of embarrassing or emotionally damaging children who take the test, (3) the extent to which community mores and values are likely to be affected by the test, (4) the potential benefits of testing, (5) the possibility of using volunteers instead of captive audiences, (6) the steps that will be taken to ensure confidentiality of results, and (7) the possibility of obtaining data without testing (using census reports or public documents, for example).

To some extent all observations and tasks (including testing) are an invasion of privacy to the person who prefers not being tested, but most students are willing and often anxious to participate in any procedure that promises some alleviation of their problems. The probability of invading privacy is high whenever testing or measurement is designed for the benefit of someone other than the person being tested or observed. A teacher who administers a test to his students solely to gather information for a professional paper, thesis, or dissertation may well be encroaching upon the rights of his students to privacy unless he obtains the informed consent of the participants, their parents, and school authorities. The base elements of informed consent include a complete description of the purposes, procedures, risks, costs, and potential values of the study. In addition, the procedures used to ensure confidentiality or anonymity should be described. "Risk," of course, refers to both physical and psychological trauma.

In research there must be a reasonable balance between the individual's desire to maintain privacy and the right of society to expand and disseminate knowledge. But what ethical problems arise when subjects refuse to be tested in spite of the need to gather important research data? Does the researcher have the right to deceive subjects who might refuse to be tested? The code of ethics of the American Psychological Association (APA 1963) addresses the issue:

> The psychologist is justified in withholding information from or giving misinformation to research subjects only when in his judgment this is clearly required by his research problem and when . . . the principle(s) regarding the protection of the subjects are adhered to.

Principles of privacy and the protection of subjects transcend those of testing. For example, some students resent any questions of a personal nature, even being asked to write a theme on "What I Did Last Summer." Some parents object strongly to required "show-and-tell" periods that presumably provide "opportunities" for children to discuss issues that parents might prefer remain in the privacy of the home. Ethical considerations require that teachers be sensitive to these matters, perhaps by allowing alternative activities and by insuring that the elements required for obtaining informed consent be followed scrupulously if the activity has little potential value to the participants or if there is any degree of risk that is not a part of everyday life. Because the teacher's main responsibility is to his students, that trust should be maintained by avoiding those situations that are potentially damaging to that relationship.

Tests Create Anxiety and Interfere
with Learning

A common criticism of tests is that they create anxiety and thus interfere with learning. Like most generalizations, this evaluation contains elements of both truth and inaccuracy. *Some* students may be hindered by test-produced anxiety, but this fact by no means implies that all or even most students are affected negatively. Indeed, a number of studies suggest that most students perceive tests as helpful.

In one study (Feldhusen 1964), for example, college students were asked to respond to a questionnaire on the effect of weekly quizzes on their attitudes and achievement. Eighty percent stated that the quizzes helped them to learn more; the remaining 20 percent stated that the quizzes helped them "no more than usual." On another item only 2 percent of the students believed that the quizzes created anxiety, and of this group 87 percent believed that the test-produced anxiety was helpful because it made learning easier.

In another study (Fiske 1967), respondents were asked to indicate how favorable they would be to taking tests. Fewer than 15 percent gave negative or critical responses to a wide variety of tests when the purpose was to gather research data. A somewhat larger percentage felt uneasy about taking tests if a crucial decision affecting their lives was involved. In this study tests were perceived as being favorable or unfavorable depending on how the results were to be used.

In an excellent summary of how tests affect students (Kirkland 1971), the following conclusions were reached on the relationship among tests, anxiety, and learning:

1. Mild degrees of anxiety usually facilitate learning, whereas high anxiety levels hinder learning in *most* instances.
2. The less able student incurs a higher level of test anxiety than does the more capable one.
3. Being familiar with the type of test to be administered reduces test anxiety.
4. Highly anxious students do better than less anxious ones on tests measuring rote recall; they perform less well, however, on tests requiring flexibility in thought.
5. Test anxiety increases with grade level.
6. Although there appears to be no relationship between sex and anxiety among elementary school children, junior high school girls indicate that they experience more anxiety than do boys at comparable grade levels.

In most studies relating anxiety to testing the procedure has been to identify subjects who admit they are anxious during examinations and to compare their performance with those who report low degrees of anxiety. None of these studies provides data on the extent to which the test itself creates anxiety among individuals who are not generally anxious. Observations of children taking examinations demonstrate some indications of nervousness (nail biting, pencil tapping, squirming). How detrimental such effects are in the long run is not clear, but certainly the way tests are used (to punish or to facilitate instruction) is an important consideration. The effective teacher creates sufficient interest and motivation in children to do their best without also creating the kind of undesirable stress demonstrated by Sally in Figure 2.1.

© 1969 United Feature Syndicate, Inc.

Figure 2.1

The following suggestions may help motivate students to prepare for and take examinations without creating unnecessary anxiety:

1. Emphasize tests for diagnosis and mastery rather than as a means of punishing students who fail to live up to the expectations of the teacher or parents.
2. Avoid the "sudden death" examination in which passing or failing is a function of performance on only one test, such as a final examination.
3. Write personal notes on each examination paper encouraging students to keep up the good work or to put forth greater effort (Page 1958).
4. Be sure each item has "face validity"—that is, it measures some important aspect of life as perceived by the student.
5. Avoid unannounced examinations.
6. Schedule personal conferences with students as often as possible to reduce anxiety and to redirect learning where necessary.
7. Avoid invidious comparisons among students.
8. Emphasize student strengths, not deficiencies.
9. Deemphasize the role of competitive examinations when some students are unable to compete.
10. Treat each student's grades and records confidentially.
11. Allow students to choose among activities of equal instructional value.

Tests Permanently Categorize Students

If educational and psychological tests are misused, they do much to scar some pupils permanently by rigidly categorizing or pigeonholing them and by allowing teachers to use these classifications relentlessly. If they know that a child's IQ score is low, some teachers may decide that the child is unteachable and may assign menial tasks to keep him occupied and "out of trouble." However, if tests are considered to be samples of behavior that do not measure fixed or unchanging traits, teachers will not be so likely to categorize students.

Any single observation of an individual's performance represents only limited information that may vary as circumstances change. The adolescent who "goofs off" during a scholastic aptitude test may take the test much more seriously when he applies for college. Only by continuous evaluation can teachers amass sufficient data to allow them to draw reasonable conclusions about typical performance.

Again, it is the misuse of examinations rather than the tests themselves that should be criticized. And not all teachers misuse test results. The evidence seems to be that when teachers are given knowledge about their pupils, they tend to assign marks on a more individualized basis (Baker and Doyle 1959). On the other hand, there is no evidence that providing teachers with knowledge about their pupils inevitably leads to higher achievement levels. In one study (Hoyt 1955), for example, it was shown that although pupil-teacher relationships improved when test results became available to teachers, achievement did not improve unless specific attempts were made to improve student learning.

Tests Penalize Bright and Creative Students

In *The Tyranny of Testing* (1962, p. 97), Banesh Hoffmann, a theoretical physicist, argues that "the tests deny the creative person a significant opportunity to demonstrate his creativity and favor the shrewd and facile candidate over the one who has something to say." As partial evidence for his position, he provides a grammar item "made by one of the leading test makers":

Among them, Tom and Dick were not able to find enough money.

Hoffmann argues, and probably correctly, that the average student who knows the rules of grammar will recognize that in a comparison of two people, *between* is the proper word rather than *among*. But the brighter and more creative student might recognize the ambiguity in the word *them,* which can refer to Tom and Dick or to some group larger than Tom and Dick to which they both belong. If the second interpretation is favored, the sentence is correct as is. Hoffmann believes that if answers were keyed to more creative responses, test results would not be so biased against those students.

In fairness to the critics of testing, it must be admitted that vague and ambiguous items sometimes do appear on tests, and nothing is gained by trying to justify their inclusion. But to claim that all or even many items discriminate against the bright or creative student cannot be justified either. Hoffmann examined over 200 items but critized only 5 percent of them, and his criticisms were leveled at sample or practice exercises, which presumably are of lower quality than those that actually appear in the tests themselves.

In a direct investigation of Hoffmann's claim of multiple-choice item ambiguity and discrimination against "creative" persons, Gilbert Sax and William Greenberg (1969) found only one student out of 357 college juniors and seniors who was able to justify answers to as many as five out of nine items called "defective" by Hoffmann using his "creative" responses rather than those provided by the test publisher. Three-fourths of the students who responded "correctly" using Hoffmann's "creative" key were unable to justify their choices, or they selected Hoffmann's choices for incorrect reasons. Evidently if tests discriminate against creative individuals, the amount of discrimination is minimal.

Tests Discriminate against Minority Students

One of the most persistent and serious allegations against tests is that they discriminate against minority groups, particularly against blacks, American Indians, Puerto Ricans, and Chicanos. Virtually all studies agree that children from disadvantaged homes attain lower intelligence and achievement test scores than do children from middle and upper socioeconomic levels. The relationships among race, ethnic background, socioeconomic status, and test scores are highly complex, and we can only attempt to introduce some of the major concerns in this text.

In 1970, 25.5 million Americans (or 13 percent) were living below poverty levels (U. S. Department of Commerce, Bureau of the Census 1971). The psychology of the disadvantaged child is permeated with a concern for obtaining the basic necessities of life (food, clothing, shelter), although there is as wide a range of individual differences among the disadvantaged as one might expect in any group. To the extent that education fails to provide these necessities, it is seen as useless and irrelevant and a force to be neutralized in the fight for survival. Many children from disadvantaged homes are not as highly motivated by the promise of *future* benefits from attending school and "doing one's best" as are middle-class and upper-class students. These children tend to put forth their best efforts when an *immediate* gain can be realized, and furthermore, they are more concerned with pleasing their peers than their parents or teachers. Their need for immediate reinforcement and their particularly strong peer-group attachments must be understood if the relationship between test performance and socioeconomic status is to be interpreted properly.

In contrast, the middle- or upper-class child strives to do his best on tests because he is convinced—with good reason—that doing well now will have important repercussions for him later. Second, he generally wants to please his parents and teachers by doing well, and test results reinforce his need to achieve. This difference in motivation is one explanation of the differential test performance of disadvantaged and advantaged pupils. As Kenneth Eels and his associates (1951, p. 21) have stated:

> [Lower class] children often work very rapidly through a test, making responses more or less at random. Apparently they are convinced in advance that they cannot do well on the test, and they find that by getting through the test rapidly they can shorten the period of discomfort which it produces.

Again, there is little criticism of testing when its purpose is diagnostic and the results are used to benefit respondents or when items are clearly related to job criteria. A typing test is manifestly fair to all applicants if the job involves only typing, since it provides an excellent sample of the respondent's on-the-job behavior. However, if tests are used to assess *potential,* their use can be unfair to many minority group members. To some teachers and employers, aptitude measures indicate a capacity to learn regardless of the opportunities available for employment. And in extreme instances, teachers may even believe that a child with low aptitude scores cannot be taught. Such an interpretation of test results is unjustified.

Test scores are never direct measures of potential or capacity; rather, they are samples of *current* behavior. Although tests can be useful in predicting success, the prediction is based on how the examinee currently responds to test items. If there is a high correspondence between current levels of test performance and how the subject will respond to criteria when on the job or at a higher grade level in school, the test is a useful predictor. Failure to do well on the predictor test implies failure on the criterion only if the test is relevant to the criterion and if it is assumed that no one will attempt to improve or train the applicant when he is on the job.

Many minority group members do not take tests well because they have not learned the skills, knowledge, and attitudes required to succeed. If disadvantaged individuals do poorly on a test that can differentiate fairly between those who are successful and unsuccessful on the job or in college, it is not reasonable to criticize the test. What such tests indicate is that low scorers are less likely to be successful than high scorers unless there is on-the-job opportunity for improvement. Criticism should be directed at employment policies or at the failure of the schools to provide students with skills needed to succeed.

However, tests are *biased* to the extent that they penalize applicants by rejecting those who have low test scores but would perform satisfactorily if employed. Thus if both blacks and whites would have performed equally well on the job or in college but only whites attained a minimum acceptance test score, the test is biased against the black applicant.

Relatively few empirical studies demonstrate the extent to which tests are biased against minority groups. In some of these studies so few individuals were selected for testing that results are questionable, and in other studies the criterion used to measure job success is controvertible. For example, if supervisory ratings determine success on the job, the foreman's possible bias makes it difficult to appraise a minority worker's actual performance. Also, under the provisions of the Fair Employment Practices Act, businesses, industries, and schools were not allowed to identify the racial or ethnic backgrounds of their personnel. Data on the extent of test bias are therefore limited and inconclusive.

One of the most carefully considered papers on testing minority children was prepared by the Society for the Psychological Studies of Social Issues (Fishman et al. 1964, pp. 137–39). One of its conclusions is particularly pertinent to the claim that tests are biased:

> In situations where minority-group members are likely to have to continue competing with others under much the same cultural handicaps that they have faced in the past, normative interpretation of their aptitude and achievement test scores will probably yield a fairly dependable basis for short-term predictive purposes. When special guidance or training is offered to help such individuals overcome their handicaps, however, achievement beyond the normative expectancies may well be obtained, and predictions should be based on expectancies derived specifically from the local situation.
>
> . . . In spite of their typical cultural bias, standardized tests should not be sold short as a means of making objective assessments of the traits of minority group children. Many bright, nonconforming pupils, with backgrounds different from those of their teachers, make favorable showings on achievement tests in contrast to their low classroom marks. These are often children whose cultural handicaps are most evident in their overt social and interpersonal behavior. Without the intervention of standardized tests, many such children would be stigmatized by the adverse subjective ratings of teachers who tend to reward conformist behavior of middle-class character.

In general, the available evidence suggests that standardized tests do not systematically discriminate against minority groups. For example, Anne Cleary (1968) could find no differences between black and white college freshmen in the extent to which the Scholastic Aptitude Test (SAT) either overpredicted or underpredicted grades in two racially integrated schools. In a third college the SAT overpredicted grades attained by the black students.

Tests Measure Only Limited and Superficial Aspects of Behavior

A common criticism of tests is that they measure only limited and superficial aspects of behavior. It is argued that the most important human traits, such as love, creativity, motivation, and character, are not evaluated by tests, whereas less important, easier to measure human traits are assessed. The implication is that the schools avoid teaching humanistic subjects for content that can be tested more easily.

While it is true that no test or battery of tests can measure all the complexities and degrees of human behavior, many tests in use today have resulted from societal needs, especially in schools, the psychological clinic, and industry, and it has been repeatedly demonstrated that when properly used, tests are a valuable adjunct to these institutions. Empirical data supporting the use of tests probably accounts for the current demand for measures of intelligence, aptitude, and achievement.

Tests are used to help make decisions and are of great value in doing so. One can only guess that few individuals would be willing to make decisions about love, marriage, and character based on test results and clinical evaluations. Except in the psychological clinic, too few people analyze and evaluate their chances for a successful marriage by any objective means, and most would reject the opportunity to do so. Nonetheless, sex knowledge inventories and scales do measure compatibility and are beginning to have wider use. Probably the most important reason for the limited use and development of tests of creativity, love, and the like is that there is little agreement on what these terms mean, and it is difficult to measure any concept with unknown characteristics. Everyone is in favor of democracy until it is clarified and delimited.

To make the best decisions, teachers must have the most complete and accurate information obtainable, and it can be empirically demonstrated that tests provide more accurate and complete information than do impressionistic, subjective evaluations. New testing procedures and new test instruments are constantly being developed, and although testing specialists still have a long way to go in refining psychometric science and practice, the value of tests for decision making cannot be denied.

Ethical and Unethical Testing Practices

Membership in any profession presumes a commitment to the public welfare. The public expects and has the right to expect that in return for its confidence and respect, the profession will protect its concerns and rights. A code of ethics defines practices that a profession, by its own consent, imposes upon itself. It also defines those acts that members should attempt to avoid in fulfilling their obligation to the public. Deliberate violations of a code can lead to dismissal from the professional society and to loss of continued employment in that profession.

The American Psychological Association (1968, pp. 357–61) has published nineteen principles of ethics, at least four of which are relevant to testing and which are applicable to teachers using tests:

Confidentiality   Because his client's welfare is his greatest concern, the psychologist recognizes his responsibility to maintain a confidential relationship with him. Only under certain prescribed conditions can this relationship be violated:

1.   Where there is a clear and immediate danger to the client, and then the psychologist may inform only other professional workers or public authorities.
2.   If the client will benefit by talking to other professionals concerned with the case.
3.   If the client gives his permission for confidential communications to be reported to others.

Test security   Tests are the professional instruments of psychologists, and as such their dissemination is restricted to those with the technical competence to use them properly. No standardized tests should ever be left unsecured.

Test interpretation   Test scores and materials should be made available only to individuals who are qualified to use them. Test results should be interpreted to parents and students in ways that ensure against their misuse and misinterpretation.

Test publication   Standardized tests should provide a manual or technical handbook describing how and by whom the test can be used most effectively. Advertisements concerning tests should be factual and descriptive, not emotional or persuasive.

While perhaps it is stated in more general terms, the Code of Ethics of the Education Profession developed by the National Education Association (NEA) (1969–70) reflects the same concerns and obligations as those faced by psychologists. Teachers are responsible for protecting their clients—the children in their classrooms—against unprofessional practices.

Because teachers are responsible for the administration and interpretation of tests they give, policy statements regarding test use have been formulated. One of the most comprehensive statements (Thompson n.d.) identifies a number of ethical and unethical testing practices directly related to teachers:

Ethical Practices

1. It is both ethical and advantageous to inform students in advance that they are about to take a standardized test and to tell them something about the nature of the test. They can be told, for example, that the test will cover social studies and arithmetic, and that items are in multiple-choice format. They can and should be told something about the advantages that such testing will have for them and how test results will be used.

2. Teachers should feel free to explain the mechanics of taking a standardized test, and students can be given practice in filling out an answer sheet by making their marks heavy and black and by erasing completely. Students should *not*, however, be given copies of the actual examination questions. It is essential that teachers *not* make these questions available.

3. It is perfectly proper to try to motivate students to do as well as they can as long as they are not threatened or made anxious about their performance.

4. It is essential that all standardized test materials be kept secure before, during, and after the examination. Leaving copies of standardized tests around for pupils to examine is unethical. All test materials and test results should be kept locked. (Thompson recommends numbering each test and making certain that all tests used have been returned.)

5. It is ethical to combine classes for testing as long as there is an adequate number of proctors to safeguard tests and to make sure students are following instructions. A reasonable proctor-examinee ratio is thirty to one.

6. Once an examination has been administered and scored, it is permissible for teachers to examine results and determine areas of student weakness. It is proper to modify the curriculum as a result of standardized achievement testing only if the teacher can demonstrate that the change conforms to overall school objectives. To modify the curriculum solely for the purpose of increasing test scores is unethical.

Unethical Practices

1. It is unethical for teachers to tutor students on the specific subject matter of an expected examination. Such "coaching" destroys the standardized procedures of test administration, and it makes scores uninterpretable and a waste of students' time. Scores on standardized tests can only be interpreted when the tests are given in exactly the same way as they were to the norm or comparison group.

2. It is not ethical for teachers to examine the content of standardized tests and to use that specific content in their classrooms. To do so violates the principle that standardized tests are *samples* of behavior

and not necessarily examples of all that a student should know at a particular grade level. Because students in the norm group were not exposed to such items prior to taking the test, the teacher's classroom curriculum need not match test content perfectly. Rather, school districts should select standardized tests that meet their general objectives, although not all items will do so. Furthermore, it is likely that teachers will include subject matter in their classrooms not tested on the examination.

3. It is unethical for teachers to use standardized test items on their own examinations. Not only is plagiarism illegal, but standardized test items are to be used only once—during the standardized testing. By making such items available to students on locally constructed tests, the teacher ruins the standardization procedures. Similarly, it is not ethical for teachers to use standardized test items as part of any instructional set of materials.

4. It is improper for teachers to try to improve pupil performance by developing items that parallel those on standardized tests. Nor is it acceptable for teachers to administer one form of an examination when the district is to administer a second form as a part of its testing program. Sometimes teachers do this to "preview" student performance on the regularly scheduled test, but the practice is unethical since it gives spuriously high scores to students having the advantage of practice.

5. It is unethical to exclude some students from participation in district-wide testing, even though the teacher expects them to do poorly. It is likely that the norm group also was composed of students who were expected to do poorly on examinations. Nor should teachers attempt to eliminate an entire section of a class from taking such tests on the grounds that they are the "low ability group." The obvious exception is students who are so mentally handicapped that they are in special classes and are not part of the "regular" school program.

6. It is not ethical to neglect the instruction of any student for the purpose of increasing test scores of other pupils. The goal of education is the maximum achievement of *each* pupil, not the attainment of high test scores. No student should be penalized in the hope that others will compensate for his performance.

7. It is unethical to alter in any way the directions, time limits, and scoring procedures of any standardized test. This includes reading items aloud when the directions specify they are to be read by the student; it includes giving extra help by answering any questions once the examination is under way unless specifically allowed in the test manual; and it further includes the insidious practice of a teacher standing over someone's shoulders and frowning when he misses an item. The value of standardized tests is that they are given under standard (uniform) conditions, and anything that violates those conditions makes the examination results more difficult or impossible to interpret.

8. It is unethical to create anxiety and rivalry about standardized tests among students and between classes or schools. Examinations are

not contests and should not be treated as such. The welfare of the student is violated when anxiety is produced.

Testing as Social Interaction and Responsibility

Testing is a form of communication and social interaction between two or more parties. Testing presumes an ethical and responsible attitude on the part of the examiner and desire to cooperate on the part of the examinee. As in all forms of social interaction, mutual trust and respect must be developed. The examinee will want to cooperate if he knows that test results will benefit him. Because a good deal of his time and effort is devoted to taking a test, he has the right to expect value from it. Anything short of this relationship of mutual trust and understanding can lead to frustration, distrust, and the inability to provide the examinee with the kind of help he expects from a professional worker.

Summary

1. Because of its widespread use and importance, testing has come under public criticism:
   a. *Tests represent an invasion of privacy*. Tests may be an invasion of privacy when they are used without the permission of examinees to obtain personal or sensitive information. An exception is the testing of students to measure commonly agreed-upon academic objectives. The administration of attitude and personality measures probably should require parental permission. Test users should fully inform students and their parents of the purpose of testing, the nature of the test items or tasks (but not specific content), and ways in which the information will be used. When tests are used for selection, students should not be required to divulge personal information that is irrelevant to performance on the criterion measure. Tests used in research studies require a balance between the individual's right to privacy and society's right to obtain knowledge. Deception is unethical unless the research topic is of such great importance that deception is warranted and necessary and danger to the individual (physical and psychological) is minimal.

b. *Tests create anxiety and interfere with learning.* Most persons do not feel threatened by examinations if personal consequences are minimized. How tests are used largely determines whether they are perceived as threatening. The relationship between the degree of anxiety and learning has several aspects:

  i. Although anxiety may facilitate learning under certain conditions, it is debilitating to many students and particularly when performing tasks requiring flexibility in thought.

  ii. Students who are familiar with specific types of tests are less anxious than those who lack experience with those tests.

  iii. More capable students are less anxious when taking tests than those who are less capable.

  iv. Test anxiety increases as students grow older.

  Students can be motivated to prepare for and to take tests without creating needless anxiety.

c. *Tests permanently categorize students.* The belief that measurements are infallible and that performance cannot be modified has had serious consequences. For example, some teachers treat children according to tested expectation levels and disregard evidence of change. A number of school districts have eliminated group intelligence tests because teachers and parents have regarded IQ scores as unmodifiable and infallible measures of what the child ought to be learning in school. Students can change, and great care should be exercised in the interpretation and use of test results. This does not, of course, imply that tests have no value.

d. *Tests penalize bright and creative students.* One of the most consistent criticisms of tests is that they are insensitive to atypical but defensible responses. This criticism seems to have little validity. While some items on standardized tests may be ambiguous, vague, or have more than one justifiable answer, the evidence is that these are the exception rather than the rule.

e. *Tests discriminate against minority groups.* Another pervasive belief is that tests penalize members of minority groups, especially blacks, American Indians, Puerto Ricans, and Chicanos. The following points should be considered:

  i. Members of minority groups that have been discriminated against may not be motivated by the future promises of education as much as they are by their immediate needs. They thus often perceive tests as irrelevant to current problems.

  ii. Working hard on tests is important for youngsters who are motivated by parental and teacher approval but is less important for those whose basic reinforcement is derived from peer-group approval.

      iii. Although children from lower socioeconomic levels generally obtain lower test scores than those from more affluent groups, this is not true for all individuals, nor does it necessarily imply that such differences are unmodifiable.

      iv. Tests may accurately predict failure on the job or in school if no attempts are made to train the individual and to help him cope with future demands. Test scores are samples of current behavior and may be excellent predictors of how the individual will perform without benefit of remediation, but such scores do not imply an inability to learn.

      v. Tests are biased against minorities whenever a prediction of failure is made when in fact the minority member would have been successful if employed or admitted. Contrary to commonly accepted beliefs, the limited evidence is that aptitude tests do not systematically penalize members of minority groups, but that they may overpredict the actual grades attained by minority students.

  f. *Tests measure only limited and superficial aspects of behavior.* A commonly recurring criticism of tests is that they cannot measure the most important human traits, such as love or creativity, but rather, they force test users into making important decisions based on tests that measure superficial and relatively unimportant criteria.

      i. The fact that tests measure samples of behavior and must of necessity be limited in content does not imply that they lack utility. The purpose of testing is to obtain relevant and accurate observations to facilitate decision making and to minimize observational errors. Tests and other measurement procedures have the advantage over impressionistic judgments providing evidence of their usefulness.

      ii. Crucial decisions regarding love, marriage, and character are not likely to be made on the basis of psychological tests even if it could be demonstrated that their use would improve decision making.

      iii. The "higher" human traits generally do not mean the same thing to everyone. Unless the universe that constitutes these abstractions can be agreed upon, it is unlikely that tests or any other procedures will be developed that attempt to measure them.

2. Everyone who uses tests must be committed to following ethical testing practices. The American Psychological Association includes four principles concerning testing in its code of ethics: provisions for confidentiality, test security, test interpretation, and test publication.

3. Testing is a form of social interaction and public responsibility which demands the mutual trust of the examinee and examiner. The responsibility of the teacher is to have a thorough knowledge of the tools of his trade and to use this knowledge to benefit his students.

Suggested Readings

Dizney, Henry. "Characteristics of Classroom Test Items Identified by Students as 'Unfair.' " *Journal of Educational Measurement* 2, no. 1 (June 1965): 119–21. The author of this article found that students had a fairly strong tendency to rate difficult items as unfair. Items rated most unfair were those judged by students as not having been discussed sufficiently in class.

Kirkland, Marjorie C. "The Effects of Tests on Students and Schools." *Review of Educational Research* 41, no. 4 (October 1971): 303–50. A detailed examination of the effects of tests on students, parents, teachers, schools, and society.

Wellingham, Warren W., ed. "Invasion of Privacy in Research and Testing." Proceedings of a symposium sponsored by the National Council on Measurement in Education and published as a supplement to *Journal of Educational Measurement* 4, no. 1 (Spring 1967): 1–31. In addition to a foreword by the editor, the proceedings include "Testing and Privacy," "Seeking a Balance between the Right of Privacy and the Advancement of Social Research," "The Privacy Issue and a Professional Response at the Departmental Level," and "Clearance of Questionnaires with Respect to 'Invasion of Privacy,' Public Sensitivities, Ethical Standards, Etc.: Principles and Viewpoints in the Bureau of Research, U.S. Office of Education." These discussions contain some of the thinking of the federal government and the reactions of professional organizations concerned with testing.

Planning the Test

*"Cheshire-Puss, . . . Would
you tell me please, which way I ought
to go from here?"*

*"That depends a great deal on
where you want to get to," said the
Cat.*

*"I don't much care where—,"
said Alice.*

*"Then it doesn't matter which
way you go," said the Cat.*

*"—so long as I get
somewhere," Alice added as an
explanation.*

*"Oh, you're sure to do that,"
said the Cat, "if you only walk long
enough."*

Alice in Wonderland (*Lewis Carroll*)

3 As long as it makes little
difference what people do, they can heed the Cheshire Cat's advice to Alice and
they will be certain to get *somewhere*. In education, however, getting "somewhere" is not a very satisfactory objective. Teachers need a sharply defined idea
of what they want to accomplish.

Like rulers, scales, and thermometers, examinations all "measure"; but just
as few of us would make the mistake of trying to measure weight with a ruler,
so we should also realize that all tests are not equally effective for all purposes.
Like Alice, some teachers construct and administer examinations without defining
what they want to accomplish. Nor are the reasons for testing always clear. Sometimes items that do not measure the test's objectives are constructed, and often
teachers fail to measure objectives accurately because they initially fail to specify
them clearly.

The Philosophical Basis of Educational Goals

A major difficulty facing educational measurement is the inability of teachers, administrators, and the public to arrive at a consistent philosophy of education that would imply specific school objectives. Currently at least two major philosophic positions are held in education: absolute positions such as realism and idealism, and relativistic positions such as pragmatism.

Realism

Realists argue that there is an external reality that is independent of man. The world is stable, orderly, uniform, and capable of being investigated scientifically. To realists, education is the means for learning about reality—about the way things "really" are. Because science is the most objective way of discovering reality, it has high priority in the school curriculum.

Generally realists tend to define educational objectives narrowly. They do not deny the values of "social adjustment" or "worthwhile use of leisure time," but they consider these objectives secondary and the responsibility of other institutions. Courses in driver education are the responsibility of the department of motor vehicles or the police department; physical education is the responsibility of the health department; and cleanliness and morality are the responsibility of the home and the church (Broudy 1961).

Idealism

Philosophical idealists also believe in absolutes, but unlike realists, they believe that *ideas* are the ultimate reality. Since the "external world" can be understood only through the mind, the mind must be developed fully to comprehend the universe. But what ideas are the most lasting and valuable? Those that have withstood the test of time. The idealist's ultimate objective is to understand what are often called the "Great Books"—the classics that have lived through the years and that contain the accumulated knowledge of mankind. According to idealists, the educated man is well acquainted with his cultural heritage and the thoughts of great men.

Pragmatism

Pragmatists deny an absolute and unchanging universe and insist that all is in a state of flux. Words such as *truth, value,* and *absolute* have no meaning beyond their *use*. Something is good if in the long run it produces consequences that are beneficial to the individual and his society.

Because the world is relative and changing, there are no eternal truths to be learned in school. The learner creates knowledge as he interacts with others in a social and open environment. Because there is no knowledge beyond what the individual has, it follows that the individual must experience and test "reality" for himself. The role of the teacher is to act as a guide, not as an informer and certainly not as an authority figure.

The pragmatist defines education broadly. Since education is life (and not preparation for life, as some realists and idealists claim), it is the school's responsibility to provide experiences in living and to foster social adjustment. If driver education creates better and safer drivers and thus prolongs life, it is a legitimate area of education.

Life is not organized around subject matter areas, so pragmatists generally prefer a curriculum based on the child's perceived "needs." Adolescents who are concerned about dating, for example, could examine appropriate aspects of psychology, hygiene, and physiology. In this way subject matter becomes a tool to solve problems, not an end in itself.

The School's "Resolution" of Conflicting Purposes

Because people hold fundamentally different views about the ultimate purposes of education, educators have had to compromise. Any school's curriculum is likely to reflect many different philosophic positions. At one time the teacher may lead students to self-discovery of scientific principles, and at another he may be the authority whose superior knowledge must be accepted.

Because the education profession and the public have not agreed on common objectives of education, long-term purposes, in order to be immune from attack, are often so broadly stated that they are unclear. In 1918, for example, the Commission on the Reorganization of Secondary Education listed the following "cardinal principles" for the public schools:

Good health
Command of fundamental processes
Worthy home membership
Vocational efficiency
Good citizenship
Worthy use of leisure time
Ethical character

This list was modified in 1938 by the Educational Policies Commission to include the following objectives (Carr 1946):

Self-realization
Human relationship
Economic efficiency
Civic responsibility

These lists state no priorities and contain goals so broad that their definition depends on individual preference. Thus in some schools the "command of fundamental processes" may have more priority than the development of "ethical character." To one person, "good citizenship" may stress conformity; to another, it may demand active dissension. The responsibility for delimiting these broad objectives has rested with individual teachers.

Although the schools have not been able to gain a consensus on all specific objectives, some of the broadly stated ones have nevertheless had a strong impact. *The Seven Cardinal Principles of Secondary Education* (Commission on the Reorganization of Secondary Education 1918), for example, helped broaden the curriculum to include more than the three Rs. Besides the "command of fundamental processes," schools were charged with the responsibility of relating the curriculum to healthful living, the student's home life, vocational adjustment, citizenship, the use of leisure time, and the building of ethical character. As points of departure from the traditional curriculum, these broad objectives had a profound impact on American education, yet the vehicle for translating these goals into classroom procedures remained the teacher.

Establishing Priorities among Objectives

The rapid expansion of knowledge has compelled schools to add new programs. In part, this has been accomplished without eliminating courses and programs; more teachers and teacher aides have been added, limits for college entrance have been lowered, materials have been improved (teaching machines, computer-assisted instruction, more effective films, etc.), and the teachers have tried to increase their effectiveness. Because of the number of goals competing for the teacher's time and the school district's funds, not all objectives can be given equal priority. But the question of *who* should determine priorities has never been clearly answered. In theory the school board usually speaks for the citizenry on policy matters, which implies that the board has an obligation to seek statements of goals and priorities from all segments of the community. The board cannot act as a completely independent agent, however, for it also has obligations legislated by the federal and state governments. Theoretically this legislation is also the wish of the public. Superintendents, curriculum experts, and teachers—all who have a voice in determining curricula—must also remain within the confines of government legislative restrictions and mandates, which vary from state to state.

Some attempts have been made to study the process of making priority decisions. Robert Stake and Dennis Gooler (1970), for example, asked teachers and laymen four questions to help establish educational priorities among objectives:

1.   How much is accomplishment of this goal worth in money?
2.   How much school time should be spent in pursuit of this goal?
3.   If this goal is not met, how much should be spent in remediation?
4.   If this goal is not met, how upset should the school people be?

They found that teachers and laymen differed considerably in how various subjects were ranked. Whereas the teachers believed that family life and sex education were most important, the laymen rated it eleventh out of a total of fifteen categories. Perhaps more interesting is the fact that teachers wanted to devote the largest blocks of time to chemistry, physical education, and book-keeping, although they did not rate these subjects as important as sex education and family life. As Stake and Gooler point out, priorities do exist within schools, but they are probably determined more by different group pressures than by careful consideration of the philosophical issues and consequences of student "needs." Even these "needs" are open to different interpretations as figure 3.1 shows.

National News Syndicate, Inc.

Figure 3.1

Various investigators have described the needs of youth. Abraham Maslow (1968) developed a hierarchy in which the satisfaction of more basic needs is prerequisite to the satisfaction of higher-order needs. Children who are hungry, for example, are not likely to attend to intellectual needs; children who do not experience love are not apt to strive for the respect of others or to be motivated to develop cognitive (knowledge) skills. Similarly, the more basic needs would ordinarily take precedence over the higher-order needs should there be a conflict between the two. Maslow's hierarchy of needs is:

Higher-order   1.   Need to know and understand (curiosity, exploration, obtaining knowledge, etc.)

         2.   Self-actualization needs (desire for independence, becoming self-sufficient, self-directed, etc.)

         3.   Esteem needs (feeling confidence, worthiness, usefulness, etc.)

         4.   Love and belonging needs (need for affection, friends, etc.)

         5.   Safety needs (avoidance of danger, disease, fear, etc.)

Basic needs   6.   Physiological needs (food, water, rest, oxygen, etc.)

To help determine the degree of emotional security adults feel, Maslow and his associates (1952) developed a test, the Security-Insecurity Inventory, that contains seventy-five items to be answered yes, no, or "?" This example illustrates how tests are developed to measure an aspect of a general theory of behavior.

Another classification system of needs is Robert Havighurst's developmental tasks (1952). At each stage of growth from infancy to adulthood certain needs must be satisfied if the individual is to be happy and is to progress to the next stage of development. Basic to the concept of developmental tasks is what Havighurst has called the "teachable moment," or the proper time for learning each task. It occurs "when the body is ripe, society requires, and the self is ready to achieve a certain task. . . ."

The developmental tasks of infancy and early childhood (birth to about age six) include learning to walk, taking solid foods, talking, controlling elimination, becoming aware of sex roles, forming simple cognitive concepts, recognizing role structures, and distinguishing elementary concepts of right and wrong. The school presumes that the child has learned these skills and functions by the time he enters school or completes kindergarten. Havighurst has also outlined developmental tasks for middle childhood (ages six to twelve) and adolescence (ages twelve to eighteen).

Dimensions of Educational Objectives

Educational objectives can be described as being process or product, behavioral or implicit, immediate or ultimate, and restricted or inclusive.

Process and Product Objectives

Process objectives describe who will be responsible for a given activity, what the activity is, and when it will be accomplished. The *who* part of a process objective usually refers to the teacher or to the students, but sometimes it may also refer to a specific administrator or parent. The *activity* is a description of what should take place, such as having students read chapters 1 through 3 or listen to various types of music, or having the teacher order films for the year. The *when* of a process objective is a specific date indicating when the activity should be completed.

Some advantages of process objectives are:

Process objectives have the advantage of specifying what someone must do by a specific time to monitor a program and ascertain whether it is on schedule. Process objectives also help the evaluator determine the prior sequencing of activities. For example, a seating plan designed to place hard-of-hearing and nearsighted students in the front of the room near the teacher presumes the capability of administering and interpreting vision and hearing tests. Assigning chapters in a textbook for students to read presumes that these books are available in sufficient quantity when they are needed. One activity depends on a preceding and prerequisite one.

The teacher is not necessarily the only person involved in a process objective. The school nurse, for example, should be consulted to assure that current and accurate health data are available for each child. The nurse, in turn, may depend on the attendance clerk to report which students are new to the school and therfore need hearing and vision tests.

Process objectives help ensure that all important steps or stages in a program have been considered and properly sequenced. They also provide the evaluator with a target date for completing each activity and inform him whether or not he is managing or monitoring the program efficiently and on time. What process objectives do *not* do is indicate the *effectiveness* of the activity. Effectiveness depends on having *product objectives*.

A *product objective* is a statement that indicates what the student must do or know as a result of instruction. Giving an assignment in a textbook is a process, but what the students are expected to do or know as a consequence of the assignment is a product. For example, a professional basketball coach may specify numerous process objectives for himself, his trainers, and the team, but the proposed product may be to win the league championship. At the elementary school level, the physical education teacher's product might be to have his students be "good sports," or more specifically, to admit to personal fouls they might commit and to cheer for the opposing team after the game.

In some instances it may not be necessary to specify a product objective at all; the process of experiencing may be sufficient. It is conceivable, for instance, that a school might want students to explore different art media, different kinds of music, or different kinds of prevocational training courses such as wood and metal shops or cooking or sewing in order to have a broader base from which to plan their futures.

It could be argued, however, that all process objectives ultimately relate to some product. That is, the exploration of various art media should have some effect on the student; doing exercises in physical education should produce a healthy "product." Subjects in which processes are not closely tied to products may be given low priority status in the competition for inclusion in the curriculum. Sports have a high priority partly because there is a clear and valued product (winning); finger painting, show-and-tell sessions, and playing games may be given a lower priority since the product may be difficult to describe and evaluate. This does not argue for or against the legitimacy of stating objectives as processes rather than as products, but it does suggest that American culture is more concerned with results than with the methods used to achieve those ends.

Behavioral and Implicit Objectives

Behavioral objectives specify an observable task (sometimes called a "terminal behavior") that the student must perform to demonstrate that the goal has been attained. Although all behavioral objectives involve student products, not all product objectives are behavioral. Some imply a covert or nonobservable response. These covert or nonobservable responses are *implicit objectives*.

In their most complete form, behavioral objectives contain three elements (Mager 1962):

1. A terminal behavior or overt activity to be performed by the student
2. A specification of the conditions under which the terminal behavior is to be manifested
3. A minimum level of acceptable performance

Consider, for example, the following behavioral objectives:

1. *Recites* the Gettysburg Address without using notes and without error.
2. Given the quadratic formula and no time limit, the student will *solve* at least eight out of ten quadratic equations correctly.
3. *Plays* "Meadowland" on the flute from memory with at least 30 percent fewer errors than exhibited at the end of the tenth week of school.

In each of these objectives the italicized verb refers to an observable response and is therefore a terminal behavior. The conditions under which these behaviors are to be demonstrated have also been specified (i.e., "without using notes," "given the quadratic formula and no time limit," and "from memory"), as have the minimum levels required for competence (i.e., "without error," "eight out of ten," and "30 percent fewer errors than exhibited at the end of the tenth week of school"). Under some conditions it may not be necessary to specify the conditions under which testing is to take place or the minimum level of acceptable performance (this will be discussed later in this section).

Implicit objectives, on the other hand, imply an inner or nonobservable state of *knowing, understanding, appreciating,* and so forth. The following are examples of implicit objectives:

1.   Is aware of his role as a citizen.
2.   Appreciates the role of labor and business.
3.   Understands the differences between socialists and communists.

Some verbs lend themselves to specifying behavioral objectives; others are used to specify implicit objectives:

Verbs Used in Writing Behavioral Objectives	Verbs Used in Writing Implicit Objectives
elects	understands
lists	appreciates
writes	is able to
compares	prepares for
contrasts	develops
solves	learns
constructs	desires
computes	comprehends
locates	is interested in
recites	knows
outlines	is aware of
omits	interprets
ranks	recognizes
counts	shows
circles	clarifies
selects	remembers
completes	is acquainted with

The verbs in the second column are not explicit or observable objectives and therefore cannot be measured unless the desired behaviors are also specified, as in the following example:

Implicit Objective: *To know the difference between implicit and behavioral objectives*

Behavioral Objectives: 1.   *Writes* three examples of behavioral and implicit objectives.
2.   *Checks* all examples of behaviorally stated objectives contained in a list.
3.   *Lists* three advantages of implicit objectives and three advantages of behavioral objectives.

Some verbs, such as *recall, identify,* or *state,* cannot be easily classified as either behavioral or implicit unless additional information is given. For example, if the teacher means that the student will *mentally recall* a given fact, the objective is implicit, but to *recall orally* is an overt behavior. Many other verbs can be used to formulate behavioral objectives if the conditions are made clear or are understood. Some examples of verbs requiring clarification are *planning, judging, criticizing, inferring, modifying, distinguishing, rephrasing, demonstrating, deducing, explaining,* and so forth. These verbs can be made more explicit by indicating the manner or media that will be used to *plan, judge,* etc. Thus *"to infer* the author's purpose" is not behavioral since the process of inferring is not directly observable. But if it is understood that the inference will be made in the form of *selecting, writing,* or *listing,* then the student's behavior is observable and the objective would therefore be behavioral. Similarly, *recognizes* is usually considered to be implicit, such as in the objective *"recognizes* the meaning of the Bill of Rights." But indicating what the student does "to recognize" can make the objective behavioral. For example, "recognizes the meaning of the Bill of Rights by writing a paragraph on each of the first ten amendments of the U. S. Constitution" is a behavioral statement since an observable response is specified. When the conditions under which testing takes place are specified, implicit terms can often be made behavioral.

Much debate in education has occurred between persons who accept only behaviorally stated objectives and those who believe that behavioral objectives are too limiting and restrictive. Rather than join this debate, it may be more instructive to specify under which conditions each type of objective is appropriate.

Conditions that call for behavioral objectives   Behavioral objectives have their greatest use under essentially the same conditions that require criterion-referenced feedback (see p. 53). If subject matter is sequentially ordered and based on the assumption that mastery of prerequisite skills is necessary to advance in the sequence, behavioral objectives provide the teacher with the specific information needed for decision making. Whether the student should be advanced to a more complex task depends on whether he has mastered prerequisite skills. Implicit objectives may not be specific enough to allow the teacher to determine whether or not a standard has been attained.

Second, behavioral objectives are useful in subjects in which a high level of proficiency is required. Before licensing an individual as a commercial airline pilot, one would want to make certain that he was capable of performing at some predetermined level of competence. Behavioral objectives specify what these minimum criteria are.

Third, accountability for student learning requires behaviorally stated objectives. Accountability presumes the ability to determine whether students have met course objectives, and this determination, in turn, presumes an observable response. For example, consider the implicit objective "The student will understand fractions." If the response, "understanding," is implicit and therefore not observable, how can the teacher determine whether he has been successful in teaching this objective? A behaviorally stated objective such as "Students will check the larger of two proper fractions" is a clearer objective since it at least specifies a terminal behavior. The conditions under which students are to manifest this behavior (i.e., given thirty pairs of fractions) and the minimal level of acceptable performance (at least twenty-five correct in thirty minutes) should also be stated.

Fourth, accurate diagnoses of students' difficulties require objectives that are stated behaviorally. For example, a teacher might develop a diagnostic test that requires the student to "add fractions with like denominators." The terminal behavior specifies an observable task ("adds"). The conditions of testing and minimal level of performance could also be specified for greater clarity.

Fifth, when teachers need to communicate on the nature of an objective with other teachers or with students, the objective should be stated behaviorally. Telling a substitute teacher to construct a test on fractions will not be of much help. Students may find it difficult to study for an examination on "repairing common household appliances" since that task is not well defined. However, if they are told that they will be expected to replace a heating element in a toaster to conform with factory specifications in thirty minutes, students can prepare more adequately.

When the conditions of testing are understood, it is not necessary to include them in a behavioral objective. In many cases these conditions are well known by the teacher and students, and nothing is gained by writing them. Most students will not expect to use notes or their textbooks when taking examinations; most will know that they will have a given amount of time to complete the test; and most will understand that they are to receive no help from others in the class. But when the conditions of testing are unique or help to clarify the student's task, they should be included.

Nor is it always necessary to specify a minimal "passing" score. On norm-referenced tests, for example, there may be no minimum level specified in advance. Instead, such tests are designed to measure individual differences, and "passing" is often a function of how well others performed on that test. Furthermore, what constitutes mastery varies greatly from task to task and perhaps from student to student. A teacher may not be willing to specify a minimum level of performance on some tasks if by doing so he creates an impossible goal for some students to attain. He may prefer to specify the terminal behavior, provide instruction, and then test students to determine how much progress they have made. If the task is not required for subsequent learning, he may choose to accept whatever progress the students have made.

Conditions that suggest the use of implicit objectives   A number of situations call for implicit objectives. First, implicit objectives may provide general guidelines or act as reminders to teachers that some goals are important even though their measurement may not be. For example, teachers may want children to learn "to think on their own." This may not be a part of any structured lesson, but it can be a by-product of how the teacher treats students and how lessons are presented even though no formal attempt is made to assess proficiency. Nothing, of course, prevents the teacher from specifying what behavior he is willing to accept as evidence that the student does "think on his own" and thus writing behavioral objectives, but the fact that he can do so does not argue that he should.

Second, some objectives are important, but their measurement may not always be feasible or necessary. Teachers often have little control over what the student does at home or what he will do as an adult, but this does not mean that teachers are concerned only with what the student does in school. The art or shop teacher, for example, may want students to learn to use leisure time wisely but may have no intention of directly measuring whether or not students have accomplished that objective. If teachers are not planning to measure student attainment of an objective, there is no purpose in stating that objective behaviorally.

Third, implicit objectives can form the basis for behavioral objectives. By beginning with an implicit objective, the teacher can generate a number of different behaviorally stated objectives that are tied together by a common element. For example, if a teacher wanted to deliberately teach students how to think for themselves and if he wanted to hold himself accountable in this regard, he could accept any one or all of the following as evidence that he had been successful:

1. The student orally defends his political and social beliefs even when they are attacked by an authority figure.
2. The student goes to the library to gather evidence to support his beliefs.
3. The student questions contradictory statements found in his textbook.

Although these objectives differ from each other, they could all be summarized by an implicit objective such as "The student thinks on his own."

Fourth, implicit objectives may be more communicable to the public than behaviorally stated objectives. An objective such as "The student will be able to read critically" may make more sense to parents than would "The student will list four facts found in a specific story." The terminal behavior, though it is more specific and measurable, does not necessarily suggest *why* the student needs to list facts at all.

Fifth, implicit objectives may be useful for writing items that operationally define the attribute being measured. In this case test performance is specified as acceptable evidence that the objective has been obtained. Instead of describing verbally what the terminal behavior is, the test itself may define the operations that were used to produce it. For example, suppose that a teacher who wanted to measure "the ability to discriminate facts from opinions" developed a series of paragraphs and asked students to list "facts" on one side of the page and "interpretations" on the other. This test describes clearly what the teacher wanted the students to do; it defines the students' task.

The difficulty with this approach is that most tests are samples of different behaviors, traits, skills, or abilities. Should the teacher provide only the test itself, it might be difficult or impossible to determine from what population or universe these items were being sampled. Consider the following ten addition problems:

$$
\begin{array}{cccccccccc}
2 & 5 & 6 & 9 & 7 & 8 & 3 & 5 & 9 & 2 \\
+3 & +4 & +2 & +0 & +1 & +4 & +4 & +6 & +6 & +4
\end{array}
$$

What do these items measure? The addition of single-digit whole numbers whose sums are equal to or less than 15? Or perhaps the addition of any two single-digit whole numbers from 0 to 9? It is important to specify what universe these ten items represent if teachers want to include more items of the same type. Given the implicit objective "The student will know how to add combinations of two-single-digit whole numbers," the universe would be delineated, and teachers could add more items to the samples and disregard whether the sums of the two numbers were equal to or less than 15.

Immediate and Ultimate Objectives

Many school activities are designed to prepare the student for future events such as marriage, employment, coping with leisure time in a four-day work week, and being able to vote intelligently. To measure the effectiveness of a curriculum in meeting these long-range objectives would require expensive and complex procedures. In some instances teachers might have to wait a considerable time before the student is ready for marriage or a job or is capable of voting. Because the school has little influence over what adults do, it usually concerns itself with more immediate objectives, over which it does have some control.

Although teachers cannot check directly on their effectiveness in teaching ultimate objectives, they can and should be certain that students have learned those behaviors within their ability and time limitations to teach. Thus although "intelligent voting" could not easily be measured by teachers, it is possible to make certain that students understand the immediate issues related to voting— the various political parties, advantages and limitations of various forms of government, the historical conditions that lead to social unrest, and so forth.

In recent years students have questioned the relevance of some aspects of the curriculum. Their charge is valid when teachers assign such tasks as "Memorize the names of all vice-presidents of the United States" or "Memorize a list of seventy adverbs" (these examples, by the way, are not contrived) without explaining their importance. Sometimes close examination confirms that an objective is picayunish; in other cases presenting the rationale for a topic's inclusion in the curriculum might make it more palatable.

Restricted and Inclusive Objectives

Some objectives are so restricted that they are practically equivalent to the test item itself; others are more broadly stated to allow for the inclusion of numerous samples of behaviors from the same designated universe. Some examples of restricted and inclusive objectives are:

Restricted Objectives

Adds 1 + 1, 2 + 1, 3 + 1, 4 + 1, 5 + 1, 6 + 1, 7 + 1, 8 + 1, 9 + 1, 2 + 1, 2 + 2, 2 + 3, . . . 9 + 9.

Orally identifies the following colors: red, yellow, blue, green, orange, and violet.

Writes the name of the inn where Long John Silver met Jim Hawkins. Writes the names of four nations visited by Lemuel Gulliver in his travels. Orally names five persons whom Dorothy met in *The Wizard of Oz.*

Inclusive Objectives

Adds groups of two single-digit whole numbers from 1 to 9.

Orally identifies primary and secondary colors.

Recalls (by writing) specific facts of stories he has read.

Examine the list of restricted objectives. Each of the three examples contains a number of objectives which, when taken separately, closely approximate a test item. Thus "adds 1 + 1" could by itself be transformed into a test item by asking the student to write his answer to that problem on a sheet of paper. However, when all of the addition objectives are considered together, they completely describe the inclusive objective "adds groups of two single-digit whole numbers from 1 to 9." The same line of reasoning applies to the second example. One could write six separate objectives to represent all the primary and secondary colors or write the more inclusive objective "orally identifies primary and secondary colors." In these two examples the inclusive objectives completely encompass their restricted counterparts.

The third example is different from the first two in a number of ways. First, the inclusive objective does not specify what facts or stories will be selected for the student to recall. Second, whichever ones are selected will not compose the universe or totality of all possible stories that could have been selected. Third, should teachers be given only the restricted objectives, they might have difficulty determining the inclusive objective.

In logic, drawing a conclusion based on complete enumeration of all facts or observations is called induction by complete enumeration. If one should describe each of 30 students in a classroom as being female, it can be inductively concluded that all students in that room are female. This is analogous to describing what the student must do for each color and then concluding that he is to "identify primary and secondary colors." The conclusion is a simple summary statement of all elements that compose it.

Sometimes, however, teachers are not provided with a complete catalogue of student behaviors from which to generalize. Instead, they may be given only partial information from which they try to draw a general conclusion. This is called induction by incomplete enumeration since all the elements that enter into the conclusion are not specified. Thus if no information were given on the number of boys and girls in a given school, it might be concluded that all were females if the first thirty selected at random were females. In this example it cannot be certain that the conclusion is right, and even one negative instance would make it necessary to modify the conclusion.

Inclusive objectives are much like general conclusions. They may completely describe everything the student must do, or they may contain selected samples of behavior. The samples themselves may not be crucial except as they act as evidence that the more inclusive objective has been reached. In some cases many different examples could have been selected for the same inclusive objective.

Only inclusive objectives need be written by the teacher if the restricted counterparts are completely enumerated, as in the first two examples on page 56, because these objectives contain all elements common to the restricted objectives. However, if the inclusive objective can be measured by many different restricted objectives, it is necessary to write the inclusive objective and then indicate what specific restricted samples will be used.

One other point should be made. If a restricted objective is not a part of a clearly defined inclusive objective, the teacher should consider its value for the student. For example, knowing the names of the four nations visited by Gulliver in his travels is not by itself a particularly important objective. Whatever importance it has is gained by being related to a more inclusive objective, such as teaching children how to read for detail.

The Cognitive, Affective, and Psychomotor Domains

Objectives may be conveniently categorized as cognitive, affective, or psychomotor. *Cognitive objectives* emphasize the attainment, retention, and development of knowledge and intellect. The acquisition of subject matter—whether it is very simple or complex in nature—is primarily a cognitive function. The *affective domain* encompasses those behaviors characterized by feelings, emotions, or values. Affect is usually positive (directed toward some goal object) or negative (directed against a goal object). Thus a student may be favorably or unfavorably impressed by his teachers, the school, or the curriculum. The *psychomotor domain* refers to muscular or motor behaviors. Running, using tools, speaking, and handwriting may be classified as psychomotor activities.

The categorizing of behaviors into domains does not necessarily imply that the domains are completely independent of each other. When a student gives a speech, for example, all three domains may be involved, although probably not equally. If the teacher is primarily concerned with the student's presentation (gestures, voice inflection, movement), he is emphasizing a psychomotor skill; to the extent that the concern is with the organization and content of the speech, it is primarily a cognitive task; concern with pleasantness or unpleasantness places the task in the affective domain. What aspect the teacher is emphasizing largely determines in which domain the behavior should be classified.

The Cognitive Domain

Benjamin Bloom and his associates (1956) have divided cognitive objectives into six categories: knowledge, comprehension, application, analysis, synthesis, and evaluation (see table 3.1). Their purpose in developing a taxonomy of educational objectives was (p. 12):

> It should be noted that we are not attempting to classify the instructional methods used by teachers, the ways in which teachers relate themselves to students, or the different kinds of instructional materials they use. We are not attempting to classify the particular subject matter or content. What we are classifying is the *intended behavior* of students—the ways in which individuals are to act [or] think . . . as the result of participating in some unit of instruction.

The behaviors in the taxonomy include implicit and overt behaviors. An attempt was made to categorize these behaviors by complexity, but the taxonomy is not entirely successful in this regard. It is difficult to examine a test item and categorize it without knowing what the students have studied previously. Also, some test items contain aspects that may refer to various levels of the taxonomy. Nonetheless, the taxonomy is important for teachers because it provides a reasonably complete description of goals that should be considered before tests are constructed. The categories help to remind teachers of the vast number of alternatives they have when developing tests.

Knowledge　According to Bloom, the simplest level of complexity is *knowledge.* The knowledge objective requires a student to answer questions solely by rote memory and to recall simple definitions, facts, rules, sequences, procedures, principles, and generalizations. Unfortunately it is probably safe to say that the great majority of items constructed by teachers are on the knowledge level and require little thinking on the part of students (or teachers for that matter). An examination that places a premium on rote knowledge and excludes thinking and reasoning can give students the impression that the sole purpose of education is memorizing facts.

Comprehension　The second level of complexity, *comprehension,* involves translating from one level of abstraction to another. This type of objective requires students to restate a problem in their own words, to give an example of a principle or concept, to qualify statements, to extrapolate trends into the past or future, or to point out implications or consequences.

Table 3.1. An Outline of Bloom's *Taxonomy of Educational Objectives: Cognitive Domain*

Level	Examples
1.00 Knowledge	
1.11 Knowledge of terminology	Simple definition required
1.12 Knowledge of specific facts	Dates, events, persons, places
1.21 Knowledge of conventions	Rules of etiquette, grammar
1.22 Knowledge of trends and sequences	Processes, directions regarding time
1.23 Knowledge of classifications and categories	Classes, sets, divisions, arrangements useful to a given field
1.24 Knowledge of criteria	Criteria to evaluate facts, principles, etc.
1.25 Knowledge of methodology	Techniques and procedures
1.31 Knowledge of principles and generalizations	Abstractions which summarize observations of phenomena
1.32 Knowledge of theories and structures	Body of principles and generalizations
2.00 Comprehension	
2.10 Translation of one level of abstraction to another; translation from one form to another form	Restating a problem, reducing size of communication, giving an example
2.20 Interpretation	Reordering and rearranging, qualifying
2.30 Extrapolation	Extension of data to past or future
3.00 Application	Applying data to new problems
4.00 Analysis	
4.10 Analysis of elements	Finding assumptions, distinguishing facts and opinion
4.20 Analysis of relationships	Relevant data, causal, finding fallacies
4.30 Analysis of organizational principles	Form and style, inferring author's purpose
5.00 Synthesis	
5.10 Production of a unique communication	Skill in writing, telling stories, composing
5.20 Production of a plan, or proposed set of operations	Proposing hypotheses, planning units, tool designing
1.30 Derivation of a set of abstract relations	Formulation of a theory
6.00 Evaluation	
6.10 Judgments in terms of internal evidence	Evaluation by logical accuracy, consistency, and other internal criteria
6.20 Judgments in terms of external criteria	Evaluating theories, judging by standards, weighing values

From Benjamin S. Bloom, *Taxonomy of Educational Objectives, Handbook I: Cognitive Domain*, pp 201–207. © 1956 by David McKay Company, Inc. Used with permission.

Application   *Application* is the third level of complexity. At this level students apply principles or concepts in new situations, such as working word problems in arithmetic or physics.

Analysis   The fourth level of complexity, *analysis,* requires students to break down information into its constituent parts. Finding assumptions, distinguishing facts from opinion, discovering causal relationships, finding fallacies in stories or arguments, specifying the style of a written or musical piece, or inferring the author's purposes are items that require analysis.

Synthesis   When a student is required to produce a story, composition, hypothesis, or theory on his own, he is synthesizing knowledge. At this level the student produces something unique; instead of breaking knowledge into simpler elements (analysis), he constructs a unique communication of his own.

Evaluation   According to Bloom, the most complex form of cognitive measurement is *evaluation,* which involves placing a value judgment on data in order to make a decision. At this level the student evaluates such information as historical evidence, editorials, and theories by their internal consistency or by external standards. Unfortunately few teachers develop test items at this level because they are often uncertain how to measure these more complex objectives.

Newton Metfessel, William Michael, and Donald Kirsner (1969) have published a sample list of verbs and direct objects to facilitate the writing of behavioral objectives from the cognitive domain of Bloom's taxonomy (see appendix 8). The first column in appendix 8, titled Taxonomy Classification, is a list of infinitives that either are behavioral (to tell, to write, to choose) or are easily converted to behavioral objectives by specifying the conditions under which testing is to take place ("to recall orally and without notes"); the last column contains examples of direct objects of these verbs, but no attempt was made to force all infinitives to fit each of the direct objects. Appendix 8 is a useful guide for writing behavioral objectives at various levels of complexity.

The Affective Domain

Five levels describing the affective domain of educational objectives have been published by David Krathwohl, Benjamin Bloom, and Bertram Masia (1956): receiving (attending), responding, valuing, organization, and characterization (see table 3.2).

Receiving or attending   If teachers are to inculcate or encourage the development of favorable affective responses, students must be ready to accept or become sensitized to stimuli. The student who refuses to listen to classical music is not likely to modify his negative preconceptions.

The lowest subcategory under *receiving* (level 1.0) is *awareness* (level 1.1), which presumes some minimum consciousness or knowledge. For example, determining whether students are aware of the projective elements of abstract paintings could be measured by asking them to observe a series of abstractions and to interpret what, if anything, they see. Those who claim they see "nothing" or who describe abstractions as "blobs" are not aware of the projective feelings such paintings attempt to convey. Or students might be asked to categorize paintings in as many different ways as possible in the expectation that some of them might eventually use an abstract-realistic continuum.

The next highest subcategory *willingness to receive* (level 1.2). Instead of simply being aware, the student is now willing to attend to or at least to not actively avoid some stimulus. Evidence for being willing to receive is usually

Table 3.2 An Outline of Krathwohl's *Taxonomy of Educational Objectives: The Affective Domain*

Level	Examples
1.0 Receiving (Attending)	
1.1 Awareness	Perceives, is aware of, takes into account
1.2 Willingness to receive	Tolerates, does not avoid
1.3 Controlled or selected attention	Differentiates, attends to certain portions and disregards others
2.0 Responding	
2.1 Acquiescence in responding	Obeys, is compliant, does what he is told
2.2 Willingness to respond	Responds voluntarily without force and on his own
2.3 Satisfaction in response	Enjoys what he is doing, gains satisfaction
3.0 Valuing	
3.1 Acceptance of a value	Highly tentative commitment to a belief, questions beliefs, identifies with a belief
3.2 Preference for a value	Actively pursues his beliefs, willing to devote time and effort in pursuing values, volunteers
3.3 Commitment	Strongly certain that his beliefs are correct, loyal to beliefs, willing to work hard for his goals
4.0 Organization	
4.1 Conceptualization of a value	Clarifies the meaning of his beliefs, shows their interrelationships, makes generalizations
4.2 Organization of a value system	Orders and organizes to make them internally consistent and compatible
5.0 Characterization by a Value or Value Complex	
5.1 Generalized set	Responds in accordance with a generalized value system
5.2 Characterization	Consistently responds in accordance with a philosophy of life

Who?	Activity?	When?
Teacher	Check each child's health records to determine which students will need special teaching considerations.	By end of first week of school *t*
Teacher	Develop a seating arrangement plan based on each child's special needs.	By end of second week of school
Teacher	Develop a method of evaluating the effectiveness of the seating arrangement.	By end of second week of school

the student's indication of whether he likes, dislikes, or is indifferent to some activity. In this example the concern is not *how much* the student likes or dislikes the activity but whether he has some minimal willingness to consider it. Presuming, for example, that a student has some *awareness* of pictorial abstractions, his willingness to tolerate that topic (despite being neutral toward it) indicates a *willingness to receive*.

The highest sublevel under receiving is *controlled or selected attention* (level 1.3). When students respond at this level, they express a preference for some activity and actively select it from among others. They are capable of controlling their own attention to attend to some favored stimulus (such as rhythm in poetry, background music in movies, examples of split infinitives, or incorrect pronunciations) "despite competing and distracting stimuli."

Responding   At level 2.0, in *responding,* the student does more than merely receive or attend to stimuli; he responds to them in various degrees of zest.

The lowest sublevel in the responding category is *acquiescence in responding* (level 2.1). The two key words that describe this level are *obedience* and *compliance.* The student participates in an activity because he submissively accepts the requirements or suggestions of his teacher. Given a choice, he might select some other alternative. The student who visits an art gallery because the teacher requires it is functioning at this level.

Level 2.2 in the affective domain is *willingness to respond.* At this level the student responds voluntarily, not out of obedience or compliance. He is under no obligation and there is no veiled or explicit threat of punishment for not responding. He engages in an activity because of his genuine interest, not because the teacher has suggested or requires it. The student who voluntarily visits an art gallery, reads books not on a required reading list, or studies some subject in greater depth than is required is responding at this level.

The highest sublevel in category 2.0 is *satisfaction in response* (level 2.3). The important consideration at this level is enjoyment or satisfaction. Not only might the student visit an art gallery but he enjoys it; not only does he read books not required but he enjoys them as well. Satisfaction in response can be measured by having students indicate degrees of enjoyment on a three- or five-point rating scale, or by using student comments, gestures, grimaces, and laughter as evidence.

Valuing   Level 3.0, *valuing,* involves placing a judgment of worthiness on some belief or attitude and implies some degree of internalization and commitment. Valuing also implies consistency in responding to a general class of objects or beliefs to the point where others recognize this general pattern.

Level 3.1 is called *acceptance of a value.* At this level the student has only a tentative commitment toward some belief or attitude he considers important and worthy; he would still rather "switch than fight." But he does regard the object of his commitment—whether belief, person, or phenomenon—as more valuable than a mere source of pleasure and satisfaction; it now possesses intrinsic value.

Preference for a value is level 3.2. The degree of commitment is greater than in level 3.1 but not yet as strong as a moral pledge to behave in a certain way. At this level the student has not only begun to accept some belief but he is willing to actively pursue the valued object, belief, or phenomenon. The difference between levels 3.1 and 3.2 is largely one of degree. The student who has a preference for a value is willing to devote greater time, effort, and (perhaps) funds in pursuing his values than is the student who merely accepts a value. The student is more involved and demonstrates this involvement by actively contributing to the valued object or phenomenon. For example, he may work for a political candidate in whom he places great value; he may volunteer his time to work with disadvantaged children; or he may engage in public debates to express his ideals.

The highest sublevel in valuing is called *commitment* (level 3.3). The student is convinced that his values are correct, and he is loyal to the point where convincing others becomes important. He not only is involved in pursuing his values but he is driven to do so. He has a devotion to a cause or belief that demands a continued and sustained effort to achieve some goal. The committed person would much rather "fight than switch."

Organization   The fourth level in the affective domain is *organization*. Values become interrelated and priorities are developed among them to form a value system. Pacifism as a value, for example, raises numerous questions related to social, economic, political, and moral beliefs. These beliefs require the elimination of inconsistencies and the development of priorities consonant with the value system.

Level 4.0 is organized into two sublevels: *conceptualization of a value* and *organization of a value system*. Admittedly conceptualization does not always follow commitment—in some instances the commitment may result from the conceptualization—but organization of a value system ordinarily requires its conceptualization.

Conceptualization of a value (level 4.1) involves an abstract and therefore symbolic set of interrelated values. These values are conceptualized by analyzing their interrelationships and by drawing generalizations that represent the value system. The student who attempts to conceptualize his interpretation of good art is operating at this level, as is the student who wants to identify the factors common to all religions or branches of science. When values are conceptualized the process is largely cognitive, but this level of conceptualization was undertaken because of a highly developed affective value system.

In level 4.2, *organization of a value system,* the values that have been conceptualized in level 4.1 are now ordered in an attempt to make them internally consistent and compatible with each other. For example, students capable of organizing their value systems can consistently rank activities related to theoretical, economic, aesthetic, social, political, or religious values (Allport, Vernon, and Lindzey 1960).

Characterization by a value or value complex   The highest level of the affective domain is *characterization by a value or value complex*. Persons at this level not only have an organized value system (level 4.2) but are capable of behaving in accordance with a consistent "philosophy of life." They know who they are and what they stand for, and they act accordingly.

The two sublevels in this category are *generalized set* (level 5.1) and *characterization* (level 5.2). *Generalized set* means that the individual is ready or predisposed to respond in accordance with his value system when he faces new problems. In effect, his values help determine what he perceives as important, what approaches he will take or consider to remedy problems, and how tenaciously he pursues a given course of action. At this level the student's mode of approach to a problem is of major concern. For example, the student who is confident of his own abilities could be expected to respond positively to a wide range of situations calling for a judgment of probable success; the pragmatist should be expected to evaluate different issues by their consequences rather than by emotional appeals or dogmatic assertions.

Level 5.2, *characterization,* is the highest level in the affective domain, according to Krathwohl and his associates. It refers to the development of a philosophy of life that is all-encompassing and that gives character to those capable of reaching this level. The philosophy is internally consistent, and the individual acts in accordance with his philosophy. Those few individuals who have reached this level are recognized as being complete persons who behaved in accordance with their ideals and beliefs. Such figures as Albert Schweitzer, Mahatma Gandhi, Joan of Arc, and Jesus Christ attained this level of integration.

Students probably cannot be expected to advance much beyond levels 2 or 3 as a result of any given experience or set of experiences in class. Level 4, if it is to be a serious goal of education, will require that teachers help students clarify and organize their own value systems. Level 5 will be attained by very few students—perhaps only by those who are capable of attaining what Maslow has called "self-actualization,"—those who "need to know and understand" (see p. 47). Like many other long-term objectives of education, the attainment of "characterization" depends on the acquisition of more immediate values and beliefs that teachers can help students acquire. Teachers interested in helping students develop in the affective domain will find the infinitives and direct objects listed in appendix 8 helpful.

The Psychomotor Domain

The psychomotor domain includes behaviors that rely heavily on the muscular system, including running, jumping, speaking, typing, hammering, drilling, and so forth. All individuals engage in psychomotor activities to different degrees. For very young children, the developmental tasks may emphasize such psychomotor activities as eating, drinking, crawling, walking, and elimination. During the early elementary grades children learn such physical activities as throwing, catching, using simple tools, and developing hand-eye coordination. As individuals mature, the psychomotor skills become more complex and may depend on stronger cognitive and affective components. In many sports activities, for example, it might be difficult to determine which domain is prepotent at any given moment.

A taxonomy for the psychomotor domain has recently been published by Harrow (1972). A number of different systems could form the basis for a taxonomy. For example, it is possible to categorize psychomotor activities by the degree of endurance, strength, and speed required. Psychomotor objectives could also be organized by function, with life-sustaining activities as the most basic and perhaps creative activities at the highest level.

Other Taxonomies

Taxonomies of objectives have been developed for specific school subjects. Thomas C. Barrett (Clymer 1968), for example, has prepared a combination cognitive and affective taxonomy for reading comprehension which is reproduced in outline form as table 3.3. Some aspects of Barrett's taxonomy could be adapted to art and music comprehension and appreciation if some leeway is granted to the interpretation of the various categories. In music, for example, level 3.3 (inferring sequence) could be used to see if students can predict how a particular refrain will end, but this category might not be particularly important in art. Conversely, students of art might consider an analogue to level 3.1 (i.e., suggesting additional ways or techniques that might have made the drawing or painting more interesting or appealing) as having somewhat greater importance. The selected readings at the end of this chapter suggest sources of objectives and taxonomies. The main advantage of the Bloom and Krathwohl taxonomies is their utility in different subjects.

Item Sampling and Selection

Examinations should be composed of items that represent important and clearly stated objectives. An examination "on chapter one" may not define what is important in that chapter or provide much of a guide for students preparing for the test. Some teachers unintentionally construct most of their test items from very few pages of an assigned chapter simply because many "facts" are presented on those pages. To develop a more representative test of the chapter as a whole, a two-way grid listing content areas on one side and level of item complexity across the top may be prepared as shown in table 3.4. In general,

Table 3.3. An Outline of Barrett's Taxonomy of Reading

1.0 Literal comprehension (concern with information stated explicitly)
   1.1 Recognition (locate specific information stated explicitly)
      1.11 Recognition of details (names of characters, places, and times)
      1.12 Recognition of main ideas
      1.13 Recognition of a sequence
      1.14 Recognition of comparison (identify similarities among characters, places, and times)
      1.15 Recognition of cause and effect relationships
      1.16 Recognition of character traits
   1.2 Recall (produce from memory ideas stated explicitly)
      1.21 Recall of details
      1.22 Recall of main ideas
      1.23 Recall of a sequence
      1.24 Recall of comparisons
      1.25 Recall of cause and effect relationships
      1.26 Recall of character traits

2.0 Reorganization (concern with analyzing, synthesizing, and organizing information that has been stated explicitly)
   2.1 Classifying (placing persons, things, and places into categories)
   2.2 Outlining (organizing a selection in outline form)
   2.3 Summarizing (paraphrasing or condensing a selection)
   2.4 Synthesizing (consolidating information from more than a single source)

3.0 Inferential comprehension (using information explicitly stated along with one's own personal experiences as a basis for conjecture and hypothesis)
   3.1 Inferring supporting details (suggesting additional facts that might have made the selection more informative, interesting, or appealing)
   3.2 Inferring main ideas (providing the main idea when it is not stated explicitly)
   3.3 Inferring sequence (conjecturing about what might have happened or will happen when no explicit statements are included in the selection)
   3.4 Inferring comparisons
   3.5 Inferring cause and effect relationships (inferring the author's intentions, motivations, or characters)
   3.6 Inferring character traits (hypothesizing characteristics of persons included in a selection)
   3.7 Predicting outcomes (predicting what will happen as a result of reading only part of a selection)
   3.8 Interpreting figurative language (inferring literal meanings from the figurative use of language)

4.0 Evaluation (judgments and decisions regarding value and worth)
   4.1 Judgments of reality or fantasy (judging whether an event is possible)
   4.2 Judgments of fact or opinion (distinguishing between supported and unsupported data)
   4.3 Judgments of adequacy and validity (judging whether or not a selection agrees with other sources of information)
   4.4 Judgments of appropriateness (determining relative adequacy of different parts of a selection in answering specific questions)
   4.5 Judgments of worth, desirability, and acceptability (decisions of good and bad, right or wrong)

5.0 Appreciation (psychological and aesthetic impact of the selection on the reader)
   5.1 Emotional response to content (verbalizing feelings about the selection)
   5.2 Identification with characters or incidents (demonstrating sensitivity to or empathy with characters or events)
   5.3 Reactions to the author's use of language (responding to the author's ability to select the most appropriate connotations and denotations of words)
   5.4 Imagery (verbalizing feelings produced by the author's selection of words that produce visual, auditory, etc., sensations or images)

the following criteria should determine the approximate number of items for each objective: (1) the relative importance or weight assigned content areas, (2) the relative emphasis given to the levels of complexity in Bloom's taxonomy, and (3) the amount of class time devoted to each topic. Many of the lower-level objectives in the taxonomy are taught not so much because of their intrinsic values but because they allow students to engage in more complex activities that are considered important. Students are taught what a dictionary is so they can use one when needed; they are taught addition not for its own sake but because it helps solve problems. Because the taxonomy is hierarchical, it can be used to remind the teacher of the importance of including these higher-order objectives on the examination.

The distribution of items on a 50-item test could look like the two-way grid in table 3.4. The numbers within the grid are estimates of the totals for

Table 3.4. Example of a Two-Way Grid Useful in Item Sampling

Major Content Areas	Specific Content Areas	Levels of Item Complexity							
		Knowledge	Comprehension	Application	Analysis	Synthesis	Evaluation	Totals	Percentage
The role of measurement, testing, and evaluation	Physical measurements (Historical background)	3	2					5	10%
Measurement, testing, and evaluation	Measurement	1						1	6%
	Testing	1						1	
	Evaluation	1						1	
Reasons for using tests	Selection	1			1	1		3	56%
	Placement	1			1	1		3	
	Remediation			1	1	1	1	4	
	Feedback								
	A. Norm-referenced			3	1	1		5	
	B. Criterion-referenced				1	1		2	
	Motivation				2	2	2	6	
	Program improvement			2	1	1		4	
	Theory development				1			1	
Types of tests	Individual and group			1		1		2	28%
	Objective and subjective	1	1					2	
	Power and speed			2				2	
	Verbal and nonverbal		1	1				2	
	Performance & pencil-&-paper		1					1	
	Sample and sign		1			1		2	
	Teacher-made & standardized	1	1				1	3	
								50	100%

each major content area according to weights established by the teacher's estimate of importance or the amount of class time devoted to each topic. These numbers are always approximations and need not be adhered to rigidly when constructing the test. The grid also provides a guideline for constructing objectives by reminding the teacher of the content and the levels of complexity that might be included on the test. The total number of items on each topic is determined by its importance; importance, in turn, can be suggested by the hierarchical categories of the taxonomy; and the taxonomy can be used, along with content, to suggest the objectives for the examination. It is important to remember that the grid lists content areas but not what the student must *do* to meet the criteria for an instructional unit. Behavioral objectives serve that purpose.

As an example of how this procedure works, consider the topic on the grid titled Objective and subjective tests. What should students be able to do as a result of reading this section in the text? The six levels of objectives from Bloom's taxonomy can help here. Here are some possibilities:

Level	Terminal Behavior
1.11	To define "objective" and "subjective" tests
1.24	To identify the criteria for an "objective" test
2.10	To restate in one's own words what an "objective" test is
2.20	To distinguish between an "objective" and "subjective" test
4.10	To identify the assumptions underlying the differences between "objective" and "subjective" tests
5.10	To originate a set of specifications for determining whether a test is "objective" or "subjective"
6.10	To assess the fallacies of categorizing tests as "objective" or "subjective"

These examples by no means exhaust the possibilities available to the teacher, but they do force him into deciding what he wants the students to learn. For example, suppose the teacher wants students "to define 'objective' and 'subjective' tests." Although the terminal behavior has been specified, the conditions under which the student is to demonstrate his ability to define these terms have not been stated. These terms could be defined orally, in writing, or by selecting a correct alternative. These conditions need not be stated formally if they are clearly understood.

In selecting a level 1.11 objective, the teacher has in effect developed a highly restricted objective. A more inclusive objective could be written which would encompass definitions of all different types of tests presented in that chapter (individual and group, objective and subjective, power and speed, and so forth). Should this be done, each type of test could be included on the examination for students to define. If this were done, fourteen items, or 28 percent of the test, would consist of memorizing definitions. An alternative might be sampling or selecting three or four terms to define; or the teacher might prefer to have students define some terms while identifying the assumptions underlying others. If objectives are derived from levels 5 and 6 of the taxonomy, the teacher will have to be satisfied with sampling fewer items since each item will be complex and time-consuming for students. Which alternatives will be selected depends in part on the kind of information the teacher wants to obtain and the reasons for giving the test (diagnosis, feedback, motivation, etc.).

For *criterion-referenced tests,* the teacher needs to specify the minimal level of acceptable performance. For a highly restricted objective such as specified by level 1.11 above ("to define 'objective' and 'subjective' tests"), the minimum passing score for the item that measures that objective would probably be set at a very high level (i.e., both terms defined correctly) since only one item can measure that objective. But as the level of complexity is increased or as the objective becomes more inclusive, the teacher is more likely to accept a lower level of achievement unless 100 percent mastery of important or fundamental skills or knowledge is required. For *norm-referenced tests,* a minimal level of proficiency is usually established after the examination has been administered.

Some Preliminary Considerations

One of the most important responsibilities of the teacher is to determine which student outcomes are to be given high priority. These decisions are rooted in one's philosophy of education and in an assessment of student needs. In most instances teachers are given wide latitude in making such decisions, although they must operate within legislated, administrative, and community regulations and mores.

In addition to questions about the establishment of objectives and selection of teaching methods and materials, teachers often raise such related questions as: When, if ever, should open-book examinations be used? How often should tests be given? Should tests be announced in advance? How should items be presented? These questions will be discussed here. The question of how difficult the test should be will be discussed in chapter 9.

Open-Book and Closed-Book
Examinations

Open-book tests allow students to use their books or notes during the examination. In courses where objectives emphasize some of the higher levels of Bloom's taxonomy, the teacher may want students to apply specific formulas, facts, or information rather than spending time memorizing them. It is common, for example, to allow chemistry students to use the periodic table when taking tests or to allow students to use maps, slide rules, blueprints, and formulas in other classes.

Open-book examinations have their greatest value when (1) the teacher wants students to apply rather than memorize information or (2) when the teacher wants students to learn how to use reference materials within a time limit. In some classes it may not be important for students to memorize formulas, symbols, or procedures even though the teacher may want students to use them in solving problems. If students are allowed to use their notes or other reference material, they can devote more time to learning to apply this information. In subjects where memorized knowledge is prerequisite to and necessary for subsequent learning, the teacher may want students to demonstrate their knowledge without using references. Whether an open-book test or a closed-book exam is administered often depends on the criterion for evaluating learning. In some instances this criterion is the amount of time that will be saved by the student when he relearns the same material in the future. The procedure for measuring the amount of time saved is to require students to demonstrate 100 percent mastery and then to relearn the same information later. The time it takes students to relearn is then compared with the time it takes students who have never learned the material. In other cases the criterion for learning might be whether the student is capable of recalling or reproducing information he has learned previously. For example, teachers would no doubt want students to reproduce the alphabet from memory and would not be satisfied if they could do so only with the aid of references. That skill is basic enough to insist upon memorization and perfect mastery.

Some teachers allow students to use references but include a large number of items on the test to discourage overuse of sources. The student who must rely heavily on his notes is penalized by not having sufficient time to look up the information he needs. Presumably this procedure requires a higher level of initial proficiency in learning than does allowing the student to be completely dependent on references. When objectives emphasize speed in using reference materials, the open-book examination may have much to recommend it.

Other claims for the open-book examination are not well founded on research data, but they appear to be reasonable from a common-sense point of view. Some persons argue that cheating and test anxiety are reduced with open-book tests since the student can use resource information, but at least one study (Kalish 1958) found little difference in the average attainment and attitudes of students taking open-book and closed-book tests.

The take-home exam is an extension of the open-book test. Students can work at their leisure and at their most comfortable rate of speed using whatever resources are available. This type of testing is most useful when students need to use a wide variety of resources that might not be available in the typical classroom. The two major disadvantages of the take-home test are the difficulty of objectively scoring long, complex answers and the possibility that students might not do their own work. Methods of scoring essay tests will be considered in chapter 5, but take-home examinations that allow for a wide variety of student responses are among the most difficult to score objectively. However, if the take-home test is used as an exercise or teaching device to indicate student strengths, weaknesses, and methods of improvement (rather than for "grading"), it can still be a valuable help for students.

There is no entirely satisfactory way of guaranteeing that students do their own work on a take-home exam. Indeed, obtaining help from others may be both a defensible and desirable method of studying if the test is a learning exercise to help students prepare for an in-class test. Some teachers encourage students to collaborate with each other or with other persons in seeking answers to take-home tests. As Robert Ebel (1965) has suggested, students may put forth a good deal of effort and may produce high-quality papers when they are given the opportunity to seek information from all available resources. But most teachers probably agree that the student should be doing his own work. In a book titled *College Days* (1923, pp. 21–22), Stephen Leacock recalls his experiences with and attitudes toward students who depended on others to do their work for them:

> But the greatest nuisance of all to the schoolmaster is the parent who does the boy's home exercises and works his boy's sums. I suppose they mean well by it. But it is a disastrous thing to do for any child. Whenever I found myself correcting exercises that had obviously been done for the boys in their homes I used to say to them:
> "Paul, tell your father that he *must* use the ablative after *pro*."
> "Yes, sir," says the boy.
> "And, Edward, you tell your grandmother that her use of the dative case simply won't do. She's getting along nicely and I'm well satisfied with the way she's doing, but I cannot have her using the dative right and left on every occasion. Tell her it won't do."
> "Yes, sir," says little Edward.
> I remember one case in particular of a parent who did not do the boy's exercise but, after letting the boy do it himself, wrote across the face of it a withering comment addressed to me and reading: "From this exercise you can see that my boy, after six months of your teaching, is completely ignorant. How do you account for it?"
> I sent the exercise back to him with the added note: "I think it might be hereditary."

The Frequency of Testing

The frequency of testing depends on the function the test is to serve. In most cases a single testing period may suffice for selection, placement and summative evaluation decisions. For diagnosis, formative evaluation, and motivation more frequent testing may be necessary or desirable.

When the purpose of testing is to provide feedback, some advantage may be gained by administering numerous examinations, particularly during the early stages of learning, when students need guidance and direction from the teacher to get them on the right track. Such tests are not necessarily graded but are given to help students acquire knowledge as efficiently as possible. The tests thus function as learning exercises.

Usually the frequency of testing is important to teachers because they want the tests to motivate student achievement. Some teachers believe that frequent testing encourages good study habits; others take the position that frequent testing takes too much time away from instruction. The empirical evidence does not point definitely to a frequency of tests that best motivates students. In an early study, Victor Noll (1939) found no relationship between achievement and frequency of testing for "average" students; for those of lower ability, frequent testing (weekly or biweekly) seemed to improve achievement. Other studies have confirmed the value of frequent tests for the less able student (Keys 1934; Ross and Henry 1939), provided that testing is not overdone (Weiden 1945). In general, it appears that frequent testing motivates students to learn, particularly the student of lower ability. Another consideration that favors frequent testing is that students prefer it (Keys 1934; Ross and Henry 1939).

The Effect of Unannounced Tests

Surprise tests are generally not recommended. First, the evidence suggests that students perform at slightly higher levels when they are informed about a forthcoming examination than when the test is unannounced (Tyler and Chalmers 1943). Second, unannounced exams may create unnecessary anxiety among students, particularly among those who are already fearful of tests. Third, they do not give students adequate preparation time. Most junior and senior high school students take five or six different subjects from different teachers and devote varying amounts of time to each subject, depending on the requirements of the class. If students are aware of a forthcoming test, they can modify their study habits accordingly. Fourth, surprise tests do not promote either efficient learning or higher achievement. Thus their use cannot be justified except on the nebulous "moral" grounds that students, like Boy Scouts, should always be prepared.

Modes of Item Presentation

Teacher-made examinations allow for alternate ways of presenting items to students. For example, the teacher can read each item aloud. Although this procedure may be necessary if students have difficulty in reading, its inefficiency severely limits its effectiveness. Students must work at the same rate of speed and are unable to review items; those with unrecognized hearing losses are further handicapped. If items must be presented orally, true-false or completion tests should be used since multiple-choice and matching items contain too many alternatives to be presented efficiently aloud. Essay questions may be written on the blackboard, but the writing must be large enough for all students to read. Reading these items aloud will reduce the possibility that some students, because of shyness or faulty vision, will misread or misinterpret them.

Some evidence shows that presenting test items through slides or closed-circuit television transparencies can be advantageous in large classes (Fargo et al. 1967; Schwarz 1967). A lengthy examination may require much time and incur high costs for stencils, paper, and assembling. These items can be placed on a transparency and presented on an overhead projector in a well-lit room and still yield results comparable to the use of test booklets for each student. When such modes of presentation are used, speed of response should be a negligible factor. Although there is some evidence (Elliott and Osburn 1965; Ferris and Nichols 1969) that slow-working students can pace themselves on examinations to keep up with the rest of the class, overemphasis on speed may detract from the student's ability to answer questions accurately.

Another consideration is the order in which items should appear. One study (Sax and Cromack 1966) has shown that (1) arranging items from easy to hard will yield higher scores than if items are arranged in other sequences, such as from hard to easy, random placement, or placement of easy items among more difficult ones, and (2) the advantage of the easy-to-hard sequence is most pronounced when time is restricted and is much less important when time limits are generous.

Whether items should be grouped by content or format (multiple-choice, essay, etc.) has not been studied empirically on teacher-made achievement tests. A study of the organization of items on standardized tests found that students attempt more items and therefore obtain higher scores when items are arranged in *spiral-omnibus format* rather than in separate subtests according to content (Sax and Carr 1962). *Spiral-omnibus format* is the arrangement of different types of items in order of difficulty. On some aptitude tests, for example, items begin with the easiest mathematics item followed by the easiest items measuring vocabulary and spatial relationships. The sequence is then repeated with the next most difficult math, vocabulary, and spatial relationships items in that order. When the same items are reorganized into separate math, vocabulary, and spatial relationship subtests (still in ascending order of difficulty), students do not perform as well. Evidently students who are poor in mathematics, for instance, tend to become discouraged when items become more difficult in that subtest. When items appear in spiral-omnibus format, students are more likely to attempt them since they have been encouraged by doing well on other types of items nearby.

However, on achievement tests there are good reasons for grouping items on the same topic and not intermixing them. A test on "language arts" may be composed of items that measure widely different topics such as spelling, reading comprehension, and application of grammar rules. For reasons to be discussed in chapter 13, each of these topics should be developed as a separate test which can be justified in its own right. In the Sax and Carr study reported in the previous paragraph, all three types of items were combined as a measure of scholastic aptitude, and it was not necessary to obtain separate scores for each part.

On teacher-made examinations, then, items should be arranged from easy to hard. If separate scores are desired on different parts of the exam, those parts should be placed together to form separate subtests. Where subtests contain different kinds of items, the order might proceed from true-false, to completion, multiple-choice, and matching, with essay questions placed last. This placement sequence exposes students first to those items requiring the least amount of time to read and answer and may discourage pupils from spending inordinate amounts of time on one essay question when they could have responded to many true-false items in the same amount of time.

Summary

1. In order to plan tests, objectives must be determined and written.

2. Objectives should be related to a consistent philosophy of education. Some philosophies are:
   a. *Realism.* Realists assume that an external reality exists independently of man. Since the world is orderly, the purpose of education is to discover universal truths primarily through the scientific method.
   b. *Idealism.* Idealists believe that ultimate reality is composed of ideas. The purpose of education is to develop the mind by studying subjects that have withstood the tests of time, particularly the "Great Books."
   c. *Pragmatism.* Pragmatists do not accept the concept of "ultimate" reality. Rather, everything is relative and in a state of flux and change. Therefore, the learning of "subject matter" is subservient to the learning of how to solve problems; matters of morality depend on consequences.

3. The schools do not attempt to resolve these philosophic positions. Instead, they combine elements from all philosophies, which often produces conflicting values and purposes.

4. Some attempts have been made to establish priorities among objectives. In some instances priorities are established by state legislatures and boards of education. Priorities can also be established by asking community members to estimate how much money the accomplishment of a goal might be worth, the amount of time that should be spent in pursuing some goal, and so forth. Maslow's hierarchy of needs and Havighurst's developmental tasks are also ways of establishing priorities among objectives.

5. Objectives may be categorized by four dimensions:
   a. *Process and product objectives.* Process objectives are used to monitor activities to make sure that someone is responsible for accomplishing an objective within specified time limitations. Product objectives indicate what the student must do or know as a result of instruction.
   b. *Behavioral and implicit objectives.* Behavioral objectives state what the student must do to demonstrate the attainment of an objective; implicit objectives refer to covert behaviors. Many implicit objectives can be

made behavioral by stating the conditions under which testing is to take place. Behavioral objectives are important in the following conditions:

   i. When the subject matter is sequential and mastery of prerequisite skills is necessary before the student can be allowed to advance in the sequence.

   ii. If subject matter requires a high level of proficiency.

   iii. If teachers are to hold themselves accountable for student achievement.

   iv. If the teacher wants to develop diagnostic tests to measure specific objectives.

   v. If maximum clarity is required for communicating objectives.

   Implicit objectives can be used in the following circumstances:

   i. If objectives need serve only as points of emphasis.

   ii. If objectives refer to a desirable goal not measurable within the limitations of the school.

   iii. If objectives are to serve as a broad base from which behavioral objectives can be written.

   iv. If objectives are to be communicated to parents.

   v. If an item pool is available to be used as a criterion to demonstrate and clarify the meaning of an objective.

c. *Immediate and ultimate objectives.* Immediate objectives are those over which the school exerts some influence; ultimate objectives are long-term goals that the school may consider desirable but which teachers cannot control directly.

d. *Restricted and inclusive objectives.* Restricted objectives are stated so specifically that they are equivalent to the items given to students; inclusive objectives are more broadly stated so as to include more than one specific item. Inclusive objectives specify the universe of items that could be asked on a topic.

6. Because measurements are samples of behavior, the test constructor needs to determine how many items he will formulate for each objective. In addition, he needs to determine how complex each item should be. Complexity of items can be defined by using a taxonomy or classification system such as that proposed by Bloom:

a. *Knowledge.* The least complex level refers to items that require simple memorization.

b. *Comprehension.* This level requires the student to translate from one level of abstraction to another by restating a problem in his own words, for example.

c. *Application.* Items in the third level of complexity require the student to relate principles or concepts in new situations.

d. *Analysis.* Students who analyze a problem critically examine information to determine the interrelationships among the parts, such as in finding assumptions or fallacies in an argument.

e. *Synthesis.* At this level students construct something unique, such as writing a story or developing a hypothesis.

f. *Evaluation.* The student makes a value judgment using internal or external criteria, such as in evaluating conflicting evidence.

7. Objectives in the affective domain can also be described:

a. *Receiving or attending.* The lowest level of this taxonomy requires the individual to be aware of something and to at least tolerate its presence.

b. *Responding.* At this level the individual responds in various degrees of zeal to stimuli.

c. *Valuing.* Valuing implies the judgment of worthiness of some belief along with some internalization and commitment.

d. *Organization.* At this level values become organized and interrelated to form a system of beliefs that is internally consistent.

e. *Characterization by a value or value complex.* At the highest level the individual has developed a coherent philosophy of life and lives according to that philosophy.

8. Objectives within the psychomotor domain emphasize activities requiring fine and large muscle groups. Hand-eye coordination tasks, typing, speech, and so forth are in this domain.

9. Barrett has constructed a taxonomy of objectives in reading comprehension that includes both cognitive and affective domains. This taxonomy could also be adapted to art and music.

10. A two-way grid can be prepared to determine if desired student behavior is being adequately sampled. Content areas might be listed along one dimension of the grid, and the six levels of Bloom's taxonomy can be listed along the other. The total number of items measuring each content area could then be allocated among various levels of complexity. The purpose of this is to make certain that a reasonable sampling of items from all levels of complexity and from all subjects is included on the test.

11. Students generally expect tests to be composed of items roughly proportional in number to importance and to the amount of time devoted to each topic in a text or in class discussions. If this is not the case, students should be informed in advance.

12. No hard-and-fast rules can be developed to determine how many items should come from each level of complexity. Some objectives can be measured only by asking students to memorize *knowledge,* such as specific facts,

places, or dates, but more complex items probably demonstrate a greater understanding of these facts.

13. Once objectives have been written, the teacher still faces a number of decisions:

   a. *Open-book and closed-book examinations.* Although most examinations do not allow students to use notes or the textbook, there are good reasons why their use might be encouraged. This decision depends on the criterion for learning. If the students are to apply information or use special reference materials, open-book exams are often a good choice. If recall of information is desirable or if the amount of time saved in relearning the material is the criterion, closed-book examinations are probably more useful.

   b. *The take-home examination.* This is an extension of the open-book test. In some cases allowing students to obtain help from others may be useful. The take-home test has been used successfully as a teaching device or exercise.

   c. When tests are used to motivate students, frequent testing seems to be of some benefit to students of lower ability.

   d. Surprise or unannounced tests are not recommended because they tend to create anxiety, reduce preparation time, and do not lead to improved learning.

   e. Reading test items aloud to students is not recommended except perhaps for true-false or completion items and only if it is necessary. Tests can be administered successfully on slides or on closed-circuit television.

   f. Items should be arranged from easy to hard if time limits are restricted. When subtest scores are wanted, items should be arranged within each subtest in ascending order of difficulty. Essay questions should be placed at the end of the examination to discourage students from spending inordinate amounts of time on one or two of these items and being penalized by not attempting a greater number of true-false and multiple-choice items.

Suggested Readings

Clark, D. Cecil. *Using Instructional Objectives in Teaching.* Glenview, Ill.: Scott, Foresman and Co., 1972, 167 pages. A comprehensive analysis of how objectives can be written and used by classroom teachers. The text is organized into sixteen "areas of concern"; an appendix summarizes the major points discussed in the text.

Coop, Richard H., and White, Kinnard P. "Objectives and Achievement Measurement: The Congruency between Students' and Teachers' Perceptions of Behavioral Objectives." *Educational and Psychological Measurement* 32, no. 2 (Summer 1972): 355–64. The authors used a list of 150 verbs and verb phrases as parts of behavioral objectives to determine if students in grades 4 to 12 were capable of understanding these objectives. The authors provide lists of verbs that students had difficulty understanding. In grades 4 to 7 some of these verbs included: *critique, perceive, analyze, think critically, categorize, contrast, distinguish,* and *compute;* for students in grades 9 to 12, *critique, perceive, formulate a generalization, infer, appraise, generate, partition,* and *give debit and credit.*

Duchastel, Philippe, and Merrill, Paul F. "The Effects of Behavioral Objectives on Learning: A Review of Empirical Studies." *Review of Educational Research* 43, no. 1 (Winter 1973), pp. 53–69. An excellent review of the effects of behavioral objectives on student learning. Although these effects are difficult to measure, some of the problems and issues related to these topics will be of interest to teachers and prospective teachers.

Harrow, A. J., *A Taxonomy of the Psychomotor Domain.* New York: David McKay Co., 1972.

Stoker, H. W., and Kropp, R. P. "Measurement of Cognitive Processes." *Journal of Educational Measurement* 1, no. 1 (June 1964): 39–42. This article reports on an evaluation of Bloom's *Taxonomy of Educational Objectives.* In general, raters could agree on the categories to which items should be classified. Evidence was also presented to show that the hierarchical nature of the taxonomy could be supported.

Principles of Test Construction: True-False, Multiple-Choice, and Matching Items

> *Dr. Ferdinand Sauerbruch (1875–1951), celebrated German surgeon, once failed six candidates for a medical degree in Zurich, Switzerland, because they failed to properly answer this question: "Why does my dog wag its tail?" The proper answer: "Because it is happy to see us!"*
>
> © *1967 King Features, Inc.*

4 Dr. Sauerbruch's dog may have been happy to see him, but chances are his students were not. One can only guess at what objective this item was attempting to measure! Writing relevant, defensible test items demands both technical and creative skills. Because many important decisions affecting students are made on the basis of test results, teachers are responsible for developing the best examinations possible.

This chapter considers methods of constructing true-false, multiple-choice, and matching tests. Chapter 5 is concerned with the completion test and the essay examination.

Constructing the True-False Test

A true-false item consists of a statement to be marked *true* or *false*. At times it may be more convenient to have students *agree* or *disagree* with a statement or answer *yes* or *no* to a question. These formats are also considered true-false items since acceptance or denial is involved.

Advantages of True-False Tests

Item sampling   Because true-false items and answers tend to be short, the teacher can examine students on more material in a time period than he can with any other kind of item. The true-false test can help ensure an adequate sample of items when a great deal of subject matter must be covered.

Ease of construction   Teachers often construct true-false examinations quickly by taking statements directly from the text and modifying them slightly to make some false, *but this should be avoided.* Not only can statements out of context be ambiguous but the practice encourages memorization without understanding. Still, it takes less time to construct a true-false item than it does to construct a multiple-choice question or an essay question.

Ease of scoring   Because on most true-false tests the student simply has to agree or disagree with a statement, scoring is relatively mechanical, and a high degree of objectivity is possible. Some practices in scoring true-false tests should be avoided. If students write _T_ or _F_ next to each item, responses may be ambiguous. One student's _T_ may look like another student's _F_. For the same reason the use of + and − is discouraged. More objectivity is gained if students circle the word *True* or *False*.

Disadvantages of True-False Tests

Emphasis on rote memorization   Modern educational practices tend to deemphasize rote memorization except in gaining prerequisite knowledge for more complex skills. Most teachers are interested in what the student can do with a skill, not simply that he has it; how a student can apply multiplication rules is considered more important than multiplication per se. In part the deemphasis of rote learning results from a complex modern life that demands of students comprehension, application, analysis, synthesis, and evaluation. If examinations test only the skill of memorization, the student may believe that memory is the most important part of education.

But the fact that most true-false items measure rote knowledge does not argue that they *must* do so. Nothing about a true-false item per se prevents the teacher from asking highly complex questions. The items on page 81, for example, require the student to apply principles of geography to a situation new to him.

Dependence on absolute judgments   The true-false test presumes a dichotomous world that is composed of truth or falsity and does not easily admit the possibility of intermediate values. Most "facts" are not entirely true or false but require qualification, and it is unfair to ask the student to guess at the teacher's criteria for evaluating the truth of a statement. Consider, for example, the following "facts":

T   F   1. The sun rose yesterday.
T   F   2. $\frac{2}{3} = .7$
T   F   3. There are only 50 states in the United States.

The first example appears to be true, but taken literally—that is, the sun moved across the sky—it is false. Whether the sun "rose" yesterday at the North Pole can also be questioned.

In the second example truth or falsity depends on how accurate the teacher wants responses to be. As an approximation to one decimal place, the item is true, but if the teacher has in mind the more precise figure of .667, the item is false.

In the third example students could be confused by the word *only*. Although there are fifty states, if the statement is interpreted to exclude territories and possessions it is false. It is extremely difficult to construct unambiguous true-false items unless statements are taken directly from the text-book, a practice, as already noted, that should be avoided.

Likelihood of guessing   Another disadvantage of the true-false item is that it allows a high degree of guessing. Since they are confronted with only two alternatives, uncertain students, like Linus in figure 4.1, can always guess and hope to answer correctly.

The *chance score* is the average score that would be obtained by students who responded randomly to all questions. On true-false tests the probability of guessing correctly is .50 for each item. That multiplied by the number of items

© 1968 United Feature Syndicate, Inc.

Figure 4.1

Figure 4.2

on the test gives the chance score. On a true-false 100-item test, for example, the chance score is $.50 \times 100 = 50$. Students who have partial knowledge or who are "lucky" will do better than chance, and students like Linus in figure 4.2 who have misinformation or who are "unlucky" will do worse. If students can get about half the items right on a true-false test without even having to read them, a relatively large number of items are wasted, and teachers will have to construct longer examinations to compensate for guessing.

Suggestions for Writing True-False Items

Construct items that measure important objectives   Requiring students to respond to new situations is one way to increase the thought content of true-false tests. For instance, the fictitious map in fig. 4.3 can encourage students to apply principles and generalizations in geography.

If objectives stress the student's ability to justify conclusions drawn from data, the suggestions offered by the Progressive Education Association's Eight-

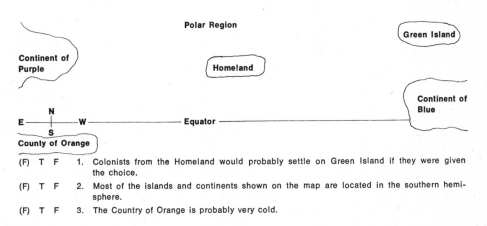

Figure 4.3

Year Study Evaluation (PEA 1938) can be used to good advantage. The student is presented with a problem situation and is asked to select one of three courses of action that is most acceptable to him. Because the selection is a matter of opinion, it is not scored. Rather, the test attempts to determine whether the student can justify whatever course of action he has chosen by checking those reasons that justify his position and by leaving blank those that do not. The following (PEA 1940) is an example of this type of item.

Labor Organizer

Tom Jones is an active leader in various workers' organizations. He criticizes the present system of private business, maintaining that it is organized for the purpose of making profits and that it subordinates human welfare to this end. He has fought for workers' rights to organize in order to be able to bargain effectively for better working conditions and higher wages. In order to help workers obtain these rights in the face of opposition from business, he has organized labor and has led strikes which have tied up business for months. This resulted in considerable losses to business.

Many people believe that the ideas and activities promoted by him and others like him are dangerous and should not be permitted.

What should be done in such cases?

> Directions: Choose the most acceptable course (or courses) of action and fill in the appropriate spaces on the answer sheet.

Courses of action: [These are not scored.]

    A.   The promotion of such ideas and activities should not be permitted.
    B.   Such persons should be allowed to express their ideas as long as they refrain from organizing others to take action.
    C.   No one should be allowed to interfere with the right of people to promote their ideas through the organization of sympathetic groups.

What reason would you use to support your course (or courses) of action?

Reasons: [These are either marked as justifying the student's course of action or are left blank.]

    1.   The right of free speech should not include the right to advocate ideas which are too radically different from the ones commonly held. [This is scored as sound for A.]
    2.   Any suppression of freedom to express and promote ideas is dangerous to democracy. [Sound for C]
    3.   Allowing freedom of speech has usually prevented violent revolutionary changes in political institutions. [Untenable for A, B, and C]

4. It is un-American to try to change our institutions by such violent actions as strikes. [Sound for A and B]

Avoid the use of specific determiners   A specific determiner is an unintentional clue to the correct answer. Examine the following true-false items:

T F 1. All large cities are connected by railways.
T F 2. No school system is supported entirely by local funds.
T F 3. It is possible to bisect any angle.
T F 4. It is impossible to run the mile in less than 3'30".
T F 5. Revolutions have always led to socially desirable goals.
T F 6. Wars are never justified in a democracy.
T F 7. Some wars could have been prevented.

Test-wise students have learned that sweeping generalizations, indicated by such absolute terms as *always, all,* and *never* (examples 1, 2, 4, 5, and 6), are likely to be keyed *false.* Item 3 would probably be marked *true* since few activities are impossible. The last statement would be keyed *true* because it implies a reasonable qualification.

A specific determiner makes it possible for the unprepared student to respond correctly. While this may encourage students to become sophisticated test takers, it will do little to measure important course objectives.

Approximately half the statements should be false   Because "true" items are easier to construct than "false" ones, they usually predominate in tests. And since students who are in doubt of the correct answer tend to mark statements *true,* they are likely to respond correctly even when they are uncertain, despite the situation depicted in figure 4.4.

Figure 4.4

Each statement should be unequivocally true or false   Consider the following examples:

T   F   1.   The census is taken every ten years
T   F   2.   Bodies fall at approximately 32.16 feet per second.

In the first example the statement can refer to the United States census or to another, unspecified census. In some European countries, for example, the census is taken every five years. As it now reads the statement is true under one condition but false under another. A better item is:

T   F   1.   The Constitution of the United States requires a national census every ten years. [T]

The second example is faulty because it too has an equivocal answer. The rate of acceleration is approximately 32.16 feet per second *if* the falling body is in a vacuum near the earth's surface. Without added clarification, the item is only partially true (or false, depending on how one looks at it). A better item is:

T   F   2.   A body falling in a vacuum near the earth's surface increases in velocity at approximately 32.16 feet per second. [T]

State each item positively if possible   Negatively stated items can be confusing, especially to young children. Two negatives in the same sentence make the item particularly difficult to understand:

T   F   1.   It is not undesirable to use double negatives inadvertently in a true-false item.

Modifications of True-False Tests

Because true-false tests yield relatively high chance scores, some modifications have been designed to reduce guessing.

Correction for guessing   When items have only two options, students can get half of them right by chance. If there are three options, they are likely to guess two wrong for each response they guess right. This suggests penalizing the student who responds incorrectly on a true-false examination by subtracting his wrong answers from his right ones. A score corrected for guessing is equal to the number of items right minus the number wrong *if* there are two options, as in a true-false test. Items omitted are disregarded in scoring. In that way the student gains a point for each correct answer, is penalized one point for each incorrect response, and is neither penalized nor rewarded if the item is omitted.

Suppose that a student responds correctly to 50 items out of 100 on a true-false examination, thus obtaining the chance score of 50. Using the formula $S_{TF} = R - W$ (corrected score on a true-false test equals the number of items marked *right* minus the number marked *wrong,* disregarding omitted items), his corrected score is 0. Correcting for guessing reduces chance scores to 0.

On a three-option test the correction for guessing is to subtract one-half point for each incorrect response from the total number of correct responses (because for every right answer there are two incorrect ones). On a four-option exam the ratio of rights to wrongs is 1 to 3, so the number of wrong responses is divided by 3 to correct for guessing. Generalizing this reasoning leads to the following equation:

$$S_{CG} = R - \frac{W}{\text{options} - 1}$$

$$\text{score corrected for guessing} = \text{number of right answers} - \frac{\text{number of wrong answers}}{\text{number of options} - 1}$$

Since there are only two options on a true-false test, the formula simplifies to rights minus wrongs. In all cases omitted responses provide neither credit nor penalty.

Should tests be corrected for guessing? The answer is debatable, but teachers should be aware of the arguments for and against this practice.

Arguments in favor of correcting for guessing   1. Under severe time limits some students work rapidly and guess on items, whereas others work more slowly and do not guess. Consider the hypothetical case of two students, Albert and Bill, who are taking a 100-item true-false test with a one-hour time limit. If Albert guesses on all items, the best estimate is that he will receive a chance score of 50. If Bill refuses to guess but has no greater knowledge than Albert, he is clearly at a disadvantage since he will have a score of 0. Correcting for guessing will reduce Albert's spuriously high score but will not penalize Bill. Another possibility, of course, is to persuade both students to attempt all items.

2. It is especially important to correct for guessing if the student is asked to check all items in a series that are right and if the teacher simply counts the number of check marks. Under these conditions the student who marks all items as true receives a "perfect" score. For example:

Check each statement that is true: *Keyed Answer*   *Student's Answer*

1. $\sqrt{25 + 25} = \sqrt{25} + \sqrt{25}$ False   √
2. $\Sigma X^2 = (\Sigma X)^2$ False   √
3. $\sqrt{X} = X^{1/2}$ True   √
4. $6(3 + 2) = 30$ True   √

Using this system of scoring, the highest possible score is 2 since there are only two items keyed *true*. Unless scores are corrected for guessing, students can mark all items true and receive a perfect score (i.e., two correct) although the first two items are wrong. Since each of the four items is scored independently, the correction is right minus wrong *for each item,* not rights minus 1/3 wrongs.

3. Students should be discouraged from guessing on both moral and pedagogical grounds. The moral argument is that students who guess and obtain high scores are being dishonest because in effect they have taken unfair advantage of the nature of true-false and multiple-choice items by guessing; they should therefore be penalized. The pedagogical argument is that guessing may become reinforced if the child learns that he can get some items right without studying. The assumption is usually made that correction formulas will deter the child from guessing and will as a consequence facilitate learning. Little evidence is available to support or deny this contention.

4. Corrected scores correlate more highly with criteria than do uncorrected ones. For example, Gilbert Sax and LeVerne Collet (1968) told a randomly selected group of undergraduate students that guessing would not be penalized (instruction I) when they took form A of a test, but when they later took form B, they were told *not* to guess because wrong answers would be penalized (instruction II). The experiment was designed to eliminate the possibility that differences in instructions, difficulty levels, or order of presentation (form A, then B or form B, then A) might affect results. Using students' grade point averages as the criterion, more accurate predictions were made when corrected scores were used than when the scores were uncorrected.

Arguments against correcting for guessing   1. Under severe time limits correction formulas may reduce differences between students who guess and those who do not. However, one difficulty with these formulas is that they may discourage only some of the examinees from guessing—probably those who are less willing to gamble even when they are reasonably certain of the correct answer. Others who are equally certain of the right answer may be more willing to take a chance and are therefore likely to respond correctly.

2. Correction formulas do not differentiate between those who guess blindly and those who have misinformation and thus penalize both.

3. Teachers complain that correction formulas require too much time because they have to count both right and wrong responses and disregard omitted items. In large classes the amount of additional time needed to correct for guessing may be great indeed.

4. Probably few students engage in blind guessing, and its effects are likely

to be small. Although true-false items are particularly susceptible to high chance scores, increasing the length of the test will minimize the effects of guessing.

To correct or not to correct?   There is no simple answer to the question of whether correction formulas should be used. These formulas will reduce the effects of chance guessing but only at the expense of increased computational labor on the part of teachers and possible negative effects on knowledgeable but cautious students.

Reducing the effects of guessing in other ways   *Encouraging students to guess*   The effects of chance guessing can be reduced by deliberately encouraging all students to guess when in doubt. Since one purpose of correction is to reduce the chance differences between guessers and nonguessers, encouraging guessing may be as effective as attempts to prevent it. Even if time limits are very restrictive, encouraging guessing will tend to equalize the scores of those who have the same amount of information. However, this "solution" is not likely to be viewed favorably by those who believe that guessing is pedagogically or morally wrong.

Increasing the number of items   Another way of reducing the effects of guessing is to increase the number of items on the test, the number of options on each item, and the time limits correspondingly. Furthermore, if items are not too difficult (see chapter 9), the need to guess should be reduced. These procedures are strongly recommended, even though they require the teacher to prepare somewhat longer examinations. The current evidence suggests that the teacher needs to construct about three to four times as many true-false items as multiple-choice items to make them equivalent in accuracy (Oosterhof and Glasnapp 1972).

Student revision of false statements   A third method of reducing the effects of guessing is to have students revise all items marked false to make them true. For example:

	Items	Corrections, if any
T (F)	1. $X^2(X^3) = X^6$	X^5
(T) F	2. $X^{1/2} = 1/X$	NONE
T (F)	3. <u>Insects</u> have 8 legs.	SPIDERS

The part of the statement to be corrected if false is underlined. This method provides more complete sampling of the students' understanding than does the more traditional true-false test. However, it does complicate scoring and reduce the number of items that can be used.

Confidence weighting   Another method of reducing chance guessing is to have the student indicate how certain he is that a response is correct. Confidence weighting assumes that the student who is sure of his correct answer deserves more credit than the one who is less certain. For example, the student is asked to indicate whether the statement $X^{1/2} = 1/X$ is true or false and then to indicate his degree of certainty.

Degree of Certainty	Student Response	Score
1. Positive	Correct	+2
2. Less certain	Correct	+1
3. Uncertain	Correct	+½
4. Uncertain	Omits answer	0
5. Uncertain	Incorrect	−½
6. Some idea	Incorrect	−1
7. Positive	Incorrect	−2

A correct response can give the student 1/2 to 2 points, depending on how certain he is of being right; penalty points of different weights are given for incorrect responses. If he omits the item, he receives no credit.

In confidence weighting the excessively brash student and the student who is uncertain of his knowledge are both penalized. Guessing may be reduced by confidence weighting, but the advantages must be weighed against the added time it takes students to answer each item.

Constructing the Multiple-Choice Item

Multiple-choice items consist of two parts: a *stem* and a number of *options* or *alternatives*. The stem is a question or statement completed by one of the alternatives. All incorrect or less appropriate alternatives are called *distracters* or *foils,* and the student's task is to select the correct or best alternative from all the options.

Advantages and Disadvantages of Multiple-Choice Tests

The multiple-choice item has numerous advantages. First, it has great versatility in measuring objectives from the rote knowledge level to the most complex level. Second, because student writing is minimized, the teacher can sample a substantial amount of course material in a relatively short time. Third, scoring is highly objective since little interpretation is needed to count the number of correct responses. Fourth, teachers can construct multiple-choice items that require students to discriminate among options that vary in degree of correctness. This allows students to select the "best" alternative and avoids the absolute judgments usually required of true-false tests. Fifth, because multiple-choice items usually have four or five options, they reduce the effects of guessing as Tanglefoot discovered much to his sorrow (see figure 4.5). And finally, the

Figure 4.5

multiple-choice format is particularly amenable to *item analyses* (see chapter 9) to detect areas of student weakness, evidence of item ambiguity, item difficulty, and the extent to which the item can measure individual differences.

The major problems with multiple-choice items are that they are time-consuming to write, and students sometimes complain that there is more than one defensible "correct" answer. This difficulty can be remedied by careful editing and pretesting of items.

Suggestions for Writing Multiple-Choice Items

The stem should introduce what is expected of the examinee   The stem delimits the student's task and makes clear the purpose of the item. Consider the following examples where the asterisk indicates the correct alternative:

Poor	*Better*
America	After whom was America named?
a. contains the world's largest population.	a. Columbus
b. is the site of the world's oldest culture.	b. Magellan
c. is a unilingual culture.	c. Ponce de Leon
d. was named after Vespucci.	*d. Vespucci

The use of incomplete stems encourages the writing of items that may have only the vaguest correspondence with specifically stated objectives. Because the stem fails to present the student with a well-defined task, the distracters tend to be a hodgepodge of any random thoughts that might have occurred to the teacher. The poor example measures four different objectives. Instead of one multiple-choice item designed to measure recognition of a specific person, the student is faced with four true-false items, each of which is related to a different objective. The better example measures a single objective; the task is clear and options consist of names only.

Stems can be written as incomplete statements or as questions. Although there is no experimental evidence to suggest which approach is superior, elementary grade students will probably have an easier time with questions than with incomplete statements. If the stem is open-ended, it should express a complete idea, and all options should measure a specific objective; that is, they should all be names of persons, examples of principles, or dates, for example.

Avoid specific determiners   Multiple-choice items should not contain clues to the correct answer. One clue is option length. The longest option is frequently the right one, perhaps because more space is required to justify it as being correct. There are two other common specific determiners in the *poor* example below:

Poor	*Better*
The type of standardized test used to measure academic achievement is called an	The type of test used to measure academic learning is called
	*a. an achievement test.
a. achievement test, since formal classroom learning is measured.	b. a case study.
b. case study.	c. a special aptitude test.
c. special aptitude test.	d. a test of intelligence.
d. test of intelligence.	

First, the word *achievement* appears in the stem and in the correct option. By using *academic learning* instead of *achievement* in the improved example, this specific determiner is avoided. Note also that the stem of the poor example ends with *an* and the correct option must thus begin with a vowel. This fault can be corrected by placing the article with the options.

Use vocabulary suited to the maturity of the students   One fourth-grade teacher administered the following *poor* item to her class:

Poor	*Better*
Magellan's primary contribution to world culture is that he was the first person to	Magellan was the first person to

Poor	*Better*

Poor

Magellan's primary contribution to world culture is that he was the first person to

a. circumnavigate the globe.
b. discover the Atlantic Ocean.
c. land on American soil.
d. look for the Fountain of Youth.

Better

Magellan was the first person to

*a. go around the world.
b. discover the Atlantic Ocean.
c. land on American soil.
d. look for the Fountain of Youth.

Although most of the students knew what Magellan had done, few understood the meaning of such words as *primary, contribution, culture,* and *circumnavigate.* The *poor* example measured vocabulary the students had not learned; the improved version is simpler and a better measure of the teacher's objectives.

Stems and options should be stated positively whenever possible   Elementary-grade pupils find negatives confusing. For older students, a negative in *either* the stem or options (but not both) is permissible.

Poor

Which of the following is not a characteristic of the gifted child?

a. He is emotionally stable.
b. He is not awkward.
c. He is not as old as his classmates.
d. He is friendly.

Better

Which of the following is a characteristic of the gifted child?

a. He tends to have many emotional problems.
b. He is awkward.
*c. He is younger than his classmates.
d. He is unfriendly.

If the word *not* is used in the stem, it should be underlined to make sure it is not overlooked.

Options should be plausible   There is no advantage in writing distracters no one will select, so each alternative should be plausible. If the test constructor puts himself into the role of the unprepared examinee, he can often predict likely errors and can incorporate better distracters into the item.

Poor	*Better*
Which of the following substances is the hardest?	Which of the following substances is the hardest?
a. Cardboard b. Glass c. Paper d. Steel	a. Concrete *b. Diamond c. Iron d. Steel

One way of preparing plausible alternatives is to have students write their answers to the question posed in the stem. Incorrect responses can later be used as distracters.

Items should have a defensible correct or best option   Unless they are given directions to the contrary, students will presume that only one answer is the correct or best one for multiple-choice items.

Poor	*Better*
Most fatalities are due to	Most accidental deaths occur in which of the following places?
a. acts of God. b. automobile accidents. c. home accidents. d. jobs. e. old age.	a. Automobiles *b. Homes c. Jobs (excluding auto and home accidents) d. Schools

In the *poor* example, can old age be considered a fatality? Is a housewife at her job when at home? Are home accidents acts of God? To avoid pitfalls each option should be examined to make sure it is either the most defensible answer or clearly wrong. It is as important to be able to justify the reasons for incorrect options as it is to be able to defend the correct one.

Avoid items measuring opinions   On multiple-choice items, one option should clearly be correct or best. An item measuring opinion is neither correct nor incorrect—all options are equally defensible.

Poor	*Better*
Which of the following persons is the best composer?	Which of the following composers was known primarily as an organist during his lifetime?
a. Bach b. Beethoven c. Brahms d. Mozart	*a. Bach b. Beethoven c. Brahms d. Mozart

Vary the placement of the correct option   Students who are uncertain of the correct answer tend to select the middle options and avoid the responses in extreme positions. Unfortunately many test constructors also select the center option as the correct one and thus give answers away. There are several ways to avoid overusing middle alternatives as correct options. One way is to allow the toss of a die to determine option position. Another approach is to alphabetize options. Numerical options, however, should always be placed in ranked sequence, either ascending or descending.

Avoid overlapping alternatives   Because multiple-choice questions should have only one right answer, synonyms appearing among alternatives must all be incorrect. Consider the following options:

a. Boy
b. Girl
c. Lad
d. Son

The correct alternative is probably *girl,* since the other options are close in meaning.

Overlapping alternatives are often inadvertently used by novice test constructors to increase the number of alternatives. For example:

Poor	*Better*
If a magnet were cut in half, what would happen to the north and south poles?	If a magnet were cut in half, what would happen to the north and south poles?
a. Both halves would have north and south poles.	*a. Each half would have both a north pole and a south pole.
b. Each half would have the opposite polarity from the other.	b. Each half would have only a north pole *or* a south pole.
c. Each half would have either a north or south pole.	c. Polarity would be lost on both halves.
d. One half of the magnet would be completely north and the other half completely south.	

In the *poor* example, options b, c, and d say essentially the same thing and must therefore be incorrect.

Use "none of the above" as an option only if there is an absolutely right answer   "None of the above" should be used only when an item is of the "correct-answer" type rather than the "best-answer" variety. One alternative only can be justified as the right answer for the former type of multiple-choice item, but for the best-answer type, one option is simply better than the others, although all contain some element of truth.

Poor	*Better*
A film depicting the life of Albert Einstein is most comparable to	X^2 times $X^3 =$
	a. X
	*b. X^5
a. an article.	c. X^6
b. a biography.	d. none of the above
c. an essay.	
d. none of the above.	

The stem in the poor example implies that the student is to find the best alternative. If he selects "none of the above," it may be that he can think of a more appropriate answer than the options provided. Since no option is absolutely right on best-answer questions, "none of the above" can always be defended as

Dave Lettick, *Saturday Review*, July 5, 1969, p. 48. Used by permission of the artist.

Figure 4.6

the correct alternative by students, particularly *after* papers have been returned to them.

The use of "none of the above" in the *better* example is justified because there is only one possible answer. If the student believes that the correct answer is not among the alternatives, he can select "none of the above."

"None of the above" is inappropriate if all possible answers have been included among the options. For example, an item could ask students if in relation to Earth, Mars were closer to, farther from, or equidistant to the sun. "None of the above" would obviously be an incorrect fourth option since all possibilities are exhausted in the first three options. A more humorous but equally inappropriate use of "none of the above" is shown in figure 4.6.

Avoid using "all of the above" as an option   "All of the above" is an inappropriate option for items requiring or implying a best answer since clearly all options cannot be best. Even when the answer is absolute, it is a weak alternative because the student simply has to find two defensible options to realize that "all of the above" must be the keyed response.

The stem should be clear and grammatically correct and should contain elements common to each option   Multiple-choice items obey standard English rules of punctuation and grammar. A question requires a question mark. There is little excuse for allowing students to take examinations containing spelling or other grammatical errors. It is difficult for parents and school administrators to discriminate between carelessness and ignorance. This *poor* example was actually given in a sixth-grade classroom:

Poor	*Better*
That swimming pool which needs cleaning most often than any other swimming pool is that swimming pool which	The swimming pool that will need the most cleaning is one filled with water from
a. is filled with water from a stream.	*a. a stream.
b. is filled with water from the ocean.	b. a well.
c. is filled with water from a well.	c. rainfall.
d. is filled with water collected from rainfall.	d. the ocean.

Note that each option in the *poor* example begins with the phrase *is filled* with water. This phrase is included in the stem of the *better* example to reduce repetition.

Suggestions for Measuring Complex
Objectives by Multiple-Choice
Items

Although most items in multiple-choice tests measure objectives from level 1 of Bloom's taxonomy (Knowledge), they need not be that restricted. The following suggestions may help increase the thought content of items, provided that is the teacher's intent.

The objective should permit the measurement of understanding   If objectives require the student to memorize a response, items will be restricted to measuring rote knowledge. The following objectives, for example, preclude testing more complex skills:

1. In response to the question "Who was the first president of the United States?" the student will write George Washington.
2. Given the question "To which class does the frog belong?" the student will select the option *amphibia*.
3. The student will write the names of three "warm" colors as given in class.

These objectives do not measure understanding because they demand answers that can be learned only through memorization.

Construct items in a form different from that originally presented   Suppose a textbook describes the problem $2\overline{)8}$ as meaning "How many groups of two are there in eight?" The same question on an examination requires only a rote response. A slightly more complex item (level 2, comprehension) could ask the student the meaning of $42\overline{)89}$, and a still more complex item is:

Which of the following represents the meaning of the 4 in the problem
$$3\overline{)12}\ \overset{4}{}\ ?$$

a. XXX XXX XXX XXX
b. XXXXX XXXXX
c. XXXXXXXXXXXX
d. XXX

In this item the student has to remember that the 4 means four groups of three.
    Suppose a student has just been taught to recognize several paintings by Picasso. Having him select those paintings from among others requires little

thinking or understanding, but showing him a series of paintings he has never seen and asking him to select those by Picasso provides better evidence of comprehension.

Use novel pictorial materials to measure principles that require students to apply knowledge   If classroom instruction heavily emphasizes verbal descriptions, the teacher can use pictures to measure complex processes. For example, if a textbook explains how glaciers flow, the item in figure 4.7 can measure how well students have understood the material.

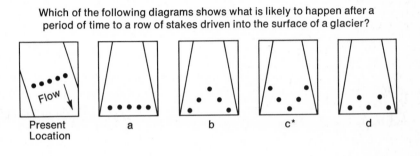

Which of the following diagrams shows what is likely to happen after a period of time to a row of stakes driven into the surface of a glacier?

Present Location   a   b   c*   d

Figure 4.7

Use analogies to measure relationships   If a student is able to derive relationships that have not been taught directly, he is giving evidence of understanding course content. A civics item, for instance, could measure the student's understanding of the relationship among four terms designated by the letters *A, B, C,* and *D:*

Governor (*A*) is to state (*B*) as president (*C*) is to

  a. his cabinet.
  b. the electoral college.
  c. the Senate.
*d. the United States (*D*)
  e. the vice-president.

The analogy should clearly demonstrate the *relationships* the teacher wants to measure. These relationships are among the four terms (designated *A, B, C,* and *D*) that form the analogy. For example, the governor (*A*) is related to the state (*B*) in the same way that the president (*C*) should be related to the correct alternative (*D*). Because the governor is the elected head of the state, the same relationship is that the president is the elected leader of the United States. In this way it could be argued that A is to B as C is to D.

Some analogies are contrived and far-fetched, as in the *poor* example below:

Poor	*Better*
Correction for guessing is to formula as true-false is to	$R - W/2$ is to $R - W$ as three = choices is to
*a. $R - W$.	a. chance.
b. $R - W/2$.	b. multiple-choice.
c. $R - W/3$.	c. one-half.
d. $R - W/4$.	d. R $-$ W/3
	*e. true-false

In the *poor* example one simply has to remember that true-false tests are corrected for guessing by using the formula $R - W$ (rights minus wrongs), but there is no necessary relationship between terms A and B (correction for guessing and formula) and C and D (true-false and $R - W$). In the *better* example the relationship between A and B is a three-option correction to a two-option correction for guessing; terms C and D express the same relationship.

In writing analogy problems it is particularly important that the distracters be related as closely as possible to term C. That is, it should not be possible to examine term C and thus immediately select the correct alternative. For example:

Iguana (A) is to lizard (B) as fox terrier (C) is to

*a. canine (D).
b. cat.
c. elephant.
d. pig.

In this case the relationship between terms A and B need not be considered by the student since there is only one option related to term C; *canine* must be the correct answer.

Have students identify assumptions and analyze criteria   Because students study for the type of examination they expect to take, having them consider assumptions as they read assignments can facilitate learning. To recall an assumption made *explicit* in a text does not measure understanding, but to find assumptions on one's own does. Having students analyze criteria can also help measure their understanding. For instance, a textbook could divide the colonial period into New England, the South, the middle states, and the frontier. A multiple-choice item could then read as follows:

What criterion was used in the text to divide the colonial period into New England, the South, the middle states, and the frontier?

*a. Economic
 b. Political
 c. Religious
 d. Social

Have students discover relationships among similar topics   Another way of measuring understanding is to have students note similarities among various topics studied. A test item for students who have studied different woodwind instruments could be:

Woodwind instruments are similar in that they all have

 a. conical bodies.
*b. tone holes.
 c. reeds.
 d. register keys.

Have students select examples of principles or concepts   One of the most effective testing procedures is to have students apply their knowledge of principles, concepts, theories, or terminology. For example:

"And, spite of pride, in erring reason's sprite,
One truth is clear: Whatever IS, is RIGHT."

This passage is a typical example of which of the following poetic styles?

*a. Classical
 b. Modern
 c. Romantic
 d. Victorian

Options need not be verbal. The example in figure 4.8 uses graphic material to test students' concept of *infinite elasticity* in economics.

Provide for a condition contrary to fact   Asking students to estimate what might have happened if an event had *not* occurred also tests their grasp of subject matter. For example, students might remember from their reading that

Which of the following graphs best represents a schedule of infinite elasticity (where D = demand)?

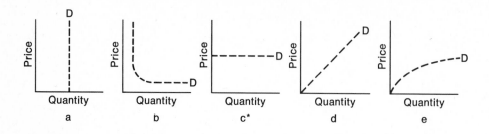

Figure 4.8

Robert Gray discovered the Columbia River, but they might have much more difficulty estimating the most likely consequence if the Columbia had not been discovered then.

If Robert Gray had not discovered the Columbia River in 1792, what country would have profited the most at that time?

a. England
b. France
c. Russia
*d. Spain

Use charts and tables   Items developed by the Progressive Education Association (PEA 1938) demonstrate the versatility of charts and tables. Test 2.2, Interpretation of Data, consists of nine statements to be marked in the following manner:

Mark space a—if the evidence given is sufficient to make the statement true.

Mark space b—if the evidence suggests that the statement is probably true.

Mark space c—if the evidence is insufficient to make a decision concerning the statement.

Mark space d—if the evidence suggests that the statement is probably false.

Mark space e—if the evidence alone is sufficient to make the statement false.

An approximate distribution of energy in the infra-red, visible, and ultra-violet portions of the radiation from different sources of light expressed in percentages is shown in the table below:

Percentage of Energy of Various Light Sources

	Sunlight	Carbon Arc	Incandescent Lamp	Quartz Mercury
Infra-red (heat)	78	85	90	53
Visible light	15	10	9	20
Ultra-violet	7	5	1	28

Statements

[d] 1. Most of the energy of sunlight is available as visible light.

[d] 2. The sunlight contains a larger percentage of energy as ultra-violet than do any of the other sources.

[a] 3. Less than 10 percent of the energy furnished by an incandescent lamp is used in giving off visible light.

[a] 4. The quartz mercury arc furnishes a larger percentage of energy as ultra-violet light than does the sun.

[a] 5. Most of the energy of all the sources of light listed is given off as heat, or infra-red rays.

[c] 6. The quartz mercury arc is more effective for health treatments than sunlight.

[c] 7. On a cloudy day the proportion of the total energy in the form of ultra-violet light from sunlight is less than 7 percent.

[b] 8. The temperature of a light source determines to a high degree the percentages of ultra-violet light, visible, and infra-red.

[d] 9. There are many other sources which emit a lower percentage of ultra-violet than the incandescent lamp.

Scoring the Multiple-Choice Test

Children below the fourth grade should probably answer questions on the test booklet itself rather than on a separate answer sheet (Gaffney and McGuire 1971). Average third-grade children evidently experience a good deal of difficulty in answering questions on a separate page. They tend to respond slowly and to lose their place easily.

There is a decided advantage in using a separate answer sheet for older children. First, scoring time can be reduced considerably because answers are all on a single sheet. Second, errors in scoring will probably be reduced since the teacher can devote full attention to the tasks and not be bothered by having to count right answers on each page of the booklet. Third, the use of a separate answer sheet greatly facilitates analyzing class responses to each item for diagnostic purposes. (This topic is discussed in greater detail in chapter 9.)

Many school districts have commercially printed answer sheets that teachers may order for their classes (see figure 4.9). These can be scored electronically if the district has the facilities or they may be scored by hand. For hand

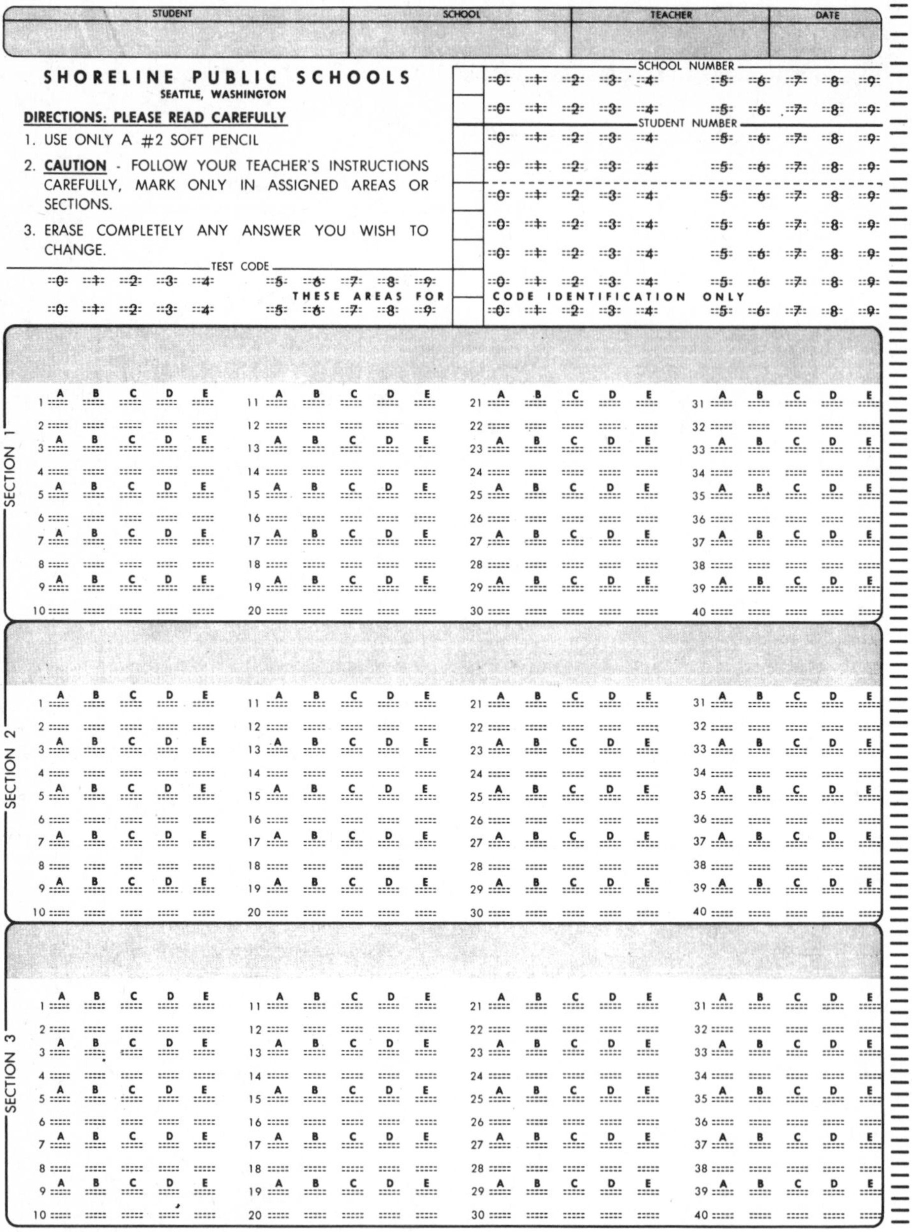

Shoreline Answer Sheet (Shoreline School District, Washington). Used by permission.

Figure 4.9. An example of an answer sheet used by the shoreline public school

scoring the easiest procedure is to prepare a scoring stencil by cutting or punching holes in the answer sheet that correspond to the correct answer. By placing the stencil over each pupil's answer sheet, the correct responses will appear in the holes. Cardboard stencils and answer-key punches are available commercially.

For most classroom purposes, counting the number of answers marked correctly is all that is required for multiple-choice examinations. Although there are some advantages to correcting multiple-choice tests for guessing (Sax and Collet 1968), most teachers will probably not want to bother with the additional labor required.

An interesting modification in scoring multiple-choice examinations has been studied by Collet (1971). Rather than penalizing a student for responding incorrectly, the suggestion has been made that students be given partial credit for every option they recognize as being *incorrect*. For a five-option test, the student receives one-fourth of a point for every answer he can identify as being wrong but is penalized one full point for eliminating a correct alternative. Thus students are given partial credit for recognizing which alternatives are wrong even though they may not be able to identify which option is the correct one. Collet stated that the major advantage of elimination scoring over traditional correction for guessing formulas is that it "permits subjects with only partial knowledge to gain credit for the discriminations they *can* make." Most students would probably welcome being given credit for having partial knowledge.

Constructing the Matching Test

The matching item is basically a multiple-choice test in which the examinee associates an item in one column with a choice in the second column. The student may associate names of individuals with their accomplishments, events with dates, or countries with their capitals. Items are usually listed in the first column and options in the second column, as in the example in figure 4.10.

Directions: In Column A are five diagrams. In Column B are the names of different geometric figures. Match the name of the figure with the diagram that best depicts it by placing the letter in Column B on the appropriate line next to Column A. Options may be used once or not at all.

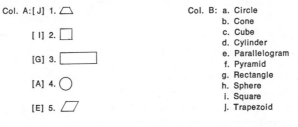

Figure 4.10

Advantages of the Matching Test

The matching exercise is simple to construct and score and is well suited to measuring *associations*. Like the multiple-choice format, it presents students with questions and alternatives. But if the example in figure 4.10 were multiple-choice format, each of the five items in column A could be followed by five options from column B, creating needless repetition.

Another advantage of the matching item is that it reduces the effects of guessing. In the example in figure 4.10 the student has only one chance out of ten of guessing correctly on the first item, one out of nine for the second, one out of eight for the third, and so on. By the time he gets to the last item there are still five alternatives from which he can select. Obviously the more options that are provided, the less chance there will be to guess correctly.

Disadvantages of the Matching Test

A major complaint about the matching test is that it tends to ask students to associate trivial information. Unfortunately most matching tests do emphasize memorization, although it is possible to construct items that measure more complex cognitive skills.

A second limitation of matching tests is that most commercial answer sheets can accommodate no more than five options, and school districts that provide electronic test scoring services for teachers generally use these commercial sheets.

Suggestions for Writing Matching Tests

Use homogeneous options and items   Failure to provide homogeneity can lead to the following types of item:

Column A	*Column B*
____1. First president of the United States	A. Columbus
____2. Discoverer of America	B. William Penn
____3. Year America was discovered	C. George Washington
____4. Beginning of the Revolutionary War	D. Washington, D.C.
____5. Founder of Pennsylvania	E. 1492
____6. Present capital of the United States	F. 1776

Items 1, 2, and 5 are concerned with the names of persons; 3 and 4, with dates; and 6, with the name of a city. The chances for responding correctly are, respectively, 1 out of 3, 1 out of 2, and 1 out of 1. The six items should be arranged in three separate sets of matching tests, each containing *only* names, dates, or places. As they are currently written, the student can éliminate irrelevant options and obtain a higher score than he may deserve.

Have more options than items   This is especially important if options can be used only once. Consider the following example:

Column A: Presidents	*Column B: Term of Office*
[A] James Madison	A. 1809–1817
[B] James Buchanan	B. 1857–1861
[C] Calvin Coolidge	C. 1923–1929

Assuming that the student responds correctly to items 1 and 2, he cannot miss the third. If the teacher provides at least four more options than items, students have only one chance out of five (as on a five-option multiple-choice test) of guessing correctly on the last item.

Arrange options and items alphabetically or numerically   If options are organized alphabetically or numerically, students do not have to waste time searching for the correct response. This is especially important if there are many options.

Limit the number of items within each set   It is usually wise to limit the number of *items* to no more than five or six per set. A longer list is difficult for students to handle and for the teacher to construct and score. A six-item subtest will probably have about ten options. Any more options will make the search for the correct answer overly difficult and time-consuming.

Place the shorter responses in column B   This time-saving practice allows the student to read the longer item first in column A and then search quickly through the shorter options to locate the correct alternative.

Provide complete directions   On some matching tests options are used only once; on others students may use any option as often as needed. In either case directions should tell the student what the ground rules are.

Directions should also advise him *how* he is to respond. Generally teachers prefer students to put the letter of the selected option on the line at the left of column A. If students are not told to do this, they may put the number of the item next to the correct option in column B.

It is also important to clarify the student's task by telling him what columns A and B represent. The dates in the previous example would not be clear without the explanation that they refer to terms of office.

Place options on the same page   On long tests time is wasted if students constantly have to flip from page to page to search through all options to locate the correct one. In addition, students are sometimes unaware that there are additional options on a subsequent page. If all options are on the same page, students will save time and the teacher will know that all options have been considered.

Avoid specific determiners   The same types of specific determiners found on multiple-choice tests are also found on matching items. For example, the matching test on page 104 asks the student to associate the founder of Pennsylvania with the name of William Penn. Even the most unprepared student is likely to answer correctly.

Suggestions for Measuring Complex Objectives with Matching Tests

Match examples with terminology   Perhaps the most direct and simplest method of increasing the thought content on matching tests is to match *examples* with terminology, provided, of course, students have not seen the examples previously.

Directions: Column A consists of five events that can be explained by one of the nine terms in column B. Place the letter of the term in column B that best explains each event on the line next to column A. Terms in column B may be used only once or not at all.

Column A	*Column B*
[E] 1. A kindergarten child calls his teacher "Mommy."	A. Conditioning
	B. Discrimination
[C] 2. Billy gives up crying for help when his mother pays no attention to his cries.	C. Extinction
	D. Forgetting
[B] 3. Carl fears dogs but not cats.	E. Proactive inhibition
[A] 4. Delbert dislikes algebra because the teacher is cruel and mean.	F. Retroactive inhibition
	G. Reversal shift
[F] 5. John studied French and then German. He found that he constantly mistook "der" for "les."	H. Serial learning
	I. Transposition

In the following questions you are asked to make inferences from the data which are given you on the map of the imaginary country, Serendip. The answers in most instances must be probabilities rather than certainties. The relative size of towns and cities is not shown. To assist you in the location of the places mentioned in the questions, the map is divided into squares lettered vertically from A to E and numbered horizontally from 1 to 4.

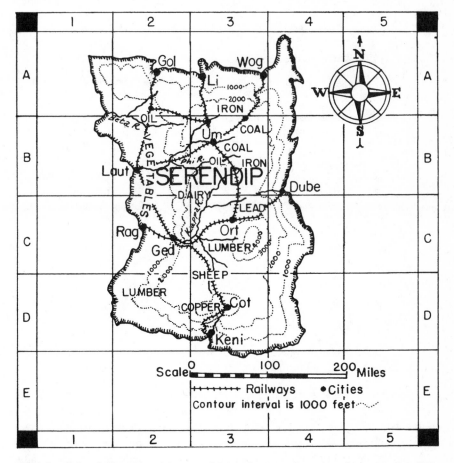

Which of the following cities would be the best location for a steel mill?

(A) Li   (3A)
(B) Um   (3B)
(C) Cot   (3D)
(D) Dube   (4B)

Figure 4.11

Use novel pictorial material   Because of the inherent similarity between multiple-choice and matching items, many of the suggestions applicable to one are also applicable to the other. The multiple-choice item in figure 4.11 can easily be converted to a matching test. To convert this item to a matching format, students will relate the names of the fictitious locations to descriptive statements about the island itself:

	Column A: Map Characteristics	*Column B: Names of Cities*
[J] 1.	Located on the highest part of the island	A. Li (3A)
[F] 2.	Probably has the largest population	B. Um (3B)
[B] 3.	Is in the best grazing area	C. Cot (3D)
[C] 4.	Located about 200 miles from Laut	D. Dube (4B)
[D] 5.	Located farthest east	E. Rag (2C)
		F. Ged (2C)
		G. Wog (3A)
		H. Gol (2A)
		I. Laut (2B)
		J. Ort (3C)

Summary

1. This chapter was designed to help students construct true-false, multiple-choice, and matching items.

2. True-false items require students to either agree or disagree with a statement. They tend to be easy to construct, take little time for students to read, and can be marked with a high degree of objectivity. Three disadvantages are: they can stress an overdependence on memorization, they force students to judge the degree of truth or falsity in a statement, and they are easily affected by guessing.

3. Suggestions for writing true-false questions include: have students respond to items that measure relatively complex objectives; avoid specific determiners, or clues to the correct answer; have an approximately equal number of items keyed *true* and *false;* make certain that the statement is unequivocally true or false; whenever possible, avoid negatively stated items.

4. Because true-false questions yield high chance scores, the effects of guessing need to be reduced. Some suggestions are:

a. Use the correction for guessing formula, which penalizes students for responding incorrectly whether they guessed or have misinformation. Arguments in favor of correcting for guessing are that such formulas

  i. Equate the scores of students who guess with those who work more carefully under restricted time limits.

  ii. Deter students from selecting all alternatives where more than one answer may be correct.

  iii. Discourage students from guessing and thus tend to facilitate learning.

  iv. Improve the extent to which tests are capable of predicting criteria.

  Arguments against the use of correction for guessing formulas are that they

  i. May discourage some students from attempting answers even though they may have some information.

  ii. Penalize students who make errors whether they guess or not.

  iii. Are laborious to use.

  iv. May not make much difference if the exam can be lengthened to compensate for guessing.

5. Chance effects on true-false examinations can also be reduced by other procedures: encourage all students to guess, increase the number of items, have students revise all false statements to make them true, weight the student's degree of certainty (confidence weighting).

6. The multiple-choice item presents the student with a stem (an open-ended statement or a question) and a number of alternatives or options from which he is to select the correct or best answer. Suggestions for writing multiple-choice items include:

a. The stem should inform the student what is expected of him.

b. Clues to the correct option should be avoided.

c. Vocabulary should be suited to the maturity level of the students.

d. Stems and options should be stated positively, if possible.

e. Options should be plausible, not far-fetched.

f. Only one answer should be considered correct or "best."

g. Items measuring opinions should be avoided.

h. The correct options should be assigned positions in the list of options at random.

i. Options that are identical in meaning should be avoided since they cannot both be correct.

j. "None of the above" is a reasonable alternative only if the item has a definite right answer and is not the "best answer" variety.

k. "All of the above" is a weak option because the students need only to recognize two defensible options to respond correctly.

l. The stem should be clear and grammatically correct and should contain elements common to each alternative.

7. Multiple-choice items can be constructed to measure more complex objectives by:

   a. Developing objectives that do not require rote responses.
   b. Presenting items in a form different from that in which the subject matter was learned originally.
   c. Using novel pictorial materials.
   d. Using analogies.
   e. Identifying assumptions and analyzing criteria.
   f. Having students show how various topics are interrelated.
   g. Asking students to select an example of a principle or concept.
   h. Having students recognize a condition contrary to fact.
   i. Interpreting charts and tables.

8. The matching test is essentially a multiple-choice examination in which the student is asked to associate terms, dates, places, events, names, or conditions. Suggestions for writing the matching test include:

   a. Items measuring widely different objectives should be kept separate.
   b. More options than items should be included on the test to reduce the effects of guessing.
   c. Items and options should be arranged alphabetically or numerically to facilitate matching.
   d. No more than about six items should be included in a given set.
   e. Options should be shorter than items, if possible.
   f. Directions should be complete.
   g. All options within a given set should be placed on the same page.
   h. Specific determiners should be avoided.

9. Matching tests can measure complex objectives by having students:

   a. Matching examples with terminology.
   b. Use pictorial material as examples of principles or concepts.

Suggested Readings

Board, Cynthia, and Whitney, Douglas R. "The Effect of Selected Poor Item-Writing Practices on Test Difficulty, Reliability, and Validity." *Journal of*

Educational Measurement 9, no. 3 (Fall 1972): 225–33. The authors found that the inclusion of unnecessary information in the stem reduced reliability. Reliability was also reduced by using incomplete stems and grammatical cues as specific determiners.

Diamond, James, and Evans, William. "The Correction for Guessing," *Review of Educational Research* 43, no. 2 (Spring 1973): 181–191. A brief but readable account of the effects of using the correction for guessing on reliability, validity, test-taking behavior, public acceptance, scoring labor, and statistical problems.

Echternacht, Gary J. "The Use of Confidence Testing in Objective Tests." *Review of Educational Research* 42, no. 2 (Spring 1972): 217–236. An excellent summary of research findings related to confidence testing. The first half of the article will be most useful to students.

Educational Testing Service. *Making the Classroom Test: A Guide for Teachers.* Princeton, N. J.: Educational Testing Service, 1961, 27 pp. An excellent summary of item-writing procedures, differences between teacher-made and standardized tests, and methods of scoring teacher-made exams.

Huff, Darrell. *Score: The Strategy of Taking Tests.* New York: Appleton-Century-Crofts, 1961, 148 pp. An interesting account of the ways in which students can learn to become more test-wise. From the perspective of the teacher, it can help demonstrate practices in writing test items that should be avoided.

Reiling, Eldon, and Taylor, Ryland. "A New Approach to the Problem of Changing Initial Responses to Multiple-Choice Questions." *Journal of Educational Measurement* 9, no. 1 (Spring 1972): 67–70. This is a difficult study to read, but the conclusions are interesting. The authors demonstrate that there are advantages in changing initial responses on multiple-choice questions if there are good reasons for doing so. One's initial impressions are not necessarily best.

Principles of Test Construction: Completion and Essay Tests

Read the following stanza and answer each of the questions below:

"The boast of heraldry, the pomp of power,
And all that beauty, all that wealth e'er gave,
Awaits alike th' inevitable hour:
The paths of glory lead but to the grave."

Boast. *How do you distinguish boast from boost? Would it be an improvement to say, "The boost of heraldry." If so, why?*

Heraldry. *What is the Greek for this?*

All that beauty. *Question: All what beauty?*

Awaits. *What is the predicate and what is predicated?*

Lead but to. *What is the difference between* but to *and* but in? *Which is preferable here?*

Final Question. *Write the life of the poet Gray, being particular to remember that his grandfather was born in Fareham, Hants, or possibly in Epsom, Salts.*

Adapted from Stephen Leacock, Funny Pieces, *New York: Dodd, Mead & Company, 1936, p. 39.*

5

For those with a philosophical bent, the following essay examination format may be more familiar.

Discuss Descartes' proposition "Cogito ergo sum" as a valid basis of epistemology.
Answer:

Something of the apparent originality of Descartes' dictum, "Cogito ergo sum," disappears when we recall that, long before him, Globulus had written "TESTUDO ERGO CREPITO," and the great Arab scholar Alhellallover, writing about 200 Fahrenheit, has said "INDIGO ERGO GUM." But we have only to turn to Descartes' own brilliant contemporary, the Abbé de Foi Grasse, to find him writing, "DIMANCHE, LUNDI, MARDI, MERCREDI, JEUDI, VENDREDI, SAMEDI," which means as much, or more, than Descartes' assertion. It is quite likely that the Abbé was himself acquainted with the words of Pretzel, Wiener Schnitzel, and Schmierkäse; even more likely still he knew the treatise of the low German Fisch von Gestern, who had already set together a definite system or schema. He writes: "WO IST MEIN BRUDER? ER IST IN DEM HOUSE. HABE ICH DEN VOGEL GESEHEN? DIES IST EIN GUTES MESSER. HOLEN SIE KARL UND FRITZ UND WIR WERDEN IN THEATER GEHEN. DANKE BESTENS."

Stephen Leacock, *Funny Pieces,* p. 6

The author of these essays assures us that he once walked into an examination room in Toronto in 1891, wrote what he thought was a paper on English philosophy, and received—much to his pleasure and surprise—a degree in ethnology.

True-false, multiple-choice, and matching items ask the examinee to *recognize* the correct or best answer. In contrast, completion and essay tests require the examinee to *recall* or *supply* information. The completion item is an incomplete sentence which the student completes from memory with a word or short phrase.

Example: America was first discovered by Columbus in the year _____.

The essay item demands a more extended answer. Essays can be relatively restricted (What is the definition of a speed test?) or much more extended (For what purposes are tests given?). In this chapter advantages, limitations, and methods of constructing completion and essay tests will be discussed.

Constructing the Completion Test

There is a minor distinction between *completion* tests and *short-answer* tests. As defined earlier, the completion test asks the student to complete a sentence with a word or short phrase. The short-answer item poses a question that can be answered with a word or phrase. For example:

What is the square root of 25?
Who discovered radium?

Both short-answer and completion tests require the student to *supply* rather than to *recognize* a correct alternative, but the responses tend to be quite short in comparison to essays. Because short-answer and completion tests tend to be similar, the following discussion applies to both.

Advantages of the Completion Test

Construction is relatively easy   One of the main reasons for the popularity of completion items is that teachers find them relatively easy to construct. In part this ease of construction is due to the low level of complexity measured by this type of item. Constructing completion or short-answer tests that measure the higher levels of Bloom's taxonomy is difficult.

Guessing is eliminated   Because completion items require recall, the student has no possibility of recognizing correct options. Students having partial information may respond correctly on recognition items (true-false or multiple-choice, for instance) but will be unable to supply the correct answer on a completion item. Hence, the role of guessing on completion tests is zero.

Item sampling is increased   Because completion items take less time to read and answer than do multiple-choice items, teachers can give students a large number of questions to sample their knowledge of the subject. This advantage is offset if responses require much computation.

Disadvantages of the Completion Test

They are difficult to score   Consider the following example:

The first president of the United States was _____.

Obviously (at least to most adults) the teacher expects to find the name of George Washington in the blank space. Unfortunately there are many other correct answers, such as *a general, born in Virginia, a man, born, alive, married, elected,* and a myriad of other possibilities that range from pleas for sympathy to genuine misunderstanding of what the teacher wanted. It is difficult to construct completion items that have only one correct answer to an unambiguous statement. And each possible answer increases the difficulty of scoring the examination objectively.

They typically measure rote objectives   Because answers to completion and short-answer tests are usually restricted to a few words, items tend to measure the recall of specific facts, names, places, and events and rarely measure more complex learning outcomes.

Suggestions for Writing Completion and Short-Answer Items

Write items that clearly imply the type of response desired   It should be clear to the student that the required answer is, for example, a date, place, event, or person's name.

Poor	*Better*
George Washington was born in _____.	George Washington was born in _____ County, Virginia.
Washington was born in the state of _____.	In what county was George Washington born? _____

Use only one blank per item   Using more than one blank for each item is very confusing.

Poor

The _____ of _____ took place in the year _____.

Here the task is so indefinite that unless the student has memorized the text, he will probably give up in despair.

Better

The Battle of Hastings took place in the year _____.

Put the blank space at the end of the item, if possible   When the blank space begins the sentence, the student may have to reread the item to discover what he is expected to do. If the blank space appears at the end of the sentence, he can more easily grasp what the task requires.

Poor	*Better*
_____ defines a test which must be administered to only one person at a time.	The type of test which must be administered to only one person at a time is called _____.

To facilitate scoring, have students place all answers in a single column
Because sentences are of unequal length, answers can be difficult to find and
score if there are a large number of them on a page. Scoring can be facilitated if
students write their answers in a column. For example:

Pi, to three decimal places, is numerically equal to _____.   1. _____
If two angles of a triangle sum to 120 degrees, it is called   2. _____
_____.

Avoid using statements taken directly from the textbook   Extracting
statements from a text encourages memorization rather than understanding,
defeating meaningful learning. An additional hazard for the student is that
statements taken out of context are often ambiguous.

Avoid specific determiners   Specific determiners can occur in completion
items if the teacher is not careful.

Poor	*Better*
If two angles sum to 120 degrees, the triangle is called an _____ triangle.	If two angles sum to 120 degrees, the triangle is called [a, an] _____ __ triangle.
The men who developed the first intelligence test were named _____.	The first intelligence test was developed under the direction of _____.

Constructing the Essay Examination

Essay examinations differ from completion and short-answer tests in degree
rather than in kind, for essays usually allow greater freedom of response to
questions and require more writing. Because of the wide (but often unjustifiable)
popularity of essay tests among teachers, the characteristics of essays will be
examined in some detail, and suggestions will be offered to improve their quality.

Advantages of Essay Tests

Essay tests give students freedom to respond within broad limits   Although writing skills can be measured by having students select the best example

of effective writing, the teacher's objectives may call for the student to write an extended paper on some topic. The essay examination allows students to express their ideas with relatively few restraints.

Guessing is eliminated   Because essays involve recall, there are no options to select from, and guessing is eliminated. The student must supply rather than select the proper response.

Essay items are practical for testing small numbers of students   Constructing and scoring a lengthy multiple-choice test for five or ten students probably takes more time than constructing and reading essay examinations. But as the number of students increases, the advantage of essay tests decreases.

Essay tests reduce assembling time   Because there are few items on most extended essay tests, less time is required for typing, mimeographing, and assembling. If only a few questions are asked, the teacher can write them on the blackboard.

Essay tests can measure divergent thinking   Divergent thinking is indicated by unconventional, creative, and relatively rare responses. Because essay tests allow greater freedom of response than other types of tests, the opportunity for obtaining unusual responses is increased.

Disadvantages and Limitations of Essay Tests

Essay tests typically suffer from a number of serious limitations, some of which can be controlled and others of which cannot.

The essay test is difficult to score objectively   Essay responses are difficult to score objectively because the student has greater freedom to write. Also, long, complex essays are more difficult to score than shorter, more restricted ones.

Many studies have investigated problems of scoring essay tests. Daniel Starch and Edward Elliott (1912; 1913; 1913) reported the results of a series of early experiments on the scoring of essay tests.

1. The first and most startling fact brought out by this investigation is the tremendously wide range of variation [of scoring papers in Eng-

lish, geometry, or history]. . . . The extremes in each case extend over nearly the entire marking scale. . . . It is almost shocking to a mind with more than ordinary exactness to find that the range of marks given by different teachers to the same paper may be as large as 35 to 40 points.

2. The variability or unreliability of marks is as great in one subject as in another. Contrary to current belief, grades in mathematics are as unreliable as grades in language or in history. The variability of marks is not a function of the subject but a function of the examiner and the method of examination.

More recent studies have reconfirmed earlier findings. For example, Jon Marshall (1967) found that even when teachers were specifically told to ignore spelling, grammar, and punctuation errors and to mark solely on content, papers having identical content received very different scores depending on the number of spelling, grammar, and punctuation errors deliberately introduced by the investigator. Furthermore, he found that experienced teachers assigned lower marks to papers containing these errors than did less experienced teachers. Another expected but interesting finding was that teachers who were well prepared in subject content were harder graders than those who were less well prepared.

The belief that disparate ratings occur because readers of essay tests are inexperienced is not supported by available evidence. One investigator (Ashburn 1938) had three qualified professors of humanities read a number of well-prepared essay questions and student responses. The author concluded:

1. The essay questions used in this experiment were more carefully prepared than is usual in many course examinations.

2. The answers were read with much more care than is usual in many course examinations.

3. In the cases covered by this experiment:
   a. About 6 percent of the students fail.
   b. About 44 percent pass.
   c. The passing or failing (not merely the difference of a letter grade but the difference between credit and no credit) of about 40 percent depends not on what they know or do not know but on *who* reads the papers.
   d. The passing of about 10 percent depends not on what they know or do not know but on *when* the papers are read.

Although suggestions for improving the objectivity of scoring essay tests are provided later in this chapter, it must be admitted that essays—particularly long, complex ones—tend to be scored much more subjectively than other types of tests.

Extended essays measure only limited aspects of student knowledge
Because extended responses require time to write, the student must have fewer
questions to answer. Thus essay tests sample limited content and are not always
a fair measure of what the student actually knows. This problem is less serious,
of course, when responses are restricted and the number of items increased.

Essay questions are time-consuming to both teacher and student   Students often spend much time answering only one or two extended-essay questions, which may severely limit sampling their knowledge. Teachers also devote
many hours to reading lengthy responses. However, if time limits are kept constant, William Coffman (1972) has shown that objectivity is improved more
by increasing the number of items than by allowing greater freedom in responding to fewer items.

The development of high-speed electronic computers has led investigators
to try to score essays electronically (Garber 1967; Page 1966). In general,
these initial attempts suggest that the computer can grade essays as well as
teachers, although neither does the job very well.

Essay responses are subject to bluffing   Although essays eliminate guessing, they do not prevent bluffing. Poorly prepared students often attempt to get
a passing grade by answering *something,* even if the responses are unrelated to
the questions asked.

Bel Kaufman's *Up the Down Staircase* (1964) provides some excellent
examples of how students attempt to bluff on essay tests. In response to the question "What have you gotten out of English so far?" one student wrote the following:

A kaleidoscope. A crazy quilt. An ever-shifting pattern. Shapes and
shadows that come and go, leaving no echo behind, no ripple on the
water where no stone was ever dropped. Such is my remembrance of the
lost and vanished years of English, from whence I arise, all creativity
stifled, yet a Phoenix with hope reborn each term anew. Will it be different this term? Will I be encouraged, guided, inspired? The question,
poised on the spear of Time, is still unanswered. (I was supposed to be in
Mrs. Schachter's Creative Writing class but because of a conflict with
Physics 2, I couldn't get in.) *

Elizabeth Ellis

Most essays require little more than rote memorization   Proponents of
the essay test claim that it promotes divergent and creative thinking. Unfortu-

---

* From the book *Up the Down Staircase* by Bel Kaufman. © 1964 by Bel Kaufman.
Reprinted with permission of the publisher, Prentice-Hall, Inc., Englewood Cliffs, N. J.

nately this is true only if questions call for that type of response. In practice, very few essay questions require originality, and most emphasize the lengthy enumeration of facts or trends.

Essay tests place a premium on writing   Students can read much more rapidly than they can write. Much of the time allotted to answering an essay question is devoted to the mechanics of writing, and there is relatively little time to think about content. On more objectively scored tests, little time is spent in writing and therefore more time can be spent in thinking about responses. If the teacher is not attempting to measure writing skills, a multiple-choice test will probably provide more information per unit of time than will an essay.

The Use of Essay Tests to Facilitate Learning

One frequently hears the argument that essay tests facilitate learning to a greater extent than do multiple-choice examinations. The prevalence of multiple-choice testing in the schools and the concomitant lack of practice in writing is often blamed for the students' inability to write. Some feel that the more essays a student writes, the higher will be the quality of that writing. Those who accept this position tend to be critical of multiple-choice tests.

Advocates of essay examinations also argue that students study in more desirable ways for essay tests than for multiple-choice tests. Students *claim* that they organize, outline, and summarize assignments when preparing for essay tests, and that they look for relationships, trends, and principles instead of the facts, dates, and details which they expect to find on true-false and multiple-choice tests. But the available empirical evidence does not support these contentions. Sax and Collet (1968), for example, found that college students who expected and prepared for a multiple-choice final examination did slightly better on essay finals and much better on multiple-choice finals than did a comparable group of students who expected to find and studied for brief essays on their final examination.

Other evidence regarding the instructional values of essay and recognition tests is meager, especially insofar as writing skills are concerned. Even if it is granted that students learn to write effectively by writing, the typical essay *examination* may not be the best way to promote this objective. Good writing requires time to think, organize, write, and revise one's work, and too seldom do essay examinations provide either the time or the encouragement for reflective thinking. Instead, the essay test might just as easily encourage inadequate expression, poor grammar, incorrect punctuation, and improper spelling as the student races with the clock to write as many ideas as possible. Perhaps students need to write *and revise* more papers, themes, and compositions under the teacher's supervision. Then the student can benefit from the errors, misconceptions, and inconsistencies that the teacher indicates but still develop his own writing style. However, expressive attention to detail can well destroy the impact of a theme, as shown in figure 5.1.

Situations that Suggest the Use of Essay Questions

No one type of test is suitable for all purposes; each test has advantages and limitations that restrict its use. Essay questions have their greatest advantage in the following situations:

The objectives specify writing or recall rather than recognition   If objectives specify that the student is to *write, recall,* or *supply* information, an essay examination may be necessary. Objectives that emphasize extended student responses suggest the use of essays, term papers, or themes.

The number of examinees is small   When the class size is small the teacher can afford to spend more time reading responses. Reading extended responses for large classes may prove excessively time-consuming.

The test will not be reused   Because multiple-choice tests are difficult to construct but easy to score, they prove most valuable when the test can be reused. If a test can be used only once, an essay examination may be more convenient than a multiple-choice test.

Suggestions for Writing Essay Questions

One reason essay tests are hard to score is that teachers often do not specify precisely what they want students to do. Sometimes the teacher is not sure what he wants; at other times he knows what he wants but fails to communicate that desire to the student. In either case the ambiguity of the essay question and the lack of scoring standards reduce the effectiveness of essay tests. The following suggestions should be useful in writing essay questions.

Specify limitations   Tell the students the length of the desired answer and the weight each question will be given in determining scores or judgments. One way to do this is to tell the student how much time he should spend on each item, the approximate number of words for each answer, the maximum number

THINK ENGLISH IS EASY HERE?

Bad start—be explicit.
Say "eighty-seven."   *"fathers"!*

Fourscore/and seven years ago, our fathers brought

forth upon this continent a new nation, conceived in lib-

erty, and dedicated to the proposition that all men are
not a good word

created equal.
"gigantic" would be better

Now we are engaged in a great civil war, testing

whether that nation, or any nation so conceived and so
You used these
3 words before.

in rule 194,   dedicated, can long endure. We are met on a great battle-
p. 6

Too many   field of that war. We have come to dedicate a portion of
parentheses

that field as a final resting place for those who here

gave their lives that that nation might live. [It is alto-
Trite

gether fitting and proper that we should do this.] *sentence*

meaning?   But in a larger sense we cannot dedicate, we cannot
??   *use another word*

consecrate, we cannot hallow this ground. The brave men,
Spelling!

living and dead, who struggled here, have consecrated it
Don't you mean "subtract"?   *awkward*

far above our poor power to add or detract. The world will
Rule 194,

p. 6   (little/note) nor (long/remember) what we say here; but it can
make up
your mind!

never forget what they did here. It is for us, the living,

awkward   rather, to be dedicated here to the unfinished work which
Too many
"heres"!

they who fought here have thus far so nobly advanced. It

tr.   is rather for us to be (here dedicated) to the great task
Trite expression   *Rule 194*
Use "tremendous"   *p. 89*

Too many   remaining before us: that from these honored dead we take
small words

& too simple   increased devotion to that cause for which they gave the

last full measure of devotion; that we here highly resolve

that these dead shall not have died in vain; that this

nation under God, shall have a new birth of freedom; and
Spelling!

that government of the people, by the people, and for the

people, shall not perish from the earth.

This theme is fair, but there is too much repetition in it. There are six
"thats" in the last sentence alone. Need more variety in word choice, and your
words are too simple. Try again—you are improving.   C—

Hugh Schram, "Think English Is Easy Here?" *Michigan Educational Journal,* February 1, 1957, p. 520.

Figure 5.1. An English Teacher's Correction of a Paper by Abraham Lincoln

of points for each item, or the maximum amount of space to be devoted to each item. Examples of directions include:

In no more than one paragraph of 100 words . . .
In no more than ten minutes . . .
In no more than one page . . .
For a maximum of three points . . .

Structure the task   Instructions to students should clearly specify the task. Many essay questions are so vague or ambiguous that the instructor's intent is lost. If students are to write an unambiguous essay, they must be told what they are to do. Asking students to *discuss, evaluate,* or *compare* without defining these terms invites subjectivity. Consider, for example, how difficult it would be to answer the following essay items:

Discuss essay questions.
Compare multiple-choice and essay questions.
Evaluate essay questions.

Any "discussion" of essay questions could involve their advantages, limitations, uses, or construction, and the student has no way of knowing which of these the teacher wants. It is also insufficient to ask students to compare or contrast unless the basis for comparison is stated.

Chapter 3 showed how objectives can be stated behaviorally to make them precise. Essentially the same procedures can be used in writing essay items. Teachers should avoid such terms as *discuss, compare,* and *evaluate* unless their precise meaning is clear. Terms such as *write, describe, list, name,* and *outline* are much more specific. The following examples show how potentially ambiguous questions can be clarified.

Ambiguous Tasks	*Clearer and More Highly Structured Tasks*
1. *Who* was George Washington?	1. *List* three accomplishments of George Washington's political career. (1 point each)
2. *Where* was George Washington born?	2. *Write* the name of the country in which George Washington was born. (1 point)
3. *What* did George Washington do?	3. *Outline* George Washington's life using the following major headings: childhood, early military career, marriage, civilian life, revolutionary activities, presidency. *List* no

more than three facts under each major heading. (1 point each; maximum: 18 points)

4. *When* was Washington born?

4. *Name* the specific year in which George Washington was born.

5. *In your opinion,* who was the best president of the United States and *why.*

5. *Rank* Washington, Adams, and Lincoln in order of importance. List five criteria you used to rank them. (Maximum: 5 points)

6. *Summarize* the first term of Washington in office.

6. *Write* a paragraph of no more than 300 words describing George Washington's recommendations to Congress concerning foreign policy. (1 point for each recommendation; (maximum: 3 points)

7. *Analyze* the reasons Washington was elected president.

7. In no more than one page, *list* three advantages and three disadvantages considered by electors in voting for George Washington for president of the United States in 1789. (Maximum: 6 points)

8. *Discuss* Washington's marriage.

8. *List* three material advantages (1 point each) marriage had for George Washington.

9. *Criticize* the statement that Washington never told a lie.

9. *List* three events (1 point each) that show the truth or falsity of the alleged claim that George Washington never told a lie.

10. *Compare and contrast* Washington with Lincoln.

10. *Compare and contrast* Washington with Lincoln *on each of the following:* (1) socioeconomic-background; (2) attitudes toward slavery. (Maximum: one page; 4 points)

Make each item relatively short and increase the number of items   Long items that require the student to tell everything he knows about some topic are vague and difficult to score. By constructing a larger number of specific items, teachers can sample students' knowledge more comprehensively and systematically. This also makes scoring essay items easier, since there is less information on each question.

Tell students how many points each part of a question is worth   A common fault of teachers in constructing and scoring essay questions is to arbitrarily assign twenty or more points to an essay without telling the student what will be given partial or full credit. Tell the student *what* you expect, *how much* you expect, and *how many points* will be accorded each part of the question.

Give all students the same essay questions if content is relevant   Sometimes teachers construct several essay questions and allow students to choose the ones they will answer. This practice is desirable when the purpose of testing is to measure writing effectiveness rather than subject matter acquistition. Students can select those questions best suited to their writing skills (style, effectiveness, grammar, and punctuation) and can avoid the frustration of having to write on an unfamiliar topic (Wiseman and Wrigley 1958).

But the situation is quite different if the purpose of the essay is to measure comprehension or understanding of subject matter. Because items differ in complexity, the least knowledgeable students could select the easier questions and in effect could obtain higher scores or ratings than those who are willing to tackle more complex topics. If subject matter is important, all students should be expected to respond to the same items. Otherwise, the choice of topic rather than the degree of knowledge could account for differences in pupil performance.

Ask questions in a direct manner   There is no need to be devious or pedantic when framing essay questions. A beautiful example of pedanticism in essay questions appeared in the *Saturday Review* (Calandra 1968). The author, a professor of physics, was asked by a colleague to judge an essay which he had graded 0 (the student was contesting the score). The question was "Show how it is possible to determine the height of a tall building with the aid of a barometer." The student answered: "Take the barometer to the top of the building, attach a long rope to it, lower the barometer to the street, and then bring it up, measuring the length of the rope. The length of the rope is the height of the building." Although the response was not what the professor wanted, it did answer the question.

The student was then asked to take a second examination to demonstrate his knowledge of physics. This time he wrote: "Take the barometer to the top of the building and lean over the edge of the roof. Drop the barometer, timing its fall with a stopwatch. Then, using the formula $S = \frac{1}{2} at^2$, calculate the height of the building." This answer, which fulfilled the letter if not the spirit of the question, earned almost a perfect score for the student.

In a later and less formal discussion with the student, the author of the article discovered that the student had many other ways to use a barometer for determining height, including the one the professor originally wanted (determine the value of g at street level and at the top of the building). The final paragraph explains the student's reasons for giving his initial unconventional answers:

> . . . [He] said that he was fed up with high school and college instructors trying to teach him how to think, to use the "scientific method," and to explore the deep inner logic in a pedantic way, as is often done in the new mathematics, rather than teaching him the structure of the subject. With this in mind, he decided to revive scholasticism as an academic lark to challenge the Sputnik-panicked classrooms of America.*

Suggestions for Rating or Scoring Essay Questions

There are two general approaches to scoring essay tests: the *point* and the *sorting* methods. The point system is especially useful for scoring a relatively large number of limited-response essay questions. Teachers using this method decide how much weight each question will have and inform students of the number of points necessary for a perfect score on each question. The student's total score is simply the sum of points awarded for each answer.

To demonstrate the effectiveness of the point system with and without explicit scoring criteria, three sixth-grade pupils were asked to "write a three- or four-sentence paragraph that explains whether or not you believe that adding any two numbers that are the same *must always* give an answer that is *smaller* than if the same two numbers are multiplied together."

Student	Response
Lisa:	If you add 10+10 you get 20, but if you mult. 10×10 you get 100. Mult. numbers mean that you add the first number how many times the second number says. Like 10×10 means you mult. 10, 10 times.
Janet:	yes when you add two numbers together it is smaller because you are adding that number only once. 5+5 is smaller than 5×5.
Donna:	No not exactly. Like 2+2=4 and 2×2=4 but I think any numbers over them is higher.

These three papers were given to thirty-eight students preparing to teach, and they were asked to assign from zero to ten points to each. They were told specifically to disregard spelling, handwriting, punctuation, neatness, grammar,

---

* Copyright 1968 by Saturday Review, Inc. Alexander Calandra, "Angels on a Pin," *Saturday Review*, December 21, 1968, p. 60. Copyright 1968 Saturday Review, Inc.

and awkwardness of expression. They were also informed that all three pupils were sixth-graders from a nearby "average" elementary school. For comparison, the pupils' teacher agreed to read the responses of all pupils in the class (who were given fictitious code names to make identification more difficult). You might find it illuminating to assign scores from 0 to 10 to each paper yourself before checking the results in table 5.1.

Table 5.1. Points Assigned to Three Papers by Thirty-eight Students Preparing to Teach and the Classroom Teacher on Two Separate Occasions

Lisa		Janet		Donna	
Points	Frequency	Points	Frequency	Points	Frequency
10	2	10	1	10	2
9	3	9	2	9	1
8	5	**8	2	8	3
7	6	7	3	7	4
*6	5	6	2	6	4
**5	8	5	10	5	2
4	1	*4	4	*4	5
3	3	3	5	3	7
2	3	2	5	**2	5
1	1	1	2	1	3
0	1	0	2	0	2
Average	5.5		4.5		4.4

* Teacher's first estimate of the pupil's score.
** Teacher's second estimate of the pupil's score.

The raters assigned all possible scores from 0 to 10 to each paper. In the absence of scoring criteria, each rater assigned scores based on his own subjective etimates of the pupil's performance. The teacher, by the way, had assigned scores of 6, 4, and 4 to the papers of Lisa, Janet, and Donna, respectively, admittedly based on her "general impressions" of the responses. It is interesting to note that when she was asked (unexpectedly) to rescore *all* papers one day later, the scores of Lisa, Janet, and Donna were reported as 5, 8, and 2, respectively. Even when the same teacher reread papers just one day later, both Lisa and Donna were rated lower, whereas Janet increased her score by four points. Therefore, it is obvious that the teacher's judgment is not necessarily an accurate criterion.

The important point to remember is that in the absence of clearly defined scoring criteria, raters tend to assign values to essay responses from their subjective impressions. Because these perspectives vary not only from person to person but also within the same individual at different times, teachers must develop criteria that they can refer to and depend on as they read each answer. If scoring criteria are made explicit, greater agreement among readers should follow.

When a point system of scoring is used, it is useful to specify the number of points to be given to each type of response *at the time the questions are being written*. This enables the teacher to inform the pupil of the maximum number of points possible for each response and to phrase questions to elicit the type of response desired. A serious situation arises when the teacher informs students that an essay is worth thirty points but later discovers that she cannot discriminate that finely among responses and is thus forced to assign points haphazardly.

It is not always necessary to anticipate criteria for every possible point allocated to a given response. If an extended essay is given a maximum value of only one or two points, it cannot differentiate among subtle differences in student responses. On the other hand, little is gained by trying to differentiate among responses to a very simple question by trying to allocate portions of 100 points to minor degrees of correctness.

The optimal number of points to be given an essay depends on how accurately the teacher can describe the nature of responses to be accorded different score values (Coffman 1972). For example, a teacher planning to assign a maximum of fifteen points to a question should be able to develop criteria for answers of three, six, nine, twelve, and fifteen points.

The reason for defining the scoring criteria *before* the test is given can be shown by reexamining the responses of the three pupils on page 126. Lisa and Janet have both given a correct example in which the sum is smaller than the product. The rest of Lisa's response describes the meaning of multiplication. Neither of them has considered the possibility that the sum may equal the product (as Donna has) or that the sum may be larger than the product ($1 + 1$ is larger than 1×1). If extra points are to be given for providing an example or for stating a principle, the student should be informed of this when he takes the test. One simple scoring criterion is:

> 1 point for a statement or example showing that a sum may be larger than a product
> 1 point for a statement or example showing that a sum and product may be equal
> 1 point for a statement or example showing that for any number larger than 2, the sums are smaller than products
> Disregard incorrect, irrelevant, or unclear statements or examples; disregard any generalization for which there are exceptions; disregard any multiple examples of the same principle.

The directions to the students could then read: "For a maximum of three points, give three reasons or examples to prove the following statement either true or false: Adding any same two numbers *must always* give an answer smaller than multiplying the same two numbers." Applying these criteria to Lisa, Janet, and Donna's responses, one point should be assigned to both Lisa's and Janet's papers and two points to Donna's.

Another possibility is to develop scoring criteria at the time responses to each item are read. This may necessitate rereading some papers to make certain that criteria are applied equitably and standards are not allowed to vary from paper to paper. The major objection to this practice is that it may encourage teachers to write vague questions but then try to "compensate" for this by developing criteria after it is too late for the pupil to modify his responses.

The *sorting* method is more appropriate than the point system for rating longer essays. Rather than examining every sentence or main idea the student writes to determine how many points he is to receive, the teacher estimates the overall quality of each answer. He places the best responses in one pile, the worst in another, and intermediate ones in between. If letter grades are given, papers may be sorted into five piles.

After the papers are initially sorted, it is a good idea to reread papers in each pile to ensure homogeneity. The purpose is to sort papers to maximize differences between groups and to minimize differences within each group.

But whether the point system or the sorting method is used, the objectivity of essay test scoring can be increased. Some suggestions follow.

Remove names from papers before scoring   This reduces the *halo effect,* the tendency on the part of a rater to allow his general impressions of a person to influence his evaluation of specific behaviors. Thus the fact that John is particularly well liked by his teachers and is generally considered to be an excellent student can make it difficult for a teacher to score John's essay objectively. By removing all names from papers before scoring them, the teacher reduces the probability that grading will be influenced by his expectations of student performance rather than by the quality of the response itself. Other clues such as writing style and handwriting may be more difficult to disguise.

Read and evaluate each student's answer to the same question before going to the next item   If an essay test contains a number of questions, the teacher may be tempted to read and evaluate all items written by one student before going on to the next student's paper. This practice has two serious consequences: if the student does well on the first question, there is a tendency for the teacher to assume equal competence on the remaining items; and if the student does well on the entire test, the teacher is likely to rate the next paper lower in comparison. (The opposite can also happen, of course. If the student does poorly on the first question, the remainder of his test might receive a lower score than it deserves. Or if the first examination is judged very weak, the next one will probably be considered better.) The first consequence is an example of the halo effect. The second consequence occurs because subsequent ratings are relative to and influenced by preceding evaluations.

The practice of reading the *same* question on all papers before reading the next has much to recommend it. It is easier for teachers to keep in mind their criteria for evaluating a single item as they rate each paper than to remember the criteria for *all* items as they read each student's entire test.

Keep scores of previously read items out of sight when evaluating remaining questions   This can help to avoid the possibility that teachers will let prior evaluations affect subsequent ratings. Perhaps the best way to do this is to keep records on a separate sheet and to shuffle papers thoroughly after all responses to the same item have been rated.

Decide on a policy for dealing with irrelevant or incorrect responses
Sometimes students include irrelevant material in their essays, or they may respond incorrectly. Teachers differ in the amount of weight they give to spelling or punctuation errors, for example. The important point is that students should be told how the teacher will score irrelevant, incorrect, or illegible responses, and the teacher should adhere to the principles he establishes. The teacher's problems are only compounded if students can attain higher scores or ratings than they deserve by ploys such as Arthur has devised in figure 5.2.

Reprinted courtesy of Mell Lazarus, Publisher's-Hall Syndicate and the Seattle Post-Intelligencer. Copyright 1972, Field Enterprises.

Figure 5.2

If possible, reread papers before returning them to students or have other teachers read the papers   Although it is time-consuming, this practice guards against gross error in scoring. It serves three purposes: (1) it gives the teacher some idea of how accurately he is able to score essay questions; (2) it guards against hasty, temporary, and unjustifiable scoring procedures; and (3) the average of two or more ratings can help to cancel atypical and idiosyncratic ratings.

Put comments on the paper   After items have been evaluated, the teacher should let students know the basis of his marking practices, especially if the examination is expected to facilitate learning. A long essay with only a grade on it cannot provide the student with the information he needs to improve. Similarly, teachers who have detailed scoring plans but only circle or point out spelling or punctuation errors lead the student to believe that these were the sole criteria for marking.

Some teachers have developed simple but useful codes with which to comment on student papers. The standard marks used for correcting proofs can be used to good advantage, and other symbols can be developed as needed. It is probably more useful to the student to receive many brief comments on his paper—such as "unclear," "good point," or "expand"—than to get extensive discussion of one or two minor points to the exclusion of the remainder of the paper.

Summary

1. This chapter discusses the principles for constructing short-answer/completion tests and essay tests (short-answer tests require the student to answer questions with a brief response; completion tests require the student to complete a sentence by supplying the correct word or phrase).

2. Completion tests have a number of advantages, including ease of construction, elimination of guessing, and increased sampling of student knowledge.

3. The disadvantages of completion tests are related to scoring and their tendency to measure only rote responses.

4. Some suggestions for writing completion items include:
   a. Indicate clearly what type of response is required.
   b. Restrict the number of blanks to be completed to a single response.
   c. Place the part of the item to be completed at the end of the item, if possible.
   d. Place all responses in a single column to facilitate scoring.
   e. Avoid taking statements directly from the textbook.
   f. Avoid specific determiners.

5. Responses to essay examinations vary in length from one or two words to many pages. The advantages of essay tests are that they:
   a. Allow the student freedom to clarify and expand upon his answers.
   b. Eliminate guessing.
   c. Are practical for use with small groups of students.

    d. Are simple to assemble and duplicate.

    e. Allow unconventional answers.

6. Some disadvantages of the essay test are that they:

    a. Are difficult to score.

    b. Reduce the number of items that can be asked in a time period.

    c. Allow the student to bluff.

    d. Overemphasize rote responses despite claims to the contrary.

    e. Depend on writing skills.

7. Essay tests may encourage students to write poorly unless they are given time to revise papers and correct grammatical errors. Themes written under the supervision of the teacher may be more effective for increasing writing skills than essay tests.

8. Essay tests are probably of greatest value when the number of examinees is small, when the test will not be reused, or when grading will be de-emphasized.

9. Suggestions for constructing essay tests include:

    a. Specify the length of response or the amount of time students should spend on each question.

    b. Provide students with explicit instructions.

    c. Obtain a larger sampling of students' knowledge by increasing the number of items asked and by reducing the length of responses for each item.

    d. Inform students of the weight or number of points each item will be given.

    e. Give all students the same essay questions unless writing skill rather than content is being measured.

    f. Ask questions in a straightforward way; inform students of the criteria that will be used to score responses.

10. Essays can be scored by either the *sorting* method, in which the teacher sorts responses into separate piles that are homogeneous in quality, or the *point system,* which involves summing the number of points students have earned for each answer. Scoring criteria should be determined before the test is administered.

11. Objectivity of essay examinations can be increased by:

    a. Removing the names of students from papers to avoid the halo effect (the tendency to allow a general but irrelevant impression of the student to influence scoring).

b. Reading each student's response to the same item before thoroughly shuffling papers and reading the next item.

c. Avoiding the temptation to examine previous responses in determining the quality of a given response.

d. Determining a policy for scoring incorrect, irrelevant, or illegible answers.

e. Rereading papers before deciding on a final grade.

f. Commenting on papers to indicate the basis for scoring.

Suggested Readings

Chase, Clinton I. "The Impact of Some Obvious Variables on Essay Test Scores." *Journal of Educational Measurement* 5, no. 4 (Winter 1968): 315–18. The author investigates the effects of handwriting, spelling, the use of a scoring key, and the order in which papers are read on essay test scores.

_____. "On the Validity of Essay Tests of Achievement." *Journal of Educational Measurement* 3, no. 2 (Summer 1966): 151–56. Coffman takes the position that essay tests can be used effectively as criteria against which to measure objective tests.

Coffman, William E. "Essay Examinations." In Robert L. Thorndike, ed., *Educational Measurements,* 2d ed., pp. 271–302. Washington, D. C.: American Council on Education, 1971. The section titled "Improving Essay Examinations" will be of value to teachers.

Huff, Darrell. *Score: The Strategy of Taking Tests.* New York: Appleton-Century-Crofts, 1961, 148 pp. Chapter 12 points out ways in which students can capitalize on improper methods used to construct essay tests.

Klein, Stephen P., and Hart, Frederick M. "Chance and Systematic Factors Affecting Essay Grades." *Journal of Educational Measurement* 5, no. 3 (Fall 1968): 197–206. A detailed analysis of how marks are assigned in a law school, where greater than average care is given to reading and evaluating essays. An interesting finding was that persons with no training in law assigned the same marks to student papers as did law professors.

6

Chapter 1 defined measurement as "the assigning of numbers to attributes according to rules." In education, these numbers usually consist of scores from pencil-and-paper tests, but they can also be obtained by observing how students respond to other kinds of tasks, such as the number of aggressive acts committed by pupils, their frequency of tardiness, or the extent to which students interact positively with the teacher. The evaluator uses a wide variety of observational techniques with his experience and knowledge to determine a course of action. Whether the course of action is optimal depends in part on the accuracy and relevance of the measurements and the background of the evaluator.

The more accurate and relevant the measurements are, the greater is the probability that appropriate decisions can be reached. All members of the scientific community—including teachers—depend on empirically derived data (measurements) to help them reach decisions. The *purpose* of testing determines the degree of accuracy required. The physicist can measure intraatomic distances with extremely precise instruments, but the carpenter would hardly demand the same degree of accuracy in measuring a strip of lumber. IQ scores need not be specified more precisely than by a whole number, but teachers would probably feel uncomfortable with a report that a student had an IQ somewhere between 80 and 140. Such imprecision would greatly limit decisions.

This chapter examines various techniques used to summarize and interpret measurements, beginning with a system of classifying measurements according to their properties and assumptions. Various "summary statistics," such as measures of central tendency, variability, and association, and their relationships will also be discussed.

Discrete and Continuous Variables

A *variable* is any quantity that can have different values. In the formula used to convert feet to inches (inches = 12 × feet), both inches and feet are variables since they can take any values assigned to them. Similarly, in the formula used to convert centigrade temperatures to Fahrenheit temperatures ($F = \frac{9}{5} C + 32$), both F and C are variables because they can be represented by different values.

A *constant* is any fixed or unvarying quantity. In the formula for changing feet to inches, the value 12 is unchangeable and is therefore a constant. In the formula for converting degrees centigrade to degrees Fahrenheit, the values $\frac{9}{5}$ and +32 are constants. Other examples of constants include pi (3.1416), $\frac{1}{12}$ when used to convert annual salaries to monthly salaries, and 60 when used for changing minutes to seconds.

Variables may be discrete or continuous. *Discrete variables* contain a limited set of frequencies that the variables can yield between any two values being counted. In contrast, *continuous variables* are measured along a continuum and are approximations accurate only to a specified degree. Weight and height, for example, are continuous variables because their measurements can, at least theoretically, yield an infinite number of values depending on the accuracy of the measuring scale.

The number of students in a room is an example of a discrete variable since the set of frequencies between 30 and 32 has only one possible value. Similarly, the number of persons who are married or single, who are citizens or noncitizens, or who earn hourly wages of $2.00, $2.01, and $2.03 is fixed for any given set of data. The variables are exact, and any number assigned to them represents a definite value having no intermediate point. (One cannot be a partial citizen or half married.) On the other hand, the states of being happy or sad, fat or thin, neurotic or normal are examples of continuous variables because any values assigned to these attributes are only approximations which could be made more precise by using more accurate measuring devices. For example, length could be measured to the nearest inch (e.g., 60, 61, 62, and so on), half inch (60.0, 60.5, 61.0, 61.5, 62.0), or quarter inch (60.00, 60.25, 60.50, 60.75, 61.00, 61.25, 61.50, 61.75, 62.00). For some types of carpentry work, accuracy to $\frac{1}{16}$ of an inch or smaller may be necessary, but in the routine measurement of pupils' heights, accuracy to the nearest inch is sufficient. Because length can always be subdivided into smaller units, it is a continuous variable.

If accuracy is required to the nearest inch, how do we classify the height of a student who measures $60\frac{3}{4}$ inches? The rule is to decide on the unit of measurement (in this case, the inch) required by the task (estimating height) and to consider any given measurement (such as 60 inches) as including all values that are *one-half unit below* to *one-half unit above* it. Therefore, 60 inches will include all values that range from 59.5 (one-half unit below 60) to 60.5 inches (one-half unit above 60); 61 inches includes all values from 60.5 to 61.5 inches; 62 inches, from 61.5 to 62.5 inches, and so on. Thus *to the nearest inch,* a student who measures 60¾ inches would be recorded as being 61 inches tall. Table 6.1 provides other examples that show how limits are established for continuous variables having different degrees of accuracy. The range of a value was determined by taking one-half the degree of accuracy and then adding that value to and subtracting it from the example value.

Table 6.1. Examples Demonstrating How Limits Are Determined for Continuous Variables Having Different Degrees of Accuracy

Variable	Unit of Measurement	Degree of Accuracy	One-Half the Degree of Accuracy	Example Value	Range
Height	Inch	Nearest inch	½ of 1 = .5	61 inches	60.5–61.5
Height	Inch	Nearest ½ inch	½ of ½ = .25	61 inches	60.75–61.25
Height	Inch	Nearest $\frac{1}{100}$ inch	½ of $\frac{1}{100}$ = .005	61 inches	60.995–61.005
Weight	Pound	Nearest $\frac{1}{10}$ pound	½ of $\frac{1}{10}$ = .05	100 pounds	99.95–100.05
Time	Hour	Nearest ½ hour	½ of ½ = .25	25 hours	24.75–25.25
Time	Seconds	Nearest $\frac{1}{1000}$ second	½ of $\frac{1}{1000}$ = .0005	30 seconds	29.9995–30.0005
Knowledge	Points correct	Nearest point	½ of 1 = .5	80 points	79.5–80.5

Test scores are also measured along a continuum that represents some attribute such as knowledge, aptitude, or interest. The unit of measurement is usually the number of items answered correctly, and the degree of accuracy is to the nearest point. Considered in this way, a score of 80 represents all intermediate values from 79.5 to 80.5 even though partial credit may not be given.

Scales or Units of Measurement

In addition to being classified as discrete or continuous, measurements may also be classified as nominal, ordinal, interval, or ratio scales.

Nominal Scales

Nominal scales assign attributes to different discrete and unordered categories. Nominal scales help distinguish between or among different class members, but because these scales are not quantitative, they are pseudomeasurements at best. The categories used to describe different makes of cars (Buick, Ford, Chevrolet, etc.) are nominal scales since they discriminate one member of a category from another.

Scales that categorize objects, persons, or places are nominal because they presume only qualitative distinctions. A *blackboard* differs from a piece of *chalk,* and *John R. Jones* is not the same as *John S. Jones.*

Numerals can also be nominal. The number on a football player's jersey simply identifies him, and that number can be exchanged for another as long as no two players on the same team have the same number. Note that it would be meaningless (but not impossible) to add, subtract, multiply, or divide these numerals, since their only function is to identify the players. Like the names of objects, these numbers are arbitrary and can be changed without violating any rules.

Nominal scales are always discrete because they involve categorization into specific groups. Measurement involves *counting* the number of objects or persons placed in each category, and those counts do not permit intermediate values. Table 6.3 summarizes the characteristics of nominal and other kinds of scales.

Ordinal Scales

Ordinal scales allow traits, attributes, or characteristics to be ranked without regard to the equality of differences. Generally the person or object that has the greatest amount of an attribute (height, intelligence, adjustment, for example) is ranked 1; the one with the next greatest amount is ranked 2, and so on until all individuals are ranked. Although the ranked numbers are discrete, the attribute they measure may be continuous.

Ordinal measurements do *not* assume that differences in rank equal the differences in the attribute being measured. For example, if height is the property being measured, the difference between the first and second ranked individuals does not necessarily represent the same difference that is between those persons ranked fourth and fifth.

Many measurements in education and psychology are ordinal—for example, letter grades and most ratings. Ordinal scales might rank Albert higher on some trait than Mary, or Bill may be described as having a more favorable attitude toward school than does Alex, but the differences between their ranks are not necessarily equal.

Interval Scales

On *interval scales,* differences between successive categories are equal in the attribute being measured. A thermometer, for example, is divided into equal units, and the difference in temperature between 100° and 101° is equivalent to the difference between 110° and 111° or between any other two adjacent points.

When data represent equal intervals, the original set of measurements can be converted to a new set having different characteristics. For example, should interval data appear as in table 6.2, the differences between successive categories could be increased by multiplying the original values of a constant such as 10; or the zero point can be changed by adding a constant such as 50 points to the product.

Table 6.2. The Effects of Multiplying and Adding Constants to Original Values on an Interval Scale

Original Value	Multiplying Original Value by the Constant 10	Adding a Constant of 50
+5	+50	100
+4	+40	90
+3	+30	80
+2	+20	70
+1	+10	60
0	0	50
−1	−10	40
−2	−20	30
−3	−30	20
−4 ⎫ 1	−40 ⎫ 10	10 ⎫ 10
−5 ⎭	−50 ⎭	0 ⎭

The important point is that differences between successive units on interval scales can be changed by multiplying or dividing these values by a constant; the zero point can be changed by adding or subtracting a constant. For example, by adding 5 points to the original values in table 6.2, the −5 would become 0, the −4 would be +1, and so forth.

The formula used to convert degrees centigrade to degrees Fahrenheit ($F = \frac{9}{5} C + 32$) is a transformation from one scale to a comparable one which has a different zero point and a unit of different size. When $\frac{9}{5}$ is multiplied by degrees centigrade, this simply changes the size of each unit by $\frac{9}{5}$, or 1.8. The unit on a Fahrenheit scale is 1.8 times as large as the unit on a centigrade scale.* The addition of 32 points changes the location of 0, just as the addition of a constant changed the 0 to 50 in column 3 of table 6.2. In that table adding 50 points to 0 provided a new scale with 50 as the midpoint. Adding 32 points to a centigrade scale equates +32°F and 0°C. This ability to convert the characteristics of one scale to characteristics of another is basic in measurement, a point which will be examined in greater detail later in this chapter.

---

* On a Fahrenheit scale water freezes at 32° and boils at 212°. The difference is therefore 180 degrees. On a centigrade scale water freezes at 0° and boils at 100°; the difference is 100°. Degrees Fahrenheit, therefore, are 1.8 times as variable as degrees centigrade (180/100 = 1.8).

Ratio Scales*

A *ratio scale* not only has interval characteristics but also has an absolute zero. Because both Fahrenheit and centigrade thermometers have arbitrary or convenient zero points, it is possible to have negative temperatures. The Kelvin thermometer, however, has ratio scale characteristics, for it is based on equal intervals *and* an absolute zero. This absolute zero represents a point below which there are no possible values. ($-273°C$ or $0°K$, for example, is the point at which molecular motion ceases in gases).

A ruler is a simple example of a ratio scale. Differences between categories (inches) are equal in length, and there is an absolute zero (i.e., negative length is meaningless).

Because ratio measurements require an absolute zero, it is not permissible to add or subtract constants from numerators or denominators of ratios; doing so might yield negative values and violate an important characteristic of ratio scales—absolute zero. But each value can be multiplied by a constant without changing the essential nature of the scale. For example, if one student is 6 feet tall and another is 3 feet tall, the ratio of their heights is 6 to 3, or $6/3$; multiplying both of these values by 12 to convert them to inches yields values of 72 and 36, which are still in the ratio of 2 to 1.

In contrast, interval scales do not permit the formation of meaningful ratios. It may *appear* that $100°C$ is twice $50°C$ and that the ratio is $100/50$ or $2/1$. If temperatures centigrade were depicted in the following way, this misconception would be perpetuated:

$$0° \qquad +50° \qquad +100°$$

In the above example the distance of $100°$ does seem to be twice as far from $0°$ as $50°$. But this is because negative values were not included in the centigrade scale. If the scale is extended to include an absolute zero ($-273°C$ or $0°$ Kelvin), the top line of the figure below shows that $100°$ centigrade is not twice as far from the absolute zero as a temperature of $+50°C$; rather, the ratio should be formed between $373°$ Kelvin and $323°$ Kelvin ($373/323 = 1.15$). Half of $373°K$ is $186.5°K$. Ratios, to be meaningful, must be measured from absolute zeros.

---

* A ratio is a proportional relationship between two numbers. A ratio of 2 to 1 may be written 2/1 and means that one value is twice the value of a second. A ratio of ½ means that one value is half the magnitude of another value.

Temperature in °C	−273	−250	−200	−150	−100	−50	0	+50	+100	+150	+200	+250

Temperature in °K	0	23	73	123	173	223	273	323	373	423	473	523

Table 6.3. Characteristics of Scales of Measurement

	Scale	Definition	Uses and Examples	Limitations
Most complex	Ratio	Scale having an absolute zero and equal intervals.	Distance, weight, temperature in degrees Kelvin, time required to learn a skill or subject.	None except that few educational variables have ratio characteristics.
	Interval	Scale having equal differences between successive categories.	Temperature (centigrade and Fahrenheit), calendar dates.	Ratios are meaningless; the zero point is arbitrarily defined.
	Ordinal	Scale involving ranking of objects, persons, traits, or abilities without regard to equality of differences.	Letter grades (ratings from excellent to failing), military ranks, order of finishing a test.	Restricted to specifying *relative* differences without regard to absolute amount of difference.
Least complex	Nominal	Scale involving the classification of objects, persons, or events into discrete categories.	License plate numbers; Social Security numbers; names of people, places, objects; numbers used to identify football players.	Cannot specify quantitative differences among categories.

Frequency Distributions

Consider the following test scores obtained by sixty students:

53	94	77	58	31	52	74	53	64	52
48	49	79	40	32	54	73	68	50	49
97	47	84	37	28	92	74	67	53	57
62	61	82	61	42	88	69	68	54	59
31	87	22	58	41	88	77	69	46	52
39	86	24	27	48	72	78	62	48	50

These "raw" or untreated scores are difficult to interpret in their present form. Try to estimate the average score, for example. What are the lowest and highest score values? How many students had scores between 90 and 100?

A *frequency distribution* is a table that summarizes how often each score occurs. Sometimes large numbers of scores are grouped into convenient intervals, and the frequency or number of scores that corresponds to each interval is determined. Figure 6.1 depicts a frequency distribution for the sixty scores. The frequency distribution shows that there are no scores lower than 20 or higher than 99. The average is probably between 50 and 59, and most of the students obtained scores between 50 and 54.

The principles and conventions below were followed in constructing the frequency distribution depicted in figure 6.1.

1. Generally there should be between ten and twenty intervals or groups of scores. The fewer the number of intervals, the greater the inaccuracy in describing the original set of scores; as the number of intervals is increased, the more computational labor there will be. Between ten and twenty intervals is optimal for accuracy and convenience.
2. To determine the width of each interval:
    a. Find the highest raw score. In the example of raw test scores, the highest score is ninety-seven.
    b. Find the lowest raw score. In the example, the lowest score is twenty-two.
    c. Subtract the lowest from the highest score. This difference is seventy-five.
    d. Divide the difference by the approximate number of intervals you want. In the example, for about fifteen intervals, each will have to be five points [difference between the highest and lowest scores divided by the number of desired intervals: $^{75}/_{15} = 5$].
    e. Begin the lowest interval with a multiple of the interval width. Since the lowest score is 22 and the interval width is 5, a score of 20 is the multiple of 5 which is closest to 22.

Scores	Tally	f (frequency)
95–99	/	1
90–94	/ /	2
85–89	/ / / /	4
80–84	/ /	2
75–79	/ / / /	4
70–74	/ / / /	4
65–69	++++	5
60–64	++++	5
55–59	/ / / /	4
50–54	++++ ++++	10
45–49	++++ / /	7
40–44	/ / /	3
35–39	/ /	2
30–34	/ / /	3
25–29	/ /	2
20–24	/ /	2

N [number of cases] = 60

Figure 6.1. A Frequency Distribution for Sixty Scores

Measures of Central Tendency

Measures of central tendency describe points on a distribution that represent the average or most typical values. The most common measures of central tendency are the mean, the median, and the mode.

The Mean

The *mean* is the arithmetic average of a set of scores. It is found by summing the scores and dividing that sum by the number of scores. In mathematics the capital Greek sigma (Σ) means "sum" whatever follows. The letter X by convention designates any score value. ΣX means add all the score values. By letting N equal the number of cases, the mean is defined as

$$\text{Mean} = \frac{\Sigma X}{N}$$

or the sum of all scores divided by the number of scores.

Figure 6.2

In figure 6.2, Nancy and Sluggo are able to impress Aunt Fritzi by describing their performance as being equal to ΣX, or 100, rather than $\Sigma X/N$, or 50. The division by N allocates the sum of scores to each person by an equal amount.

For the sixty raw scores presented earlier, the mean is $3537/60 = 58.95$. Appendix 2 describes methods of computing the mean directly from a frequency distribution.

The mean has a number of important characteristics:

1. All scores in a distribution help determine the mean. It can be demonstrated mathematically and empirically that the mean of a random (pure chance) sample of scores taken from the total number of available scores varies less from sample to sample than does any other measure of central tendency. The mean is a very stable measure of central tendency that can be depended on not to vary much from samples selected from the same population.

2. If the mean is subtracted from each score in a distribution and these differences are summed, the sum will equal 0. For example:

X (Scores)	Minus the Mean =	Differences
8	−5	+3
2	−5	−3
7	−5	+2
3	−5	−2
5	−5	0
Sum = 25		0
Mean = 5		

This implies that the mean is particularly sensitive to scores at the extreme ends of a distribution. Note that should more values of 5 be added to the scores above, the mean remains unchanged. But the mean does change when the preceding distribution is altered by changing the 8 to 88:

X	Minus the Mean =	Differences
88	−21	+67
2	−21	−19
7	−21	−14
3	−21	−18
5	−21	−16
Sum = 105		0
Mean = 21		

The mean is now 21, but the sum of the differences remains 0. The mean will increase if high scores are added and will decrease if low scores are included.

The Median

The *median* is the point that divides the number of ordered scores in a distribution into two equal parts. It is found by arranging the scores in order of magnitude and selecting the value that separates the scores into equal halves. For example, when the scores 8, 2, 7, 3, and 5 are placed in order, they become 2, 3, 5, 7, and 8. The score 5 is the median; it divides the distribution so that there are two scores below it and two above it.

If there is an even number of scores, the median is halfway between the two middle values. For example, 2, 3, 5, and 7 have a median of 4 since that value is halfway between the two middle numbers, 3 and 5. If the scores are 2, 3, 6, and 7, the median is 4.5. (Appendix 3 contains instructions for computing a median directly from a frequency distribution.)

Characteristics of the median include:

1. Extreme scores do not affect the size of the median. The two distributions of 8, 2, 7, 3, and 5 and 88, 2, 7, 3, and 5 have *means* of 5 and 21, respectively. But the *medians* are 5 for both distributions.
2. The value of the median is determined entirely by the middle scores when they are arranged in order. The median is a less stable measure of central tendency than the mean and can be expected to vary more from sample to sample selected from the same group. This instability occurs because only partial knowledge about the entire distribution is being used.

The Mode

The *mode* is the score that appears most frequently in a distribution. In the distribution 4, 6, 9, 10, 10, 10, 10, 12, for example, the mode is 10. Sometimes two or more scores appear more frequently in a distribution than do others, and in these cases the distribution is called *bimodal* or *multimodal*. If all scores appear with equal frequency, there is no mode, but this would be an atypical occurrence.

In a frequency distribution the mode is the midpoint of the interval that has the most scores. For the frequency distribution on page 141, the mode is the midpoint of the interval 50–54. When the scores of that interval are arranged in order (50, 51, 52, 53, 54), the mode is 52.

The mode has the following characteristics:

1. It is the easiest measure of central tendency to compute.
2. It is highly unstable since its value may be drastically changed by the inclusion or elimination of a single score.
3. It is particularly useful for nominal data. For example, in some elections the winner is the person who receives the modal number of votes.

Relationships among Means, Medians, and Modes

A frequency distribution may be *symmetrical* or *skewed*. If it is symmetrical, the lower half of the distribution mirrors the upper half (see figure 6.3). In a skewed distribution (see figures 6.4 and 6.5) scores are piled up at either the high or the low end of the distribution, and there is a "tail" at the other end. The direction of the tail determines whether the distribution is *positively* or *negatively skewed*. If the tail points toward the high end, the distribution is positively skewed; if it points to the low end, the distribution is negatively skewed. The distribution in figure 6.3 is symmetrical because the frequencies are distributed equally around the center of the distribution.

Easy examinations yield negatively skewed distributions, whereas the scores of difficult examinations cluster at the low end with a tail to the right (positively skewed). Symmetrical distributions are equivalent in shape on both sides of the midpoint.

Because the mean is greatly influenced by extreme scores, it will have a more extreme value than the median or mode if the distribution is skewed. In a symmetrical distribution the mean, median, and mode will coincide. If the distribution is skewed, the median will lie between the mean and the mode (figures 6.4 and 6.5). The highest point on the curve is always the mode because it has the largest frequency. The relationship among means, medians, and modes can be seen by examining figures 6.3, 6.4, and 6.5. In figure 6.4, for example, the tail points to the high end of the distribution, and the mean is larger than the median or mode. The opposite situation exists in figure 6.5. In figure 6.3, a symmetrical distribution, the mean, the median, and the mode coincide.

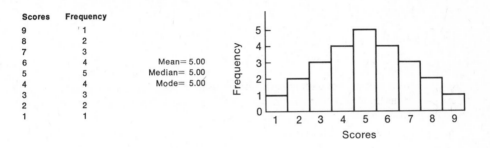

Scores	Frequency
9	1
8	2
7	3
6	4
5	5
4	4
3	3
2	2
1	1

Mean= 5.00
Median= 5.00
Mode= 5.00

Figure 6.3. Showing the Mean, Median, and Mode in a Symmetrical Distribution

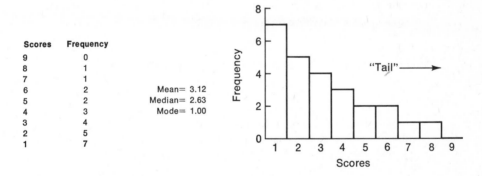

Scores	Frequency
9	0
8	1
7	1
6	2
5	2
4	3
3	4
2	5
1	7

Mean= 3.12
Median= 2.63
Mode= 1.00

Figure 6.4. Showing the Mean, Median, and Mode in a Positively Skewed Distribution

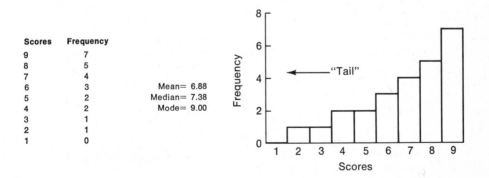

Scores	Frequency
9	7
8	5
7	4
6	3
5	2
4	2
3	1
2	1
1	0

Mean= 6.88
Median= 7.38
Mode= 9.00

Figure 6.5. Showing the Mean, Median, and Mode in a Negatively Skewed Distribution

The characteristics of means, medians, and modes determine which should be used.

Use the mean under the following conditions:

1. If sampling is important. The mean varies less from sample to sample selected from the same group than does either the median or the mode. Should teachers have to compute some measure of central tendency from a large number of cases, it is possible to *randomly* select a sample of these cases and reduce computational effort.
2. If other statistics (such as the standard deviation, which is discussed in the next section) require or call for a mean. Because the mean is stable, other statistics are often computed from it.
3. If there are no extreme scores in the distribution or if the teacher wants the extreme scores to play a significant role in determining central tendency. The mean is the preferred measure of central tendency unless extreme scores will have an undesirable effect by giving a distorted picture of the distribution. For example, if scores all cluster around some point in the distribution, teachers usually prefer the central tendency measure to reflect those values, and any extreme score may have an unwanted effect.

Use the median under the following conditions:

1. If distributions contain extreme scores whose effects the teacher wants to minimize. Because only the number of scores affects the median, extreme scores do not change its value. For example, if a student received five grades of A (excellent) and only one D (poor), the median would be an A but the mean would be a B (good).
2. If the data exist only as ranks. For example, if teachers were asked to rank students on some attribute (e.g., cooperation), the middle individual would be the median pupil on that attribute.
3. If a rapid measure of central tendency is required. Generally it will take less time to list scores from high to low and select the middle one than it will to sum these scores and divide by N to obtain a mean. This is especially true if the scores themselves are relatively large.

Use the mode under the following conditions:

1. If the most typical value is desired. This will occur particularly with nominally scaled data.
2. If the central tendency must be estimated very quickly. Simply finding the most frequently occurring score requires little time. However, the mode is the least stable measure of central tendency.

The most complete information about a distribution is obtained when all three measures of central tendency are reported. Each provides a different kind of information that the teacher may need to better understand class performance.

Measures of Variability

Variability is the extent to which scores are spread out or dispersed. Distributions differ in variability as well as in central tendency. Two groups of children may have the same mean IQ, but one group's IQs may range from 80 to 130, whereas the other group's may range only from 90 to 110.

The following distributions all have three scores and a mean of 4.*

	A	B	C	D
	0	4	0	2
	0	4	4	4
	12	4	8	6
Mean =	4	4	4	4

Clearly the mean and the number of cases only partially describe a distribution. A more complete description includes a measure of variability such as the range or standard deviation.

The Range

The *range* is the difference between the high score and the low score in a distribution. In distribution A of the previous example, the range is 12; for B, it is 0; for C, 8; and for D, 4. Although it is easy to compute, the range is of limited use since its value is determined only by the extreme scores. The addition or elimination of a single extreme case can drastically change the value of the range.

The Standard Deviation

The variability measure most often used in measurement is the standard deviation (abbreviated as *s*, sigma, σ, or *SD*). The *standard deviation* is a

---

* The small number of cases was designed to demonstrate the meaning of variability. In practice N should be much larger.

measure of the extent to which scores vary around the mean. The greater the variability of scores around their mean, the larger will be the standard deviation. When distributions all have identical scores (distribution B), the standard deviation is 0.

Since all scores are used to obtain the standard deviation, it is a more representative measure of variability than the range. The standard deviation varies less from sample to sample than does the range, and greater confidence can be placed in the standard deviation than in the range.

Subtracting the mean from each score in a distribution determines how far *each* score differs from the mean. In the distribution below Ann's score of 2 is two points lower than the mean, and Cindy's score of 6 is two points higher than the mean. The Score Minus Mean column indicates each score's distance from the mean.

Student	Score	Mean	Score Minus Mean
Ann	2	4	−2
Betty	4	4	0
Cindy	6	4	+2
	Sum = 12		
	Mean = 4		

It would be useful and convenient to express the degree of variability or differences among scores in a single positive number. One possibility might seem to be to take the mean of these differences. But because the sum of the differences always equals 0, the mean of these differences will also be 0. Another possibility is to disregard the sign of the differences and treat them all as positive values. This procedure has little to recommend it, and it is generally not used.

Another way of eliminating negative differences is to square them and then take the mean or average of these squared differences as a single measure of variability. This value is called the *variance,* and it is of great importance in measurement; it will be referred to throughout the text. *The square root of the variance is the standard deviation.*

Figure 6.6a depicts the variability or distance of each of the three students' scores from the mean of their scores. Ann's score is 2 points below the mean; Betty's score does not vary from the mean at all; and Cindy's score is 2 points above the mean. To obtain a *variance,* square the differences of each student's score from the mean. For Ann, the squared difference from the mean is 4; for Betty it is 0; and for Cindy it is 4.

The area of a square is determined by squaring either its length or its width. Ann's score, for example, is represented by an area which is −2 units long and −2 units high (figure 6.6b), yielding an *area* of 4 square units. Cindy's score is 2 points above the mean and (squaring this value) has an area of 4 square units also. Because Betty's score is at the mean, the distance from it is 0. The variance is the mean of these squared distances for all individuals: $4 + 0 + 4 = \frac{8}{3} = 2.67$. The sum of the squared values represents a

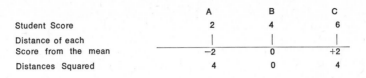

Figure 6.6a. Variability of Student Scores from the Mean

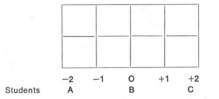

Figure 6.6b. Demonstrating that the Square of Each Student's Score from the Mean is Represented by an Area

total area of 8 units; by dividing by N to obtain a mean, this is equivalent to allocating an equal portion of the total area to the three students. The *variance* is therefore the mean number of square units or area apportioned to each person.

The variance is represented by the algebraic formula

$$\text{variance} = \frac{\Sigma(X - M)^2}{N}$$

The numerator is the sum of the squared differences of each score from the mean, or using the previous example, the sum of $(-2)^2 + (0)^2 + (+2)^2$, or 8. N, the number of scores, is 3, and the variance therefore is $\frac{8}{3}$ or 2.67.

The square root of the variance (the standard deviation) is the length of one side of the square, which determines the total area. Squaring the difference between the mean and each score eliminates all negative values but results in a number representing an area; taking the square root of this area yields a one-dimensional measure of the extent to which scores vary around the mean.* Symbolically the standard deviation is

$$SD = \sqrt{\frac{\Sigma(X - M)^2}{N}}$$

Using the previous example, the square root of 2.67 is 1.63, which is the standard deviation.

---

* Technically the square root of the variance may be a positive value or a negative value, but the standard deviation is defined as the positive root of the variance.

To summarize the computation of the standard deviation:

1. Subtract the mean from each score in the distribution: $X - M$.
2. Square these differences and sum them: $\Sigma(X - M)^2$.
3. Divide by the number of cases; this is the variance:

$$\frac{\Sigma(X - M)^2}{N}$$

4. Take the square root of the variance; this is the standard deviation:

$$\sqrt{\frac{\Sigma(X - M)^2}{N}}$$

PIXies ®   by Wohl

Figure 6.7

Appendix 5 demonstrates the method of determining the variance and standard deviation directly from a frequency distribution. Appendix 1 describes a procedure for extracting a square root. Taking each step one at a time can avoid the situation shown in figure 6.7.

Students typically ask, "What does a standard deviation of 1.63 mean?" Essentially the standard deviation is a *standard* for measuring *deviations* or differences between the mean and each score in a distribution. It is a summary statistic that increases when the variability in scores increases, and it is 0 when all scores in a distribution are identical. The value 1.63 represents a relative degree of variability and should be so interpreted. The four distributions on page 147 have standard deviations of 5.66, 0, 3.27, and 1.63, respectively.* The 1.63 therefore identifies the distribution with the least amount of variability (excluding distribution B). How standard deviations are used is explained in the next section, "Standard Scores."

Standard Scores

The mean and standard deviation describe the central tendency and variability of scores in a distribution. To compare an individual on different distributions, it is convenient to know *how many* standard deviations he is above or below the mean of each distribution. When scores are expressed in standard deviation units, they are called *standard scores*. The most commonly used standard scores are z scores and T scores.

z Scores

Suppose that a student received the following scores on tests having different means and standard deviations:

Course	Score	Mean	Standard Deviation
History	35	35.0	5.0
Algebra	45	50.0	3.0
Psychology	70	65.0	10.0
Art	70	65.0	2.0

On which test did the student do best relative to the mean of the scores of the students in his class? In history he is at the mean of his class; he is five points below the mean of his class in algebra; and he is five points above the mean in psychology and in art. Considering only the student's scores and the means, it might appear that he did equally well in psychology and art because both are five points above the mean.

---

* A more convenient raw score formula for SD is $\sqrt{\dfrac{\Sigma X^2 - \dfrac{(\Sigma X)^2}{N}}{N}}$. Using the example on p. 148, add the three scores, 2, 4, and 6, which sum to 12 ($\Sigma X = 12$); hence, $(\Sigma X)^2 = 144$. Square each score to yield the values 4, 16, and 36; thus $\Sigma X^2 = 56$. N, the number of cases is 3. The formula then becomes $\sqrt{\dfrac{56 - \dfrac{144}{3}}{3}}$. The standard deviation is therefore $\sqrt{\dfrac{8}{3}}$, or 1.63.

Note, however, the standard deviations. The psychology scores were the most variable, and art, the least variable. If scores tend to cluster closely around the mean (that is, if the standard deviation is small), a very high score is atypical and represents a high standard of performance. However, if the scores tend to spread out, an identically high score does not represent an equally high standard of performance in relationship to the other scores on the test.

Suppose that the lengths of the arrows in figure 6.8 represent the variability of scores in psychology and art, respectively, and that both have means of 65. A score of 70 in art places the student at about the top of that distribution. A score of 70 is not nearly as high in psychology since the scores are more variable. Therefore, the student's score in art represents a relatively higher level of performance than does his psychology score. Clearly a consideration of the standard deviation is necessary when comparing scores on one distribution with scores on another.

Figure 6.8. Showing the Meaning of Identical Raw Scores on Distributions that Differ Markedly on Variability

The number of points a person scores above or below the mean in relationship to the standard deviation of scores in the distribution is called a *z score*. In history, for example, the hypothetical student was at the mean and the standard deviation was five points. He is therefore no standard deviations from the mean, and his *z* score is 0. In algebra he is five points *below* the mean and the standard deviation is 3. His *z* score is therefore, $-\frac{5}{3}$, or -1.67. On the psychology test the student is five points above the mean, and because the standard deviation is 10.0, he is $\frac{5}{10}$ of a standard deviation above the mean. His *z* score is $+.5$. In art his *z* score is $+2.5$ because he is $2\frac{1}{2}$ standard deviations above the mean. On the basis of *z* scores, he did best in art, followed by psychology, history, and algebra, in that order.

Symbolically a *z* score is defined as

$$z = \frac{X - M}{SD}$$

The $X - M$ tells how many points the student scores above or below the mean. When this difference is divided by the standard deviation, the number of standard deviations above or below the mean results. *z* is a positive value for scores above the mean and is a negative value for scores below the mean.

The principle to remember is that scores on different examinations should not be directly compared with each other unless both the means and standard deviations of the two distributions are the same.* If either the means or the standard deviations differ, scores must be converted to standard scores (such as z scores) before the relative standing of students can be compared.

Except for the amount of computational labor involved, it is helpful for teachers to convert all scores to z scores so that they can be compared. A teacher's record book might resemble the following:

Student	Social Studies	Math	Science	Art	Music
Amy A.	2.9	2.1	1.8	2.5	1.6
Betty B.	.3	.7	.4	1.2	−.1
Carl C.	.0	−1.4	− .3	−2.5	.1
Dorothy D.	1.3	1.1	1.9	1.0	1.6
Elizabeth E.	−2.7	3.2	.8	2.4	−2.1
Frank F.	.5	−.3	.6	−.4	.6
Gertrude G.	1.4	1.2	1.9	2.1	1.6
⋮					
Zelda Z.	.8	2.4	1.4	.9	1.2

By using standard scores (in this case z scores), the teacher can compare each child's progress in several subjects and can also compare one child with another. For example, Amy A. received the highest score in social studies, and Elizabeth E., the lowest. Carl is average (at the mean) in social studies and is very weak in art. Over all subject areas Amy seems to be the best student, and Carl, the weakest.

The rationale behind the use of z scores is analogous to the conversion of temperatures from one type of scale to another (see pages 137 to 140). Multiplying all values by a constant changes the size of each interval, and adding a constant changes the arbitrary nature of the 0 point by an amount equal to the value of the constant.

T Scores

One objection to z scores is that they can be both negative and fractional. T scores eliminate these objections. Like z scores, T scores are standard scores based on the number of standard deviations that a person falls above or below the mean; but unlike z scores, they are neither fractional nor negative.

The rationale behind the use of T scores is simple. By multiplying each z score by 10, the decimal is eliminated. By adding +50 points to that product, negatives are eliminated. For example, Amy A.'s z score in social studies was 2.9. Multiplying 2.9 by 10 eliminates the decimal and yields a value of 29. By adding 50 points to 29, Amy's T score equals 79. Carl C. has a z score of 0 in social studies. Ten times that value still equals 0, and adding 50 points gives him

---

* Technically the shapes of the distributions should also be equal.

a T score of 50. Carl also has a z score of -1.4 in math. His T score is $10 \times (-1.4) + 50 = -14 + 50 = 36$. Symbolically $T = 10z + 50$. The relationship between z and T scores (and other standard scores to be discussed) can be seen in table 6.4.

Other Standard Scores

While z and T scores are most commonly used, there are other standard scores. On some of the tests published by Educational Testing Service (such as the College Entrance Examination Board and the Graduate Record Examination), z scores are multiplied by 100, and 500 points are added to that product. Thus a z score of 0 (the mean) will correspond to 500, and a z score of $+1$ will correspond to 600. There is no particular advantage of this system over T scores except that they are recognizable as Educational Testing Service scores and eliminate decimals if z scores are carried out to two places. Any other values could have been selected just as easily.

Many intelligence tests convert scores to *deviation IQs,* which have means of 100 and standard deviations of 16.* Thus on tests making this conversion, a deviation IQ of 132 always represents a score falling two standard deviations above the mean; an IQ of 84 is one standard deviation below the mean. See table 6.4 for the relationship among z, T, ETS, and deviation IQ scores.

The decision to set the mean at 500 or 100 is arbitrary. Similarly, the standard deviation can be set at any convenient value. The manuals accompanying standardized tests usually provide information about the mean and standard deviation of scores.

To summarize:

Standard Score	Formula	SD	Mean
z	$\dfrac{\text{score minus mean}}{\text{standard deviation}}$	1.0	0
T	$10z + 50$	10	50
ETS	$100z + 500$	100	500
Deviation IQ	$16z + 100$	16	100

Note that in each case multiplying z by a different value changes the size of the standard deviation by that value (i.e., z scores have standard deviations of 1.0 and means of 0; T scores have standard deviations of 10.0; ETS scores, 100.0; and deviation IQs, 16). By adding a constant to the z score, the mean is changed by the value of the constant (i.e., z score means are 0; T scores have means of

---

* Some intelligence tests set the standard deviation at 15 rather than 16. The decision to use a standard deviation of 15 or 16 points grew out of long use with certain tests that yielded standard deviations close to those values.

Table 6.4. The Relationships among Various Standard Scores and Percentiles*

z Scores	T Scores	ETS Scores	Deviation IQs	Percentiles	Stanines	%	Boundary
+3.0	80	800	148	99.87			
+2.9	79	790	146	99.81			
+2.8	78	780	145	99.74			
+2.7	77	770	143	99.65			
+2.6	76	760	142	99.53			
+2.5	75	750	140	99.38			
+2.4	74	740	138	99.18		4.01%	
+2.3	73	730	137	98.93	9		
+2.2	72	720	135	98.61			
+2.1	71	710	134	98.21			
+2.0	70	700	132	97.72			
+1.9	69	690	130	97.13			
+1.8	68	680	129	96.41			95.99
+1.7	67	670	127	95.54			
+1.6	66	660	126	94.52			
+1.5	65	650	124	93.32	8	6.56%	
+1.4	64	640	122	91.92			
+1.3	63	630	121	90.32			89.43
+1.2	62	620	119	88.49			
+1.1	61	610	118	86.43			
+1.0	60	600	116	84.13	7	12.06%	
+ .9	59	590	114	81.59			
+ .8	58	580	113	78.81			77.37
+ .7	57	570	111	75.80			
+ .6	56	560	110	72.57			
+ .5	55	550	108	69.15	6	17.50%	
+ .4	54	540	106	65.54			
+ .3	53	530	105	61.79			59.87
+ .2	52	520	103	57.93			
+ .1	51	510	102	53.98			
0.0	50	500	100	50.00	5	19.74%	
− .1	49	490	98	46.02			
− .2	48	480	97	42.07			40.13
− .3	47	470	95	38.21			
− .4	46	460	94	34.46			
− .5	45	450	92	30.85	4	17.50%	
− .6	44	440	90	27.43			
− .7	43	430	89	24.20			22.63
− .8	42	420	87	21.19			
− .9	41	410	86	18.41			
−1.0	40	400	84	15.87	3	12.06%	
−1.1	39	390	82	13.57			
−1.2	38	380	81	11.51			10.57
−1.3	37	370	79	9.68			
−1.4	36	360	78	8.08			
−1.5	35	350	76	6.68	2	6.56%	
−1.6	34	340	74	5.48			
−1.7	33	330	73	4.46			4.01
−1.8	32	320	71	3.59			
−1.9	31	310	70	2.87			
−2.0	30	300	68	2.28			
−2.1	29	290	66	1.79			
−2.2	28	280	65	1.39			
−2.3	27	270	63	1.07			
−2.4	26	260	62	.82	1		
−2.5	25	250	60	.62			
−2.6	24	240	58	.47			
−2.7	23	230	57	.35			
−2.8	22	220	55	.26			
−2.9	21	210	54	.19			
−3.0	20	200	52	.13			

* The percentiles correspond to points along a normal curve.

50; ETS scores, 500; and deviation IQs, 100). Remember also that T scores, ETS scores, and deviation IQs are computed from the z scores, and the z scores are computed from the test scores themselves.

Locating Individuals on a Normal Curve

The *normal curve* is a mathematically defined theoretical distribution often approximated in educational and psychological measurement (see figure 6.9). The curve is symmetrical—the left side is a mirror image of the right side. Most of the scores are in the center of the distribution, and the number of scores decreases at the extremes. On a normal curve (or any other perfectly symmetrical curve), the mean, the median, and the mode are identical.

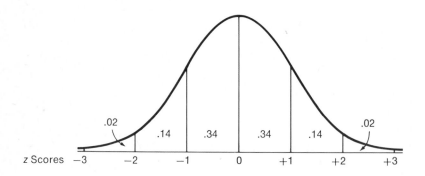

Figure 6.9. A Normal Distribution Showing the Approximate Percentage of Cases between Various z Scores

Some properties of the normal curve are shown in figure 6.9. The curve never touches the baseline. It extends infinitely, although fewer than 1 individual in 10,000 will fall above or below 3.7 standard deviations from the mean.

In all normal curves the percentage of individuals falling between different z scores is constant. Through calculus it can be demonstrated that approximately 34 percent fall between the mean and one standard deviation above or below the mean. About 14 percent fall between z scores of $+1$ and $+2$ or between -1 and -2. About 2 percent of individuals fall above $+2$ and the same percentage is lower than 2 standard deviations below the mean. In a normal distribution almost all scores fall between -3 and $+3$ standard deviations from the mean.

Percentiles, Deciles, and Quartiles

A *percentile* is a point on a distribution at or below which a given percentage of the individuals fall. The 50th percentile, for example, is the point that divides a distribution into equal halves. The median, whether in a normal distribution or not, is always the 50th percentile since half of the individuals are always at that point or lower.

Examine the normal curve in Figure 6.10. A student with a z score of +1 is one standard deviation above the mean and falls at the 84th percentile. This is because in a normal distribution 50 percent of the cases are below the mean and 34 percent are between the mean and + one standard deviation. Similarly, a z score of +2 equals a percentile of 98. Because the normal curve extends infinitely, percentiles on these curves do not range from 0 to 100 but from less than 1 percent to greater than 99 percent. The percentiles corresponding to various z scores as given in figure 6.10 hold only for normal distributions. (See appendix 4 for methods of computing and graphing percentiles for distributions of any shape.)

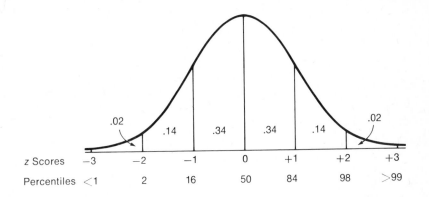

Figure 6.10. Percentile Equivalents of Selected z Scores

In a normal distribution z scores are interval measurements since the differences between them are equal. The distance between a z score of 0 and a z score of +1 is the same as between z scores of −1 and −2. This relationship does *not* hold for percentiles. The difference between the 50th and 84th percentiles is equivalent to a gain of one standard deviation. But there is only a 14 percent increase in the percentage of cases between z scores of +1 and +2. Percentiles are ordinal measurements and should not be added, subtracted, multiplied, or divided. This is important to remember when interpreting percentiles to parents or students. A difference of two percentile points near the center of the distribution means much less then does the same difference at the extremes. A child who improves from the 1st to the 5th percentile is making about as much gain as the child who increases from the 50th to the 70th percentile.

Points that divide frequency distributions into equal fourths are called *quartiles*. The first quartile (abbreviated Q_1) is the 25th percentile, Q_2 is the 50th percentile or median, and Q_3 is the 75th percentile. A quartile is a point on a distribution below which are 25, 50, or 75 percent of the scores. It is therefore incorrect to refer to someone as being in Q_1, Q_2, or Q_3. Q_1 is a *point*, not a range of scores. However, someone can be described as being at Q_1, below or above that value, or between Q_1 and Q_2.

Percentiles can also be categorized by tenths, yielding *deciles*. Ten percent of the cases fall below the first decile, 20 percent below the second decile, 90 percent below the ninth decile. Like quartiles, deciles are points, never ranges.

Some test publishers describe variability of scores using *interquartile* or *semi-interquartile ranges*. The difference between the score values that corresponds to Q_3 and Q_1 is the *interquartile range*. Half of that distance [i.e., $(Q_3 - Q_1)/2$] is the *semi-interquartile range*, usually symbolized by Q. Q is a measure of the average difference between score values that correspond to Q_3 and Q_1. In a distribution with a small range of scores, the difference between Q_3 and Q_1 will also be small; in more variable distributions, larger differences will be found between these two values.

The interquartile and semi-interquartile ranges are not often used because standard deviations are more accurate measures of variability. The exception perhaps occurs in badly skewed distributions. The interquartile and semi-interquartile ranges involve only the middle portion of the distribution. Standard deviations, in contrast, are affected by extreme scores since they require squaring the difference between each score and the mean. The most extreme deviation scores, when squared, strongly affect the value of the standard deviation but will not affect Q.

Stanines

A standard score is based on the number of standard deviations a person is from the mean. Stanines are also standard scores based on the principle that there are fixed percentages between various standard deviations on the normal curve. A *stanine score* (the word is a composite of the words *standard* and *nine*) is found by dividing the normal curve into nine equal segments—each having an interval representing half a standard deviation—and assigning to each of these segments an ordered number from 1–9. The major advantages of using stanines are that they are easy to compute and that all measurements are represented by a single-digit whole number from 1 to 9. If recording space is limited, this is particularly important.

Figure 6.11 shows the relationship between z scores, the percentages of cases under the normal curve, and stanines. Beginning at the mean (where the z score is 0), the percentage of cases falling between standard deviations one-half a unit wide can be mathematically derived. The middle stanine (5) extends from one-fourth of a standard deviation below the mean to one-fourth of a standard deviation above the mean. Approximately 20 percent of the cases fall between these two values. Figure 6.11 shows the approximate percentages of cases corresponding to each stanine. Stanine 9 includes the highest 4 percent of cases; stanine 8, the next lower 7 percent, and so on.

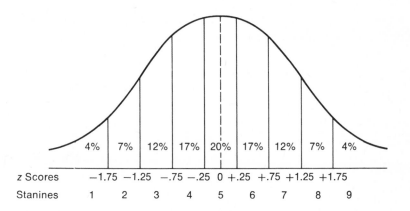

| | 4% | 7% | 12% | 17% | 20% | 17% | 12% | 7% | 4% | |

| z Scores | | −1.75 | −1.25 | −.75 | −.25 | 0 | +.25 | +.75 | +1.25 | +1.75 | |
| Stanines | | 1 | 2 | 3 | 4 | 5 | 6 | 7 | 8 | 9 | |

Figure 6.11. Approximate Percentages of Cases Corresponding to Various Stanines

Converting scores to stanines—no matter how skewed the original distribution—forces the distribution to be normal. Other standard score distributions (z scores and T scores, for example) do not change the shape of the original measurements.* However, by using the percentage of cases in a normal distribution between various standard deviations, the distribution is normalized. This procedure is probably most justifiable when the *population* of scores is assumed to be distributed normally and the *sample* is not badly skewed. For example, the random selection of individuals on standardized tests often results in a slightly skewed distribution. Normalizing the distribution makes it correspond more to what the theoretical distribution might be if an infinite number of individuals could be tested.

Table 6.4 summarizes the relationships among the various standard scores discussed in this chapter. For example, a z score of +3.0 is equivalent to a T score of 80, an ETS score of 800, a deviation IQ of 148, and (assuming a normal distribution) a percentile of 99.87, which is in stanine 9.

---

* In this text the term T *score* will refer to a nonnormalized transformation defined as $10z + 50$. In other contexts T scores might refer to distributions that have been normalized.

Expressing the Relationship between Two Sets of Scores

Measures of central tendency, variability, and relative position (standard scores, percentiles) are used to describe distributions and the position of individuals within these distributions. Sometimes it is useful to describe the extent to which scores on one distribution approximate scores obtained by the same individuals on another distribution. For example, a teacher might want to examine the relationship between students' reading and intelligence test scores or determine whether students' absentee rate is associated with family income.

Correlation is the statistical procedure used to measure the degree of relationship between two variables. This relationship is expressed by a number called the *correlation coefficient* and is symbolized by the letter *r*.

Because variables are often expressed in different units (for example, pounds and inches), correlation coefficients take this into account by converting all values on the two variables into *z* scores. Whether the distribution is height in inches, weight in pounds, or scores on tests is of no consequence.

Magnitudes and Signs of Correlations

Correlation coefficients differ in sign and magnitude. A *positive correlation coefficient* means that individuals who obtain a positive or negative *z* score on one variable obtain a *z* score of the same sign on the other variable. A positive correlation means that individuals who are above the mean on one distribution will tend to be above the mean on the second distribution. Those who fall below the mean (have negative *z* scores) on one distribution will tend to do the same on the other. A *negative correlation* occurs when those who are *above* the mean on one distribution tend to be *below* the mean on the other.

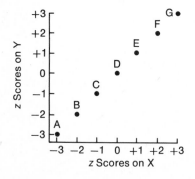

Figure 6.12a. Graph Showing a Positive Correlation

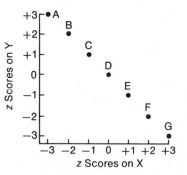

Figure 6.12b. Graph Showing a Negative Correlation

Height and weight are positively correlated, since tall people tend to weigh more than short ones; those who are below average in height *tend* to be below average in weight. Reading scores and intelligence are also correlated positively; good readers tend to be above average in intelligence, and poor readers tend to have lower IQs.

A negative correlation occurs when low scores on one variable tend to be associated with high scores on another. The *greater* the amount of alcohol a person consumes, the *poorer* will be his coordination. Another example of a negative correlation is the tendency for communities with lower delinquency rates to have above average numbers of playgrounds.

Figures 6.12a and b depict the z scores of individuals A through G on two distributions (X and Y). In figure 6.12a, individual A had z scores of -3 on both the horizontal (X) and vertical (Y) axes; others who received negative z scores on one variable also did so on the other; those who obtained positive z scores did so on both variables. The opposite situation exists in figure 6.12b. Here those with negative z scores on X, the horizontal axis, tend to have positive z scores on the Y, the vertical axis. Figure 6.12a is an example of a positive correlation; figure 6.12b depicts a negative correlation. Correlations are positive or negative depending on whether the corresponding z scores on the two variables have the same or different signs.

Correlations also vary in magnitude. When all the paired z scores fall on a straight line (called a *regression line;* thus the symbol r), as in figures 6.12a and b, the correlation is perfect and is represented by a coefficient of 1.00. If the teacher knows a student's z score on one variable, he can predict with certainty his z score on the other. A correlation of $+1.00$ would be expected if the teacher correlated students' heights measured both in inches and centimeters. If the correlation is -1.00, a positive z score on one axis will correspond to a negative z score of the same value on the other axis.

Correlations range in magnitude from 0 to 1.00. A 0 correlation means that there is no relationship between the scores on the two distributions except that which might be expected by chance. For example, if cards numbered from 1 to 100 were thoroughly shuffled then randomly paired, no systematic relationship between them would be expected. Because this relationship is due to chance, the correlation will be 0.

Some correlations of different magnitude are presented below:

Variables	Correlation
Weight in kilos and weight in pounds	+1.00
Height of identical twins reared together	+ .93
IQs of identical twins reared together	+ .91
IQs of identical twins reared apart	+ .67
Weight of fraternal twins	+ .63
IQ and spelling ability	+ .60
Performance and verbal IQ	+ .50
Aptitude test scores and grades	+ .50
Vocabulary and socioeconomic status	+ .40
Honesty ratings among siblings	+ .30
Height and intelligence	+ .20
Weight and intelligence	+ .10
Intelligence of randomly paired children	.00

Graphic Descriptions of Correlations

When correlations are not perfect, the paired z scores do not fall along the regression line but depart from it as shown in figures 6.13a, b, and c. In figure 6.13a the dots form a circular pattern, whereas they form elipses in figures 6.13b and c. The more circular the plotted z scores are, the closer the correlation is to 0; if the paired z scores all fall on the regression line, the correlation is either $+1.00$ or -1.00.

A careful examination of figure 6.13a shows why circular plots yield correlation coefficients of 0. Suppose that many students are randomly paired and given an intelligence test. The IQ of each student and his counterpart could be converted to z scores. Teachers can arbitrarily agree to plot the IQ of the younger member of each pair on the X axis and the IQ of the older member on the Y axis. Each dot represents the younger student's z score on the X variable *and* the corresponding score of the older student on Y. Now consider an

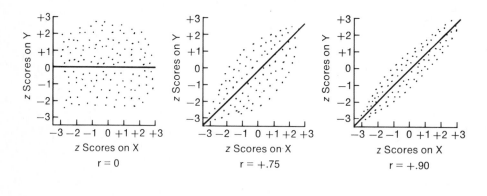

Figure 6.13a   Figure 6.13b   Figure 6.13c

unknown student whose *z score* on X is $+1.0$. What z score should the teacher predict for this student's partner? That prediction would necessarily be inaccurate since the z scores on Y vary all the way from -3 to $+3$ for *any* given z score on X. In figure 6.13a the regression line was plotted parallel to the X axis and across from 0 (the mean) on Y to minimize errors in predicting Y from X. That location for the regression line means that teachers should predict a z score of 0 (i.e., the mean on distribution Y) for any added values of X. If there is no relationship between X and Y, the teacher's best prediction of Y should be the mean of Y because an error in overpredicting is just as likely as an error in underpredicting. If the regression line were placed across from $+3$ on the Y axis, the teacher would consistently predict higher values than are warranted by the data. By drawing the regression line through the center of scores on the Y axis, the line that best fits the data is plotted.*

Figures 6.13b and c again show the regression line drawn to minimize the distance of all paired z scores from that line, but because the dots are closer to the regression line, fewer errors are likely in estimating scores on Y. As noted earlier, there can be no errors in predicting Y if all points fall on the regression line as in figures 6.12a and b. Although they are not necessary for the purposes of this text, there are formulas that can be used to plot the exact regression line without resorting to "eyeball" approximations (see, for example, Ferguson 1971).

Figures 6.13a, b, and c portray regression lines used to predict Y from known values of X. Where this is so, only one regression line is necessary. How-

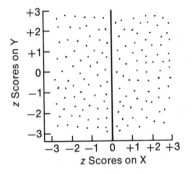

Figure 6.14a. Regression Line Used To Predict X from Y Where the Correlation is Zero

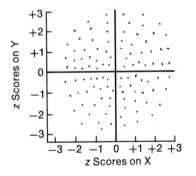

Figure 6.14b. Regression Lines Used To Predict X from Y and Y from X Where the Correlation Is Zero

---

* Technically the regression line is drawn to minimize the sum of the squared differences of each paired z score from the regression line. The reason for this is that the regression line is like a mean, and the sum of differences of scores around the mean is always 0. If each difference is squared, however, negative values are eliminated, and the sum of squared differences can be used to measure variability around the regression line.

ever, what if teachers want to predict in the opposite direction (predict X from knowledge of Y)? If the correlation were 0 between X and Y, a *vertical* regression line would be needed, as drawn in figure 6.14a. For any given value along the Y axis, the best prediction would be a z score of 0 for X. To predict in both directions (X from Y and Y from X), two regression lines are needed. These cross at right angles to each other when the correlation is 0 (see figure 6.14b), and they coincide only when the correlation is $+1.00$ or -1.00.

The Numerical Definition of Correlation as Related to z Scores

The *correlation coefficient* is the average product of z scores. Algebraically this is equivalent to

$$r_{xy} = \frac{\Sigma z_x z_y}{N}$$

where z_x is each student's z score on the X variable ($z_x = \dfrac{X - M}{SD}$) and z_y the corresponding z score on the Y variable. Each person's z score on X is multiplied by his z score on Y; these products are then summed and divided by the number of cases. Note that correlation coefficients are computed for groups (usually no less than twenty or thirty in number because the stability of r depends on the number of cases), and each person in the group has two values to be compared.

To illustrate, suppose that five individuals each take two examinations, and the teacher wants to know the correlation between these two measures. He computes the means and standard deviations of the scores in the two distributions and transforms the scores on the two tests into z scores:

Individuals	X (Math Scores)	Y (History Scores)	z Scores Math z_x	z Scores History z_y	Product $z_x z_y$
Albert	8	13	+1.5	+1.5	2.25
Betty	6	9	+ .5	+ .5	.25
Carl	4	7	− .5	0.0	.00
Dan	2	5	−1.5	− .5	.75
Ellen	5	1	0.0	−1.5	.00
Sums =	25	35	0.0	0.0	3.25
Means =	5.0	7.0	0.0	0.0	.65
SDs =	2.0	4.0	1.0	1.0	

$$r_{xy} = \frac{\Sigma z_x z_y}{N} = \frac{3.25}{5} = .65$$

In this example Albert's z score in math is $(8-5)/2$, or $+1.5$; his z score in history is also $+1.5$; and the product is 2.25. This operation is repeated for

"If only 6 plus 2 equalled 9!"

Figure 6.15

each student to yield a product of all z scores. The sum of these products is 3.25, and the mean of these products—the correlation coefficient, r—is 3.25/5, or +.65. Other ways of computing correlation coefficients that can reduce labor and the possibility of error are presented in appendix 6.

Some Cautions in Interpreting Correlations

Correlations should not be interpreted as percentages   A correlation coefficient of .65 does not mean and should not be referred to as "65 percent"; it is simply described as "point six five."

When correlations are squared and multiplied by 100, the resulting values are called *coefficients of determination*. These indicate the hypothetical percentage of factors associated with the two variables being correlated. For example, although a correlation of +.50 between aptitude test scores and grades *cannot* be called 50 percent, the coefficient of determination obtained by squaring .50 yields a value of .25, which when multiplied by 100, *can* be interpreted as a percentage. It means that 25 percent of the factors that are associated with aptitude test scores are also associated with grades. Using the same reasoning, a correlation (r) of .65 yields a coefficient of determination ($100r^2$) of 100 (.65 × .65), or 42.25. For the data presented on page 164, this means that 42.25 percent of all factors associated with the students' math scores are also associated with their history scores. Although it is not possible to specify exactly what these factors are, there is an overlap of 42.25 percent of whatever is measured by these tests (knowledge, reading ability, intelligence, motivation, and so forth).

By converting correlation coefficients to coefficients of determination, their relative magnitudes may be compared more directly. For example, by examining table 6.5, it can be seen that *correlations* of 1.00 and .50 correspond to *coefficients of determination* of 100 percent and 25 percent, respectively. A correlation of 1.00 is four times as strong as a correlation of .50, *not* twice as strong, as it might appear from comparing the correlations.

Table 6.5. Relationship between Correlations (*r*) and Coefficients of Determination (100*r*^{2})

Correlation (*r*)	Determination (100*r*^{2})
1.00	100%
.90	81
.80	64
.70	49
.60	36
.50	25
.40	16
.30	9
.20	4
.10	1
.00	0

Correlations are ordinal indices   Differences between successive values of *r* do not represent equal differences in degree of relationship. The difference between a correlation of .40 and one of .50 does not represent the same difference as that between correlations of .90 and 1.00. This can be seen more clearly by examining the *coefficients of determination* in table 6.5. There is a much greater difference between correlations of .90 and 1.00 than there is between .40 and .50 when the corresponding coefficients of determination are compared.

Correlations do not necessarily imply causal relationships but only that a relationship of some direction and magnitude exists   For example, there probably exists a high positive correlation between the amount of beer consumed and the number of automobile accidents over each year from 1900 to the present. Rather than believe that beer consumption and the number of auto accidents are causally related, however, it is more reasonable to suggest that some condition such as an increase in population accounted for the increase in beer consumption and in automobile accidents.

In education numerous misinterpretations of correlations have resulted from implying causality. For example, a high correlation between intelligence and achievement test scores does not necessarily mean that one is the cause of the other (they could simply be measuring the same factors in much the same way that inches and centimeters both measure length). Similarly, the number of playgrounds and the incidence of juvenile delinquency in different communities generally correlate negatively, but the correlations do not mean that building playgrounds will reduce delinquency any more than it supposes that increases in delinquency *must* reduce the number of playgrounds. The correlation only provides a measure of relationship; it does not mean that the relationship is necessarily causal.

   To interpret correlations meaningfully, compute them from data that can best be represented by a straight line   The graphs on page 162, figures 6.13a, b, and c, all best express the relationship between X and Y as a straight line plotted to minimize the sum of squared differences of the paired scores around the regression line (see footnote, p. 163). In contrast, figure 6.16 shows a hypotheti-

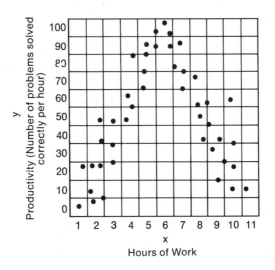

Figure 6.16. Showing the Curvilinear Relationship between Two Variables

cal relationship between productivity and the number of hours of work. Productivity steadily increases in the early hours of work, levels off, then declines near the end of the work day. The regression line used to predict Y from X in figure 6.16 would be represented by a horizontal line parallel to the X axis; the second regresssion line used to predict X from different values of Y would be approximately at right angles to the first regression line. As noted on page 162, when regression lines cross at right angles, the correlation is 0. But in figure 6.16, although a definite relationship exists between X and Y, the computed correlation will be close to 0 because the data are best represented by a curved line, not by a straight line. For example, the correlation between X and Y for the first six hours of work is $+.85$; for the last five hours, the correlation is $-.79$; yet over the entire eleven hours of work the correlation is only $+.13$.

The moral is simple: correlation coefficients are capable of describing relationships between two variables meaningfully when those relationships are best expressed by a straight line. When the relationships are curvilinear, correlation coefficients will be misleading. This is an important point. If a teacher correlates two sets of data and the resulting coefficient is low, it could mean (1) that there really is little relationship between X and Y, as in figure 6.13a, or (2) that there is a relationship but the data are curvilinear, as in figure 6.16. Which of these two explanations is most reasonable can be determined by plotting the scores and noting whether there is a decided bend or flattening of the curve or whether scores generally appear to be best represented by a straight line. All of the formulas presented in this chapter regarding correlation presume a linear relationship between X and Y, and these formulas should not be used unless this assumption can be defended.

The number of cases is important in interpreting correlations   Consider, for example, one student who takes tests X and Y. No correlation can be computed for a single individual because correlations are defined as an *average* product of z scores. With only one case, the student's score will be identical to the mean, and there can be no variability on either X or Y. Since dividing by 0 is not a defined operation, no correlation can be computed.

If two students each have different scores on X and Y, the correlation must be either $+1.0$ or -1.0 because their z scores will be identical and of the same sign or opposite signs. If student A is below the mean on both X and Y, student B must be equally above the mean on those distributions. In this example the correlation will be $+1.0$ since the signs are the same for both students. Correlations computed from small numbers of cases need to be interpreted with caution.

In the previous example of the two students, the correlation must be either $+1.0$ or -1.0 since they had different scores on X and Y. What would happen if their scores on X or on Y were identical? In that case the correlation is indeterminate. If all students obtain the same scores, as, for example, on a criterion-referenced mastery test, the standard deviation of those scores would be 0, and a z score could not be computed since division by 0 is undefined. Correlations assume some variability of scores on both X and Y.

Summary

1. This chapter helps students understand and use various statistical concepts needed to describe and interpret distributions of scores.

2. Discrete variables contain a finite set of frequencies that the variable can yield between any two values being counted; continuous variables, in contrast, are approximations accurate to a specified degree. Continuous variables are measured along a continuum having an infinite set of values that could be measured, for example, between 1.5 and 2.0 inches.

3. Four scales of measurement—nominal, ordinal, interval, and ratio scales—have the following characteristics:

   a. *Nominal.* Nominal scales are qualitative and are used to assign different attributes of objects or events to different categories.

   b. *Ordinal.* Ordinal scales rank attributes, traits, or characteristics without regard to equality of differences.

   c. *Interval.* Interval scales have equal differences between successive categories. Thus the size of each unit can be varied by multiplying or dividing by a constant; the origin or zero point can be modified by adding or subtracting a constant from the original measurements.

   d. *Ratio.* Ratio scales have interval properties and an absolute zero. Constants cannot be added or subtracted from numerators and denominators of ratios, but they may be multiplied or divided by constants without changing the value of the ratio.

4. Frequency distributions simplify the presentation of data. To reduce computational labor with little loss in accuracy, from ten to twenty intervals is the recommended optimum.

5. Means, medians, and modes are measures of central tendency.

   a. *Mean.* The mean is the "arithmetic average" found by summing all scores and dividing by the number of scores. When the mean is subtracted from all scores, the sum of the differences is 0.

   b. *Median.* The median is the point on an ordered distribution that divides the frequencies in equal halves. The median is less stable than the mean, but it is not influenced as much by extreme scores.

   c. *Mode.* The mode is the most frequently occurring score. It is the least stable measure of central tendency.

6. The range, standard deviation, and variance are measures of variability.

   a. *Range.* The range is the difference between the highest and lowest values in a distribution. It tends to be an unstable statistic and is used only if a rough measure of variability is warranted.

   b. *Standard deviation.* The standard deviation is the most common method of describing variability. It measures variability by using the mean as the reference point. The more the scores vary around the mean, the larger the standard deviation is. The standard deviation is 0 if all the scores in a distribution are the same.

    c. *Variance.* The variance is the standard deviation squared. Variances are measures of area rather than of distance from the mean.

7. Standard scores include:

    a. *z scores.* The z score is the number of standard deviations a person is from the mean of a distribution. It can be positive or negative. A z score of 2.1 means that the student is 2.1 standard deviations above the mean.

    b. *T scores.* The T score is obtained by multiplying a z score by 10 (to eliminate decimals) and adding 50 points (to eliminate negative numbers).

    c. Any other set of standard scores can be obtained by multiplying the z score by any number and adding a constant. Thus ETS scores multiply the z score by 100 and add 500 points. The amount added will be the mean of the new distribution and the multiplier will be its standard deviation.

8. Some characteristics of the normal curve are:

    a. For any normal curve, the percentage of individuals below a given z score is fixed and constant. Percentiles, quartiles, and the semi-interquartile range are described in relationship to the normal curve.

    b. Stanines divide the normal curve into nine equal areas. Unlike the other types of standard scores described, the conversion to stanines forces the original distribution to be normal.

9. Correlations are either positive or negative. They are positive if corresponding z scores are of the same sign and negative if they differ. The strongest correlation is represented by 1.0 (whether positive or negative), and a purely chance relationship is represented by 0.

10. The extent to which scores vary around a regression line can be used to estimate the degree of correlation. The more scores spread out from the regression line, the lower the correlation is. The regression line is drawn to minimize the differences between predicted and obtained values.

11. Correlations are the average product of z scores.

12. Cautions in interpreting correlations include:

    a. Correlations are not percentages.

    b. Correlations are ordinal indices.

    c. Correlations do not necessarily imply causal relationships.

    d. Correlations are reasonable indices of the relationship between two variables when those variables are best represented by a straight regression line. If this assumption is not true, correlations will be spuriously low.

Suggested Readings

Bartlett, C. J., and Edgerton, Harold A. "Stanine Values for Ranks for Different Numbers of Things Ranked." *Educational and Psychological Measurement* 26, no. 2 (Summer 1966): 287–89. The authors provide a table for determining stanines when data are ranked. Be sure to read the assumptions.

Chase, Clinton I. *Elementary Statistical Procedures*. New York: McGraw-Hill Book Co., 1967, 245 pp. The first seven chapters describe most of the concepts presented in this chapter.

Diederich, Paul B. *Short-cut Statistics for Teacher-made Tests*. 2d ed. Princeton, N. J.: Educational Testing Service, 1964, 37 pp. See p. 23 for a simplified approximation to finding the standard deviation. Correlations can be simplified computations by a procedure described on pages 34ff.

Edwards, Allen L. *Statistical Analysis*. 3d ed. New York: Holt, Rinehart and Winston, 1969, 244 pp. Chapters 1–6 are an introduction, "Variables and Scales," "Frequency Distributions," "Central Tendency," and "Measures of Variability."

Magnusson, David. *Test Theory*. Reading, Mass.: Addison-Wesley Publishing Co., 1966, 270 pp. See pp. 1–13 for a discussion of scales of measurement and the normal curve. Pp. 32–44 describe correlations and the regression line.

Wesman, Alexander G. "The Three-Legged Coefficient." *Test Service Bulletin of the Psychological Corporation,* no. 40 (December 1950): 20–22. The term *three-legged coefficient* refers to a three-legged stool of which one leg is the use of correlations to predict; another is the relationship of correlations to criteria; and the third is the group taking the test and the criterion. Wesman's conclusions deserve repeating: "He who uses a three-legged stool without ascertaining that all three legs warrant confidence is very likely to be floored."

The Reliability of
Measurements

7

The preceding chapter discussed various statistical techniques used to summarize and interpret test scores. This chapter is concerned with the concept of reliability. *Reliability* describes the extent to which measurements can be depended on to provide consistent, unambiguous information.

Measurements are *reliable* if they reflect "true" rather than chance aspects of the trait or ability measured. To the extent that chance or random conditions have been reduced, reliability will be high, and measurements will provide dependable knowledge. Chance factors include conditions within the examinee (fatigue, boredom, lack of motivation, carelessness), characteristics of the test (ambiguous items, trick questions, poorly worded directions), and conditions of scoring (carelessness, disregard or lack of clear standards for scoring, and counting and computational errors).

Obtained, True, and Error Scores

An *obtained or raw score* is the number of points an individual receives on a test. A poorly constructed test or unmotivated examinees affect these test scores. When such factors are present, teachers cannot assume that the raw scores represent an accurate picture of the student's ability or knowledge.

A *true score* represents an individual's obtained score uninfluenced by chance events or conditions.* It is a theoretical value that can be depended on to yield consistent knowledge of individual differences. In practice, the best *estimate* of a person's true score is his obtained score. Yet chance conditions can sometimes underestimate or overestimate corresponding true scores.

The difference between an obtained score and its theoretical true value is called an *error of measurement* or *error score*. The greater the difference is between an obtained score and the corresponding true score, the greater is the amount of error. (Error is 0 if obtained and true scores are identical.) The chance factors that contribute to unreliability are errors of measurement.

An obtained score may be thought of as having two components—a *true* component that represents true knowledge or ability and an *error* component that reflects chance. This relationship can be symbolized by

obtained score = true score + error score

Sometimes obtained scores are too high because error or chance operates in favor of the examinee. For example, he could guess at an answer and respond correctly. At other times chance operates to depress the obtained score. In the long run, the "laws of chance" predict that the positive and negative effects of measurement errors will cancel each other.

Table 7.1 shows the hypothetical relationships between *obtained, true,* and *error scores*. Student A, for example, obtained a score of 3, had a true score of 5, and therefore had −2 points of error. Student F's obtained score was not in error at all since he received the score he deserved. Keep in mind that these

Table 7.1. Hypothetical Distributions of Obtained, True, and Error Scores and Their Means, Variances, and Standard Deviations

Student	Obtained Score	=	True Score	+	Error Score
A	3		5		−2
B	17		15		+2
C	16		20		−4
D	23		25		−2
E	27		25		+2
F	25		25		0
G	35		25		+10
H	26		30		−4
I	33		35		−2
J	45		45		0
Sums	250		250		0
Means	25.0		25.0		0
Variances	120.2		105.0		15.2
SDs	10.9		10.2		3.9

Fundamental Statistics in Psychology and Education. © 1965 by McGraw-Hill Book Company. Used with permission.

* As Julian Stanley (1971) has so aptly put it: "As used, true score is not the ultimate fact in the book of the recording angel. Rather, it is the score resulting from all systematic factors one chooses to *aggregate*, including any systematic biasing factors that may produce systematic incorrectness in the scores."

distributions are entirely hypothetical because empirical knowledge of true scores is unknown.

The means, the variances, and the standard deviations of obtained, true, and error scores also appear in table 7.1. As stated earlier, error scores are assumed to obey the laws of chance and cancel each other; the mean amount of error is therefore 0. However, because there is variability among the error scores, variance and standard deviation will not be 0. These two values are, respectively, 15.2 and 3.9. (Remember that the square root of the variance is the standard deviation.)

Two other important relationships are shown in table 7.1. First, the mean obtained score is equal to the mean true score because the mean amount of error is assumed to be 0. In other words, the best estimate of the mean true score of a class is its mean obtained score. Second, the obtained score variance (120.2) is equal to the sum of the true score variance (105.0) and the error variance (15.2), but this relationship does *not* hold for the standard deviations ($10.9 \neq 10.2 + 3.9$).

Ideally, obtained and true scores should be identical. If they are, obtained and true score variances will be identical and error variance will be 0 because there would be no variability in the error column (all scores having 0 error). Reliability is then perfect since chance factors are not operating to produce differences between obtained and true scores.

The standard deviation of the error column is called the *standard error of measurement*. Fortunately it is possible to estimate this value without having direct knowledge of true scores. (This procedure will be demonstrated later in this chapter.) It is important to understand that reliability is perfect if the standard error of measurement is zero; and that this occurs when obtained and true scores are the same. When *reliability* is 0, the standard error of measurement is maximum because obtained and true scores have only a chance relationship to one another.

A Technical Definition of Reliability

Technically *reliability* is defined as a ratio of true to obtained variance. In practice, true variance will, of course, have to be estimated since it cannot be computed directly. If the true and obtained variances are the same, the ratio will be +1.0, and no chance or error is operating. In table 7.1 the true variance is 105 and the obtained variance is 120.2. The ratio 105/120.2 is .87, which is the reliability of these measurements. In other words, 87 percent of the obtained variance is attributable to true variance. If the ratio were +1.0, the obtained variance would be entirely attributable to the true variance; if the ratio were 0, there would be no relationship between obtained scores and corresponding true scores.

The *correlation* between obtained and true scores can be estimated by taking the square root of the reliability coefficient. Using the previous example, the square root of .87 (the reliability coefficient) is .93. This value, .93, is the estimated correlation between obtained and true scores. When this value is +1.0, it indicates perfect correspondence between each pupil's obtained and true score; when it is 0, there is no relationship between obtained and true scores, a situation previously shown to occur with maximally *unreliable* measures.

Empirical Methods of Estimating Reliability

Because teachers do not know an individual's true score, they cannot know how much effect chance has in determining any given obtained score. Still, it is possible to estimate the effect of chance on measurements in general. To the extent that error can be eliminated, reliability will be high; reliability will be low to the extent that chance affects obtained scores.

Conditions affecting individuals consistently cannot (by definition) be due to chance and therefore cannot contribute to error variance. Consistency of measurements means high reliability since chance has been reduced. The *degree of consistency* can be determined by a correlation coefficient. *Correlation* is the generic term for all measures of relationships, and *reliability* may be thought of as a special type of correlation that measures consistency of observations or scores. Measurements are consistent (i.e., reliable) when they reflect nonchance, or true, relationships—the same nonchance relationships that enter into the technical definition of reliability (the ratio of true to obtained variance). When error variance is high, there must be a corresponding decrease in reliability. Similarly, when error variance is reduced, true and obtained variance will more closely approximate each other, thereby increasing reliability.

Several empirical procedures have been devised to estimate reliability: (1) the correlation between scores on the same test taken twice, (2) the correlation between scores on two forms of the same test taken concurrently, (3) the correlation between scores on two forms of the same test taken at different times, and (4) the correlation among the items on a single test. These reliability coefficients have been called (1) stability, (2) equivalence, (3) stability and equivalence, and (4) internal consistency (homogeneity), respectively (APA 1954).

Stability

Stability is measured by correlating test scores obtained from the same individuals over a period of time. If individuals respond consistently from one test administration to another, the correlation between scores will be high.

Suppose that students take an intelligence test every year in one school district and every two years in another. The first district probably assumes that intelligence test scores remain stable (consistent) over a one-year period but that retesting is necessary because individuals are likely to respond inconsistently if longer periods of time exist between tests. The second district assumes that scores do not fluctuate markedly over a one-year period and that it is therefore unnecessary to test more frequently than every two years. Which of these two school districts is "correct" depends in part on the correlation between intelligence test scores obtained one year and two years apart. Typically these correlations are about .80 or .90, and remain relatively constant (Bayley 1949). Thus it is probably unnecessary to test children more often than once every two years.

A second consideration is the age of the children. As might be expected, many more chance factors enter into the measurement of young children than of older ones. More frequent testing may thus be necessary in the lower grades.

Still a third consideration is the use to be made of test results. If decisions are crucial, teachers may be satisfied only with reliabilities in the .90s. On the other hand, for routine matters they may be satisfied with much lower reliabilities. Practical limitations may, of course, force teachers to make decisions even when reliability is low.

One factor strongly affecting stability is the amount of time that elapses between successive administrations of the same test. If an examination is immediately repeated, students are likely to mark the same answers twice. Short-term memory may produce highly consistent test scores, but the usefulness of high reliabilities over very short periods of time is questionable. Generally teachers want to know how stable measurements are over periods of time ranging from several months to several years.

Another factor affecting stability coefficients is scorer reliability. Stability coefficients may be low because raters use different criteria at different times. This can be prevented by developing more objective scoring systems.

The use of stability as a measure of reliability assumes that the traits or factors being measured remain constant. Because intelligence scores, for example, are most useful if they remain fairly consistent, high stability coefficients are desirable. However, stable scores are *not* desirable if the test is supposed to measure an unstable trait. A test that measures mood, for example, should yield highly *unstable* measures because mood is expected to fluctuate.

Different time intervals between initial and subsequent testings usually lead to different coefficients of stability. If time intervals are short, stability coefficients are likely to be high; over longer periods of time, stability coefficients decrease. That is why it is more accurate to talk about the reliability of *measurements* (data, scores, and observations) than the reliability of *tests* (questions, items, and other tasks). Tests cannot be stable or unstable, but observations can. Any reference to the "reliability of a test" should always be interpreted to mean the "reliability of measurements or observations derived from a test." An accurate description of how stability should be reported for standardized tests is: "For a sample of sixty-five fourth-grade children tested on the Z Intelligence

Test, a stability coefficient of .89 was found for an interval of ten months." Data from other samples of children over different time intervals should also be reported if available.

Equivalence

Equivalence is determined by constructing two or more forms of an examination and administering them to the same persons at about the same time. To eliminate transfer or practice effects, half of the individuals take one form followed by the other, and the sequence is reversed for the other half. The correlation between scores on the forms is a measure of their equivalence.

Many standardized tests are available in parallel or equivalent forms, and their publishers should provide data on how nearly equivalent those forms are. The higher the degree of equivalence is, the more justified teachers are in substituting one form for another. Students who miss a regularly scheduled examination, for example, can take the parallel form. If the scores are equivalent, it makes little difference which form students take.

Because they are so time-consuming to construct, most teachers will not attempt to develop parallel or equivalent forms. If equivalent forms are constructed, a detailed table of specifications should be prepared. Items that differ in content but meet the criteria listed in that table can be constructed. Those that measure the same objective are assigned randomly to the two forms (by flipping a coin, perhaps). Correlating student scores on the two or more forms determines the degree of equivalence.

Parallel forms are never perfectly correlated or reliable. If items fail to measure the same objectives equally well, correlations will be low. Errors of measurement occur because items on two forms of a test are likely to differ. The more they differ, the greater will be the amount of *unreliability*. However, since equivalence is determined by correlating scores on tests designed to be parallel, the lack of reliability must come from differences in item sampling and not—as in measures of *stability*—from changes in the individuals themselves.

Stability and Equivalence

When there is a relatively long delay between the administration of two parallel forms, a coefficient of *stability and equivalence* can be obtained. This coefficient includes those errors of measurement that occur because individuals change (stability) and because parallel forms are not perfectly equivalent. Because temporal changes and changes in performance on the two forms are both likely to affect coefficients of stability and equivalence, this is the most stringent test of reliability.

Coefficients of stability and equivalence are particularly suitable to the measurement of gain or improvement. A teacher might want to administer a personality inventory now and readminister a parallel form of the examination later to estimate the degree of personality change. The use of parallel forms avoids the problem that students will remember earlier responses and simply answer the same way twice. Yet changes in scores should not reflect *chance* variations from one testing period to the other because chance conditions lower reliability. Measures of stability and equivalence provide teachers with knowledge of the extent to which chance variations occur as a result of temporal stability and the degree of equivalence of items on parallel forms of tests.

Internal Consistency or Homogeneity

The preceding techniques of estimating reliability are most practical for *standardized* tests. However, although standardized tests should provide this information, few teachers will want to take the time and effort to administer the same test twice (stability) or to construct two forms of an examination to be administered over short (equivalence) or longer (stability and equivalence) periods of time. In most cases teachers want to estimate reliability from a single administration of a test. This desire has led to measures of *internal consistency* or *homogeneity*. The *split-half technique* and the *Kuder-Richardson method* are most often used for this purpose.

The Split-half Technique

Suppose, for purposes of demonstration, that a teacher constructs a ten-item examination. Using the split-half method, he scores the odd-numbered items separately from the even-numbered ones. If scores on the even- and odd-numbered items are then correlated, the internal consistency of the measures can be obtained. Consider, for example, a student's responses to the ten-item exam (correct answers are credited with a $+$, and incorrect responses with a $-$):

1. $+$ 2. $+$ 3. $-$ 4. $+$ 5. $+$ 6. $-$ 7. $-$ 8. $-$ 9. $+$ 10. $-$

The student has earned a total score of 5—three correct responses on the odd-numbered items, and two correct responses on the even-numbered items. The teacher proceeds the same way for each student in the class. In the example below (the small number of cases is used only to illustrate a point), the correlation between odd and even scores is $+.92$ (see chap. 6 for the method of computing a correlation).

Student	Score on Odd-Numbered Items	Score on Even-Numbered Items
Carl	3	2
Amos	5	5
Anne	4	4
Mary	1	1
Bill	4	5

The correlation of $+.92$ means that one-half of the test measures nearly the same traits or abilities as does the other half. Measurements are therefore consistent between the two halves.

Tests can be split other ways, but those are generally not recommended. For example, scores on the first half of the test could be correlated with scores on the last half. However, on most achievement tests, items are arranged in ascending order of difficulty, and the scores on the first half of a test may not correlate well with the scores on the second half, where such factors as fatigue and item difficulty are most pronounced. By using an odd-even split, this difficulty can be resolved.

The split-half method has three limitations. First, the major source of error is the items themselves; any changes in the examinee over time do not affect this type of reliability. Unreliability therefore results from the differences in item sampling on the two halves of the test. Because temporal conditions are not reflected in split-half reliabilities, this technique generally yields rather high coefficients.

Second, for a ten-item examination, the maximum score on each half of the test is 5. Later in this chapter it will be shown that reliability will increase—other factors being equal—as more items are added to the test. A longer test provides a more adequate sample of whatever trait or ability is being measured and therefore tends to be more reliable than a shorter test. The split-half method correlates only one-half the responses with the other half. Such correlations provide a measure of reliability for half a test but not for the test as a whole. To estimate the reliability of the whole test from knowledge of the correlation between the halves, the *Spearman-Brown formula* must be used:

$$\text{Spearman-Brown* formula} = \frac{2 \text{ times the correlation between the halves}}{1 \text{ plus the correlation between the halves}} \text{ or } \frac{2r}{1+r}$$

This formula estimates reliability when the number of items is doubled. If the correlation between halves is .92, this value is multiplied by 2 and then divided by $1 + .92$ (i.e., $1.84/1.92 = .96$, rounded). The split-half reliability should be reported as .96, *not* .92 (the correlation between the halves).

A third caution concerns the use of split-half reliabilities with speed tests. Chapter 1 defined a speed test as one which consists of such simple items that virtually no one misses any item he has had time to attempt. The following example shows what will happen on a *pure speed test* consisting of 100 items:

---

* The formula $2r/(1+r)$ is used to estimate the reliability of a test *doubled* in length. The more general Spearman-Brown formula, $\frac{kr}{1+[(k-1)r]}$ can be used to estimate reliability for a test increased or decreased any number of times. When the test is doubled, $k = 2$; if tripled, $k = 3$; if halved in length, $k = .5$, and so forth.

Individual	Number of Items Attempted	Number of Odd Items Correct	Number of Even Items Correct
Mary	50	25	25
Belle	84	42	42
Bernie	54	27	27
Marge	36	18	18
Lois	28	14	14

Mary attempted 50 items and obtained a perfect score. Half of these items are odds and half are evens. When these odd- and even-numbered items are correlated on a pure speed test, the correlation will be spuriously high because all items attempted will be correct. Individuals would then receive identical scores on odd- and even-numbered items. *Split-half reliabilities should be computed for power tests only.* To the extent that speed plays a part in determining scores, split-half methods will yield spuriously high coefficients.

Kuder-Richardson technique

The Kuder-Richardson reliability—like the split-half method—is determined from a single administration of a test. However, unlike the split-half method, it is not necessary to score each half of the test separately. An advantage of the Kuder-Richardson method is that it avoids the problem of deciding in which way a test should be split.

The Kuder-Richardson method provides an estimate of the average reliability found by taking all possible splits without actually having to do so. It is therefore a more generalized procedure than the odd-even split-half technique. Because the test is not split into parts for separate scoring, there is no need to use the Spearman-Brown formula. Like other reliability coefficients, Kuder-Richardson reliabilities range in value from 0 to 1.0.

Although Frederic Kuder and M. W. Richardson (1937) developed a number of formulas for estimating reliability, formula 20 is most often used and recommended. It is particularly simple to use if the difficulty level of each item (the proportion of students who respond correctly) has been determined by means of an *item analysis* (see chap. 9), from which each student receives a score of 1 or 0 for each item. The Kuder-Richardson formula 20 is:

$$KR_{20} = \frac{n}{n-1}\left(\frac{SD^2 - \Sigma pq}{SD^2}\right),$$

where n = the number of items on the test

SD^2 = the variance of scores (the standard deviation squared)

p = the difficulty level of each item or the proportion of the group that responded correctly

q = the proportion that missed the item, or $1 - p$

The computation of a Kuder-Richardson formula 20 reliability estimate is shown below for a 5-item test (the small number of items is provided solely to demonstrate the procedure) administered to 30 students.

Item	Number of Students Responding Correctly	p Proportion Responding Correctly	q (or $1 - p$) Proportion Responding Incorrectly	(pq) Product
1	15	$15/30 = .50$	$1 - .50 = .50$	$.50 \times .50 = .2500$
2	10	$10/30 = .33$	$1 - .33 = .67$	$.33 \times .67 = .2211$
3	12	$12/30 = .40$	$1 - .40 = .60$	$.40 \times .60 = .2400$
4	20	$20/30 = .67$	$1 - .67 = .33$	$.67 \times .33 = .2211$
5	6	$6/30 = .20$	$1 - .20 = .80$	$.20 \times .80 = .1600$

Number of students in class = 30
Number of items in test   = 5
Variance = SD^2 = 2.5

$\Sigma pq = 1.0922$

1. Find the p value, or difficulty level, for each item. This is the number of students responding correctly to each item divided by the total number of students taking the test. On item 1 above, for example, 15 out of 30 students responded correctly, and the proportion is .50. Omitted items are counted as wrong.

2. Multiply the value of p found in step 1 by q, the proportion of the class missing the item. If p is the proportion responding correctly, q is $1 - p$. Using item 1 as an example, if .50 respond correctly, .50 must have responded incorrectly. Note that $p + q$ always $= 1.0$, since everyone responds either correctly or incorrectly to each item.

3. Compute the variance (the square of the standard deviation). Computation of the variance, of course, requires the distribution of scores. For the example above this value is given as 2.5.

4. Add all of the pq values to give Σpq. Subtract Σpq from the variance.

5. Divide the value found in step 4 by the variance and multiply this quotient by $\dfrac{n}{(n-1)}$, where n is the number of items on the examination. Do not confuse n (the number of items) with N (the number of students).

Substituting the values in the example into the Kuder-Richardson formula 20 yields the following:

$$KR_{20} = \frac{n}{n-1}\left(\frac{SD^2 - \Sigma pq}{SD^2}\right) = \frac{5}{4}\left(\frac{2.5 - 1.0922}{2.5}\right) = \frac{5}{4}\left(\frac{1.41}{2.5}\right) = .71$$

It is not necessary to be able to derive the Kuder-Richardson formula 20 (KR_{20}) mathematically to understand its meaning and to learn how to use it. SD^2 has already been defined as the variance of a test (the standard deviation

$$pq = \frac{\Sigma(x-M)^2}{N}$$

squared). Just as a distribution of test scores can have variability, so can each of the items. If everyone responds correctly or incorrectly to an item, its variance will be 0 since there is no variability. In the formula pq is the variance for a single item, and the Σpq is the sum of the individual item variances. Note that KR_{20} will be 0 if SD^2 and Σpq are the same. Also, KR_{20} increases in magnitude as the difference between SD^2 and Σpq increases because the total test variance (SD^2) is composed not only of the sum of the individual item variances (Σpq) but also of what are called *covariances* (C) or the correlations among the various items constituting the test. Only when the covariances among items are 0 will $SD^2 = \Sigma pq$. Note again from the formula for KR_{20} that when SD^2 does equal Σpq the reliability *is* 0. In other words, when the items are all unrelated to each other such that the covariances are 0, each item measures something distinct from all other items, and the measurements are maximally heterogeneous. Then KR_{20} will be 0.

How does the teacher create a homogeneous or internally consistent set of measurements? The answer is to construct items that measure the same objectives to increase the covariance or correlation among these items. A high correlation among items means that they measure the same trait or ability and are thus internally consistent.

The numerator for KR_{20} ($SD^2 - \Sigma pq$) actually yields the covariance terms, which, as stated earlier, involve the correlations among items. When items correlate with one another, they are measuring nonchance factors or *true scores* (see pp. 172–173). Thus the numerator for KR_{20} is an estimate of true variance which when divided by the obtained variance satisfies the technical definition of reliability.

The Kuder-Richardson formula 20, like the split-half technique, assumes that the test is designed to measure power rather than speed. It is easy to see what would happen if the Kuder-Richardson method were used with a pure speed test. Since each item attempted will be correct, its p value will be $+1.0$. Items near the end of the test will have p values of 0 since no one will attempt them. In either case the product of pq will be 0, and $\Sigma pq = 0$. This leaves the variance divided by the variance, which of course will equal $+1.0$—a spuriously high value.

Kuder-Richardson reliabilities also assume that items should measure the same trait, factor, or attribute. When the teacher recognizes and accepts this assumption, the Kuder-Richardson formula provides a meaningful way of estimating reliability from a single administration of a test. A student who performs well on such a test has demonstrated his knowledge on a set of items all measuring the same attribute.

This last sentence demonstrates an important difference between the split-half technique and the Kuder-Richardson method. It is possible, for example, for item 1 on form A of a test to measure the same trait as the first item on form B. Item 2 on forms A and B could also be parallel items but measure a different ability than does item 1. In this admittedly extreme case, where items are parallel *between* forms but differ widely in what they measure *within* each form, the split-half reliability could be perfect whereas the Kuder-Richardson reliability obtained on each form could be 0 (Thorndike 1951).

Conditions Affecting Reliability Coefficients

The most common conditions that affect reliability are: (1) objectivity in scoring, (2) the variability of the group tested, (3) the number of items on the test, and (4) the difficulty level of the test.

Objectivity in Scoring: Scorer Reliability

Scorer reliability refers to the extent to which different observers or raters agree with one another as they mark the same set of papers. The higher the degree of agreement is, the higher the scorer reliability will be. An example of dubiously high scorer reliability is shown in figure 7.1. Scorer reliability is neces-

© 1969 United Feature Syndicate, Inc.

Figure 7.1

sary if measurements are to be reliable. For example, if raters disagree on the number of points to be accorded a given paper or observation, factors unrelated to the student's ability are being measured. The inconsistency in scoring will reduce the correlation between what students deserve and what they receive.

Scorer reliability places an upper limit on the reliability of the measurements themselves. Whatever the scorer reliability may be, other forms of reliability must be equal to or lower than that value. This is important because it suggests that one of the teacher's first considerations is to construct examinations that can be marked objectively. (Many of the suggestions offered in chaps. 4 and 5 were designed to help improve upon this phase of test construction.) To the extent that there is *subjectivity* in scoring, reliability coefficients are likely to be low. Subjectivity means that inconsistencies are being allowed to create random error which in turn lowers reliability coefficients.

In most cases, because multiple-choice, true-false, and matching items have a high degree of objectivity in scoring, there is probably no reason to estimate how consistently or reliably different scorers will mark the same papers. However, there are advantages in allowing two or more scorers to evaluate the same essay responses independently and then correlating the assigned scores. This tells the teacher how reliably papers have been scored. If the reliability in scoring is only .60, for example, the reliability of measurements will be even lower. Perhaps the best the teacher can do in this case is to develop more adequate (objective) scoring systems by specifying more clearly the number of points to be accorded different responses.

Variability of the Group Tested

One of the most important conditions affecting reliability is the *true variance* of scores in the group tested. In general, the larger the true variance or spread of scores is, the greater will be the reliability. Keeping in mind that reliability refers to the consistency of measuring true individual differences, the greater these differences are, the easier it will be to obtain consistent results from one testing to another or from one form of a test to a parallel form.

Figure 7.2 illustrates this point. Suppose that a rater were given the task

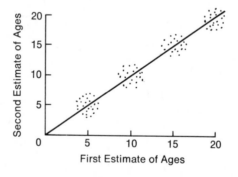

Figure 7.2. Reliability of Estimating Ages of Students of Widely Different Grade Levels

of guessing the ages of four different groups of people: kindergarteners, sixth-graders, tenth-graders, and college seniors. The rater was assigned this task in September, and two weeks later was asked to reestimate their ages without the benefit of notes or any other memory aids. Because there is great variability in the physical characteristics of students in these various categories, he would be expected to accurately predict which persons were in each age group. As seen in figure 7.2, the regression line appears to show great rater reliability in discriminating among age groups, but within each age group, his predictions are far less reliable because it is difficult to determine whether a child is 5.5 or 6 years old or whether a college senior is 20 or 21. Within each subgroup the correlation of first and second age estimates is close to 0, but when the estimates are made from kindergarten through age 21, there is great *consistency* in determining that an individual belongs to one of the four reference groups.

Another way to consider the effects of variability on reliability is to see what happens when variability is 0. In that extreme case all individuals receive the same score, and the standard deviation is 0. Each person is then at the mean of his group and has a z score of 0. Since correlations (and reliability coefficients) are defined as the average product of z scores, the product of z scores and the reliability coefficient are both 0. Only when there is some variability is correlation and reliability possible.

On mastery tests teachers generally expect all students to perform at a relatively high level. In this case any estimate of reliability will be spuriously low since the variability of that group would be close to 0. The classical concept of reliability assumes variability in student performance; if that variability is lacking, reliability estimates will be low or 0.

To further illustrate that reliability depends on the amount of variability, consider the equivalence of two forms of an examination given to two groups of students. The scores of the first group are highly variable, and those of the second group are restricted in range. These values are shown in table 7.2.

Table 7.2. Equivalent Form Reliability Coefficients Derived from Two Groups Having Large Variabilities (Group 1) and Small Variabilities (Group 2)

	Group 1			Group 2	
Student	Scores on Form A	Scores on Form B	Student	Scores on Form A	Scores on Form B
A	180	175	F	100	102
B	140	162	G	99	101
C	100	120	H	101	99
D	60	80	I	98	87
E	0	30	J	100	88
Means	96.0	113.4		99.6	95.4
SDs	62.5	53.4		1.0	6.5
Reliability	.99			.44	

The reliability is almost perfect for group 1, but it is low for group 2 because of that group's limited variability. When an individual in group 1 receives a different score on form B than on form A, his relative rank on the two forms changes little, and since student scores are still so far apart, consistent individual differences remain fairly intact. In contrast, a very small change in group 2 from form A to form B may change an individual's rank within the group. This leads to decreases in the reliability coefficient since reliability depends on the consistency of z scores.

This principle has some interesting applications. For example, if students in grades 4–6 are tested, a high degree of reliability is more likely than if students at a single grade level are tested because the variability of scores is smaller in a single grade than when three grades are combined. It is misleading, then, to report reliability coefficients for children at more than one grade level for such coefficients are likely to be spuriously high. Teachers should also not be surprised to learn that the reliability of measurements for a particular class is lower than that reported in standardized test manuals for the same grade level because the range of ability in a single class is generally smaller than the range for a national sample of students, even at the same grade level.

A second application of this principle is in testing groups with different ability levels. An honors class is typically composed of students who are reasonably close together in ability. In contrast, a "regular" class is often composed of students with widely differing backgrounds. If reliability coefficients are computed for the two groups, the honors class will probably have lower reliabilities than will the regular one. Teachers will find it more difficult to measure individual differences in homogeneous classes than in heterogeneous groups.

Number of Items on the Test

The number of items on a test also affects reliability, other things being equal. The more items there are, the higher the reliability will be. In part this is because an increase in the number of items is accompanied by an increase in the potential variability of students within the group. A one-item test cannot have much variability, since scores can be only 0 or +1. Longer tests also provide a better (more consistent) sample of the students' knowledge or ability than shorter ones.

The increase in reliability as a function of test length is given by the Spearman-Brown formula (p. 179). This formula estimates the reliability if the length of tests is increased. If a test initially has a reliability of .50, doubling the number of items increases the reliability to .67. If the length of the test is again doubled, the estimated reliability increases to .80, assuming, of course, that the quality of items remains constant.

Robert Ebel (1972) has shown that doubling the length of a test quadruples true variance while only doubling error variance.* If the following relationship are kept in mind, the implications of this principle will be clear:

1. obtained variance = true variance + error variance (see p. 174)

2. reliability = $\dfrac{\text{true variance}}{\text{obtained variance}}$ (see p. 174)

---

* Those students interested in the rationale for this concept are referred to the original article.

Given a test of twenty-five items with an obtained variance of 40 and a reliability of .50, the second formula above can be used to estimate the true variance (20.00). This value satisfies the equation

$$.50 = \frac{\text{true variance, or 20}}{40}$$

Using the first formula above, the values 40 and 20 can be substituted for the obtained and true score variances, respectively. The error variance must therefore be 20 to satisfy that equation $(40 = 20 + 20)$.

Now suppose that the number of items is doubled. According to the Spearman-Brown formula (p. 179), the reliability for a fifty-item test would be .67 if the twenty-five-item test had a reliability of .50. According to Ebel, because the length of the test was doubled, the true variance increased fourfold. Since that value was 20, true variance increases to 80, whereas error variance only doubles (from 20 to 40). Using formula 1 above, obtained variance $= 80 + 40$. To satisfy this equation, the obtained variance must be 120. Thus $120 = 80 + 40$. Also, the reliability (from formula 2 above) will be $80/120$, or .67, the same value that would have been computed from the Spearman-Brown formula.

Suppose test length is again doubled to 100 items. Using the same reasoning, true variance will increase fourfold, from 80 to 320, while error variance will double (from 40 to 80). The obtained variance (see formula 1) will be $320 + 80$, or 400, and the reliability will increase from .67 to .80 $(320/400 = .80)$. In other words, increasing the number of items strongly increases true variance and reliability, whereas error variance increases at a much slower rate. The moral is both simple and important. To increase reliability, increase the number of good-quality items. Table 7.3 illustrates this point.

Table 7.3. Table Showing the Relationship between Length of Test and Reliability

n (number of items)		True Variance	Obtained Variance	Error	Reliability
Original test	25	20	40	20	.50
Test doubled in length	50	80	120	40	.67
Test quadrupled in length	100	320	400	80	.80

Increasing the number of items on a test is one of the most effective ways to improve the reliability of measurements. A very short test cannot adequately sample behavior, but a long test is no guarantee of high reliability. The Spearman-Brown formula indicates that reliability will increase as long as the items added to the examination are equivalent to those of the original test. Adding poor items (ambiguous or vague items, for example) can lower reliability.

Because a total score includes a greater number of items than any given subtest, total scores usually have higher reliabilities. Highly *unreliable* information will come from a single item, and any decision based on very short tests is likely to lead to many wrong conclusions.

Test Difficulty Level

A very easy or very hard test is incapable of measuring individual differences since examinees all tend to respond uniformly.

The difficulty level of a test may be defined at M/n, where M is the mean of the scores in a distribution and n is the number of items. As the mean approximates the number of items on the test, the test becomes progressively easier. On a maximally simple test the mean is equal to the number of items (assuming that one point is allowed for each item). In that case everyone responded correctly to all items, and there can be no variability among students; when variability is 0, reliability will be 0 also.

Other conditions being equal, teachers would probably do better to construct easy rather than hard examinations to improve reliability. Difficult tests encourage guessing, which creates *random error,* and this contributes to *unreliability.* On easier tests there is no need to guess (or at least its effects are reduced), and that source of error is diminished.

The development of criterion-referenced tests* has led to a number of measurement problems, particularly problems of determining reliability. These difficulties have been pointed out by James Popham and T. R. Husek (1969, pp. 5–6):

> But although it may be obvious that a criterion-referenced test should be internally consistent, it is not obvious how to assess the internal consistency. The classical [correlational and Kuder-Richardson methods] procedures are not appropriate. This is true because they are dependent on score variability. A criterion-referenced test should not be faulted if, when administered after instruction, everyone obtained a perfect score. Yet, that would lead to a zero internal consistency estimate, something measurement books don't recommend.
>   . . . If a criterion-referenced test has a high average inter-item correlation, this is fine. If the test has a high test-retest correlation, that is also fine. The point is *not* that these indices cannot be used to support the consistency of the test. The point is that a criterion-referenced test could be highly consistent, either internally or [temporally], and yet indices dependent on variability might not reflect that consistency.

---

* A *criterion-referenced test* attempts to measure the attainment of some minimum level of competency, such as 80 percent or 100 percent of the number of items on the test. *Norm-referenced tests,* in contrast, attempt to measure individual differences. If students attain a high level of competence, the mean score will be high relative to the number of items, and there will be little variability in scores and low reliability when measured by correlations and Kuder-Richardson formulas.

For the teacher the dilemma is constructing criterion-referenced tests that yield high reliability indices. Unfortunately no completely satisfactory resolution of this problem has been proposed, although a number of suggestions hold promise. Samuel Livingston (1972, p. 139) has argued that the difference between the criterion score and the mean can be considered as "'true variance' for criterion-referenced purposes, and it may be substantial even when there is little or no variation among the observed scores." The supplementary readings at the end of this chapter contain a number of other suggestions. Perhaps the best that teachers can do at present is to construct tests that are closely tied to course objectives and to construct enough items *for each objective* to improve decision-making ability.

The Standard Error of Measurement

Because reliability coefficients depend on group variability, it would be useful to have a measure of consistency that is not so affected by score variability. The *standard error of measurement* (the standard deviation of error) provides an absolute rather than a relative measure of the extent to which raw and true scores are equivalent. If the standard error of measurement is 0, all the scores in the error column must be 0, and individuals' obtained and true scores must be identical (see table 7.1). If some error scores are high positive values while others are low negative values, the standard error will be large, and there must be a lack of correspondence between true and obtained scores. As previously noted, any nonsystematic difference between true and obtained scores lowers reliability.

Fortunately true scores are not needed to estimate the standard error of measurement. The formula for the standard error of measurement is

$$SE_{\text{meas}} = SD\sqrt{1 - \text{reliability}}$$

where *SD* equals the standard deviation of obtained scores. To use this formula, subtract the reliability coefficient from 1.0, take the square root of the resulting value, and multiply it by the standard deviation. For the example in table 7.1, $SE_{\text{meas}} = 10.9\sqrt{1 - .87}$, or 3.9, the same value as the standard deviation of the error column. In the example on p. 173 the reliability of .87 was the ratio of true variance (105.0) to obtained variance (120.2), but in practice, this value is estimated by using a coefficient of stability, equivalence, stability and equivalence, or internal consistency—the selection should be determined by the purposes served by each type of reliability.

The formula for the SE_{meas} indicates that the standard error of measurement must be 0 when the reliability is +1; when reliability is 0, the SE_{meas} is equal to the standard deviation. This means that if measurements are entirely unreliable (0 reliability), the spread of obtained scores (as measured by the standard deviation) is due to chance conditions—equivalent to drawing numbers out of a hat to determine test scores.

The standard error of measurement is expressed in the same unit as is the standard deviation. If the standard deviation is computed from IQ scores, the standard error of measurement will also be expressed as IQ units; if computed from raw scores, the standard error will be in raw score units. This means that the standard errors of tests that yield different kinds of norms should not be compared. The standard error of measurement may be seven points for an IQ test but only three points on raw score measurements. If teachers want to compare tests having different norms, they should compare the reliability coefficients.

Using the Standard Error of Measurement

The SE_{meas} is used to estimate the variability of scores around a hypothetical "true" value. Consider the following example, in which the raw scores for all students have a true component of 10. The sample consists of five students for illustration, although the theory attains greater credibility as the sample size increases.

The best estimate of the group's true ability on this test is 10, the mean of the five measurements. To estimate the amount of error, subtract the true score (10) from each of the obtained scores. The difference is an error of measurement, and the standard deviation of these errors is the SE_{meas}, or 1.4.

Student	Obtained Score	=	True Score	+	Error
Albert	10		10		0
Betty	11		10		+1
Carl	9		10		−1
Don	12		10		+2
Ed	8		10		−2
	Sums = 50		50		0
	Means = 10.0		10.0		0
	SDs = 1.4		0		1.4

The mean amount of error is zero, since errors of measurement are random—sometimes yielding too high a score and sometimes too low a score. Because all five students have the same true score, the standard deviation of true scores is 0.

Now make another assumption—namely, that the error scores are normally distributed around the mean error of 0. This assumption is theoretically reasonable since error scores are produced by chance and can be expected to be normally distributed. Since the standard error of measurement is the standard deviation of the error column, the SE_{meas} for these five students is 1.4.

How can teachers interpret and apply this information? Draw a normal curve with a distribution of error scores having a mean of zero and a standard error of 1.4 (see figure 7.3). This means that if an infinite number of students took the same test, 68 percent would be 1.4 score units too high or too low from 0 error or the true score of 10; 96 percent would be 2.8 points too high or too low; and it is most unlikely any student would score more than 4.2 points higher or lower than his true score.

The SE_{meas} may also be used to estimate the amount of error or chance fluctuations around an individual's true score. A given obtained score on an examination is only one possible value an individual might receive if the test were readministered or if an equivalent form of the examination were given. Thus on a particular intelligence test a student might have an IQ of 115. To make effective decisions, teachers need test scores that are stable or comparable from form to form. If the student were to receive IQs that varied greatly each time the test were retaken, teachers could place little value in any decision they might make.

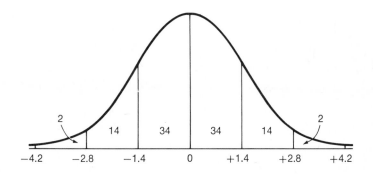

Figure 7.3. A Normal Curve With a Distribution of Error Scores Having a Mean of Zero and a Standard Error of 1.4

On most intelligence tests the standard deviation of scores is sixteen points. If the reliability coefficient is .91, the SE_{meas} will be 4.8 ($SE_{meas} =$ SD$\sqrt{1 - \text{reliability}} = 16\sqrt{1 - .91} = 4.8$). For simplicity, round this to 5.0. The SE_{meas} provides the degree of fluctuation to be expected should a student retake the same examination or if he were given a parallel form. Thus the teacher could say that the student obtained an IQ score of 115 ± 5.0 (read plus or minus five points). This means that the student's score will be expected to fluctuate within a range of five points on either side of his *true* score 68 times out of 100. Note that the assumption is *not* made that his true score is 115, although that is a possibility. The IQ of 115 represents his performance on this one administration and could be higher or lower the next time. How much higher or lower depends on the SE_{meas}.

The Cooperative Test Division of Educational Testing Service has made another practical use of the SE_{meas} on the School and College Ability Tests (SCAT). This test is composed of verbal, quantitative, and total scores and is designed to measure academic aptitude. Instead of reporting student performance in percentiles on the two subtests and total score, it considers each score as a band or range of student performance that extends from one standard error of measurement below to one SE_{meas} above the student's *actual* score. The *true* score, with a probability of .68, is assumed to be within the confines of the band.

In figure 7.4, the shaded band on the verbal scale covers the range from the 75th to the 89th percentile; quantitative, from the 65th to the 82nd percentile; and total, from the 79th to the 86th percentile. The length of each band is determined by a conversion table that provides the teacher with the lowest and highest percentiles included within one SE_{meas} from the student's actual score. Note that the length of the band for the total score is smaller than for either the verbal or quantitative subtests. This is because the total is composed of items from both subtests, and more items increase reliability and lower the SE_{meas}.

In figure 7.4 Richard Smith's "score" is between the 75th and 89th percentiles on the verbal subtest of the SCAT. Should he retake this test, the chances

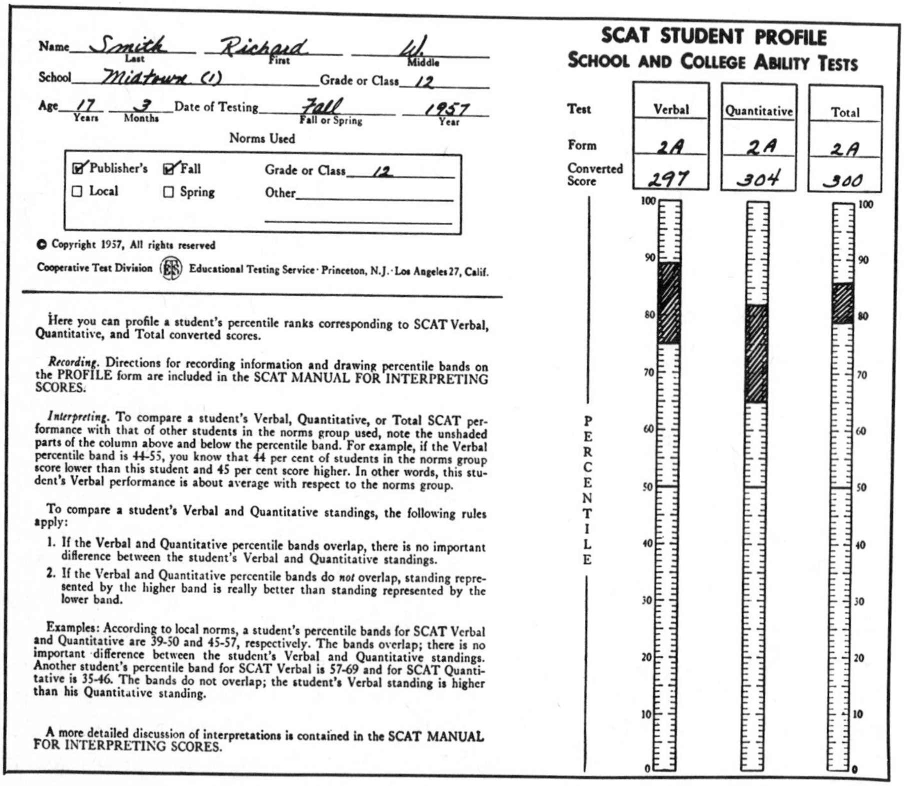

Name Smith (Last) Richard (First) W. (Middle)
School Midtown (1) Grade or Class 12
Age 17 (Years) 3 (Months) Date of Testing Fall (Fall or Spring) 1957 (Year)

Norms Used

☑ Publisher's ☑ Fall Grade or Class 12
☐ Local ☐ Spring Other

© Copyright 1957, All rights reserved

Cooperative Test Division Educational Testing Service · Princeton, N.J. · Los Angeles 27, Calif.

Here you can profile a student's percentile ranks corresponding to SCAT Verbal, Quantitative, and Total converted scores.

Recording. Directions for recording information and drawing percentile bands on the PROFILE form are included in the SCAT MANUAL FOR INTERPRETING SCORES.

Interpreting. To compare a student's Verbal, Quantitative, or Total SCAT performance with that of other students in the norms group used, note the unshaded parts of the column above and below the percentile band. For example, if the Verbal percentile band is 44-55, you know that 44 per cent of students in the norms group score lower than this student and 45 per cent score higher. In other words, this student's Verbal performance is about average with respect to the norms group.

To compare a student's Verbal and Quantitative standings, the following rules apply:

1. If the Verbal and Quantitative percentile bands overlap, there is no important difference between the student's Verbal and Quantitative standings.
2. If the Verbal and Quantitative percentile bands do *not* overlap, standing represented by the higher band is really better than standing represented by the lower band.

Examples: According to local norms, a student's percentile bands for SCAT Verbal and Quantitative are 39-50 and 45-57, respectively. The bands overlap; there is no important difference between the student's Verbal and Quantitative standings. Another student's percentile band for SCAT Verbal is 57-69 and for SCAT Quantitative is 35-46. The bands do not overlap; the student's Verbal standing is higher than his Quantitative standing.

A more detailed discussion of interpretations is contained in the SCAT MANUAL FOR INTERPRETING SCORES.

SCAT STUDENT PROFILE
SCHOOL AND COLLEGE ABILITY TESTS

Test	Verbal	Quantitative	Total
Form	2A	2A	2A
Converted Score	297	304	300

Figure 7.4

are 68 out of 100 that he would fall between those two percentiles. Note that the verbal and quantitative subtest percentile bands overlap. Since these bands reflect chance or random responses, teachers cannot be sure that there is an "important difference" between them. As the bands become farther apart on the two subtests, to that extent a "significant" difference exists.

Figure 7.4 is a sample *profile* or graph of an individual's performance on SCAT. By reporting scores as a band, the temptation to interpret any given percentile as fixed and uninfluenced by errors of measurement is reduced. The wider the band is, the greater the error is. Only on perfectly reliable tests ($r = 1.0$) are there no errors of measurement.

Percentile bands can be interpreted to mean that the chances are 68 out of 100 that the student's true score lies somewhere between the limits marked by the percentile band. Although teachers can never be certain just where the true score is, they can obtain closer approximations to it when the SE_{meas} is small.

The Reliability of Individual and Group Scores

It seems reasonable even on a priori grounds to assume that decisions involving a single individual will require a much higher degree of reliability than is necessary for evaluating the behavior of groups. As early as 1927, Truman Kelley suggested that reliabilities of at least .94 were needed for making decisions regarding any given student; for decisions about groups of students, he recommended reliabilities of not less than .50.

Ideally, of course, reliability should be $+1.00$, but in practice, teachers may have to settle for whatever they can get. Certainly, other conditions being equal, it would be better to select a test having higher rather than lower reliability, but in some situations there may be only one test, or all tests may yield equally low reliabilities, or the cost required to increase reliability may be prohibitive.

The relationship between the magnitude of the reliability coefficient and the number of cases can be seen by examining table 7.4 (Thorndike and Hagen 1969). This table shows the probability that two individuals or groups, one at the 75th percentile and the other at the 50th percentile, will reverse their relative positions on repeated testings with instruments having different reliabilities. For example, when scores of single individuals are being considered, the probability is .50 that the individual at the 50th percentile will surpass the one at the 75th percentile on a repeated testing when the reliability is 0. Even when the reliability is .80 ,there is about 1 chance out of 5 that the reversal will take place or 4 chances out of 5 that the two individuals will maintain their relative positions. For a reliability of .95, there are only 2.2 chances in 100 that a reversal will occur.

Table 7.4. Percentage of Times Direction of Difference Will Be Reversed in Subsequent Testing for Scores Falling at the 75th and 50th Percentile

Reliability Coefficient	Percentages of Reversals with Repeated Test		
	Scores of Single Individuals	Means of Groups of 25	Means of Groups of 100
.00	50.0	50.0	50.0
.40	40.3	10.9	0.7
.50	36.8	4.6	0.04
.60	32.5	1.2	
.70	27.1	0.1	
.80	19.7		
.90	8.7		
.95	2.2		
.98	0.05		

From Robert L. Thorndike and Elizabeth Hagen, *Measurement and Evaluation in Psychology and Education*, Third Edition (New York: John Wiley & Sons, Inc., 1969), p. 194.

When sample sizes of 25 are selected, the same probability (2.2) can be obtained with reliability coefficients between .50 and .60. When the sample size is increased to 100, there is about the same probability of a reversal occurring when the reliability is .50 as when the reliability is .98 for individual comparisons. Thus tests yielding low reliabilities can be useful if decisions are applicable to groups rather than to individuals.

The Reliability of Difference Scores

Sometimes teachers want to compare *differences* between pretest and posttest scores or to compare intelligence and achievement test scores. In both cases it is necessary to know how reliable these difference scores are because the *reliability of difference scores* tends to be lower than the reliability of either test considered alone.

The reliability of a difference score depends on the reliability of each test and the correlation between them. If it is assumed that all scores have been expressed as z scores and that the two tests being compared are equally reliable, the following formula can be used to estimate the reliability of the difference scores (Gulliksen 1950):

$$\text{reliability of difference score} = \frac{\text{reliability} - \text{correlation between tests}}{1 - \text{correlation between tests}}$$

For example, if the reliability of two tests is .90 and they correlate .80 with each other, the reliability of the difference score drops to .50:

$$\text{reliability of difference score} = \frac{.90 - .80}{1 - .80} = .50$$

It is apparent that when test reliability equals the correlation between the tests, the reliability of the difference score will be 0, and that when the reliability of each test is $+1.0$, the reliability of a difference score will also equal $+1.0$ no matter what the correlation might be between tests.

The reason for typically low reliabilities of difference scores is that each of the two tests being compared contains some unreliability or errors of measurement. The difference score, which contains error or chance factors from *both* tests, is less reliable than either test alone because chance reduces reliability. To make matters worse, if the two tests correlate perfectly with one another, they measure the same true scores. Assuming that reliability remains constant, the difference scores would contain only errors of measurement on each of the two tests. The combination of these errors of measurement suggests that the teacher determine for himself the reliability of difference scores before attempting to make decisions based on them.

Teachers can increase the reliability of difference scores by selecting or constructing highly reliable tests. As noted previously, one of the most effective ways of improving reliability is to increase the number of items in the test, but there is not much one can do to lower the correlation between the two tests if student *gain scores* are being compared. Gain scores presume that pretest and posttest scores measure different stages of learning on two tests of similar or identical content. This similarity in content means that the test scores will correlate highly with one another. In addition, because student knowledge is common to both measures, this will increase the correlation between them. Gain scores therefore tend to be unreliable measures.

Where scores do not measure improvement but merely try to compare scores on two different tests, the correlation between the two tests is usually lower than the correlation obtained with gain scores. The classic example is comparing IQ scores with achievement test scores to yield what Raymond Franzen (1920) has called an *accomplishment quotient*. This was obtained by dividing the student's achievement by his "intelligence," where both measures were expressed in similar units. Ratios smaller than 1.00 (usually reported as 100 to eliminate decimals) supposedly meant lower achievement than ability. Although few teachers still formally compute accomplishment quotients, IQ scores and achievement test scores are still improperly compared despite the abundance of data showing that these tests correlate almost as highly with each other as they do with themselves. Under such conditions, difference scores will have reliabilities close to 0.

Difference or gain scores suffer from other deficiencies:

1. Gain scores do not necessarily measure improvement in knowledge. Maturation and practice often account for observed differences. Using a control or comparable group that has not been subjected to

the same treatment (instruction) allows the teacher to compare their posttest scores. To the extent that *initial* differences between the two groups were random, maturation and practice effects would be equal, and differences, if greater than chance, would be due to instruction.

2. Students who initially perform at a high level cannot be expected to make gains equal to those made by students in the middle or lower parts of the distribution. The extreme example would be students who initially received scores of 0 or 100 percent. Unless they maintain their positions, students in the upper group could only register losses, whereas those on the bottom could only "improve." Data reported by Frederic Lord (1958) of gains made by five groups of college students who differed on initial scores on science reasoning and understanding confirmed these expectations. The mean gains for the five groups (from low to high initial scores, respectively) were 6.26, 5.16, 2.93, 2.04, and .31. As Lord pointed out, a gain of one or two points for those in the initially high group represents as much true gain as a gain of five or six points in the initially low group.

3. The *regression effect* can account for differences among pupils, especially when they are initially selected on the basis of exceptionally high or low scores. The regression effect is the tendency for true scores to lie closer to the mean than their corresponding obtained scores. The reason for this phenomenon (first described by Sir Francis Galton) is that error tends to increase at the extremes of a distribution. When a student is selected because of an extreme score, part of that value is determined by his true ability but part is also determined by chance—in his favor if his obtained score is high and against him if it is low. When that test is repeated, some of the chance conditions that helped place him at the extreme will no longer be present, and his scores will regress toward the mean. The implication for the teacher is to guard against attributing the regression effect (particularly on unreliable tests) to "true" improvement. Only on perfectly reliable tests (those free from error) will the regression effect be absent.

Sources of Error

Reliability coefficients provide estimates of error that vary in magnitude depending on the conditions allowed to influence them. Because these sources of error are multitudinous, attempts to catalog them have not been entirely successful. Nonetheless, at least three major sources of error can be examined:

1. Characteristics of the students
2. Characteristics of the test
3. Conditions affecting test administration and scoring

Characteristics of the Students

Some characteristics of students are consistent either from test to test or from occasion to occasion and therefore contribute to true variance. The true level of a student's knowledge or ability is an example of a *desired* source of *true* variance. Other consistent (reliable) characteristics of students that contribute to true variance may be irrelevant and unwanted, including being "test-wise" or being able to recall previous answers on a retest, which may be consistent with the student's ability and therefore a part of a true variance (Stanley 1971).* The teacher's role is to reduce the effects of these unwanted but consistent tendencies by improving instruction. Then reliable tests would measure knowledge rather than knowledge systematically influenced by test-wiseness, consistent illness, or lack of motivation. But as Stanley has observed, this accomplishment will be difficult because these attributes may be closely related to ability and true level of knowledge.

Characteristics of students that contribute to error and therefore to unreliability should be reduced or eliminated if possible. These characteristics are usually temporary and undesirable conditions that detract from the relationship between true and obtained scores, such as inconsistent recall of information, inability to concentrate, mood fluctuations, and so on. Although many of these student characteristics are not under the direct control of the teacher, the type of reliability coefficient should measure the effects of only those conditions that satisfy the purposes of measurement. For evaluating the effects of instruction, for example, teachers will want to make sure that measured gains are not being produced by unreliable measurements. A reliability coefficient that takes time into consideration (stability or stability and equivalence) can ascertain the reliability of the measurements.

Characteristics of the Test

Tests themselves may be a source of unreliability if they contain trick questions, ambiguous items, confusing formats, excessively difficult items, too few items, or dissimilar item content. Each of these conditions encourages guessing, which in turn lowers reliability. Teachers who want to measure attributes reliably must construct and select tests that contain items that avoid these deficiencies. (Many of the suggestions in chaps. 4 and 5 for writing good test items were designed to improve reliability.)

Because tests are samples of behavior selected from a given population, even equivalent forms of the same test will not yield identical results. Students

---

* In the next chapter it will be pointed out that these consistent but irrelevant characteristics will reduce *validity,* or the extent to which measurement relates to some criterion.

who are proficient in arithmetic in general may fail more multiplication items on one form of a test than on another because of differing item content. These differences in content should be considered as contributing to error variance since they affect individuals differently.

Conditions Affecting Test Administration and Scoring

Potential sources of error can occur from the administration of a test. The *physical environment,* for example, can affect student performance adversely and usually contributes to error variance. For that reason teachers must be concerned about temperature and humidity control, lighting, seating conditions and arrangements, and the avoidance of distractions. Other factors of test administration involve the *instructions given to examinees* (e.g., their clarity, complexity, consistency, or ambiguity), *adherence to specified timing requirements,* and the *relationship of the examiner and the students* (age differences, idiosyncratic mannerisms, appearance, race and ethnic background). To the extent that any of these conditions affect students in different ways, reliability is decreased.

Many sources of error enter into test scoring, particularly with extended-answer essays that use poorly defined scoring criteria. The scorer himself is a source of error when he makes arithmetic errors, is unmotivated, or fails to understand or abide by scoring criteria. Mistakes in recording scores also contribute to error variance. Any biasing factors that are consistent will of course contribute to true variance but will lower validity. For example, teachers may intend to measure content but might be highly influenced by such irrelevant factors as penmanship, spelling, grammar, and prior knowledge about the student. Establishing and abiding by clear scoring criteria can help avoid some of these problems.

Error Components of Different Reliability Coefficients

Four empirical methods of estimating reliability were discussed in this chapter: stability, equivalence, stability and equivalence, and internal consistency (split-half method and Kuder-Richardson formula 20). Each of these coefficients is useful under certain circumstances; under others, reliability may be spuriously low if measured by a coefficient that includes unimportant sources of error. Conversely, some reliability estimates will be spuriously high because important sources of error have not been allowed to affect them. This section will examine the relationship between the three major sources of error (characteristics of students, tests, and administration and scoring) and the four empirical approaches to estimating reliability.

Stability

Different stability coefficients will be obtained over different time intervals. Over short periods of time, the students are unlikely to change, but as the time interval increases, true changes are more likely to occur. Furthermore, although memory will be consistent and will lead to increases in true variance over short time intervals, it can be expected to dissipate and have little or no effect over more extended intervals. As far as individuals are concerned, then, stability coefficients over short ranges of time are affected by memory, which increases true variance; over longer times, stability coefficients are minimally affected by memory and are influenced much more by actual changes occurring in students. These true but fluctuating changes will contribute to error and unreliability because they are inconsistent.

The characteristics of the test itself will increase error if items are ambiguous and encourage guessing. Because only a single form of a test is administered twice, no error variance can be attributed to differences in item sampling.

Conditions of test administration and scoring contribute to error variance if they occur on only one of the two test administrations; systematic errors that occur on both administrations of the test are treated as true variance that improves reliability but decreases validity.

Coefficients of short-term stability are likely to be quite high because so few sources of error are allowed to influence them: individuals and test content remain equal and memory effects increase reliability. The only conditions that might lower short-term stability coefficients are differences in test administration and scoring, which, at least on objectively scored tests, would be minimal. For these reasons teachers should always ask how much time elapsed between the first and second administrations of the test.

Equivalence

Whenever one form of a test may be substituted for another, the equivalence of the forms should be known. Usually this requires students to take the two tests within a short time period. Changes in individuals are unlikely, but because there are two forms of a test instead of one, memory effects will not spuriously affect coefficients of equivalence.

The major source of error with equivalent forms is attributed to differences in the items constituting the two forms. Each of the two forms is considered to be composed of items randomly drawn from the same population or universe. When this universe is well defined (e.g., addition of single-digit integers from 0 to 9), parallel forms probably measure the universe quite well. But when the universe is more complex and less well delineated, the test forms may not be parallel or equivalent. It would be much more difficult, for example, to construct two forms of a test with a high coefficient of equivalence if the universe was extensive (addition of any set of integers), complex (ability to evaluate the effects of social change on school boards), or vague (ability to evaluate).

As with any two administrations of a test, differences in giving the two forms will reduce reliability. Reliability will also be reduced if scoring criteria are allowed to vary for each of the two forms.

Coefficients of equivalence are likely to yield lower estimates of reliability than do measures of stability. The same sources of error affect both except that equivalence is affected by an additional source of error—the use of two forms.

When a relatively long time separates the administration of two forms of a test, all the potential sources of error in *both* stability *and* equivalence will be present. The individuals may change, the items may not be equivalent, and the opportunity for differences in administering and scoring the two forms is increased. When coefficients of stability and equivalence are reported, most of the potential sources of error have been allowed to influence reliability. Although such coefficients tend to be lower than estimates of reliability using *either* stability *or* equivalence, they may also be more important.

Internal Consistency or Homogeneity

For most teacher-made tests, split-half or Kuder-Richardson reliabilities will be most practical. Split-half coefficients indicate how equivalent two halves of the same test are, and many persons who are knowledgeable in measurement prefer to think of such coefficients as a type of equivalent form reliability rather than as a measure of internal consistency. In this text the split-half method is considered a measure of internal consistency because (1) both are inappropriate with speed tests, but separately timed alternate forms are appropriate, and (2) both are obtained from a single test administration.

Measures of internal consistency coefficients tend to be higher than long-term stability since the possibility that students will change is small; internal consistency tends to be higher than equivalence because there is only one form of the test. Thus internal consistency is often used to set the upper limit for long-term stability and for equivalence. If internal consistency is low, other types of reliability coefficients will be lower still.

All tests should be internally consistent, that is, they should measure the same trait or ability and not attempt to include items uncorrelated with each other. On a test that measures many different traits or attributes, there is a serious question regarding what the test does measure and what the sum of the item scores means. The split-half method can still yield a high reliability coefficient if the two halves contain an equivalent "hodgepodge" of items (see p. 183). Because the Kuder-Richardson formula 20 yields the mean reliability for all possible splits, it is clear that the split-half provides an estimate of KR_{20}.

Kuder-Richardson methods derive their sources of error from the number of items on the test and the correlation among items. Anything that lowers the correlation among items lowers Kuder-Richardson reliabilities. It is important to make sure that guessing, item ambiguity, difficulty levels, directions, and scoring criteria and methods are as highly controlled as possible.

Summary

1. Measurements are reliable if they measure nonchance aspects of the trait, ability, or attribute being measured.

2. An obtained score is composed of true and error components. The relationships among these terms include:
   a. An error of measurement is the difference between a true score and an obtained score.
   b. The true score is the hypothetical score a person would get if errors of measurement were 0.
   c. The obtained score is equal to the true score plus errors of measurement.
   d. Obtained variance is equal to true variance plus error variance.
   e. If obtained variance and true variance are equal, error variance must be 0 and reliability must be perfect.
   f. The mean obtained score is assumed to equal the mean true score; thus the mean error score is assumed to be 0.
   g. Reliability is the ratio of true variance divided by obtained variance.

3. Teachers do not have a direct measure of true variance, but they can estimate the amount of chance that influences scores by using one or more of the following approaches:
   a. *Stability*. Stability coefficients are obtained by correlating a set of measurements with a retest at some later point in time.
   b. *Equivalence*. Equivalence can be estimated by correlating two or more sets of measurements presumed to measure the same universe of items.
   c. *Stability and equivalence*. Stability and equivalence can be estimated by correlating two or more sets of measurements over different periods of time.
   d. *Internal consistency or homogeneity*. Internal consistency can be estimated by determining the extent to which measurements on a single form are intercorrelated.

    i. The split-half method is one way to estimate internal consistency.

    ii. The Kuder-Richardson formula 20 is a second way to estimate internal consistency.

4. Measures of internal consistency or homogeneity should be computed for power tests rather than for speed tests.

5. Reliability can be improved by the following practices:

    a. Develop items that measure the same trait or ability on each test given.

    b. Be sure that scorers have clear and unambiguous instructions.

    c. Increase the number of items on a test since true variance increases more rapidly than error variance when tests are increased in length. The Spearman-Brown formula is used to estimate the reliability of a set of measurements when the number of items is increased.

    d. Keep the difficulty level of the test moderate for all items.

6. The standard error of measurement is the standard deviation of error scores. It can be computed directly from a formula (given in the text) even though true scores may be unknown. The larger the standard error of measurement is, the more error there is around the true score. When the standard error of measurement is 0, then each student will receive his true score. Perfectly reliable tests have standard errors of measurement of 0.

7. Some publishers of standardized tests report scores in the form of percentile bands. The length of the band is computed from one standard error of measurement above to one standard error of measurement below the actual percentile the student received.

8. If teachers are concerned about individual performance, they should require higher reliability coefficients than if group progress is being assessed.

9. Most difference or gain scores tend to be unreliable because pretests and posttests each contain a certain amount of error which accumulates in the difference between them. The reliability of difference scores can be increased by using tests that are each highly reliable.

10. Some sources of error are:

    a. *Characteristics within students.* Stable but undesirable characteristics of test scores (e.g., being "test-wise") increase the consistency of scores but should be eliminated because they reduce the validity of measurements.

    b. *Characteristics within items.* Some items are tricky, ambiguous, confusing, or excessively difficult, all of which tend to reduce reliability.

    c. *Administration and scoring of items.* Any factor that increases the role of chance will reduce reliability. For that reason teachers must administer standardized tests under the conditions specified in test manuals. Scoring must also be conducted according to the rules specified by the test publisher.

11. The error components of each type of reliability are:

   a. *Stability*. True changes in individuals are more likely to occur over long periods of time; over short periods of time, memory of previous responses will probably transfer to the retest situation and will keep responses constant. Thus over short periods of time stability coefficients are spuriously high.

   b. *Equivalence*. Because students do not take the same test twice, the effect of memory is negligible. However, differences in item content between the forms contribute to error.

   c. *Stability and equivalence*. The lowest reliabilities are likely to come from coefficients of stability and equivalence since all the error factors common to both stability and equivalence will be present.

   d. *Internal consistency or homogeneity*. These coefficients tend to be relatively high since individuals do not change much when responding to different items within a test and because there is only one form of a test. Both the split-half and the Kuder-Richardson methods derive sources of error from within the items themselves. Items that do not measure the same trait or ability as others tend to lower the internal consistency of the measurements.

Suggested Readings

Cronbach, Lee J. *Essentials of Psychological Testing.* 3d ed. New York: Harper & Row, 1970, 752 pp. See in particular pp. 151–93. Cronbach describes reliability as a "coefficient of generalizability." This will not be an easy chapter for most readers, but the concept of the "signal-noise" ratio is becoming more widely used.

Ebel, Robert L. "The Value of Internal Consistency in Classroom Examinations." *Journal of Educational Measurement* 5, no. 1 (Spring 1968): 71–73. Ebel takes the position that classroom examinations should be internally consistent whether they are used to predict some criterion or to assess current behavior. Horn's rejoinder appears in the same issue.

Magnusson, David. *Test Theory.* Reading, Mass.: Addison-Wesley Publishing Co., 1966, 270 pp. Chapters 4–9, while rather technical, provide an excellent description and mathematical derivation of formulas such as the Kuder-Richardson.

Wesman, Alexander G. "Reliability and Confidence." *Test Service Bulletin of the Psychological Corporation,* no. 44 (May 1952): 2–7. A brief but excellent description of reliability and the factors that affect it.

The Validity of Measurements

THE FAMILY CIRCUS   **By Bil Keane**

"Mommy, what time is my foot?"

Family Circus by Bil Keane reprinted courtesy of The Register and Tribune Syndicate, Inc.

Figure 8.1

8 Few persons would try to measure time with a scale or weight with a ruler. Clocks measure time and scales measure weight, no matter how badly constructed they are. Obviously some instruments are more precise (i.e., reliable) than others, but no one would deny that all clocks measure time.

The teacher's instruments often consist of samples of items or behaviors rather than direct measures. From these limited samples he attempts to infer something about the student's performance outside of the test situation. How well the student performs on the test represents *to some degree* how he might be expected to respond elsewhere. Generally persons who have high aptitude scores are expected to do well in some occupational or educational skill being measured by the test. Similarly, it would be hoped that a social studies test in fact measures knowledge of social studies rather than some extraneous characteristic such as reading ability or intelligence.

Effective instruction depends in part on the teacher's ability to diagnose learning difficulties and to select the most appropriate remedial methods and materials. To do this, the teacher needs dependable, relevant knowledge about student progress. Valid information can help teachers modify instruction to meet individual differences and promote changes in the curriculum based on empirical relationships rather than subjectivity.

Validity can be defined as the extent to which measurements are useful in making decisions relevant to a given purpose. Placement decisions, for example, can be improved upon if the teacher can estimate the student's likelihood of "success" in different curricula. To the extent that measurements fail to improve effective decision making by providing misleading or irrelevant information, they are *invalid*. No matter how *reliable* they are, measurements are useless if they are not *valid* for some purpose.

Validity is not established by declaration but by evidence. Many standardized tests present little or no evidence on how useful they are for the purpose implied by their titles. Even a fairly innocuous test title such as the Borman-Sanders Elementary Science Test requires a thorough evaluation by the teacher before the test is used. Read one reviewer's comments (Olson, in *Seventh Mental Measurements Yearbook,* p. 1217) on what *he* believes the test measures:

This test, containing 75 multiple choice and 25 matching items, allegedly measures the achievement of "elementary principles and facts of physical science with which the elementary school pupils should be familiar."

Despite the catalog claims, the Borman-Sanders is a prime example of a test that measures practically nothing of consequence but does it with high reliability. The failure of the test authors to provide important technical information—such as the distribution of the norming population, the methods used in computing reliabilities, and substantiating evidence to support claims of validity—is important, but it becomes secondary when one reviews the test content.

While the format is awkward and difficult to read, it may be the best feature of the test. It certainly helps to conceal the fact that most of the test items suffer from the molehill-out-of-the-mountain syndrome, asking for what may be the least important information about significant science concepts. In addition to being obsolete, the remainder of the test items are *insignificant* (e.g., "Inflate a balloon and release it, open end toward you. The principle it exemplifies was worked out by: 1. Sir Isaac Newton 2. Henri Becquerel 3. Alexander Graham Bell 4. J. Bjerknes"), *provincial* (e.g., "A wild flower sometimes called the 'Kansas Gay Feather' is really a: 1. sunflower 2. smartweed 3. spiked blazing star 4. snow on the mountain"), and *trivial* (e.g., "The space capsule of the Redstone rocket that carried the United State's [sic] second astronaut was named: 1. Monarch 2. Angel 3. Liberty Bell 4. Trieste").

In all fairness, it must be noted that the multiple choice items as exemplified above are superior to the matching section of the test.

There is not a single item that requires student cognition above the level of recall or which appears to be relevant to modern science curricula. If the Borman-Sanders has any use, it is as a convenient compendium for instructors of measurement courses. In it they will find examples of nearly every error in test development and construction that it is possible to commit, all arranged in one convenient unattractive package.

Other examples of tests whose titles imply validity include the following:

Test	*Implied Decision*
1. Army General Classification Test	Classification of individuals
2. Test for Organic Brain Damage	Identification of brain-damaged persons
3. Analysis of Reading Difficulty	Diagnosis of reading problems
4. Culture-Fair Inventory	Ability to make decisions regardless of a person's background
5. Adjustment Inventory	Screening of maladjusted individuals or diagnosis of adjustment problems

However, many standardized tests do not imply validities by their titles. For example, the D 48 Test is particularly conservative in not suggesting what it can or cannot do by its title. Similarly, the titles of Progressive Matrices and the Quick Word Test give few clues as to their content. The manuals for standardized tests should provide data on how valid their measurements are for various purposes, and titles should not claim or imply more than the evidence warrants. This topic will be developed more fully in chapter 10.

Empirical Methods of Determining Validity: Content Validity

Decisions based on *content validity* determine whether students have mastered, excelled in, or failed items or tests measuring specific course objectives. Chapter 3 discussed the development of two-way grids and procedures for writing items to correspond with desired goals. *Items* have content validity if they ask students to demonstrate those skills and competencies required by the objectives. *Tests* have content validity if the behavior and subject matter called for in the items correspond to the behavior and subject matter identified in the specific objective. The inclusion of items that are unrelated to objectives or the failure to include items required by an objective contribute to content *invalidity*.

Some tests purport to measure objectives directly, although the skill or ability may be measured only tangentially, if at all. An example is measuring spelling ability by having students *select* misspelled words from among others that are correctly spelled. The ability to identify misspelled words may be much different from the ability to spell dictated words correctly. Another example is the Mathematics Reading Vocabulary subtest of the California Achievement Tests, which requires the student to define such words as *start* and *choose* along with vocabulary more relevant to mathematics, such as *divisor, reduce,* and *quotient.* The ability to define mathematics vocabulary should be judged on terms that clearly measure that objective.

An admittedly stringent criterion for content validity is to require two independent groups or individuals to construct an examination using the same objectives and criteria. Each would be given such information as (1) a description of the universe from which items are to be constructed; (2) a set of behavioral objectives; (3) the number of items to be constructed for each objective; (4) the format (multiple-choice, completion, essay, and so forth); (5) the nature of the students for whom the test is being prepared (age, reading ability, socioeconomic background, and other relevant data); and (6) directions for test administration and scoring. When the two tests have been constructed, both "forms" would be given to the same group of students; the correlation between the two sets of measurements would indicate how well the items measure the same trait or ability. However, as Lee Cronbach (1971) has stated, the difficulties inherent in validating an examination by this procedure have discouraged most individuals from attempting to do so, and the few attempts that have been made have not been entirely satisfactory.

Usually the teacher will have to evaluate the content validity of his own tests, and this should begin at the planning stage. Because the teacher is intimately involved with his own test, there are advantages in asking other teachers to compare items with objectives, thereby avoiding problems of bias. Having to defend the inclusion of an item in a test or to explain its absence when an objective requires it encourages teachers to construct more meaningful examinations. Sometimes studying the objectives reveals problems in the nature of the subject matter and in what students are expected to learn. The process of evaluating content validity can produce a closer relationship between teaching and testing.

Establishing validity by determining the correspondence between items and objectives is applicable primarily to *achievement tests* or measures of student attainment of subject matter. Most teacher-made examinations do not purport to measure any criterion other than the teacher's own objectives. The test itself is—or at least it should be—a direct measure of course or unit objectives. But not all tests are constructed to measure classroom achievement, and a criterion more relevant than the teacher's objectives may be required. For example, one cannot determine whether a test is capable of measuring "neuroticism" simply by examining its content. Empirical evidence is required to demonstrate that the test does in fact measure that attribute.

Criterion-Related Validity

The term *criterion-related validity* was introduced in the 1966 edition of *Standards for Educational and Psychological Tests and Manuals* (APA 1966, p. 13) and means the correlation of measurements with an external criterion. If the measurements are used to predict future behavior (e.g., grades, ratings, scores on other tests, and so forth), these correlations are called *predictive validity coefficients;* if validity is estimated by correlations of measurements with currently obtainable criteria, these correlations are called *concurrent validity coefficients.* Concurrent validity is of value in determining whether a newly developed test can be substituted for a more complex or costly assessment procedure, for example.

Predictive Validity

Predictive validity is used to *predict* or estimate how the individual will perform on some subsequent *criterion task.* Prediction implies a time difference between the obtaining of measurements on a predictor test and the criterion against which the test is to be validated. The *criterion* is a standard which is accepted as a direct measure of the trait or ability to be predicted. Since a C average is required of most college graduates, grade point average is often used as a criterion or standard of "success." Success on the job could be measured by salary increments, recommendations by supervisors, years of service, and so forth.

There may be disagreement over what the criterion for success should be. Dissatisfaction with grades as a criterion has caused some schools to substitute such criteria as attendance or participation in community events for the traditional letter grade. Because each predictor is likely to correlate differently with each criterion, there can be many different predictive validity coefficients. Consequently no single predictive validity coefficient represents *the* validity of a set of measurements. Different predictive validity coefficients can be obtained, depending on what *criterion* is agreed upon and what *predictors* are selected.

A *predictive validity coefficient* is the correlation between predictor test scores and subsequently obtained criterion measurements. Predictor tests are constructed or selected to sample the skills, attributes, or traits required by the criterion. A high predictive validity coefficient means that the predictor measures the same traits as the criterion; if the coefficient is low, there is little relationship between the two. Predictive validity coefficients vary considerably, but correlations of .60 or .70 are considered to be quite high. Table 8.1 presents reported predictive validity coefficients for several predictors, criteria, time intervals, and subjects.

Table 8.1. Some Examples of Predictive Validity Coefficients

Predictor	Criterion	Time	Subjects	Coefficient	Source
California Test of Basic Skills					
Language	English grades	1 year	Representative	.60	
Language	Math grades	(grades	samples	.40	Nolan &
Reading	English grades	8–9)		.55	Jacobson
Reading	Math grades			.28	1972
Total battery	English grades			.63	
Total battery	Math grades			.46	
California Test of Mental Maturity, Short Form (IQ)	English grades			.46	
California Test of Mental Maturity, Short Form (IQ)	Math grades			.34	
American College Test	Grade point average	1 year	Low socioeconomic college students:		Merritt 1972
			Females	.50	
			Males	.32	
			Total	.71	
Ratings of artistic achievement	Leadership ratings	1 year	Male National Merit Scholarship students who were high social achievers in college	.26	Holland & Astin 1962
Number of honors in high school	Leadership ratings	4 years	Same as above	.15	

Concurrent Validity

A *concurrent validity coefficient* can be determined when measurements on the predictor and criterion tests are obtained at about the same time. If the teacher wants to know how well measurements *predict* a criterion, predictive validity is appropriate. At other times, however, the teacher wishes to know whether the test is capable *now* of discriminating between successful and unsuccessful persons on some criterion task. A high *concurrent validity coefficient* indicates that the test is currently capable of discriminating among individuals on a criterion such as success as measured by salary, grade point averages, and the like; a high *predictive validity coefficient* indicates that the test is capable of predicting which individuals will become successful.

An example may help to clarify the difference between concurrent and predictive validity. Suppose that a school psychologist wants to develop a test for predicting which students will eventually require psychiatric treatment. He first gives his test to a large group of high school students and plans to wait five years to measure their "adjustment." Of course, he would have the usual difficulties in keeping informed of the current location of the students, but when he eventually completes his study, he would be able to report on the effectiveness of his test in *predicting* which persons required treatment. In this example there is a time lapse (five years) between predictor (his test) and criterion (numbers of students who required psychiatric care); therefore, he will have obtained a predictive validity coefficient.

Few persons have the patience to wait this long; most wish to know what the *current* relationship is between test scores and the criterion. To avoid the five-year wait, the school psychologist could have given the test to persons currently receiving psychiatric treatment and to those judged to lack symptoms of emotional maladjustment. The correlation between the test scores (the predictor) and some criterion of adjustment obtained at about the same time would be a measure of concurrent validity. High scores on the experimental test should be associated with a high degree of adjustment (or maladjustment) and vice versa.

If a test cannot distinguish between maladjusted and normal individuals now, it is not likely to do so more accurately in the future. Concurrent validity coefficients provide a maximum value for predictive validity coefficients. If the concurrent validity coefficient is .60, the predictive validity will probably be lower, assuming that the same criterion measure is used both times.

Construct Validity

Validity has been defined as the extent to which measurements are useful in making decisions relevant to a given purpose. It was shown that some test titles imply validity, and that neither the titles nor the manuals of other tests provide information on the type of validity presented.

The validiy of test titles should be supported by evidence in the test manual. A test of "motivation," for example, should present evidence that it does in fact measure motivation and can be used in situations that call for a decision regarding that construct.* Determining the validity of a construct is important when the "test user wishes to infer the degree to which the individual possesses some hypothetical trait or quality (construct) presumed to be reflected in the test performance" (APA 1966). For example, decisions regarding pupil performance on a test designed to measure "creativity" can be improved if the teacher understands how these scores are related to such constructs as "achievement" or "intelligence." Construct validity would also be important in determin-

---

* A *construct* is a hypothesized trait, ability, or characteristic that is abstracted from a variety of behaviors but which is presumed to have educational or psychological meaning. The trait or construct might be aggressiveness, introversion, adjustment, mechanical ability, verbal fluency, or social intelligence, to name only a few.

ing what traits or abilities a newly developed test measures. A test designed for one purpose may, upon analysis, be found to be a better measure of something quite different or a measure of nothing of consequence.

Another purpose for determining construct validity concerns the development and refinement of educational and psychological theory.* Empirical observations (e.g., measurements) provide input data to help clarify and define the theory. A theory that argues that frustration produces aggression must have some way of measuring both frustration and aggression. If different measures of frustration correlate positively and highly among themselves, this suggests that *frustration* is a single trait—although measured by different approaches—in much the same way that *length* can be measured with different measurement instruments. One would also have to show that *nonfrustrated* organisms remain *unaggressive*. The theorist obtains as much information as possible to understand the meaning of the hypothesized construct. The evidence will either *support* or *fail to support* a given construct, but it cannot *prove* a given proposition. Other evidence obtained under different conditions and with different subjects might require some modification of the construct.

Personality and intelligence tests typically attempt to measure a theoretical construct or trait. For instance, a theory of intellect could gain support if a test could be developed to measure whatever behaviors the theory would predict. J. P. Guilford (1967) has hypothesized that intelligence comprises 120 separate abilities, and he has undertaken extensive studies to validate this position. Some of his evidence consists of low correlations among various tests of intelligence (the theory would require that they be low); other evidence involves comparisons of student achievement as predicted by tests derived from Guilford's theory and other tests derived from different theoretical considerations. In a study in which grade point averages and scores on the Cooperative Mathematics Tests (algebra) were used as criteria, Keith Holly and William Michael (1972) found that tests constructed under the requirements of Guilford's theory were consistently better predictors of both criteria and were less time-consuming to administer than commercially available mathematics tests or previous grades in mathematics. To clarify the meaning of intelligence, more studies must be conducted using other criteria and tests that measure different aspects of Guilford's theory of intelligence. (See pp. 295-297 for a more thorough description of Guilford's theory.)

Generally the process of validating constructs involves at least six steps:

1. An explicit justification that the construct has important educational or psychological properties is required. Developing constructs unrelated to theory or to the advancement of educational practice serves little purpose. To justify the need for a theory of intellect, Guilford (1959) has demonstrated the value of an integrated theory of intel-

---

* A *theory* is a unified system of principles, definitions, postulates and observations organized to most simply explain the relationships among variables (Sax 1968, p. 13).

ligence and has pointed out the implications of his theory for psychological theory, vocational testing, and educational practice.

2. A distinction must be made between the hypothesized construct and other constructs that may appear similar. For example, Guilford has attempted to show that what is typically called "creativity" is better defined as *divergent thinking*. One reason for making this distinction is that "creativity" often involves long-term efforts resulting in a novel product or idea. *Divergent thinking*, however, makes no pretense of measuring sustained effort, for that would more logically belong to the realm of motivation rather than intellect.

3. The hypothesized construct must be measurable. Guilford's theory of intellect postulates that there is a measurable difference between "figural" and "symbolic" divergent thinking. Figural divergent thinking requires the construction of a test that measures a variety of different responses using content such as size, color, form, location, or texture. In contrast, symbolic divergent thinking requires the use of letters, numbers, or other conventional signs. Tests that seem to measure many of Guilford's hypothesized constructs have been constructed.

4. Evidence should be obtained from different sources to support the construct. Usually the investigator tries to develop different tests that independently measure the same trait. Figural divergent thinking, for example, should be capable of being measured by different tests that have size, color, form, location, and texture in common. When different tests all measure the same construct, the construct has *convergent validity* (Campbell and Fiske 1959).

5. Evidence should be obtained to demonstrate that constructs do not correlate with irrelevant factors. That is, the construct should have *discriminant validity*. For example, a test of divergent or novel thinking should not correlate highly or positively with a measure of rigidity because the two traits are logically incompatible. Demonstrating what the construct does *not* represent is as important as showing what it does represent.

6. The construct is modified to conform with additional information. As new evidence accumulates, the investigator should modify the nature of the construct. Wherever the construct is deficient or fails to predict as hypothesized, it requires modification. New evidence will modify expectations, which in turn suggest new approaches for the investigator to pursue.

Factors Affecting Predictive Validity Coefficients

Because predictive validity coefficients are expressed as correlations, they are affected by some of the same factors that affect reliability, including the amount of time that elapses between measurements of the predictor and criterion and the number of items in the predictors.

The Time between Measurement of Predictor and Criterion

Predictions tend to be more hazardous over long periods of time than over short periods since many chance factors can affect both predictors and criteria, producing low correlations. Over short periods of time chance effects are reduced and predictive validity coefficients are increased.

Practical difficulties limit the usefulness of long-term prediction. Predictive validity coefficients are usually obtained for *selection* and *placement* purposes, and a test constructor may be unable to wait long periods of time to correlate predictor and criterion measures. Test constructors prefer to develop predictive validity coefficients over shorter periods of time, realizing that long delays will probably result in even lower coefficients.

Another practical limitation is the need to test large numbers of persons to ensure that an adequate number will be available when it is time for the criterion to be measured. To validate a college entrance examination, for example, it may be necessary to test thousands of high school students because many will fail to attend the college where the validation study is being conducted and others will drop out before criterion measures are obtained. Because of attrition, criterion data will probably be obtained at the end of the freshman year.

The Effects of Reliability

The *maximum validity coefficient* is directly related to reliability. The formula that expresses this relationship is

$$\text{maximum validity} = \sqrt{\text{reliability}}$$

In other words, if the reliability of a set of measurements is .70, its validity cannot be higher than $\sqrt{.70}$, or .837. It is possible (but not likely) that a test will correlate more highly with an external criterion (validity) than it does with itself (reliability).

Group variability   On pages 184-186 it was shown that correlations tend to increase with increases in group heterogeneity, and one might expect this relationship to hold for both reliability and validity since they are expressed as correlations. However, because reliability is the ratio of true variance to obtained variance, and obtained variance is the sum of true variance plus error variance, reliability may be defined as true variance divided by true variance plus error variance:

$$\text{reliability} = \frac{\text{true variance}}{\text{obtained variance}} = \frac{\text{true variance}}{\text{true variance} + \text{error variance}}$$

Increasing the obtained variance (by adding more items to the test or by administering it to a more heterogeneous sample) affects reliability, depending on whether the increase in variability is due to true or error variance. If the increase in obtained variance is due to true variance, reliability will increase; if it is due to error variance, reliability will decrease. If one were capable of determining each examinee's true score, those true scores would be perfectly reliable. Should a different and randomly selected number be added to each of these true scores, the variability of the raw scores would increase, but reliability would decrease since the error was increased. Increasing the variability of the group will increase all correlations including reliability and validity coefficients only if the increase in variability is due to increases in true score variance or reduction in error variance.

Reliability of the criterion   Criteria, like predictors, are fallible measurements. Whether they are grade point averages, teacher ratings, or the number of problems solved correctly, they are all subject to errors of measurement and unreliability. A student who solves fifty problems correctly today may produce only forty tomorrow. The mean of his obtained scores is still the best estimate of his "true" performance, and any difference between this value and what he does on any other equivalent test is an error of measurement.

Because these errors of measurement are random (i.e., due to chance), no variable can correlate with them. Correlations assume consistency from one variable to the next, and errors of measurement are, by their nature, inconsistent. Predictive validity coefficients are low to the extent that either predictors or criteria are unreliable or are composed of errors of measurement.

If errors of measurement could be eliminated, the resulting correlations would be between true scores. Errors of measurement *attenuate,* or lower, correlation coefficients. Although criteria themselves are fallible, they should be standards of excellence against which predictor measures are evaluated. Scores on a predictor test may appear to be invalid when in fact the criterion is unreliable. Fortunately it is possible through statistical techniques to estimate the correlation between a fallible test with an infallible, or perfectly reliable, criterion. This is a reasonable correction since a test should not be judged invalid when the criterion itself is unreliable.

In reporting validity coefficients it is important to distinguish between uncorrected and corrected values. The uncorrected coefficients are always empirically determined by correlating a fallible predictor with a fallible criterion. Hence they contain errors of measurement and whatever true variance is common to both. In practice, a predictor is not free of error, and its lack of reliability should be reflected in the validity coefficient. Criteria, on the other hand, should be perfectly reliable, and it is reasonable to correct a criterion for attenuation as long as it is made clear that the correlation is a corrected and theoretical value rather than an uncorrected coefficient.

The formula for *correcting the criterion for attenuation* is

$$r = \frac{\text{validity coefficient}}{\sqrt{\text{criterion reliability}}}$$

Consider a criterion measure with a reliability coefficient of .80 and a predictive validity coefficient of .40. If the teacher wants to estimate the predictive validity by correlating test scores with an errorless criterion, the formula would be

$$\frac{.40}{\sqrt{.80}} = .44$$

It is also possible to correct both predictor *and* criterion for attenuation. This would provide a *maximum* predictive validity coefficient since the effect of errors of measurement would be eliminated from both predictor and criterion. However, these coefficients should not be used in making practical prediction decisions regarding individuals because they eliminate error in what are actually fallible measures.

The formula for *correcting both the criterion and the predictor scores for attenuation* is

$$r = \frac{\text{validity coefficient}}{\sqrt{\text{predictor reliability} \times \text{criterion reliability}}}$$

Again, assuming that the predictive validity coefficient is .40, the predictor reliability is .70, and the criterion reliability is .80, the maximum correlation between predictor and criterion is

$$\frac{.40}{\sqrt{.70 \times .80}} = .53.$$

This is the correlation between a perfectly reliable (errorless) predictor and a perfectly reliable criterion. Compared with .44 (the predictive validity estimated by correcting the criterion for attenuation), it would appear that little would be gained by trying to increase the reliability of the predictor or the criterion in this example since making them both perfectly reliable (by correcting both for attenuation) would result in a correlation of only .53. If the teacher wants a more valid test, he had best begin anew by constructing a predictor that measures more of the true variance in the criterion.

Keep in mind that two measures may each be perfectly reliable and yet not correlate with one another because they measure different attributes or abilities; also, two measures may fail to correlate with each other because of the unreliability of one or of both. By correcting both measures for attenuation, the teacher can determine the advisability of increasing reliability or developing a new predictor. The rule is: if correcting both the predictor and criterion for attenuation leads to a marked increase in validity, the teacher should devote greater effort to increasing the reliability of both measures, if that is practical; however, if the same correction does not appreciably increase validity, a new predictor that more closely matches the skills or knowledge required by the criterion should be developed.

As an example, if the predictive validity coefficient is .30 and the reliabilities of the predictor and the criterion are .20 and .90, respectively, correcting both measures for attenuation leads to an estimated validity of .70 $\left(\dfrac{.30}{\sqrt{.20 \times .90}} = .70 \right)$. If only the criterion is corrected, the estimated validity will be $\dfrac{.30}{\sqrt{.90}}$, or .31. Correcting the criterion for attenuation when it is already reliable has little effect on validity; correcting predictors and criterion has a marked effect when the reliability of the predictor is low.* Then increasing the reliability of the predictor would be of value unless the test is already excessively long or time-consuming, making an increase in length impractical. In that case it would be better to construct a new test containing items that more closely resemble the knowledge and skills required on the criterion.

Number of Items in the Predictor

Increasing the length of an examination usually increases both reliability (see pp. 186-188) and validity because the maximum validity increases as a function of reliability. This increase in validity will occur only if the added items are comparable to those on the original test, however. Furthermore, the assumptions are that the criterion and the individuals tested remain unchanged.

---

* The same statement holds for a criterion with low reliability. In that case, however, there is considerable doubt whether the measure should be considered a criterion. One distinction between a predictor and a criterion, other than the obvious fact that there is a temporal difference, is that the criterion should be a standard of excellence and should therefore be reliable.

Adding new items to an examination will probably have a greater effect on reliability than on validity, as can be seen in table 8.2. If the original thirty-item examination had a reliability coefficient of .700 and a validity coefficient of .400, increasing the length of the examination affects reliability much more

Table 8.2. Reliability and Validity Coefficients for Tests of Various Lengths

Number of Items	Reliability	Predictive Validity
30	.700	.400
60	.824	.433
90	.875	.447
120	.903	.454
150	.921	.459
180	.933	.462
210	.942	.464

than validity, and the greatest increases occur with the more moderate coefficients. Again, the assumptions are that the criterion and individuals remain constant.

Cross-Validation

Suppose that a high school counselor is interested in predicting dropouts. The typical procedure would be to construct items that discriminate between graduates and nongraduates and to eliminate those items that fail to distinguish between these two groups. Suppose that the "test" constructed by the counselor consists of ten true-false items so difficult that students have to guess on all of them. To simplify matters, assume that the counselor used just one graduate and one dropout. Their "scores" follow; + means a "correct" answer and − means an incorrect response.

Item 1	2	3	4	5	6	7	8	9	10	Total Score
Graduate −	+	+	+	+	−	+	−	−	−	5
Dropout +	−	−	+	−	+	−	−	+	−	4

Items 1, 6, and 9 are not included on the final edition of the test because the dropout did better than the graduate; items 4, 8, and 10 fail to discriminate or measure individual differences and are also excluded. However, items 2, 3, 5, and 7 discriminate perfectly; thus these items will be retained to predict graduate versus dropout status.

All four items will correlate perfectly with the criterion since they were selected for their "ability" to do so. Of course, the scores of the fictitious graduate and dropout were pure guesses, although this was unknown to the counselor.

All "responses" are therefore completely random, and the four items that were retained simply reflect the effects of chance. Nonetheless, if the counselor indicates the extent to which these "items" predict graduate status for these two students, they would appear to be perfectly valid predictors.

Because chance plays a part in determining which items discriminate and which do not, items should be *cross-validated*. *Cross-validation* is a procedure whereby a test constructor reexamines his data by administering his test and a new criterion measure to a new group of persons. It is an attempt to substantiate or refute findings derived from the original item selection procedure by applying items to other groups of subjects. An item which initially discriminates because of chance is unlikely to discriminate when the test is readministered. If cross-validation achieves results similar to those found in the administration of the original test, it offers some evidence that the relationship between predictor and criterion is genuine and not due to chance. Conversely, if cross-validation procedures do not substantiate earlier findings, the test constructor must develop new items that do correlate with the criterion. In the previous example the four items that discriminated by chance would probably fail to do so when readministered to another group of students, and a new test would need to be constructed.

Criterion Contamination

Criterion contamination is the unjustifiable procedure of allowing individuals whose judgments are used as criteria to examine predictor scores, thereby "contaminating" their judgments with prior knowledge of predictors. Sometimes, for example, teachers' judgments or ratings are used as criteria in validating a new test. The "correct" procedure is to administer the experimental test to students and then to ask teachers to rate students before they examine the students' scores. Criterion contamination would occur if teachers were allowed to see these scores because they might modify their judgments to correspond more closely with test results. This would, of course, increase the correlation between experimental test scores and the now "contaminated" criterion measures or judgments.

Face Validity

The *face validity* of a test is the extent to which it appears relevant, important, and interesting to the examinee. Teachers want students to enjoy taking tests and to feel that they have not wasted their time. More important is whether students are in fact wasting their time on invalid or unreliable tests—no matter how relevant the test may *appear* to be. Nonetheless, for motivation and for good relations, it is important that students and parents perceive the test as important. Complaints to school principals can be reduced if tests do not appear to be trivial in content or do not use language that "talks down" to students.

Some items may have face validity but lack empirical validity. That is, it is possible for students to enjoy taking an empirically useless test. Also possible are measurements that are empirically valid but that have little face validity. Often rewriting these items can make them appear more relevant. An elementary arithmetic test for "slow" high school students should use adult examples; a reading test for selecting secretaries should utilize practical examples and avoid literary ones; a mathematics test in a physics class should employ physics examples.

It should be clear that face validity is secondary to other forms of validity. If possible, however, items should appear relevant to examinees because if a test appears trivial and childish, empirical validity may be impaired.

Validity and Reasons for Using Tests

Selection

Predictive and concurrent validity coefficients provide evidence of the usefulness of measurements for predicting or distinguishing between successful and unsuccessful applicants. In general, the higher these coefficients are, the more useful the measurements are. Although most validity coefficients are below .65, teachers might have to make decisions from data with validity coefficients as low as .20. When validity coefficients are that low, the teacher will misclassify (incorrectly reject or accept) many individuals, yet the test could still provide practical data: low validity coefficients are better than none at all.

Expectancy tables   Teachers must base selection decisions on the number of available positions and the number of applicants. If teachers *must* select only ten or fifteen students, the best and simplest approach is to rank them and take the top ten. If the number to be selected is flexible, an *expectancy table* can help make selection decisions. An expectancy table usually has predictor scores along one axis and criterion measures on the other. In the expectancy table in figure 8.2, one person had a grade point average of 4.00 and a predictor score of 100. In this example there is a tendency for high grade point averages to accompany high predictor scores. The correlation (predictive validity coefficient) between predictor and criterion is .67.

Grade point averages above 2.0 are passing grades; those below 2.0 represent failures. The total group includes 185 students; 133 of them received passing grades $(37 + 96 = 133)$, and 52 received failing grades $(31 + 21 = 52)$. If all 185 students were admitted, 133 out of 185 would have been successful (about 72 percent), and 28 percent would have failed. If all students with predictor scores of 65 and higher were admitted, 117 students $(96 + 21)$ would have been admitted, and 96 would have been successful. The ratio of 96 to 117

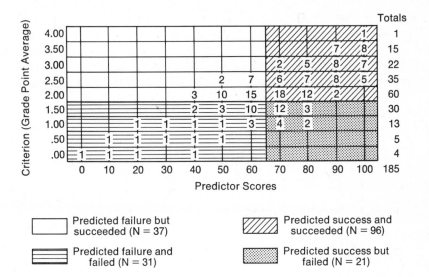

Figure 8.2. Hypothetical Expectancy Table Relating Predictor Scores to Grade Point Average $(r = .67)$

represents the percentage (82 percent) of successful students who were admitted. The ratio of the number successful to the number admitted is referred to as the *success ratio*. In the example the success ratio is 82 percent. Note that if the cutting score were set at 85 rather than 65, 46 students would have been selected, and none would have failed. The success ratio would then have been 100 percent, but very few students would have been admitted.

The ratio of the number of persons selected to the number of applicants is called the *selection ratio*. With the cutting score set at 65, 117 $(96 + 21)$ out of 185, or 63 percent, would have been selected. Notice that as fewer students are selected, the cutting score moves to the right and the success ratio increases. An increase in the selection ratio means that the cutting score is moved to the left and more students are admitted. As more of these students are admitted, however, the success ratio becomes lower.

Figure 8.3 shows what happens to the selection and success ratios if the validity coefficient is 1.0—all the scores fall along a straight line, and by knowing the predictor score, the criterion score can be predicted perfectly. No matter where the cutting score is placed above 55, the success ratio is 1.0. Below 55, the success ratio is 0. With validity coefficients of 1.0, there is no risk of failure for each person selected; those who were refused admission would have failed had they been admitted.

The relationship among success ratios, selection ratios, and validity can be seen from the Taylor-Russell tables (table 8.3). Developed as an aid to effective selection decisions, the Taylor-Russell tables demonstrate how these decisions are improved depending on test validity, selection ratios, and the proportion of students who are successful without being selected by the test.

Selection ratios from .05 to .95 are located at the top of the table. Validity coefficients ranging from .00 to 1.00 are located along the side of each group of figures where .05, .50, .70, and .95 of students are found who are rated as satisfactory *without* the use of the test. The main body of the table consists of the success ratios or the proportions of students judged successful *after* administering tests with different validities.

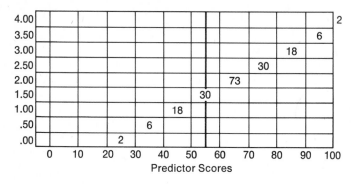

Figure 8.3. Expectancy Table Where r = 1.0

The table indicates the amount of improvement in making selection decisions that results from a knowledge of test scores. For example, if .50 of the students are satisfactory without having been selected by a test, the administration of a test with 0 validity means that testing produced no gains regardless of the selection ratio. However, still assuming that .50 of the students are rated satisfactory without being selected by a test, if teachers select .05 of applicants (the selection ratio), the administration of a test having a validity coefficient of .20 would improve the success ratio from .50 to .67. The test therefore helped teachers select 17 percent more individuals who succeeded than who did so without the test.

The Taylor-Russell tables demonstrate that when the validity of a test is 0, the success ratio is directly proportional to the selection ratios. For example, if .05 of students are satisfactory without the use of a test to select them, and a test with a validity of 0 is introduced, the success ratio will still be .05. With validities of 0, teachers can select no better than the proportion of students who are judged to be satisfactory without the test.

Second, notice that when the selection ratio is low, there is rapid improve-

Table 8.3. Proportion of Successful Students Selected as a Result of Using Tests of Different Validities under Different Selection Ratios When .05, .50, .70, and .95 of Students Are Successful without the Use of the Test

		Selection Ratios										
		.05	.10	.20	.30	.40	.50	.60	.70	.80	.90	.95
		If .05 of Students Are Satisfactory without Use of Test										
V	.00	.05	.05	.05	.05	.05	.05	.05	.05	.05	.05	.05
A	.20	.11	.09	.08	.08	.07	.07	.06	.06	.06	.05	.05
L	.40	.19	.16	.12	.10	.09	.08	.07	.07	.06	.05	.05
I	.60	.31	.24	.17	.13	.11	.09	.08	.07	.06	.06	.05
D	.80	.50	.35	.22	.16	.12	.10	.08	.07	.06	.06	.05
I T Y	1.00	1.00	.50	.25	.17	.13	.10	.08	.07	.06	.06	.05
		If .50 of Students Are Satisfactory without Use of Test										
V	.00	.50	.50	.50	.50	.50	.50	.50	.50	.50	.50	.50
A	.20	.67	.64	.61	.59	.58	.56	.55	.54	.53	.52	.51
L	.40	.82	.78	.73	.69	.66	.63	.61	.58	.56	.53	.52
I	.60	.94	.90	.84	.79	.75	.70	.66	.62	.59	.54	.52
D	.80	1.00	.99	.95	.90	.85	.80	.73	.67	.61	.55	.53
I T Y	1.00	1.00	1.00	1.00	1.00	1.00	1.00	.83	.71	.63	.56	.53
		If .70 of Students Are Satisfactory without Use of Test										
V	.00	.70	.70	.70	.70	.70	.70	.70	.70	.70	.70	.70
A	.20	.83	.81	.79	.78	.77	.76	.75	.74	.73	.71	.71
L	.40	.93	.91	.88	.85	.83	.81	.79	.77	.75	.73	.72
I	.60	.98	.97	.95	.92	.90	.87	.85	.82	.79	.75	.73
D	.80	1.00	1.00	.99	.98	.97	.94	.91	.87	.82	.77	.73
I T Y	1.00	1.00	1.00	1.00	1.00	1.00	1.00	1.00	1.00	.88	.78	.74
		If .95 of Students Are Satisfactory without Use of Test										
V	.00	.95	.95	.95	.95	.95	.95	.95	.95	.95	.95	.95
A	.20	.98	.98	.97	.97	.97	.97	.96	.96	.96	.95	.95
L	.40	1.00	.99	.99	.99	.98	.98	.98	.97	.97	.96	.96
I	.60	1.00	1.00	1.00	1.00	1.00	.99	.99	.99	.98	.97	.96
D	.80	1.00	1.00	1.00	1.00	1.00	1.00	1.00	1.00	.99	.98	.97
I T Y	1.00	1.00	1.00	1.00	1.00	1.00	1.00	1.00	1.00	1.00	1.00	1.00

Taylor and Russell, 1939.

ment in the proportion of persons judged successful even with modest gains in validity. For example, if .50 of students are satisfactory without the use of a test to select them, an increase in validity from .20 to .40 increases the success ratio from .67 to .82. However, if the selection ratio is high (meaning that almost everyone who applied is selected), the success ratio increases only from .51 to .52. An extremely high selection ratio forces colleges or teachers to accept a large proportion of applicants, some of whom are bound to be unsuccessful. Even if the validity is 1.00, they would still have to accept persons who would later be judged unsuccessful. The exception is where everyone or a very large proportion of persons is judged to be satisfactory students even without the use of a selection test.

Placement and Remediation

Selection is necessary to but not sufficient for placement and remediation decisions. One could recommend special classes for the gifted student, the retarded child, or the slow reader, or classes to aid the student offset some of his current difficulties.

Generally selection is simpler than placement or remediation. Selection implies a dichotomous decision of admission or rejection. If he is admitted, the student has to be assigned to an optimal program, and there might be several possibilities. The responsibility of the school counselor is to know what opportunities exist within the school and to recommend or place individuals in classes where they are most likely to be successful.

Measurements are valid for placement and remediation decisions to the extent that they exhibit *incremental validity*. The *incremental validity* of measurements is the increased efficiency of prediction over information already known. An examination of the Taylor-Russell tables (table 8.3) shows that incremental validity is greatest when 50 percent of those selected are rated as satisfactory because improvement in prediction is greatest at that point. Even when the validity of the placement test is 0 and 5 percent are selected, the success ratio is .50. A test with a validity of .20 raises the success ratio to .67. The difference between .50 and .67 is the *incremental validity* of the test. It demonstrates how the success ratio increases as a function of the increase in test validity.

Cronbach (1970) has provided an excellent example of the role of incremental validity in making placement decisions. Suppose that test A correlates .40 with success in class 1 and in class 2. Test A would probably be considered a general ability test that is as useful in predicting success in one class as in the other, but it exhibits 0 incremental validity since it cannot differentiate between those who will be successful in one class but not in the other. If the decision is made to place those in the upper half of test A, 25 percent would randomly be assigned to class 1 and the other 25 percent to class 2. The other half would be rejected for either class.

Now suppose a different situation with two tests B and C. Test B correlates .40 with success in class 1 and 0 with success in class 2; test C correlates 0 with success in class 1 and .40 with success in class 2. In this example there is high incremental validity. Once again the decision is to place all those who score in the upper half of *either* test B or C into class 1 or class 2. These relationships are shown in figure 8.4. All those to the *right* of the vertical line are in the upper half for test B; those *above* the horizontal line are in the upper half for test C. Because test B correlates with performance in class 1, those who are to the right of the vertical line are accepted in that class. Those above the horizontal line on test C will be placed into class 2 since only test C correlates with performance in that class. The only students who are not placed are those in the lower left quadrant since they are rejected for class 1 and class 2 because of low scores on both tests B and C. Those in the upper right quadrant did equally well on test B and test C, and the best prediction is equal success in classes 1 and 2. Teachers can either randomly assign half of that group to each of the classes or try to develop tests that will differentially place those persons into class 1 *or* class 2. In any case they could place 75 percent of the students by having tests B and C correlate differentially with success in different classes, whereas they could only place 50 percent by using test A, which was unable to differentially predict suc-

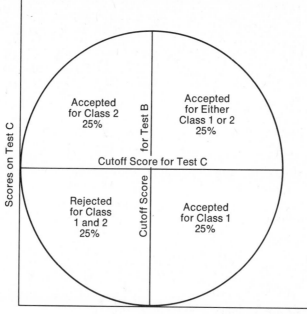

Figure 8.4. Regions of Acceptance and Rejection for Two Tests, B and C, Differentially Predicting Success in Classes 1 and 2 (adapted from Cronbach, 1970, p. 447)

cess in the two classes. For placement decisions teachers prefer tests that correlate positively with success on one criterion but 0 or negatively with another. In that regard, tests B and C are useful for placement.

Another criterion for placement is that the correlation among various predictor tests be as close to 0 as possible. Each test should correlate with success in a specific job or task, but tests should not correlate with each other. If tests correlate highly with each other, they measure the same traits or abilities and one provides little information not available from the other. If both tests correlate with a particular criterion but not with each other, each test contributes independent information to making valid placement decisions.

Summary

1. Validity is the extent to which measurements are useful in making decisions relevant to a given purpose. Types of validity are:

a. *Content validity*. Content validity is the extent to which items on a test ask students to demonstrate skills and competencies required by the objectives. Content validity is crucial for achievement tests.

b. *Criterion-related validity*. Criterion-related validity refers to two types of coefficients: (1) the correlation of a set of measurements with an external criterion measured concomitantly, and (2) the same type of correlation where there is a time lapse between measurements and a criterion. The former is called concurrent validity; the latter, predictive validity. Concurrent validity coefficients will be higher than predictive validity coefficients.

c. *Construct validity*. Construct validity is the extent to which measurements justify or support the existence of psychological traits, abilities, or attributes. This justification often involves obtaining evidence regarding convergent validation (this provides evidence that various tests are capable of measuring the construct) and by discriminant validation (this provides evidence that irrelevant tests are incapable of measuring the construct).

2. Predictive validity coefficients are affected by a number of conditions:

a. The longer the amount of time between measurements obtained from the predictor and the criterion is, the lower the predictive validity is likely to be.

b. Reliability places a limit on validity. The maximum validity is equal to the square root of the reliability coefficient.

c. Increasing the number of items in the predictor has a greater effect on reliability than on validity.

3. The correction for attenuation can be applied to criterion measures to make them perfectly reliable; or the "correction" can be applied to both the predictor and the criterion to estimate the relationship between perfectly reliable predictors and a perfectly reliable criterion.

4. Cross-validation is the procedure used to make sure that items originally selected to correlate with some criterion in a predictor test do so for some reason other than chance. By readministering items to a new sample of students, the effects of chance on item selection can be determined.

5. Criterion contamination refers to the improper procedure of allowing judges whose ratings are to be used as a criterion to examine test data of those persons whom they are supposed to rate. The criterion (judges' ratings) thus becomes contaminated with prior knowledge of examinees' test scores.

6. Face validity is the extent to which a test appears relevant, important, and interesting to an examinee. Face validity can be increased by including items on tests that measure important content as judged by the examinees.

7. Expectancy tables are ways of interpreting validity to students and parents.

The criterion measure is usually listed on the vertical side of the table and predictor scores along the horizontal side. Each row consists of the number of persons having different scores on the criterion; each column contains the number of students having different predictor scores.

8. The success ratio is the number of successful students divided by the number of students admitted into a program. The higher the success ratio is, the fewer are the students who will fail a program.

9. The selection ratio is the number of persons selected divided by the number of applicants. As teachers or schools become more selective, they also increase the success ratio, but they do so at the cost of selecting fewer individuals.

10. The Taylor-Russell tables are ways of improving selection decisions. The tables provide the incremental validity or the increase in efficiency of prediction over information already available. Incremental validity is greatest when 50 percent of the students selected are rated as satisfactory without the benefit of tests.

11. Tests are most effective for placement decisions if they correlate positively with success on one criterion and have a 0 or negative correlation with success on another.

Suggested Readings

Astin, Alexander W. "Criterion-Centered Research." *Educational and Psychological Measurement* 24, no. 4 (Winter 1964): 807–22. A discussion of the nature and role of the criterion, its use in test construction, and the nature of criterion-centered research.

Ebel, Robert L. "Must All Tests Be Valid?" *American Psychologist* 16, no. 10 (1961): 640–47. Ebel's answer to the title of his article is no if a criterion "better than" the test itself is a necessary condition for validity. This article is readable and interesting.

Cronbach, Lee J. "Test Validation." In Robert L. Thorndike, ed., *Educational Measurement,* 2d ed., pp. 443–507. Washington, D. C.: American Council on Education, 1971. A detailed and somewhat technical (especially the second half of the chapter) discussion of the nature of validity.

Kendall, L. M. "The Effects of Varying Time Limits on Test Validity." *Educational and Psychological Measurement* 24, no. 4 (Winter 1964): 789–800. An interesting account of how validity was increased by *reducing* time limits on an examination. Kendall found that tripling time limits beyond the point where validity was at a maximum value was ineffective.

Item Analysis Procedures and Interpretation

Out of the Mouths of Babes

(Gleaned, reputedly, from sixth-grade test answers)

Geography

The general direction of the Alps is straight up.

Most of the houses in France are made of Plaster of Paris.

Manhattan Island was bought from the Indians for $24 and I don't suppose you could buy it now for $500.

Science

Iron was discovered because someone smelt it.

Q. What happens when there is an eclipse of the sun? A. A great many people come out to look at it.

The four seasons are salt, pepper, mustard, and vinegar.

Physiology

The spinal column is a long bunch of bones. The head sits on top and you sit on the bottom.

The stomach is a bowl-shaped cavity containing the organs of indigestion.

To prevent colds, use an agonizer to spray nose until it drops into your throat.

A person should take a bath once in the summer and not so often in the winter.

Miscellaneous

One of the main causes of dust is janitors.

9

Unique responses to questions are not amenable to analysis by the procedures described in this chapter. They usually result from ambiguous questions that provide little direction as to how students are to respond. Most of the suggestions for item writing in previous chapters were designed to improve reliability and validity. Nonetheless, even the most carefully prepared items are susceptible to human error and on analysis may prove to be ambiguous, too simple, overly difficult, or nondiscriminating (incapable of measuring individual differences when that is the purpose of the test). Many of these problems can be detected and at least partially resolved by item analysis procedures. Although the procedures discussed in this chapter are particularly useful for multiple-choice tests, they can be adapted to other item formats.

Reasons for Analyzing Items

Examinations that greatly influence students' course grades (such as midterms and finals) or that serve other important decision-making functions should be as free from deceptive and ambiguous items as possible. Unfortunately it is often difficult to recognize problems before the test has been administered. Item analysis procedures allow the teacher to discover items that are:

1. Ambiguous
2. Miskeyed
3. Too easy or too difficult
4. Nondiscriminating

Item analyses can enhance the technical quality of an examination by pointing out options that are nonfunctional and that should be improved or eliminated.

Still another purpose of item analysis is to facilitate classroom instruction. In diagnostic testing, for example, the item analysis identifies areas of student weakness, providing information for specific remediation. Coupled with clear objectives and an adequate sampling of important student behaviors, item analyses can do much to help teachers prepare better examinations and in the long run can save teachers' time. In one study (Lange et al. 1967) the investigators found that it took five times longer to construct new multiple-choice items for college students than it did to revise and improve old items by taking advantage of an item analysis.

A Simplified Item Analysis Form

The item analysis procedures described in this text are designed to minimize labor but still provide dependable, useful information. Because it is necessary to tally student responses to each item on the examination, a separate answer sheet facilitates scoring and counting, especially if the test consists of many pages. A simple answer sheet for true-false or multiple-choice items can use the slant bars on a typewriter, or students can circle what they believe is the correct alternative, as in the examples below.

	T	F
1.	/ /	/ /
2.	/ /	/ /

1. A   B   C   D   E
2. A   B   C   D   E
3. T   F

Table 9.1 presents a convenient form that can serve as a guide in an item analysis. The steps are:

1. Score each test by counting the number of answers marked correctly, and place that number on the answer sheet.
2. Arrange the scored test papers or answer sheets in order from high to low scores.
3. Remove the lowest and highest 27 percent of the papers, leaving intact the middle 46 percent. Truman Kelley (1939) has shown that using the extreme 27 percent groups reduces labor without seriously reducing the accuracy of the data. However, if the item analysis is used for a small number of students, there is some advantage in subdividing scores at the median to include more cases in the upper and lower groups.
4. Count the number of students in the *upper portion* of the class who responded to *each* option; include that information in column (1) of the item analysis form (table 9.1). In column (2) indicate the number of students in the *lower portion* who responded to each alternative. If a test has been administered to 100 students, for ex-

Table 9.1. Item Analysis Form

Item	(1) Upper 27%	(2) Lower 27%	(3) Difference	(4) D	(5) Middle 46%	(6) Total	(7) p
1.							
a.	5	3					
*b.	15	7	8	.30	25	47	.47
c.	0	12					
d.	0	0					
e.	7	5					

* Note that the correct alternative is marked by an asterisk (*).

ample, the distribution of responses to item 1 made by the upper and lower 27 percent would appear in columns (1) and (2).

5. Subtract the number of students in the lower group who selected the correct alternative (marked with the asterisk) from the number of students who responded correctly in the upper group. Place the difference in column (3). In table 9.1 the difference is 8, although it is possible for the difference to be negative if more individuals in the lower group responded correctly than in the upper group.

6. Divide the difference found in column (3) by the number of students in the upper (or lower) group. There are 100 students in the example; 27 percent of 100 is 27; and 8 divided by 27 is approximately .30. This value is the *discrimination index, D,* which will be discussed later in this chapter. The discrimination index is written in column (4) of the item analysis form.

7. Count the students in the *middle group* who responded to the correct option, and place that value in column (5). If the upper and lower groups each contain half the class, there will, of course, be no middle group, and column (5) can be omitted. In this example, 25 students in the middle group responded correctly.

8. Add the number of individuals who responded correctly in the upper, lower, and middle groups. These values are found in columns (1), (2), and (5) of the item analysis form. The sum of these three values represents the total number of students who answered the item correctly. This sum is placed in column (6).

9. Divide column (6) by N, the total number of students taking the test, and enter this value in column (7). This is the *proportion* of students in the total group who responded correctly (often abbreviated p), and it is a measure of the difficulty level of the item. Since 47 students responded correctly out of a total of 100 who took the test, $p = .47$. Approximately half the class responded correctly to this item.

Although the item-analysis procedures may at first appear to be complex, Quincy's "solution" serves little purpose (see fig. 9.1). A better approach is to learn how to keep records and to use data more wisely.

Counting the number of students in the upper and lower groups who responded to each option is the most time-consuming aspect of performing an item analysis. If there are many items or students, this clerical chore can take much

Figure 9.1

time. Some public schools and most universities have electronic data-processing equipment that can be used for this purpose. Teachers can also reduce labor by using only 27 percent of the students in each extreme group rather than counting responses made by the entire sample. But if N is small (some authorities define *small* as less than 100 in *each* extreme group, or a total of 370), the accuracy of the item analysis data is greatly reduced. Another possibility is for the teacher initially to count only correct responses. If the item discriminates well and is of average difficulty or easier, there is no need to count *incorrect* responses. Difficult items or those that fail to discriminate among students in the upper and lower groups should be analyzed further by counting responses to all options in the two extreme groups.

Albert	Betty	Key
1. A	1. A	1. A
2. C	2. B	2. B
3. A	3. A	3. A
4. D	4. D	4. D
5. E	5. E	5. E
6. B	6. C	6. B
7. D	7. D	7. D
8. C	8. C	8. C
9. E	9. B	9. C
10. B	10. A	10. B

Figure 9.2. Responses of Two Students in Comparison to Keyed Answers

A typewriter can also help simplify the counting of responses. The hypothetical answers of two students on a ten-item examination are shown in figure 9.2. It is easy to type the letter *A, B, C, D,* or *E* corresponding to an examinee's response to each of the ten items. Teachers can then prepare a work table like the following:

Item Number	1	2	3	4	5	6	7	8	9	10
Albert	A	C	A	D	E	B	D	C	E	B
Betty	A	B	A	D	E	C	D	C	B	A

On item 1 both students chose option *A;* on item 2 one student selected *C* and the other selected *B,* and so on. By using this procedure, teachers can quickly count the number of students who responded to each option on every item. *Be sure to separate the responses of students composing the upper and lower groups before tallying responses.*

Interpreting Item Analysis Data

Ambiguity

One measure of item ambiguity is the extent to which students in the *upper group* select an *incorrect* option with about the same frequency as they select the *correct* one. *Ambiguity* defined in this way is the inability of the highest-scoring students on the test to discriminate between a "correct" alternative and one judged by the teacher to be "wrong." From the students' point of view, the item is ambiguous. An ambiguous item could also be defined as one that allows for more than one "correct" alternative as judged by a group of experts, although a question that is clear to experts may be ambiguous to students who lack understanding of the item's content. Asking other teachers to take the test can help identify items that are ambiguous according to this second definition. Unfortunately the item analysis cannot reveal if ambiguity results from the students' lack of knowledge or from poorly written items.

Consider the following examples:

1. $4 + 3 \times 6 =$ *Upper 27%*

      *a. 22   11

       b. 27   2

       c. 42   11

       d. none of the above   1

2. Which of the following is a standard score?

                                                         Upper 27%

       a. Deviation IQs   11

       b. Percentiles   2

      *c. z scores   11

       d. None of the above   1

In the first example students were supposed to remember that the order of arithmetic operations is first multiply, then divide, add, and subtract if there are no parentheses or brackets to indicate that a different order is required. If the purpose of the item is to measure knowledge of arithmetic sequencing, it should not be ambiguous to students who know the rule. The fact that eleven students incorrectly added and then multiplied (option *c*) simply means that they did not remember or know the rule. The item appears to be ambiguous because students lack knowledge, not because the item is defective.

However, the second item would be ambiguous to experts since two options can be justified. As indicated in chapter 6, both deviation IQs and z scores are standard scores. In this example options *a* and *c* are both defensible, and the most knowledgeable students (those in the upper part of the class) were unable to tell which answer the teacher wanted. This item is defective; option *a* should be replaced.

When students in the *upper* portion of the class select a "correct" option and an "incorrect" option with about equal frequency, the item is ambiguous either because students lack knowledge or because the options are poorly written. Which of these reasons is applicable to a given item is determined by examining the highly selected but "incorrect" options to see if more than one answer can be justified. If more than one answer can reasonably be considered "correct," the teacher should give credit for all such options. To avoid haggling over points in class, credit should be given before students' papers are returned to them.

Miskeying

Miskeying is another common error that can be corrected before students' papers are returned. One way of detecting potentially miskeyed items is to examine the responses of the students in the *upper* portion of the class. An "incorrect" option selected by a large number of these students suggests a keying error, as in the following example:

Who was the first president of the United States?

		Upper Group
*a.	John Adams	3
b.	Abraham Lincoln	1
c.	Franklin Roosevelt	0
d.	George Washington	12

Because the majority of the most capable students selected Washington as the correct alternative and so few agreed with the "keyed" answer, the teacher should check the key for a possible error.

Guessing

Sometimes items inadvertently contain information students have not yet studied; others may be so difficult or so trivial that students have no idea how to respond. When any of these conditions occur, students in the *upper* portion of the class are likely to respond randomly to the choices since all alternatives will seem equally plausible. Consider the following item:

A zamindar is a (an)	Upper Group
a. small sword.	6
b. African plant.	5
*c. property owner.	6
d. native warrior.	6

If students have no idea of the correct answer, they tend to distribute their choices with about equal frequency among all options. This type of responding can help teachers detect subjects that are not clearly understood by students. If an item is confusing to those in the upper portion of the class, it is usually even more confusing to those in the lower group.

Discrimination Indices

Discrimination indices measure the extent to which items are capable of measuring individual differences. If "successful" and "unsuccessful" students respond equally well on an item, it has a discrimination index of 0 and is useless for measuring individual differences. On the other hand, if most successful students respond correctly to an item and most unsuccessful ones miss it, the item discriminates in the proper direction.

The criterion used to determine successful and unsuccessful students on academic achievement tests is usually the total score on the examination itself. Successful students receive the highest total scores, and unsuccessful ones, the lowest scores. When this total score is used as the criterion, it is referred to as an *internal criterion*. When grade point averages or teacher ratings are used to differentiate between successful and unsuccessful individuals, these are referred to as *external criteria*.

Which of these criteria should be used will be discussed later in this chapter. Whatever the criterion, however, the number or percentage of individuals who compose the successful (upper) and unsuccessful (lower) groups must be decided. Sometimes the upper and lower halves are used; at other times upper and lower thirds, quarters, or other values are used. If halves are used, discrimination indices are based on the responses of all individuals taking the test rather than just the responses of a portion of them. The disadvantages are that such indices require a good deal of labor, and differences between upper and lower groups are smaller than they would be if only the extreme scores were used.

If teachers choose to compare the responses of students in the upper and lower 27 percent groups, they can reduce their labor by about half, but the smaller groups may also produce unreliable data. An extreme example makes this clear. Suppose a teacher chooses the *one* highest-scoring pupil and the one lowest-scoring pupil on a test and compares their individual item responses. Differences between the two students on each item will be maximal, but their responses might not be typical of those of the other students in their respective groups. As more students are added to each criterion group, differences will be reduced between them, since more marginal pupils will be included in "successful" and "unsuccessful" categories. Chance differences will be reduced, but at the cost of greater labor and lower discrimination indices.

Kelley (1939) has recommended using extreme 27 percent groups to maximize discrimination and minimize labor, and this suggestion is most often used when N is large. Discrimination indices on standardized tests frequently have at least 100 students in each of the extreme 27 percent groups, or a minimum of about 370 persons, in order for the indices to remain stable from sample to sample. Of course, teachers do not have classes that large, but they may be able to give the same examination in other classes and obtain more accurate and representative data. In any case, not much can be done about small samples except to increase the percentage of students in each extreme group and to remember the highly tentative nature of any results such data may yield.

Numerous techniques have been suggested for measuring item discrimination, but no index appears to have great technical advantages over the others (Engelhart 1965). However, some indices are more laborious to compute than others and are therefore less practical.

D, the "upper minus lower difference," appears to be the simplest measure of item discrimination, and it is often used in analyzing teacher-made tests. D is defined as the difference between the proportion of individuals responding correctly in extreme groups; it ranges in value from $+1.0$ to -1.0. If everyone in the upper group responded correctly to an item that is failed by all those in the lower portion of the class, the difference is 100 percent, or $+1.0$ expressed as a proportion. A D index of .70 would result if 85 percent and 15 percent of students in upper and lower groups, respectively, responded correctly to a given item.

When a larger proportion of students in the lower group do better on an item than those in the upper group, the D index is negative, and the item *negatively discriminates*. Negatively discriminating items are usually poorly written or ambiguous. Because negatively discriminating items favor those individuals who have the least knowledge (as measured by internal or external criteria), they do not contribute to the trait or ability being measured.

Sometimes the suggestion is made to eliminate the effects of all negatively discriminating items by omitting them or by giving everyone credit. But the number of students composing upper and lower groups on many teacher-made examinations is often so small that chance could account for at least some of these negative differences, particularly when the D value is small. Furthermore, each item should be designed to measure a specified objective, and its elimination may reduce content validity. Ideally, for each concept being taught, the teacher would have a large pool of items—each having high content validity—from which to choose. Those items that are most discriminating should be selected for use. If there are no surplus items, and if each item is an important contributor to the content validity of the test, the item analysis may help to improve the quality of the items by reducing ambiguity or by increasing the plausibility of the alternatives.

Before they are readministered, negatively discriminating items may be modified by revising options to increase the probability that the correct one will be selected more frequently by those in the upper group. If an *incorrect* option is overselected by the students in the upper group, it can either be eliminated or revised to make it less attractive. Another possibility, of course, is to improve the quality of instructions so that students will be less likely to select incorrect responses.

As a rule of thumb, items that discriminate from 0 to +.30 contribute relatively little to measuring individual differences and should be revised to make them more discriminating before they are reused. Items that discriminate between 0 and −.30 should be omitted if D is based on a large number of individuals (a total of 400 or more is often recommended), *and* if the test contains other *positively discriminating* items measuring the same objective. Items that *negatively discriminate* more than about −.30 are probably deficient in other ways and should be eliminated from the item pool if possible.

One reason for the desirability of high, positive D indices is that reliability increases as the average value of D increases. Because D is a measure of the difference between portions of a group, the standard deviation of scores is increased by increasing D. If this increase measures true differences, an increase in *reliability* can be expected.

Similarly, negatively discriminating items tend to lower reliability since they measure something other than what the test as a whole measures. As stated earlier, it may be necessary to include some items with negative D indices if they measure important objectives not covered by other items on the test. In this case some degree of reliability is forfeited to maintain the content validity of the test.

Discrimination indices and homogeneity of item content   Most teacher-made examinations try to measure a single area of competence or ability such as spelling, handwriting, or arithmetic. When test content is *homogeneous* (measures only one area, trait, or ability), the total score is a reasonable criterion for separating examinees into successful and unsuccessful criterion groups. Items that discriminate positively correlate with the total score and measure whatever the total score measures.

Because the best estimate of a student's knowledge is his total score on the test, each item should contribute to or correlate with that total. Each positively discriminating item is a subsample of whatever the test as a whole measures. If the test as a whole measures trivial or irrelevant knowledge, a positively discriminating item simply contributes to trivia and irrelevance. The assumption to be satisfied is that the test as a whole does in fact meet important course objectives.

Sometimes tests measure different skills or traits and are composed of *heterogeneous* samples of items. An achievement test may (but should *not*) contain items on spelling, arithmetic, English, science, *and* social studies. The total score on such an examination measures widely different objectives and is analogous to adding apples and orange crates to determine the total number of apples. If discrimination indices are based on *heterogeneous internal criteria,* items are contributing to a meaningless total score.

What should the teacher who has a heterogeneous criterion but still wishes to evaluate item discrimination do? One solution is to develop different tests, each of which is homogeneous in one subject, such as spelling or arithmetic. Items *on each test* should yield high, positive D indices with *their own total score* used as the *internal criterion.* Each test should therefore be a reliable measure of part of the heterogeneous criterion and might best be considered as an independent subtest. Instead of computing a meaningless total score, the teacher could report that Albert has scores of X in spelling, Y in English, and Z in mathematics.

Discrimination indices and criterion-referenced tests   Unlike *norm-referenced tests,* which are designed to measure individual differences, *criterion-referenced* or *mastery tests* specify some minimum level of competence which all students are expected to attain. Instead of trying to emphasize the variation among students, teachers using criterion-referenced tests try to achieve a high degree of *homogeneity.* Instead of constructing items to compare one person with another, on criterion-referenced tests teachers design items to measure whether students have attained "mastery" of knowledge or skills. Individual differences are unimportant for mastery tests.

Suggestions have been offered to help select items for mastery tests, but they all suffer from serious deficiencies. One possibility, for example, is to compare the item responses of pupils who have been exposed to a specific unit of instruction with the responses of a comparable group that has not been taught the knowledge or concepts measured by the criterion test. Differences between the two groups would be attributed to the effects of instruction. This type of evidence provides some support for the hypothesis that the items measure desired content. But suppose that no differences are found? The reason could be poor instruction or poor item quality.

A second suggestion is to compare item responses of students before and after they are introduced to a unit of instruction. This procedure has the obvious advantage of not requiring two groups. The disadvantage is that exposure to items on the pretest might carry over to the posttest. Differences, then, could be explained, at least in part, by familiarity with pretest content rather than by the quality of the items.

The position taken in this text is that neither of these suggestions answers the question of how items should be selected for mastery tests. If students are to print correctly all the letters of the alphabet in sequence, the task is set. If students fail to improve or if their performance is no better than that of a comparable group that was not taught these skills, the fault should probably not be placed on the items. Poor instruction, lack of maturity, or the simplicity (or difficulty) of the task could account for the failure to obtain differences in test scores. Perhaps the best approach to the construction of mastery tests is for teachers to define their objectives as clearly as possible and to write items that have high content validity.

Difficulty Levels

The *difficulty level* (p) is usually defined as the proportion of students responding correctly to an item. The higher this proportion is, the easier the item is. The maximum value of p, $+1.0$, occurs whenever everyone responds correctly; the lowest value of p, 0, means that everyone missed the item or failed to respond to it. Note that on the item analysis form (table 9.1, p. 231) the difficulty level (p) is indicated in column (7).

Unless there is evidence of ambiguity, miskeying, or other deficiencies, the value of p is usually not sufficient to justify the inclusion or rejection of an item *after* it has been administered. The p level does not indicate that an item is good or bad, only that it is hard or easy. For instance, mastery test items usually have high values of p, which means that scores tend to pile up at the high end, creating a negatively skewed curve (discussed in chap. 6). Negatively skewed tests are valuable in helping to identify those who fail to reach mastery. Hard tests, in contrast, can help to identify those who excel in relation to the other members of the test group. Whether p values should be high or low depends in part on how the test will be used.

The difficulty level of an item is also important because of its relationship to D, the discrimination index. An item that is extremely easy or hard cannot effectively discriminate among students. For maximum discrimination, everyone in the upper portion of the group must respond correctly to the item, whereas all those in the lower portion of the group must miss it. The difficulty level of a perfectly discriminating item would be .50 *if the effects of guessing could be disregarded*. It is important to realize that this value of .50 could result from items that discriminate perfectly or from those that do not discriminate at all. For example, it is possible for the difficulty level of an item to be .50 but the discrimination index (the extent to which the item measures individual differences) to be 0. A D index of 0 would occur if half the upper group and half the lower group responded correctly to an item. *High discrimination indices require some optimal level of difficulty, but optimal difficulty levels do not assure high D indices.* However, because it is usually easier to estimate item difficulty (p) than it is to judge how well an item will discriminate (D), a rationale for establishing an optimal level of difficulty will be discussed.

On a true-false test there are two alternatives for each item. Assuming a 100-item test, the most likely score a student would receive by responding randomly to all items should be 50. This value is the *chance score*. If students did respond randomly to all items, the reliability of measurements would be 0 even though item difficulty is .50. Clearly this test is too difficult to measure individual differences reliably.

Table 9.2. Optimal Difficulty Levels for Items Having Different Numbers of Options as Determined by Two Different Procedures

Number of Options	Optimal Difficulty Using Formula: $\dfrac{CS + (1.00 - CS)}{2}$	Optimal Difficulty According to Lord
0 (completion, essay)	.50	.50
2	.75	.85
3	.67	.77
4	.63	.74
5	.60	.69

Adapted from Lord 1952.

The *optimal difficulty level* of a test depends on the chance score and number of items making up the test. One way of estimating optimal difficulty level is to compute the chance score and to add to that value one-half the difference between a perfect score and the chance score. Using this procedure, a 100-item true-false examination would yield an optimal difficulty level of .75:

$$\text{chance score} + \frac{\text{perfect score} - \text{chance score}}{2} = .50 + \frac{1.00 - .50}{2} = .75$$

That is, 75 percent of the students would respond correctly to each item. On completion or essay tests, where the chance score is 0, the optimal difficulty level would be .50. These "optimal" values assume that discrimination is equally important at all ability levels. (See pp. 246-247 for a discussion of how the difficulty level is related to analyzing grades.)

Frederic Lord (1952) has argued, however, that these estimates of difficulty levels are systematically too low because difficult items introduce more guessing or errors of measurement than easier items. The values suggested by Lord tend to be about ten points higher than those determined by using the formula described in the preceding paragraph, and they are probably better estimates. Both values are presented in table 9.2, and teachers would do well to aim for difficulty levels as close as possible to those suggested by Lord.

Item Improvement

By examining the responses of students in the upper and lower groups on each option, teachers can revise items to make them more discriminating (again assuming that the purpose is to measure individual differences), less ambiguous, and more functional. Any option that is not selected by students in either the upper group or the lower group violates the principle that each alternative in a multiple-choice item should be plausible, and it should be revised before it is used again.

A second principle for improving items is that all *distracters* (incorrect alternatives) should, if possible, discriminate negatively. This means that incorrect options should be selected less frequently by the upper group than by the lower group. Option *e* in the example below violates this principle:

Options	Upper Group	Lower Group
a.	0	8
b.	0	0
c.	3	8
*d.	15	9
e.	9	2

Note that the correct option, *d,* discriminates positively and that options *a* and *c* discriminate negatively. These are desirable characteristics since those in the upper group tend to agree with the keyed answer. However, option *b* is implausible because it is selected by no one in either group; it should therefore be modified before being used again. Option *e* requires modification since it discriminates positively (attracts the upper portion of the class more than the lower) although it is incorrect. Option *e* should be examined carefully to determine whether it is definitely a wrong answer. If it can be justified as a "correct" alternative, all pupils who selected that item should be given credit for it. Again, it is to the teacher's advantage to give credit *before* the tests are returned to the students.

Developing an Item File

The item analysis not only shows the test constructor the quality of each item but it also allows him to select those that meet his particular needs. It may be desirable, for example, to use relatively simple items if the general ability level of the class is low. By keeping a record of item characteristics (such as the difficulty level and the discrimination index), teachers can select items that will be most useful for a specific purpose.

The suggestion that an item file be developed implies that test items will be reused. As more items are accumulated, teachers will not have to administer the same ones frequently. Beginning teachers, however, may find it necessary to reuse the same items until they have a chance to develop new ones.

Because feedback improves learning, students should have the opportunity to examine their tests and to clarify any misunderstandings they might have.

Test papers should then be collected by the teacher to prevent students from developing their own item files. This is important for two reasons: (1) item files in the hands of students give unfair advantage to those who have access to them and penalize those who do not; (2) tests can be improved only through the process of rewriting and modifying items. The teacher who constructs entirely new examinations for each class may find it difficult to improve the quality of his examinations. Instead of a pool of items of demonstrated quality, the teacher will have only the present examination of unknown quality.

Generally an item file consists of items on 5 x 8 inch cards. The item is typed (or cut and pasted) on one side of the card with its objective, level of complexity from Bloom's taxonomy, grade and general subject content, and the source of the item. Figure 9.3 depicts the front side of an item file card.

Objective: Given a list of five definitions of an objective test, the student will select the definition provided in the textbook.

Topic: Objectivity of tests

Level of Complexity: I (Knowledge)

Which of the following is the best definition of an "objective test" as defined in your textbook?

    a. A true-false or multiple-choice test.
    b. A test in which students generally agree on the correct answer.
    c. A test containing items whose truth or falsity are not in question.
  *d. A test in which raters can agree on assigned points.
    e. A test having a clearly stated purpose or objective.

Course: Education 308

Source: Sax, pp. 15 to 16

Figure 9.3. Front Side of a 5 x 8 Card Used in an Item File

If each card contains a single item, it is easy to collect and duplicate those that are to appear on a test or to substitute one item for another. Items selected for final inclusion in the examination can be compared with the desired item distributions of the two-way grid described in chapter 3 to make certain that the test corresponds to desired specifications. The teacher can also provide students with the objectives and number of items meeting each objective if he wishes. Listing the source of the item makes it easy to refer back should questions arise later.

The reverse side of the 5 x 8 card can contain such information as: the number of students in specified groups (such as the upper and lower 27 percent groups) selecting each option, the discrimination index (D), the difficulty level (p), the date of administration, and the section or type of class. (A record of the date of administration and identification of classes helps prevent overuse of an item.) A completed back side of an item analysis card is presented in figure 9.4. There is some advantage to filling in the reverse side of the item card with pencil. Item data can then be erased and new information accumulated with a minimum of effort.

Date:	Class & Section:		N		
10/25/73	308 a		122		
	Upper 27%	Middle 46%	Lower 27%		
a	5		8		
b	2		9		
c	1		6	$D = .45$	
*d	25	42	10		
e	0		0	$p = .63$	

Comments: Replace option e. Difficulty and discrimination adequate. No evidence of ambiguity, guessing, or miskeying.

Figure 9.4. Reverse Side of a 5 x 8 Card Used in an Item File

Relating Item Analyses to the Purposes of Testing

Whether items should be difficult or easy and should discriminate or not depends on the purposes of testing. This section examines the uses of item analyses for selection and placement, for diagnosing student and class learning difficulties, for marking (grading), for mastery, to facilitate learning, and to evaluate curricula.

Use of Item Analyses in Selection and Placement

Item analyses can be used to identify items that will most effectively discriminate among individuals who will be "successful" and those most likely to fail. The criterion of "success" can be grade point average, teacher ratings, or the number of assignments completed by students.

Controlling the difficulty level of items is one way to help improve selection and placement decisions. Figures 9.5a and b depict negatively and positively skewed distributions, respectively. In a negatively skewed distribution, the scores tend to pile up at the high end (as would be true on mastery tests), and few students receive low scores. It is just the opposite for positively skewed distributions. Since it is not possible to discriminate among individuals who receive the same score, the most accurate discriminations occur at the tails of the distribution, where fewer individuals receive tie scores. Other things being equal, relatively easy items (negatively skewed distributions) are favored if the purpose of testing is to place individuals in schools or classes for the low-ability child or if teachers want to detect those students who have not mastered course objectives. If teachers want to select or place high-ability students, the items should be so hard that only the brightest students will attain high scores.

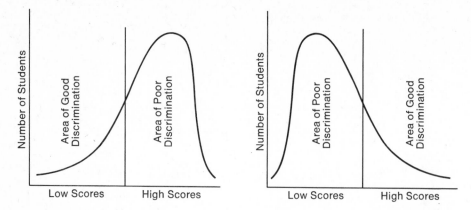

Figure 9.5. (a) Negatively and (b) Positively Skewed Distributions Showing Areas of Good and Poor Discrimination

When the purpose of testing is selection or placement, each item should contribute not only to the total score (that is, be positively discriminating) but also to some criterion *external* to the test. It is important to know that students who answer an item correctly are different from those who respond incorrectly not only with regard to their test score (internal criterion) but also that they are more likely to be successful on some external criterion (receive higher grades or complete more assignments, for example). The discrimination index based on an *internal criterion* indicates how well the item contributes to the test as a whole, but not whether the test is a good predictor of an external criterion. The ideal situation is a test in which all items yield high, positive discrimination indices (contribute to internal-consistency reliability) and also correlate highly with external criteria (have high criterion-related validity). In practice, of course, some items may correlate with external criteria but may not contribute to reliability; others may contribute to reliability but have little to do with the external criterion.

As stated earlier in this chapter, it is probably more defensible (and certainly simpler) to construct items with high discrimination indices based on an internal criterion than it is to develop items that individually relate to some aspect of a heterogeneous criterion but not to each other. Consider, for example, a heterogeneous criterion such as grade point average, which depends on achievement in different school subjects. It is far better to construct highly discriminating but separate tests for each subject than to construct one test containing items that measure a multitude of different objectives. Each test should be composed of items measuring the same trait or ability to be able to stand on its own merits. If a student is selected, it is because he has demonstrated competence on a variety of relatively independent measures; if he is rejected, the teacher knows which tests he failed.

A second point to consider is that *in practice* items tend either to be highly discriminating *and* related to some criterion *or* to yield low discrimination indices and be related to nothing of consequence (Nunnally 1967). Compared to building a single test with items measuring different aspects of some external criterion, it is relatively easy to construct separate tests containing discriminating items. One might as well, then, use the simpler approach.

The third point relates to the often vague nature of the criterion itself. For example, teachers may have to rate students on "friendliness" or "citizenship." The criterion measure for selection and placement may be less carefully thought out than the tests used to predict it. This implies that it might be more fruitful to develop separate tests, each containing highly discriminating items, than it is to worry about the extent to which each item measures some external criterion. Whether these tests can in fact predict the criterion is, of course, an empirical question.

Use of Item Analysis for Diagnosis

Item analyses of both teacher-made and standardized tests can help teachers understand the strengths and weaknesses of individual students and of the class as a whole. By examining the *incorrect* options selected by students, teachers can detect misunderstandings or lack of knowledge. Consider the following example:

In dividing .18 by 2, there are

	Upper Group	Middle Group	Lower Group
a. two nineteens in eighteen hundredths.	0		1
b. two nine-tenths in eighteen hundredths.	2		3
*c. two nine-hundredths in eighteen hundredths.	5	5	2
d. two nine-thousandths in eighteen hundredths.	0		1

Note that most of the *errors* are in response to option *b*. These errors occurred because students had difficulty locating the 0 as a place holder. With this information, the teacher is in a better position to reteach this concept.

To be most useful for diagnostic purposes, each option should measure a plausible source of student misunderstanding. Each distracter should appeal to someone who has failed to meet the objective measured by the item. The teacher can then find the reasons for student failure and do something about it.

Item analyses of standardized achievement tests can also be used to identify student strengths and weaknesses. Some test manuals provide item analysis data, including item difficulty levels and discrimination indices. Suppose that a test manual reports that 65 percent of fourth-grade students selected randomly throughout the United States responded correctly to an item. Using his own classroom data, the teacher can compare *class* difficulty levels with *national* data. Two cautions about making these comparisons should be mentioned: (1) the teacher's class may be atypical and could therefore be expected to perform at a lower or higher level than the national sample; (2) not every item on a standardized test will measure objectives the teacher considers important for *his* students. *If* the class is fairly typical in background and ability, and *if* the items are considered important, a comparison of class and national norms will suggest areas that need further work.

Use of Item Analyses for Marking

Norm-referenced tests should discriminate maximally among students. Items that fail to discriminate among students cannot measure individual differences and should be eliminated from the item pool. The problem in selecting items for marking is to determine for which portion of the distribution those items should maximally discriminate.

The difficulty level of an item determines, at least in part, how that item can best be used. If the teacher is particularly concerned with accurately discriminating between students who will be required to repeat an entire course and those who "barely pass," relatively easy items can best fulfill this purpose. In general, the percentage of individuals who are expected to fail a course (as determined by school policy, previous records of failure, or the school's philosophy of education) should determine the difficulty level of items. For example, if 5 percent of the students typically have failed a course—and assuming that the purpose of testing is to maximize differences at the low end of the scale—the difficulty level of the items can be represented by 1 minus the proportion of expected failures, or in this example, a difficulty level of .95. Because the items are all very easy, only a few students would be expected to fall at the low end of the scale. Similarly, if maximum discrimination is desired to separate "honor" students from those rated as "excellent," items will have to be difficult. At the upper end of the distribution the average item difficulty should equal the proportion of students to be judged as excellent. If that proportion was expected to be .10, items having a difficulty level of .10 should be selected. *Because of the role of guessing on true-false and multiple-choice tests, this value of .10 should be added to the chance score.* Where the purpose of testing is to maximize individual differences at all ability levels rather than at one extreme or another, the discussion of the optimal level of difficulty on pages 239-240 becomes relevant. Again, the type of decision determines what the "ideal" distribution of scores will look like.

The extent to which items correlate with one another also influences the type of marking decisions possible. Consider, for example, a test in which all items have D indices of 1.0 and all items are perfectly intercorrelated (i.e., a perfect Kuder-Richardson reliability of 1.0). In this extreme example all students composing the upper criterion group would respond correctly to each item, whereas those in the lower group would respond incorrectly. The only two scores on the examination would be perfect ones and 0s; no intermediate marks could be obtained. The problem is further complicated by the fact that attempts to lower the correlation among items will also lower internal consistency reliability. The total test score for each student would be meaningless since there would be no relationship among the items. What, then, does the teacher do?

The "solution" of this dilemma is to accept a compromise between high reliability and the desire to have D indices of 1.0 for each item. In practice, this compromise provides few problems since it is rare for all items to intercorrelate perfectly and for all D indices to fall at the maximum value. If teachers want to discriminate maximally along the entire range of ability, they should select items that approximate the optimal values discussed on pages 239-240. When items are selected with this criterion in mind, reliability tends to *increase*. It might be thought that the spread or variability of scores would be increased by selecting items having a wide range of difficulty levels, but this is not the case. Rather, the easiest and most difficult items do not contribute to variability; the ones that do are those that meet the criteria for optimal difficulty. Having a large number of items with extreme difficulty levels may facilitate discrimination at the two ends of the distribution, but the reliability of the measurements as a whole will suffer. In general, the larger the variability of D indices is, the smaller the standard deviation will be, and small standard deviations lead to low reliability coefficients. The teacher should therefore allow some variability in the difficulty level of each item but try to keep this variability relatively low around the optimal value.

Use of Item Analyses for Mastery or Criterion-Referenced Tests

The intent of mastery tests is to assure the teacher that students have obtained at least some minimum degree of competence following instruction. The ideal situation is for all students to respond correctly to each item. The p value or difficulty level would then be 1.0 for each item, and the mean score on the test as a whole would equal the number of items. For example, if all students responded correctly to each item on a fifty-item test, each person would have a score of 50, and the mean of these items would also be 50. As a matter of fact, the sum of the p values for each item always equals the mean of the test because p is obtained by summing the number of students who respond correctly to an item and dividing by the number of students. This is the same procedure one would follow to compute the mean of a test. *Remember that the difficulty level of each item determines the test mean.* The average difficulty level of the test can be determined either by summing all p values and dividing by the number of items or by dividing the mean score for the test as a whole by the number of items. As indicated previously, to demonstrate that mastery has been accomplished, this ratio of the mean to the number of items on the test should be high.

One difference between mastery tests and examinations designed to measure individual differences is the relative importance of p and D. On mastery examinations p should be high, but discrimination (D) is of less importance. Conversely, obtaining high reliability coefficients is necessary for marking. As noted, reliability can be increased by adhering to optimal levels of difficulty and discrimination, but these optima depend on what range of scores requires maximum discrimination.

A test designed for mastery may, of course, be an excellent measure of individual differences. No matter what the intentions of the teacher are, the item characteristics of a test (particularly p and D) determine the efficacy of measuring individual differences. Furthermore, it is conceivable that mastery be set at some predetermined level (e.g., 85 percent), while marks are assigned to students at various levels of accomplishment. The problem with this approach is that mastery tests are most often used to make certain that students have reached at least some minimal level of competence no matter how long it may take. If the purpose of the test is to measure individual differences, time is usually kept constant while test scores are allowed to vary. Hence at the end of some specified period of time (such as at the end of a unit of instruction), all students are required to take the test, and the differences among them reflect not only the inherent difficulty and discrimination of items but also the degree to which the student is prepared to take the test. A student may not "master" test item content but still be "passed" and allowed to proceed to the next unit of instruction. This is most justifiable if there is no apparent hierarchy of complexity that requires the student to learn prerequisite skills.

It is important to note that there is no necessary relationship between student performance on a test designed to measure individual differences and the evaluation decision of the teacher in assigning marks. For example, no psychometric principle requires that low-ability youngsters receive lower marks than more talented students. The number of students receiving letter grades or marks (A = excellent, B = good, and so forth) is primarily based on philosophical and psychological principles. It is conceivable that a test could be designed to measure individual differences but still have each pupil receive marks of A or F (fail). The fact that the test was capable of measuring individual differences does not dictate the number or percentage of passes or failures.

Use of Item Analyses to Facilitate Learning

Learning is improved when students are given specific feedback regarding their progress. In general, the more specific this feedback is, the greater is the probability that students will improve. By reviewing the test with students when the papers are returned, teachers can help students discover their errors and misconceptions. Another method teachers can use to facilitate student learning is to administer pretests. An item analysis of the pretest can alert the teacher, who can then advise students about their misconceptions.

Tests used for *formative evaluation* can also guide students *before* they take a final examination. By keeping records of student performance, teachers can modify their teaching strategies to help increase student knowledge. Items that reflect a high degree of guessing require the intervention of the teacher. Low p values (i.e., difficult items) can also mean that students lack the necessary knowledge. Here again the item analysis can be of great value to teachers and students.

At least among college students, difficult examinations throughout the course lead to higher student achievement on a final examination than do easy examinations (Sax and Reade 1964; Sax, Eilenberg, and Klockars 1972). Students who expected a hard, rote final examination (as measured by using Knowledge or level 1 type items from Bloom's taxonomy) outperformed students who expected easy and/or complex items (levels 2–6 of Bloom's taxonomy). For college-age students, difficult and rote items given during a course generally led to higher student performance on a final examination that consisted of equal numbers of easy, difficult, rote, and complex items. The dilemma facing the teacher is that it may not always be possible to construct easy items to help discriminate among lower ability students and at the same time to increase motivation by constructing difficult tests. Whether these findings hold for students in elementary and secondary schools is now unknown, but even if difficult tests did motivate these students to learn, the teacher also has the responsibility to make sure that tests are not so difficult that students become frightened or overly anxious.

Item analyses can also help to improve learning by having each student record and compare his improvement either with his previous performance or with the p value for the whole class. For example, if only 25 percent of the class responded correctly to a given item, its p value would be .25, and it would be considered difficult. All individuals who responded correctly to that item, therefore, did so either because of chance ("luck") or because they were particularly well prepared. Responding correctly to an item that is so easy that virtually no one misses it should be less rewarding than responding correctly to an item that is very difficult for most members of the class.

Use of Item Analyses to Evaluate the Curriculum

Item analysis data can help teachers evaluate areas of a curriculum or unit that need improvement. For example, the knowledge that students perform at a low level on items designed to measure some particular course objective may persuade the teacher to devote more time and effort to clarifying the objective. The p index, or difficulty level, warns the teacher that the content measured by an item or group of items has not been taught effectively. Conversely, the data may suggest that the teacher is spending too much time teaching concepts that most students already know.

There is a growing tendency for schools to keep records of item analysis information, particularly of item difficulty. With this information, student achieve-

ment can be compared before and after a curricular innovation has been introduced to provide feedback to teachers and administrators regarding the effectiveness of the innovation.

For example, consider the hypothetical data depicted in figure 9.6. Suppose
that one objective of teachers in a particular school district is that students
learn to divide fractions correctly. Figure 9.6 is a graph showing the proportion
of national and local students who responded correctly to an item on a standardized test that measures division with fractions (data are fictitious). Increasing
the number of items would be desirable, but unfortunately most standardized
tests are used for gross screening purposes, and only a few items that measure
a specific objective can be included. Should any student miss those items, the
teacher would probably have to develop additional items if a better sampling of
student knowledge is desired.

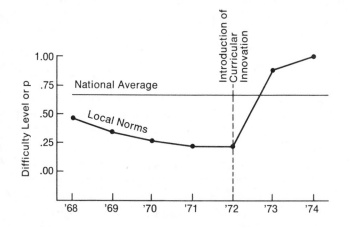

Figure 9.6. p Values of National and Local Students Before
and After a Curricular Innovation (data are hypothetical)

Figure 9.6 shows that the p value obtained from a national sample of
sixth-grade students was approximately .65 from 1968 to 1974. Usually this
information is provided in the accompanying test manual, but if not, it probably
could be obtained from the test publisher. Between 1968 and 1971, students in
this hypothetical school district were considerably below the national norm on
this item. Then starting in 1972, teachers modified the curriculum in mathematics, and student performance improved markedly. Because there is some
variability in student performance from year to year, student performance
should be plotted for several years preceding and following the innovation. Although these data do not *prove* that the innovation was responsible for increasing
student performance (events or conditions other than the introduction of the
innovation could explain the increase in p values), it may be possible to rule

out some competing explanations (such as the possibility that generally brighter sixth-graders began entering the district in 1972).

Summary

1. Item analyses help teachers discover which items are ambiguous, miskeyed, overly difficult or too easy, and nondiscriminating. Item analyses can also help point out options that are nonfunctional and the kinds of errors students are making.

2. Ambiguity is determined by examining the responses of individuals in the upper extreme group (usually 27 percent). If these students respond with about equal frequency to an incorrect alternative as to a correct one, the item is ambiguous from their point of view.

3. Miskeying is also determined by examining the responses of students in the upper extreme group. An item should be examined when students in the upper portion of the class respond to what has been marked as "incorrect" by the teacher. If students respond with about equal frequency on all alternatives, guessing may be suspected. This could occur if the item is too difficult or if it covers content not discussed in class or in the text.

4. Items fail to discriminate when the same proportion of students in the upper and lower extreme groups respond with equal frequency to the correct alternative. The discrimination index described in this text is D, the "upper minus lower difference." An item discriminates perfectly if everyone in the upper group responds correctly and everyone in the lower group responds incorrectly. Under those conditions, D will be equal to 1.0. Items discriminate negatively if more students in the lower group respond correctly than in the upper group.

5. Because the total score on an examination is a reasonable criterion of the degree of student knowledge, it can be used to separate students into lower and upper criterion groups. Items that discriminate well contribute to the internal consistency of the test; negatively discriminating items reduce reliability but because validity is more important than reliability, some negatively discriminating items may be retained if eliminating them would reduce validity.

6. The difficulty level of an item is defined as the proportion of students who respond correctly to it. The higher this proportion (p) is, the easier the item

is. It is obtained by counting the number of students responding to the correct alternative and dividing by the total number of students. Difficulty levels do not by themselves make items good or bad, just hard or easy.

7. On criterion-referenced tests one should expect D indices to be low and p indices to be high. Although replacements for the D index have been suggested the position taken here is that current indices of discrimination are not meaningful for criterion-referenced tests. Indeed, if objectives have been written clearly and if items have high content validity, no discrimination index is needed.

8. On norm-referenced tests items that are too hard or too easy do not discriminate well. Discrimination indices depend on items with optimal difficulty levels, although optimal difficulty levels do not ensure high discrimination indices.

9. The optimal difficulty level for an examination is halfway between the chance score and a perfect score. However, because difficult items introduce more guessing than easy items, these "optimal" values are too low by about .10.

10. Items can be improved by eliminating alternatives that are unselected by students in either the lower or the upper extreme group and by replacing them with better distracters. All *incorrect* alternatives should be negatively discriminating.

11. An item file is an efficient way to accumulate and organize test items. The front side of the item file card contains the item, the correct answer, the objective the item was designed to measure, the level of complexity, the general topic, the course number, and the source of the item. Information from item analyses can be placed on the back of the card.

12. When a test contains "easy" items, the scores will tend to pile up at the high end of the distribution, and there will be few students at the low end. "Easy" items thus help discriminate among the lower members of the group. Conversely, "difficult" items discriminate among the higher scoring members of the group.

13. Item analyses can be used to diagnose class difficulties by examining the number of errors on each distracter.

14. There is some advantage in not having all items discriminate perfectly even if it were possible to construct such items. If all items did discriminate perfectly, students would either have a perfect score or a score of 0, assuming that items were perfectly correlated with one another. The "solution" to this problem is generally simple: virtually no test will have all items with D indices of 1.0.

15. On mastery tests p values should be high, but discrimination is not important; on norm-referenced tests D is more crucial than p.

16. There is an apparent relationship between test difficulty and student motivation, at least among college students. Difficult tests tend to motivate students (particularly those in the upper half of the group) more than easier tests. The effects of test difficulty on the motivation of younger students is unknown.

17. The difficulty level of an item can also be used to evaluate the effect of instruction. On a standardized achievement test, for example, the failure of students to do as well as students in the norm group may indicate that students have not been as well prepared. By keeping records of student performance on each item of the examination, teachers can form a reasonably accurate picture of how much progress students are making in comparison with the norm group. Although responses to a single item tend to be unreliable, they can still give the teacher some general idea of how well students are doing from year to year.

Suggested Readings

Cureton, Edward E. "Simplified Formulas for Item Analysis." *Journal of Educational Measurement* 3, no. 2 (Summer 1966): 187–89. Cureton presents some indices of discrimination other than D and describes their relationships to D.

Fan, Chung-Teh. *Item Analysis Table*. Princeton, N. J.: Educational Testing Service, 1952. The Chung-Teh Fan tables can be purchased from the publisher. By using the proportion responding correctly in upper and lower 27 percent groups, the table provides an estimate of the item's difficulty level without having to count responses in the middle group.

Henrysson, Sten. "Gathering, Analyzing, and Using Data on Test Items." In Robert L. Thorndike, ed., *Educational Measurement,* 2d ed., pp. 130–59. Washington, D. C.: American Council on Education, 1971. A comprehensive and technical discussion of item analysis procedures; alternative approaches to those described in this text are described.

Ryan, James J. "Teacher Judgments of Test Item Properties." *Journal of Educational Measurement* 5, no. 4 (Winter 1968): 301–6. Fifty-nine mathematics teachers were asked to evaluate items by indicating their relevance and by estimating their difficulty, how well they would discriminate, and their validity. Item relevance was a major determiner of how teachers judged items.

Sax, Gilbert; Eilenberg, Enid G.; and Klockars, Alan J. "Achievement as a Function of Test Item Complexity and Difficulty." *Journal of Experimental Education* 40, no. 4 (Summer 1972): 90–93. The authors found that college students given two training tests that were both difficult and rote performed at a higher level on a final examination than did those students given easy and "complex" training tasks.

Weitman, Morris. "Item Characteristics and Long-Term Retention." *Journal of Educational Measurement* 2, no. 1 (June 1965): 37–47. Weitman found that long-term achievement was facilitated if items that are highly discriminating and do not emphasize rote memory are administered. Such items may, however, measure "common sense" or general information.

10

Because such a large number and variety of standardized tests are currently available, teachers must develop the skills to select those that are appropriate for their needs. So many tests are available, even within specific categories such as character and personality or mathematics (see table 10.1), that the beginner may find it difficult to locate the "best" one. This chapter provides criteria for locating and evaluating published information on standardized tests.

Practical Considerations in Selecting Tests

Tests can be evaluated *technically* and *practically*. Technical recommendations—particularly those related to reliability and validity—are discussed later in this chapter. The first part of this chapter examines factors related to cost and ease of administration, scoring, and interpretation.

Cost

Cost limits the selection of standardized tests. Although no test should be selected solely because it is inexpensive, it might be necessary to disregard an excellent test because it is too costly. The cost includes not only the initial outlay of funds to purchase test booklets but also the expenses needed to replace them. At the lower grades pupils typically write or mark directly on the test booklet, whereas older students can reuse text booklets by using inexpensive separate answer sheets.

Added to the cost of booklets and answer sheets is the cost of test scoring. In some school districts tests are scored by the teacher; other districts have electronic test scoring facilities. Many school districts prefer to use the services

Table 10.1. Number of Tests Available by Major Classification

Classification	Number of Entries	Percentage of Entries
Character and Personality	306	14.4
Vocations	287	13.5
Intelligence	238	11.2
Miscellaneous	233	11.0
Mathematics	198	9.3
English	192	9.0
Reading	159	7.5
Social Studies	113	5.3
Science	106	5.0
Foreign Languages	92	4.3
Sensory-Motor	55	2.6
Business Education	53	2.5
Achievement Batteries	45	2.1
Fine Arts	29	1.4
Multi-Aptitude Batteries	20	0.9
Total	2,126	100.0

Buros 1961, p. xix.

of test publishers, who can provide not only the scores for each pupil but also school or district-wide statistical summaries of data. If students or parents are given copies of test scores, the preparation cost of those must also be included in the total price of testing.

Time Limits

Another factor that affects test selection is the length of the examination. Time limits for testing that conflict with established class periods will require class schedule changes and will cause administrative inconveniences. But although a short test may be both economical and convenient, the consequence of using shorter examinations is reduced reliability. Since there is no purpose in giving unreliable tests—no matter how convenient or inexpensive—time restrictions should not be heavily weighted in selecting tests.

Ease of Administration

The more complete the directions for administering the test are, the more uniform test administration can be. Detailed directions to both the student and the test administrator facilitate test taking and giving. Directions should include the following information: time limits, if any, for each section of the test; seating arrangements; suggested or recommended proctor-student ratios; the type of marking instrument (pencil, crayon); methods of correcting errors (erase, cross out); minimum lighting, temperature, and ventilation requirements; procedures for excusing students from the examination room; emergency procedures (fire, illness); the method of distributing and collecting test answer sheets and pencils; and procedures for correcting and scoring answer sheets or booklets.

The manual (1966) for the Differential Aptitude Tests contains some sixteen pages of detailed directions needed to administer these tests properly. The directions include:

1. A description of the test booklets given to each student
2. A description of the various kinds of answer sheets that may be used
3. A reminder of the type of pencil to be used with each type of answer sheet
4. A statement that all subtests should be completed within two weeks' time.
5. A reminder that testing should be scheduled in the morning and when no other distracting events are occurring in the school
6. Suggested time schedules for testing to be completed in two, four, or six sessions
7. Methods of training staff to administer and proctor examinations (A proctor-examinee ratio of 1 to 20 or 30 is recommended.)
8. Methods of accurately timing examinations by using an interval timer, stop watch, wall clock with sweep second hand, or wrist watch with sweep second hand (listed in order of preference)
9. A warning that one subtest requires extreme accuracy not attainable with inexpensive timers
10. Specific recommendations on how to distribute all materials
11. The physical conditions of the room
12. The exact words the administrator is to say when distributing, administering, and collecting all materials

Although they are very specific and understandable, the directions for the Differential Aptitude Tests do not tell the test administrator what to do if testing is interrupted during a timed section. Without that information, subjective judgments enter into test administration, and standardization procedures are weakened.

Format

A pleasing test format can motivate students to do their best on standardized tests. Too little space between items or print that is too small may affect students adversely. Acceptable format specifications include type size commensurate with student maturity, clear and unambiguous pictures, and items that are neither too crowded nor carried over to the next page. Directions to the examiner should be organized so that all information necessary for test administration is together. The manual for the Differential Aptitude Tests clearly separates administration directions, scoring information, and norms. Boldface type that indicates the exact words to be used by the examiner is a useful feature.

Availability of Alternate Forms

Multiple forms of an examination allow teachers to retest students at different times to evaluate progress without having them retake the same test. It also allows teachers to test students in different sections of a class without being concerned about test security. Students in a morning class, for example, could be given form A of a test and afternoon students, form B. Some tests have three or four alternate forms. The Miller Analogies Test, often used to select college seniors for graduate schools, has four forms. The use of all these forms makes it difficult for a student to recognize items from a previously administered test or to help another person planning to take the same test.

Multiple-Level Examinations

When examinations are used to evaluate student progress over extended periods of time, there is some advantage in using several levels of the same test (e.g., primary, elementary, junior high, senior high) rather than switching from one test to another. Using the primary level on Test X and the elementary level on Test Y makes judging student progress difficult. If different levels of the same test are available, this improves comparability of test content, norms, and norm groups. Should markedly different tests be used at various levels, changes in scores could be attributed to changes in test content, to the use of different norms (age, grade, standard scores), and even to the types of students that compose the norm group (black students, midwesterners, students from upper and lower socioeconomic groups, and the like).

Availability of Answer Sheets and Simple Scoring Procedures

As suggested previously, using separate answer sheets for older children can reduce booklet replacement costs substantially. Scoring is also simplified since all responses are on a single page.

Separate answer sheets can be either hand or machine scored. Hand-scored answer sheets are of three types—those employing stencils, carbon-backed keys, or pinprick keys. A stencil is usually a sheet of cardboard with holes corresponding to the location of the correct responses (see figure 10.1). If the student's response appears in the hole when the stencil is placed on the answer sheet, the answer has been marked correctly.

The carbon-backed answer sheet consists of a sheet of carbon paper sealed between two pieces of paper. The student marks his answers on the outer sheet and carbon paper transfers them to the inside of the second sheet, where circles or squares correspond to the correct answers. Scoring consists of tearing apart the two outer sheets of paper, removing the carbon paper, and counting the number

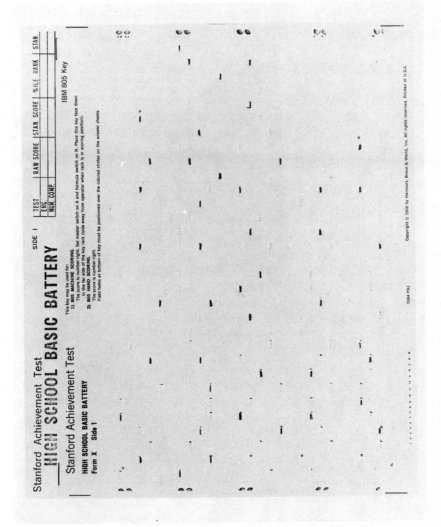

Figure 10.1

of marks located in the boxes or circles (see figure 10.2). Although carbon-backed answer sheets are expensive, the cost can probably be justified by the convenience and saving of time.

The pinprick key uses the same principle as the carbon-backed answer sheet except that a pinhole indicates the subject's choice. This type of scoring is used with the Kuder Preference Record: Vocational, which measures different broad areas of interest such as outdoor, mechanical, scientific, computational, and so forth. Because a pinprick can pierce more than one sheet of paper, it

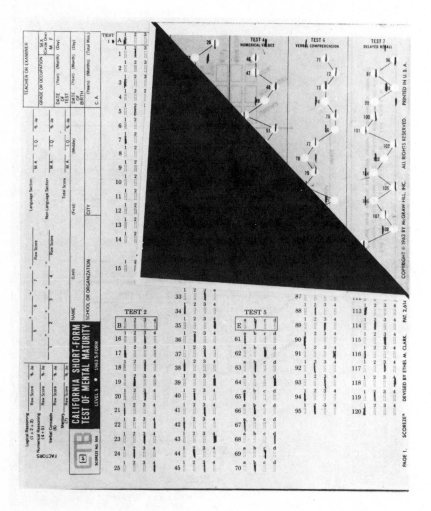

Scoreze No. 559, devised by Ethel M. Clark. Copyright © 1963 by McGraw-Hill, Inc. Reproduced by permission of the publisher, CTB/McGraw-Hill, Del Monte Research Park, Monterey, California, 93940. All rights reserved. Printed in the U.S.A.

Figure 10.2

records student responses to all interest areas at the same time. A backing pad is provided to ensure that the pinpricks do no damage to furniture.

In general, scoring by machine involves *contact* or *light scanning* principles. In contact scoring the student uses a special electrographic pencil that contains a conductive material that can be sensed by contact points in the machine. The contact points are set to correspond to the correct answer. As each answer sheet is fed into the machine, a dial indicates the number of correct responses. This process is relatively slow in comparison to that of light-scanning machines and is also affected by changes in temperature and humidity.

In recent years light-scanning equipment has become popular. A sensor in the machine electronically "reads" marks made by any pencil. The Measurement Research Center (MRC) at the State University of Iowa had developed a light-scanning machine which in the 1950s and 1960s was capable of the following (from E. F. Lindquist, *Testing Today,* Boston: Houghton Mifflin, First Issue, pp. 2–3):

> The machine accepts a stack of about 2,000 answer sheets at a time, and then automatically:
>
> 1. Passes the sheets under its photoelectric "eyes" at the rate of 100 answer sheets per minute
> 2. Senses the marks on both sides of the sheet by means of light transmitted through the sheet
> 3. Compares the marks made by the examinees with the right answer key which has been stored in its "memory" (if desired, the same marks may be scored by different keys simultaneously)
> 4. Counts (at the rate of 10,000 per second) the number of right answers to each of as many as fourteen different tests on each answer sheet, or adds the weights for the right answers if weighted scoring is desired
> 5. Exercises its "judgment" while counting to ignore bad erasures and disallow multiple marks, thus eliminating the need for a preliminary visual scanning of the answer sheets
> 6. Converts each of the raw scores to one or more scaled scores according to conversion tables it has previously memorized
> 7. Computes as many as four *weighted* composites of various combinations of scores on each answer sheet
> 8. If necessary, in turn converts these composite scores to scaled scores comparable to the subtest scaled scores.
> 9. Reads the examinee's name from each answer sheet
> 10. Writes (types) the examinee's name, scaled scores, and composites on a multiple-carbon continuous report form
> 11. Notes, and records opposite each examinee's name, whether or not he has attempted all of the tests in the battery
> 12. Notes, and records after each examinee's name, whether or not the answer sheet was in perfect registration and all sensing circuits were performing properly, during the scoring of that particular sheet
> 13. Punches all of this information about each examinee in an electronic

accounting machine card which may be fed to other "brains" for subsequent processing if desired.

Recent advances have increased the scanning speed from about 6,000 answer sheets per hour to about 60,000—a tenfold increase! The addition of a small computer to the system allows the MRC to process many different kinds of answer sheets (Baker 1971). Optical scanners that read handwritten or typed messages are also available, but these devices tend to be too slow for test scoring.

Ease of Interpretation

Test manuals should provide specific information to facilitate test interpretation. A description of all norms reported on the test together with their advantages and limitations should be included. Also useful would be examples of possible misinterpretations with warnings of what *not* to do. Some case studies—particularly typical ones—should be provided as examples of proper test use and interpretation.

Many of the factors that lead to faulty interpretations of test results are of a technical nature related to reliability and validity. These concepts will be considered in greater detail.

Technical Considerations in Selecting Tests

In 1966 the American Psychological Association published *Standards for Educational and Psychological Tests and Manuals.* Prepared by a joint committee of the American Psychological Association, the American Educational Research Association, and the National Council on Measurement in Education, the report included a list of *essential, very desirable,* and *desirable* features that should be included with any published test and manual. *Standards* provides very comprehensive criteria by which tests may be evaluated.*

Standards is divided into six major categories: Dissemination of Information, Interpretation, Validity, Reliability, Administration and Scoring, and Scales and Norms. This chapter discusses only those criteria listed as essential.

* A revision of the guidelines was published early in 1974.

Dissemination of Information

Principle: When a test is published for operational use, it should be accompanied by a manual . . . that makes every reasonable effort to follow the recommendations in this report.

Not every principle in *Standards* applies to all tests; however, it is the responsibility of the test publisher to follow the recommendations whenever possible. If information is unavailable when the manual is published, the manual should clearly state this deficiency. Furthermore, information published separately from the manual should meet the same criteria as the manual. An implication of this principle is that promotional materials should not mislead or exaggerate.

Principle: The test and its manual should be revised at appropriate intervals. While no universal rule can be given, it would appear proper in most circumstances for the publisher to withdraw a test from the market if the manual is 15 or more years old and no revision can be obtained.

The purpose of this recommendation is to keep test information current. An outdated manual may lead to faulty interpretations. Furthermore, as new information is obtained, the manual should be revised or supplemented. The degree of comparability between new and old forms of a test should also be readily available.

Interpretation

Principle: The test, the manual, record forms, and other accompanying material should assist users to make correct interpretations of the test results.

A subcategory of this principle is that names of tests and subtests should not presume more than can be justified from the available evidence (see pp. 206-207). Common misinterpretations of the test, if known, should be clarified in the manual. For example, intelligence test scores should warn the reader against assuming the measurement of native ability.

Principle: The test manual should state implicitly the purposes and applications for which the test is recommended.

It is the responsibility of the test publisher to inform the potential user of the test's validity for different purposes. Some tests are used for research only and are not suitable for other purposes. The manual should also state test limitations and deficiencies.

Principle: The test manual should indicate the qualifications required to administer the test and to interpret it properly.

Three levels of competence have been recognized by the American Psychological Association in the use and interpretation of tests. Level A involves those tests that can be administered and interpreted with the aid of a manual. Most educational achievement tests fit into this category. Level B requires some technical knowledge of test construction, such as that provided by this text, as well as background in statistics, individual differences, adjustment, and personnel work. Aptitude tests and adjustment inventories applicable to normal populations fit this category. Level C, the administration of individual intelligence tests and projective techniques, requires a substantial background in testing and psychology. The manuals for all tests should indicate how competent the individual must be to administer and interpret the test. If a test serves a variety of purposes, the amount of training necessary for administering and interpreting the test for each purpose should be specified.

Principle: Statements in the manual reporting relationships are by implication quantitative and should be stated as precisely as the data permit. If data to support such statements have not been collected, that fact should be made clear.

A statement in the manual such as "A high score is necessary for college success" violates this standard because it fails to state how high a score is necessary and for what degree of success. Test manuals should also indicate whether data are applicable to groups or to individuals. Some tests yield measurements that are reliable enough to be used for interpreting group performance but are unreliable for individual interpretation.

Validity

Principle: The manual should report the validity of the test for each type of inference for which it is recommended. If the validity for some suggested interpretation has not been investigated, that fact should be made clear.

Validity is specific to given purposes, and no test manual should simply report that measurements are valid without stating what they are valid for and to what extent they are valid for these purposes. The fact that 70 percent of the persons who respond to a certain item are neurotic does not necessarily mean that John, a person who responds to that item, is neurotic. He may well be an exception, and that possibility should be clear from reading the manual.

> *Principle:* If a test performance is to be interpreted as a sample of performance or a definition of performance in some universe of situations, the manual should indicate clearly what universe is represented and how adequate is the sampling.

This principle refers to *content validity*. Content is validated by demonstrating that items measure specific objectives. Since no test can contain all possible items on a topic, the manual should report the basis and procedures used to select the items contained in the test.

A subprinciple states that when content is selected from courses of study or from textbooks, the manuals should specify the dates the texts were published. An excellent sampling of material may soon be outdated.

> *Principle:* All measures of criteria should be described completely and accurately. The manual should comment on the adequacy of the criterion. Whenever feasible, it should draw attention to significant aspects of performance that the criterion measure does not reflect and to irrelevant factors that are likely to affect it.

If measurements are recommended for a particular purpose, their validity for that purpose should be included in the manual. When tests are used for prediction, the correlation between scores and criteria should be reported for different situations and institutions. This recommendation reminds the reader that a high validity coefficient as reported in a manual may be inadequately low in another situation or in another school.

If the criterion is *corrected for attenuation* (see pp. 215-217), both the corrected and uncorrected coefficients should be reported in the test manual. As noted earlier, the criterion is usually corrected to make it error free, but not necessarily the test scores since they are fallible measures.

For predictive validity, the time that elapsed between the test administration and the obtaining of criterion data should be reported. Over very short time intervals correlations are likely to be higher than those obtained over longer periods of time. If concurrent validity is used as an estimate of predictive validity, it should be made clear that these coefficients are likely to be overestimates of predictive validity.

Efforts made to avoid criterion contamination (see p. 226) should be reported in the manual. If contamination could have occurred, the manual should so indicate.

The correlation of test scores with course grades should be accompanied by a detailed description of the course, the teaching methods used, and grading procedures. When the same course content is taught differently, validity coefficients may vary considerably.

> *Principle:* The sample employed in a validity study and the conditions under which testing is done should be consistent with the recommendations made in the manual. They should be described sufficiently for the user to judge whether the reported validity is pertinent to his situation.

The manual should report how the sample employed in determining validity was selected. Means and standard deviations of all scores should be reported to help the teacher judge the extent to which his students have characteristics similar to those of the norm group. These characteristics include age, grade, sex, and socioeconomic level. Information pertaining to school or other institutional policies that restrict the types of individuals admitted and retained should also be included in the manual. Obviously the teacher's class should be comparable to the norm group if scores are to be interpreted properly.

> *Principle:* Any statistical analysis of criterion-related validity should be reported in the manual in a form from which the reader can determine what confidence is to be placed in judgments or predictions regarding the individual.

This principle attempts to guard against using esoteric and unjustifiable statistics in the interpretation of predictive and concurrent validity coefficients. Easily understood correlations between scores and criteria are most commonly used, but expectancy tables may also be of value.

The manual should report the extent to which the test *misclassifies* individuals. The misclassification should not merely be between normal and abnormal groups, for example, but between subclassifications of abnormals if the test was designed for that purpose.

The incremental validity (see p. 224) of a test should also be reported whenever such data can be obtained. In other words, the fact that a test is useful for a given purpose must be qualified by stating how much better it is than other already available data.

> *Principle:* If the author proposes to interpret the test as a measure of a theoretical variable (ability, trait, or attitude), the proposed interpretation should be fully stated. The interpretation of the theoretical construct should be distinguished from interpretations arising under other theories.

A test designed, for example, to measure *introversion-extroversion* not only should clearly define those terms but should also differentiate them from terms of a similar nature derived from other theories. This provides some uniformity in evaluating construct validity.

Reliability

Principle: The test manual should report evidence of reliability that permits the reader to judge whether scores are sufficiently dependable for the recommended uses of the test. If any of the necessary evidence has not been collected, the absence of such information should be noted.

This principle applies to every score or subscore for which the manual states or implies some use or interpretation. The methods of obtaining reliability coefficients and standard errors of measurement should be described with sufficient detail to determine whether they are applicable to any specified groups. As with validity, the test user should be told what procedures were followed to select the persons for whom reliability data are being reported.

Because reliability is affected by the variability of scores, it is essential that reliability coefficients be reported for a single grade only and not for a grade span of several years. The reliability for a single grade is almost always smaller than the reliability for two or more grades combined.

Principle: Reports of reliability studies should ordinarily be expressed in the test manual in terms of . . . standard errors of measurement, or product-moment reliability coefficients.

Chapter 7 has described the standard error of measurement and the use and interpretation of correlation coefficients to express reliability. The correlations described in chapter 6 are product-moment correlations. The use of unconventional statistics may lead to misinterpretations of reliability coefficients; all statistics and coefficients therefore need to be explained in detail.

The manual should also make clear that reliable measurements are not necessarily valid. Reliability is requisite to validity but is not an assurance of it. Since many tests fail to report validity, the absence of these data might give the impression that reliable data are necessarily valid. High reliability coefficients indicate that the test is measuring *something* consistently but do not indicate what that something is.

Principle: If two forms of a test are published, both forms being intended for possible use with the same subjects, the means and variances of the two forms should be reported in the test manual along with the coefficient of correlation between the two sets of scores. If necessary evidence is not provided, the test manual should warn the reader against assuming comparability.

This principle warns the test user against assuming the comparability of two or more forms of a test unless there is evidence to support equivalence. That the forms have equal means and variances (the standard deviation squared) is not sufficient to assume comparability of forms unless the correlation between scores on the alternate forms is high.

> *Principle:* If the test manual suggests that a score is a measure of a generalized, homogeneous trait, the evidence of internal consistency should be reported.

Internal consistency reliability should be reported using the split-half method or the Kuder-Richardson technique. If another technique is used, it should be explained thoroughly in the manual. Because both split-half and Kuder-Richardson reliabilities assume *power* tests, evidence should be included in the manual to show that speed of response is inconsequential. Internal consistency reliability will be spuriously high to the degree that speed is emphasized.

> *Principle:* The test manual should indicate to what extent test scores are stable, that is, how nearly constant the scores are likely to be if a test is repeated after time has elapsed. The manual should also describe the effect of any such variation on the usefulness of the test. The time interval to be considered depends on the nature of the test and on what interpretation of the test scores is recommended.

Stability coefficients should be accompanied by the means and standard deviations of both sets of scores. It is possible for correlations to be high between two sets of measurements and still have a large difference between their means. The manual should explain how stable scores are for a specified period of time. Ordinarily scores remain fairly constant over short periods of time and are less constant over longer time periods. A *very desirable* feature of a test manual would be to report coefficients of stability over different time periods.

Administration and Scoring

> *Principle:* The directions for administration should be presented in the test manual with sufficient clarity and emphasis that the test user can duplicate, and will be encouraged to duplicate, the administrative conditions under which the norms and the data on reliability and validity were obtained.

In particular, the manual should stress the importance of following instructions rigidly and without improvisation. Time restrictions should be followed *exactly* because the difference of a second or two could easily modify scores drastically.

Manuals should also make clear to the examinee what he is supposed to do. On interest inventories that ask students to express preferences for different activities, for example, the student needs to know if he is to select those activities with or without regard for practical considerations such as time or expense. He should also be told if his responses mean that he would enjoy that activity *occasionally* or *regularly*. A student might occasionally like to repair cars but might not want to do so for a living.

> *Principle:* The procedures for scoring the test should be presented in the test manual with a maximum of detail and clarity so as to reduce the likelihood of scoring error.

It would be *very desirable* for the manual to stress the need to double-check for clerical errors in both scoring and recording test data. In one study the investigators found that 28 percent of standardized tests corrected by a group of third- and fourth-grade teachers contained scoring errors (Phillips and Weathers 1958).

The test manual should clearly specify to the examinee and the examiner whether or not a correction for guessing formula will be applied. If the test has severe time limits, either a correction formula should be used or students should be encouraged to respond to every item even though they may have to guess on some. If a correction formula is used, examinees should be instructed to omit items only if the answer would be a pure guess.

Scales and Norms

> *Principle:* Scales used for reporting scores should be so carefully described in the test manual as to increase the likelihood of accurate interpretation and the understanding of both the test interpreter and the subject.

Standard scores such as z scores, T scores, and stanine scales are preferred to norms that do not have fixed means and standard deviations. The manual should indicate how the scales were derived and should explain their advantages and disadvantages.

> *Principle:* If scales are revised, new forms added, or other changes made, the revised test manual should provide tables of equivalence between the new and the old forms. This provision is particularly important in cases where data are recorded on cumulative records.

Most schools keep files or records on each student as he progresses through the grades. Improvement is difficult to measure unless old and new norms have the same meaning or unless a conversion table is provided to facilitate interpretation.

Principle: Norms should be reported in the test manual in terms of standard scores or percentile ranks which reflect the distribution of scores in an appropriate reference group or groups.

Means and standard deviations of all raw-score distributions should always be reported in the manual. If various distributions of scores are presented for different groups, standard scores or percentile ranks should be reported for each along with the raw-score means and standard deviations.

Principle: Norms presented in the test manual should refer to defined and clearly described populations. These populations should be the groups to whom users of the test will ordinarily wish to compare the persons tested.

In using tests to *select* students for colleges and universities, for example, it should be possible to compare an individual with other applicants for admission, with those who have been admitted, or with those who have demonstrated excellence. The comparison group should be clearly identified to reduce errors of interpretation since a person may receive a high percentile score when compared with unselected applicants but be low in comparison to students who are performing successfully.

Because it is not possible to test *all* applicants, trainees, or successful students, it is necessary to sample persons who can adequately represent these groups. If a test publisher gathers norm data by asking administrators to mail in the scores of their students, selectivity is likely to bias these data. Scores might not be returned because of embarrassment over poor student performance or a lack of clerical assistance. Such selection factors yield unrepresentative norms. Publishers can avoid this difficulty by selecting schools that closely resemble census data. If 15 percent of school children in the population are black, the test publisher should strive for the same percentage in his sample.

Normative data provided in test manuals should include the number of cases involved and their age, sex, and educational status. The number of cases is important because more accurate results are obtained with larger numbers *provided* that the sample is representative of the population. An oversampling of older children or females (especially on verbal tests) generally yields relatively high norms and gives a biased picture of the population.

If norms are based on a small number of cases, the test user should be warned of the possible errors that may be made in interpreting data. Furthermore, the manual should report whether or not scores differ for various age, sex, or ethnic groups.

Norms should be provided in a manual only after their validity and reliability have been assessed because their inclusion often leads users to assume their validity.

Since norms depend on the conditions of testing (noise, interruptions, seating arrangements) and the motivation of examinees, these conditions should be described in the test manual.

A Brief Evaluation Form

Standards for Educational and Psychological Tests and Manuals (APA 1966) contains principles which—at least to date—no test publisher has met completely. In part this is because the recommendations were set at a very high level and because test publishers are not legally obligated to meet these standards. But even though the implementation of the principles contained in *Standards* is voluntary, test publishers have complied with many of these recommendations.

Although there have been attempts to evaluate tests and manuals by assigning points to various technical and practical criteria, these efforts have not met with much success because validity always takes precedence over other considerations. Any rating form that assigns a high value to a test or manual simply because of practical considerations is doing the teacher a disservice. Invalid measurements, no matter how reliable, inexpensive, or convenient they are, serve no purpose and should not be used.

On the other hand, a test that is too expensive for a school district is not particularly useful either, even if it would yield valid measurements. The best the teacher can do is to select tests that meet as many of the recommendations as possible, particularly those regarding reliability and validity. Cost may prevent a test from being used, but it should never be the sole basis for selecting a test.

Table 10.2 lists many of the practical and technical criteria that should be considered when selecting or evaluating a standardized test. The Boehm Test of Basic Concepts is used as an example of how this form can be utilized.

Table 10.2. An Evaluation of the Boehm Test of Basic Concepts Using a Test Analysis Form

I. Reference data
   A. *Title:* Boehm Test of Basic Concepts (BTBC).
   B. *Author:* Ann E. Boehm, Teachers College, Columbia University.
   C. *Publisher:* The Psychological Corporation.

Table 10.2 (*Continued*)

D. *Type of test:* School "readiness."

E. *Description of test and subtests:* The BTBC consists of two booklets, each of which contains twenty-five items plus three practice exercises. Each item consists of at least three pictures, and the student marks the one he believes is correct by making an *X* on it. The items are designed to measure the understanding of such concepts as *top, farthest, most, always,* and so forth. The fifty items are categorized as "space," "quantity," "time," and "miscellaneous" concepts.

II. Practical considerations

A. *Costs:* Package of thirty tests with directions and class record sheet with scoring key $5.90
Ten or more of the above packages, each   5.40
Manual, separately   .50
Directions, separately for each of two booklets   .20
Class record sheet and scoring key, separately   .15
Directions in Spanish   .40
Specimen set   1.00

B. *Time limits:* Untimed; requires from fifteen to twenty minutes for each of two booklets when used with kindergarten children; time includes the reading of instructions to class and monitoring pupil responses on three practice items.

C. *Format:* Generally clear pictures with little, if any, crowding of items; each booklet contains twenty-five sets of pictures plus three practice problems; a few drawings are ambiguous; one item appeared ambiguous because the object referred to could either be a doll or a girl (the *p* value for that item as reported in the manual, however, was very high, suggesting that it was not ambiguous to the children); drawings include figures of black and white children and adults.

D. *Alternative forms:* Two booklets each to be administered in a single session but not designed to be comparable.

E. *Levels:* Designed for children in grades K–2 with three socio-economic groups identified at each level.

F. *Availability of answer sheets:* Students mark items directly on test booklet.

G. *Simplified scoring procedures:* Clear and detailed; two scoring "plans" are presented, depending on whether booklets 1 and 2 are to be scored separately or together; the class record form contains a picture of all items and the correct answer.

III. Technical considerations

A. Dissemination of information

1. *Availability of a manual:* Yes, a manual is available.

2. *Copyright date of manual and test booklets:* 1969.

3. *Presumption of validity by test title:* Little evidence available in test manual to support Boehm's position that the concepts measured are "basic."

Table 10.2 (*Continued*)

4. *Purpose of the test:* To measure the child's understanding of concepts needed to follow instructions in school.

5. *Required qualifications:* None stated in the manual; no special skills appear to be necessary for administering, scoring, or interpreting the test; the manual provides specific suggestions for helping children overcome conceptual errors or misunderstandings.

B. Validity

1. *Validity for each recommended use:* Because the purpose of the test is to identify concepts misunderstood by children, and because these concepts are supposed to be "basic" to or necessary for the ability to follow directions, one would expect some evidence to support these contentions. Such evidence is not contained in the manual.

2. *Type of validity reported:* The author of the test claims that *content validity* is the appropriate way to validate items. Information regarding content validity, however, should accompany evidence of *criterion-related validity* since claims are made that require empirical support. But even evidence for content validity is weak because the procedures used to select items were subjectively determined by examining "relevant curriculum materials" not described in the manual. Other vague criteria used to select items, such as "occurred with considerable frequency," "seldom if ever explicitly defined," and "relatively abstract," are not satisfactory. Content validity, in particular, demands a basis for selecting those items included in the final form of a test. Of the fifty items in this test, twenty-three are classified as measuring spatial concepts, eighteen are quantitative, four refer to time, and five fall into the "miscellaneous" category. Item content should correspond with the most frequent and important student deficiencies, but no data are presented in the manual to support this contention. If each of these four types of concepts is independent of the others and does measure different abilities, it would have been advisable to separate the items by subtest. Evidence favoring this separation could be demonstrated if each item contributed to its own classification but not to others. What was done, however, was to use the total score as an *internal criterion* and to include items that were discriminating on the basis of this total score rather than on any subclassification.

3. *Time elapsing between test administration and measurement of the criterion:* Not applicable except for criterion-related validity.

4. *Possibility of criterion contamination:* Not applicable except for criterion-related validity.

5. *Adequacy of selecting persons used in the validation sample:* Not applicable to content validity.

Table 10.2 (*Continued*)

6. *Statistical procedures used to describe validity:* No validity data are presented.

C. Reliability

1. *Reliability for each recommended use:* Coefficients of *stability* and *internal consistency* should be reported for this test. No coefficients of stability are reported. Split-half reliabilities corrected by the Spearman-Brown formula range from .68 (for a sample of 349 middle-class second-graders) to a high of .90 (for 453 middle-class kindergarteners). Split-half coefficients are reported for low, middle, and upper socioeconomic groups in grades K, 1, and 2. When the socioeconomic groups were combined at each grade level, the coefficients were .90, .85, and .81 for the three groups, respectively.

2. *Means, standard deviations, and correlations between forms:* Not relevant since there is only one form with two booklets.

3. *Time elapsing between the administration of parallel forms:* Not applicable.

D. Administration and scoring

1. *Clarity and completeness of instructions:* Test administration directions are clear and easy to follow. Boldface type is used to separate instructions to be read aloud to students from general information. The manual recommends using small groups of students with proctors or teachers' aides because each pupil's responses have to be checked on the practice items. The manual makes no statements about guessing.

2. *Clarity and completeness of scoring directions:* Scoring directions are clear and explicit. Omitted items or those marked ambiguously are treated as errors. The manual also provides clear instructions on how to complete the class record form.

3. *Safeguards against clerical errors in scoring:* The class record form has internal checks against making errors in summing each pupil's total score. The manual should provide a warning concerning the necessity for accurate scoring, particularly for second-graders from high socioeconomic levels. For example, if the student deserved a score of 49 but received only 47 points because of scoring errors, the percentile would decrease from 70 to 30.

E. Scales and norms

1. *Types of norms provided:* The class record form allows teachers to compute the number of items missed by each pupil and the number of pupils who miss each item. The manual provides p values (difficulty level, or the proportion of pupils in the standardization group responding correctly) for each item by grade and socioeconomic level. Percentiles are also provided.

Table 10.2 (*Continued*)

2. *Difficulty level of items:* A serious weakness of the BTBC is that items tend to be too easy, particularly at the upper grades and with students from the higher socioeconomic levels. At grade 2, for example, the means for low, middle, and high socioeconomic groups are 43.5, 46.7, and 47.8, respectively. Considering the fact that there are only fifty items on the test, the test appears to be too simple if interpretations regarding individual differences are desired. Even among first-graders from high socioeconomic levels the mean is 45.6. As a norm-referenced test, the BTBC seems to be most useful at the kindergarten level or for students from low socioeconomic groups in grade 1.

3. *Comparability between old and revised norms:* Not applicable.

4. *Description of the population used to select norm group:* The manual states that norms should serve "as an informal guide" on the BTBC since its purpose does not require representative norms. As a means of identifying students in need of remedial services, however, normative *and* criterion-referenced data would be helpful. The interpretation of the percentile norms, for example, presumes the desirability of comparing students with a population having known characteristics. The procedure followed in norming the BTBC was to select five cities (Fresno, Calif.; Atlanta, Ga.; Highland Park, N. J.; New Rochelle, N. Y.; and Tulsa, Okla.) and to ask "school officials" to nominate three schools to represent low, middle, and high socioeconomic groups. Because administrators were allowed to select schools, there is serious doubt that the population is unbiased. To complicate matters, the Highland Park schools did not provide children from low socioeconomic levels. In addition, the definition and characteristics of *low, middle,* and *high socioeconomic groups* are not included in the manual. To the author's credit, many of these limitations are recognized in the manual, but acknowledging a problem does not remedy it.

5. *Methods used to select the norm group from the population:* Here again the manual is unclear about which students eventually formed the norm or standardization group. Therefore, the adequacy of the sample used to develop norms is unknown. The manual does provide some information that can help to determine the adequacy of the sample. For example, a table of *p* values is provided for each item. Generally students identified as coming from high socioeconomic homes tend to do better than those from lower or middle-class backgrounds, and students in the upper grades do better than younger children. Unfortunately these findings would be expected on almost any measure. If the older children performed *less* well than the younger ones, this could be used as an argu-

Table 10.2 (*Continued*)

ment *against* using the BTBC, but the fact that they performed better contributes little to an understanding of the characteristics of the standardization group.

6. *Time of year standardization data were obtained:* Most teachers planning to use the BTBC will probably want to do so at the beginning of the school year since one of its purposes is to help identify students who are likely to have trouble understanding concepts. The manual states, however, that normative data were obtained in the middle of the school year, presumably after students had received instruction. The norms therefore were obtained from students who were somewhat advanced over those most likely to be given the test. Beginning- and end-of-school-year norms would facilitate test interpretation and the measurement of improvement.

Published Sources of Information about Tests

Sources of information about tests are catalogs, bulletins, yearbooks, indices, and journals. The teacher contemplating which test to select should be familiar with at least the most commonly used sources.

Publishers' Catalogs

Publishers of standardized tests usually provide free catalogs to qualified persons. These catalogs typically include a brief description of the tests, the purposes for which they were developed, the age or grade levels for which the tests are recommended, the number of alternate forms, types of norms provided (percentile, stanine, etc.), time limits (if any), scoring methods (hand and machine), costs for test booklets, answer sheets, and accessories (class record forms, special pencils), and the availability and cost of a *specimen set*. A specimen set usually includes a test booklet, an examiner's manual, an answer sheet, and available technical reports. Many universities and school districts maintain a file of specimen sets for teachers to examine. Specimen sets are generally available only for pencil-and-paper tests and can range in cost from $.50 to over $3.00 per set. Before ordering multiple copies of any test for class use, the teacher should obtain a specimen set.

In addition to describing available tests, catalogs also describe the services publishers perform, such as providing technical advice to industrial concerns and schools, statistical and research services for individuals and institutions, and test scoring services.

Information on who may purchase tests is often printed in test catalogs. One of the large test publishers, The Psychological Corporation, makes the following statements concerning qualifications needed to purchase tests:

Who May Purchase Tests

The tests in this catalog are instruments which must be used with professional care. The sale of tests is therefore restricted in accordance with the principles stated in *Ethical Standards for Psychologists,* published by the American Psychological Association. Eligibility to purchase tests is determined on the basis of training and experience. Registration forms are available on request. Members of the American Psychological Association and certain other established professional users of tests are exempt from formal registration procedures. The rules governing the sale of tests to various classes of purchasers are stated below.

1. Schools, colleges, and governmental agencies   Orders for tests received on official purchase order forms or by officially signed letters will be filled promptly. *Individual staff members* may purchase tests only if the individual establishes his personal qualifications.

School teachers and counselors may purchase tests by official purchase order with the written authorization of the superintendent, principal, or guidance director. Authorization is required for *each* order.

Graduate students may purchase tests for study, research, or practice only if the order is countersigned by the professor of psychology who assumes responsibility. Authorization is required for *each* order.

2. Business and industrial firms   Business and industrial firms using tests for selection, training, and promotion of their own employees are asked to note the *a, b, c* symbols accompanying test descriptions in this catalog.

Level a: Company purchase orders for test marked *a*—those commonly used for employment purposes—will be filled promptly. Registration is required for the purchase of *b* and *c* level tests.

Level b: Available to firms having a staff member who has completed an advanced level course in testing in a university, or its equivalent in training under the direction of a qualified superior or consultant.

Level c: Available to firms only for use under the supervision of qualified psychologists, i.e., members of the American Psychological Association or persons with at least a Master's degree in psychology and appropriate training in the field of personnel testing. The qualified person may be either a staff member or a consultant.

3. Consultants to business and industry, employment agencies, vocational counselors and psychologists in private practice   Registration is required. An organization is qualified to purchase tests if its testing services and/or consultation on testing are under the full-time staff member who is a member of the American Psychological Association or who has demonstrated equivalence in professional training and experience. A Master's degree in psychology with at least a year of experience under professional supervision is the minimum requirement for individuals and organizations who use tests in advising clients.

Approval for test purchase is withheld or withdrawn where there is evidence of violation of the principles and practices of testing and counseling commonly accepted by professional psychologists. No tests are sold for self-guidance, nor to any individual or organization engaged in testing and counseling by mail.

Test users are urged to guard against the improper use of tests and to protect their value by keeping tests and scoring keys in locked files or storage cabinets accessible only to authorized personnel.*

---

* The Psychological Corporation Test Catalogue, 1972, p. 50.

Although there are literally hundreds of test publishers (individuals, universities, publishing companies, and associations), most tests are published by the following groups:

The Bobbs-Merrill Company, Inc., 4300 West 62nd St. Indianapolis, Ind. 46268

American Guidance Service, Inc., Publishers' Building, Circle Pines, Minn. 55014

California Test Bureau (CTB)/McGraw-Hill Book Company, Del Monte Research Park, Monterey, Calif. 93940

Consulting Psychologists Press, Inc., 577 College Ave., Palo Alto, Calif. 94306

Cooperative Test Division, Educational Testing Service, Princeton, N. J. 08540

Harcourt Brace Jovanovich, Inc., 757 Third Ave., New York, N. Y. 10017

Houghton Mifflin Company, 110 Tremont St., Boston, Mass. 02107

Personnel Press, Inc., 20 Nassau St., Princeton, N. J. 08540

Institute for Personality and Ability Testing, 1602 Coronado Dr., Champaign, Ill. 61820

The Psychological Corporation, 304 East 45th St., New York, N. Y. 10017

Psychometric Affiliates, Box 3167, Munster, Ind. 46321

Scholastic Testing Service, Inc., 480 Meyer Rd., Bensenville, Ill. 60106

Science Research Associates, Inc., 259 East Erie St., Chicago, Ill. 60611
Sheridan Psychological Services, Inc., P.O. Box 837, Beverly Hills, Calif. 90213
Stoelting Company, 424 North Homan Ave., Chicago, Ill. 60624
Western Psychological Services, 12031 Wilshire Blvd., Los Angeles, Calif. 90025

A complete list of all test publishers as of 1972 is available in *The Seventh Mental Measurements Yearbook* (Buros 1972). The *Test Collection Bulletin,* published quarterly by Educational Testing Service, lists new addresses, publisher changes, new test scoring services and systems, and addresses of all publishers referred to in its listing of new test acquisitions.

Bulletins

Educational Testing Service, Harcourt Brace Jovanovich, Inc., The Psychological Corporation, and California Test Bureau have over the years published free bulletins on testing. Since 1932, for example, The Psychological Corporation has published unusually well written bulletins on a variety of testing topics. Bulletins 36–57 are available at no cost. The groupings below indicate which *Test Service Bulletins* are printed in a single booklet:

No. 36. *What is an Aptitude?* Regardless of its title, what makes a test an aptitude test?

No. 37. *How Effective Are Your Tests?* A survey of methods of validating selection tests in business-industrial settings.

No. 38. *Expectancy Tables—A Way of Interpreting Test Validity.* Description of a simple, easily-understood device for appraising and demonstrating the usefulness of tests for selection, guidance, and some clinical purposes.

No. 39. *Norms Must Be Relevant.* On the importance of having the right reference group for interpretation of tests.

No. 40. *The Three-Legged Coefficient.* How to tell what a correlation coefficient means.

No. 41. *Human Resources and the Aptitude Inventory.* Application of aptitude test results in pupil classification and in curriculum planning.

No. 42. *Does Testing Cost Too Much?* A look at the costs of testing vs. the costs—both apparent and hidden—of the mistakes which testing can help avoid.

No. 43. *The Search for Talent.* On the identification of special abilities among high school students.

No. 44. *Reliability and Confidence.* The meaning of reliability coefficients—and some common misconceptions.

No. 45. *Better Than Chance.* How large must the validity coefficient be to justify use of a test in personnel selection?

No. 46. *The Correction for Guessing.* The logic and illogic of using penalty formulas in scoring multiple-choice tests.

No. 47. *Cross-Validation.* The importance of an independent check on the effectiveness of tests and test items.

No. 48. *Methods of Expressing Test Scores.* On the equivalence of popular standard score systems and percentiles, with chart.

No. 49. *The D.A.T.—A Seven-Year Follow-Up.* A research report on the subsequent education and occupation of persons who took the *Differential Aptitude Tests* while they were high school students.

No. 50. *How Accurate Is a Test Score?* The standard error of measurement as an indicator of how large a margin of error to allow for in interpreting test scores.

No. 51. *Aptitude, Intelligence, and Achievement.* Differences and similarities among these three types of tests, and the purposes for which each kind is most useful.

No. 52. *Watch Your Weights.* How to check on the mixture obtained when scores on parts of a battery are combined to make a total score.

No. 53. *Comparability vs. Equivalence of Test Scores.* When and to what extent a new test or an alternate form can safely be substituted for an older one, and what underlies comparisons of scores on two or more different tests.

No. 54. *On Telling Parents about Test Results.* Problems and techniques of explaining the meaning of test results to students and their parents.

No. 55. *The Identification of the Gifted.* Problems and methods of finding *both* the students who are extremely able in one area *and* those having high capacity in several different abilities.

No. 56. *Double-Entry Expectancy Tables.* A convenient and easily understood procedure for displaying predictions based on two tests or on a test and another variable such as age, school marks, years on the job, or the like.

No. 57. *Testing Job Applicants from Disadvantaged Groups.* A discussion of aspects of test usage which require special attention in the appraisal of disadvantaged applicants.

No. 58. *Local Norms—When and Why.*

No. 59. *Restriction of Range: Questions and Answers.*

Harcourt Brace Jovanovich, Inc., has published a series of reports called *Test Service Notebook,* which includes the following titles:

A Glossary of Measurement Terms
Fundamentals of Testing
Innovation in the Assessment of Individual Differences
Testing: Bond or Barrier between Pupil and Teacher?
Using Stanines to Obtain Composite Scores Based on Test Data and Teachers' Ranks

Educational Testing Service (ETS) is another excellent source of free bulletins. Since 1967 ETS has published its *Test Collection Bulletin,* which contains the most up-to-date listings of new tests published in the United States and foreign countries. The *Bulletin* also contains information on new testing programs, tests that have gone out of print, publisher changes, new test publishers, test scoring services and systems, new test reference materials, sources of test reviews in journals and books, and current addresses of all test publishers referred to in that issue of the *Bulletin.*

ETS provides a Tests and Measurement Kit, at a nominal cost. It includes:

Multiple-Choice Questions: A Close Look
Selecting an Achievement Test: Principles and Procedures
Making the Classroom Test: A Guide for Teachers
Short-cut Statistics for Teacher-made Tests

It also publishes *TM News* in association with Rutgers University Graduate School of Education. These publications contain up-to-date reports about measurement topics. *TM Reports,* published by the same organization, periodically summarizes conference papers presented at national meetings of the American Educational Research Association (AERA). One set, for example, includes the following topics:

I. *Evaluation: The State of the Art*
II. *Criterion Referenced Measurement*
III. *Educational Statistics*
IV. *Test Development, Interpretation, and Use*
V. *Innovations in Measurement*

Other *TM Reports* are on such topics as developing criterion-referenced tests, a bibliography of test bias, ability grouping, developing performance tests, a bibliography of tests of basic learning for adults, an overview of state educational assessment programs, a bibliography of criterion-referenced measurements, and bibliographies pertaining to measurement relating to tobacco smoking, drugs, and alcohol.

California Test Bureau has published a glossary of ninety-six measurement concepts, an inventory or checklist of steps to follow in administering standardized tests, and a very useful discussion of ethical considerations to follow in selecting, administering, and using standardized tests. These are all available free of cost.

The National Council on Measurement in Education (NCME) publishes quarterly reports concerned with "the practical implications of measurement and related research and their application to educational problems of individuals, institutions, and systems."

Yearbooks

A number of organizations and individuals publish yearbooks of value to educators. The National Society for the Study of Education (NSSE), for example, publishes yearbooks on a variety of subjects concerning education. Some of those most relevant to testing include:

Fourteenth Yearbook, 1915, Part II: Methods of Measuring Teachers' Efficiency

Fifteenth Yearbook, 1916, Part I: Standards and Tests for the Measurement of the Efficiency of Schools and School Systems

Seventeenth Yearbook, 1918, Part I: The Measurement of Educational Products

Twenty-first Yearbook, 1922, Parts I and II: Intelligence Tests and Their Use

Twenty-second Yearbook, 1923, Part I: English Composition: Its Aims, Methods, and Measurements

Thirty-fourth Yearbook, 1935: Educational Diagnosis

Thirty-seventh Yearbook, 1938, Part II: The Scientific Movement in Education

Forty-fifth Yearbook, 1946, Part I: The Measurement of Understanding

Sixty-second Yearbook, 1963, Part II: The Impact and Improvement of School Testing Programs

Sixty-eighth Yearbook, 1969, Part II: Evaluation: New Roles, New Means

Each NSSE yearbook contains chapters written by different experts in the topic under discussion. Almost every university library contains a full set of these volumes.

Probably the most useful source of information for selecting tests is a series of yearbooks edited by Oscar K. Buros. Although one of these volumes was published as early as 1933, it contained only lists of available tests and did not review or evaluate their quality. Buros's second volume did contain evaluations of many of the currently available tests. In 1938 and 1940 Buros published *The 1938 Mental Measurements Yearbook* and *The 1940 Mental Measurements Yearbook*. The *Third Mental Measurements Yearbook* was published in 1949, the *Fourth* in 1953, the *Fifth* in 1959, the *Sixth* in 1965, and *The Seventh Mental Measurements Yearbook* in 1972.

These yearbooks contain critical evaluations of tests by outstanding reviewers and synopses of test reviews that have been published in other sources. Current costs of tests, grade and age levels for which each test was designed, the name of the test publisher, the amount of time required for administration, names of subtests, and the availability of alternate forms are included.

Each *Mental Measurements Yearbook* also contains lists of books and monographs related to testing, of test publishers, of journals that have published test reviews, and an index listing names of persons who have published or reviewed tests. Although this information tends to be outdated—the *Test Collec-*

tion Bulletin referred to previously (published by Educational Testing Service) is more up to date—no source compares with the yearbooks for the quality of its test evaluations.

Buros has also published monographs titled *Reading Tests and Reviews* (1968) and *Personality Tests and Reviews* (1969), which contain excerpts from the first six *Mental Measurements Yearbooks* in addition to new information.

One weakness of the *Yearbooks* is that each new publication covers only tests that have appeared since the publication of the preceding *Yearbook*. A test may be reviewed in the *Sixth Yearbook* but not in the *Seventh*.

To help locate information about available and out-of-print tests, Buros published *Tests in Print* in 1961. Each entry consists of the test title, appropriate levels, publication dates, names of subtests, authors, publishers, and references to entries in yearbooks that reviewed the test.

Certainly teachers should examine the *Mental Measurements Yearbooks* before they select tests. Some of the more popular tests may be reviewed three or four times; others may be listed but not reviewed. Extensive bibliographies accompany many entries, making it possible for the reader to study related literature.

Another excellent yearbook is the *Annual Review of Psychology*. Each edition contains a major article on at least one aspect of testing. The *Review* attempts to summarize new developments in such fields as personality measurement and statistical theory. It also contains an excellent bibliography on recent developments in testing.

Indices

Both the *Education Index* and *Psychological Abstracts* are published monthly and contain listings of newly published tests, sources of information about testing practices, and research reports on the use of tests. Because they are published monthly, both sources are current. The *Education Index* provides an exhaustive list of articles related to testing, but since abstracts are not given, the reader will have to judge the relevance of an entry by its title. *Psychological Abstracts* contains a brief review or abstract of each published article, usually including at least the major findings of each study reported. It helps save time by suggesting which articles are most relevant for a given purpose. A yearly index is also available for rapid location of information. Virtually all university and college libraries contain complete sets of both.

Journals

The most current information about tests is found in professional journals in education and psychology. Although many journals mention tests and studies of testing practices and theory, the following journals are especially relevant:

Journal	Dates of Publication	Description of Articles
Journal of Educational Measurement	Quarterly	Original research and reports; test reviews in each edition.
Review of Educational Research	Five times a year	Until February of 1968, trends and new developments in testing were published in a separate edition every three years. The last issue devoted entirely to measurement appeared in April 1970. More recent issues contain critical reviews of research literature, some of which are relevant to measurement.
Psychological Bulletin	Monthly	Comprehensive and critical reviews of different topics, including measurement and testing.
American Educational Research Journal	Quarterly	Original experimental and theoretical studies, some of which concern measurement.
Educational and Psychological Measurement	Quarterly	Discussions, research, measurement theory, descriptions of testing programs, and suggestions relating to test usage; articles tend to be technical. Contains a validity section published twice a year.
American Psychologist	Monthly	Timely articles of interest to counselors and psychologists; periodical discussions of ethics, standards, test usage, and similar topics.
Measurement and Evaluation in Guidance	Quarterly	Empirical articles on the use of tests in guidance; since the fall of 1970 has included reviews of new tests; contains lists of reviews in other journals, lists of new tests used in counseling, and critical commentaries on testing practices.

Summary

1. This chapter develops criteria for evaluating standardized tests and suggests sources of information about these tests.

2. Both practical and technical considerations are important in evaluating tests. Practical considerations include:

   a. *Cost.* Costs include the initial outlay of funds for tests, answer sheets, stop watches, and so forth. Continuing costs include answer sheet replacement and test scoring services.

   b. *Time limitations.* Time limitations must be considered since class schedules may be upset if more time than one class period is necessary to administer tests.

   c. *Ease of administration.* Administration of tests is facilitated if the test manual includes full information. Because standardized tests are designed to be given and scored under uniform testing conditions, failure to describe these conditions fully is a potential source of invalidity.

   d. *Format.* Tests should be pleasing to look at and not so overcrowded that they produce confusion. Format can also refer to the directions that are to be read by the examiner to the examinees. If these directions are set in boldface type, the test administrator can find them quickly and easily read them exactly as they are given in the manual.

e. *Alternate forms.* Alternate forms of a test make it easier for a teacher to retest students when this is desirable or necessary.

f. *Multiple levels.* Multiple-level examinations provide comparability of norms over widely different grade levels. Their purpose is to allow teachers to compare student progress with the progress made by the norm group from the elementary through the secondary grades.

g. *Answer sheets and simple scoring procedures.* The use of separate answer sheets is encouraged for students above the fourth grade. Hand-scored answer sheets include those that use stencils, carbon-backed keys, and pinprick keys. If large numbers of tests must be scored, there is some advantage in using electronic data-processing equipment. Contact and light-scanning are two methods of "reading" answer sheets.

h. *Ease of interpretation.* Test manuals should include case histories and examples of typical errors made in interpreting test scores. Examples of what the teacher should and should not do should also be included.

3. *Standards for Educational and Psychological Tests and Manuals,* published in 1966, contains a number of important requirements for standardized tests. Those listed as *essential* include:

a. All tests should be accompanied by a manual.

b. The test and its manual should be revised periodically.

c. The manual should state the purposes for which the test is recommended.

d. The qualifications needed to administer, score, and interpret the test should be clearly stated.

e. Minimal criteria for specific purposes should be included.

f. The validity of the test for different purposes should be stated.

g. If content validity is appropriate, the nature of the universe from which items were selected should be made clear.

h. The criterion against which the test is validated should be described completely.

i. The sample employed in a validity study should be described completely and should include means and standard deviations of all scores and descriptions of various groups that might have been employed (e.g., their ages, grades, sex distributions, and so forth).

j. Correlation coefficients between predictors and criteria should be reported along with evidence of the degree of misclassification and the degree to which the test provides incremental validity.

k. For construct validity, the manual should clearly define the construct and differentiate it from similar constructs.

l. Evidence of reliability should be presented for each type of interpretation for which the test is designed.

m. Reliability should be presented by correlations or by the standard error of measurement.

n. If equivalent-form reliability is being reported, the manual should contain the means and standard deviations of the forms and the correlation between them.

o. For stability coefficients, the manual should state the amount of time that elapsed between the test and the retest.

p. The directions for administering the test should encourage uniformity.

q. Principles and procedures for scoring tests should be stated to reduce scoring errors.

r. All norms provided in the manual should be carefully explained.

s. Revised manuals should indicate the equivalence of the new with the old forms.

t. Norms should be reported in reference to appropriate groups.

u. All norms should clearly state the populations of individuals to which they are relevant.

4. An evaluation of the Boehm Test of Basic Concepts shows the use of a test analysis form that contains many of the requirements listed in *Standards for Educational and Psychological Tests and Manuals.*

5. There are many sources of information about educational and psychological tests, including:

a. *Publishers' catalogs.* Catalogs from publishers of standardized tests include such information as brief descriptions of the tests, their costs, purposes, appropriate age or grade levels, number of alternate forms, norms, time limits, scoring methods, and cost of a specimen set.

b. *Bulletins.* Many publishers of standardized tests publish bulletins relating to norms, test administration, scoring, and so forth. Most of these are free or inexpensive.

c. *Yearbooks.* The yearbooks of the National Society for the Study of Education, the *Mental Measurements Yearbooks* edited by Oscar K. Buros, and the *Annual Review of Psychology* are examples of helpful yearbooks. In particular, Buros' *Mental Measurements Yearbooks* are highly recommended for anyone planning to purchase a test.

d. *Indices.* The *Education Index* contains lists of new tests and information about testing practices on a monthly basis. The monthly *Psychological Abstracts* also lists tests and reviews of tests and testing practices and provides brief abstracts of content as well.

e. *Journals.* Professional journals in education and psychology often review tests or contain articles related to testing practices.

Suggested Readings

Buros, Oscar Krisen. *The Seventh Mental Measurements Yearbook.* Highland Park, N. J.: Gryphon Press, 1972. Anyone seriously contemplating using any standardized test would do well to examine the reviews included in one or more of these *Yearbooks.*

French, John W., and Michael, William B., cochairmen. *Standards for Educational and Psychological Tests and Manuals.* Washington, D. C.: American Psychological Association, 1966, 40 pp. This is the single best source of criteria to be applied in evaluating standardized tests and their manuals.

Katz, Martin. *Selecting an Achievement Test: Principles and Procedures.* Princeton, N. J.: Educational Testing Service, 1961, 34 pp. Free copies of this booklet are available from the publisher. Although reprinted in 1969, the references are dated by the 1961 copyright. Nonetheless, many of the concepts are of value in helping to select an achievement test.

Sax, Gilbert. *Empirical Foundations of Educational Research.* Englewood Cliffs, N. J.: Prentice-Hall, 1968, 443 pp. See chapter 7, "Reliability and Validity of Psychometric Measures," for a discussion of the principles of test selection for research purposes.

The Nature and Measurement of Intelligence

© 1973 King Features Syndicate, Inc.

Figure 11.1

11 The first systematic studies of individual differences were begun in 1796, the year the astronomer Maskelyne dismissed his assistant, Kinnebrook, for failing to observe stellar transits as accurately as he. Twenty years later an astronomer named Bessel read of the dismissal and began a series of studies which eventually led to the concept of the "personal equation," or the idiosyncratic differences in reaction time to a stimulus. Bessel showed that individuals differ in reaction time and that such differences varied from occasion to occasion.

Sir Francis Galton gave the study of individual differences its greatest impetus. As early as 1869 Galton said:

> I have no patience with the hypothesis occasionally expressed, and often implied, especially in tales written to teach children to be good, that babies are born pretty much alike, and that the sole agencies in creating differences between boy and boy, and man and man, are steady application and moral effort. It is in the most unqualified manner that I object to pretensions of natural equality.

Not only did Galton recognize individual differences but he was also certain that such differences were hereditary. The debate between the hereditarians and the environmentalists raged between 1920 and 1935, only to be resurrected in somewhat different form by Arthur Jensen's controversial article in the 1969

Harvard Educational Review, "How Much Can We Boost IQ and Scholastic Achievement?" Later in this chapter the hereditary-environment issue will be examined in greater detail.

In 1882 Galton was given space in the South Kensington Museum to test, for a small fee, individuals who wanted their "abilities" measured. Most of the tests were simple reaction time and association tests based on the assumption that complex mental functioning could be studied by investigating simpler sensory processes. By 1888 Galton had worked out a measure of correlation to show how "mental" and "physical" attributes were related. But in 1901 Clark Wissler demonstrated "that the physical tests show a general tendency to correlate among themselves but only to a very slight degree with mental tests." (The term *mental tests* was first used by James McKeen Cattell in 1890.) If complex mental processes were to be measured, simple sensory tasks would have to make way for more sophisticated techniques.

The Binet Tests

Compulsory education in France led to the development of the first intelligence test. In 1904 the French minister of public instruction named a commission to determine which children would not benefit from instruction in regular classes. The commission decreed that children be admitted to special classes only after a medical and psychological examination; unfortunately there were no tests available for measuring the ability to profit from regular public school.

By 1905 Alfred Binet had tried numerous methods of measuring intelligence—simple sensory tasks as well as phrenology and palmistry—and had decided that such attempts were useless and unrelated to school achievement. If intelligence were measurable, it would have to be measured by tasks that bright children could pass and less able ones would fail. Many of the tasks developed in 1905 by Binet and his assistant, Theo Simon, are still used in the 1960 revision of the Binet-Simon tests.

By the time Binet died, in 1911, the same year in which he published his second test revision, educators throughout the world were clamoring for further information about the measurement of intelligence. Henry Goddard published his English translations of Binet's 1908 and 1911 revisions for use in the United States. In 1916 Louis M. Terman restandardized the Binet tests for use with American children and adults. Norms and items were revised again by Terman in 1937 and by Maud Merrill in 1960.

World War I produced the impetus to develop group intelligence tests. Again, a practical need to deploy men optimally led to such tests as the Army Alpha and Army Beta examinations. The success of these tests in the military encouraged educators and psychologists to create group intelligence tests applicable to civilian populations.

Since World War I the history of intelligence testing has focused on (1) the construction of new and more accurate batteries of tests, (2) improvement in the norming and standardization of these tests, (3) the development of new theoretical positions on the meaning of intelligence, and (4) improved utilization of these tests in education, business, and the psychological clinic.

The Meaning of Intelligence

Intelligence is the ability of an organism to adjust itself adequately to its environment.

Intelligence is the hereditary capacity to learn.

Intelligence is the ability to reason.

The intelligent person is one who can solve a wide variety of difficult questions rapidly.

These four definitions of intelligence are only a small sample of the many that have been suggested. Some of these definitions emphasize the *function* of intelligence to help the individual survive or adjust. Other definitions stress the *origin* of intelligence, some emphasizing its hereditary nature and others that intelligence is learned. Still other definitions refer to the *structure* of intelligence by describing component traits or abilities. None of these definitions is necessarily "right" or "wrong." Rather, they represent differences in approach and emphasis.

An Operational Definition of Intelligence

However teachers may choose to define intelligence, the definition will have to be related to the procedures or operations used to measure it. If intelligence is defined as a "hereditary capacity to learn," then some way of measuring hereditary capacities must be devised or the definition serves little purpose.

The measurement of intelligence consists of administering a series of tasks (stimuli) and observing responses to them. The nature of the items determine— at least in part—who will pass and who will fail these tasks. From these responses teachers *infer* something about the intelligence of the examinee. Note that intelligence itself—whatever that may be—is not measured directly but is inferred from the responses to test items. Each different set of tasks imposed may well lead to different responses and to different inferences. Thinking of intelligence in this way implies that each person may have as many different measured intelligences as there are different kinds of tasks or tests and that intelligence varies, depending on the nature of these tasks.

An *operational definition* describes the procedures or operations needed to measure a term such as *intelligence*. The rules for constructing, administering, and scoring any given intelligence test operationally define the meaning of intelligence as measured by the test. If tests are constructed using different item selection rules, an IQ of 100 on a test that contains many vocabulary items need not contradict an IQ of 120 on a different test that emphasizes hand-eye coordination. Reporting that Johnny is average in intelligence or has an IQ of 95 is not as precise as saying that he received a Binet IQ of 95 or a Lorge-Thorndike IQ of 100. A Binet IQ of 95 has meaning because the procedures used to develop that test are well known. The statement that "intelligence is whatever is measured by an intelligence test" may appear to be trite and uninformative, but it does point out the need to define intelligence in relationship to some specific test.

The Structure of Intelligence

Spearman's *g*, or General-Factor Theory of Intelligence

The history of measurement has not neglected the search for a universally acceptable *and* quantifiable meaning of intelligence. If all intelligence tests shared certain common properties, teachers could justifiably refer to intelligence without differentiating among various intelligence tests. The first scientific attempt to describe the elements common to all intelligence tests was formulated by Charles Spearman in 1904 and again in 1927. From his studies of the correlations among scores obtained from different intelligence tests, Spearman postulated a *general-factor theory of intelligence*. According to the theory, intelligence tests share with each other a "general factor," *g*, which he defined as the general ability to educe abstract relationships. Some tasks require more *g* than others, but all cognitive tasks involve *g* to some extent.

If *g* alone could account for intelligence, one would expect the correlation among various intelligence tests to be close to 1.0. Spearman realized that in practice the correlations were much lower and that some factor other than *g* must be present to account for these lowered correlations. These factors he named *s*, for "specific factors." In addition to *g*, every intelligence test has, then, numerous factors specific only to it and to no other test. *g* therefore contributes to the correlation among intelligence tests, while *s* prevents correlations from reaching 1.0. Tests based on a unifactor theory yield single intelligence scores that attempt to be as pure a measure of *g* as possible. Little would be gained by trying to measure specific factors since they are not present in any other measurements.

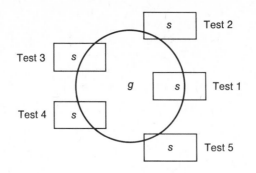

Figure 11.2. Graphic Depiction of the General-
Factor Theory

Figure 11.2 depicts Spearman's general-factor theory. Each rectangle corresponds to a test which to some degree is a measure of g. The extent to which the test measures g is indicated by the amount of the rectangle in the g circle. Those parts of the rectangles outside the circle represent the amount of s, or specific factors.

Each of the tests in figure 11.2 contains or is saturated with different amounts of g. Tests 1, 3, and 4 will correlate highly with each other because they all contain relatively large amounts of the g factor and therefore measure the same general ability. In contrast, tests 2 and 5 have little g and will therefore correlate only slightly with each other.

In later years Spearman found it necessary to modify his general-factor theory to account for the presence of factors not explainable by either g or s. For example, when subjects are given the task of crossing out all the a's and e's on a page, not only is g measured but each task also yields its own specific factor, or s (e.g., one specific factor for canceling the a's and one for canceling the e's). Spearman found that these two tasks correlated with each other as depicted in figure 11.3, where tests 6 and 7 contain common elements of g. The specific factors also overlap, demonstrating that they correlate with each other. These correlated specific factors were called *group factors*. They are not as broad as g or as specific as s but are somewhere between the two. All tests contain differing amounts of g and s, but fewer tests yield group factors.

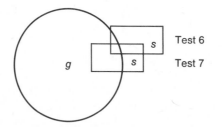

Figure 11.3. Graphic Depiction of Group
Factors

Two of the group factors Spearman identified were *verbal ability* and *numerical ability.*

Teachers often assume the validity of a general-factor theory of intelligence when they refer to children as being "bright," "average," or "dull" without stating in what subjects the child excels or does poorly. The "bright" child is thought of as excelling *in general.* Other theoretical positions would argue against this belief.

The following statements summarize Spearman's unifactor theory:

1. The most important element of intelligence is the *g* factor, defined as the ability to educe abstract relationships. Individuals differ in the amount of *g* they possess.
2. The meaning of intelligence is synonymous with *g.* Specific factors, *s,* are unique to each test and are therefore of lesser value than *g.*
3. Although *s* factors were supposed to be unique to each test, some appeared to correlate with each other. These correlated specific factors were called *group factors.*

Multiple-Factor Theories of Intelligence

Spearman defined intelligence as the ability to form abstract relationships. The concept of *g* represents a kind of "mental energy" or intellectual power. To measure *g*, tests should contain items that require abstract and complex reasoning abilities.

In contrast, multiple-factor theorists conceive of different types of intelligence. For example, a person might have a high verbal intelligence, be average in spatial intelligence, and be below average in numerical intelligence. The number of different kinds of intelligence postulated depends on the particular statistical methods used to derive these basic abilities, called *factors,* as well as on the beliefs of the theorists.

Thorndike's position   E. L. Thorndike is generally considered to be the "father of educational psychology." In 1898 Thorndike published *Animal Intelligence,* which demonstrated methods of studying complex behavior of animals in the laboratory. Six years later he published *Theory of Mental and Social Measurements,* which gained for him recognition as a leader in educational and psychological measurements.

Thorndike's learning theory was called *Connectionism.* Learning was conceived of as the development of new stimulus-response connections occurring at the point where impulses pass nerve cells. Memory was simply the maintenance or persistence of these neural connections.*

---

* Thorndike's *Connectionism* was a refinement of stimulus-response psychology, which had had a long history and a recent impetus from Pavlov's studies in conditioning.

Thorndike believed that the intelligent person is capable of making a large number of connections. Thought only appears complex because of the inability to separate and identify all the numerous connections that compose complex intellectual behavior. If different mental tasks utilize the same stimulus-response connections, then the identical elements in these tasks produce high correlations.

Thorndike recognized that some mental functions could be classified into separate types of ability—numerical ability, verbal reasoning, and so forth. On Thorndike's test, called the CAVD (from the initial letters of the words *completion, arithmetic, vocabulary,* and *directions*), intelligence exhibits itself in the ability to perform four types of complex acts, such as the ability to complete sentences, to reason *a*rithmetically, to use *v*ocabulary, and to follow *d*irections. Thorndike attempted to measure the number and variety of tasks (graded according to difficulty level) a person could complete.

Thurstone's position   Another multiple-factor theory which has contributed greatly to the understanding of intelligence was formulated by L. L. Thurstone at the University of Chicago. According to Thurstone, intelligence is represented neither by *g* nor by a multitude of highly specific connections, as claimed by Thorndike, but is somewhat intermediate between the two positions. Thurstone (1938) identified a relatively small number of "primary mental abilities" which are independent of each other. Although he modified the exact number of primary mental abilities from time to time, the ones that are most often reported are:

(*N*) *Number:* The ability to do calculations accurately and rapidly

(*V*) *Verbal:* Primarily measured by vocabulary and other verbal tests

(*W*) *Word fluency:* Measured by the number of words related in some way (such as ending in *ion*) that can be produced in a specific period of time

(*S*) *Space:* The ability to visualize patterns and objects when they are rotated or when they are part of a configuration change

(*M*) *Memory:* The ability to memorize rote material

(*R*) *Reasoning:* Primarily inductive reasoning

(*P*) *Perceptual speed:* The ability to note visual details rapidly

Figure 11.4 demonstrates the essence of Thurstone's multiple-factor theory. Each circle represents a completely independent factor. Test 1 measures to a small degree both *N* and *R* factors; test 2 measures to a greater degree both *V* and *M;* test 3 is a very good measure of *V* and a less useful measure of *S;* test 4 measures only factor *W;* test 5 measures both factors *M* and *S,* although it is more heavily saturated with the *M* factor; tests 6 and 7 are both excellent measures of *R;* and test 8 is almost a pure measure of *P.*

The first attempt to measure intelligence using Thurstone's theory was in 1938. The most recent standardization of his Primary Mental Abilities Test

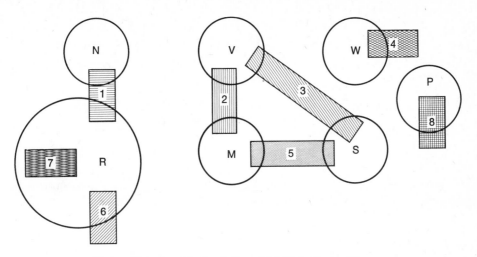

Figure 11.4. Graphic Depiction of Multiple-Factor Theory

(PMA), in 1962, consisted of five factors: verbal, number, reasoning (grades 4–12 only), perceptual speed (K–6 only), and spatial.

The belief in separate primary mental abilities assumes a negligible correlation among factors. Although some of these correlations at the upper grade levels are low (.13 for space and memory, for example), others are too high for independence to be assumed (.59 for verbal and reasoning). Some additional conditions or traits must account for these high correlations. Thurstone later argued that the "primary mental abilities" could be further analyzed to produce "second-order general factors" to explain the moderate correlations among factors (the median correlation is about .35). Advocates of Spearman's general-factor theory have been quick to argue that the presence of correlated factors could be explained by a general intelligence factor, or g. Some correlations at the lower grade levels are as high as .70, demonstrating the similarity among factors and arguing against their independence. Thurstone's theory predicts the relationships shown in figure 11.4, but the findings suggest a series of circles that all overlap to some extent.

Guilford's position   In 1967 J. P. Guilford published *The Nature of Human Intelligence,* in which he postulated a "structure of intellect" composed of operations, products, and content (see figure 11.5). Each of these facets of intelligence was analyzed and separated into subcategories: five for operations, six for products, and four for content, making a cube of $5 \times 6 \times 4 = 120$ cells. These categories and subcategories may be described in the following way:

> *Operations:* Basic intellectual processes of thinking used by individuals
> C 1. Cognition: Discovery, rediscovery, recognition of information or understanding

M	2. *Memory:*	Retention, or the ability to bring forth information learned previously
D	3. *Divergent production:*	Searching for multiple, creative, or novel solutions to a problem
N	4. Co*N*vergent production:	Searching for a "correct" solution to a problem
E	5. *Evaluation:*	Placing a value judgment on knowledge and thought

Content: Type of material or content on which operations are performed (i.e., the contents of thought and intelligence)

F	1. *Figural:*	Concrete material as perceived through the senses
S	2. *Symbolic:*	Letters, digits, and other conventional signs
M	3. Se*M*antic:	Verbal meanings or ideas
B	4. *Behavioral:*	Knowledge regarding other persons

Products: Results of performing operations on content (i.e., the form of thought produced by individuals)

U	1. *Units:*	Production of a single word, definition, or isolated bit of information
C	2. *Classes:*	Production of a concept or the noting of similarities
R	3. *Relations:*	Production of an analogy, an opposite, or any other form of relationship
S	4. *Systems:*	Production of an internally consistent set of classifications of various forms or content
T	5. *Transformation:*	Production of a change of meaning, arrangement, or organization
I	6. *Implications:*	Production of information beyond the data given

Theoretically each cell in the cube should be measurable, and over 100 factors have been identified. In Guilford's theory each cell in the cube is identified by a trigram or three-letter code that refers to an *operation,* a *content* and a *product,* in that order. With the exception of *convergent operation* and *semantic content,* which could be confused with *cognition operation* and *symbolic content,* the first letter determines what abbreviation will be used. The letter *N* is used to refer to convergent production and *M* for semantic content. For example, the cell marked *CFU* represents the joining of three dimensions of the cube, the *c*ognition of *f*igural *u*nits. A test designed to measure *CFU* might consist of tachistoscopically presented figures to be recognized by the examinee. Similarly, *DFU* (*d*ivergent production of *f*igural *u*nits) could be measured by the number of different combinations of figures an examinee can make from a short straight line and a curved line.

Perhaps of greatest interest to the teacher is the use being made of the Guilford model (Meeker 1969) in the curriculum. If intelligence is composed of 120 separate abilities, the responsibility of the teacher is to systematically develop the most important and relevant abilities to their maximum. Mary

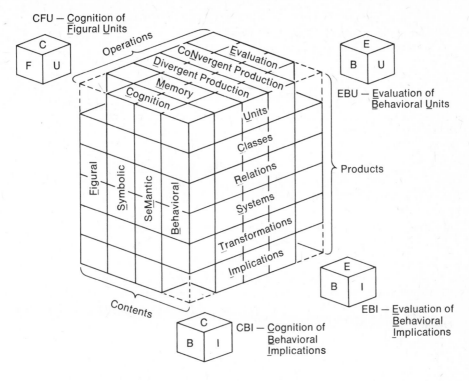

Adapted from Guilford, 1967.

Figure 11.5. Guilford's Structure of Intellect

Meeker (p. 52), for example, has suggested that teachers use a form of the shell game (a small object is hidden under one of three walnut shells) to teach memory for figural units (*MFU*). One can teach and measure memory for convergent semantic systems (*NMS*) by having the student order a set of four pictures into a meaningful sequence.

The assumption behind this approach is that intelligence can be taught and that the skills learned will transfer to or facilitate learning similar skills. Some preliminary evidence to support this position and a method for validating the extent of transfer have been published by Paul Jacobs and Mary Vandeventer (1972). The implications of their study are far-reaching because they offer suggestions for improving specific facets of intellect related to identifiable tasks. But when one considers the complexity of a skill such as reading and the current inability to identify the cells that are relevant to reading, it becomes clear that Guilford's model requires a good deal of research before it can be of practical value. Nonetheless, the search for tasks that can be used to develop reliable data for each of the 120 cells is progressing, and a few studies support the efficacy of Guilford's approach.

The Origins of Intelligence: The Heredity-Environment Issue

The years between 1920 and 1935 were marked by vigorous debates between those who claimed that intelligence was entirely a result of heredity and those who were equally certain that individual differences in intelligence were due to the effects of environment. Most educators believed that heredity and environment interacted to produce intelligence, although they disagreed over the relative contributions of each.

The exact percentages that heredity and environment contribute to intelligence are no longer considered important questions. First, these percentages are difficult to determine because the effects of environment are present even at the time of conception. Second, even if intelligence test scores do measure innate capacity, one would have to argue that academic achievement or learning also measures innate abilities since the two correlate very highly. Third, the consequences of heredity or environment are of less importance than the amount of change in intellectual functioning possible through training and education. Height, for example, can be modified by drugs even though it is genetically determined.

Co-Twin Control Studies

One method of studying the relative effects of heredity and environment is by investigating the intelligence of identical twins raised in different environments. Because identical twins have exactly the same heredity—resulting from the splitting of a single fertilized egg—large differences in IQ scores would be evidence of environmental effects.

In one study the correlation of IQ scores for identical twins reared together was .91; for twins reared apart it was .67 (Newman, Freeman, and Holzinger 1937). The average difference in IQ points between identical twins reared together was about 5 points; for identical twins reared apart, the difference was slightly more than 8 points. These differences represent the effects of environment as well as errors of measurement, present on all tests. In a sense these data are equivocal since most separated twins are placed in similar environments; rarely is one twin placed in a stimulating, enriched environment and the other in a culturally impoverished home. In the cases that showed the largest differences in IQ-between separately reared identical twins (24 points), the differences were attributed to the differential effects of schooling. For identical twins reared apart with equal educational backgrounds, the average difference in IQ was the same as that found for separated identical twins in general—5.2 points. However, the separated twins with the greatest differences in education had average IQ differences of 16 points.

Foster Children Studies

Most studies have shown that the correlation between the IQs of parents and their offspring is approximately .50, a figure which represents the contributions of both heredity and environment. But since there is no hereditary relationship between children and foster parents, any correlation between their IQs should reflect the role of environment. These correlations are about .20; presumably heredity accounts for the differences in the two correlations. This conclusion assumes that foster children have the same kind of environment as children raised with their biological parents. Although there is not much evidence on this point, what little there is argues that the correlation between the IQs of foster children raised together is somewhat higher than the correlation between the IQs of a foster child and a biological child reared together.

Environmental Change Studies

If changes in the environment lead to changes in IQ scores for the same individuals, these changes must be due to the role of environment. One authenticated example of an individual who lived in an extremely restrictive environment was Kaspar Hauser, who was isolated from all human contact in a small, dark cell until he was seventeen years old (Singh and Zingg 1966). Although initially he was unable to talk or walk, Kaspar was tutored and reached normal intelligence. At least in this isolated instance a marked improvement in environment led to great intellectual gains. More moderate gains have occurred in children who were reared by animals. The difficulty with many of these studies is that the extent of retardation before the children were abandoned is difficult to ascertain (Singh and Zingg 1966).

There is some evidence that a deteriorating environment leads to a decrease in IQ scores. In 1930 Lester Wheeler (1932) found that the intelligence level of six-year-old Tennessee mountain children was about 95, close to national averages. However, sixteen-year-olds, who had been in the impoverished environment longer, had a mean IQ of only 74. Ten years later, the mean IQ of six-year-olds had increased from 95 to 103 and that of sixteen-year-olds from 74 to 80. Between 1930 and 1940, Wheeler reported, great improvements were made in industrialization and in educational opportunities in that part of the country. Still, the longer the children remained in the relatively sterile environment, the lower their IQs tended to be. Similar findings were reported with canal-boat children in England (Gordon 1923).

A Summary of the Role of Heredity and Environment

Generally co-twin control studies suggest the importance of heredity as a determiner of intelligence. However, where twins have been separated into vastly different environments, intelligence seems to be related to the amount and quality of education. Studies of foster children also suggest that heredity is an important component of intelligence.

On the other hand, marked changes in the environment lead to changes in performance on intelligence tests. A deteriorating environment tends to lower IQ scores, whereas environmental improvement often leads to higher IQ scores.

Most psychologists and geneticists would probably argue that intelligence is a function of the interaction of heredity and environmental factors and that pure measures of either are currently not attainable. Environment is always present to modify genetic factors, and heredity may well place limits on the amount of improvement that the environment can effect. Teachers should understand this interdependence, but they need not take an inflexible position until conclusive evidence is available.

Some Correlates and Uses of Intelligence Test Scores

Intelligence not only has structure and origin but also performs certain functions (i.e., purposes and uses). The Binet tests were originally developed to select individuals who were unable to function adequately in regular classrooms so that they could be placed in special programs. Indeed, intelligence tests are still used for this purpose, but they have also been applied to diagnosing adjustment and personality disorders. Intelligence can be better understood by relating test scores to other conditions, such as social class, ethnic background, and sex differences, which allegedly affect test scores. Each of these contentions will be examined briefly.

Intelligence and Education

Most of the studies relating intelligence to education have correlated IQ scores and such variables as highest grade completed, grade point average, and learning rate. Because correlations do not necessarily involve a causal relationship, one can only demonstrate the extent to which these variables are associated with one another; one cannot be certain that high IQs cause students to continue their education, or if education increases IQ scores. Nonetheless, correlations between final grade completed and IQ tend to be substantial (in the .70s), and those who continue their education tend to be brighter than those who drop out.

Some evidence supports the hypothesis that continuing education raises IQ test scores. Generally these studies agree that individuals who initially score low on IQ tests tend to score even lower on subsequent tests when they are no longer attending school. For those who continue their education, IQ scores tend to increase significantly (Husen 1951; Adjutant General's Office, Army General Classification Test 1945).

School marks also correlate substantially with IQ scores. How high these correlations are depends on (1) the nature of the intelligence and achievement measuring test, (2) the nature of the subject matter, and (3) the nature of the students. In general, group tests seem to correlate with school marks as well as or better than individual tests of intelligence, perhaps because reading is instrumental both in determining course grades and in the ability to succeed on group tests.

IQ tests tend to correlate more highly with achievement tests than they do with school marks; some of the correlations between standardized achievement tests and IQ measures are in the .90s. Clearly the distinction between achievement and intelligence is all but eliminated when correlations are that high. Whatever certain achievement tests measure is measured equally well by tests of intelligence. The correlations are highest if achievement tests emphasize verbal reasoning skills; they tend to be lower in handwriting and commercial subjects.

IQ tests tend to be better predictors of grades and achievement test scores in the lower grades than in college, a finding that can be attributed partially to the greater restriction of the range of test scores, which tends to depress correlations at the upper grade levels. The highest correlations of IQ with achievement typically are in reading at the lower grades and with English at the college level. These subjects allow great variability in individual differences, which increases correlation coefficients.

Group intelligence tests emphasizing verbal skills tend to be excellent predictors of school achievement, particularly when these tests are administered to elementary school children. Verbal skills are precisely what is stressed in the child's early school years.

Intelligence and Clinical Diagnosis

The school psychologist most often uses individual intelligence tests to screen for clinical abnormalities and to help differentiate one form of clinical abnormality from another. A diagnosis of mental retardation is usually based on a total IQ score of less than 80 on an individual intelligence test. The ability of the intelligence test to estimate the *degree* of retardation is also important because placement decisions must be made. Special classes for the retarded often require that the child be unable to function without the services of a specially trained teacher, for example.

Two categories of mental retardation have been proposed. The *educable mentally retarded* child was defined by Samuel Kirk* as

> one who, because of subnormal mental development, is unable to profit sufficiently from the program of the regular elementary school, but who is considered to have potentialities for development in three areas: (1) educability in academic subjects of the school at a minimum level, (2) educability in social adjustment to a point where he can get along independently in the community, and (3) minimal occupational adequacies to such a degree that he can later support himself partially or totally at the adult level.

Kirk defines the *trainable mentally retarded* child as

> one who is not educable in the sense of academic achievement, ultimate social adjustment independently in the community, or independent occupational adjustment at the adult level. This is what differentiates a trainable mentally retarded child from an educable mentally retarded child. The trainable mentally retarded child, however, has potentialities for learning: (1) self-help skills, (2) social adjustment in the family and in the neighborhood, and (3) economic usefulness in the home, in a residential school, or in a sheltered workshop.

Whether a child is placed into a class for the educable or one for the trainable is determined by the cooperative efforts of the school psychologist, the child's teachers, and his parents. Although the intelligence test is of greatest value in estimating the degree of retardation, it also provides clues regarding the child's ability to cope with the specific kinds of tasks that appear on such tests. Two children may have equally low IQs, but one may be able to put forth a sustained effort without frustration in attempting to answer difficult questions, whereas the other may have a short memory and attention span which, when coupled with his inability to tolerate frustration when faced with new tasks, makes him a candidate for special class instruction.

Intelligence tests can also help identify gifted pupils, although there is less agreement on what constitutes giftedness than on what retardation is. Giftedness may be perceived as either a highly developed talent in one particular area, such as music or science, or a general ability. These two conceptions are not necessarily contradictory since measures of general intelligence seem to correlate with many specific talents. Contrary to popular belief, gifted children

---

* From Samuel A. Kirk, *Educating Exceptional Children*, 2nd ed., © 1972 by Houghton Mifflin Company. Used with permission.

seem to surpass the average population on practically all measures. In the most extensive investigation of gifted children conducted, Lewis Terman (1929–59) found that gifted children were heavier, taller, and in better health, lived longer, had fewer divorces, talked earlier, walked earlier, were functioning two full grade levels above their actual grades, graduated earlier, participated to a greater extent in extracurricular activities, were more emotionally stable, cheated less, and entered professional and semiprofessional occupations at a much higher rate than children of average intelligence.

Some attempts have been made to use intelligence tests to locate emotionally disturbed individuals and those suffering from organic brain disease. On the Wechsler Adult Intelligence Scale, schizophrenics are said to score high on general information and vocabulary but low in perceiving similarities and in discovering missing parts of pictures (Wechsler 1958, p. 171). Organic brain disease is characterized by high vocabulary scores but poor ability to recall digits, assemble puzzles, and code symbols.

The use of differential responses on intelligence tests to discover emotional or physical maladjustment has not been particularly successful. First, group characteristics do not necessarily apply to an individual, yet individual diagnosis is what is desired in the psychological clinic. Second, many of the terms in clinical psychology and psychiatry have not been universally agreed upon. Studying the responses of *schizophrenics* presumes that there is some agreement on the meaning of this term. Third, an increasing number of psychologists and psychiatrists no longer accept the position that diagnosis is necessary for treatment, and they therefore spend little or no time using diagnostic instruments. The clinical applications of tests are discussed in greater detail in chapter 15.

Intelligence and Socioeconomic Status

Socioeconomic status (SES) has variously been measured for children by considering the father's occupational level, the family income, social values, type of dwelling, and the individuals with whom the family identifies and with whom they are at ease. Since World War I extensive studies showing the relationship of SES to intelligence have been reported. The trends for parents and children are similar: the higher the SES, the higher the IQ.

The most extensive study of the IQs of children according to father's occupational level was published by Quinn McNemar (1942). From the data obtained in the standardization of the 1937 revision of the Stanford-Binet test, he found that the child's IQ declined steadily at all age levels as the father's occupational level "decreased" from professional to day laborer. Exceptions were semiskilled laborers, minor clerical personnel, and businessmen, whose children had higher IQs than children whose parents were rural owners. (The difference between the IQs of children whose fathers were in professional occupations and those who were laborers was about twenty points.)

In a study involving almost 19,000 white enlisted men in World War II, T. W. Harrell and M. S. Harrell (1945) reported the means and ranges of white men belonging to various civilian occupations on the Army General Classification Test (AGCT) (see table 11.1). Although these data do not include officers or those eliminated from the service because of discharges, rejections, or misconduct, it is still one of the most ambitious undertakings of its kind. The mean of the AGCT is 100, and the standard deviation is 20 points.

Table 11.1 shows that the highest AGCT scores were made by accountants, with a mean of 128.1 but with a range of 94–157. This finding indicates the necessity of defining intelligence as a function of the specific types of tasks presented to examinees. The AGCT contains arithmetic, vocabulary, and spatial relationship items. Presumably these are the tasks in which accountants excel. Tests containing other types of items might well yield different rankings of occupations. Nonetheless, those in the professions tend to score highest, followed by the semiprofessionals, clerical employees and businessmen, semiskilled workers, and unskilled laborers.

Table 11.1. Means and Ranges of AGCT Scores Corresponding to Selected Civilian Occupations

Occupation	Mean	Range
Accountant	128.1	94–157
Teacher	122.8	76–155
Bookkeeper	120.0	70–157
Clerk, general	117.5	68–155
Salesman	115.1	60–153
Stock clerk	111.8	54–151
Machinest	110.1	38–153
Sheet metal worker	107.5	62–153
Auto serviceman	104.2	30–141
Plumber	102.7	56–139
Laborer	95.8	26–145
Teamster	87.7	46–145

Harrell and Harrell 1945, pp. 231–32.

Perhaps more important than the means are the ranges of scores, which overlap greatly from occupation to occupation. Differences *within* each group are much greater than are differences *between* groups. Ranges, of course, tend to be unreliable since their values depend only on the lowest-scoring and highest-scoring individuals, and some of the low scores probably reflect a lack of motivation among draftees.

Ethnic Background and Intelligence

Probably no subject has aroused such heated debate as the interpretation of differences in IQ among various ethnic and racial groups. Note that the debate is not whether such differences exist on intelligence tests, but rather how these differences are to be accounted for and what changes should be made to counteract their social effects.

Almost all investigations agree that on intelligence tests placing a heavy emphasis on verbal reasoning, black persons *on the average* score ten to fifteen points lower than white persons. Studies also agree that the overlap in IQ scores between blacks and whites is probably somewhere between 12 and 35 percent. An overlap of 25 percent would mean that a fourth of the blacks would surpass the median IQ of whites. Any presumption that the IQ of one individual selected randomly exceeds the IQ of another of a different race would be in error by the percentage of overlap.

The debate on the causes of racial differences on intelligence tests lay relatively dormant until an article by Arthur Jensen in the *Harvard Educational Review* (1969) rekindled the flames of controversy. Anti-integrationists used the Jensen article to support their position that environmental changes in educational opportunity would do little to improve the status of blacks. Egalitarians saw the Jensen article as an attack on civil rights and a step backward for black equality.

Neither of these reactions is justified from a careful, unbiased reading of the Jensen article. Three major conclusions were developed:

1. About 80 percent of intelligence is attributable to heredity.
2. Compensatory educational programs have been tried, and they have failed.
3. Educators should redesign the curriculum to take advantage of the particular strengths of each racial group.

Nowhere does Jensen argue that attempts to reduce differences between races should be abandoned. In fact, he strongly urges that innovations intervene in the environments of disadvantaged youngsters and suggests that there are programs superior to such large-scale interventions as Head Start. Nowhere does Jensen advocate differential treatment of children except in terms of their own "characteristics." He points out that on some tasks—primarily those involving rote learning—differences between races are virtually nonexistent. He advocates a search for additional factors and skills that could be used to help disadvantaged children and reminds his readers that intelligence tests typically measure a relatively restricted range of abilities, primarily involving abstract and verbal reasoning.

Jensen's conclusions have not gone unanswered. Advocates of programs such as Head Start have indicated that, contrary to Jensen's conclusions, initial gains are continued throughout the elementary grades. Furthermore, the critics point to the difficulty in attempting to separate the effects of heredity from environment and express the fear that genetic explanations of intelligence tend to dissuade educators and the public from trying to remedy these differences.

A still broader issue may be raised regarding the Jensen controversy.

Should educators, as a matter of policy, teach some children simple rote associations, in which they tend to perform well, whereas children of different genetic backgrounds are taught more complex concepts and principles? Ethical considerations and the great variability within each racial group argue against restricting any kind of learning to some favored portion of society. It should also be remembered that racial extraction and socioeconomic status are related and that blacks and other minority groups tend to be drawn from the lower SES levels.

Evidence of group or individual differences carries with it no necessary implications for differential treatment. None of the studies on the modifiability of intelligence is exempt from procedural weaknesses, and bias in one direction or the other is not likely to benefit those in the greatest need of educational intervention. The role of measurement is to discover individual and group differences and similarities and to help evaluate the effectiveness of programs designed to maximize the growth of all individuals.

Intelligence and Sex Differences

Whether or not there are differences in intelligence between males and females depends almost entirely on the nature of the items used to measure intelligence. On tests such as the Stanford-Binet, items that showed large sex differences were excluded on the assumption that they reflect the experiential backgrounds of men and women. For example, one would expect that the ability to define such words as *awl* and *bobbin* is related more to experience than to different abilities. However, some tasks on intelligence tests tend to favor females, and others tend to favor males. For example, females are superior to males on tasks requiring verbal skills such as word fluency, vocabulary, and speech; and males seem to excel in mechanical, spatial, and numerical ability. These tasks are usually balanced so that sex differences are negligible on overall IQ scores.

Norms on Intelligence Tests

The raw score an individual receives on a standardized test is almost always compared with scores made by some reference group having known characteristics. Typically this reference group is selected to represent the essential characteristics of the United States population as determined by census reports. These essential characteristics often include geographical regions, urban-rural distinctions, occupational groupings, and age classifications.

On intelligence tests the scores individuals obtain may be converted to age, grade, quotient, or standard score norms. Knowing that a student responded correctly to thirty-two items on an intelligence test does not by itself indicate how he compares with other individuals selected to represent the characteristics of his age or grade level. A score is high, average, or low depending on how others of a similar background perform on the same tasks. This section examines the nature of the norms used on intelligence tests.

Age Norms

The chronological age level at which a person performs on an intelligence test is called his *mental age*. A person who obtains the same number of points as the average ten-year-old is said to have a mental age, or MA, of 10-0; should he equal the performance of the average twelve-and-a-half-year old, his MA would be 12-6. Two individuals of widely differing chronological ages can have the same MA if they both obtain the same number of correct items. Thus if three children with chronological ages (CA) of five, six, and seven all received the same score as the average six-and-a-half-year-old, their MAs would all be 6-6.

The use of age norms presumes that test performance increases with chronological age. Older individuals are expected to get higher scores and therefore have higher MAs than younger persons. Although this relationship should hold true on the average, some bright younger children will surpass the performance of less capable older ones.

The relationship between MA and CA depends largely on the type of item administered. Figures 11.6a and b show the percentage of ten- and twelve-year olds passing a picture absurdity and vocabulary task, respectively, on the 1960 revision of the Stanford-Binet. These are called *mental age curves* because they show the relationship between performance on an intelligence test and chronological age. The "typical" mental age curve shows either an S-shaped figure or one depicted by a great increase in performance at the lower age levels and a flattening out or "plateau" at the upper levels.

This tendency for mental age curves to flatten out at the upper age levels is typical and violates the assumption that performance should improve with age. On many tests this plateau is reached at about age sixteen, while on others, depending on the nature of the items, it may not appear until the early twenties or even later. This plateau was at one time called the *age of arrest* to imply that intellectual development was arrested or retarded at those ages. The age of arrest is now recognized as an artifact of the item and not necessarily a characteristic of examinees. It is easy to construct items that discriminate between the average five-year-old and six-year-old, but it is virtually impossible to think of a task that an average forty-one-year-old could pass but an average forty-year-old could not pass. This problem is encountered on many items at much earlier ages. Figure 11.6 b, for example, shows that the curve is almost perfectly flat

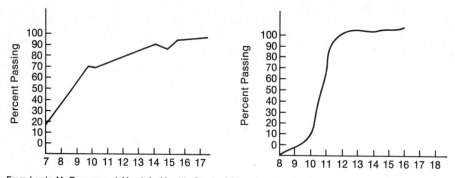

From Lewis M. Terman and Maud A. Merrill, *Stanford-Binet Intelligence Scale*, © 1960 by Houghton-Mifflin Company. Used by permission.

Figure 11.6a. Percent Passing Picture Absurdity Problem at Different CAs on 1960 Revision of Stanford-Binet

Figure 11.6b. Percent Passing Vocabulary Items at Different CAs on 1960 Revision of Stanford-Binet

by age twelve, which means that twelve-, thirteen-, fourteen-, and fifteen-year-olds all attain the same score on the vocabulary items. Mental age is not a useful concept beyond the age of arrest because age groups above that level do equally well. The Stanford-Binet provides different tasks at half-year intervals between the ages of two and five because between those ages it is possible to construct items that can discriminate at six-month intervals. From age five through age fourteen, items are placed at yearly intervals. At age fourteen even cruder norms are developed to discriminate between Average Adult, Superior Adult I, Superior Adult II, and Superior Adult III.

When performance on intelligence tests is examined throughout the age span from seven to sixty-five, psychologists typically find a curve such as shown in figure 11.7. There is a rapid increase in test performance at the lower age groups, a flattening effect in the teens and early twenties, followed by a gradual decrease in performance. The average sixty-five-year-old does about as well on the test as the average ten-year-old. This again demonstrates the weakness of mental age norms to describe the performance of adults.

Mental age can be computed by either of two procedures. On tests such as the Stanford-Binet, where tasks are arranged by age, the scoring depends on the number of items passed at each age level. The subject is tested from the lowest age at which all items are passed (called the *basal age*) to the age level at which all items are missed (*ceiling age*). Between the basal age and the ceiling age various months of credit are given, depending on the number of items that appear at each of these levels.

Table 11.2 shows how the MA is computed on the 1960 revision of the Stanford-Binet. Unless the examinee is known to be very bright or very dull, testing usually begins one age level below the subject's CA or chronological age. The testing of a four-year-old child would begin at level 3-6; an eight-year-

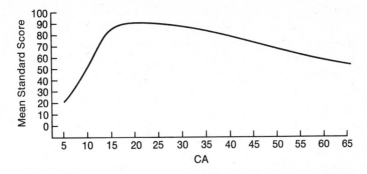

From David Wechsler, *The Measurement and Appraisal of Adult Intelligence*, Fourth Edition, p. 31, © 1958 by The Williams and Wilkins Company, Baltimore.

Figure 11.7. Increases and Declines in Mental Functioning from Ages 7–65 on the *Wechsler-Bellevue Scale*

old would start at the seven-year-old level. To illustrate, assume that the testing of a four-year-old child commenced at level 3-6. That age level has six items, and the child responded to five correctly. Items are arranged in half-year intervals from ages two through five, and because each one corresponds to one-sixth of the six-month interval, a correct response is given one month of credit. Since only five months of credit were earned at level 3-6, a basal age was not established, and the next lower level, level 3, was administered. At that level the subject responded correctly to all items, thus establishing a basal age of 3-0. indicating that he did at least as well as the average three-year-old.

Table 11.2. Computation of Mental Age on the 1960 Revision of the Stanford-Binet

Age Level	Number of Items	Number of Items Passed	Credit Years	Credit Months
8	6	0 (ceiling)		0
7	6	1		2
6	6	1		2
5	6	2		4
4-6	6	4		4
4	6	6		6
3-6	6	5		5
3	6	6 (basal)	3	—
		Total	3	23

Mental age = 4 years, 11 months

At age 4-0, the next level (the child already took level 3-6 and earned five months of credit), he responded correctly to all six items, giving him six months of additional credit beyond his basal age of 3-0. Beginning at age five, the six items for each age level, each worth two months' credit, are spread over a twelve-month period. At age five the subject had two items correct, yielding four months of credit. This process is continued until the subject misses all items at some age level. Two assumptions of this test are that additional testing beyond the ceiling age would only encourage frustration and would not result in additional credit and that the subject would respond correctly to all items *below*

Table 11.3. Age, Grade, and Deviation IQ Equivalents of Raw Scores on the Lorge-Thorndike Intelligence Test (1964), Verbal Battery, Form I, Level H (for CA 14–0)

Raw Score	Mental Age	Mental Age Grade Placement	Deviation IQ
1	8-6		62
2	8-8		64
3	8-11		65
4	9-1		67
5	9-4		68
6	9-6	4.1	70
7	9-8	4.3	72
8	9-11	4.6	73
9	10-1	4.8	75
10	10-4	5.0	77
11	10-6	5.2	78
12	10-9	5.4	80
13	11-0	5.7	82
14	11-3	5.9	83
15	11-6	6.2	85
16	11-9	6.4	86
17	12-0	6.7	88
18	12-3	7.0	91
19	12-6	7.2	93
20	12-8	7.4	94
21	12-11	7.6	95
22	13-1	7.8	96
23	13-4	8.0	97
24	13-6	8.2	98
25	13-9	8.4	99
26	14-0	8.6	100
27	14-3	8.9	101
28	14-6	9.1	102
29	14-8	9.3	103
30	14-11	9.5	105
31	15-1	9.6	106
32	15-4	9.7	107
33	15-6	9.9	108
34	15-8	10.0	109
35	15-10	10.2	111
36	16-0	10.4	112
37	16-2	10.6	113
38	16-4	10.8	114
39	16-6	11.0	115
40	16-9	11.2	116
41	17-0	11.5	117
42	17-3	11.7	118
43	17-6	12.0	119
44	17-10	12.2	119
45	18-2		120
46	18-6		121

Lorge, Thorndike, and Hagen 1964, pp. 56 (deviation IQ), 62 (mental age grade placement, 64 (mental age).

his basal age if these were administered. Generally these assumptions are reasonable since tasks are graded according to difficulty level, but exceptions do occur.

On all group tests and on some individual tests of intelligence, mental age is determined directly by tables that convert the number of correct responses to the average chronological age of persons obtaining that score. For example, if the average CA of persons obtaining thirty correct items on an intelligence test is 14-11, any other person who attains thirty correct items will have an MA of 14-11. Table 11.3 shows how age, grade, and deviation IQ norms relate to various raw scores on the Lorge-Thorndike Intelligence Test for fourteen-year-olds. A raw score of twenty-six corresponds to an MA of 14-0, a mental age grade placement of 8.6, and a deviation IQ of 100.* Other tables on the Lorge-Thorndike provide CA norms other than 14-0.

In summary, MA norms have the following characteristics:

1. They represent a level of attainment and not a relative index of brightness unless they are compared to the individual's CA.
2. They assume increases in test performance as a function of age.
3. Mental age curves flatten out when the tests are given to adults and decrease among older persons. At those age levels these norms do not meet the assumption of increasing performance with increases in age.
4. Mental age may be computed by giving credit to all items passed above a basal age or by using a norm table that provides age equivalents for different scores.

Grade Norms

The grade level at which a person is functioning on an intelligence test is called his *mental age grade placement* (MAGP) or *intelligence grade placement* (IGP). MAGP or IGP is simply a way of indicating the grade level in school that corresponds to a given mental age. Referring to table 11.3, teachers could report that a child has an MA of 10-4 or that he is performing at the fifth-grade level on an intelligence test. Since most children start school when they are five or six years old, teachers can usually estimate MAGP or IGP by subtracting five and one-half years from the child's MA.

Table 11.3 is a typical example of how test manuals present age and grade norms on intelligence tests. Because the two types of norms are derived in almost identical ways, they can be easily interchanged. Age norms, of course, can be developed before the child enters school, whereas grade norms encompass only the years that children attend school. All the difficulties inherent in age norms on intelligence tests are also present with grade norms.

One distinction between age norms and grade norms is that age norms

---

* The meaning of *mental age grade placement* and *deviation IQ* will be described later in this chapter.

are based on a twelve-month year, whereas grade norms are divided into ten parts, each corresponding to a month of the academic year. To help distinguish between these norms, MA is usually represented by a number such as 12-4, meaning that the child obtained the same number of items correct as the average child of twelve years, four months of age. Grade norms, in contrast, are represented by a number such as 4.7 where the number to the left of the decimal stands for year in school (i.e., fourth *grade*), and the number to the right stands for months. In the fourth grade, for example, the range of grade equivalents would be 4.0, 4.1, . . . , 4.8, and 4.9.

Quotient and Standard Score (Deviation IQ) Norms

Whether a child with an MA of 6-0 is "bright" or not depends on his chronological age. Many older intelligence tests directly compared MA with CA to yield an *IQ,* or *intelligence quotient.* In formula form, the intelligence quotient was given as

$$IQ = \frac{MA \text{ (mental age)}}{CA \text{ (chronological age)}} \times 100$$

Multiplication by 100 eliminated decimals.

The simplest way to use the formula is to convert both MA and CA to months. A child with an MA of 10-5 who is eight years and ten months old has an IQ of

$$\frac{125}{106} \times 100 = 118$$

(carried out to two places and rounded).

For a number of good reasons, the use of quotients has all but disappeared on newer intelligence tests. On some older tests, such as the 1937 revision of the Stanford-Binet, the means and standard deviations varied greatly at each age level. For example, at age two and one-half, the mean IQ was 105 and the standard deviation was 20 points; at age six, the mean was 100 and the standard deviation 13. These different means and standard deviations at each age level made interpretation difficult. At age levels two and one-half and six, a child who was two standard deviations above the mean would obtain IQs of 145 and 126, respectively. The limitations inherent in mental age norms also suggested the need to modify the traditional intelligence quotient, which led to the development of *deviation IQs.*

Deviation IQs are standard scores that yield a constant mean and standard deviation. The mean on all deviation IQ scales is 100, and depending on the test, the standard deviation is either 15 or 16. By keeping the mean and standard deviation equal at all age levels (Terman and Merrill 1960, pp. 27–28):

(a) a given IQ now indicates the same relative ability at different ages,
(b) a subject's IQ score, ignoring errors of measurement, remains the same from one age to another unless there is a change in ability level, and
(c) a given change in IQ indicates the same amount of change in relative standing regardless of the ability level of the subject.

Table 11.3 shows some of the deviation IQs that correspond to various raw scores on the Lorge-Thorndike Intelligence Test for children having CAs of 14-0. For example, twenty-six items correct is average for fourteen-year-olds and is equivalent to a deviation IQ of 100.

Some Examples of Individual Intelligence Tests

Individual Tests

The 1960 revision of the Stanford-Binet Intelligence Scale   The latest revision of the Stanford-Binet was published in 1960. Some items from earlier editions were eliminated or modified, and other items were relocated at different age levels. The greatest change was the replacement of quotient IQs with deviation IQs. Six items appear at half-year age levels from ages two through 4-6, at each year level from ages five through fourteen, and at Superior Adult I, Superior Adult II, and Superior Adult III levels, and eight items appear for Average Adult.

Table 11.4 samples items at different age levels from the 1960 Stanford-Binet. The manual indicates to the examiner what materials to use, what procedures to follow in administering items, the criterion for successful item performance, and scoring standards.

Administering the Stanford-Binet is the responsibility of a qualified psychologist or school counselor. Many universities have courses that instruct advanced students in education and psychology in methods of administering, scoring, and interpreting individual tests of intelligence. Unless testing is conducted under the same conditions faced by the norm group, test scores will have little meaning. Not only must the examiner be thoroughly familiar with the test itself, but supervised practice is necessary. Since the test is given orally, the examiner must score each response as "passed" or "failed" and in some instances (where allowed or required), he must question the subject for additional information. It is important that the teacher be able to understand psychological reports of students tested with the Stanford-Binet.

Table 11.4. Examples of Items Appearing at Different Age Levels on the 1960 Revision of the Stanford-Binet

Year IV

1. **Picture Vocabulary:** Subject (S) is asked to name at least fourteen objects out of eighteen. Each object is on a 2" × 4" card.
2. **Naming Objects from Memory:** Three small objects are placed in front of S and each is identified. S closes his eyes, one object is hidden, and S is asked to name the hidden object.
3. **Opposite Analogies I:** S is to respond correctly to two out of five opposite analogies such as "Brother is a boy; sister is a . . ."
4. **Pictorial Identification:** S must identify at least three out of six pictures on a card such as "Show me the one that we cook on."
5. **Discrimination of Forms:** S must match at least eight out of ten forms with those on a card.
6. **Comprehension II:** S must respond correctly to questions such as "Why do we have houses?" and "Why do we have books?"

Year VIII

1. **Vocabulary:** S must define at least eight words.
2. **Memory for Stories:** "The Wet Fall": S must recall the answers to at least five out of six questions asked about a story just read.
3. **Verbal Absurdities I:** S is asked to indicate what is foolish about four sentences such as "A man had flu (influenza) twice. The first time it killed him, but the second time he got well quickly."
4. **Similarities and Differences:** S indicates how at least three pairs of two terms each are the same and how they are different.
5. **Comprehension IV:** See year IV, item 6. At year VIII the questions are more difficult, such as "What makes a sailboat move?"
6. **Naming the Days of the Week:** S must name the days of the week in correct sequence and indicate which day comes before three that are named by the examiner.

Year XII

1. **Vocabulary:** S must define at least fifteen words.
2. **Verbal Absurdities II:** More complex statements of the type at year VIII, item 3.
3. **Picture Absurdities II:** "The Shadow": S must indicate the absurdity of a picture showing a shadow pointed in the wrong direction from the sun.
4. **Repeating Five Digits Reversed:** S must repeat backward five digits given one second apart.
5. **Abstract Words I:** S must define an abstract word such as *pity*.
6. **Minkus Completion I:** S is to fill in one word in a blank to complete a sentence such as "The streams are dry . . . there has been little rain."

Superior Adult II

1. **Vocabulary:** S must define at least twenty-six words.
2. **Finding Reasons III:** S must give three reasons that justify an act or deed.
3. **Proverbs II.** S must tell the meaning of proverbs.
4. **Ingenuity I:** S is required to solve "water jar" problems—i.e., given two containers of different sizes, he is to bring back a certain amount of water from a river.
5. **Essential Differences:** S must indicate the essential difference between two abstract words such as *work* and *play*.
6. **Repeating Thought of Passage I:** Value of Life: S must repeat at least four out of seven essential points made in a paragraph from memory.

Terman and Merrill 1960, pp. 343, 344, 345.

Table 11.5. Distribution of the 1937 Standardization Group

IQ Ranges	Percent	Classification
160–169	.03	Very superior
150–159	.2	
140–149	1.1	
130–139	3.1	Superior
120–129	8.2	
110–119	18.1	High average
100–109	23.5	Normal or average
90–99	23.0	
80–89	14.5	Low average
70–79	5.6	Borderline defective
60–69	2.0	Mentally defective
50–59	.4	
40–49	.2	
30–39	.03	

Terman and Merrill 1960, p. 18.

The interpretation of Stanford-Binet scores reflects the interaction of clinical judgment and knowledge about the reliability and validity of the measurements. Clinical classifications for Stanford-Binet IQs were included in the 1937 revision (see table 11.5). Note that about half (46.5 percent) the population have IQs in the average range and that almost 65 percent have scores between the low and high average categories.

The reliability of the Stanford-Binet is highly satisfactory. As with most intelligence tests, reliability is higher for older children than for younger children and higher for duller persons than for brighter ones. In other words, the greatest degree of reliability is obtained if the child is both below average in IQ and older. For example, the stability and equivalence (over a week's time) was reported as .83 for IQs between 140 and 149 and .91 for IQs between 60 and 69 at ages two and a half to five and a half; at ages six to thirteen, the reliability varies from .91 for the higher IQs to .97 for the lower scores. Over a ten-year period retest correlations are about .65.

The Stanford-Binet is a very good predictor of school performance since most of the correlations are somewhere between .40 and .75, depending on the grade level and subject being correlated. Correlations are somewhat higher for English and reading than for mathematics (Anastasi 1968).

The Wechsler Adult Intelligence Scale (WAIS)

Dissatisfaction with the use of age norms for adults on the earlier revisions of the Stanford-Binet led David Wechsler to construct an adult scale utilizing deviation IQs. In 1939 he published the Wechsler-Bellevue Intelligence Scale, named after Bellevue Hospital, where he was chief psychologist. The purposes of the scale were (1) to avoid the use of the MA, (2) to reduce the effect of speed, which tends to handicap adults, (3) to devise tasks more interesting to adults, and (4) to increase the diagnostic usefulness of the scale by yielding both verbal and performance scales.

In 1955 the Wechsler-Bellevue was revised and retitled the Wechsler Adult Intelligence Scale (WAIS, pronounced Wāce). It was specifically designed for persons sixteen years of age and older. Items are arranged by separate subtests rather than by ages, and scores are converted to deviation IQs by the use of tables.

The *verbal scale* of the WAIS is composed of six subtests:

1. *Information:* General knowledge questions on a wide variety of topics arranged in ascending order of difficulty. Designed to measure knowledge generally available to most segments of the population.
2. *Comprehension:* A test designed to measure practical judgment and information; for example, "Why should people pay taxes?"
3. *Arithmetic:* Word problems requiring a minimum amount of computational skills.
4. *Similarities:* Consists of thirteen pairs of words; the examinee is required to indicate how each pair is the same.
5. *Digit span:* Repetition from memory of digits repeated both forward and backward.
6. *Vocabulary:* Examinee is required to define general terms.

The *performance scale* consists of five subtests:

1. *Digit symbol:* A code-substitution task where the examinee is required to insert an abstract symbol in a blank space that is underneath a numeral within one and one-half minutes. A key showing which symbol corresponds to each of nine numerals is given at the top of the page.
2. *Picture completion:* The examinee must indicate what part of a picture is missing.
3. *Block design:* The examinee must copy designs by arranging blocks having white, red, and diagonally bisected red-white sides to correspond with examples in a booklet.
4. *Picture arrangement:* Consists of eight different series of cartoon strips, each of which is presented in disarranged order; the examinee must rearrange the cards into a correct sequence.
5. *Object assembly:* Consists of puzzles of different degrees of complexity.

The following are typical of Wechsler questions.*

General information: How many nickels make a dime?
General comprehension: Why is copper often used in electrical wires?
Arithmetic: Three men divided eighteen golf balls equally among them-
    selves. How many golf balls did each man receive?
Similarities: In what way are a lion and a tiger alike?

The WAIS yields a verbal, performance, and full scale IQ. Raw scores on each subtest are converted to standard scores having a mean of 10 and a standard deviation of 3, making it possible to compare the various subtest scores. The six standard scores on the verbal scale and the five on the performance scale can then be summed and converted to a full scale deviation IQ.

Generally the internal consistency reliability is higher for the verbal scale than for the performance scale. Wechsler (1955, p. 103) reports reliabilities as low as .65 for object assembly to .94 for vocabulary for a sample of eighteen- to nineteen-year-olds. The internal consistencies are given as: verbal IQ, .96; performance, .93; and full scale, .97. These values are highly satisfactory.

The use of separate verbal and performance scales assumes a low correlation between them. Wechsler reports verbal-performance correlations of .77 for eighteen- to nineteen-year-olds and .81 for forty-five- to fifty-four-year-olds. These values are much too high to assume that the two scales are independent.

Relatively little evidence is available on the validity of the WAIS. The full scale seems to be the best predictor of the amount of education, the correlation being .72 for forty-five- to fifty-four-year-olds. It also appears that the WAIS correlates highly with the 1937 edition of the Stanford-Binet (.85 with full scale WAIS; .80 with verbal WAIS; and .69 with the performance scale) (Wechsler 1955, p. 105). If the WAIS has any advantage over the Stanford-Binet for young persons aged sixteen to twenty-six, it is probably that it has a performance scale that can correlate with nonverbal criteria. However, the relatively high correlation between verbal and performance IQs probably obviates most of this advantage.

The Wechsler Intelligence Scale
for Children (WISC)

In 1949 Wechsler adapted the Wechsler-Bellevue test to measure the intelligence of children between the ages of five and fifteen. The Wechsler

---

* Examples courtesy of The Psychological Corporation, New York, N.Y. The student should understand that many psychological tests must be kept secure to avoid their becoming invalidated. These examples, therefore, are similar but not identical to those found on the WAIS.

Intelligence Scale for Children (WISC, pronounced wĭsk), like the WAIS, yields a verbal, performance, and full scale IQ. The verbal and performance scales contain the following subtests (see figure 11.8 for an example of a WISC-type picture arrangement test and figure 11.9 for an example of a WISC-type picture completion test):

Verbal	Performance
1. General information	1. Picture completion
2. General comprehension	2. Picture arrangement
3. Arithmetic	3. Block design
4. Similarities	4. Object assembly
5. Vocabulary (digit span)	5. Coding (or mazes)

Figure 11.8. Example of WISC–type Picture Arrangement Test

Figure 11.9. Example of WISC–type Picture Completion Test

Digit span is an alternate or supplementary test that may be used when a verbal subtest has been invalidated (perhaps because of administrative error). Maze tracing may be substituted for coding, added as a supplementary test, or used instead of any invalidated performance subtest. The scoring, however, uses only five verbal and five performance subtests. Scoring on the WISC is identical to that on the WAIS.

The reliability coefficients (split-half) tend to be higher for the verbal IQ than for the performance IQ and for older subjects than for younger. At age thirteen and one-half, the full scale reliability is .94.

In a review of twenty-one correlations between WISC verbal, performance, and full scale IQs and Stanford-Binet IQs, William Littell (1960, p. 136) found median correlations of .80, .66, and .81, respectively.

Almost no investigations have been conducted on the predictive validity of the WISC. Indeed, the WISC manual does not even mention the word *validity*. In Littell's summary of studies conducted on the WISC, the median correlations with standardized achievement tests were .62, .53, and .66 for verbal, performance, and full scale IQs, respectively. These values compare favorably with validities reported on the Stanford-Binet (Littell, 1960, p. 142).

The Wechsler Preschool and Primary Scale of Intelligence (WPPSI)

In 1967 Wechsler developed the Wechsler Preschool and Primary Scale of Intelligence (WPPSI, pronounced wĭp′sē) for children between four and six and one-half years of age. With the exception of a few scales, the WPPSI and the WISC are very similar in construction, administration, and scoring. Some evidence has indicated that the WISC is too difficult for retarded children at ages five and six. The fact that the WISC has not been revised since 1949 makes it difficult to interpret WISC IQ scores.

One improvement of the WPPSI over the Binet is the inclusion of non-whites in the norm group. This is particularly valuable when the test is administered to preschool and primary minority children. Unfortunately the items appear too difficult for below-average four-year-olds, no matter what their racial extraction is. For diagnosing mental retardation, the Binet still holds the advantage at the lower age and grade levels.

The reliabilities (split-half) of the verbal, performance, and full scale IQs on the WPPSI are in the low .90s, indicating a high degree of internal consistency for each of the three scales. Stability over a three-month period was in the upper .80s and lower .90s for a group of five-year-olds. At ages five and six WPPSI scores correlated .76 with the 1960 revision of the Stanford-Binet, suggesting that both tests measure essentially the same factors.

Group Tests of Intelligence

No attempt will be made to describe all the group tests of intelligence now available—Buros (1961) reported the availability of 170 different ones—but summary data and information on tests most often used in education are given.

Reliability and Validity of Group Intelligence Tests

Most manuals for group intelligence tests provide information concerning reliability, particularly internal consistency. These values are typically around .90, the correlations being somewhat higher for secondary students than for elementary school students. Alternate-form reliabilities (equivalence) are often in the .90s, indicating a high degree of correspondence between forms. Usually less adequate information is provided for stability.

Manuals for group tests of intelligence—like those for individual tests—tend to provide little information about validity. Much information concerning reliability and validity appears in technical supplements that are not readily available to teachers or administrators.

Group intelligence tests usually correlate highly with each other (.70 to .90) and less highly with teacher grades (.40 to .70), depending on the maturity of students and the nature of the subject. Total scores are almost always more valid than part or subtest scores. Verbal scores tend to correlate higher with English, science, reading, and social studies grades, whereas nonverbal scores correlate higher with mathematics grades.

Uses of Group Tests of Intelligence

Group intelligence tests are usually used for screening individuals who may be in need of special educational or psychological services. Low scores on these tests can mean that (1) the child has a low level of ability, (2) he is unable to read the items on the examination, or (3) he is unmotivated to take the test. Problems of motivation and reading can sometimes be eliminated by the oral administration of individual tests. Thus low performance on a group IQ test coupled with low school performance usually calls for the administration of the Stanford-Binet or one of the Wechsler tests.

Types of Items on Group
Intelligence Tests

Many group intelligence tests use similar types of items. At the lower age and grade levels these items are usually pictorial. The teacher reads directions for each item to the children and students respond by circling or putting an X on the correct alternative. At the upper grade levels the teacher may read the directions but the students are expected to read items on their own. Marks may be made on the test booklet or on answer sheets designed for machine scoring.

The following types of items are found on many group intelligence tests:

1. *Vocabulary:* Selecting the correct meaning of a term from several choices
2. *Sentence completion:* Selecting a word or phrase that best completes a sentence
3. *Arithmetic:* Solving word problems
4. *Verbal similarities:* Showing how two or more words are the same
   calf : cow*
   A. puppy : dog   B. nest : bird   C. horse : bull   D. shell : turtle
5. *Verbal opposites:* Showing how two words differ
6. *Verbal sequencing:* Indicating what precedes or follows a day of the week, month of the year, and so forth
7. *Discrimination of differences:* Selecting a word or picture that does not belong in a series (see figure 11.10)

---

* Example 1, SCAT, Series II, Form 3A. Copyright © 1966 by Educational Testing Service. All rights reserved. Reprinted by permission.

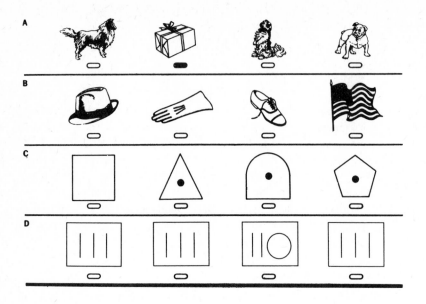

Figure 11.10. Example of Otis-Lennon Elementary I Test, Form J

8. *Proverbs:* Interpretation of proverbs
9. *Sentencing arrangement:* Rearranging scrambled words to make a sentence
10. *Inference:* Deducing the correct conclusion from a major and minor premise
    L. All four-footed creatures are animals.
       All horses are four-footed.
       Therefore,
       1. creatures other than horses can walk.
       2. all horses can walk.
       3. all horses are animals.*
11. *Delayed recall:* Answering a series of questions after a story has been read
    N. The story read to you a while ago was concerned with
       1. politics.
       2. conservation.

---

* From California Test of Mental Maturity, Level 3, devised by Elizabeth T. Sullivan, Willis W. Clark, and Ernest W. Tiegs. Copyright © 1961 by McGraw-Hill Book Co., Inc. Reproduced by permission of the publisher, CTB/McGraw-Hill Book Co., Del Monte Research Park, Monterey, California 93940. All rights reserved. Printed in the U.S.A.

3. fire prevention.
4. international relations.**

12. *Following directions:* Performing an act in accordance with directions

13. *Deducing consequences:* Judging the most likely consequence of an act

14. *Figure relationships:* Selecting a figure that logically completes a sequence

00.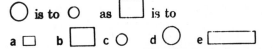

Lorge-Thorndike Intelligence Tests, Level 5, Form B, NonVerbal Battery, Houghton Mifflin Company, 1954. Reproduced by permission of the publisher.

Figure 11.11. Example of an item from Lorge-Thorndike Intelligence Tests. Find the drawing at the right that goes with the first three.

15. *Figure analogies:* Perceiving relationships among forms of different shapes and sizes

Sample Z

○ **is to** ○ **as** ☐ **is to**

a ☐ b ☐ c ○ d ○ e ▭   Z

The right answer is choice a so the answer space under a in row Z has been marked.

Reproduced from Otis-Lennon Mental Ability Test, copyright © 1967 by Harcourt Brace Jovanovich, Inc. Reproduced by special permission of the publisher.

Figure 11.12

** Ibid.

16. *Right and left:* Judging whether a picture shows a right or left part of an object or person

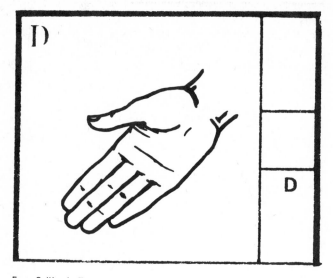

Figure 11.13

17. *Number series:* Indicating which number is misplaced in a series or which number completes a sequence (2, 4, 6, 8, . . . ?)
18. *Manipulation of areas:* Counting the number of objects in three-dimensional space

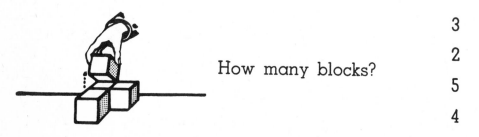

How many blocks?

3

2

5

4

Figure 11.14

Except for number series, sensing right and left, and manipulation of areas, all these types appear at some age level on the Stanford-Binet. These examples do not exhaust the variety of items, most of which require some form of reasoning and language ability. Many group intelligence tests are similar in format to individual tests.

Table 11.6 describes five of the best known and most often used group intelligence tests. It is assumed that before *any* test is selected or interpretations of scores are offered a thorough review of the test and its manual will have been made using the criteria developed in chapter 10.

Table 11.6. Descriptions of Representative Group Intelligence Tests

Test	Grade Levels	Norms	Number of Forms	Subtests
California Test of Mental Maturity (CTMM)	K to adult	MA, dev. IQ, percentiles, stanines, T scores	1	Language, nonlanguage, total
Cooperative School and College Ability Test (SCAT)	4–14	Percentile bands	2	Verbal, quantitative, total
Henmon-Nelson Tests of Mental Ability	3–12	MA, dev. IQ, percentiles, MAGP	2	Total score only
Lorge-Thorndike Intelligence Tests	3–12 or 13	MA, dev. IQ, percentiles, MAGP	2	Verbal, nonverbal
Otis-Lennon Mental Ability Test	K-12	Dev. IQ, percentiles, stanines	2	Total score only

Summary

1. The systematic study of individual differences began with the dismissal of the astronomer Kinnebrook for failing to observe stellar transits accurately. In 1816 another astronomer, Bessel, began to study individual differences in reaction time. Sir Francis Galton's study of individual differences in "abilities" is often considered the beginning of the study of intellectual differences.

2. Compulsory education in France led Alfred Binet to develop intellectual tasks that could be used to differentiate among those who needed special classes for the retarded from those who could profit from regular classroom

instruction. Binet's first test was published in 1905 and was revised in the year of his death, 1911. Henry Goddard published English translations of the Binet scales in 1908 and 1911; Louis M. Terman of Stanford University restandardized these tests in 1916 and in 1937. The last standardization was by Maud Merrill in 1960. Since World War I the demand for group tests has increased rapidly.

3. Intelligence may be defined by function (the purpose of intelligence), by origin (whether intelligence is hereditary or produced by environment), and by structure (the abilities that compose intelligence).

4. Operationally, intelligence is an inferred ability and is not measured directly by any test. Since each intelligence test contains different items or tasks, an individual may have as many "intelligences" as there are tests unless it is possible to discover the factors that are common to all intelligence tests.

5. Charles Spearman, a British psychologist, was the first person to study mathematically the elements of intelligence that seemed common to all tests. According to his "general-factor theory of intelligence," intelligence could be accounted for primarily by what he called *g*—the general ability to educe relationships. To account for the lack of a perfect correlation among different tests of intelligence, Spearman postulated *s,* or specific factors unique to each intelligence test. The *s* factors simply accounted for differences among tests of intelligence, but it was *g* that determined "mental capacity." Spearman later modified his theory to include "group factors," which were thought of as being correlated specific factors.

6. Three major multiple-factor theories of intelligence have been described.

   a. E. L. Thorndike's position regarding intelligence developed out of his theory of learning. Each stimulus-response connection yields a slightly new aspect of learning, and since there are many such connections, no single factor can account for them all. The intelligent individual is one who is capable of making a great number of connections.

   b. L. L. Thurstone's position, which has been most widely held among American psychologists, is that intelligence can be accounted for by a relatively small number of "primary mental abilities."

   c. J. P. Guilford has proposed a "structure of intellect" theory. According to this position, intelligence consists of 120 separate traits or abilities. These are usually represented by a cube, where one side consists of five types of "mental operations," another side consists of four types of "content," and the third side of six types of "products."

7. Whether intelligence is primarily attributable to hereditary or environmental factors has been the subject of much debate. The evidence is often of the following types:

a. *Co-twin control studies.* In these studies identical twins (i.e., those having identical heredity) who are reared in different environments are compared on intelligence tests. Results of these studies are equivocal because it is rare that identical twins are placed in different environments. When they have been, however, differences are greatest among twins having vastly different educational backgrounds.

b. *Foster children studies.* There is some evidence that the correlation between the intelligence of foster children and that of their foster parents is somewhat lower than the correlation between the intelligence of children and that of their biological parents when they have been raised by their biological parents. Although this argues for a hereditary component to intelligence, there might be differences in the ways that foster parents and biological parents raise their children.

c. *Environmental change studies.* There is evidence that marked changes in the environment can modify intelligence test scores. Individuals who had been isolated from all human contact since the time of birth showed marked increases in mental functioning when the environment was improved. But the data from many of these studies are suspect because accurate records were not kept. There is some evidence that improving environmental conditions leads to higher intelligence test scores and that sterile environments reduce these scores. The position taken in this text is that intelligence probably depends on both heredity and environment, but that the exact contributions of each are unknown.

8. Some correlates of intelligence are:

a. *Intelligence and education.* Relatively high correlations are found between IQ scores and the highest level of education completed. There is some evidence that attending school increases IQ scores. Because of the high correlations between IQ and achievement test scores (particularly in the secondary grades), there is doubt whether there is much difference between the two measures at those levels.

b. *Intelligence and clinical diagnosis.* Intelligence tests have been used successfully as an adjunct to clinical diagnosis of mental deficiency. Sometimes, however, scores on these tests have been used as diagnostic "signs" to differentiate subjects in special clinical categories, such as "brain-damaged," from "normal" subjects. Intelligence tests have not been particularly beneficial for these purposes.

c. *Intelligence and socioeconomic status.* Socioeconomic measures and intelligence test scores correlate positively. In general, the higher the socioeconomic level of the parents is, the higher will be the IQ scores of the children. Although the mean IQ differs depending on one's occupation, the variability within each occupation is much greater than differences between occupations.

d. *Intelligence and ethnic background.* Although there are tested differences in the mean IQs of blacks and whites, there are disagreements on what these differences mean. Arthur Jensen's recent arguments on the hereditary nature of intelligence have raised both procedural and ethical questions regarding the meaning of such differences.

e. *Intelligence and sex.* Items that tend to favor one sex over another are usually eliminated on intelligence tests or are balanced to make test results equal for the sexes.

9. Intelligence tests yield age, grade, quotient, and standard score norms. Age norms are called mental ages (MA); they assume that students will attain higher scores as they increase in age. MA tends to increase rapidly and then to flatten out at the "age of arrest." MAs can be computed either by giving partial credit for items responded to correctly between a person's basal age and ceiling age or by examining a norm table. Grade norms have many of the same characteristics as age norms, with the following exceptions: grade norms on intelligence tests are based on a ten-month school year rather than on a twelve-month year, and grade norms can encompass only those years in which children are in school. The traditional IQ as a ratio of MA/CA times 100 has been abandoned on virtually all the newer intelligence tests in favor of deviation IQ norms, described in chapter 6.

10. The 1960 revision of the Stanford-Binet tends to have very high reliability coefficients and satisfactory validity coefficients. Only a total score is reported on the Stanford-Binet.

11. The Wechsler Adult Intelligence Scale is designed for persons of sixteen years of age or older. It contains verbal and performance Scales, but these tend to correlate highly with each other.

12. The Wechsler Intelligence Scale for Children was developed in 1949 and has not been revised. It is designed for children from ages five to fifteen years. Reliabilities and validity coefficients are satisfactory.

13. The latest test developed by Wechsler is the Wechsler Preschool and Primary Scale of Intelligence, which was designed for children between four and six and one-half years of age. It therefore overlaps with the Stanford-Binet; however, the Wechsler test includes blacks in the norm group. For below-average four-year-olds, the Binet is recommended over the Wechsler.

14. The various group tests of intelligence that are available contain similar types of items. The reliabilities of these tests tend to be high, although much less information is provided regarding their validity. Most of these tests correlate highly among themselves but less highly with more subjective ratings such as teachers' marks. Group tests are often given to discover persons who should be given individual tests.

Suggested Readings

Albert, Robert S. "Genius: Present-Day Status of the Concept and Its Implications for the Study of Creativity and Giftedness." *American Psychologist* 24, no. 8 (August 1969): 743–53. Summarizes the history and current status of studies on genius. The bibliography is extensive.

Burt, Cyril. "Inheritance of General Intelligence." *American Psychologist* 27, no. 3 (March 1972): 175–90. Cyril Burt was a British psychologist who, in the Spearman tradition, was an advocate of a *g,* or general ability factor. This article is rich in history.

Jenkins, James J., and Paterson, Donald G., eds. *Studies in Individual Differences: The Search for Intelligence.* New York: Appleton-Century-Crofts, 1961, 774 pp. Perhaps the best compendium of original articles written on the measurement and understanding of intelligence from Francis Galton to J. P. Guilford.

Light, Richard J., and Smith, Paul V. "Statistical Issues in Social Allocation Models of Intelligence: A Review and a Response." *Review of Educational Research* 41, no. 4 (October 1971): 351–67. Except for the appendix, this is a highly readable article on the nature-nurture question as it relates to intelligence. Students interested in this problem may want to read Jensen's article in the *Harvard Educational Review* 39 (1969): 1–123. William Shockley's article in the *Review of Educational Research* immediately follows the one by Light and Smith. Shockley's position has been a major source of controversy.

McNemar, Quinn. "Lost: Our Intelligence? Why?" *American Psychologist* 19, no. 12 (December 1964): 871–82. Another article in favor of a general intelligence factor by a highly respected statistician and psychologist.

The Measurement of Aptitudes

12 Tests have developed from man's need to solve practical problems in the clinic, in industry, and in the schools. The preceding chapter discussed how intelligence tests were originally devised to place children into special classes for the retarded. When they are used to predict general academic achievement, intelligence tests are often called tests of *scholastic aptitude.*

The purpose in administering aptitude tests is to predict how an individual will perform on some criterion before training or instruction is begun or before selection or placement decisions are made. Aptitude tests are cognitive measures used to predict success in specific courses (algebra, foreign languages, music) or in specific jobs (mechanic, stenographer, welder). High aptitudes may not always be either sufficient or desirable, as shown in the news article below.

Aptitude? Yes;
Trustworthy? No

MEMPHIS, Tenn.—(AP) —County penal farm officials wanted to find out how smart one of their prisoners was and he promptly showed them.

They sent [one inmate] to the Board of Education offices yesterday to take an aptitude test. While there, he escaped.*

---

* January 1, 1968. Used by permission of The Associated Press.

The differences between the terms *intelligence* and *scholastic aptitude* are not universally agreed upon. The position taken here is that when intelligence tests are used to predict academic achievement, either *scholastic aptitude* or *intelligence* may be used.

Tests such as the Stanford-Binet Intelligence Scale and the Wechsler Intelligence Scale for Children, which were designed to sample a wide variety of behaviors important in most cognitive tasks, are considered *global* or *general* aptitude measures; tests designed to predict success in more limited subjects (welding, music, and so forth) are *specific* aptitude measures.

Many tests used for prediction make no assumption of subsequent training or are not cognitive measures; therefore, these are *not* aptitude tests. Any test may be used for prediction, but aptitude is measured only if the test measures a cognitive skill and is used primarily for prediction, selection, or placement.

The Use of Aptitude Tests

Aptitude tests are used widely in schools. The counselor is concerned with the possibility that a child may have difficulty learning how to read, learning to do algebra, or being successful in foreign languages. Knowing which students are likely to experience problems in learning can help teachers plan remedial programs. Or teachers of art, music, and science may want to identify students who have high potentials in those subjects so that they can be offered advanced instruction.

"Well, since you put all the square pegs in the round holes, I'd suggest something requiring brute strength."

© Sidney Harris, used by permission.

Figure 12.1

Specific aptitude tests are particularly useful in making *placement* decisions (see figure 12.1). While global measures may be sufficient to indicate that a student has the general intellectual ability to succeed in many academic programs, measurement of more specific abilities, such as success in engineering, carpentry, or art, may require the construction or use of more specific aptitude tests.

The Differential Nature of Aptitudes

In general, aptitude measures are of value only if they correlate highly with criteria. These correlations between test scores and criteria indicate high predictive validity, a necessity for any aptitude test. But a practical consideration in selecting aptitude tests is the correlation of subtest scores with each other. High correlations mean that subtests measure the same abilities and thus duplicate each other. The ideal situation is to have each subtest correlate highly with a criterion but zero or negatively with the other subtests.

This chapter will frequently mention the Differential Aptitude Test (DAT) not only because it is widely used in junior and senior high schools but also because its manual provides much more information than most. A particularly refreshing feature of the manual is its detailed, candid analyses of the test's strengths and weaknesses.

The DAT provides a table showing the average intercorrelations among subtests (see table 12.1). Note, for example, that although some of the subtests have low correlations (.19 between clerical speed and accuracy [CSA] and verbal reasoning [VR]), other correlations are quite high (.74 between grammar [GR] and verbal reasoning). At least on the criterion of low subtest intercorrelations, the clerical speed and accuracy subtest seems highly desirable. But the primary criterion for the differential measurement of aptitude is high predictive

Table 12.1. Mean Intercorrelation Coefficients of the DAT for Boys, Form L (*N* = 913)

	NA	AR	CSA	MR	SR	SP	GR
Verbal reasoning (VR)	.70	.68	.19	.55	.58	.59	.74
Numerical ability (NA)		.66	.36	.50	.53	.60	.66
Abstract reasoning (AR)			.33	.59	.63	.41	.58
Clerical speed and accuracy (CSA)				.16	.28	.29	.21
Mechanical reasoning (MR)					.62	.27	.46
Space relations (SR)						.31	.46
Spelling (SP)							.65
Grammar (GR)							

validity. On this criterion the weakness of the subtests is most apparent. Clerks should obtain high CSA scores, yet they perform no better on this subtest than do other kinds of workers.* In addition, the verbal reasoning and numerical ability subtests seem to differentiate best among various *levels* of performance, no matter what the occupation, and this combination is included in almost all intelligence tests.

Reliability of Aptitude Measures

Generally measures of internal consistency reliabilities (split-half and Kuder-Richardson) tend to be quite high for aptitude measures. On the DAT most of the split-half reliabilities are in the upper .80s and lower .90s. Reliabilities tend to increase with increasing grade levels (from grade 8 to grade 12 on the DAT), and differences in reliability are small between the sexes. The highest reliabilities are obtained for space relations, spelling, verbal reasoning, and numerical ability; the lowest is for mechanical reasoning.

Even over relatively long periods, stability coefficients on the DAT tend to be rather high. These coefficients vary from .59 (space relations) to .87 (verbal reasoning) for boys over a three-year interval between the ninth and twelfth grades.

Validity of Aptitude Measures

The crucial question for all aptitude measures is *predictive validity,* or the extent to which measures can predict a criterion. The problem, of course, is to find a reliable criterion. In education, grade point average is often used as a criterion, but the difficulty is that grades vary in meaning and emphasis between schools and among teachers within schools. If course content and grading standards parallel test content, the likelihood that tests will yield high validity coefficients will increase. But in another school and with different teachers the same test could yield negligible or even negative correlations with grades.

Again, the greatest amount of information on predictive validity using grades as the criterion comes from the DAT. Table 12.2 summarizes the median correlations between DAT subtest scores and grades in various school subjects

---

* It is possible, of course, for the CSA subtest to discriminate between good and poor clerical workers even though it does not differentiate among workers in different occupations. The manual for the DAT provides no evidence for or against this supposition, however.

for students in grades 9–12. The amount of time that elapsed between testing and marking varied from about three to nine months. The DAT manual also provides the various predictive validity studies for each subtest, which range from .83 to −.01. In almost every instance the best predictor was the combination of verbal reasoning and numerical ability—exactly the same types of items that appear on most intelligence tests. Evidently no matter what subtests are available, intelligence or scholastic aptitude is the best predictor of course grades.

Table 12.2. A Summary of Predictive Validity Coefficients between DAT Subtests and Course Grades for Boys and Girls in Grades 9–12*

Course	VR	NA	VR + NA	AR	CSA	MR	SR	SP	GR
English									
Boys	.49	.47	.54	.38	.27	.16	.29	.45	.50
Girls	.55	.52	.60	.45	.28	.28	.31	.48	.55
Mathematics									
Boys	.38	.50	.50	.39	.20	.23	.28	.27	.38
Girls	.41	.53	.54	.43	.20	.26	.32	.32	.40
Science									
Boys	.45	.44	.52	.38	.24	.29	.34	.36	.44
Girls	.54	.51	.59	.42	.25	.28	.34	.40	.48
Social studies									
Boys	.46	.46	.52	.34	.24	.16	.27	.38	.48
Girls	.52	.52	.58	.40	.28	.27	.33	.45	.50
Languages									
Boys	.44	.42	.54	.24	.13	.15	.22	.49	.50
Girls	.48	.40	.53	.26	.19	.19	.18	.48	.49
Commercial									
Boys	.37	.44	.42	.24	.28	.11	.21	.34	.39
Girls	.42	.49	.47	.40	.25	.22	.28	.45	.49

DAT manual, pp. 5-6 to 5-27. Copyright 1947, 1952, © 1959, 1963, 1966, 1968 by The Psychological Corporation, New York, N. Y. Reproduced by permission. All rights reserved.
* Time periods vary between three and nine months.

Even in the so-called nonacademic courses it appears that the VR+NA combination is one of the best predictors of course grades. In art, for example, the highest predictive validity coefficient for boys is .62 for the VR+NA combination, whereas the next best predictor is AR (.57). Essentially the same findings are relevant for girls.

Variations of programs among schools make it difficult to generalize, especially when some correlations are based on very small numbers of students. Still, it appears that the VR+NA combination is the single best score to use for predicting scholastic success in most courses. This seems to be true not only for relatively short-term predictions but also for predictions over a period of three and one-half years.

Correlations higher than those reported in table 12.2 are typically found when DAT scores are correlated with standardized achievement tests. Again, the VR+NA combination yields the highest correlations; the lowest correlations come from clerical speed and accuracy, mechanical reasoning, and space relations. But spelling and grammar are also good predictors if the criterion is a standardized achievement test rather than grades.

Generally predictive validity coefficients increase as the reliability of the criterion increases. Standardized tests of achievement, because they are more reliable than most teacher grades, tend to yield higher validity coefficients; subjective ratings are often so unreliable that few predictors can correlate with them. This implies that the validity is as dependent on the criterion as on the predictors.

When interpreting validity coefficients for aptitude measures, one must remember that restricting the range of ability lowers correlation coefficients. It is difficult for a test to predict when examinees are homogeneous with regard to the trait being measured, and correlations obtained from such a group are likely to be low. If only the top 5 percent of students are selected, for example, the range may be so restricted that validity coefficients might be close to 0. On the other hand, a policy of selecting everyone may yield high validity coefficients, but only for a group so divergent that almost any measure might distinguish the best from the least well prepared applicants.

Although most predictive correlations fall below .40, these correlations may have value in placing or selecting students. Figure 12.2, for example, shows the percentages of applicants who failed to complete and who successfully completed a training program for pilots and flight engineers, although previously

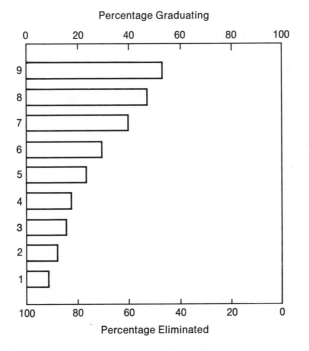

Figure 12.2. Percentage of Men Graduating from Pilot Training Related to Aptitude Score on Mechanical Principles (Flanagan, 1948. Face p. 83, No. 1) (N = 1017; r = .43)

obtained interview data indicated that all were qualified. The men with the highest aptitude scores successfully completed training to a much greater extent than those with lower stanine scores. Not only were training costs considerably reduced by selecting the more qualified trainees, but more effective decisions were made.

Norms on Aptitude Tests

Most aptitude tests provide percentiles and standard score norms such as stanines. Many provide separate norms for males and females, and others have norms for applicants and for those eventually hired.

Percentiles are useful norms as long as one considers the group with whom the subject is being compared. To argue that Johnny is at the 70th percentile on an engineering aptitude test has little meaning unless the teacher or counselor knows whether the comparison group is composed of applicants admitted into an engineering school who were eventually successful there or of applicants who later failed the engineering curriculum.

If sex is relevant to performance on the criterion, sex norms should be presented in the manual. For example, males typically score higher than females on mechanical reasoning and space relations on the DAT, whereas girls usually surpass boys on clerical speed and accuracy, spelling, and grammar. If separate norms were *not* provided, a boy might appear to be average in mechanical comprehension even though his percentile would be much lower if he were compared only with boys.

Reasons for Using Aptitude Tests

Selecting Individuals Using Aptitude Measures

One of the most important uses of aptitude tests is for *selection*. No method will guarantee either that all potentially successful persons will be admitted to a program or that all potential failures will be rejected. Errors in decision making are to be expected, but (hopefully) they will be minimized.

The *composite method* and the *cutoff method* are most often used in making selection decisions. A *composite selection strategy* means that scores from a number of tests are combined to maximize their correlation with a criterion. The test scores are combined by assigning weights that maximize the contribution of each score in predicting the criterion. The procedures for assigning weights are beyond the scope of this text, but the rationale is straightforward. Tests are included in a battery to measure different aspects of the criterion. A battery predicting teaching aptitude, for example, might include tests that measure skill in interpersonal relations, job-related knowledge, intelligence, interest, and other factors that correlate with teaching success. Concomitantly, tests that correlate with each other are excluded to prevent duplication of effort. The *regression formulas* used to assign these weights maximize the correlation between the composite test scores and criterion measures. Typically, including more than three or four predictors in a battery yields negligible gains.

If the composite method is used for selection, each individual is given a single value that represents a weighted composite score from all measures included in the battery. These scores are then ranked, and as many individuals as needed are selected.

With the cutoff method, scores for each individual are kept separate for each subtest that correlates with the criterion. Minimum passing scores are determined for *each* predictor test. Only individuals who pass every test—no matter what their total score is—are selected.

The decision to use one method of selection over another depends on a number of factors. Less effort and mathematical sophistication are required by the cutoff method. However, this method assumes that an individual who fails one subtest will not be successful no matter how well he performs on the remaining subtests; compensatory behavior is disregarded. This might be justifiable for some purposes. Consider commercial airline pilots: they must have good vision, be relatively immune to air sickness, have good spatial abilities, and be able to fly a plane. A serious deficiency in any one of these characteristics should justify the elimination of that person as a pilot.

For many other purposes, however, it is possible to compensate for a deficiency on one subtest by proficiency on another. A school might retain a faculty member who is known to encourage lively discussions among students even though his relationship with his peers might leave something to be desired. If the composite method is used for selection, an individual can be selected if he can compensate for low scores on some variables by high scores on others.

What constitutes minimum performance on an examination is largely a matter of judgment and practical considerations. If the number of applicants is small relative to the number needed, it may be necessary to take everyone who applies. If there is a large supply of individuals to select from, one can afford to be more selective.

The cutoff score is also affected by political, ethical, and social considerations. Setting a high cutting score for admission to a state university might eliminate those who are most likely to fail and could therefore reduce public expenditures for higher education. However, this monetary saving would come at a social cost to the state, particularly when social equality is a major national goal.

Advocates of low cutoff scores propose that everyone should have a chance to succeed regardless of test performance. Since tests are fallible measures, a low cutoff score will give some individuals the opportunity to surpass their predicted behavior. But this gain for a few individuals must be weighed against the probability that more students will fail.

Placing Individuals through the Use of Aptitude Measures

Many of the problems of making selection decisions are also present when aptitude tests are used for placement purposes. Placement decisions assume that individuals have been selected into the institution or organization and that some decision must be made regarding their optimum deployment.

It is instructive at this point to distinguish between two different attitudes toward placement. Some individuals take the position that placement decisions are entirely for the benefit of the organization, whether that organization is a school, a business, or a government agency. Individuals judged most capable for a job are forced into accepting positions that they may not particularly enjoy and that may not be the best for them. In times of national emergency, when men must be deployed optimally in short periods of time, this attitude is understandable and defensible, but at other times it is less defensible. An alternative approach is to consider placement decisions as the joint responsibility of the organization and the individual. This attitude is often expressed (and just as often disregarded) in counseling, where the responsibility of the teacher or counselor is to *interpret* the meaning of test scores without making decisions for the student. The predictive validity of most aptitude tests for placement purposes is too low to be used as a mandate for an examinee's course of action. The teacher or counselor might suggest alternatives to a student, but the ultimate responsibility for that decision is the student's.

Using Aptitude Tests for Diagnosis

If teachers know that students are likely to experience difficulty in learning, they can plan remedial exercises to increase the probability of success. Similarly, knowing that students already possess prerequisite knowledge can prevent teachers from wasting students' time by reteaching well-developed skills.

Aptitude tests have great applicability to the diagnosis of student problems. At the primary grades, for example, *readiness tests* are often administered to determine which children will probably experience difficulties in learning specific school subjects such as reading or arithmetic. At the high school level, foreign language aptitude tests may help determine which individuals possess the skills necessary to learn foreign languages.

Analyzing the errors students make on aptitude tests can help determine the best remedial procedures. A child who understands stories read to him and who can match vocabulary words with their corresponding pictures but who cannot differentiate between such letters as *p, d, q,* and *b* can be taught to make finer discriminations among letters and to attend to such factors as shape, size, upward and downward extensions, and direction.

Many carefully structured learning "packages" consist of a pretest, programmed learning sequences, and a posttest. To the extent that the pretest serves as a predictor of the level at which the student is functioning, it is serving as an aptitude measure. If it is also diagnostic in function, it should enable the teacher to select the most appropriate type of remediation for each child.

Using Aptitude Tests for Feedback

Aptitude tests have long been used by teachers and school counselors to inform students of their potential in such fields as medicine, art, and auto mechanics. Perhaps the best way to report such scores to students is by using expectancy tables (pages 220 and 221). Criterion measurements are listed along one dimension of the table (either across the top or on one side); predictor scores are listed along the other. In table 12.3 cell entries consist of

Table 12.3. Expectancy Table Showing Space Relations Scores and End-of-Course Grades in Watch Repairing

Number Receiving Each Grade						Raw Score	Pecentage Receiving Each Grade				
N	E	D	C	B	A		E	D	C	B	A
9				3	6	80–99				33	67
33			7	19	7	60–79			21	58	21
43	1	8	17	17		40–59	2	18	40	40	
14	3	5	4	2		20–39	21	36	29	14	
12	4	3	4	1		0–19	33	25	33	9	

the number and percentage of students earning different grades in a watch-repairing course predicted from raw scores on the spatial relations subtest of the Differential Aptitude Test. The correlation between spatial relations scores at the beginning of the course with final course grades is .69 for this particular group of 111 students.

Suppose that a student obtains a spatial relations raw score of 50. The teacher can show the student the expectancy table, can locate the raw score in the interval 40–59, and can note that *in the past* 80 percent of students with scores in that interval received grades of B or C in the course. As the teacher is able to gather more relevant information about the student (his motivation to become a watch repairer, his ability to manipulate small objects, obligations and responsibilities that might not allow him to complete the course), the student will be better able to decide whether or not he should attempt the program and his likelihood of success.

It should be noted from table 12.3 that 2 percent of the students in the range 40–59 did fail the watch repair program. With a larger number of cases, predictor scores should be grouped in intervals of less than 20 points, providing the teacher with more accurate predictions of criterion scores.

Another way of interpreting aptitude scores is to predict the most likely criterion score a student will earn based on knowledge of his aptitude test score. This prediction uses what is called a *regression equation,* which, in the following example, involves a single predictor* (e.g., spatial relations scores) used to estimate this student's most likely criterion score. The following information is needed to use a regression equation (figures in parentheses were computed from data in table 12.3):

1. r_{pc}, or the correlation between predictor and criterion scores (.69)
2. SD_c, or the standard deviation of criterion scores (1.08)
3. SD_p, or the standard deviation of predictor scores (21.6)
4. X_p, or any student's predictor score (50)
5. M_p, or the mean of the predictor scores (51.84)
6. M_c, or the mean of the criterion scores (2.32 where 4.0 = A, 3.0 = B, etc.)

The regression equation to predict X_c (the student's criterion grade point average) is

$$X_c = r_{pc}\left[\frac{SD_c}{SD_p}(X_p - M_p)\right] + M_c, \text{ or } X_c = .69\left[\frac{1.08}{21.6}(50 - 51.84)\right] + 2.32$$

This simplifies to $.69[.05(-1.84)] + 2.32 = .69[-.0920] + 2.32 = -.06 + 2.32 = 2.26.$†

The best prediction is that the student will receive a grade point average

---

* Regression equations employing more than a single predictor can also be used, but they are beyond the scope of this text.
  † The steps in computing the predicted criterion score are:
  1. Divide SD_c (1.08) by SD_p (21.6). This equals .05, rounded.
  2. Subtract M_p (51.84) from X_p (50). This equals −1.84.
  3. Multiply .05 (answer to step 1) by −1.84 (answer to step 2). This equals −.0920.
  4. Multiply −.0920 by r_{pc} (.69). This product is −.06, rounded.
  5. Add −.06 to M_c (2.32). The best prediction of the student's criterion score, X_c, is 2.26.

of 2.26. Notice that if the validity of the predictor (r_{pc}) is 0, the best prediction of the criterion will always be M_c, or the mean of the criterion group. If they have no knowledge at all about a person, teachers will make fewer errors if they estimate that a student is average than if they estimate any other value.

To compute criterion scores for more than one student, remember that all values in the regression equation remain constant except X_p. Since the order of multiplication is irrelevant, .69 can be multiplied by .05 (which is .0345), and that product can be multiplied by the value in the parentheses. For each individual, then, the regression formula simplifies to $X_c = .0345 (X_p - 51.84) + 2.32$. A student with a score of 95, for example, would be expected to have a grade point average of .0345 $(95 - 51.87) + 2.32$, or 3.8, rounded.

The amount of error in prediction can be estimated by using the formula for the *standard error of estimate* (SE_{est}). Only two values are required for its computation, the standard deviation of the criterion scores (SD_c) and the square of the predictive validity coefficient (r^2_{pc}, the correlation between the predictor and the criterion score). The formula is

$$SE_{est} = SD_c\sqrt{1 - r^2_{pc}}$$

For the data in table 12.3, the $SE_{est} = 1.08 \sqrt{1 - .69^2}$, or .78, rounded.* The value .78 refers to the variability of actual or obtained scores around the corresponding predicted values. The larger the SE_{est} is, the less accurate the predictions will be. Note that if r^2_{pc} is 1.0, then SE_{est} will be 0. In other words, a validity coefficient of 1.0 means that teachers are predicting perfectly (i.e., without error). On the other hand, if r^2_{pc} is 0, then the amount of error will be equal to the standard deviation of criterion measures. This means that errors in prediction are as great as the variability of the criterion measures themselves.

The standard error of estimate is a standard deviation and may be so interpreted. The SE_{est} measures the variability, spread, or dispersion of obtained scores around the *regression line* that best relates the criterion (X_c) to predictors (X_p). The regression line is drawn to minimize errors in predicting X_c values.† Note that if all scores fall on that line, the correlation would be 1.0 and prediction would be perfect (i.e., zero errors of estimate). Whenever correlations are not perfect, however, some students will receive higher or lower criterion scores than the regression line would predict. As the variability of scores increases around the regression line, the SE_{est} becomes greater and the predictors become less accurate.

---

* The computation proceeds as follows:
1. Square .69. This is .69 times .69, or .4761.
2. Subtract .4761 from 1.000. This is .5239.
3. Take the square root of .5239 (see appendix 1). This is .72.
4. Multiply .72 times 1.08. This is .78.
† Recall (from chap. 6) that the regression line is drawn so as to minimize the sum of the squared differences of paired scores around that line.

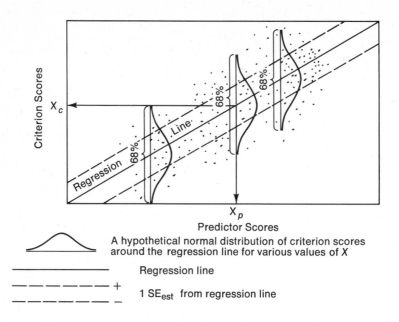

Figure 12.3. Regression Line Showing How Criterion Scores (X_c) Are Predicted from Different Values of X_p Assuming That Actual Scores Are Normally Distributed Around the Regression Line.

The SE_{est} is an overall measure of the variability of criterion scores around the regression line for all values of the predictor. In figure 12.3 the standard deviations of scores around the regression line are equal, and the SE_{est} will closely approximate these separate standard deviations. Figure 12.4, in contrast, demonstrates extreme differences in variability around the regression line. If the SE_{est} is computed from this distribution, it will underestimate the variability of scores for X_{50} (where the variability is large) and will overestimate the variability for X_{10} (where the variability is small). Only if the variabilities are equal (or at least approximately so), can the SE_{est} represent variabilities for all predictor scores.

Furthermore, it is assumed that scores around the regression line are normally distributed for *each* predictor score, as depicted in Figure 12.3. If so, then 68 percent (approximately two-thirds) of all actual criterion scores will vary between +1 SE_{est} and −1 SE_{est} from the regression line. Approximately 96 percent of all scores will fall between +2 SE_{est} and −2 SE_{est}. For the data in table 12.3, it was predicted that students with a predictor score of 50 would have a grade point average of 2.26. But since the SE_{est} is .78, that value can be subtracted from and added to 2.26. Therefore 68 percent of all students will obtain criterion scores between 3.04 and 1.48.

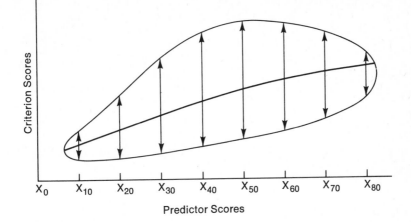

Figure 12.4. Showing the Unequal Spread of Raw Scores Around a Regression Line for Various Values of a Predictor

Examples and Types of Aptitude Tests

Aptitude tests vary in specificity (see figure 12.5). The most global measures are derived from such tests as the Standford-Binet, which sample a wide variety of tasks. At the other end of the continuum are those that measure specific sensory aptitudes, such as vision and hearing tests.

Multiaptitude Batteries

The two most often used and best understood multiaptitude batteries are the Differential Aptitude Test (DAT) and the General Aptitude Test Battery (GATB). The former is designed for grades 8–12; the latter, for adults (over seventeen years of age).

Multiaptitude batteries have the advantage of being standardized on the same individuals, making comparison across subtests feasible. The use of such batteries assumes that several different abilities constitute each criterion and that each ability is measurable. Some economy is gained by using batteries and by combining their subtests to predict different criteria rather than having to purchase a different test for each course or vocation.

| Measures of g | (Stanford-Binet) | Differentiated Intelligence Tests | (Wechsler, California Test of Mental Maturity) | Multi-Measures of Intelligence | (Primary Mental Abilities Test) | Multi-Aptitude Batteries | (Differential Aptitude Test) | Specific Aptitudes | (Bennet Mechanical Comprehension Test) | Vocational and Professional | (Graduate Record Examination-Advanced Test, Education) | Sensory Tests (Snellen E Chart) |

◄──────Global   Specific──────►

Figure 12.5. Degrees of Specificity as Measured by Different Kinds of Tests

Currently the GATB consists of the following subtests:

(*G*) *Intelligence:* A composite of three subtests: vocabulary, arithmetic reasoning, and three-dimensional space

(*V*) *Verbal:* Vocabulary using synonyms and antonyms

(*N*) *Numerical:* Computation and arithmetic reasoning

(*S*) *Spatial:* Ability to visualize objects in three dimensions presented in two dimensions (see figure 12.6a and b)

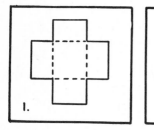
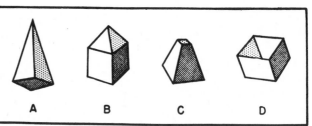

From General Aptitude Test Battery, Bureau of Employment Security, U.S. Department of Labor, Washington, D.C.

Figure 12.6a

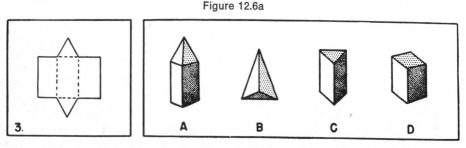

Figure 12.6b

(P) *Form perception:* Matching drawings of tools and of geometric forms (see figure 12.7a, b, and c)

From General Aptitude Test Battery, Bureau of Employment Security, U.S. Department of Labor, Washington, D.C.

Figure 12.7a

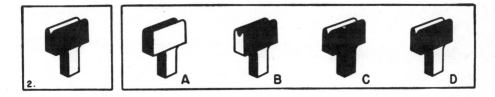

Figure 12.7b

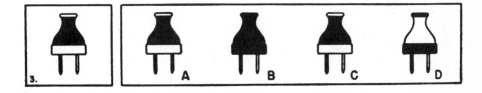

Figure 12.7c

(Q) *Clerical perception:* Matching names

(K) *Motor coordination:* Measures ability to put specified marks into a number of squares

(F) *Finger dexterity:* Ability to assemble and disassemble rivets and washers

(M) *Manual dexterity:* Ability to transfer and turn pegs in a pegboard

Many of the highly speeded GATB subtests are of greatest value when predicting criteria requiring rapid movements such as hand-eye coordination tasks, although the validity of these measures is low. As with other multiaptitude batteries, the intelligence, verbal, and numerical scores tend to correlate most highly with criteria.

Although the DAT has been described in detail in this chapter, a new edition has been prepared. Two new forms, S and T, employ the same 8 subtests as do the earlier editions. Items have been revised on verbal reasoning, numerical ability, mechanical reasoning, spelling, and language usage (formerly the grammar subtest). Over 60,000 students comprised the new standardization group and special care has been taken to include minority students. An interesting innovation is the optional DAT/Career Planning Report which provides the student with a personalized computer interpretation of the appropriateness of his occupational choices as they relate to his abilities, course preferences, and educational and vocational goals.

Other aptitude test batteries include the Flanagan Aptitude Classification Test (FACT), the Guilford-Zimmerman Aptitude Survey, Multiple Aptitude Tests, and Academic Promise Tests.

Specific Aptitude Tests

Specific aptitude tests are used to predict the probability of artistic, musical, creative, clerical, and mechanical success. Even when multiaptitude batteries contain a mechanical reasoning subtest (such as the Differential Aptitude Test), a specific aptitude test on the same topic may be longer and better normed and validated. In other instances a specific aptitude test might be less costly than an entire battery of tests.

Clerical aptitude tests   A widely used clerical aptitude test is the Minnesota Clerical Test. The test is designed for students in grades 7–12, but norms are also available for adults in occupations where clerical skills are important (e.g., accountants, inspectors, office workers, clerks). The test is composed of two parts: number comparison and name comparison. In each part the subject compares two long numbers or names (such as of industrial concerns) and indicates whether the two are the same or different (see fig. 12.8). Each part is separately timed, and a correction for guessing formula is applied to discourage random responding. The Minnesota Clerical Test is often given along with a measure of intelligence to select clerical supervisors.

Because males and females perform differently on this test, separate percentile norms are provided for each sex. Stability coefficients over a few months are high, generally above .70. Validity data also support the use of the test. For example, scores on the Minnesota Clerical Test correlated .47 with college accounting grades in one study. Other studies demonstrate that the test correlates well (about .50) with production records of bookkeepers and less well with supervisory ratings (about .28).

Now try the samples below.
66273894————66273984
527384578————527384578
New York World————New York World
Cargill Grain Co.————Cargil Grain Co.

Figure 12.8. Example of Minnesota Clerical Test

Although the Minnesota Clerical Test is generally considered to be better standardized and validated than many clerical tests, other tests have somewhat different emphases in content and predictive validity. Some include spelling items, alphabetization, unscrambling sentences, and items measuring simple computation. Tests are also available for measuring stenographic and typing aptitude.

Mechanical aptitudes   Mechanical aptitudes have been described as being both global and differentiated. Those advocating the global approach conceive of mechanical aptitude as a single trait that differs in amount from person to person. Opposing them are those who believe that mechanical aptitudes consist of a number of relatively independent abilities. Most authorities today tend to support the latter position, implying that an adequate measure of mechanical aptitude may require administration of several tests or subtests rather than just one.

Mechanical assembly tests   Some mechanical aptitude tests require the examinee to assemble parts; his score is based on the number of parts he can assemble in a given period of time. The Minnesota Assembly Test, one of the best known, consists of thirty-three unassembled mechanical objects to be put together within a specified time period; the number of correctly assembled parts is the score.

The greatest problems with mechanical assembly tests are their high initial cost and their low validity. Scores on the Minnesota Assembly Test, for example, correlate negligibly with grades. Also, because norms were obtained with adolescents, information about the test's ability to predict job success is virtually nonexistent.

Information tests   Tests can also measure an examinee's information about or experience in mechanics. Such tests could be of value in selecting trainees who have had some exposure to mechanical objects and procedures.

One of the best-known mechanical information tests is the O'Rourke Mechanical Aptitude Test. On part 1 the examinee matches pictures of tools, such as a screwdriver, with pictures of objects used in conjunction with them, such as a screw (see figure 12.9). Part 2 consists of multiple-choice items that measure knowledge about tools and their use. Both parts contain a wide variety of questions measuring knowledge about carpentry, electricity, painting, printing, and other occupations.

The O'Rourke manual offers little information concerning reliability or validity. A few very high validity coefficients are reported, but these are admittedly atypical.

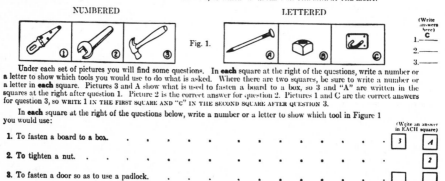

Each of the three pictures marked with a number is **used with** a picture at the right marked with a letter. Look at the picture marked 1. Then look at the pictures marked A, B, and C and decide which is **used with** 1. Write the letter of the picture which goes with 1, on the line marked 1 at the right of the pictures. Then find the picture that is **used with** picture 2, and write the letter of that picture after 2 on the line at the right. The first sample is done correctly. Picture C is **used with** picture 1, so "C" is written after 1 on the line at the right. B is **used with** 2, so WRITE "B" ON THE LINE AT THE RIGHT AFTER 2. "Nail," marked A, is used with "hammer" marked 3, so WRITE "A" AFTER 3 ON THE LINE AT THE RIGHT.

Fig. 1.

Under each set of pictures you will find some questions. In **each** square at the right of the questions, write a number or a letter to show which tools you would use to do what is asked. Where there are two squares, be sure to write a number or a letter in **each** square. Pictures 3 and A show what is used to fasten a board to a box, so 3 and "A" are written in the squares at the right after question 1. Picture 2 is the correct answer for question 2. Pictures 1 and C are the correct answers for question 3, so WRITE 1 IN THE FIRST SQUARE AND "C" IN THE SECOND SQUARE AFTER QUESTION 3.

In **each** square at the right of the questions below, write a number or a letter to show which tool in Figure 1 you would use:

1. To fasten a board to a box.

2. To tighten a nut.

3. To fasten a door so as to use a padlock.

Figure 12.9. Example of O'Rourke Mechanical Aptitude Test

Mechanical reasoning tests   Another aspect of mechanical aptitude is mechanical reasoning or comprehension. One of the most widely used tests in this category is the Bennett Mechanical Comprehension Test (BMCT). Designed primarily for eleventh and twelve-grade students, industrial applicants, and industrial employees, the test consists of pictures of familiar objects. The examinee might be asked to indicate which of two pairs of shears would best cut metal and which of two rooms with different amounts of furniture would have more of an echo (see figure 12.10).

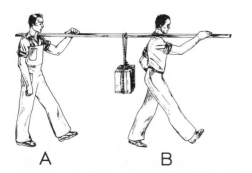

X

Which man carries more weight?
(If equal, mark C.)

A   B

Figure 12.10

According to the manual, validity coefficients range from .30 to .60 in predicting success in engineering-type occupations. A separate test is available for women, but there appears to be little information about its validity, despite the fact that it has recently been revised (1970) and new norms developed.

Dexterity tests   Many occupations require finger and hand dexterity. Studies have demonstrated that manual dexterity involves multiple skills and is not a unitary ability. Thus, one needs a particular type of dexterity test for a watchmaker but a different type for an automobile mechanic. Some tests require the examinee to use the tools necessary on the job (e.g., *Bennett Hand-Tool Dexterity Test*) whereas others require the ability to discriminate, sort, and place discs as rapidly as possible (e.g., *Stromberg Dexterity Test*). Still others require the ability to use tweezers in moving small objects (The *O'Connor Finger and Tweezer Dexterity Tests*). These dexterity tests are administered individually.

Spatial relations tests   Virtually all multi-aptitude test batteries and many intelligence tests contain a spatial relation subtest. Data indicate that they are useful predictors of success in many occupations and school subjects.

For example, spatial relations abilities are involved in engineering, drafting, and art.

One of the most widely used group of spatial relations tests is the Revised Minnesota Paper Form Board Test. The test consists of sixty-four disarranged parts of a geometric figure. The examinee is required to select the correctly assembled figure from among different numbers of options (see figure 12.11).

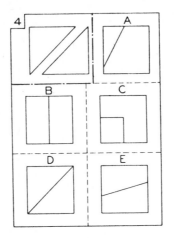

Figure 12.11

The test may be given to students in grades 9–12 and to adults. "Percentiles for educational and industrial groups including apprentices, applicants, and engineers" are available (the Psychological Corporation Test Catalog 1973, p. 13).

Musical and Artistic Aptitudes   The most commonly used musical aptitude test is the Seashore Measures of Musical Talent, which consists of a phonograph record or tape presenting six aspects of auditory discrimination: pitch, loudness, time, timbre, rhythm, and tonal memory. The test is designed for grade 4 through high school and college. Percentile norms are provided for each subtest.

All items on the Seashore consist of pairs of stimuli. In measuring pitch, the examinee must judge whether the second stimulus sound is higher or lower than the first. Timbre is measured by asking the examinee to determine whether two notes differ in quality. The time subtest asks which of two intervals is the longest. On the tonal memory subtest, the examinee must indicate whether two sequences of notes are the same or different.

According to some studies, musical aptitude (as measured by the Seashore) seems to mature at about the age of fifteen. Atlhough high aptitude test scores are probably necessary for success in music, the Seashore does not measure other, perhaps equally important, aspects of musical talent, such as creativity or appreciation.

The major criticism of the Seashore is that it is highly atomistic; that is, each subtest measures a very narrow aspect of musical talent. In an attempt to remedy this situation, the Wing Standardized Tests of Musical Intelligence was developed in England. The test consists of seven subtests: chord analysis, pitch discrimination, memory for pitch, harmony, intensity, rhythm, and phrasing. The Wing test differs from the Seashore primarily in that the last four subtests require the examinee to evaluate the aesthetic quality of different chords.

Although validity data on the Seashore are conflicting and fragmentary, the data on the Wing test seem quite promising. Correlations with teacher grades, for example, are reported to be .60 and higher. Evidence indicates that musical aptitude is a unitary ability; therefore, a total score may be a more useful predictor than separate subtest scores.

Artistic aptitudes are of two types: *aesthetic judgment* and *aesthetic production*. The former may be necessary for the art critic; the latter, for the artist himself. Aesthetic production no doubt requires the ability to form an aesthetic judgment, but the converse is not necessarily true.

The best known aesthetic judgment test is the Meier Art Judgment Tests. It consists of 100 pairs of black and white plates. One member of each pair is a masterpiece, and the other is a slight modification of the original. The examinee is told how the pair drawings differs but not which is the classic; his task is to decide which he prefers (see figure 12.12).

The Meier test is capable of discriminating among groups that have known differences in art training (concurrent validity). Evidence of predictive validity comes from correlations of the Meier with ratings of art students made by their instructors. These correlations vary from about .40 to .70 and are satisfactory.

The Horn Art Aptitude Inventory is a test that measures aesthetic production. The test consists of two parts: a "scribble and doodle" exercise and "imagery." In part 1 the examinee is required to sketch twenty different but familiar objects, such as a tree, a book, and a fork. Each must be completed in a short time period (three to ten seconds). The imagery section consists of twelve rectangles containing several lines from which a representational picture must be drawn.

The manual for the Horn test contains examples of excellent, average, and poor drawings and suggests criteria for scoring. Relatively high correlations were obtained when two raters evaluated the same drawing, suggesting that scoring criteria are adequate. Validity coefficients also seem to be high. A correlation of

From the Meier Art Judgment Test (University of Iowa, Iowa City, Iowa: Bureau of Educational Research and Service). Reproduced by permission of the publisher.

Figure 12.12. In this example, the foreground differs.

.53 was obtained between test scores and an instructor's mean ratings of drawing in an art course; for thirty-six high school seniors taking art, test scores correlated .66 with instructor evaluations at the end of the course.

Creativity measurement   Currently no standardized tests of creativity can be recommended, although a number of experimental and research forms are available. The preceding chapter referred to Guilford's structure of intellect model, in which the difference between convergent (i.e., conformity, getting the "right" answer) and divergent thinking was explained. Divergent thinking is characterized by novel, original responses. All the divergent thinking tests produced by Guilford and his associates are measures of creativity *if* one is willing to equate creativity with novelty. For example, one test might require the examinee to list the purposes a newspaper might be used for other than as a source of information or amusement. While this may be an excellent measure of novelty, the validity of such data to predict the long-term achievement usually associated with highly creative persons is lacking. The dedication to persevere until a task is completed is probably not measured well by these tests either.

Another battery of "creativity" tests was developed by Torrance (Torrance Tests of Creative Thinking). It consists of ten tests that are laborious to score since each yields up to four different scores (fluency, flexibility, originality, and elaboration).

Both the Guilford and Torrance tests have low correlations with traditional measures of intelligence, which has led some persons to conclude that intelligence tests are of little value in selecting "creative" persons. Central to the issue is whether or not the Guilford and Torrance tests measure creativity or even whether experts can agree on a definition of the term.

Readiness tests   At the elementary and primary grades aptitude tests are called *readiness tests*. This has been an unfortunate selection of a word, since *readiness* implies that the child is prepared to begin formal instruction in a subject or skill such as reading. Too many teachers have thought they must delay learning until the child was "ready." However, a low score on any aptitude test does not indicate a lack of learning ability as much as it designates which students need help in mastering concepts necessary *to begin* formal instruction. A child who cannot discriminate between the letters *p* and *q* may obtain a low reading readiness score. This tells the teacher that unless specific remedial action is taken, the child is likely to experience difficulty in learning how to read. A low score does not mean that the teacher should give up teaching the child.

Readiness tests are available for both reading and arithmetic. The Metropolitan Readiness Tests, for example, consist of six subtests and an optional Draw a Man Test:

1. *Word meaning:* The child selects a picture of a word stated by the examiner.
2. *Listening:* The child selects the picture depicting the meaning of the sentence read by the examiner (see figure 12.13).
3. *Matching:* The child finds similarities and differences among figures and word forms (see figure 12.14).
4. *Alphabet:* The child selects the correct letters read by the examiner.
5. *Numbers:* The child counts and applies simple numerical concepts.

Figure 12.13. Sample Item from Metropolitan Readiness Test, Listening. "Put your finger on the first row of pictures. I am going to say something about one of these pictures. See if you can find the right picture and make a mark on it. Ready, listen. This is something we take pictures with."

a

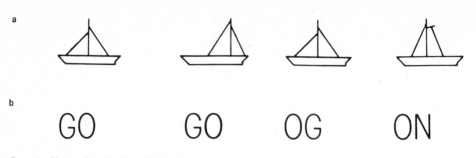

b

GO   GO   OG   ON

Figure 12.14. Sample item from Metropolitan Readiness Tests, Matching. "Put your finger on the row of pictures at the top of the page. Look at the picture of a sailboat at this edge of the page—by itself, before the green line. Find another picture in the same row that is just like it and make a mark on that one. . . . Look at the letters in the box at the beginning of the row. . . . find exactly these same letters."

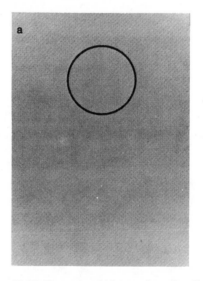

Figure 12.15. Example of Metropolitan Readiness Test, Copying. ". . . find the box with the circle on it. Take your pencil and in the same box draw another circle just like the one that is already there."

6. *Copying:* The child copies different forms in the test booklet (see figure 12.15).

To avoid boredom and restlessness, the tests are given in three sessions to kindergarten and first-grade children. Percentile and stanine norms are provided.

Highly satisfactory reliability coefficients (equivalent form and split-half) of over .90 are reported in the test manual for the Metropolitan Readiness Tests.

As might be expected from an examination of the test content, such scores are likely to correlate with intelligence tests given at the same grade levels. For example, the correlation with the Pinter-Cunningham Primary Intelligence Test was reported to be .76, indicating that both tests measure the same activities to some extent. Nonetheless, there is some evidence that readiness tests are somewhat better predictors of reading success than are general intelligence or scholastic aptitude measures, although the difference in most instances is small.

At the high school level aptitude tests are available in different subject areas. For example, tests are available to predict success in mathematics (algebra, geometry) and in foreign languages. The Modern Language Aptitude Test (MLAT) has been designed to predict success in learning either modern or ancient languages for high school students, college students, and adults. It contains five parts: aural number learning, audio-visual phonetic script, spelling clues, words and sentences, and paired associates. (See figure 12.16 for an

1. tik tiyk   tis tiys

From the Modern Language Aptitude Test, Part II, Phonetic Script. Copyright 1955, © 1958, 1959 by The Psychological Corporation, New York, N.Y. Reproduced by permission. All rights reserved.

Figure 12.16. Example of Modern Language Aptitude Test, Phonetic Script

example of phonetic script). Part of the test is on tape to measure the student's "ear for language." According to the manual, scores on the MLAT correlate more highly with foreign language success than do intelligence tests. Percentile norms are available for grades 9–11, college freshmen, and adults.

Professional and vocational tests   Aptitude tests have also been developed to select individuals into specific professions and vocations. Many graduate programs, for example, require applicants to submit scores on the Graduate Record Examination (GRE) or the Miller Analogies Test (MAT) for admission. The GRE consists of verbal and quantitative subtests with means of 500 and standard deviations of 100. It is a scholastic aptitude measure and does not attempt to discriminate among individuals planning to enter different professions. It is therefore useful for selection into graduate school but not for differential placement. For the latter purpose it is possible to use the GRE advanced tests, which are available in such subjects as psychology, education, physics, and chemistry. The advanced tests measure subject matter knowledge.

The Miller Analogies Test is also used as a scholastic prediction test. It "consists of 100 analogies items based on many areas of knowledge: vocabulary, literature, social sciences, chemistry, biology, physics, mathematics, mythology, and general information."* The MAT is generally administered and scored by testing centers at universities, and like the GRE, is not available for public examination. Percentile norms are provided for different graduate departments and professional schools.

In general, graduate school examinations demonstrate high reliability but only moderate validity coefficients. On the MAT, for example, split-half reliability is reported as about .92 on each of the four forms; equivalent form reliability is over .85. Validity, however, yielded coefficients from −.31 (using peer ratings as the criterion) to .73 (course grades in elementary school supervision). Most of the coefficients reported in the manual are between .30 and .50. As would be expected, validity coefficients increase if the criterion is another test rather than a grade or rating.

In many instances undergraduate grades are as good predictors as professional and vocational aptitude tests. Sometimes, however, using grades as predictors may be unfair. Students with good undergraduate grades from "easy" schools have an initial advantage; departments also differ in the number of high and low grades they give. The advantage of a test is that everyone is compared on the same basis.

Graduate school tests are probably best classified as relatively difficult intelligence or scholastic aptitude tests. However, some aptitude tests have been developed to predict success in specific occupations such as stenography, clerical work, typing, accounting, engineering, nursing, teaching, sales, and a host of other vocations. If collegiate level education is a prerequisite for the occupation, a broad scholastic aptitude test is probably indicated. More specific aptitude tests are needed as greater differentiation is required.

Sensory tests   Some courses and jobs require a high degree of visual and auditory aptitude or ability. A navigator who is hard of hearing or a pilot with visual difficulties is a danger to himself and to others. The child in school who cannot hear will probably not learn to read easily if his condition remains undetected.

In education, visual and auditory tests detect children whose potential handicaps may prevent them from learning. Many elementary schools routinely give eye and ear tests to screen out those children who need more sophisticated testing by clinics, physicians, or optometrists.

The most commonly used vision test in schools is the Snellen Chart. For children unable to recognize letters, the chart consists of the letter *E* in different sizes and pointing in different directions. The child can point to the direction the *E* faces. For older children or those able to recognize letters, the chart consists of different-sized letters.

The Snellen Chart is particularly useful for detecting nearsightedness and to a lesser extent, farsightedness. Since the examinee has one eye closed when

---

* W. S. Miller, *Miller Analogies Text Manual, 1960 Revision,* The Psychological Corporation, p. 3.

the test is given, it does not measure eye coordination; nor can it measure astigmatism or a variety of other conditions affecting reading. School nurses are often trained to give other vision tests to supplement Snellen Chart findings. Many alert teachers have detected signs of visual difficulty in children and have saved them years of suffering. These signs including squinting, holding books too far from or too close to the eyes, eyes that tear, continual rubbing of the eyes, oversensitivity to light, inability to distinguish colors, and getting up from the seat to look at the blackboard.

In an average classroom four or five children will experience some difficulty with hearing. The hearing loss may manifest itself in such behavior as tilting the head, cupping the hands to the ears, the inability to distinguish letter sounds, the inability to pronounce words accurately, a refusal to participate in group activities, and poor spelling performance. Although these behaviors could signify problems other than a hearing loss, any of these signs should be reported to the school nurse. Earaches, running ears, or complaints about head noises should be investigated immediately.

Two hearing tests are commonly used for gross screening in schools. In the first the child is seated with his back to the nurse or teacher, who places a running watch near each of the child's ears in random order. The child is asked to indicate when he hears the sound. A second method is to whisper questions to the child from a position where he cannot read lips. The whisper should be loud enough so that a person who had no hearing problem would be able to respond to the question.

It should be emphasized that these auditory tests are for rough screening only. For example, some people can hear sounds at some frequencies but not at others. Many school districts have hearing specialists who are trained to give more accurate tests under more controlled conditions.

Summary

1. Aptitude tests are cognitive measures designed to predict how well an individual will succeed before he is trained, selected, or placed. The terms *intelligence* and *scholastic aptitude* are used interchangeably in this text. Aptitude tests that predict success in specific programs are called specific aptitude tests.

2. Differential aptitude tests should provide subtests that correlate highly with criteria but low with each other.

3. Reliability coefficients on aptitude tests tend to increase with increases in age. Split-half and Kuder-Richardson reliabilities are generally high, but the more specific the measured ability is, the lower the reliability is.

4. All aptitude measures should have high predictive validity. The best predictors are usually subtests that relate to scholastic aptitude or intelligence—verbal and numerical abilities. Over a three-year period most predictive validity coefficients on the DAT are below .40.

5. Aptitude tests are used for selection and placement. The composite method and the cutoff method are used to make selection decisions.

   a. The composite method brings together a number of predictor tests to maximize each test's contribution in predicting some criterion. The best tests for this purpose are those that meet the criteria stated in item 2.

   b. Using the cutoff method, each test score is kept separate; if a student fails any of the tests he is eliminated no matter how well he compensates on another test.

6. In placement decisions tests must be capable of discriminating among persons who have already been selected. Constructing good placement tests is more difficult than constructing selection tests. Because validity coefficients for placement tend to be lower than those used for selection, greater caution is required when tests are used for placement.

7. Aptitude tests may also be used for diagnostic purposes. On readiness tests, for example, it is possible to measure the kinds of errors students are likely to make when they are formally taught reading or arithmetic. Item analysis procedures are useful for this purpose.

8. Expectancy tables can be used to inform students of the probability of success in different programs. Regression equations can help predict the most likely score a student will receive on a criterion.

9. The amount of error in predicting a criterion can be computed by using the formula for the standard error of estimate. The larger the SE_{est} is, the more the scores spread out on either side of the regression line. If the SE_{est} is 0, all actual scores will equal their predicted values, and the predictive validity will be perfect.

10. Aptitude tests can be placed on a continuum from the most global, or general (the Stanford-Binet, for example), to the most specific (sensory tests). Specific aptitude tests include clerical, mechanical, musical, artistic, and creative aptitude tests.

    a. *Clerical aptitude tests.* The Minnesota Clerical Aptitude Test contains two parts requiring the student to compare numbers and names. Each part is separately timed and corrected for guessing. Stability coefficients are usually above .70 (over a few months' time); validity is about .50, with production records as the criterion.

    b. *Mechanical aptitude tests.* Mechanical aptitudes may be measured by different approaches. Mechanical assembly tests require the examinee to assemble an object, usually with some time restriction; information tests measure the individual's information or experience with specific skills; mechanical reasoning tests are usually included in engineering batteries or where fairly complex reasoning is required; dexterity tests require rapid hand-eye or finger-eye coordination; spatial relations tests are included on almost all multiaptitude test batteries since the ability to visualize objects in three dimensions is important in many types of jobs and school subjects.

c. *Musical aptitude tests.* Muscial aptitude is usually measured by the Seashore Measures of Musical Talent or the Wing Standardized Tests of Musical Intelligence. The former consists of pairs of different stimuli (on a record or tape) to determine whether the individual is capable of making fine musical discriminations. The Wing test attempts to measure appreciation as well as discrimination ability.

d. *Artistic aptitude tests.* Artistic aptitude can be measured by judgments or products. On the Meier Art Judgment Test the examinee indicates which of each pair of 100 plates is a masterpiece and which is a modification; the Horn Art Aptitude Inventory compares the drawings made by the examinee with standardized products that have been previously rated for quality. Scoring tends to be relatively objective, but validity data are often lacking or meager. What evidence is available indicates relatively high agreement with ratings made by art instructors.

e. *Tests of creativity.* Some standardized tests of creativity are in experimental form. Although both Guilford and Torrance have developed tests, they probably measure novelty rather than long-term commitment to a project leading to a product or idea of great social, technical, or artistic value.

11. Readiness tests are scholastic aptitude tests used in the primary grades, particularly in arithmetic and reading. They measure the types of skills students must have acquired to begin formal instruction in these subjects. Low readiness test scores suggest that the child has not learned these skills on his own and that the teacher should help him acquire them. Readiness does not necessarily refer to some specific biological time when the child is mature enough to begin a formal program of instruction. Of course, much depends on the way in which the child is instructed.

12. Professional and vocational aptitude tests are also available. The Graduate Record Examination and Miller Analogies Test are used to predict success in graduate programs. Both tests are "secure" in the sense that they are not available for public examination. Although their reliability coefficients tend to be high, predictive validity coefficients tend to vary between .30 and .50, depending on the nature of the criterion and the sample of individuals taking the test.

13. Sensory tests are highly specific and measure vision and hearing defects. Such tests as the Snellen E Chart and the "watch-tick" test are usually administered by the school nurse for rough screening purposes only. Teachers should watch for and report symptoms of visual and auditory problems.

Suggested Readings

Bracht, Glenn H. "Experimental Factors Related to Aptitude-Treatment Interactions." *Review of Educational Research* 40, no. 5 (December 1970): 627–45. A good summary of the relationships between different levels of aptitude and instruction.

Crites, John O. *Vocational Psychology: The Study of Vocational Behavior and Development.* New York: McGraw-Hill Book Co., 1969, 704 pp. Chapters 9–11, in particular, are related to the use of aptitude tests in the measurement of vocational choice and success.

Doppelt, Jerome E., and Seashore, Harold G. "How Effective Are Your Tests?" *Test Service Bulletin of the Psychological Corporation,* no. 37 (June 1949): 4–10. The authors show how expectancy tables and graphs can be used to evaluate tests.

Horrocks, John E. *Assessment of Behavior: The Methodology and Content of Psychological Measurement.* Columbus, Ohio: Charles E. Merrill Books, 1964, 736 pp. See chapters 11–14 ("Aptitudes and Special Abilities," "Measurement of Aptitudes," "Maturation and Readiness: Tests of Physical-Motor Development," and "Maturation and Readiness: Tests of Subject-Matter Readiness").

Jackson, Douglas N., and Messick, Samuel, eds. *Problems in Human Assessment.* New York: McGraw-Hill Book Co., 1967, 873 pp. An excellent book of readings. In particular, see part 4, "Assessment for Selection," which includes nine relevant articles.

Michael, William B. "An Interpretation of the Coefficients of Predictive Validity and of Determination in Terms of the Proportions of Correct Inclusions or Exclusions in Cells of a Fourfold Table." *Educational and Psychological Measurement* 26, no. 2 (Summer 1966): 419–25. This brief article presents a simplified interpretation of expectancy tables as they relate to correlation coefficients, coefficients of determination, and the proportion of valid placements.

Wesman, Alexander G. "Expectancy Tables—A Way of Interpreting Test Validity." *Test Service Bulletin of the Psychological Corporation,* no. 38 (December 1949): 11–15. Demonstrates a variety of expectancy tables.

13

Standardized academic achievement tests measure the degree of student learning in curriculum areas that are common to most schools. Unlike teacher-made examinations, standardized achievement tests are administered and scored under uniform conditions, making it possible to compare the achievement level of one group against that of a norm or reference group.

Academic achievement tests differ from academic aptitude tests in both purpose and method of validation. Aptitude tests are given to predict success in a program *prior* to selection, placement, or training, whereas achievement tests are usually given *after* students have received instruction. This distinction implies that *content validity* is crucial for academic achievement tests because they are constructed to sample those objectives that appear regularly in most curricula; in contrast, academic aptitude tests require *predictive validity coefficients* since the goal is to predict the degree of student success. Academic achievement tests, then, typically measure knowledge obtained from formal learning situations; academic aptitude tests *may* measure not only school-acquired knowledge but also behaviors (such as finger dexterity or spatial relationships) usually not formally taught in school.

It would be difficult to tell the difference between achievement and aptitude items if the purpose of testing were unknown. For example, some tests could reflect the attainment of knowledge but also be used to predict future success. As a measure of previously acquired knowledge, the test is a measure of *achievement;* when the same examination is used for prediction, it is an *aptitude* measure. This text follows the convention of classifying tests by their function rather than by their *content* or title. If a cognitive test is used to predict success, it will be classified as an aptitude measure; if the test is used to measure knowledge learned as the result of instruction, it will be called an achievement test.

The Construction of Standardized Achievement Tests

The construction of a standardized achievement test consists of the following steps: (1) determining test rationale and objectives, (2) writing test items that meet these objectives, (3) analyzing items, (4) constructing final forms of the test, and (5) standardizing the final forms. The procedures used to construct the Stanford Achievement Test (High School Battery), considered one of the better standardized achievement tests, will be examined.

Determining Test Rationale and Objectives

The first step in constructing a standardized achievement test is to develop a test rationale and measurable objectives. The purpose of the Stanford Achievement Test (High School Battery, grades 9–12) is to survey both basic and specialized courses common to most high school programs. The developers also wished to produce tests at the high school level that were built on the accomplishments of pupils in the junior high schools. Then, according to the manual (p. 9), "a high school can . . . continue measurement of students in subject-matter fields taught in both junior and senior high schools."

From their analyses of various school systems and high school curricula, the authors of the Stanford Achievement Tests developed both a "basic" and a "complete" test battery. The basic battery consists of seven subtests: English, numerical competence (fractions, decimals, percentages, graph reading), mathematics (algebra, geometry, modern math), reading, science (physical and life), social studies, and spelling. The complete battery contains all the basic subtests plus arts and humanities, business and economics, and technical comprehension.

To determine specific test content, the authors examined textbooks and courses of study "in common use" and also asked subject-matter specialists and teachers what topics should be included on each subtest. The manual contains a list of all topics included on the final examination form; the science test, for example, consists of the following topics (p. 26):

Physics
1. Matter
2. Heat, light, sound
3. Magnetism and electricity
4. Force
5. Motion

Chemistry
1. Acids and bases
2. Atomic structure and properties
3. Chemical reactions
4. Miscellaneous

Earth and space
1. Geology
2. Weather and climate
3. Astronomy
4. Conservation

Life science
1. The cell
2. Plant life
3. Animal life
4. Reproduction
5. Health
6. Ecology

Scientific method
1. In physical science
2. In life science

Writing the Test Items

Item writing for standardized achievement tests is usually a cooperative effort of subject-matter specialists and testing experts. For the Stanford Achievement Test, teams of teachers and specialists constructed four forms of a test, each with 20 to 50 percent more items than would be required for the final version. All items were in multiple-choice format and were administered to small groups of high school students to estimate difficulty levels, the adequacy of time requirements, and the functional value of each option. Items were reviewed, tried out on new groups, and revised again until all appeared clear, unambiguous, and justifiable.

Analyzing Items

In the preceding step items were analyzed on relatively small groups of students simply to get some indication of their effectiveness. Because item analysis data reflect the characteristics of the group tested, it was necessary to complete an item analysis on a much larger sample of high school students. The national sample consisted of 26,009 students in grades 9–12 from nineteen school systems in seventeen different states. Separate analyses were run for students at each grade level, for students who had continually studied a given subject since entering the ninth grade, and for students who were enrolled in special curriculum programs or projects.

Constructing the Final Test Forms

Construction of the final test forms was a compromise between item sampling (maximizing content coverage) and administrative convenience. Because many high school classes meet for fifty minutes, it was considered desirable that no subtest take longer than forty minutes to complete. However, it was soon discovered that forty minutes was too long for spelling and too short for mathematics and science, so the first parts of science and of mathematics were combined to form a forty-minute test.

Standardizing the Final Test Forms

The norm sample used for standardizing the Stanford Achievement Test consisted of 22,699 students attending fifty-eight schools in thirty-nine different districts. To obtain reasonable norms, the authors decided that all students in grades 9–12 in a particular school had to be tested on both the basic and complete batteries. All students were also required to take a group intelligence test. Demographic data from the participating schools were compared with records compiled by the U. S. Office of Education to determine the representative nature of the sample. Two socioeconomic measures (median number of years of schooling by persons twenty-five years of age or older and median family income) showed that data from six of the eight geographical regions sampled were very similar to 1960 census reports. Statistical adjustments in data were made for the other two regions.

The norms were derived from the analysis of data obtained from the 22,699 students who participated in the standardization. Means and standard deviations for each sex and grade level are reported in the manual, and percentiles, stanines, and T scores on each subtest are provided for each grade level.

Norms on Standardized Achievement Tests

Most standardized achievement tests use such norms as percentiles, age and grade equivalents, quotients, and standard scores. In recent years the trend has been to discourage the use of age, grade, and quotient norms in favor of percentiles and standard scores.

Percentile Norms

Virtually all standardized achievement tests provide percentile norms at each grade level tested. Tables convert raw scores directly to percentiles or in some instances into standard scores, which are then converted to percentiles. Many tests also contain separate norms for boys and girls.

Age Norms

The age level at which a child functions on an achievement test is his educational age, or EA. A child who has the same number of items right on an achievement test as the average twelve-and-one-half-year-old has an EA of 12-6, no matter what his chronological age might be. The number to the left of the hyphen represents the age in years; the number to the right represents months.

The term *educational age* (EA) is generally used when referring to total scores on an achievement test battery. When a specific subtest is being referred to, it is necessary to name the subtest (e.g., reading, arithmetic, spelling). For example, one can refer to a reading age of 12-6 or state that a student has an "EA of 12-6 in reading."

Age norms on achievement tests present the same difficulties as mental age norms on intelligence tests. An increase of a year at one age level may not be equivalent to a year's gain at another. Like mental age curves, EA curves tend to flatten out at the upper age levels, making it difficult to measure achievement at those levels.

Grade Norms

Because of their *apparent* simplicity, grade norms are widely used, but they are not well understood by many teachers. In recent years a number of test publishers have tried to explain the problems of grade norms in their test manuals; nonetheless, teachers still misinterpret these norms.

The grade level at which the child is functioning on an achievement test is called his *grade placement* (GP) or *grade equivalent* (GE) score. Because most school systems operate on a ten-month basis, GEs are expressed as decimals, such as 5.4 or 11.9. The number to the left of the decimal refers to the grade level; the number to the right refers to the school month. The Stanford Achievement Test, for example, uses table 13.1 to convert decimal equivalents to school months.

Table 13.1. Grade Equivalents Corresponding to School Months

	Sep. 1 Sep. 15	Sep. 16 Oct. 15	Oct. 16 Nov. 15	Nov. 16 Dec. 15	Dec. 16 Jan. 15	Jan. 16 Feb. 15	Feb. 16 Mar. 15	Mar. 16 Apr. 15	Apr. 16 May 15	May 16 Jun. 15
Grade equivalent	.0	.1	.2	.3	.4	.5	.6	.7	.8	.9

The highest value at any grade level is .9 (such as 3.9, 4.9, or 5.9).

GE norms can be better understood if the manner in which they are obtained is examined:

1. Tests are administered to large numbers of students in different grades. Generally the same examination is given to no more than three or four grade levels at the same time of the year. A particular test might be devised for grades 1–2 or for grades 10–12.
2. The mean, median, or modal scores (depending on the test) are computed for students at each grade level tested.
3. Graph paper is used to plot the average number of items correct against the grade level (such as 4.5, 5.5, or 6.5) in which the testing took place (see figure 13.1). Lines are drawn to connect the points

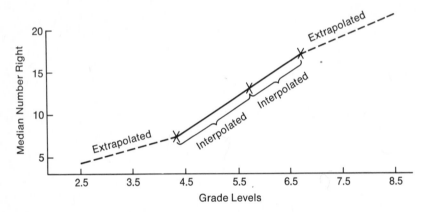

Figure 13.1. An Example of an Interpolated and Extrapolated Grade-Equivalent Curve

corresponding to the average number right. In figure 13.1 students were tested simultaneously in the fifth month of grades four, five, and six, and average scores of 8, 13, and 16, respectively, were obtained. Connecting these points by a line gives the impression that progress was continuous between grade levels, although no students were tested except at grades 4.5, 5.5, and 6.5. Intermediate values are obtained by interpolation (the process of locating intermediate values between two measured points).

4. The dotted lines correspond to the test constructor's notions of how students might have performed had the test been administered below grades 4.5 and above 6.5. These *extrapolated* portions of the curve are purely conjectural, but their use encourages teachers to make such erroneous statements as "Although Johnny is only in the fourth grade, he is doing as well as the average child in the fifth month of the eighth grade"—and this in spite of the fact that the test was never

given to anyone except those in grades 4.5, 5.5, and 6.5! GE norms that are reported beyond tested grade limits are meaningless. They imply only that the test was too easy or too difficult for students scoring at those levels and that the next higher or lower form should be administered.

In addition to being interpolated and extrapolated, GE norms also suffer from the following deficiencies:

GE norms are ordinal measurements   That is, differences between grade equivalents are not necessarily equal. Frederick Davis (1964), for example, has shown that the difference between GEs of 6.9 and 7.9 on the Stanford Achievement Test represents thirteen times more improvement than does a gain from 1.9 to 2.9

Grade norms are difficult to interpret to parents and students   No tenth-grade student wants to be told that he is functioning at a third-grade level. Nor is it easy to explain to a parent why the school refuses to place a third-grader in the seventh grade when the student obtains a GE of 7.0. Percentiles compare a child's achievement with other students of his own age or grade level, but the interpolations and extrapolations of GE norms give students and parents erroneous impressions of the degree of achievement attained and make counseling difficult.

Grade and age equivalents are not appropriate unless older students obtain higher scores than younger ones   In most areas of the curriculum this is a reasonable assumption, but if a test requires knowledge that is taught only in the lower grades, the younger students are likely to do better than the older ones. For example, many fifth-graders can define such terms as *mixed fraction, proper fraction,* and *improper fraction.* Assume that fifth- and twelfth-graders take a short test on the meaning of various types of fractions and that the average numbers right are 4 and 3, respectively. To summarize:

Grade Level	Average Score
5.0	4
12.0	3

This means that those who get four items correct would receive a GE of 5.0, whereas those who do less well would obtain a GE of 12.0. Obviously GE norms are appropriate only if more advanced students obtain higher scores than those at the lower levels.

GE norms assume that the same subject is taught continuously at the various grade levels for which the test is designed   A GE of 3.5 in reading is understandable because teachers have some idea of what reading skills children have at this grade level. But a GE of 6.5 in chemistry is meaningless since chemistry is not often taught in the sixth grade. GE norms in social studies would be difficult to obtain considering the variable nature of the social studies curriculum in different school districts.

GE norms at the upper grade levels are often meaningless   Most of the basic skills are taught by the end of the eighth or ninth grade, and courses beyond those levels are remedial or offered as advanced electives. A GE of 11.3 in reading, for example, would be extremely difficult to interpret.

Interpolated curves do not take into effect losses or decreases in knowledge over the summer vacation nor the fact that students may make more gains at some times of the year than at others.

Teachers often misinterpret GE norms as standards or criteria to be reached by all students   It is easy to forget that GEs are averages (usually *medians*) and therefore that half the students will perform below and half above their actual grade level. Furthermore, one *should* expect more from bright students than from those who are less able.

Means and standard deviations of GE norms often vary among subtests   A GE of 4.5 on one subtest could be equivalent to a GE of 4.2 on another. Standard deviations also tend to differ, depending on the nature of subtest content. In general, arithmetic and mathematics subtests tend to have relatively small standard deviations, probably because these subjects are taught sequentially and without encouraging diversity. Reading subtests, in contrast, usually have larger standard deviations because individual differences increase after students have learned the basic skills.

Table 13.2 shows the means and standard deviations of GE norms on the various subtests of the California Achievement Tests for 200 fourth-graders. From an examination of table 13.2 it can be seen that a GE of 4.5 in *reading vocabulary* is equivalent to the arithmetic fundamentals subtest value of 4.2 since both have z scores of 0. (Remember that the mean always has a z score of 0.) Furthermore, if students were two standard deviations above the means on these subtests, their GEs would be 7.1 and 5.8, respectively. Clearly GE norms can be misleading unless one knows their means and standard deviations.

Table 13.2. Means and Standard Deviations of Grade Equivalent Norms on the California Achievement Tests for 200 Students in Grade 4

Subtest	Mean GP	Standard Deviation of GP
1. Reading vocabulary	4.5	1.3
2. Reading comprehension	4.3	1.2
Total reading	4.4	1.2
3. Arithmetic reasoning	4.2	1.0
4. Arithmetic fundamentals	4.2	.8
Total arithmetic	4.2	.8
5. Mechanics of English	4.3	1.2
6. Spelling	4.4	1.4
Total language	4.4	1.2

From Technical Report on the California Achievement Tests, 1957. Reproduced by permission of the publisher, CTB/McGraw-Hill Book Co., Del Monte Research Park, Monterey California 93940.

Quotient Norms

On achievement tests quotient norms are called *educational quotients* or EQs. They are ratios of educational age to chronological age multiplied by 100 ($EQ = EA/CA \times 100$). EQ values above 100 supposedly mean that the child is functioning at a higher level on the achievement test than is expected for children of his CA. Similarly, values below 100 would indicate a lower level of test performance than that obtained by other children of comparable age.

Quotient norms have all the problems of age norms and a few of their own. For example, EQs have different means and standard deviations at different ages, depending on the particular tests taken. For that reason they are not comparable either from age to age or from test to test. These are the same criticisms that have been leveled at quotient IQ norms and that led to the development of deviation IQs.

Standard Scores

Most of the newer tests provide standard score norms such as *T* scores and stanines. Standard scores facilitate comparisons of student performance at different age or grade levels and comparisons on subtests within the same battery. For example, a *T* score of 60 on all subtests is always one standard deviation above the mean.

Developing Local Norms

Manuals report norms for national samples, and for most purposes national norms are satisfactory. However, in atypical districts where there is a much higher or lower percentage of bright or dull students, local norms can be constructed. Separate local norms could be established for different socioeconomic groups, for college and noncollege preparatory groups, or for separate racial groups. These local norms can be very useful for intragroup or intraschool comparison but are not, of course, substitutes for national norms.

Individual and School Average Norms

On a test of given length a sampling of students is likely to yield scores ranging from some that are below chance to some that are almost perfect. The variability or standard deviation of scores for individuals tends to be relatively large. However, the variability of school averages is smaller than that for individuals. That is, although the individuals from school to school can be expected to vary considerably, much less variability can be expected among schools. While some students will obtain extremely low scores, the distribution of *averages* for schools will be much more restricted. *If the raw scores obtained for a school are averaged, that average should be compared to other average scores and not to individual norms.* The best school, for example, would fall at the 99th percentile in comparison to other schools, but when compared to the greater variability of individual scores, the corresponding percentile would be lower than 99. It is therefore unreasonable to obtain the mean raw score for a school and compare it against individual norms.

Norms Derived at Different Times

Obviously students will receive different scores if they take standardized achievement tests at different times. Norms developed for students at the middle of the school year are inapplicable to students tested at the beginning or the end of the school year. For example, if students take tests in September but are compared with norms developed in February or March, their percentile and other norms will systematically be too low; if students take the test in June, their scores will be high in comparison with norm data. To be meaningful, tests should be given at times that correspond with norming dates.

Reasons for Using Standardized Achievement Tests

Selection and Placement

Success (or failure) in some programs depends largely on previous knowledge of related materials. Entrance to medical school could be based on tests measuring competence in related undergraduate courses or a school could *place* a student in an honors program depending on demonstrated competence in prerequisite courses. Many graduate schools admit or deny entrance to students depending on their undergraduate achievement. Similarly, it is possible to base college admission on high school achievement tests.

Achievement tests at the high school level tend to predict college success at least as well as scholastic aptitude tests. However, considering the time it takes to administer a battery of achievement tests, many school districts prefer to give students a single scholastic aptitude test.

High school grades are also good predictors of college success. Indeed, there is evidence (Travers 1949) that the single best predictor of college grades is the high school grade point average. The student's rank in his high school graduating class is also a very good predictor.

Achievement tests can be used as criterion measures as well as predictors. Since marking standards vary from school to school, from department to department, and from teacher to teacher, the use of standardized achievement tests as a criterion could facilitate the interpretation of scores. The problem, of course, is that standardized test items might not reflect a particular instructor's course objectives, and validity would therefore be forfeited for comparability.

Diagnosis

Most standardized achievement tests can be used for *screening*—that is, to make rough decisions about whether a student or class needs remedial help in a particular subject. Teachers using such data must recognize that the test provides very small samples of some kinds of behavior. There might be only one or two items measuring a given objective, and teachers may want to sample the students' knowledge more completely by constructing other items of the same type. The manual for the Comprehensive Test of Basic Skills (CTBS) provides an example of diagnostic information using standardized achievement tests. For grades 4–10 the CTBS measures:

	Items	Time
Reading		
1. Vocabulary	40	11
2. Comprehension	45	30
Language		
3. Mechanics	25	11
4. Expression	30	16
5. Spelling	30	8
Arithmetic		
6. Computation	48	36
7. Concepts	30	15
8. Applications	20	14
Study skills		
9. Reference materials	20	10
10. Graphic materials	30	19

Since tests 1–10 provide norms and reliability data, it is possible to determine whether a child is weak on any or all of these subtests. For diagnostic purposes, however, the terms *arithmetic computation* and *reading comprehension* are broad and fail to indicate specific areas of difficulty. Other tables indicate what skills each item measures. On test 6, for example, items 1–4 measure the addition of integers; items 18–20, the addition of decimals; items 33–36, the addition of fractions. By examining which items the student misses, it is possible to estimate the student's strengths and deficiencies.* On the other hand, some skills are measured by a single item. Such small samples of performance are of little diagnostic value; they place too much responsibility on the decision-making abilities of the teacher unless he constructs additional items to obtain a better sampling.

An interesting diagnostic feature of the CTBS is that a computer printout or response record is available, indicating which children responded correctly, incorrectly, or omitted each item on the test (figure 13.2). The name of the test is printed in the top row; in the second row is the broad classification of items described more fully on the bottom of the record; and in the third row is the item number (two-digit numbers are printed vertically, i.e., $\frac{1}{7}$ is 17).

A + is placed under each correct item; a − indicates an incorrect response; a blank space means the item was omitted. By reading across each row, the teacher can determine student responses or omissions. By reading down each column, the teacher can examine class performance on each item. Once again, it is necessary to remember that the reliability of a single item is likely to be very low.

Feedback

Students and parents should be informed of achievement test results. Students are in a good position to improve when they are told the reasons for their errors. Parents, too, have a right to know the specific strengths and weaknesses of their children. Many school districts routinely make standardized achievement test scores available to parents and encourage them to come to the school for personal conferences with the teacher or school counselor.

A common confusion faced by parents is the difference between standardized achievement test scores and the grades their children receive. A high percentile on the CTBS, for example, indicates that the student is performing at a higher level than most other children on a national standardized test that measures broad aspects of achievement. However, the child may be functioning at a much different level in comparison with other children *in his class.* Sometimes grades represent the amount of improvement, and a child who does well on a standardized achievement test may not, in the teacher's judgment, be mak-

---

* Reliability can be increased by constructing additional items.

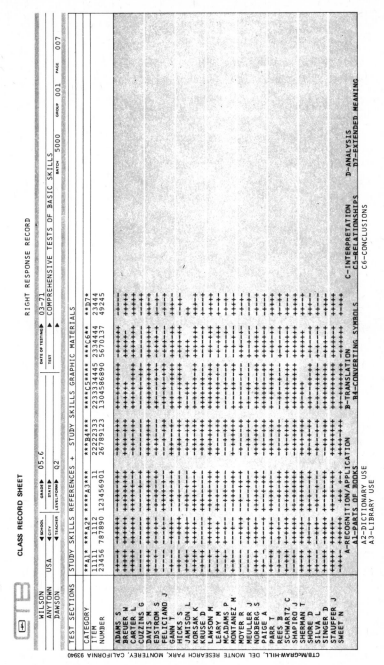

Right Response Record for use with Comprehensive Tests of Basic Skills. Reproduced by permission of the publisher, CTB/McGraw-Hill, Del Monte Research Park, Monterey, California, 93940.

Figure 13.2

ing the progress expected of him. Then the child will receive low marks although he may have high achievement test scores.

Percentiles and standard scores should be reported on achievement tests. The inequality of percentile units should be explained to parents and students, who may be disappointed if gains in percentiles near the median are compared with those at the extremes of a distribution (see table 13.3). Students and parents should also be reminded that percentiles and standard scores have meaning only in reference to some specified group, such as seniors at Elmville High School or third-graders selected nationally. It is not unusual, for example, to find a percentile decrease for students who take the same tests in both grades 9 and 12. In the lower grades a student's performance is compared with virtually all youth who are required to attend school under the provisions of compulsory education laws. But the dropout rate increases at the upper grades, particularly among lower socioeconomic groups, and by the twelfth grade a student is competing against a more select group.

Program Evaluation

One of the most important uses of standardized achievement tests is to evaluate and improve curricula. Curriculum evaluation can be extensive, such as evaluating the progress of an entire school district, or it can be restricted to a single classroom or instructional unit.

The purpose of evaluation is to improve decision making—that is, to achieve objectives at a minimum cost. This presumes that (1) there are specifiable objectives for the program; (2) there is agreement on objectives *at least* among those responsible for the program; (3) there are alternative ways of achieving these objectives; and (4) costs differ depending on which alternative is selected.

Some teachers incorrectly believe that it is necessary to complete a unit of instruction before it can be evaluated. This belief unnecessarily delays evaluation. Nothing prevents the teacher from evaluating a program's effectiveness while it is underway.

Evaluations of a completed program are called *summative evaluations;* those that provide continuous feedback throughout the program are called *formative evaluations.* One advantage of formative evaluation is that it allows the teacher to review and modify teaching methods and materials throughout the course. Item analyses can point out students' misconceptions and misunderstandings; and formative evaluation can provide students with feedback and can help improve motivation. Summative evaluation, on the other hand, usually considers the program in its entirety; it is most useful in helping the directors to decide whether a program should be continued or eliminated. Nothing, of course, prevents the evaluator from using both formative and summative evaluations to improve student learning. Chapter 18 describes a number of evaluation models and designs useful in curriculum evaluation.

Reliability of Standardized Achievement Tests

Most manuals for standardized achievement tests include extensive data on reliability. The Stanford Achievement Test provides tables of split-half and Kuder-Richardson reliabilities for single grade levels. For example, the Primary I Battery is designed for grades 1.5–2.5 and consists of six subtests: word reading, paragraph meaning, vocabulary, spelling, word study skills, and arithmetic. Reliability coefficients for grade 1.6 were computed from a sample of 1,000 cases drawn randomly from seventy-six school systems. The lowest reliabilities at this grade level, using both split-half and Kuder-Richardson estimates, were on the vocabulary subtest (.79 and .83, respectively); the highest reliability was .95, on the arithmetic subtest. Standard errors of measurement are also provided in grade equivalent units.

On the High School Battery of the Stanford Achievement Test (grades 9–12), similar analyses are provided for each grade level and for all grade levels combined. Reliabilities computed over the four grade levels are inflated values (see pp. 156-157) since correlations are influenced by group heterogeneity. Moreover, the standard errors of measurement are given only for standard scores derived from studies in grades 9–12 combined; the inclusion of standard errors of measurement for each grade level would have been a more defensible procedure. Both the Kuder-Richardson and split-half coefficients— most of which are between .87 and .92—are satisfactory for each grade tested.

All levels of the Stanford Achievement Test have four forms (W, X, Y, Z) except the High School Battery, which has only three (W, X, S). Form S is a secure form, meaning that it is not available except under high test security conditions. The manual does not provide correlations between alternate forms or for stability, although these coefficients are essential for test interpretation.

Validity of Standardized Achievement Tests

Standardized achievement tests typically provide less information on validity than on reliability, probably because it is relatively difficult to obtain validity data. The Stanford Achievement Test, like other achievement measures, should be evaluated by content validity. According to the test manual, the authors of the Stanford Achievement Test tried to construct items that reflected the goals and important objectives of the public schools. This was done by examining school textbooks and consulting subject-matter experts to determine which skills and understandings are basic at each grade level. For schools or programs that are atypical (such as schools teaching "new math" in the intermediate grades), the Stanford arithmetic subtest may not be valid, and other tests measuring knowledge of "new math" (such as the Stanford Modern Mathematics Concepts Test) can replace invalid subtests. Item analysis data are improperly used as evidence of validity, particularly so when the criterion is internal (i.e., the total score on the test). Discrimination indices and measures of item difficulty relate more to reliability than to validity.

The Stanford Achievement Test presents ten tables for the High School Battery that compare the difficulty level of each item for each subtest. In many cases these item difficulty levels vary greatly among the three forms. However, norms are "adjusted" to compensate for these differences.* Discrimination indices are not included in the manual.

Further evidence of the construct validity of the Stanford Achievement Test is a table showing the correlations among the subtests for grades 9–12 and the correlation of each subtest with the Otis Gamma IQ Test (table 13.3). As with most standardized achievement tests, subtests correlate substantially with general intelligence measures and with each other. But this table identifies another problem common to many standardized achievement tests—titles of tests and subtests can be misleading. The reading test, for example, is as good a measure of science as it is of arts and humanities. If subtest titles are to have different meanings, the intercorrelations among them should be low. Note also the substantial correlations between the subtests of the Stanford and Otis IQ scores.

Additional useful information in the Stanford Achievement Test manual is a table of *factor loadings* (see table 13.4). These factor loadings represent the correlation of each subtest with hypothetical factors or traits labeled *A, B,* and *C*. These factors are determined by *factor analysis*—a mathematical procedure used to identify the number of traits, abilities, or factors that determine the test scores. A test, for example, could be described as measuring a single factor, such as "general knowledge," or that same test, on analysis, could measure a number of factors that could be labeled *A, B, C,* and so on. Ideally each test subtest should correlate with one factor but not with any others. By examining the content of the subtests that correlate most highly with each factor, it is possible to educe the nature of each factor.

Table 13.4 shows the presence of three factors labeled *A, B,* and *C*.† The English subtest correlates .80 with factor *A* but only .26 and .31 with factors *B* and *C,* respectively. Whatever factor *A* measures, the English subtest measures it best. The next highest correlation with factor *A* is spelling, followed by reading, arts and humanities, Otis IQ, and social studies. Since all these tests have language in common, it is reasonable to call factor *A* a language factor.

---

* The adjustment is most easily accomplished by making the means and standard deviations equivalent. See pages 137-138 and 153-155.

† The mathematical procedure used to extract factors is beyond the scope of introductory texts.

Table 13.3. Correlations among Subtests of the Stanford Achievement Test between Otis Gamma IQs and the Stanford Achievement Test, Grade 9

Variable Test	2	3	4	5	6	7	8	9	10	11	12	13
1 English	.72	.67	.63	.80	.65	.64	.71	.73	.71	.64	.28	.81
2 Numerical competence		.75	.71	.72	.69	.68	.70	.55	.58	.68	.46	.77
3 Mathematics—part A			(.94)*	.68	.64	.65	.67	.52	.58	.61	.40	.71
4 Mathematics—total				.65	.60	.62	.64	.50	.57	.60	.39	.67
5 Reading					.76	.75	.79	.65	.76	.69	.41	.81
6 Science—part A						(.97)*	.73	.45	.63	.64	.60	.72
7 Science—total							.73	.45	.63	.69	.62	.71
8 Social studies								.55	.71	.69	.46	.75
9 Spelling									.62	.52	.13	.63
10 Arts and humanities										.63	.36	.70
11 Business and economics											.46	.68
12 Technical comprehension												.41
13 Otis Gamma IQ												

( )* These correlations are artificially high since subtest scores are correlated with their own total scores.

Table 13.4. Factor Loadings: Stanford Achievement Test, Grade 9

Test	Factor A	Factor B	Factor C
English	.80	.26	.31
Numerical competence	51	.44	.44
Mathematics—part A	.39	.32	.83
Mathematics—total	.37	.32	.80
Reading	.74	.44	.30
Science—part A	.42	.81	.26
Science—total	.40	.83	.29
Social studies	.61	.49	.32
Spelling	.75	.08	.25
Arts and humanities	.71	.36	.23
Business and economics	.53	.43	.31
Technical comprehension	.08	.66	.19
Otis Gamma IQ	.68	.39	.36

Adapted from High School Battery manual, table II, p. 22. Reproduced from Stanford Achievement Test, copyright © 1964–1966 by Harcourt Brace Jovanovich, Inc. Reproduced by special permission of the publisher.

Factor *B* has its highest correlations or loadings with science and technical comprehension and can be called a science-technical factor. Similarly, factor *C* seems to be a mathematics factor. Although not all the subtests are unambiguous measures of a single factor (e.g., numerical competence appears to be more closely related to the language factor than to the mathematics factor), most of the subtests correlate with factors that make sense educationally. These data can be used to analyze the *construct validity* of the Stanford Achievement Tests. Instead of referring to twelve separate subtests and assuming that each is an independent measure, the factor analysis shows that the Stanford Achievement Tests are best described as measuring three factors labeled language, science-technical, and mathematics.

Profiles

Profiles are graphic depictions of student or class performance. Because a profile expresses all scores in a common unit (such as percentiles, grade or age equivalents, or standard scores), it is possible to compare one score with another. Figure 7.4 is a profile in which a band extending from one standard error of measurement below to one standard error above the student's actual score value indicates the probable range of student performance.

Sometimes teachers prepare profiles for their own students. On the Comprehensive Test of Basic Skills (CTBS), for example, teachers may complete profiles for each student. The completed profile for Susan Blake (figure 13.3)

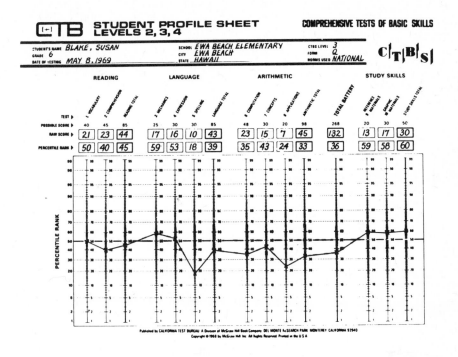

Figure 13.3. Student Profile Sheet

indicates fairly average performance except for that in spelling, which is only at the 18th percentile.

Many test publishers can provide very complete information about each child's performance. The California Test Bureau, for example, has developed an individual test record (figure 13.4). For each subtest of the CTBS there is a raw score (RS) and a grade equivalent (GE) or standard score (SS). Also, the *anticipated achievement*—a value predicted from the student's age, grade, and sex and from subtests of the California Short-Form Test of Mental Maturity—is given either in grade equivalents (AAGE) or standard scores (AASS). In addition, the record provides the difference between actual and anticipated achievement, and it plots the student's national percentile which is located in the upper right-hand corner of the profile. The band extends one standard error of measurement above and one below the student's actual percentile, indicating that the "true score" is probably somewhere between the two extremes.

The lower half of the individual test record indicates which items the student answered correctly and incorrectly on each subtest. The profile for

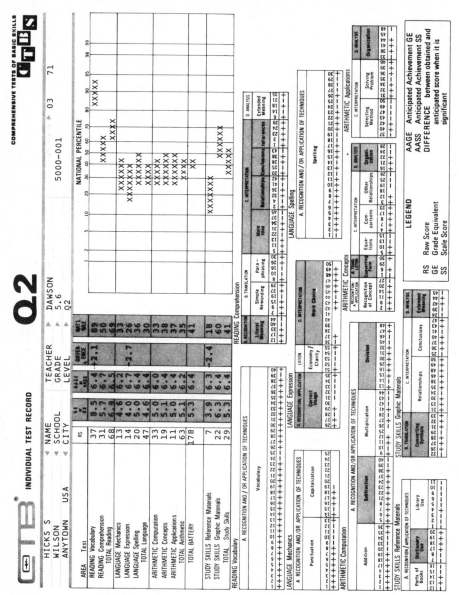

Individual Test Record for use with Comprehensive Tests of Basic Skills. Reproduced by permission of the publisher, CTB/McGraw-Hill, Del Monte Research Park, Monterey, California 93940.

Figure 13.4

S. Hicks (figure 13.4) shows that he performed at a high level on the vocabulary subtest, missing only three out of forty items. His performance is average in reading comprehension, and he is clearly below average on language expression, on language mechanics, and on study skills reference materials. A remedial program is particularly called for in the use of reference materials and language expression.

The Concepts of Underachievement and Overachievement

Educators are understandably interested in knowing whether a student is working up to his ability. The term *underachiever* refers to a student who is working below his ability; an *overachiever,* in contrast, is working above some expected level of performance. Early attempts to measure underachievement and overachievement often used an *accomplishment quotient* (AQ), or the ratio of mental age to educational age multiplied by 100 to eliminate decimals. A child with a mental age of 120 months and a reading age of 160 months would have an accomplishment quotient of 75 and would therefore be an underachiever. Any ratio above 100 indicated overachievement.

For good reasons the AQ is no longer used. First, the means and standard deviations on intelligence and achievement tests differ, making direct comparisons between such norms hazardous at best. Second, the AQ relies on intelligence test scores both as a measure of *capacity* (which they are not) and as a standard indicating the level at which a child *should* be functioning. No test score measures the *maximum* or *optimal* level of performance for any given person. Use of the AQ presumes that an intelligence test can serve that purpose.

The notion that an intelligence test should be used as the criterion for achievement fails to consider the fallible nature of all tests. If an intelligence test is used to predict achievement test scores, a discrepancy between these two measures simply means that the test has failed to predict accurately. It does not necessarily mean that the child is above or below where he should be functioning. If mastery were considered the criterion instead of scores on an intelligence test, there would obviously be a greater number of "underachievers." The "optimal" level of achievement could be determined as easily by prior achievement as by IQ, but there is no good reason to use either. One could argue that all students are "achieving below their capacity" since no one works and studies twenty-four hours a day. Similarly, one could take the position that teachers should strive for *maximum* learning among students and should not be content simply because IQ and achievement measures are equal.

"Anticipated achievement" scores such as those described on page 379 are open to many of the same criticisms that can be leveled at the AQ. For example, they fail to consider errors of measurement by which students can attain higher or lower predictor or criterion scores based simply on the effects of chance. But because of the high correlation that typically exists between intelligence and achievement scores, virtually all students fall within predicted ranges on achievement test scores when chance is accounted for. Only about 4 percent of the population are expected to be as far as two standard errors of estimate (see pp. 342-343) from their predicted values. For that reason, underachievement and overachievement really present problems of developing tests that are better able to predict achievement than those now employed (Thorndike 1963). If the correlation between IQ and achievement scores were + 1.0, every student would achieve at his "capacity" level; if the correlation were 0, the greatest number of prediction errors would occur, and more students would be classified as underachievers and overachievers. The concepts of overachievement and underachievement will be discussed further in chapter 17.

Some Examples of Standardized Achievement Tests

Diagnostic Achievement Tests

Reading   Diagnostic reading tests can be administered individually or to groups. Individually administered tests usually contain paragraphs graded in difficulty which the examinee reads aloud. The examiner marks the kinds and number of errors committed.

The Gilmore Oral Reading Test is an example of an individually administered diagnostic reading test. It consists of ten paragraphs, each accompanied by five comprehension questions. The test measures accuracy (substitutions, omissions, and disregard of punctuation), reading rate, and comprehension. Figure 13.5 is an example of a paragraph, questions, and error record from the Gilmore Oral Reading Test.

Another individually administered test is the Gates-McKillop Reading Diagnostic Test. Designed for children in grades 2 and higher, its two forms each contain the following subtests: oral reading (paragraphs), word pronunciation (flash and untimed), phrases (flash), knowledge of word parts (word attack, recognizing and blending common word parts, giving letter sounds, naming capital letters, naming lowercase letters), recognizing the visual form or word equivalents of sounds (nonsense words, initial letters, final letters, vowels), auditory blending, and supplementary tests (spelling, oral vocabulary, syllabification, auditory discrimination). Unlike the Gilmore test, the Gates-McKillop test contains no measures of comprehension or reading rate. The manual explains how to use the Gates-McKillop in considerable detail, but no evidence of

Mother likes to cook for her family. She prepares delicious meals for them. On certain holidays she cooks special foods which are family favorites. In the warm summer season, there are numerous picnics in the back yard. Father often builds the fire for these outdoor meals. Mary and Dick assist him by gathering wood. The entire family insists that food tastes much better when it is cooked and eaten in the fresh air.

TIME_____Seconds

1. What does Mother like to do?
2. When does Mother cook special foods?
3. How does Father prepare for the outdoor meals?
4. How do Mary and Dick help Father?
____ 5. Why does the family like food cooked outdoors?

ERROR RECORD	Number
Substitutions	
Mispronunciations	
Words pronounced by examiner	
Disregard of punctuation	
Insertions	
Hesitations	
Repetitions	
Omissions	
Total Errors	

From the *Gilmore Oral Reading Test, Form B.* Copyright © 1968 by Harcourt Brace Jovanovich, Inc. Reproduced by special permission of the publisher.

Figure 13.5. Gilmore Oral Reading Test Item

validity or reliability is presented. Content validity, however, seems to be satisfactory.

Still another individually administered reading diagnostic test is the Durrell Analysis of Reading Difficulty (grades 1–6), which contains graded paragraphs

3. Time _____ Memories _____

GRADE	2			3		
	L	M	H	L	M	H
TIME	62	50	35	30	23	16
MEMORIES		7			10	

Three boys.......................

built a house....................

in the woods. ....

They put a table.................

and two old chairs in it. ....

There was a basket...............

full of apples...................

under the table. ....

One afternoon...................

they went away..................

and left the door open. ....

When they came back, ...

they found two little pigs........

eating the apples. ....

Figure 13.6a. Example of *Durrell Analysis of Reading Difficulty* Paragraph.

Imagery Questions (OPTIONAL)

PARAGRAPH 3

1. *Did you see in your mind the three boys who built the house in the woods? Tell me how they looked to you.* Then ask: *How old were they? How were they dressed?* etc.
2. *Did you see the house in your mind? Tell me about how it looked to you.* Then ask: *How big was it? Did it have any windows? How many? What kind of roof did it have? Could you draw a picture of how the house looked to you?* etc.

Figure 13.6b. Example of *Durrell Analysis of Reading Difficulty* Imagery Questions

for measuring oral and silent reading, word analysis, listening comprehension, phonetics, faulty pronunciation, writing, and spelling. Listening comprehension is a measure of the ability to remember details rather than a measure of understanding. No data on reliability or validity are presented. Figures 13.6a and b present an example of a paragraph and Imagery questions from the Durrell Analysis of Reading Difficulty.

Many of the diagnostic reading tests for older children are of the pencil-and-paper variety. Most assume that the child is capable of word-attack skills and emphasize such abilities as reading for different purposes, comprehension, word meaning, study skills, and reading rate.

It is questionable whether there is an advantage to having norms on diagnostic reading tests. Teachers should know what kinds of errors students are making; it is less important to know that someone is at the third-grade level in reading. High reliability coefficients on independent subtests are more important than the availability of norms.

Diagnostic reading tests differ widely on the type of content sampled (speed, comprehension, decoding skills) as well as on administrative procedures (oral or pencil-and-paper, for example). Also, some tests sample many different types of reading errors, whereas others restrict themselves to one or two topics.

Arithmetic Numerous tests exist to help diagnose problems in arithmetic. Some tests, such as the Buswell-John Diagnostic Test for Fundamental Processes in Arithmetic, are given orally, and the examiner carefully notes the process used as the student attempts each item. A more common procedure is to allow the student to work at his own speed using a pencil-and-paper format.

One of the most ambitious attempts to measure various aspects of arithmetic attainment is the Diagnostic Tests and Self-Helps in Arithmetic, published by the California Test Bureau for students in grades 3–12. Three screening tests help discover which students need help in fractions, decimals, and whole numbers (see figure 13.7). Another test contains more difficult problems used to screen more advanced pupils in need of remedial help. Based on the results of these screening tests, any or all of the twenty-three diagnostic tests can then be administered.

Test II. Screening Test in Fractions $6\frac{1}{5} \div 4 =$

Test IV. Screening Test in Arithmetic: Decimals $100 \times .027 =$

Figure 13.7. Examples of items from the Diagnostic Tests and Self-Helps in Arithmetic.

These tests are also cross-referenced. In performing any complex mathematical operation, errors can be made on division facts, multiplication facts, subtraction of whole numbers, and division of decimals, for example. Each of these is represented by a separate subtest that can help locate the child's specific problem. Once a student is screened, exercises show him how to solve each type of problem. In addition to pointing out student errors, the materials also encourage the child to solve his own problems.

Specific Subject-Matter Achievement Tests

Standardized achievement tests are available for practically every subject taught in the elementary and secondary grades. These tests are often used at the end of a course to evaluate student performance against national norms. This can help the teacher evaluate teaching methods or discover areas of pupil strength or weakness. The crucial factor in using these tests is close correspondence between the teacher's objectives and test item content.

Because so many achievement tests are available, a careful search will usually produce one that corresponds at least reasonably well to the teacher's objectives. New tests have even been developed to meet the new objectives of some modern curricula in mathematics, science, and social studies. For example, The Psychological Corporation has published a final examination for pupils using the Biological Sciences Curriculum Study materials; other tests are available to measure achievement at the end of each unit of instruction.

The Modern Math Understanding Test (MMUT), published by Science Research Associates, Inc. (SRA), is a good example of a specific subject-matter achievement test (see figure 13.8). Designed for grades 1–9, each test measures three areas of mathematics: foundations, operations, and geometry and measure-

S1. Which numeral must be placed in the box to make the following sentence true?

$$3 + \square = 7$$

A. 2   C. 7

B. 4   D. 10

S2. Which set contains exactly two elements?

E. $\{\triangle, \square, \bigcirc, \text{❋}\}$ G. $\{\text{❋}, \triangle\}$

F. $\{\square, \bigcirc, \triangle\}$ H. $\{\bigcirc\}$

Figure 13.8. Example of Modern Math Understanding Test

ment. Each of these areas, in turn, is analyzed into four types of understanding: knowledge and computation, elementary understanding, problem solving and application, and structure and generalization. Grade equivalents and percentiles are presented for the total score; stanines are presented for each content area, each type of understanding, and total math understanding. School districts may substitute the MMUT for the more traditional arithmetic subtest that appears on the SRA Achievement Series.

Standardized Achievement Test Batteries

An achievement test battery consists of a number of tests in different subjects. Because all the tests are standardized on the same population, comparisons across different tests are possible for the same student. A typical battery consists of six or more separate tests, and a total battery score (the mean of all tests included in the battery) may or may not be provided.

Since publishers want wide use of their tests, subjects commonly taught in most schools are likely to be included in a battery. Because all schools teach language, reading, and mathematics, these are included in all test batteries; but home economics, for example, is not. Science, social studies, and reference and study skills appear in some batteries.

The philosophy underlying a test battery helps to differentiate it from other batteries. The Sequential Tests of Educational Progress (STEP), for example, stresses application and interpretation of knowledge (see figure 13.9), whereas the Metropolitan Achievement Test emphasizes the ability to recall important but specific information (see figure 13.10). The selection of one battery over another rests on careful consideration of both the technical requirements for a test and the goals of the school district.

The fact that two tests have the same title does not necessarily mean that they measure the same functions. A "spelling" subtest in one battery may require the student to select a misspelled word from among those correctly spelled;

The policeman told the boy that the candy store was right around the corner.

The policeman was

A mean.
B helpful.
C big.
D important.

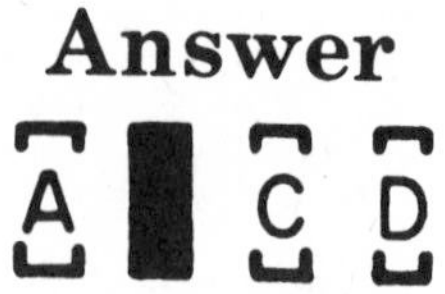

Answer

⌐A⌐ ■ ⌐C⌐ ⌐D⌐

Figure 13.9. Example of a STEP Item

In Disneyland, California, there is a street called Main Street, U.S.A. Over one shop on Main Street there is a big sign. It tells us that this is a lock shop. Inside the shop there are all kinds of locks, but they are not for sale. Visitors see *great* locks and tiny locks. Some of the locks are new and others are hundreds of years old. This shop is a lock museum.

A The locks in the lock shop are—
  A all old   C all small
  B never sold   D never cleaned

B In this story, the word *great* means—
  E nice   G famous
  F good   H large

Figure 13.10. Example of a Metropolitan Achievement Test Item

on a different test the student may not only have to find errors but correct them as well. One test might emphasize knowledge of reading vocabulary in mathematics, social studies, and natural sciences; another could yield a single vocabulary score or none at all.

The tests in table 13.5, in alphabetical order, are probably the most extensively used achievement batteries.

Remember that the final selection of any examination depends on the purpose of testing, the technical characteristics of the tests, and the practical considerations of tests as described in chapter 10.

Table 13.5

Test	Publisher	Appropriate Grade Range	Grade Levels	Forms	Subtests
Adult Basic Learning Examination, 1967	Harcourt Brace Jovanovich, Inc.	Adults			Vocabulary, reading, spelling, arithmetic
California Achievement Test, 1970	CTB/McGraw-Hill Book Co.	1.5–12	1.5–2	1	Language (auding, mechanics, usage and structure, spelling)
			2–4	2	Reading (vocabulary, comprehension), mathematics (computation, concepts and problems), language (mechanics, usage, structure, spelling)
			4–6	3	
			6–9	4	
			9–12	5	(Same subtests used on forms 2–5)
Comprehensive Tests of Basic Skills, 1968	CTB/McGraw-Hill Book Co.	2.5–12	2.5–4	1	Reading (vocabulary, comprehension), language (mechanics, expression, spelling), arithmetic (computation, concepts, applications), study skills (reference materials, graphic materials)
			4–6	2	
			6–8	3	
			8–12	4	(Same subtests used throughout forms)
Comprehensive Tests of Basic Skills, 1973		K–12	K	A	Pre-reading, language skills, elementary concepts of math
			1	B	Reading, language, mathematics
			2	C	Similar to 1968 series, with the addition of social studies and science subtests
				1–4	Similar to 1968 series, with addition of social studies and science subtests
Iowa Tests of Basic Skills, 1964	Houghton-Mifflin Co.	3–9	3–9	1	Vocabulary, reading comprehension, language skills (spelling, capitalization, punctuation, usage), work-study skills (map reading, reading graphs and tables, knowledge and use of reference materials), arithmetic skills (arithmetic concepts, arithmetic problem solving)
				2	
				3	
				4	
				(Each form contained in a single booklet)	(Same subtests used throughout forms)

Table 13.5 (Cont.)

Test	Publisher	Appropriate Grade Range	Grade Levels	Forms	Subtests
Iowa Tests of Educational Development, 1959	Science Research Associates, Inc.	9-12	9-12	X = 5 Y = 5 (Are parallel forms)	Reading (comprehension, vocabulary), language arts (usage, spelling), mathematics (problem solving, abstract concepts), social studies background (understanding concepts, general knowledge of current problems), science background, use of sources (Same subtests used in both forms)
Metropolitan Achievement Test, 1970	Harcourt Brace Jovanovich, Inc.	K-9	K.7-1.4	Primer	Listening for sounds, reading, numbers
			1.5-2.4	Primary I	Word knowledge, word analysis, reading, mathematics computation, mathematical concepts
			2.5-3.4	Primary II	Word knowledge, word analysis, reading, spelling, mathematics computation, mathematical concepts, mathematics problem solving
			3.5-4.9	Elementary	Word knowledge, reading, language, spelling mathematics computation, mathematical concepts, mathematics problem solving
			5.0-6.9	Intermediate	Word knowledge, reading, language, spelling, mathematics computation, mathematical concepts, mathematics problem solving, science, social studies
			7.0-9.5	Advanced	Word knowledge, reading, language, spelling, mathematics computation, mathematical concepts, mathematics problem solving, science, social studies
Sequential Tests of Educational Progress Series II (STEP), 1969	Educational Testing Service	4-14	4-6 7-9 10-12 13-14	4A, 4B 3A, 3B 2A, 2B 1A, 1B	English expression, reading, mechanics of writing, mathematics computation, mathematics basic concepts, science, social studies (Mechanics of writing, mathematics basic concepts for levels 2-4 only)
SRA Achievement Series, 1971	Science Research Associates, Inc.	1-9	1-2	Primary I	Reading (word verbal-picture association, sentence picture association, comprehension, vocabulary), mathematics (concepts and computation), language arts (alphabetization, capitalization, punctuation, spelling and usage)

Table 13.5 (Cont.)

Test	Publisher	Appropriate Grade Range	Grade Levels	Forms	Subtests
SRA Achievement Series, 1971 (Cont.)			3-4	Primary II	Reading (word verbal-picture association, sentence picture association, comprehension, vocabulary), mathematics (concepts and computation), language arts (alphabetization, capitalization, punctuation, spelling and usage)
			3-5	Blue Level	Reading (comprehension, vocabulary, and total), language arts (usage, spelling, and total), mathematics (concepts, computation, and total), social studies, science, uses of sources
			5-7	Green Level	Reading (comprehension, vocabulary, and total), language arts (usage, spelling, and total), mathematics (concepts, computation, and total), social studies, science, uses of sources
			7-8	Red Level	Reading (comprehension, vocabulary, and total), language arts (usage, spelling, and total), mathematics (concepts, computation, and total), social studies, science, uses of sources
Stanford Achievement Test, 1969	Harcourt Brace Jovanovich, Inc.	1.5-12, College	K.1-1.8	Stanford Early School Achievement Test (SESAT)	Environment, mathematics, letters and sounds, aural comprehension, word reading, sentence reading
1973			1.5-2.4	Primary I	Vocabulary, reading comprehension, word study skills, mathematics concepts, mathematics computation, spelling, listening comprehension
			2.5-3.4	Primary II	Vocabulary, reading comprehension, word study skills, mathematics concepts, mathematics computation, mathematics application, spelling, social studies, science, listening comprehension
			3.5-4.4	Primary III	Vocabulary, reading comprehension, word study skills, mathematics concepts, mathematics computation, mathematics application, spelling, language, social science, science, listening comprehension

Table 13.5 (Cont.)

Test	Publisher	Appropriate Grade Range	Grade Levels	Forms	Subtests
Stanford Achievement Test, 1973 (Cont.)			4.5–5.4	Intermediate I	Vocabulary, reading comprehension, word study skills, mathematics concepts, mathematics computation, mathematics application, spelling, language, social science, science, listening comprehension
			5.5–6.9	Intermediate II	Vocabulary, reading comprehension, word study skills, mathematics concepts, mathematics computation, mathematics application, spelling, language, social science, science, listening comprehension
			7.–9.5	Advanced	Vocabulary, reading comprehension, mathematics concepts, mathematics computation, mathematics application, spelling, language, social science, science
			9.–10	Task I	Reading comprehension, mathematics concepts, language
			11–12	Task II	Reading comprehension, mathematics concepts, language

Summary

1. Achievement tests differ from aptitude measures in their intent and method of validation. The purpose of aptitude tests is prediction; the purpose of achievement tests is to measure scholastic accomplishment. Aptitude tests require predictive validity, whereas achievement tests require content validity.

2. The procedure used to develop standardized achievement tests includes the following steps:

   a. Developing test rationale and objectives.

   b. Writing test items that meet these objectives.

   c. Analyzing items.

   d. Constructing final forms of the test.

   e. Standardizing (norming) the final forms.

3. Norms on standardized achievement tests consist of percentile, age, grade, quotient, and standard scores.

   a. *Age norms.* Age norms on achievement tests are called educational ages (EA). An EA of 6-0 means that the child has performed as well as the average six-year-old on the test. EA norms are ordinal variables.

   b. *Grade norms.* The grade level at which a student is performing on an achievement test is called his grade placement (GP) or grade equivalent (GE). A GE of 6.0 means that the student is doing as well as the average student who has just entered the sixth grade. The procedures used to develop GE norms, include the processes of interpolation and extrapolation of norms. GE norms are ordinal, are difficult to interpret to parents, assume that higher scores will be obtained by students in higher grade levels, and are incorrectly thought of as standards of achievement to be attained by each student.

   c. *Quotient norms.* The educational quotient (EQ) is computed by dividing the EA by the CA and multiplying by 100. EQs above 100 indicate that the student is performing at a higher level than students of his chronological age. EQs are not comparable from age to age because the means and standard deviations are not constant.

   d. *Standard score norms. T* scores and stanines are commonly reported on standardized achievement tests.

4. Many school districts have developed their own norms (called local norms). Although they are useful for intragroup comparisons, they do not permit comparisons with other districts.

5. Norms can be developed for individuals and for schools. These two will not be the same because the variability from school to school is likely to be smaller than the variability of individual performance.

6. Norms on achievement tests vary depending on what time of the year they are given. It is important for teachers to use norms appropriate to the time of year when the tests are administered to a class.

7. Standardized achievement tests can be used for several purposes:

   a. *Selection and placement.* Achievement tests can be used either as predictors or as criteria. As predictors, they serve as aptitude tests, but they may be less efficient than scholastic aptitude tests because they contain more subtests. For college selection, the high school grade point average is the single best predictor. To be used as criteria, achievement tests must match school objectives.

   b. *Diagnosis.* Achievement tests can be used for diagnosis, but more accurate diagnoses may require the teacher to construct additional items on a specific topic than are present on the standardized test.

   c. *Feedback.* Percentiles or standard scores will have to be interpreted to parents and students, but percentiles will be easier for parents to understand. In conferences with the teacher, parents and students can be told the content of the specific items that were missed.

   d. *Program evaluation.* Standardized achievement tests can be used for formative and summative evaluation provided that the program's objectives are comparable to the types of items contained in the test.

8. The reliability of standardized achievement tests tends to be satisfactory. Reliability coefficients should be provided for each grade level for which the test is designed.

9. The validity of achievement tests is best determined by examining how items were selected (content validity). Item analysis data are more related to reliability than to validity. Correlations among subtests, however, should be low; otherwise the subtests measure the same traits or abilities. Factor analysis procedures can be used to demonstrate which factors or traits are measured by the test regardless of their apparent content.

10. Because student profiles express scores in comparable units, it is possible to indicate the areas in which the student shows strength as well as the areas in which he has deficiencies.

11. The early attempts to relate achievement to "ability" led to the incorrect use of the accomplishment quotient, or the ratio of educational age to mental age, multiplied by 100 to eliminate decimals. The accomplishment quotient should not be used because norms on achievement and intelligence tests are not comparable and because the intelligence test does not necessarily

measure "capacity" for learning. Anticipated achievement norms are also used, but they often fail to consider errors in predicting achievement from intelligence scores. Since no tests correlate perfectly with one another, little is gained by referring to students as underachievers or overachievers; rather, the intelligence test predicted higher or lower scores than were actually attained.

12. Some examples of achievement tests are:

   a. *Diagnostic achievement tests.* Diagnostic reading and arithmetic tests are available. The number and types of subtests vary considerably from test to test. Although norms are not particularly important for diagnosis, the reliability of each subtest should be presented in the test manual with tables showing the intercorrelations among subtests.

   b. *Specific subject-matter achievement tests.* Tests are available to measure achievement in almost all curriculum subjects. If schools are teaching the "new math," for example, tests containing items that measure relevant course objectives should be selected.

   c. *Standardized achievement test batteries.* These tests typically contain items that measure the most commonly taught school subjects (language, reading, and mathematics, for example). Because the philosophies behind achievement batteries differ, it is important to select the most valid battery by examining the items in the test or, if available, factor analyses of the test scores.

Suggested Readings

Anastasi, Anne. *Psychological Testing.* 3d ed. New York: Macmillan Co., 1968, 665 pp. Chapter 15 contains an excellent description of the many achievement tests and batteries in common use.

Angoff, William H. "Scales, Norms, and Equivalent Scores." In Robert L. Thorndike, ed., *Educational Measurement,* 2d ed., pp. 508–600. Washington, D.C.: American Council on Education, 1971. The first half of this chapter is an excellent summary of various kinds of norms, with emphasis on those found on many achievement tests. The second half is rather technical.

Ingle, Robert B., and De Amico, Gerald. "The Effect of Physical Conditions of the Test Room on Standardized Achievement Test Scores." *Journal of Educational Measurement* 6, no. 4 (Winter 1969): 237–40. The authors found that when students were given ample time to take standardized tests, lighting conditions and the size of the writing surface appeared to make little difference. However, girls performed at a higher level than did the boys, suggesting differences in maturation levels among adolescents. The authors suggest that if time restrictions were not ample, the conditions of testing would have affected test results.

Thorndike, Robert L. *The Concepts of Over- and Underachievement.* New York: Bureau of Publications, Teachers College, Columbia University, 1963, 79 pp. Thorndike analyzes the concepts of overachievement and underachievement and suggests ways of conducting research in this area. Particularly important is the notion that these terms can have different meanings depending on the nature of the measurements used.

The Measurement of Interests and Attitudes

14 Effective evaluation presumes valid measurement. To counsel or help a youngster in the classroom requires an understanding of his *affective* or *noncognitive behaviors,* such as interests, attitudes, and personality, as well as his cognitive skills and knowledge.

Whether the public schools should concern themselves with the child's affective *and* cognitive development is a matter of both philosophy and the extent to which it is possible to emphasize one while avoiding the other. Some persons take the philosophical position that the public schools exist solely to "develop the mind"; in opposition are those who place greater emphasis on "adjustment." But perhaps more important are the questions of whether it is possible to teach intellectual skills independent of their effects on student attitudes and whether attitudes and interests will facilitate or hinder cognitive learning.

Interests and attitudes are learned responses. The art teacher who is concerned exclusively and mechanically that students memorize color combinations is not likely to engender any "appreciation" for art. Mathematics can be intriguing or intimidating, depending on teaching methods. The learning of almost any intellectual task carries with it elements of interest and attitude which may either facilitate or hinder additional learning. Whatever teaching methods one uses will affect both subject-matter acquisition and student interests and attitudes.

The Meaning of Interest and Attitude

An *interest* is a preference for one activity over another. This definition emphasizes two points. First, interests involve the selection and ranking of activities along a like-dislike dimension. One student may prefer listening to records to working arithmetic problems, for example. Second, interests involve activities or behaviors engaged in by individuals. Interests are expressed by action verbs, such as *reading* a book, *playing* a phonograph, or *planting* flowers.

Regardless of the method used to measure interests, the components of indicating preferences for activities along a like-dislike dimension will be present. The test constructor's responsibility is to develop instruments that indicate which activities are preferred over others and if possible, to what extent. By emphasizing preferences for activities rather than preferences for groups, institutions, or objects, a distinction can be made between *interests* and *attitudes,* although admittedly the two terms are not entirely independent. One may have an *interest* in arranging flowers and a positive *attitude* toward flowers (objects) in general. Some persons may have an *interest* in teaching but have a negative *attitude* toward children (groups).

Distinctions between interests and attitudes are neither universally agreed upon nor entirely satisfactory. Some authors prefer to make no distinction between the two terms, and Gordon Allport (1935) has listed sixteen different definitions of attitude alone. According to many theorists, attitudes are "predispositions" to behave in a certain way, whereas interests involve preferences but not necessarily any commitment to behave in accordance with those preferences. For example, a positive *attitude* toward children may predispose citizens to vote for school appropriations, whereas a *preference* for or interest in skydiving would not necessarily require active participation. In this text *attitude* is defined as a generalized response to a particular group, institution, concept, or object along a favorable-unfavorable dimension.

Types of Interests

Interests may be expressed, manifest, or inventoried (Super and Crites 1962), depending on the method employed to evoke responses.

Expressed Interest

An interest is *expressed* whenever an individual states his preference for one activity over another. This is the simplest and most direct way of obtaining information about interests, but it has a number of serious weaknesses. Young or immature individuals tend to express interests that conform to socially desirable or romanticized expectations, such as an interest in becoming an astronaut or reading classical books. Sometimes individuals express interest in an activity solely for its shock value.

Manifest Interest

An interest is made *manifest* when an individual voluntarily participates in an activity. The student who joins the stamp club or the housewife who attends yoga classes demonstrates interest in these activities.

Sometimes it is difficult to discern the "true" reasons a person engages in an activity. Joining the stamp club could suggest an interest in stamp collecting, but it could as easily reflect the need to belong to a social group, the desire to avoid some other activity, or simply the fact that the stamp club is the only after-school activity.

There is no necessary relationship between expressed and manifest interests, although in most instances they do coincide. Everyone engages in some activities they claim to dislike; conversely, people may refuse to engage in activities which they claim to enjoy. Nonetheless, most individuals who voluntarily devote time to some activity express a preference for it.

Inventoried Interest

Inventoried interests are those measured by tests that compare interests in different activities. Sometimes—as on the Kuder Preference Record (Form C: Vocational)—the individual must indicate which of several activities he most and least prefers. Responses are then combined to yield a profile of strong and weak interests. Another inventory, the Strong Vocational Interest Blank (SVIB), requires one of three responses ("like," "indifferent," or "dislike") to such items as occupations; school subjects; various amusements and hobbies; occupational activities such as adjusting a carburetor or repairing a clock; different kinds of people, such as military personnel or conservatives; and extracurricular activities, such as clubs or athletics. The examinee is also required to rank in importance various work conditions; to express preferences for different club (organization) offices; to state preferences between two items, such as "airplane pilot" versus "airline ticket agent"; and to select appealing personal and social traits (used for self-rating).

Each inventory emphasizes the measurement of a limited sample of interests. The SVIB is often used to help mature adolescents and college students select among semiprofessional and professional occupations (see profile, figure 14.1a and b, pp. 410 and 411). The Kuder General Interest Survey (KGIS), in contrast, measures the relative strengths of interest in broad categories such as outdoor, mechanical, scientific, computational, persuasive, artistic, literary, musical, social service, and clerical activities. Unlike the SVIB, the KGIS may be administered to children as young as seventh-graders and is a much better inventory for students interested in occupations requiring limited education.

It is important to remember that interest inventories, like all tests, can only sample limited aspects of a person's total interests. Each inventory is designed for specific age groups and for selected occupations.

Levels and Areas of Interest

Occupations and professions are characterized by *levels* and *areas*. Medicine, engineering, music, and business are *areas* or broad activities under which many different vocations are subsumed. If a college degree or highly specialized training is required, the *level* is considered professional; semiprofessional levels usually require some college or advanced training; managerial and official levels typically involve high degrees of competence learned on the job; skilled levels usually require apprenticeship training; and unskilled levels typically require little or no special competence.

The failure to distinguish between *levels* and *areas* of interest can lead to faulty decisions. For example, a student may indicate that he wants to go into medicine, but he has an IQ of only 92. Medicine, however, is an *area,* and it is possible that he could perform at the skilled level (medical technician, practical nurse, or X-ray technician). On the other hand, if a student indicates he wishes to become a physician, this term implies both an area (medicine) and a level (professional).

Table 14.1. Occupational Groupings or Areas on the Strong Vocational Interest Blank for Men and Women

Men		Women	
I	Biological science	I	Music/performing
II	Physical science	II	Art
III	Technical supervision	III	Verbal-linguistic
IV	Technical and skilled trades	IV	Social service
V	Social service	V	Verbal-scientific
VI	Aesthetic-cultural	VI	Scientific
VII	CPA owner	VII	Military/managerial
VIII	Business and accounting	VIII	Business
IX	Sales	IX	Home economics
X	Verbal-linguistic	X	Health-related services
XI	President, manufacturing concern	XI	Nonprofessional

Reprinted with the permission of the publisher from *Handbook for the Strong Vocational Interest Blank* by David P. Campbell (Stanford: Stanford University Press, 1971), p. 276.

Interest areas are defined on the SVIB by "occupational groupings" (eleven for men and eleven for women, see table 14.1) and "basic interest scales" (twenty-two for men and nineteen for women). Areas and levels are combined in most of the "occupational scales" (fifty-four for men and fifty-eight for women). Theoretically, grouping occupations makes possible the estimation of interests not specifically measured by the inventory. For example, an interest in horticulture might be suggested if a student received high scores in the biological science and aesthetic-cultural areas. In practice, however, this interpretation is hazardous because of apparent discrepancies of occupations within some of the areas (funeral director and accountant are both listed in group VIII, and policeman and carpenter are both in group IV, to name just a few). By using the basic interest scales (see profile, figure 14.1a and b) a more accurate picture of interest areas can be obtained. The basic interest scales, a relatively recent development, are currently used along with the occupational groupings. Eventually, according to David Campbell (1971, p. 277), the basic interest scales will replace the occupational groupings. Until then, however, some confusion can be expected when areas of interest are interpreted on the SVIB.

The Kuder General Interest Survey measures only *areas* of interest. However, its manual suggests appropriate occupations for various patterns and levels of interest (see table 14.2). Other Kuder tests (Form DD, for example) measure interests in specific vocations and college majors.

Table 14.2. Suggested Occupations for High Computational and Artistic Interests by Level on the Kuder Preference Record

Level	Computational Area	Artistic Area
Professional	Accountant, auditor, general accountant, professor or instructor (math, statistics, accounting), chemical engineer, civil engineer, industrial engineer, methods engineer, teacher (arithmetic), statistician	Actor, actress, architect, artist, sculptor, teacher of art, occupational therapist, curator of art gallery
Semiprofessional	Surveyor, specifications writer, estimator	Decorator and window dresser, commercial artist, designer, draftsman, photographer, taxidermist
Personal service		Barber, beautician, manicurist
Clerical and kindred	Bookkeeper and cashier (except bank cashier), bookkeeping machine operator, clerk (general office), clerk (financial institutions), office machines operator, statistical clerk, compiler	
Skilled and Semiskilled		Furrier, worker in fabrication of fur goods, milliner, dressmaker, seamstress, tailor, tailoress, photoengraver, engraver, painter, construction and maintenance

From Kuder Preference Record Vocational Form C. Copyright 1951, 1953, 1956 by G. Frederic Kuder. Reproduced by permission of the publisher, Science Research Associates, Inc.

The Relationship between Aptitudes and Interests

In general, the median correlations between all area scores on interest inventories and aptitude measures tend to be low. An analysis of these relationships on the Differential Aptitude Test and Kuder Preference Record in the DAT manual (p. A-17) shows a *median* correlation of only $+.05$ for a sample of twelfth-grade boys. However, median values disregard the more extreme correlations. For example, the correlation was $+.54$ between computational interest and numerical ability and +.48 between artistic interest and spatial relations ability. These correlations obtained from cognate activities are moderate in magnitude. Some of the correlations were negative (e.g., −.37 between social service interests and mechanical aptitude). For a group of twelfth-grade girls, the median correlation between interest and aptitude scores was −.01. The strongest positive correlation (+.48) was between artistic interest and spatial relations ability; the strongest negative correlation (−.37) was between social service interest and mechanical aptitude. Evidently, knowing a student's aptitude scores will not, at least in most instances, allow teachers to estimate his degree of interest with great accuracy. And conversely, teachers could not predict the *level* of work a student is capable of performing from a knowledge of his interest score. There would be some advantage in administering both kinds of tests simultaneously to obtain complementary data.

The typically low to moderate correlations between aptitude and interest scores may seem surprising. However, the instructions in most interest inventories ask examinees to disregard their abilities and possible lack of training as they select one activity over another. Inventoried interests therefore tend to be idealistic and independent of such realities as time and availability of funds necessary for training, the amount of income expected, motivation to succeed, and the like. They measure what the examinee would *like* to do but not necessarily what he is capable of doing.

Constructing Interest Inventories

Interest inventories are constructed using one of three approaches: rational, internal consistency, and empirical. The *rational approach* involves choosing some logical basis for categorizing interests and writing items that appear to measure each interest area. Teachers who construct their own inventories often follow this procedure. Students might be asked to check activities in which they have some interest. If a large number of science activities were chosen, the teacher assumes an interest in this area. The Lee-Thorpe Occupational Interest Inventory was developed by this "logical" approach.

The *internal consistency method* develops items from "logical" considerations; later scales are constructed so that each area of interest is internally consistent or homogeneous. Often a *factor analysis* (see pp. 377-378) is used to determine how the items can best be grouped or categorized to form homogeneous subscales. Items that correlate highly with each other measure a single factor or interest area (scientific interest, for example); items that fail to correlate with or load on any factor measured by the inventory are eliminated or new items are added to develop a new homogeneous subscale.

The *empirical approach* also begins with an experimental pool of items, but each item is selected for its ability to discriminate between successful persons and persons in general. The SVIB, for example, defines a successful person as one who has remained in the occupational field for at least three years, has indicated a liking for that work, has achieved some recognition or status for his work, and is between twenty-five and fifty-five years of age (Campbell 1971, p. 29).

If an item on the SVIB is unable to differentiate between successful chemists and men in general, it is given a weight of 0. A weight of $+1.0$ is given for each response in which successful men in a given occupation respond with greater frequency than men in general. A weight of -1 is accorded each response in which men in general respond more frequently than do men who are successful in a given occupation. The score an individual receives for each occupation is the sum of the positive and negative scores he has accumulated on that scale.

Norms on Interest Inventories

Constructors of interest inventories may wish to compare intraindividual interests on different subtests or scales. On most tests individuals are compared against external normative groups, but many interest inventories measure the individual's preferences for one activity over another, and the comparison is within the individual himself. This type of intraindividual comparison is called *ipsative* in contrast to interindividual, or *normative,* comparisons.

Ipsative scales are derived from inventories on which the individual must select one activity over another. On the Kuder General Interest Survey (KGIS), for example, the subject is given a *forced-choice format* in which he must indicate which of three activities he prefers and which he likes least. The acceptance of one activity and the concomitant rejection of another means that some scales must be high and others low. Because the number of preferred and rejected activities cancel each other out, the mean amount of interest over all subscales of an inventory is the same for everyone. *Ipsative measures fail to reflect the degree or intensity of an individual's interests because positive interests on one scale are canceled by negative interests on others.*

An example will help clarify why ipsative measurements are difficult to interpret. Suppose that a teacher is asked to rank each of several students on typing, filing, and shorthand skills and does so in the following way:

	Typing	Filing	Shorthand	Mean Rank
Alice	1	2	3	2
Betty	2	1	3	2
Charlene	3	2	1	2
Donna	1	3	2	2
Eileen	2	3	1	2

Each student's mean rank is the sum of her ranked values divided by three, the number of activities ranked. No matter how these three activities are ranked, the average or mean rank must always be 2.0. When the skills of several persons are ranked, there is no basis of comparison among them because they will all have the same mean rank. An ipsative scale could not be used to select the best all-around secretary. Similarly, just because Alice and Donna received the same rank in typing does not necessarily mean they are equally competent. For example, Alice might be inept in all secretarial skills, whereas Donna might be superb. Nonetheless, both are given ranks of one in typing. Alice's rank of 3 in shorthand could still mean that she was more competent in that skill than someone who received a rank of one. The advantage of ipsative scales is that the relative proficiencies or interests for each individual will differ; no one can be high or low on all activities.

Another difficulty in interpretation arises if percentiles are used as norms on interest inventories. Persons who receive high percentiles in comparison with the normative group have selected a greater number of activities in an interest area than those obtaining lower percentiles. If the normative sample is composed of individuals who generally dislike clerical work, for example, an individual who scores at the 99th percentile in clerical interests would be at the top of a largely disinterested group. A person at the 30th percentile in mechanical interests may enjoy repairing machines but he does so to a lesser extent than others in the normative sample. High, average, and low interests have only relative meaning if interests are expressed as percentiles.

Reasons for Using Interest Inventories

Selection

The available evidence strongly argues *against* using interest inventories for selection because they are highly susceptible to dissimulation. The usual procedure for studying faking on interest inventories is to ask subjects to respond to items under two different circumstances: (1) as if they were applying for a job and (2) as if the results were to be used in a nonthreatening situation (such as a research study). Virtually all studies agree that faking is possible, that it does occur when inventories are used for selection, and that it is difficult to prevent (Green 1951; Kuder 1954).

Kuder (1966) found that subjects who try to impress others select a large proportion of socially desirable alternatives. Some of his inventories provide V, or *verification,* scores, which are useful for detecting carelessness, misunderstanding of directions, inability to read or comprehend items, and insincerity.

Attempts to detect faking on interest inventories have not been entirely satisfactory. Some people claim that the forced-choice format discourages faking because the subject is often incapable of discerning which choice is most socially favored. However, the evidence for this contention is primarily speculative and has not been supported by empirical data (see Dickens 1959).

Another way in which test constructors attempt to reduce faking is to disguise the nature of the test. The Michigan Vocabulary Profile Test, consisting of cognitive items in human relations, commerce, government, the physical sciences, the biological sciences, mathematics, fine arts, and sports, utilizes this approach. The test assumes that one can measure interests by measuring the amount of accumulated information in an area. Insufficient data have been accumulated for evaluation, but preliminary results indicate that this tactic is promising (Super and Crites 1962, p. 379).

Placement

Interest inventories are a useful means of clarifying and confirming vocational goals. At the intermediate and high school grades they can help guide the student into the most appropriate curriculum; at the college level they can suggest vocations and professions the student may wish to consider in greater detail; for adults, they can verify or suggest jobs or hobbies the individual might find rewarding.

Interpretation of interest inventories as placement tools should follow these principles:

1. Expect some differences between expressed, manifest, and inventoried interests. Although some examinees may want to impress the examiner, most differences between expressed and inventoried interests can be attributed to the examinee's misinformation about certain vocations, to the tendency of inventories to disregard such realities as costs, time, and motivation, to the fact that inventories must restrict themselves to a limited number of vocations or areas of interest, and to differences in the examinee's frame of reference when he responds to inventory items. Some examinees may be interested in an activity but as a hobby or avocation rather than as a career.

2. The responsibility of the teacher or counselor is to provide information, not to make decisions. At best, a test or inventory can only provide information for the student to accept or reject as he sees fit. The teacher can suggest alternative solutions to problems, can help the student interpret scores completely and accurately, and can act as a sounding board for the student's beliefs and attitudes, but the final decision must be made by the student and his parents.

3. Interest inventories often yield ipsative measures, and scores should be so interpreted. One might say to a student, for example: "You seem to have a *relatively* strong interest in X but lower interests in Y. Does this seem to be the way in which you view your own interests?" This question may help clarify differences between expressed and inventoried interests. The teacher can also ask: "How much effort would you make to find a job of this kind (move to

another city, take special training, and so forth)? Would you probably accept an offer of this type of job if it were offered?" (Terwilliger 1970). Such questions help clarify the degree of preference the student has for one occupation over another.

4. Interest inventory scores do not correlate highly with aptitude measures. The teacher must remember that interests are not good predictors of the student's abilities. But as supplementary tools, particularly when they are used with aptitude scores, interest inventories can be useful for placement and guidance.

5. The interest areas measured by different inventories may differ even though terminology may be the same. The "farmer" scale on the SVIB, for example, contains norms derived in 1936 from 241 men, 75 percent of whom were graduates of agriculture colleges in California and Oregon. On the KGIS half the farmers were college graduates selected from twelve states. The sample of "farmers" therefore refers to a rather select group, particularly on the SVIB. Only by being thoroughly familiar with the inventory can the counselor or teacher interpret scores properly.

6. Almost all interest inventories require the ability to read. The Kuder tests require a reading grade level of from 6.0 to 9.0, depending on the form taken; the SVIB is even more difficult to read (a grade equivalent of about 11.0). Pictorial interest inventories are available for nonreaders.

7. The choice of an occupation is influenced by a complex interaction among various conditions: societal roles and priorities; rural-urban population shifts; abilities and aspirations; pressures from friends and family; the amount and cost of training; and personal values and interests. Rather than pressuring the student into making hasty decisions, the teacher can help him consider the *patterns* of behavior required for different "job families." The student will benefit more from being informed of the extent to which his interests and abilities match the characteristics and demands of a given occupation than from being told that he would make a good social worker, truck driver, or teacher.

8. To some extent the scales on interest inventories are based on stereotyped sex roles (compare figure 14.1a with 14.1b, for example). A woman interested in "adventure" or a man interested in "homemaking" on the SVIB will experience equal problems. The teacher or counselor needs to be cognizant of these problems by knowing something about the examinee before routinely administering any test. In some instances it might be advantageous for a person to take an inventory designed for someone of the opposite sex.

Remediation

Interest inventory results may be used to reduce learning difficulties. Administered early in the academic year, they can help identify students who need special attention because of a dislike or fear of a subject. Teachers can also capitalize on a student's interests to teach potentially disliked subject matter. For example, a child who dislikes mathematics may overcome his initial fears if mathematics can be related to areas of the curriculum he enjoys. The teacher might suggest that the student write a paper on the history of mathematics or study the geometric patterns in a painting if the student is interested in history or art.

Program Evaluation

Sometimes interest inventories are administered to determine program effectiveness if improved student interest is used as a criterion along with achievement. Other criteria that might be used include some absolute value (such as a mean of 4.0 on a scale of 5), a specified minimum percentage of students who express interest in a specified subject, or the number of books on a given topic checked out of the library.

A number of colleges and universities encourage the faculty to use student evaluations of their teaching to improve instructional efficiency and enjoyment. Students typically rate instructors on both cognitive and noncognitive factors, including the amount of student interest the faculty member was able to engender and maintain.

Reliability of Interest Inventories

Most studies attest to the unreliability of interest scores among elementary and junior high school students. Interests tend to become stable in the late teens and to change little after the age of twenty-five.

On the Strong Vocational Interest Blank (SVIB) median stability coefficients of about .62 have been reported over a twenty-two-year period when the initial testing was conducted with college seniors and graduate students (Campbell 1971, p. 118). The range in stability was from .31 (religious activities) to .76 (science). With high school seniors, however, the correlations drop to about .53 when the individuals were retested eight to ten years later (p. 116). These high coefficients attest to the stability of interests over long periods of time, especially for adults. Interestingly, the lowest stability coefficient for adults (.32) was on the teaching scale. Stability has not been as thoroughly investigated on the Kuder tests as on the SVIB, but available data suggest coefficients of about .50 through the high school years. For long-term prediction, the SVIB appears to be much more stable.

Many interest inventories are constructed to yield homogeneous scales, but this is of less importance than high stability coefficients. On the SVIB, for example, split-half reliability is about .70; on the Kuder tests these coefficients are somewhat higher.

Validity of Interest Inventories

Scores on interest inventories are not very useful in predicting subjective criteria such as course grades. This is not surprising, considering the low reliability of grades and their lack of variability, particularly with students who have been admitted to professional schools. Validity coefficients are improved (but are still low) if the criterion (e.g., standardized achievement scores) is more reliable.

Interest inventories seem to be better predictors of those who will complete training than they are of student grades. On the SVIB, for example, over 90 percent of freshmen dentistry students who obtained high interest ratings on the dentist scale graduated, compared to 25 percent of those with low interests (Strong 1943, p. 524). Students elect and complete courses in which they have some interest, although aptitude may be more important than interest in predicting success in required courses.

Interest inventories can also be used to predict job attractiveness and satisfaction. Indeed, this is probably the most important reason for using them. Although satisfaction can be measured in different ways (length of time spent working in an occupation, production records, or expressed pleasure), the evidence shows that interest inventories are good predictors of all these criteria. Strong (1955), for example, has shown that two-thirds of the college men tested with the SVIB who had high interests in engineering actually entered an occupation related to that field. Studies also support the use of the Kuder tests in predicting job satisfaction.

Some Examples of Standardized Interest Inventories

Although there are over forty standardized interest inventories available (Buros 1961), only the Kuder and SVIB inventories have been sufficiently investigated and used to warrant detailed discussion. Other inventories—notably the Minnesota Vocational Interest Inventory (MVII)—have shown some potential and will be reviewed briefly.

Strong Vocational Interest Blank (SVIB)

The SVIB has been more thoroughly investigated than any other interest inventory. The Men's Form was first published in 1927, and the Women's Form in 1933. The Men's Form has been revised twice — in 1938 and again in 1966; the Women's Form was revised in 1946 and 1969. Relatively little information is available concerning the adequacy of the Women's Form scale, probably because there was less demand for that scale than for the men's. Because women are becoming a more potent labor force, a new 'merged form' of the Strong has been published to reduce sex bias, but it is too early to determine how effective this change will be.

The SVIB is designed for mature high school and college students and for adults who desire help in selecting among fairly high level occupational interests (see figure 14.1a and b). The items on the SVIB presume a high level of reading competence.

Interests on the SVIB are expressed as standard scores (T scores) or letter ratings for each occupation listed on the profile sheet* (see figure 14.1a and b). At the top of the profile sheet is a list of basic interest scales. The vertical line corresponding to a T score of 50 represents the average score obtained from a sample of fifty-two-year-old men (see figure 14.1a); their scores at age sixteen are plotted for each basic interest scale. According to Campbell (1971, p. 157), T scores above 57 or 58 mean that the individual has stronger preferences for those areas than does the "average person." Underneath the basic interest scales are listed the various occupational scales, divided into eleven occupational groupings (see figure 14.1a). The eleven categories will eventually be replaced by the basic interest scales.

The shaded area in each row shows the performance of approximately the middle third of "men in general" on the items relevant to that occupation. Scores to the right of the shaded area indicate that the examinee shares interests more in common with samples of successful men in that vocation than with a sample of men in general. A rating of A, for example, indicates that the examinee shares the same pattern of interests as demonstrated by the highest 69 percent of successful persons in a vocation; a B rating is obtained by about 98 percent of successful men in that occupation; and a C rating is obtained by the lowest 2 percent of successful individuals. These percentages were arrived at by using cutoffs of .5 and 2.0 standard deviations below the mean score obtained by each "successful" group. Approximately 69 percent of that group scored at or above $-.5$ SD; about 98 percent scored at or above -2 SD; a rating of C is given when scores are below two standard deviations from the mean.

The supplementary occupational scales listed near the bottom of the

---

* Stanford University has licensed various agencies to provide electronic data processing of SVIB answer sheets. The profile forms therefore differ somewhat from agency to agency, as do the amount and type of information reported.

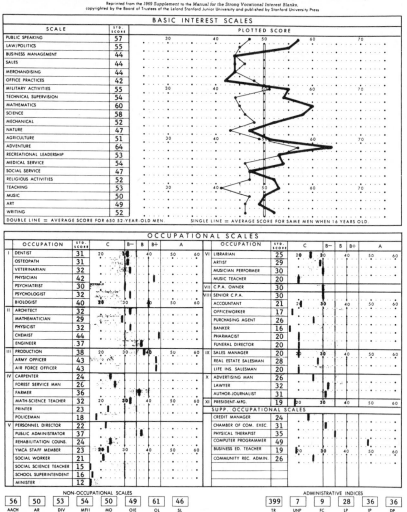

PROFILE— **STRONG VOCATIONAL INTEREST BLANK** —FOR MEN (Form T399)

Reprinted from the 1969 Supplement to the Manual for the Strong Vocational Interest Blanks,
copyrighted by the Board of Trustees of the Leland Stanford Junior University and published by Stanford University Press

Excerpted with permission of the publishers from *Manual for the Strong Vocational Interest Blanks, 1969 Supplement,* by David P. Campbell (Stanford: Stanford University Press, 1969) Fig. 2, p. 4.

Fig. 14.1a. Completed Profile for Strong Vocational Interest Blank for Men

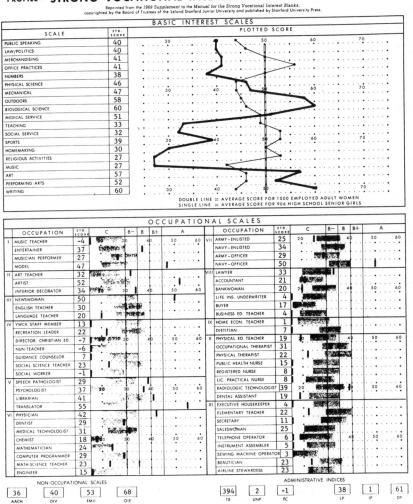

Figure 14.1b. Completed Profile for Strong Vocational Interest Blank for Women

profile sheet have all been constructed since 1956 and have not as yet been classified into one of the eleven occupational groups.

Eight "nonoccupational scales" are also reported on the men's form of the SVIB. These scales are defined and used in the following way:*

Scale	Meaning	Purpose
AACH	Academic achievement	To differentiate between patterns of interests related to high and low scholarship
AR	Age relations	To differentiate between interests popular to teenagers and mature adults
DIV	Diversity of interests	To measure breadth of interests
MFII	Masculinity-femininity (revised scale)	To differentiate between interests in art, music, and verbal activities and outdoors, adventure, and business
MO	Managerial orientation	To measure managerial and nonmanagerial interests
OIE	Occupational-introversion-extroversion	To differentiate between occupations selected by introverts and extroverts as measured by a personality scale
OL	Occupational level	To differentiate between unskilled workers and men in general
SL	Specialization level	To differentiate between specialists and non-specialists in a given field

From Campbell 1971, pp. 194–247.

Six administrative indices are also available on the SVIB:

Index	Meaning	Purpose
TR	Total responses index	To determine the number of items omitted
UNP	Unpopular index	To determine random responses by counting the number of items which almost no one selects

Index	Meaning	Purpose
FC	Form check index	To determine whether the individual was using the correct form of the SVIB
LP, IP, DP	Like, indifferent, and dislike percentages indices	To detect persons who responded to one option and disregarded others.

The SVIB is best utilized to help relatively mature high school or college students decide which vocation to prepare for or pursue. It is not designed for routine group administration, where it may be more important to indicate areas of student interest than to help a student consider some specific occupation. Relatively high scoring costs (over a dollar for each answer sheet) also prevent the SVIB from being routinely administered.

---

* The eight nonoccupational scales require validation; the column titled "Purpose" indicates intent, not evidence.

Kuder Tests

Kuder has approached the measurement of interests from two different points of view. In the first method the examinee receives a percentile score in each of ten areas (outdoors, mechanical, computational, scientific, persuasive, artistic, literary, musical, social service, and clerical). Extensive item analyses and revisions have provided scales that have high internal consistency. The Kuder Preference Record: Vocational and the Kuder General Interest Survey were designed using this approach. In the second approach Kuder has turned to empirical keying techniques similar to those used by Strong except that there is no "men in general" category. Rather, each individual's score is compared directly with those obtained by members of different occupations. The greater the number of men in an occupation who agree with the examinee's responses, the more points he receives on that scale. The Kuder Occupational Interest Survey uses this approach (see figure 14.2).

Kuder has published six tests for the measurement of interest (see table 14.3), which take from thirty to forty-five minutes to administer. The latest two forms of the Kuder (Form DD and Form E) were published in 1964 and 1966, respectively, and little information is available about their validity. Although Form DD is similar to the SVIB in design and intent, the reading level is lower and the test content includes more skilled and semiskilled occupations. The Kuder Form E can measure interest at the seventh-grade level, but validity is derived principally from association with its older edition, Form C. Although few validity studies on Form C are reported in the test manual, rather extensive literature has accumulated attesting to its value as a counseling tool. Whether the newer Form DD and Form E will yield equal or higher reliability and validity coefficients is open to conjecture.

Minnesota Vocational
Interest Inventory (MVII)

The MVII, published in 1965, measures interests in twenty-one semi-skilled and skilled occupations, making it useful in testing noncollegiate students. The MVII measures interests in such occupations as baker, stock clerk, machinist, painter, warehouseman, milk wagon driver, food service manager, retail sales clerk, printer, tabulator, pressman, carpenter, and electrician.

The MVII has been empirically keyed, using as the reference group "tradesmen in general," which is similar to Strong's "men in general." With lower-level occupations, however, there appear to be fewer differences among men engaged in different occupations. This makes it more difficult to discriminate between successful plumbers and "tradesmen in general" than between college graduates in a given occupation and "men in general."

Report of Scores ***Kuder Occupational Interest Survey*** ***(Form DD)***

NAME________ LOCATION________ DATE OF SURVEY________

OCCUPATIONAL SCALES WOMEN		COLLEGE MAJOR SCALES, WOMEN	OCCUPATIONAL SCALES MEN		Optometrist	Psychology Professor	COLLEGE MAJOR SCALES MEN	
Accountant	Nurse	Art & Art Education	Acc't, Certified Public	Engineer, Electrical	Osteopath	Radio Station Manager	Agriculture	Foreign Languages
Bank Clerk	Nutritionist	Biological Sciences	Architect	Engineer, Heating/ Air Cond.	Painter, House	Real Estate Agent	Animal Husbandry	Forestry
Beautician	Occupational Therapist	Business Ed & Commerce	Automobile Mechanic	Engineer, Industrial	Pediatrician	Sales Eng, Heating/Air Cond.	Architecture	History
Bookkeeper	Office Clerk	Drama	Automobile Salesman	Engineer, Mechanical	Personnel Manager	Science Teacher, High School	Art & Art Education	Law (Grad School)
Bookstore Manager	Physical Therapist	Elementary Education	Banker	Engineer, Mining & Metal	Pharmaceutical Salesman	School Superintendent	Biological Sciences	Mathematics
Computer Programmer	Primary School Teacher	English	Bookkeeper	Farmer	Pharmacist	Social Caseworker	Business Acc't & Finance	Music & Music Ed
Counselor, High School	Psychologist	Foreign Languages	Bookstore Manager	Florist	Photographer	Social Worker, Group	Business & Marketing	Physical Education
Dean of Women	Psychologist, Clinical	General Social Sciences	Bricklayer	Forester	Physical Therapist	Social Worker, Psychiatric	Business Management	Physical Sciences
Dental Assistant	Religious Education Director	Health Professions	Building Contractor	Insurance Agent	Physician	Statistician	Economics	Political Science & Gov't
Department Store Saleswoman	Science Teacher, High School	History	Buyer	Interior Decorator	Plumber	Supv/Foreman, Industrial	Elementary Education	Premed, Pharm & Dentistry
Dietitian, Administrative	Secretary	Home Economics Education	Carpenter	Journalist	Plumbing Contractor	Travel Agent	Engineering, Chemical	Psychology
Dietitian, Public School	Social Caseworker	Mathematics	Chemist	Lawyer	Podiatrist	Truck Driver	Engineering, Civil	Sociology
Florist	Social Worker, Group	Music & Music Education	Clothier, Retail	Librarian	Policeman	Television Repairman	Engineering, Electrical	U.S. Air Force Cadet
Home Demonstration Agent	Social Worker, Medical	Nursing	Computer Programmer	Machinist	Postal Clerk	University Pastor	Engineering, Mechanical	U.S. Military Cadet
Home Ec Teacher, College	Social Worker, Pyschiatric	Physical Education	Counselor, High School	Mathematician	Printer	Veterinarian	English	
Interior Decorator	Social Worker, School	Political Science	County Agricultural Agent	Math Teacher, High School	Psychiatrist	Welder		
Lawyer	Stenographer	Psychology	Dentist	Meteorologist	Psychologist, Clinical	X-Ray Technician		
Librarian	X-Ray Technician	Sociology	Electrician	Minister	Psychologist, Counseling	YMCA Secretary		
Math Teacher, High School		Teaching Sister, Catholic	Engineer, Civil	Nurseryman	Psychologist, Industrial			

OCCUPATIONAL SCALES WOMEN		COLLEGE MAJOR SCALES WOMEN		OCCUPATIONAL SCALES MEN		COLLEGE MAJOR SCALES MEN	
Title	Score	Title	Score	Title	Score	Title	Score

V ________

M ______	S ______
MBI ______	F ______
W ______	D ______
WBI	MO

From the Kuder Occupational Interest Survey Form DD Profile Sheet. © 1965, 1968, 1970, Science Research Associates, Inc. Reproduced by permission of the publisher.

Figure 14.2

The MVII consists of 158 items of three choices each. As on the Kuder tests, the examinee selects the activity he likes *most* and *least* from each triad. Empirically keyed scales weight each choice, depending on the frequency with which members of a given occupation select a response in comparison with tradesmen in general.

Table 14.3. Comparisons among Various Kuder Inventories

Inventory	Grade Ranges	Scoring*	Content	Comments
Form A: Personal	9–12, adult	Student, machine	Participation in group activities, familiar and stable situations, working with ideas, avoiding conflict, directing and influencing others	Measures personal and social preferences rather than vocational interests
Form B: Vocational	9–12, adult	Student, machine	Older edition of Kuder Form C but without an outdoor scale	Rarely used any longer; Form C a newer and improved version of Form B
Form C: Vocational Interest Survey	9–12, adult	Student, machine	Outdoor, scientific, mechanical, computational, persuasive, artistic, literary, musical, social service, clerical	Useful as an exploratory instrument of students' vocational interest areas
Form D: Occupational	9–12, adult	Hand, machine	Measures interests in 52 occupations such as printer, mechanic, minister, X-ray technician, physician	Allows counselors to develop local keys for other occupations or student groups
Form DD: Occupational Interest Survey	11–12, college, adult	By publisher only	Measures interests in various occupations (79 for men and 57 for women) in a wide range of levels; includes interests in 29 college majors for men and 27 majors for women	Empirically keyed; 32 of the women's scores normed on males in occupations where both sexes are consistently employed
Form E: General Interest Survey	7–12	Student, hand, machine	Same as Form C	A lower-level edition of Form C, but longer to compensate for unreliability obtained with younger children

*Note: Student scoring is accomplished by the use of a pin-punch system. The student punches a hole on an answer pad with a pin. The inside of the answer pad contains circles. By counting the number of pinpricks in circles within each interest area, a raw score can be obtained. In this way students can easily score their own inventories.
Hand scoring requires special stencils. Scoring is usually done by clerks or teachers.
Machine sorting refers to the use of electronic data-processing systems.

In addition to the twenty-one occupational scales, the MVII also contains nine *area scales,* which help the examinee identify the general areas of his interests (see figure 14.3). These scales, expressed as standard scores, were determined by selecting items that correlated highly with one another (internal consistency).

A crucial factor related to interest inventories is whether they demonstrate a high degree of stability (reliability) over relatively long periods of time. Because the MVII was designed for use at the ninth grade and above, test interpreters need to know possible interest changes that may occur as the student becomes older. The only data on stability presented in the manual for the MVII (Clark and Campbell 1965) are for a sample of ninety-eight students from an industrial institute in Minneapolis over a thirty-day interval. These correlations range from .64 (pressman) to .88 (retail sales clerk), with a median correlation of .82. Similar data are presented for the area scales, but no information is provided on internal consistency reliability.

The manual presents evidence for concurrent validity—that is, the extent to which the inventory is capable of distinguishing among various occupational groups. Ideally members of any given occupation would respond entirely differ-

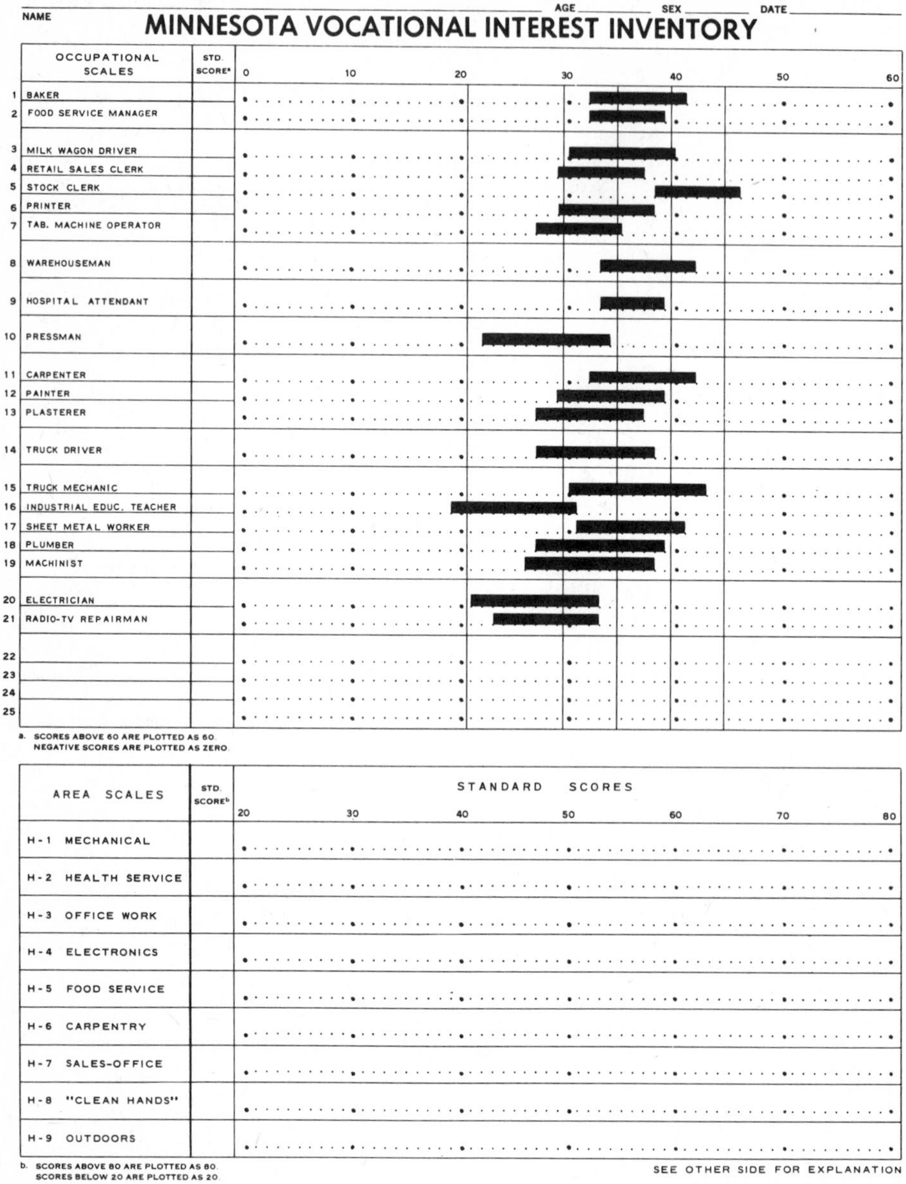

Minnesota Vocational Interest Inventory. Copyright © 1965 by the Psychological Corporation, New York, N.Y.

Figure 14.3

ently from men in other occupations and from tradesmen in general. To the extent that responses overlap, the inventory is incapable of distinguishing interests in different occupations. Here the MVII seems to have some deficiencies. The percentage of overlap between men in a given occupation and tradesmen in general ranges from 27 percent (radio-TV repairman or industrial education teacher) to 63 percent (stock clerk), with a median overlap of about 40 percent. The greatest amount of misclassification occurs for occupational groups that require the least amount of training.

The concurrent validity of the MVII can also be evaluated by examining the mean scores of different occupational groups on the various scales. For example, food service managers score higher on the baker's scale than they do on their own scale. Hospital attendants obtain their highest scores on the stock clerk scale. However, these are isolated extremes that occur infrequently. Radio-TV repairmen (an occupation that has a low overlap with tradesmen in general) do obtain their highest scores on their own scale, as do seventeen out of the twenty-one occupations tested. On the area scales bakers obtain their highest scores in food service and "clean hands"; retail sales clerks do best in the office work and sales office areas. But there are some irregularities. The second highest area scale for painters is food service; the highest area for pressmen is health service.

The MVII manual presents almost no evidence regarding predictive validity —a serious deficiency. The one study reported involved U. S. Navy electronics students who took the radio-TV repairman scale of the MVII. Inventory scores correlated .30 with course grades, but the amount of time that elapsed between the two measures is not reported.

Constructing Interest Measures for Classroom Use

Teachers will find it advantageous to construct their own interest inventories when standardized instruments are either invalid for the teacher's purposes or unobtainable because of costs or other factors. Teacher-made interest measures are of greatest value when they are used to help evaluate programs or units of study. For predicting job success or satisfaction, standardized tests are likely to be much more effective because norms are usually available.

Checklists

A simple technique for measuring interests is to have students check the activities or subjects in which they have some interest. The teacher decides on the areas of interest he wants to measure. These areas may be either extensively sampled and include activities in many different areas of the curriculum or narrowly defined and restricted to one aspect of a single course. The following example could be used to measure interests in various aspects of a tests and measurements course:

> Directions: Place a check (√) next to the *three* activities you most enjoy doing or learning about in tests and measurements.
> _____ 1. Computing various statistics such as means and standard deviations
> _____ 2. Constructing test items and questions
> _____ 3. Discussing ethical and unethical testing practices
> _____ 4. Studying how standardized tests are used for various purposes
> _____ 5. Writing behavioral objectives for a course or unit of instruction
> _____ 6. Interpreting case studies using the results of testing
> _____ 7. Evaluating the reliability and validity of standardized tests
> _____ 8. Studying the theory of such topics as reliability and validity
> _____ 9. Discussing the social impact of testing on minority groups
> _____10. Learning about the history of testing

Variations in the checklist approach could include having the student check as many of the statements as he wants or allowing him to write in an activity not included in the list. However, by restricting the number of checks allowed, a measure of *relative* strength of interest is obtained.

Rankings

In another approach to classroom measurement of interests, students rank various activities in order of preference. Younger or immature pupils might be capable of ranking only a few activities, whereas older students might be able to rank many more, depending on the similarities of the options. In the typical procedure the student places the numeral 1 next to the activity he most enjoys, a 2 next to the second most enjoyed activity, and so on. The average rank accorded each activity by class members can help evaluate class preferences. As with checklists, rankings provide only a relative degree of interest. Two persons who each assign a rank of 1 to an activity are not necessarily equally interested.

Rating Scales

In another approach to interest measurement students indicate which activities they like or dislike or indicate the *degree* to which they enjoy or dislike an activity. A five-point rating scale, for example, could be constructed in the following manner:

> Directions: For each activity listed below, circle the choice that best represents how you feel about the activity in question. SL means strongly like; L means like; I means indifferent to; D means dislike; and SD means strongly dislike.
> 1. Playing a musical instrument
>   SL L I D SD
> 2. Attending a rock concert
>   SL L I D SD

The most favorable response to each item is given five points, and the least favorable, one point. If all items measure interests in the same area, such as various aspects of music, student scores on each item may be summed and averaged to provide an estimate of general preference. However, if the items refer to activities in different areas (e.g., 1. Playing a musical instrument; 2. Constructing houses; 3. Using a microscope), scores should not be summed or averaged. Rather, the class average may be determined for each statement.

Free-Response Techniques

Free-response techniques allow the student some freedom in expressing the areas and strengths of his interests. Teachers might ask students to write an essay on their hobbies or on the activities they most enjoy. Responses can be more structured by asking students to complete sentences, which limits the range of possible answers. The following examples of free-response items vary in degree of specificity from relatively unstructured to highly restricted:

> 1. In what sorts of activities are you interested?
> 2. In my spare time I like to _____.
> 3. The one subject I disliked most in junior high school was _____
>   _____.

The interview is another form of a free-response technique. The amount of freedom is limited by the interviewer's questions. The question "What are you most interested in?" allows for a wide range and depth of answers that can be probed and clarified by both parties in the course of the interview. For young children or illiterates, the interview might be the only feasible approach to measuring interests.

The Measurement of Attitudes

In the beginning of this chapter an *attitude* was defined as a preference along a dimension of favorableness to unfavorableness to a particular group, institution, concept, or object. A person with a favorable attitude toward art, for example, is likely to rate artists (group), museums (institutions), color (concept), and paintings (objects) as favorable. An unfavorable attitude presumes a tendency to reject various aspects of art.

Sometimes a distinction is made between attitudes and opinions. *Opinions* have been defined as the "verbal expression of attitude" (Thurstone 1928). When a person states that "all men are created equal," his statement constitutes an opinion which, if he is honest and self-perceptive, will adequately reflect his attitude. The most practical application of the measurement of opinion has been the prediction of election results and the solicitation of consumer responses to various products.

Characteristics of Attitudes

Attitudes vary in (1) direction, (2) intensity, (3) pervasiveness, (4) consistency, and (5) salience. The *direction* of an attitude refers to whether an individual views a class of objects with favor or disfavor. A student who has a favorable attitude toward school is *positively* directed to some aspect or aspects of schooling, such as groups (students, teachers, or organizations), the curriculum, or perhaps the subject matter he is studying. The student who avoids school or school-related activities is *negatively* directed. It is unlikely that adults, at least, can be completely indifferent toward anything since awareness without understanding often produces fear or distrust.

Attitudes also differ in *intensity* or strength. One individual might have a *slightly* favorable attitude toward a social policy, whereas another might be *strongly* antagonistic. The understanding of an attitude should reflect how strongly one feels.

A third characteristic of attitudes is *pervasiveness* or range. One person might strongly dislike one or two aspects of schooling, whereas another might dislike almost everything concerning public and private education. Negative attitudes toward minority groups might be highly restricted (to young, "revolutionary" black men perhaps) or might include all persons of ethnic, racial, and religious backgrounds that are different from one's own.

A fourth distinguishing feature of attitudes is *consistency*. Some persons respond to an attitude scale in a perfectly consistent manner; others give both favorable and unfavorable responses to the same subject. An individual may state that he believes that *all* politicians are dishonest but at the same time argue that a *particular* politician has few or no faults.

Salience, the degree of spontaneity or readiness to express an attitude, is a fifth dimension of attitudes. Salient attitudes are often those in which the individual places great importance or about which he has a good deal of knowledge. Salience can only be measured if the attitude is *expressed* without probing of any sort. Most attitude scales comprise statements requiring a specific response such as "agree" or "disagree" and thus cannot measure salience. However, salience can be measured by interviews or by observations in which opportunities are provided for the expression of attitudes.

The Scaling of Attitudes

The measurement of attitudes presumes the ability to differentiate individuals along continua that vary in direction, intensity, pervasiveness, consistency, and (in the case of free-response questions) salience. The characteristics of four scales of measurement—nominal, ordinal, interval, and ratio—were described in chapter 6. Nominal scales are qualitative in nature and are unordered with regard to degree, but knowing that an individual has changed categories (from one political party to another, for example) could be important information.

Ordinal Scaling

Ordinal scaling involves the ranking of individuals or responses without regard to the equality of differences between the ranked variables, as in the example below:

Directions: Check the *one* statement that best describes your attitude toward education.
_____1. Education means more to me than anyone or anything in this world.
_____2. Education is one of the most important and worthwhile activities to me.
_____3. Education is of little importance to me.
_____4. People would be better off without education.
_____5. Anyone involved with education in any way should be banished from the country.

Suppose that five students (A, B, C, D, and E) each select a different option, with A selecting statement 1, B selecting 2, and so forth. Is there as much difference between the attitudes of students A and B as there is between those of students B and C or D and E? Figure 14.4a depicts the degree of favorableness (numbered 1–5) for individuals A–E. There is a slight difference in favorable-

Degree of Favorableness	Most Favorable				Least Favorable
Student Rankings	1	2	3	4	5
	A	B	C	D	E

Figure 14.4a. Showing the Inequalities in Ranks of Five Students Responding to Five Statements Concerning Education

ness between individuals A and B, but there is a great difference between individuals B and C, even though all students are just one-ranked unit apart. An individual who changes his attitude by moving from 2 to 1 has *not* made as great a change as someone who changes from 3 to 2 or from 5 to 4. If the differences between rankings were equal, differences in attitude would be more meaningful.

Interval Scaling

In interval scaling items are constructed so that the differences between successive or adjacent categories are equal, as depicted in figure 14.4b. Gains or losses of 1.0 or more units of favorableness are equal throughout the distribution and therefore indicate accurately the *amount* of change. Various types of interval scales will be examined later in this chapter.

Degree of favorableness	1	2	3	4	5
Student Rankings	A	B	C	D	E

Figure 14.4b. Showing Equalities in Differences in Attitude of Five Students to Five Statements Concerning Education

Ratio Scaling

In addition to equal intervals, ratio scales have absolute zeros. An absolute zero represents that point below which there are no values. An absolute zero on an achievement test would indicate that the student had no knowledge whatsoever regarding test content. The meaning of an absolute zero on attitude scales has been vigorously debated. Some theorists believe that absolute zero would mean that respondents completely lacked any attitude toward the topic in question. However, most respondents have attitudes in *some* direction even when they have little information on which to base judgments. Even when individuals are presented with nonsense syllables or names of fictitious ethnic groups, they tend to make those stimuli meaningful by associating them with past experiences or with other stimuli that have meaning for them. The position taken in this text is that zero refers to the point at which an attitude changes from favorable to unfavorable.

Techniques for Measuring Attitudes

Attitude scales may be classified according to whether the items disguise the nature and purpose of the scale and the extent to which the scale is structured or unstructured (Campbell 1950; 1957). A *disguised* attitude scale contains items that appear to be innocuous but which are actually designed to yield information concerning personal attitudes that might be withheld from the examiner. An *unstructured* task allows for great freedom in responding (but complicates scoring procedures), whereas a *structured* task restricts responses (but facilitates scoring).

Nondisguised Structured and Unstructured Techniques

Most attitude scales do not attempt to disguise their purpose from the respondent. The questions are direct and their purposes understood by examiner and respondent within the same frame of reference. The examiner engages in no deceit, although the respondent may or may not hide his true feelings, depending on his willingness to cooperate.

Ethically teachers and counselors should not resort to deception except in highly unusual circumstances in which the benefits to society are great and the respondent is clearly not threatened or where the threat is minimal but the expected benefits to society are important.

Responses to many attitude scales are structured or restricted to facilitate scoring and data analysis. A teacher who has to read long essays about the students' attitudes toward school, for example, has set a formidable task for himself if he eventually wants to treat class attitudes statistically. An advantage of structured scales is that each respondent faces essentially the same task. He can be asked to agree or disagree with a statement, to rank them in importance, or to select the option that best matches his beliefs or feelings. The freedom of unstructured items may not easily permit comparisons among individuals.

Disguised Structured and
Unstructured Techniques

At least three types of disguised structured techniques have been identified: information tests, perception and memory tests, and judgment tests.

Information tests   Information tests appear to measure knowledge, but they actually measure attitudes. They are based on the supposition that individuals tend to answer cognitive-type items in accordance with their underlying and often subconscious beliefs. Consider the following *structured* items:

1. In 1966, how many billions of dollars *after taxes* went to corporate profits in the United States?
   a. 30 billion dollars
   b. 70 billion dollars
2. What percentage of the students in high school believe that smoking marijuana should be legalized?
   a. 0 to 19%
   b. 20% to 39%
   c. 40% to 59%
   d. 60% to 79%
   e. 80% to 100%

The first item presents options that are equally incorrect; the correct answer to the second item is unknown. Presumably those who select option *b* in the first item believe that corporate profits are excessive, whereas those who select option *a* believe that profits are too low. In item 2 the hypothesis is that the larger the percentage selected, the more in favor the respondent is of legalizing marijuana. A serious danger in these interpretations is that some persons may actually respond to the face value of the item rather than according to their attitudes or prejudices. For example, someone may believe that a large percentage of students want to legalize marijuana but be vigorously opposed to such legislation. To be accurate, interpretations would probably have to take into consideration the responses to additional, more direct questions regarding attitudes toward corporate profits and the legalization of marijuana. Such data can indicate the meaning of various choices for the group as a whole.

Perception and memory tests   If memory and perception are selective, individuals with different attitudes should respond differently to various stimuli. One technique is to display briefly a detailed picture containing elements of the attitude that is to be measured. For example, to study attitudes toward women's liberation, a detailed picture of men and women in an office might be shown to a group for two or three seconds. Structured or unstructured questions could then be asked about the activities and roles engaged in by members of the two sexes. It is even possible to ask questions that have no answers determinable from the picture itself (e.g., "Who was sitting behind the desk?" when no desk was portrayed). Again, the interpretation of responses is more difficult than with direct or undisguised techniques.

Judgment tests   It is also possible to measure attitudes indirectly by requiring respondents to make a judgment using one set of criteria that appear to be nonthreatening while actually measuring more subtle aspects of attitude. Attitudes toward communists, for example, have been investigated (Hsü 1949) by asking three female graduate students to sort photographs of 120 men into "handsome" and "homely" categories. Later the students were asked to indicate which men were communists and which were not. The two women who were anticommunist tended to classify as "homely" those whom they judged to be communists. The procommunist graduate student rated the communists as "handsome." Evidently attitudes affect judgments.

Watson (1925) studied moral judgments by describing to his respondents two situations that were identical except that in one instance an unwarranted search was made of the headquarters of a suspected radical while in the other a business corporation suspected of dishonesty was searched. Differential responses to the two situations provided the basis of scoring.

Another form of judgment test consists of a series of arguments in the form of statements for and against some proposition. In one study (Brigham and Cook 1970) attitude scales were developed to study integration, the role of federal intervention in desegregation, and the rights of minority groups. Each scale consisted of fifteen arguments for or against a position. Respondents were told (p. 285):

> This is a test of your ability to tell good arguments from poor arguments on both sides of controversial issues. Since race relations are very much in the news these days, we have selected arguments which are relevant to three issues within this general area. For each of these issues, arguments on both sides will be presented. . . . Your task is as follows: Imagine that you are judging a debate between two teams on each of the three issues. Acting as an impartial judge, you are to rate each argument presented by either side in terms of its effectiveness. . . . Ask yourself, "How plausible is this statement? How good an argument is it? How effective is this argument?"

These argument statements, along with an undisguised scale measuring attitudes toward intermarriage and blacks, were given to three groups of students: students active in civil rights groups, students taking an elective course in minority group problems, and students belonging to groups judged to be anti-Negro. The investigators found, as hypothesized, that the ratings of arguments as to plausibility and effectiveness were directly related to the attitudes of the groups. The highest scores (most favorable attitudes) were obtained by students in civil rights groups and the lowest by the anti-Negro groups.

Evaluation of Disguised Techniques

The evidence regarding the usefulness of disguised techniques is meager. The reliability of these methods seems to be comparable to that of the more direct methods; but the problem, as might be expected, is with validity. The criteria for disguised methods are often responses on undisguised but anonymously obtained data for the same persons. Such correlations range from almost .90 to close to 0. These correlations indicate only the extent of agreement between disguised and undisguised measures and do not attest to their ability to differentiate one group from another or to predict behavior.

Studies of concurrent and predictive validity—particularly studies that compare disguised with undisguised methods—are not as yet available in sufficient numbers to draw any firm conclusions. In the Brigham-Cook study described earlier the variable that correlated highest with group membership was an undisguised measure of attitude toward blacks. However, the authors felt that respondents were under few pressures to distort their responses since they were anonymous. They suggested (but presented no evidence) that disguised methods would be better predictors than undisguised measures if there were pressure to make responses more socially acceptable.

If attitude scales are to be used in counseling, there is probably little justification for using disguised techniques. The relationship between teacher and student demands honesty and openness, and deceit is unnecessary and destructive of this relationship.

Constructing Nondisguised Attitude Scales

Three nondisguised methods of measuring attitudes will be described in this chapter: social distance scales, Likert scales, and Thurstone scales.

Social Distance Scales

One of the earliest types of attitude measurement was described by Emory Bogardus (1925), who was interested in measuring the degree of social distance that individuals placed between themselves and members of various ethnic and racial groups. He postulated that the greater the amount of social distance an

Social Distance

According to my first feeling reactions I would willingly admit members of each race (as a class, and not the best I have known, nor the worst members) to one or more of the classifications under which I have placed a cross (X).

Social Distance	To close kinship by marriage	To my club as personal chums	To my street as neighbors	To employment in my occupation in my country	To citizenship in my country	As visitors only to my country	Would exclude from my country
	0	1	2	3	4	5	6
Armenians							
Chinese							
English							
Germans							
Jew-German							
Jew-Russian							
Negroes							
Turks							

From Emory S. Bogardus, *Journal of Applied Sociology*, 9, No. 4 (March 1925), by permission.

Figure 14.5. An Example of the Social Distance Scale

individual created, the less favorable his attitude was toward a specific group. A modified version of Bogardus's social distance scale is shown in figure 14.5.

Bogardus found that the seven categories of acceptance and rejection (labeled 0 to 6, respectively) were in serial order. That is, exclusion from one's country is seen as worse than being allowed to enter only as a visitor, and so forth through the other five categories. Yet no pretense is made that differences between successive categories represent equal amounts of social distance. Social distance scales therefore yield *ordinal* measurements.

Many modifications can be made to adapt social distance scales to other groups and circumstances. The important point is to be able to accurately order the categories. Harry Triandis and Leigh Triandis (1960), for example, used some of the Bogardus categories but included others such as "I would marry this person" and "I would be willing to participate in the lynching of this person." The first and last categories were added to extend the minimum and maximum degrees of social distance, but these are not absolute; marriage and lynching are not necessarily the most extreme positions one can take. An interesting finding by the Triandises was that more information could be obtained from social distance scales if respondents were given additional information about members of various groups, such as their social class, religion, and nationality. They found a great difference in how white Americans respond to "Negro physicians" and to "Negro unskilled laborers." One of the weaknesses of the original Bogardus scale was that individuals who respond negatively to the Irish might have done so more because of religion than nationality. To American respondents, nationality is least important. More important are race, occupation, and religion in rating social distance.

Likert Scales

Rensis Likert (1932) developed a technique which has been widely and successfully used to measure attitudes. A Likert scale employs five choices expressing different degrees of agreement or disagreement (see table 14.4). Items are internally consistent so as to measure attitudinal differences along a single dimension. Each individual's total score places him along a continuum of favorableness to unfavorableness toward a homogeneously defined attitude.

Table 14.4. Examples of Likert-Type Items and the Numerical Scores Assigned to Options of Differing Degrees of Favorableness (High Scores Favorable)

Example 1 Numerical Score	How far in our educational system (aside from trade education) should the most intelligent Negroes be allowed to go?
1	(a) Grade school.
2	(b) Junior high school.
3	(c) High school.
4	(d) College.
5	(e) Graduate and professional schools.
Example 2	In a community where the Negroes outnumber the whites, a Negro who is insolent to a white man should be:
5	(a) Excused or ignored.
4	(b) Reprimanded.
3	(c) Fined and jailed.
2	(d) Not only fined and jailed, but also given corporal punishment (whipping, etc.).
1	(e) Lynched.
Example 3	All Negroes belong in one class and should be treated in about the same way.

	STRONGLY APPROVE	APPROVE	UNDECIDED	DISAPPROVE	STRONGLY DISAPPROVE
Scores	1	2	3	4	5

Example 4	Where there is segregation, the Negro section should have the same equipment in paving, water, and electric light facilities as are found in white districts.

	STRONGLY APPROVE	APPROVE	UNDECIDED	DISAPPROVE	STRONGLY DISAPPROVE
Scores	5	4	3	2	1

From Likert 1932, p. 52.

Likert scales, like social distance scales, yield ordinal measurements because differences in numerical values are not equal. In the second item in table 14.4, for example, there is a great difference between the meaning associated with a one-point response ("lynched") and a two-point response ("corporal punishment"), whereas there might be little difference between a four-point response ("reprimanded") and a five-point one ("excused or ignored").

In addition to their relative simplicity in construction, it is easy to perform item analyses on Likert scales. Items that fail to discriminate between upper and lower internal criterion groups usually are eliminated from the item pool. Sometimes items are ambiguous or respondents may accept part of a statement (e.g., "Education should be encouraged") but reject another ("and taxes raised for its support"). The item analysis procedures described in chapter 9 can be applied to Likert scales. The highest and lowest scoring groups (usually 27 percent in each) are based on the sum of the numerical scores assigned to all items. Each item should positively discriminate between upper and lower 27 percent groups. Another procedure is to count the proportion of persons in the upper group who have scores of 3 *or less* on a given item and the proportion of those in the lower criterion group who have scores of 3 *or more* on the same item. High proportions for either group indicate a poorly constructed item.

Thurstone Scales

Louis Thurstone (1928) developed the method of equal-appearing intervals, and in 1929 he and E. J. Chave published *The Measurement of Attitude,* in which a scale for the measurement of attitudes toward the church was presented.

In constructing a Thurstone scale, about 200 items are written expressing widely differing degrees of favor toward the attitude to be measured. These items are edited to make them short, unambiguous, capable of being described as favorable or unfavorable, and not "double-barreled" (one part of an item is favorable but the other part is unfavorable). Each statement in the pool is typed separately on a card and given to raters (it is common to use fifty or more), who are each requested to sort the cards into eleven categories.* Category 1 represents those items judged to be highly favorable; items assigned to category 11 are unfavorable. The assumption behind equal-appearing interval scaling is that the raters are capable of assigning items to categories along a favorable-unfavorable dimension independent of their own attitudes.

Once all items have been categorized, a distribution of the judges' ratings is prepared for each item. This distribution will indicate the number of judges who placed a given item into categories 11, 10, 9, . . . 1. The median rating by all judges on a given item is called the *scale value* of that item.

Out of the original item pool, twenty to twenty-five statements are selected that have different scale values. To the extent that these scale values represent equal increments, interval measurements have been obtained. Another criterion for selecting statements for final inclusion on the scale concerns the variability of the ratings on each item. This is usually measured by the interquartile range (the difference between the category numbers corresponding to the 75th and 25th percentile). The interquartile range is simply a measure of the extent to which the judges are capable of agreeing with one another as they sort each statement into one of the eleven categories. A small interquartile range means

---

* Some Thurstone scales have been developed using fewer items, raters, and categories. The values given here were recommended by Thurstone.

that the judges agree. The larger the interquartile range is, the more variable the judges are in assigning category numbers to the item.

Alternate forms are usually constructed by randomly placing pairs of statements having the same scale and interquartile range into two forms. Within each form items are presented in random order, and the respondent is asked to check (✔) those statements with which he agrees and to put a cross (X) next to those with which he disagrees. The median of the scale values for each statement checked is the attitude score for the individual.

Table 14.5 presents the scale values for the twenty-four items comprising the original Thurstone-Chave attitude scale toward the church. Again, the scale values are median judgments made by raters who sorted the statement into one

Table 14.5. Statements and Their Corresponding Scale Values on Attitudes toward the Church

Scale Values	Statements
0.2	I believe the church is the greatest institution in America today.
0.8	I feel the church perpetuates the values which man puts highest in his philosophy of life.
1.2	I believe the church is a powerful agency for promoting both individual and social righteousness.
1.7	I feel the church services give me inspiration and help me to live up to my best during the following week.
2.2	I like to go to church for I get something worthwhile to think about and it keeps my mind filled with right thoughts.
2.6	I think the church keeps business and politics up to a higher standard than they would otherwise tend to maintain.
3.1	I do not understand the dogmas or creeds of the church but I find that the church helps me to be more honest and creditable.
3.3	I enjoy my church because there is a spirit of friendliness there.
4.0	When I go to church I enjoy a fine ritual service with good music.
4.5	I believe in what the church teaches but with mental reservations.
4.7	I am careless about religion and church relationships but I would not like to see my attitude become general.
5.1	I like the ceremonies of my church but do not miss them much when I stay away.
5.6	Sometimes I feel that the church and religion are necessary and sometimes I doubt it.
6.1	I feel the need for religion but do not find what I want in any one church.
6.7	I believe in sincerity and goodness without any church ceremonies.
7.2	I believe the churches are too much divided by factions and denominations to be a strong force for righteousness.
7.5	I think too much money is being spent on the church for the benefit that is being derived.
8.3	I think the teaching of the church is altogether too superficial to have much social significance.
8.8	I respect any church-member's beliefs but I think it is all "bunk."
9.2	I think the church seeks to impose a lot of worn-out dogmas and medieval superstitions.
9.6	I think the church is a hindrance to religion for it still depends upon magic, superstition, and myth.
10.4	The church represents shallowness, hypocrisy, and prejudice.
10.7	I think the organized church is an enemy of science and truth.
11.0	I think the church is a parasite on society.

From Thurstone and Chave 1929, pp. 33–34.

of eleven categories. Although table 14.5 presents items in order of scale value, in practice these are randomly presented to subjects.

Evaluation of Nondisguised Techniques

The Likert and Thurstone methods of constructing attitude scales have often been compared. Allen Edwards and Kathryn Kenney (1946), for example, found that Likert scales were simpler to construct and yielded somewhat higher reliability coefficients. They also found the correlations between scores on Likert and Thurstone scales to be .72 in one instance and .92 in another. The writing and judging of hundreds of items is a time-consuming task that can be reduced by constructing Likert rather than Thurstone scales. Sometimes the choice is based on whether subjects or judges are more readily available. The techniques can also be combined by including Likert alternates to each Thurstone statement. As figure 14.6 demonstrates, however, having to make numerous decisions can be frustrating.

© 1971 Washington Star Syndicate, Inc.

Figure 14.6

Furthermore, Thurstone scales assume that judges are capable of rating statements independently of their own attitudes. Although a number of studies support this contention, most used judges who did not hold extreme positions. One study (Hovland and Sherif 1952) which used groups who differed widely in attitudes toward blacks found that the scale values accurately reflected the extremists' attitudes by placing a disproportionate number of items in upper and lower categories and disregarding the middle ones. "Average" subjects, however, responded more uniformly over the range of the eleven categories.

Literally hundreds of Likert and Thurstone attitude scales are available on a wide variety of topics (Shaw and Wright, 1967; Miller 1970). Before constructing an attitude scale it would be well worth the effort to determine whether an appropriate scale had already been published. (Remember that no published test should be duplicated or used without the written permission of the publishers.)

Uses of Attitude Scales

Selection and Placement

Attitude scales as formal evaluation techniques are more useful for placement than for selection. The two most important reasons for not using attitude scales for selection are (1) the ease in faking responses and (2) ethical considerations. If a particular attitude is relevant to job performance, no ethical questions arise; however, faking is a serious problem for nondisguised measures. It is doubtful that a teacher applying for a position would willingly admit to harboring negative attitudes toward children and public education. Whether disguising the true nature of the scale would reduce faking is an unresolved empirical question, but the ethics of doing so is questionable.

The courts have usually sided with the plaintiffs when employment or educational decisions have been based on irrelevant attitudes. When an individual is selected for a position in which political beliefs are irrelevant, his attitudes should not be a matter of concern to employers. In practice, however, it is difficult to judge the weight employers give to what they consider significant signs or overt manifestations of an attitude. While everyone is probably influenced to some extent by appearance, mannerisms, and other individual characteristics, their possible prejudicial nature should not be overlooked.

Sometimes attitude scales are administered as part of the counseling interview. *Study of Values: A Scale for Measuring the Dominant Interests in Personality* (Allport, Vernon, and Lindzey 1960), for example, measures the relative importance of theoretical, economic, aesthetic, social, political, and religious values for high school, college, and adult populations.

For grades 7 and above, *The Survey of Study Habits and Attitudes* (Brown and Holtzman 1965) has been widely used in counseling. This is a Likert-type scale consisting of 100 statements yielding seven scores:

1. Delay avoidance: willingness to complete assignments on time
2. Work methods: efficiency and knowledge of study methods
3. Teacher approval: opinions of student toward teachers and their methods

4. Education acceptance: attitude toward educational goals and requirements
5. Study habits: a combination of delay avoidance and work methods scales
6. Study attitudes: a combination of teacher approval and educational acceptance scales
7. Study orientation: a combination of study habits and study attitudes scales to provide a total measure of attitudes and habits

Scores are reported as percentiles, and it is possible to identify the critical items that differentiate between good and poor students.

Remediation

Attitude scales can be important in diagnosing the reasons for student "failure." The student who believes that education is not meaningful, that teachers and schools exist for the purpose of creating conformity, and that any form of social organization is an infringement upon his individual rights is not likely to devote the time and effort necessary to be "successful" in that type of institution. Alternative programs to traditional schooling might be recommended for and made available to these persons.

Program Improvement

Attitude scales are often used to help evaluate the effectiveness of programs, films, courses of study, or curriculum innovations. Social studies teachers, for example, might be teaching a unit about Afro-Americans and might want to evaluate student change in attitudes toward this group; similarly, a new film might be evaluated by determining student attitudes toward its content. Use could be made of social distance, Likert, or Thurstone scales.

An important use of attitude scales is in measuring school morale. Sometimes these scales are administered to students currently attending school; at other times graduates of a school or district might be asked to evaluate the practices, programs, methods, and facilities they believed were of greatest and least value. Keeping annual summaries of student morale can help point out school deficiencies and improve morale.

Reliability of Attitude Scales

Reliability estimates of attitude measurements may be obtained by stability, equivalence, stability and equivalence, or internal consistency techniques. The reliability of Thurstone scales usually involves equivalence, or the extent to which scale values on one form of the scale correlate with corresponding values on a second form. Coefficients of equivalence for Thurstone scales generally range between .60 and .85, although somewhat lower coefficients of stability have been reported, even when test-retest time lapses are only a few weeks.

On Likert scales the most common form of reliability is the split-half co-efficient (corrected by the Spearman-Brown formula). These typically range in value from .80 to .95, with retest correlations over two or three weeks in the .80s and .90s. These are somewhat higher values than those reported for Thurstone scales. Alternate form reliability estimates, while not often reported for Likert scales, are in the .90s.

Validity of Attitude Scales

One of the most difficult aspects of attitude measurement is establishing criteria to determine validity. In a classic study, Richard LaPiere (1934) demon-strated the usual lack of congruence between verbal statements of attitudes and behavior. In LaPiere's travels with a Chinese student and his wife throughout the United States, only one "auto-camp" refused to accommodate the couple when they applied in person. Six months later, however, over 90 percent of those who had actually served the Chinese couple indicated on a questionnaire that they would not accept members of the "Chinese race."

If attitude is defined as a "predisposition" to act in accordance with a favorable-unfavorable scale toward some group, institution, or object, there seems to be some discrepancy between the definition and the ability to correlate attitudes with behaviors. However, if attitude is defined as a generalized response rather than as a "predisposition" (Doob 1947), the relationship between attitude and behavior is more easily resolved. For example, while attitude scales usually measure nonverbalized reactions toward an object or a group, what one does about these verbalizations may be inconsistent. Two individuals might have equally strong negative attitudes (as measured by an attitude scale) toward segregation, for example, but one may have learned to respond by participating in riots and sit-ins, whereas the other might refuse to participate in such activities.

The most common methods of validating responses on attitude scales are by content and concurrent validity. Predictive validity is most important in public opinion polling since its purpose is often to predict election results.

Content validity is easily determined on Likert and Thurstone scales. Items can be rewritten and revised until raters agree that they are clear and unam-biguous. Ambiguity can be measured by item analysis on Likert scales and by the interquartile ranges of items on Thurstone scales.

Concurrent validity is usually estimated by determining the extent to which the attitude scale is capable of discriminating between members of groups having known and different attitudes. People who attend church should have different attitudes from those who do not.

Another method of determining concurrent validity is to correlate responses on one attitude scale with those on a different scale designed to measure similar concepts. One would expect some positive correspondence, for example, between scales measuring attitudes toward religion and attitudes toward God, but these correlations vary greatly, some being as high as .90 and others being much lower. An aesthetic attitude scale, for example, correlated .38 with aesthetic values on Allport, Vernon, and Lindzey's *Study of Values* (1960). The median correlation between different scales that purportedly measure the same attitude is about .35 (Shaw and Wright 1967, p. 291).

Polling and Questionnaire Construction

Polls or attitude surveys are usually constructed by teams working in research centers, particularly when extremely accurate, unbiased data are required, such as in political forecasting or in studying consumer preferences. National and large-area surveys require the services of organizations capable of conducting large-scale investigations. More restricted polls and questionnaires, however, are within the capability of teachers.

Six steps should be followed in conducting a poll:

1. Determining objectives   The first step in conducting a poll is to determine exactly what type of information is required and for what purposes. In studying attitudes toward a breakfast cereal, questions of price, taste, convenience, nutrition, packaging (color, size, shape, lettering, information), inducements (prizes, contests), and a host of other issues could be considered. Unless one understands the purpose of the information, the remaining steps will be meaningless.

2. Determining the population   A population is defined as the total of all persons about whom the information is desired. It may be small and accessible (all the students attending a given school) or large and inaccessible (all persons in the United States over the age of four). It may be restricted by location, sex, age, religion, socioeconomic status, race, or any other characteristic deemed important. These characteristics of a population must be specified.

3. Determining the sample   A *sample* is defined as a limited number of individuals selected from the population in some unbiased manner. Where populations are small and accessible, selecting samples may be unnecessary; all individuals in the population could be studied. Sampling is necessary where populations are large, where they are relatively inaccessible, and where the cost per unit of information obtained is high.

A sample is *biased* if all elements of the population do not have an equal opportunity to be selected. Selecting potential jury members from property tax records, for example, yields a biased sample of adults because this procedure eliminates citizens who do not own property. Polls of parent attitudes will be biased if information is obtained by calling telephone numbers during the day, a procedure that systematically excludes those who do not own a telephone and those who work during the day.

Eliminating bias in sampling is a highly technical subject, but it is possible to describe a few methods. One method is to place the names of all members of the population into a container and select the desired number blindly. A simpler procedure is to use a *table of random numbers,* available in many statistics books. These tables consist of randomly assorted digits which may be read in any order beginning in any part of the table. Each individual in the population is given a number from 1 to N, N being the total number in the population. As a number is read, the corresponding person is included in the sample. Numbers in the table that are larger than N are disregarded. Sampling from a hat or using a table of random numbers is called *simple random sampling*. Samples so obtained are *unbiased* since no one is systematically excluded.

Another method of selecting samples is to select every third, fifth, or tenth person from a list containing all members of the population. If the lists are arranged alphabetically, some amount of bias may be present since this procedure may eliminate from the sample individuals who are listed next to each other (brothers or sisters, for example, who have the same last names). This procedure, called *systematic sampling,* usually yields results similar to simple random sampling and generally with much less effort.

For more complex sampling tasks, one might *stratify* the population into subgroups based on some relevant criterion such as age, sex, or socioeconomic status and then select randomly or systematically within each stratum. Or where elements of the population are widely dispersed, *area sampling* may be preferred. These techniques have been described by Sax (1968) in some detail. The same source also provides a discussion of the number of individuals that should be selected for inclusion in the sample to gain various degrees of accuracy.

4. Writing the items   Sometimes it is possible to find existing attitude scales that contain items suitable for one's purposes. Often, however, it will be necessary to write original items. These items might require written responses, might provide choices to check or select, or they might be asked orally in an interview. Interviews allow probing and clarification of the respondent's position, but they are time-consuming and expensive. Questionnaires are cheaper and easier to disseminate, but they usually do not permit the depth of response of interviews. For young children and illiterates, the interview is obviously the recommended form. Remember that if questionnaires are mailed, every one not returned is a potential source of biased sampling. Those who take the time and trouble to answer and return a questionnaire often differ significantly from those who fail or refuse to respond.

Although there are many suggestions for writing good questionnaire or interview items, no set of rules replaces empirically verifying items on sub-samples of individuals to ensure that items are unambiguous, unprejudiced, and representative of the opinions of the sample members. A newspaper poll of attitudes toward mandatory busing of students to reduce racial imbalance in the public schools contained this item: "If the school board were more responsive to public demands, would you be willing to support the proposed levy?" Clearly this item (and others) forced individuals to respond affirmatively since everyone wants "more responsive" school boards. At the very least, the phrasing of an item or question should not allow respondents to discern the attitude of the item writer.

Before items are administered in final form they should be checked for content validity and item analyses should be performed to eliminate ambiguity and to increase discrimination among individuals with different attitudes. All re-worded items should be checked again for content validity, clarity, and discrimination.

As with cognitive items, the reliability of attitude scales is a function of test length. A single question requiring a yes or no answer cannot measure the various aspects of attitude, such as intensity, pervasiveness, and consistency. A better picture of a respondent's attitude can be obtained by increasing the number of items or the number of alternatives, although there are obvious limits (see figure 14.7).

Figure 14.7

5. Administering the items   Mailed questionnaires should contain the signature of the sponsor and should be accompanied by a brief letter of explanation showing their importance. An addressed and stamped return envelope should always be provided. Respondents should be told whether their responses will be kept anonymous or under what circumstances they will be made public.

Anonymous returns do not permit the sending of follow-up letters to persuade nonrespondents to return their forms. When respondents know that they are being identified only for this purpose, they are usually willing to be identified. If code numbers are used for identification, respondents should be informed of this fact.

The interview presents some interesting administrative problems. Interview responses depend highly on the age, sex, race, and physical characteristics of the interviewer. White teachers who interview black children may not get the same responses as black teachers. One advantage of the questionnaire is that it eliminates the sometimes biasing effect of the interviewer.

6. Data analysis and interpretation   Questionnaires, interviews, and polls are usually analyzed by determining the percentage of individuals who favor or oppose some issue. The accuracy of such data—assuming unbiased samples—is determined principally by the number of cases selected for inclusion in the sample and the variability of attitude in the population. If everyone in the population has the same attitude (i.e., zero variability), a sample of one case would accurately reflect the population attitude. As variability in attitude increases, more cases will be needed to compensate for this divergence. This increase in sample size assumes, of course, that the sample was selected in an unbiased manner. If the sample is biased, increasing the number of cases just yields a greater number of biased cases.

If one is trying to determine the percentage of individuals who hold a relatively rare belief, a very large sample will have to be selected. If only one person in ten thousand believes that the earth is flat, it may take a sample many times that size before that type of person will be found.

Although chapter 17 of this text is concerned with the problem of reporting and disseminating pupil information, one point should be emphasized here. In presenting the results of a poll, questionnaire, or interview, it is important to provide the reader with such information as the number of individuals in the population who were approached, the number who responded, the number who failed to respond, and the number who responded but for some reason invalidated their responses. These numbers should also be converted to percentages to facilitate comparisons.

How data will be analyzed must be considered before items are written. If responses are to be reported by subcategories (sex, race, age, etc.), this information must be requested on the final draft of the questionnaire.

Summary

1. *Interest* is defined as a preference for one activity over another; *attitudes* are preferences for groups, institutions, or objects.

2. Three types of interest are: expressed interests—those that a person states as having interest for him; manifest interests—inferred from the kinds of activities in which a person engages; and inventoried interests—those that are measured by responses on a test or inventory.

3. Interests in various occupations differ by area—the type of occupation (medicine, engineering), and level—the amount of training required.

4. The median correlation between aptitude and interest is close to 0, but in cognate areas the correlations are moderately high. Numerical interest and numerical aptitude, for example, tend to correlate in the .50s.

5. Interest inventories have been constructed from three approaches:
   a. In the rational approach items that logically appear to measure each area of interest are constructed.
   b. In the internal consistency approach item analysis procedures are followed to make each area as homogeneous as possible.
   c. In the empirical approach items are selected to discriminate between "successful" persons and randomly selected persons.

6. Norms on interest inventories are ipsative or normative. Ipsative norms compare various areas of interest within the individual but do not permit comparisons between persons.

7. Interest inventories are used to best advantage in making placement decisions. They are too easily faked to be used for selection, although some disguised techniques appear promising for that purpose. The following suggestions will help students better understand their interest inventory scores:
   a. Obtain information about expressed, manifest, and inventoried interests.
   b. Point out realistic alternatives, but leave the final decision to the student.
   c. State alternatives in relative terms on ipsative scales to allow the student to choose among these alternatives.
   d. Use aptitude test scores along with inventoried interest measures.
   e. Learn how each scale was developed on an inventory because scales can have different meanings.
   f. Make sure the student is able to read the inventory questions before attempting to interpret scores to him.

g. Help students understand the patterns of behavior needed to enter some occupation.

h. Be cognizant of the sex role stereotyping present on some tests.

8. Interest inventories have been used to find areas of student interest in order to help those who are fearful of a subject. By capitalizing on student interests, teachers can motivate students to work in areas they might not otherwise try.

9. Inventoried interests tend to be relatively stable in the late teens and change little after the age of twenty-five.

10. Although aptitude is probably a better predictor of success in required courses, interest inventories can also be used for this purpose. They are especially useful in predicting job satisfaction.

11. The Strong Vocational Interest Blank is designed for high school and college students who are likely to enter professional and semiprofessional occupations. Some characteristics of the SVIB are:

a. Interests are shown as standard scores or letter ratings in each of a number of specific occupations.

b. Individual scores are compared with the scores of "men in general" for each occupation. High scores mean that the individual has the same interest patterns as men who are successful in that field.

c. Eight nonoccupational scales are also provided to measure such variables as interests relating to high and low scholarship, breadth of interests, and so on.

d. The SVIB is scored by licensed scoring centers, and the cost is relatively high.

12. The Kuder Preference Record: Vocational, the Kuder General Interest Survey, and the Kuder Occupational Interest Survey are other popular interest inventories. Empirical keying is used on the KOIS (as it is on the SVIB), except that the score an individual receives on a scale is determined by the number of men in an occupation who agree with the examinee's responses. The Kuder Preference: Vocational and the KGIS measure interest in ten areas, each yielding percentile norms.

13. The Minnesota Vocational Interest Inventory attempts to measure interests in semiskilled and skilled occupations and is keyed against "tradesmen in general." Nine interest area scales are provided.

14. Classroom interest inventories can employ various approaches.

a. Various activities can be listed and students can be asked to check those in which they have greatest (or least) interest.

b. Instead of simply checking items, students can be asked to rank each item from those enjoyed most to enjoyed least.

    c. Rating scales can be developed by having students indicate how much they enjoy some activity.

    d. Students can be asked to write a theme on the kinds of activities they enjoy. These can be structured or unstructured.

15. Attitudes vary in direction, intensity, pervasiveness, consistency, and salience.

16. Attitude scales may be ordinal or interval. Ordinal scales are ranked without regard to the equality of differences among the ranked variables; interval scales, in contrast, have equal units of measurement. Although the meaning of *zero* in attitude measurement has been widely discussed and debated, it was defined here as the point at which an attitude changes from favorable to unfavorable.

17. Some attitude scales are nondisguised in the sense that their intent is readily apparent to examinees; others are disguised since the examinee believes he is responding to a cognitive task although in reality he is providing information about his attitude. Disguised techniques include information, perception, and judgment tests:

    a. Information tests appear to measure knowledge, but all alternatives are equally incorrect or have no known answers. The examinee's responses reflect his attitude rather than knowledge.

    b. Perception tests briefly present stimuli (a picture, for example), and the examinee is told to report everything he can remember seeing. The assumption is that attitude determines perceptions.

    c. Judgment tests require the individual to evaluate two positions (such as on a debate). The judgment is assumed to be derived from attitudes toward the content of the debate rather than from the qualities of the debate itself.

18. Three types of nondisguised attitude scales are social distance scales, Likert scales, and Thurstone scales.

    a. Social distance scales ask the respondent to indicate the degree of social distance he places between himself and members of minority or ethnic groups.

    b. On Likert scales, items that measure different degrees of intensity toward some object, person, or institution are constructed. Each item consists of a statement that is to be answered by strongly agree, agree, undecided, disagree, or strongly disagree. Item analysis procedures are used to select items that discriminate among individuals who have different opinions on a topic.

    c. Thurstone scales are called "equal-appearing interval scales." Judges are asked to rate a large number of items on their favorableness. The median rating assigned to each item by the judges is the item's scaled value. The final Thurstone scale consists of items that have been judged to be equidistant from each other in favorableness.

19. Attitude scales are not used widely for selection, but they are sometimes used to help individuals understand themselves. Understanding a student's attitudes can be useful in providing remedial or alternative programs to traditional schooling. Attitude scales are also used to evaluate the effects of films, programs, new curricula, and so forth.

20. The reliability of an attitude scale is determined by the nature of the scale. Thurstone scales are usually constructed to yield equivalent forms. The correlation between scores on these forms can then be determined. Since Likert scales are developed from item analysis procedures, the split-half reliability (corrected by the Spearman-Brown formula) is most often used.

21. The validity of attitude scales is particularly difficult to document. In part this results from the fact that individuals may have feelings that are inconsistent with the ways in which they might act or behave.

22. Surveys of student attitudes can be conducted. This usually involves six steps:

 a. Objectives of the survey need to be determined.

 b. The population of individuals has to be identified.

 c. The sample of individuals has to be selected from the population in an unbiased manner so that all members of the population have an equal opportunity of being selected.

 d. Items are written to meet the objectives of the survey and the backgrounds and ability levels of the individuals sampled.

 e. The items are administered to ensure the largest return possible.

 f. Data are analyzed, usually by determining the percentage of persons who hold certain beliefs. The objectives largely determine how data will be analyzed.

Suggested Readings

Campbell, David P. *Handbook for the Strong Vocational Interest Blank*. Stanford, Calif.: Stanford University Press, 1971, 516 pp. The most complete summary of the work done on the SVIB.

Dolliver, Robert H. "Strong Vocational Interest Blank versus Expressed Vocational Interest: A Review." *Psychological Bulletin* 72, no. 2 (August 1969): 95–107. Reviewed are studies that indicate that the SVIB and expressed interests do not correlate highly with each other and that expressed interests are often better predictors than the SVIB. The implications for counseling are discussed.

Fishbein, Martin, ed. *Readings in Attitude Theory and Measurment.* New York: John Wiley & Sons, 1967, 499 pp. An excellent source of original articles on attitude measurement and theory. The articles vary widely in difficulty.

Katz, Martin, and Norris, Lila. "The Contribution of Academic Interest Measures to the Differential Prediction of Marks." *Journal of Educational Measurement* 9, no. 1 (Spring 1972): 1–11. The authors found that interest measures added appreciably to incremental validity among high school students when these tests were used to predict marks or grades.

Shaw, Marvin E., and Wright, Jack M. *Scales for the Measurement of Attitudes.* New York: McGraw-Hill Book Co., 1967, 604 pp. In addition to some excellent sections on the nature of scaling, the authors have brought together examples of attitude scales on many topics. Evidence of reliability, validity, scoring, and so forth are also presented. The authors remind the reader that most of the scales do not have sufficiently high reliabilities to warrant their being used for individual selection or diagnosis.

The Measurement of Personality

15 Although everyone is familiar with the concept of personality, the word defies simple definition. Some people appear to be outgoing and friendly and others moody and introverted; some are achievement-oriented, and others are easy-going, unassertive, and noncompetitive. Indeed, the number of *traits* or characteristic ways in which individuals behave has been estimated to be in the thousands (Allport and Odbert 1936). Obviously any attempt to measure that number of traits would be a dismal failure. Even with the exclusion of synonyms, Raymond Cattell (1964) has estimated that over 170 traits exist.

Attempts to measure personality must therefore be selective. In principle this does not differ from testing achievement, intelligence, attitude, or any other area since tests are samples of behavior and are necessarily limited in content. The determination that one trait will be included in and another excluded from a personality inventory depends on the theoretical beliefs of the test constructor and whatever empirical evidence he may have to support his theory. Personality theorists who are oriented to *psychoanalysis* will want to use inventories revealing the interrelationships among the ego (reality), superego (conscience), and id (basic drives). The *typologists,* in contrast, will want inventories that permit typing or categorizing of individuals into basic personality groups such as normals, schizophrenics, manic-depressives, and so forth. *Field theorists* are concerned with the individual's current perception of his "life space," and they believe that if pencil-and-paper tests are used at all, they will have to measure these perceptions. Still another approach is to use the statistical technique of *factor analysis* (see pp. 377-378) to mathematically determine the nature and number of traits. In addition to this approach, however, the factor analyst usually accepts some personality theory he wishes to validate by demonstrating that the hypothesized traits are measurable.

Pseudoscientific and Quasi-Pseudoscientific Approaches to Personality Measurement

Man's need to judge personality has resulted in some practical techniques of differentiating among individuals. Solomon's "test of nurturance" in the Old Testament (1 Kings 4:29) helped him determine which of two women was the real mother of a child each had claimed as her own. The "test" consisted of Solomon's command that the child be "divided" into two parts. The "real" mother was the one who cried out, "O my lord, give her the living child, and in no wise slay it," whereas the other said, "Let it be neither mine nor thine, but divide it." Solomon's "test," although it proved valid in that instance, could hardly qualify as the basis of a theory of personality. Systematic theories of personality probably began with Aristotle's belief in physiognomy.

Physiognomy

Physiognomy is the belief that personality characteristics can be determined by a person's physical appearance. Aristotle took the position that character could be read by observing such attributes as color of hair, gait, and voice. A person with a bulbous nose had "piggish" characteristics, whereas pointed noses represented such "doglike" traits as irascibility.

Evidence does exist that some aspects of physiognomy correlate with personality characteristics, particularly gait (Allport and Vernon 1933). Evidently energetic individuals tend to walk rapidly, whereas the dull and uninspiring tend to be slowpokes. In the past few years renewed interest in the study of body signs, now called *kinesics,* by both the scientific community and popular literature resulted in publication of Ray Birdwhistell's *Introduction to Kinesics* (1952) and Julius Fast's best-seller, *Body Language* (1971). However, unlike the exaggerated and unverified claims made by physiognomists, Birdwhistell warns that there is no one-to-one correspondence between a particular body movement and psychological traits.

Although many studies indicate that individual's often agree on various personality traits judged by physical appearance, this simply indicates widespread cultural stereotypes. The redhead is expected to have a "flaming" personality and the intellectual to be (literally) a highbrow. There is no good evidence on which to base these conclusions, but one can always find an example to "prove the point."

One personality test currently in limited use (and in general disrepute) is the Szondi Test, which consists of individual photographs of homosexuals, sadists, epileptics, hysterics, catatonics, paranoics, depressives, and manics. The subject, unaware of the clinical diagnoses, is given six sets of eight cards and must select from each set the two pictures he likes and dislikes most. The

Szondi Test assumes that clinical subgroups differ in facial characteristics which can be recognized by individuals who possess some of the same characteristic traits (overt or latent). At least in theory, an overt homosexual would select pictures of other homosexuals; however, if pictures of homosexuals are rejected, supposedly this is an indication of latent homosexuality. As might be expected, there is little empirical research data to support Szondi's contentions, although there is some evidence that raters can correctly identify homosexuals and manics but not any of the other groups (Borstelmann and Klopfer 1953).

Phrenology

In the early 1800s F. J. Gall and J. G. Spurzheim proposed a system for identifying personality and cognitive factors by measuring protuberant parts of the skull, which they believed were related to corresponding parts of the brain. Specific brain locations were reserved for each of thirty-five separate attributes, such as amativeness, concentrativeness, combativeness, and secretiveness. The capacity to recognize faces, for example, was thought to be located on either side of the top part of the nose. The theory was that any highly developed trait would produce a protuberance on that portion of the skull where the attribute was located; an underdeveloped trait could be detected by locating depressions on the skull.

Different parts of the brain do serve different functions. The brain stem (located at the top of the spinal cord) regulates involuntary responses such as respiration and blood pressure; the upper part of the brain stem regulates such drives as fear, sex, and hunger; and the top part of the cerebral cortex controls the ability to restrain and control basic drives. The current evidence is that various areas of the brain regulate body *functions,* not *traits.*

Other Pseudoscientific Approaches

The number of ways man creates for self-deception are endless. Palmistry, astrology, and numerology are among the oldest of the pseudosciences. Many newspapers print horoscopes that provide advice and predictions based on astrological signs. Probably few persons take such advice seriously, but simply enjoy them as harmless diversions.

A fascinating account of gullibility among college students was published by Bertram Forer (1949), who constructed a Diagnostic Interest Blank (DIB) consisting of a list of hobbies, job duties, secret ambitions, personal characteristics, and ambitions from which the respondent was to choose the attributes of the ideal person. Scoring was qualitative. From the "results" of the inventory, Forer prepared a brief outline on each student's personality. The students did not know that each received identical personality sketches containing the following generalities (p. 120):

1. You have a great need for other people to like and admire you.
2. You have a tendency to be critical of yourself.
3. You have a great deal of unused capacity which you have not turned to your advantage.
4. While you have some personality weaknesses, you are generally able to compensate for them.
5. Your sexual adjustment has presented problems for you.
6. Disciplined and self-controlled outside, you tend to be worrisome and insecure inside.
7. At times you have serious doubts as to whether you have made the right decision or done the right thing.
8. You prefer a certain amount of change and variety and become dissatisfied when hemmed in by restrictions and limitations.
9. You pride yourself as an independent thinker and do not accept other's statements without satisfactory proof.
10. You have found it unwise to be too frank in revealing yourself to others.
11. At times you are extroverted, affable, sociable, while at other times you are introverted, wary, reserved.
12. Some of your aspirations tend to be pretty unrealistic.
13. Security is one of your major goals in life.

Each student was asked to indicate on a five-point scale how effective the DIB was in revealing his true personality and how accurately the thirteen statements revealed basic characteristics of his personality. Of the thirty-nine students in the class, only one gave the DIB a rating below 4 (0 was poor, 5 was perfect). Only five rated the accuracy of the sketch below 4. The mean number of items on the sketch judged to be accurate descriptions was 10.2. Evidently even college students are impressed by generalizations and are willing to overrate the diagnostic value of personality descriptions.

Sources of Error in Personality Assessment: Response Biases

When an individual responds to a statement regarding some personality trait, his response is usually assumed to be either candid or deliberately deceptive. According to some psychologists, however, a person might have subconscious tendencies to answer questions systematically, independent of item content. These tendencies, called response sets, response styles, or response biases, have been the subject of vigorous debate. The three major response biases are *acquiescence, social desirability,* and *deviant response.*

Acquiescence

Perhaps the response bias that has received the most attention is *acquiescence,* which refers to the tendency to respond "true," "yes," or "agree" on both personality and cognitive tests. Scores obtained by such persons are invalid because they presumably do not measure responses to item content as much as they measure this subconscious tendency to mark items *true.*

A second definition of acquiescence has sometimes been confused with the first (this seems to be one source of difficulty between psychologists who accept the notion of acquiescence and those who do not). This second meaning defines *acquiescence* as a personality characteristic of individuals who tend to be agreeable or to respond affirmatively on personality, attitude, or interest inventories. Whether an individual possesses this response tendency can be determined by asking the same question in reverse form ("I love mankind" versus "I hate mankind"). If respondents pay attention to item content, the scores on the two forms will have a negative correlation. However, if a positive correlation is found, the scales apparently are measuring only the tendency to acquiesce.

Which of these two hypotheses is most justifiable is the heart of the debate. First, it is difficult to write items that are exact opposites. Is the statement "I love mankind" exactly opposite to "I hate mankind"? If not, correlations between the two forms are not easily interpreted. Second, most of the correlations obtained are low but positive, indicating only the possibility of acquiescence. Third, there is little evidence that measures of acquiescence correlate with behavioral manifestations of conformity. That is, there is little support for the notion that those who acquiesce on personality inventories also acquiesce in their everyday behavior.

In summary, it appears that *acquiescence,* defined as a tendency to mark more answers true than false, probably does occur with personality inventories, but the extent to which it occurs is unclear. But acquiescence, conceived of as a valid personality trait that should be measured by personality inventories, is still a matter of controversy. In the interpretation of personality measures, teachers should keep in mind the possibility that test scores are affected by acquiescence and not based solely on test content.

Social Desirability

Most individuals will respond positively to an item such as "I honestly try to avoid trouble." Allen Edwards (1970) has taken the position that individuals subconsciously try to heighten their social desirability by endorsing such items. This is not "faking" since the social desirability (SD) response set is subconscious, whereas faking is deliberate.

In one of Edwards's early studies (1953) raters judged the social desirability of a series of 140 items on a nine-point scale. The mean rating for each item became a measure of the social desirability of that item. He then asked another group of subjects to endorse the items that described themselves. Edwards found a correlation of .87 between the judges' mean rating on each item and the proportion of subjects endorsing these items. Evidently responses to personality inventory items are strongly affected by SD—so much, in fact, that one author (Nunnally 1967) has questioned the value of "self-report" inventories for any purpose because he believes that individuals differ systematically in their tendencies to respond in a socially desirable manner.

Not all psychologists accept the position that SD is as pervasive as Edwards claims. Warren Norman (1967) has concluded that SD plays a relatively minor role in personality assessment on self-report inventories and cites five studies to demonstrate his point. His arguments are partially based on the fact that Edwards correlated averages (means of judges' ratings) with group endorsements and that individual differences were not measured.

In an attempt to reduce the effects of SD, Edwards used forced-choice inventories on the Edwards Personal Preference Schedule (EPPS). A forced-choice inventory presents equally socially desirable statements that have different validities. That is, the options look equally inviting, but each correlates differentially with criteria. When an individual selects an item he believes is most self-descriptive, he receives a point if the item correlates with the criterion. He receives no points if he selects items that do not correlate with the criterion.

Many different kinds of options can be included in forced-choice inventories. On the EPPS, for example, subjects are presented in pairs of statements such as the following:*

1. A. I like to talk about myself to others.
   B. I like to work toward some goal that I have set for myself.
2. A. I feel depressed when I fail at something.
   B. I feel nervous when giving a talk before a group.

An individual who selects option *A* in item 1, for example, might be credited with one point on the exhibition scale; the selection of *B* might produce one point on the achievement subtest.

Some evidence shows that forced-choice inventories can be faked, although with more difficulty than is required on other formats. Furthermore, two items that separately are rated equal on SD may differ on SD when they are placed next to each other on a scale. The juxtaposition of options evidently makes it simpler to estimate SD. However, forced-choice inventories are ipsative measures, which makes comparisons of individuals difficult.

Deviant (Atypical) Responses

A third type of response bias is the tendency of individuals to respond atypically on personality test items. Abnormal individuals are expected to respond abnormally on content, but according to the *deviant response hypothesis* (Berg 1955), abnormal individuals tend to give unorthodox and atypical answers to test items *independently of item content*. Berg thus hypothesizes that abnormality can be detected simply by counting the number of atypical responses selected—disregarding test content—on personality inventories.

Most of the studies investigating deviant responses require the subject to select choices constructed along a strongly like–strongly dislike dimension. According to Berg, atypical individuals select options that are not selected by most persons. Moreover, Berg's position is that this tendency will appear on all tests. To eliminate the role of content (or at least to reduce its effects), Berg developed a Perceptual Reaction Test (PRT) and a Word Reaction Test (WRT). The PRT, for example, consists of sixty geometrical drawings which subjects are to rate on a like-dislike dimension.

The reaction to Berg's deviation hypothesis has been both favorable and unfavorable. In a generally favorable review, David Hamilton (1968) indicated that deviant responses are stable over time, that they are internally consistent, that there is a tendency for individuals who give deviant responses on one test to do so on another, and that these tendencies correlate significantly with measures of rigidity and intolerance for ambiguity. However, other investigators, such as Lee Sechrest and Douglas Jackson (1963), have taken the position that item content *is* important and that such measures as the PRT and the WRT are *not* free of content. Nunnally (1967) argues that virtually any test can discriminate between hospitalized psychiatric patients and nonhospitalized "normals." A person who is so confused that he responds in a random manner is likely to respond more "atypically" than do better adjusted individuals.

Observational Methods of Measuring Personality

Observational methods are procedures in which the emphasis is directed to the overt behavior of subjects. One way of obtaining data about personality is to unobtrusively observe the behavior of a student interacting "naturally" with his peers. Because *naturalistic observation* (observation in which the situation is *not* created by the observer) is most often used to observe *typical* behavior of individuals in group situations, this topic is considered in chapter 16, "The Measurement of Social Development and Participation."

Controlled Observational Techniques

Controlled observation places the individual in a situation structured to evoke particular behavior or responses. If the teacher or school psychologist wants to determine how a child will respond to frustration, he can create a stressful situation and observe the child's responses to it. The observers may take either an active or an inactive role in interacting with the student.

This chapter examines two forms of controlled observation: the interview and the situational test. The *interview* may be thought of as a nondisguised, controlled observation of an individual's behavior in a one-to-one situation. In contrast, the *situational test* disguises the purposes of evaluation by forcing the subject to respond to realistic problems.

The Interview

The *interview* consists of oral interactions between a respondent and an interrogator. The questions posed may be highly structured ("How many times have you had headaches in the last week?") or unstructured ("Tell me how you feel"), but they are always determined by the kind of information the interviewer desires. Although structured questions might simplify the categorization and summarization of responses, they might restrict what the subject is permitted to say. Unstructured interviews allow the respondent more freedom but make categorizing responses more difficult. Interviews often contain both types of questions.

The *defensive-response* or *stress interview* is sometimes used in situations where the respondent may attempt to withhold personal information about personal behavior. Such questions as "When was the first time you stole something?" are asked. This type of interview requires a good deal of training because it can easily create hostility and anger in the interviewee.

Structured interviews are probably most advantageous if a specific type of response is desired and if the interviewer and respondent "share a common vocabulary relevant to the issues and alternatives to be included in the interview" (Dohrenwend and Richardson 1963, p. 482). Unstructured interviews are called for in ambiguous situations or when the respondent and interviewer can be expected to experience difficulty understanding each other. The lack of structure permits each to clarify and pursue topics as they arise.

Other advantages of the interview include the ability of the respondent to ask questions, the relative ease in questioning young children and illiterates, and the opportunity for the interviewer to judge nuances of expression as well as interview content. Disadvantages include the difficulty in analyzing and categorizing unstructured responses, and the relatively high cost of training interviewers, meeting with respondents individually, and obtaining reliable and valid responses.

Interviews, like other data collection procedures, are evaluated by their

reliability and validity. Some common sources of error that affect both reliability and validity have been summarized by Robert Kahn and Charles Cannell
(1957). They include *errors in asking questions* (asking questions that fail to
satisfy the purpose of the interview), *probing errors* (failure to allow time for
the respondent to answer or the anticipation of answers before they are given),
errors in motivating (failure to obtain trust and confidence in the interviewer),
and *recording errors* (failure to report or categorize responses properly).

Another potential source of invalidity is *interviewer bias.* Untrained or
poorly trained interviewers are likely to hear what they want, what they expect,
or what they are "expected" to hear. Respondents in turn are affected by such
interviewer variables as age, sex, race, socioeconomic level, and personal characteristics.

Just as the reliability of tests generally increases with the addition of more
items, the reliability of an interview can be increased by including a larger
number of interviewers (see pp. 186-187); idiosyncratic ratings tend to cancel
out and reliability increases as a function of the Spearman-Brown formula (see
p. 179). Thus if two interviewers obtain data that correlate .70, adding two
more *equally competent* interviewers or observers will yield a reliability of
about .82. The extent to which interviewers obtain the same data is called the
interrater reliabiilty.

The reliability of interview responses can be estimated using coefficients
of stability, equivalence, and stability and equivalence. Stability is measured by
having interviewers collect data at two different times from the same respondents.
Equivalence is estimated by having two or more forms of interview questions
when data are obtained from the same respondents. Equivalence will be high
if the forms yield comparable results. Stability and equivalence can be obtained
by having different interviewers question respondents over time using two or
more forms.

The reliability of interviews depends on such factors as the degree of
structure, factualness, and clarity of questions; the willingness and ability of
the respondent to cooperate; the training of the interviewers; the extent to
which interviewers are capable of separating their own attitudes and beliefs
from the respondent's; and the amount of time that elapses between successive
interviews.

Predictive and concurrent validity coefficients have been reported for many
different types of interviews. In one study, for example, the investigators found
that respondents were willing to disclose their age and telephone ownership,
but were either unable or unwilling to accurately report ownership of a library
card and whether or not they had contributed to the Community Chest (Parry
and Crossley 1950). Questions that threaten a person's ego are more likely
to lead to invalid responses than nonthreatening ones.

Generally data obtained from interviews have not been an accurate
predictor of such diverse criteria as grades, supervisory ratings, production
records, and clinical prognoses of some forms of psychopathology. However,
because validity coefficients are obtained for specific purposes (selection,

diagnosis, and so forth), further discussion of the validity of the interview will be postponed until a later section of this chapter.

Situational Tests

One of the earliest studies designed to observe personality and character traits in lifelike situations was conducted by Hugh Hartshorne and Mark May (1928), who were interested in measuring the degree to which students would cheat when given the opportunity. In one of their investigations students were allowed to score their own examinations, which, unknown to them, had already been scored by the investigators. Differences in the two sets of scores were used as evidence of cheating. In another study by the same investigators money was placed in boxes and distributed to children who believed that their box would not be identified. The amount of money taken was the measure of dishonesty. These studies were carried out in different classrooms, during athletic contests and parties, at home, in Sunday school, and at club meetings to determine the extent of cheating, lying, falsifying, stealing, and self-aggrandizement that actually takes place when the opportunity presents itself.

The conclusions reached by Hartshorne and May were that (1) cheating was *task-specific*—what a student did at home was relatively unrelated to what he might do at school; (2) the correlations between different forms of behavior (lying and stealing, for example) were also low; (3) the reliability of measurements derived from most situational tests was low (the average was about .40); and (4) there was practically no correlation between different tests taken in different places.

Another classic use of situational tests was by the U. S. Office of Strategic Services (OSS) (1948) during World War II. In one test potential candidates for military intelligence work were to construct a large cube from poles, pegs, and blocks within ten minutes. Because of the complexity of the job, each candidate was given two "helpers" who, unknown to him, were psychologists trained to cajole, interfere, ridicule, and generally make the task impossible to complete. The leadership ability of each candidate was observed and rated.

Some situational tests depend on deliberate deception, whereas others simply set the stage for the individual to react to a contrived situation. In deception studies the individual is fooled, lied to, or tricked. Zick Rubin (1970) has written a popular account of some of these studies, including one in which thirty-two out of thirty-seven coeds were duped into accepting a date with a handsome graduate student. The purpose of the investigation was to determine the relationship between self-esteem and the tendency to fall in love. "Self-esteem," by the way, was also created artificially. Half the girls were given highly favorable reports on a personality test taken earlier, whereas the other half were given negative results. It was found that the women in the "negative results" group were more in love with the graduate student than those in the high self-esteem group.

Another situational test involving deception was conducted by Stanley Milgram (1963) at Yale University. Subjects were presented with a device that could deliver electric shocks ranging from 14 to 450 volts to a person trying to learn word pairs. To demonstrate how the electrical device worked and to make the experiment appear realistic, Milgram gave each "teacher" a shock with 45 volts. Then the "teacher" was told to increase shocks each time the "learner" made an error. To increase the reality of the experiment, the learners and teachers were acquainted, and their respective roles were determined by drawing straws. However, the drawing was fixed so that the learners were always Milgram's confederates. Although the responses (groans, screams) to the shocks were on tape, the teachers believed that they were inducing excruciating pain. According to Milgram, 60 percent of the teachers continued to increase the shocks according to directions even when they believed that potentially lethal doses were being administered! Kilman (1967) has argued that some of the Milgram subjects were severely traumatized by the knowledge that they were willing to acquiesce to authority despite the fact that they violated their consciences. To Milgram's credit, however, it should be noted that all subjects were carefully screened before the experiment and were followed up by a psychiatrist after the study.

Situational tests yield samples of behavior obtained under specific conditions that approximate nontest situations. Because situational tests are disguised, however, some participants may never realize that they have participated in a test. The deceptive nature of such tests usually makes them unsuitable for selection except perhaps when conducted by the military in times of national emergency. For research purposes their use might be justified if it can be demonstrated that (1) the participants will not suffer physical or emotional stress; (2) the research is of scientific significance; *and* (3) it is not practicable to conduct the investigation in any other way (American Psychological Association 1963).

Situational tests tend to be task-specific, and behavior elicited under preplanned conditions might not be duplicated under other simulated or nonsimulated conditions. This is a serious weakness and disadvantage. In the Hartshorne and May studies, for example, cheating in a classroom situation correlated only .10 with cheating in an athletic contest. Any attempt to measure cheating *in general* might well be prohibitive in cost, time, and effort.

Test-retest correlations of various tasks conducted by Hartshorne and May over a six-month period averaged about .50 despite the fact that many of the tasks were objectively scored. This implies that the participants themselves might have changed.

The validity of situational tests is difficult to assess, partly because criterion measures are difficult to obtain and may themselves be unreliable. In the Office of Strategic Services (OSS) studies, for example, individuals selected for military intelligence work were often assigned to different jobs when their training was completed, thus making comparison with criterion tasks difficult. In the Hartshorne and May studies teacher ratings of student honesty correlated about .35 with observational measures.

Considering the expense, time, and ethical questions raised by the use of situational tests, it is unlikely that they will be employed widely in education except perhaps as a research tool.

Self-reports

The *self-report inventory* usually consists of questionnaire-type statements requiring a limited form of response such as might be found on true-false or multiple-choice items. For example, respondents might have to answer "yes," "no," or "don't know" to a question such as "Do you have problems falling asleep at night?" Or the item might be in the form of a Likert scale, such as "I have trouble falling asleep at night," with choices varying from "strongly agree" to "strongly disagree." Another form of self-report asks respondents to check all the traits that characterize themselves.

As with many other group tests, the first self-report inventory was developed in response to military needs during the First World War. In 1918 R. S. Woodworth published the Personal Data Sheet. Instead of having a psychiatrist interview each man in the military, Woodworth asked items that were used by psychiatrists to characterize neurotics. Eventually 116 items were developed to empirically differentiate neurotics from normals. Individuals with high scores (indicative of neuroticism) could then be referred to a psychiatrist for an individual interview.

Woodworth's Personal Data Sheet was the beginning of a long series of self-report inventories. Some, like the Mooney Problem Check List, yielded no scores and no norms. Every "problem" checked by an individual represented some perceived difficulty in such areas as health and physical development, home and family, boy and girl relations, morals and religion, courtship and marriage, economic security, school or occupation, social and recreational, and so forth. Others, such as the Bell Adjustment Inventory, provided subscores and norms in such areas as home, health, social, occupational, and emotional problems.

Self-report inventories have been constructed using three different techniques: rational, empirical, and factor analysis (Hase and Goldberg 1967).

The rational technique   The *rational* or *logical approach* to personality assessment begins with the selection of items that appear to measure some personality trait or traits. Woodworth's initial selection of items for his Personal Data Sheet involved looking through texts on psychiatry, speaking to psychiatrists, and examining case histories. The items for the Mooney Problem Check List were devised by asking students to write descriptions of their problems. Mooney also checked case histories and interviews to yield a wide range of problems faced by individuals at different age levels. The rational approach attempts to logically sample items from some universe, such as "problems faced by adolescents."

The empirical technique   The *empirical approach* to personality assessment requires that items discriminate among various criterion groups, such as normals, neurotics, and psychotics. Woodworth, for example, selected only items that discriminated between neurotics and normals. While the empirical approach almost always begins with a rational selection of items, it empirically checks to ensure that each item does in fact discriminate among various groups.

The A-S Reaction Study (Allport and Allport 1939) is an early empirically derived inventory. Designed to measure *ascendence* and *submission,* the inventory consists of multiple-choice items with two to five options each. Each item depicts a common situation such as having someone step in front of you in a line. Choices indicate what the respondent might do about the situation (fight back, argue, leave, and so forth). By obtaining self-ratings and peer ratings of ascendence and submission, it is possible to eliminate all nondiscriminating items from the inventory.

Certainly the most widely used empirically keyed personality inventory is the Minnesota Multiphasic Personality Inventory (MMPI), published by The Psychological Corporation. Probably more research has been conducted on this scale than on any other self-report personality inventory. It consists of ten clinical scales: hypochondriasis, depression, hysteria, psychopathic deviate, masculinity-feminity, paranoia, psychasthenia, schizophrenia, hypomania, and social introversion. It also includes four "validity" keys used to detect test-taking attitudes. The question score, for example, is obtained by counting the number of responses marked "cannot say" and is usually thought of as a measure of evasiveness. The lie score consists of fifteen items distributed throughout the inventory. Individuals who endorse a large number of these items are trying to make themselves appear socially acceptable. An example of this type of item is "I have never taken anything that does not belong to me." The validity or F score was designed to detect random responding, faking in order to appear ill, carelessness, or any combination of these. This scale has sixty-four items selected infrequently by normal subjects. The correction or K score was devised to improve the discriminating power of some of the clinical scales. The K scale consists of thirty items that measure subtle degrees of defensiveness to responding candidly. For example, a person who is cautious about admitting to certain physical complaints may receive a low hypochondriasis score. However, if his K score is high, a proportion (in this case, 50 percent) of the items contributing to his score on that scale is added to his hypochondriasis score. The percentages of K to be added to the clinical scores were determined empirically to maximally differentiate one clinical type from another.

The MMPI consists of 550 statements to be marked "true," "false," or "cannot say" by persons sixteen years of age or older (see figure 15.1). Because

414. I am apt to take disappointments so keenly that I can't put them out of my mind.

289. I am always disgusted with the law when a criminal is freed through the arguments of a smart lawyer.

Figure 15.1. Items from Minnesota Multiphasic Personality Inventory

a number of the items may be considered "offensive" and personal, the MMPI is definitely *not* designed for routine screening, particularly in elementary and secondary schools. Test interpretation is particularly difficult, even though an "atlas" has been prepared (Hathaway and Meehl 1951) as an aid to interpreting profiles. By looking up a person's profile "codes" in the atlas, one can obtain brief case histories of individuals with the same pattern of profile scores.

The reliability and validity of the MMPI have been extensively investigated. The stability of the MMPI with college students is generally in the .60s over a week's interval. Internal consistency (split-half) reliabilities have also tended to be low, with a range of from 0 to .80, depending on the scale in question.

The validity of the MMPI has also been questioned. Because the original group used to key the MMPI was small (fewer than fifty in each clinical group, with some as low as thirteen), some of the items were probably assigned to a particular scale largely on the basis of chance. Factor analysis studies, for example, have not supported the organization of the inventory, nor have cross-validation studies. Concurrent validity, or the extent to which the MMPI is capable of discriminating between various clinical and normal groups, has never been satisfactory, and to their credit the authors of the MMPI have been among the first to recognize its limitations.

Many other inventories have been developed using the MMPI items or procedures based on those developed originally by the authors of the MMPI. These include the California Psychological Inventory (for use with normal subjects aged thirteen or older) and the Taylor Manifest Anxiety Scale. This latter inventory was originally developed for research purposes but has been widely used as a measure of anxiety. Items for this inventory were taken directly from the MMPI.

Factor analysis   Self-report inventories have been developed using *factor analysis* both as an aid to selecting items and for labeling the factors (traits or personality types) that can account for the correlation among items or scales. When factor analysis is used to verify the existence of certain hypothesized traits or personality types, it can provide evidence for the construct validity of the scale.

Factor analyses of existing self-report inventories are unclear both with regard to the number of factors that account for personality and what labels should be applied to these factors. A factor that can be identified with one group of subjects may not be apparent with another.

J. P. Guilford has been one of the leading proponents of developing personality inventories using factor analysis. The Guilford-Zimmerman Temperament Survey (GZTS)—Guilford's latest inventory—is composed of items from three earlier inventories developed by factor analysis procedures. The GZTS contains 300 statements divided equally into ten factors: general activity (liveliness versus slowness), restraint (seriousness versus carefreeness), ascendence (leadership versus submissiveness), sociability (having many friends versus having few friends), emotional stability (evenness of mood and composure versus erratic moods and pessimism), objectivity (realistic versus hypersensitivity), friendliness (tactfulness and respect versus hostility and the desire to dominate), thoughtfulness (reflective and mentally poised versus mental disconcertedness), personal relations (faith in people and institutions versus suspicion and fault-finding), and masculinity (interest in masculine activities and the inhibition of emotion versus feminine interests and the expression of emotion).

If each scale of the GZTS was factorially "pure," one would expect intercorrelations among the ten scales to be quite low, and this is the case except for a few scales. The median intercorrelation is only about .22, but emotional stability and objectivity correlate +.69, ascendence and sociability, +.61, and friendliness and personal relations, +.50. These correlations are moderately high and indicate that the traits measured overlap to some degree.

Another widely used factor analytic personality inventory is the 16-PF, or Sixteen Personality Factor Questionnaire, prepared by R. B. Cattell and associates at the Institute for Personality and Ability Testing (IPAT) (see figure 15.2 for sample 16-PF items. IPAT also publishes an Anxiety Scale (for persons aged fourteen and over), a Children's Personality Questionnaire (for ages eight to twelve), and a High School Personality Questionnaire, among others.

The 16-PF was designed for persons of sixteen years of age and older. The sixteen factors include such traits as aloof versus warm-outgoing, dull versus bright, emotional versus mature, and submissive versus dominant. A seventeenth factor can be used to measure motivational distortion. The 16-PF

1. I like to watch team games.
   a. yes,   b. occasionally,   c. no.

2. I prefer people who:
   a. are reserved,
   b. (are) in between,
   c. make friends quickly.

3. Money cannot bring happiness.
   a. yes (true),   b. in between,   c. no (false).

4. Woman is to child as cat is to:
   a. kitten,   b. dog,   c. boy.

Figure 15.2. Example of 16-PF Item

reflects the personality theory of its author, R. B. Cattell, who began by logically reducing a list of 18,000 trait names first formulated by Allport and Odbert (1936) to 171 traits. Through factor analysis these 171 traits were reduced to twelve basic characteristics. Four traits identified in later research were added to form the 16-PF.

Self-report inventories are widely administered because they are inexpensive, require little time to administer, and are easy to score. In comparison with cognitive measures (achievement, intelligence, and aptitude), however, they are susceptible to response biases, easily faked, and difficult to intrepret, and they thus tend to be unreliable. They have been criticized on the basis that they encourage "snooping" and violate the right of privacy when, for example, they are forced on job applicants or involuntary subjects.

No method of constructing self-reports—rational, empirical, or factor analysis—seems to hold a consistent advantage over another. In a study by Harold Hase and Lewis Goldberg (1967), the authors constructed self-report inventories using the three approaches described in this text and a fourth method called *theoretical*. Rational and theoretical approaches are identical except that in the *theoretical* approach the selection of items is suggested by the implications of some personality theory, whereas "no formal psychological theory is explicitly followed" in the *rational* method. The conclusions of the investigation (pp. 242–43) are worth repeating:

> The principal finding from this study was that sets of scales constructed by each of the four primary strategies of scale construction . . . were equivalent in their validity across 13 diverse criteria. Moreover, since all four outperformed the two [methods of construction] used for control purposes, their uniformity in predictive validity cannot be considered a function of chance-level prediction.
>
> This finding, that strategies make little difference, may have profound implications for personality assessment. On the one hand, it indicates that dogmatic assertions of the superiority of one strategy over another are premature. In addition, the findings from this study suggest that procedures of item grouping are probably *not* a cause of the relatively low validity coefficients typically reported in the psychometric literature, and therefore that the guilty culprits might well be the inventory items themselves.

Projective Techniques

Projective techniques are relatively unstructured stimuli or tasks usually administered individually by experienced psychologists to measure personality dynamics and motivation. They assume that individuals faced with ambiguous stimuli will *project* or transfer their beliefs, attitudes, and personality characteristics onto these stimuli or tasks. These unstructured tasks allow greater response flexibility and are more disguised than self-report inventories.

This section on projective techniques was included in a text primarily designed for teachers to introduce some of the basic terminology, concepts, and tests used by psychologists to diagnose student personality problems. Psychological reports are often based on the administration of projective techniques, and teachers should be prepared to read and understand them. It is unethical for teachers or counselors to administer, interpret, or report the results of projective methods unless they have advanced training and supervision in their use. However, if they can understand psychological reports which include descriptions of projective techniques, teachers can gain a better understanding of their students.

Five types of projective techniques have been identified (Lindzey 1959): association, construction, completion, choice or order, and expressive.

Association techniques   *Association techniques* require the subject to respond as rapidly as possible to such stimuli as words or pictures. A *word-association test,* for example, presents the student with a list of terms that are loaded with emotions or are neutral and instructs him to respond with the first word or idea that comes to mind. The psychologist records the amount of time it takes the respondent to react, the response itself, and any evidence of embarrassment or hesitation. Long delays in responding supposedly indicate inner turmoil. The Kent-Rosanoff Free-Association Test is a standardized list of commonly used words (such as *table, cold, hand*). Responses to these words by 1,000 "normals" have been compiled, and responses not included among these may be signs of psychopathology.

The most widely used association technique is the Rorschach Inkblot Test, which consists of ten bilaterally symmetrical stimuli shown one at a time to respondents. Each card contains an inkblot (see figure 15.3) with various degrees of structure and color. The examiner records response latency, the amount of time spent examining each picture, the position in which the card is held by the respondent, and the response content.

Scoring of the Rorschach is complex, and the details depend on which of several scoring systems is being used. Most scoring systems use the *location* (the portion of the inkblot referred to), *determinants* (form, color, movement, shading), and *content* (humans, animals, blood, and so forth).

Although scoring tends to be objective, interpretation is questionable. Responses to *location,* for example, are thought to represent intelligence if the whole inkblot is referred to; reference to uncommon details supposedly indicates compulsiveness. Responses to color (a *determinant*) are thought of as emotionality. A response including a wide range of different types of *content* suggests high intelligence; the inability to differentiate male from female stimuli might indicate sexual difficulties. Evidence for these contentions is meager, impressionistic, subjectively determined, and often contradictory.

Construction techniques   *Construction techniques* require the respondent to tell a story after examining a picture depicting a scene, a person, or a

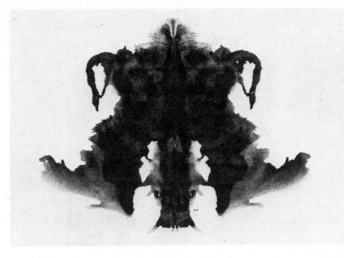

From Rorschach: PSYCHODIAGNOSTICS: Copyright 1921 (renewed 1948) by Hans Huber—Medical Publisher, Bern, Switzerland. Used by permission.

Figure 15.3. Example of a Rorschach Inkblot

social situation. No record is kept of time, but the respondent's theme and mode of responding are considered relevant.

The Thematic Apperception Test (TAT) is the most widely used construction technique. It consists of thirty pictures, each on a separate card, plus a blank card. Pictures may be given to adults or adolescents. In practice, individuals respond to no more than twenty cards, often in two or more sessions. Pictures on the TAT vary from those that are highly structured (see figure 15.4) to the blank card, which is completely unstructured. The respondent is directed to construct a story indicating what happened before, what is happening now, and how things will turn out. Scoring depends on the particular system used, but most scoring systems involve identifying the "hero" (i.e., the projection of the respondent's personality), determining his or her needs, and analyzing the "press" or social forces acting on the hero or heroine.

Some modifications of the TAT have used figures of blacks instead of Caucasians; others have used animals or drawings. These modifications assume that blacks will identify more readily with members of their own race and that children will project their own personalities more easily with animals than with human figures, but neither of these assumptions has been supported by empirical data.

In addition to their use in the psychological clinic, TATs or modifications of them have also been used to measure prejudice (authoritarianism), the need to achieve, and classroom morale. There appears to be no limit to the kinds of

From Thematic Apperception Test, reproduced by permission of Harvard University Press.

Figure 15.4. Example of a TAT item

problems (marriage, relationships among workers, family relationships, phobias, and so forth) that can be investigated through relevant pictures. As might be expected, however, *interpretation* of responses is complex. For example, subjects frequently construct protocols that remind them of movies they have seen or stories they have read.

Completion techniques   *Completion techniques* consist of incomplete sentences, stories, cartoons, or other stimuli which the respondent is to complete. Sentence completion tests are most often used and can vary from specific statements ("My most difficult subject in school is . . .") to general ones ("I believe . . .). Many of these completion techniques are "homemade" devices with no norms and no consistent scoring system; others, such as the Rotter Incomplete Sentences Blank, have both norms and specific scoring criteria.

Stories can also be used as projective devices. The Madeleine Thomas Completion Stories Test (Mills 1953), for example, consists of fifteen stories which may be administered individually to children aged six to thirteen. Some examples of these stories are:

1. A boy (or girl) goes to school. During a recess he does not play with other children. He stays all by himself in a corner. Why?
3. A boy is at the table with his parents. Father suddenly gets angry. Why?

8b. This boy has a friend whom he likes very much. One day his friend tells him, "Come with me, I am going to show you something but it is a secret. Don't tell anybody." What is he going to show him?

Each response is recorded verbatim for future analysis and interpretation. Story 1, for example, supposedly reveals adjustment, school behavior, and the desire to escape.

The Rosenzweig Picture-Frustration Study (Rosenzweig 1949) is another example of a completion technique (see figure 15.5). The test consists of

Copyright 1964 by Saul Rosenzweig. Reproduced by permission.

Figure 15.5

twenty-four cartoons at two levels (ages four to thirteen and adults). Each cartoon depicts an individual who is creating a frustrating situation and a person who must respond to it. The examinee indicates (either orally or in writing) his reaction to the frustration. Reactions are scored as *extrapunitive* (aggression vented outward to other objects or persons), *intropunitive* (aggression directed toward the respondent himself), or *impunitive* (frustration evaded). A "conformity rating" may be obtained by comparing the respondent's answers with those obtained from a norm group.

Choice or ordering techniques *Choice* or *ordering techniques* provide the respondent with a number of options to select from or to rank. The Szondi test described on pages 445–446 is an ordering technique since respondents must rank sets of pictures along a like-dislike dimension. A multiple-choice form of the Rorschach would also fit into this category since the *best* response to an inkblot must be selected.

A major advantage of choice or ordering techniques is scoring simplicity and objectivity, but this is offset by the restriction of the examinee's responses. Another disadvantage is the ipsative nature of ranked scores (see pp. 403-404).

Expressive techniques   *Expressive techniques* allow the respondent an active role in drawing, painting, dramatics, or play as a means of expressing his personality. How the respondent acts is usually considered to be as important as the product he develops.

Doll play has been widely used as an expressive technique, especially for young children. The child may be given dolls to represent family members, or his reactions may be noted as he plays with dolls of different colors, sexes, or physical abnormalities. The dolls may be placed on the floor or in doll houses, play schools, or nurseries. Some tests are highly structured and complex, whereas others might simply ask the child to select the doll he likes most and least (an ordering technique).

A complex but structured expressive technique is the Toy World Test. Depending on the form used, the test contains from 160 to 300 objects such as people, animals, houses, war implements, enclosures, and vehicles. The examiner counts the number of different types of objects played with by the child and determines how the child categorized those elements played with and the degree of aggression and distortion.

Psychodrama has also been widely used to express feelings. While it has often been used as a form of therapy in which individuals are allowed to act out different roles, it has also been used as a diagnostic aid. Married couples, for example, may be given a problem to solve (such as what they would do if their son should fail in school), and the clinician observes the roles and responses of the two parties. Psychodrama has also been used in schools and in counseling to improve intergroup relations.

Drawings and paintings may also be used as expressive techniques. The Machover Draw-A-Person Test, for example, requires the respondent to draw a person and then someone of the opposite sex. Notes are taken on drawing sequences and the respondent's statements about each drawing. Although there are no norms, case studies interpreted largely within a psychoanalytic framework are provided for different kinds of drawings. Erasures, for example, are interpreted as conflict; large heads reflect intelligence. Agreement among judges tends to be low, but there is some evidence (Swensen 1968) that the most valid indicators of pathology are global or overall ratings rather than such signs as height, head size, or shading.

Evaluation of projective techniques   The major advantage of projective techniques is the relative freedom for both the respondent and the clinician, who can probe and clarify for himself the meaning that a task has for his client. Many of these techniques are disguised and may be difficult to fake since the respondent may not be familiar with scoring and interpretation procedures. Most require little or no reading ability and can be used with illiterates and young children.

However, these methods have numerous difficulties. Most must be given individually and are expensive to administer, score, and interpret. More serious, perhaps, is the lack of evidence to justify their use. Reliability and validity studies are often nonexistent, and selected case studies too often replace "hard data."

The use of projective techniques, particularly the less structured techniques such as the Rorschach and TAT, psychodrama, doll play, and drawing tests, must be restricted to persons who possess at least a master's degree with specialized training and supervision in the use and interpretation of these techniques.

Reasons for Using Personality Measures

Selection

Attempts have been made to use observational methods (the interview and situational tests), self-report inventories, and projective techniques as selection devices, particularly in military and industrial settings. Criteria have included ratings by supervisors, job productivity, success in training schools, and grades. Validity coefficients tend to be quite low, particularly for civilian groups (Ellis and Conrad 1948).

In an excellent review of the literature on the use of interviews for selection, Lynn Ulrich and Don Trumbo (1965) reported that the highest predictive validity coefficients were obtained from highly structured rather than from unstructured interviews, but that data obtained from credentials and personality inventories were even more predictive than data obtained from interviews alone. Credential data correlated in the low .20s with on-the-job proficiency ratings, and the correlation was increased only slightly by including interview data. Considering the cost of interviews, some serious questions were raised as to their value for selection. Ulrich and Trumbo also concluded that interviews could best be employed for clarifying questions that other, less expensive methods failed to answer. The employee's motivation to work, for example, was cited as one topic for which interviews might be profitably used.

The validity of situational tests for selection also tends to be low, partly because of inadequate and unreliable criteria (often in the form of on-the-job ratings) but also because the tests are highly task-specific. The OSS situational tests, for example, correlated from 0 to slightly over .50 depending on the nature of the group tested and the criterion. Because of their cost and the elaborate preparations required for their use, they have not been used extensively.

Projective techniques have also been used for selection, but generally with unsatisfactory results. Many of the studies suffer from methodological deficiencies (small numbers of cases, lack of control or comparison groups, and so forth). But difficulties associated with unreliable criteria are also widespread. Little is known about the nature of the personality traits that are necessary for different occupations. Differences in personality appear to be as great within occupations as between occupations.

Diagnosis

No clear distinctions have been made between the use of personality measures for placement and their use for diagnosis. When cognitive tests are used, placement decisions indicate the type of program suitable for an individual within the school or organization, whereas diagnosis may be necessary if the school wishes to provide remedial services. In personality measurement the diagnosis often implies the treatment.

The entire concept of personality diagnosis is undergoing reconsideration in psychology and education (Arthur 1969). Personality diagnosis developed from a medical model which emphasized the determination of the nature of an illness from a consideration of symptoms. The treatment follows this determination. This medical model has not been accepted by all clinical psychologists. Their refusal stems largely from objections to the theory of "mental illness." Instead of accepting bed-wetting as a *symptom* of some underlying pathology, for example, behavior-oriented clinicians prefer to think of bed-wetting as the *problem*. Their argument is that—unlike "physical" symptoms—the elimination of a psychological symptom leaves no other problems, and no other pathological condition necessarily rises to take its place, as more traditional psychoanalysis would argue. In addition, these psychologists oppose the medical model on such grounds as (1) the inability to form diagnoses without knowledge about the individual's circumstances (shyness may be pathological among some groups but not among others); (2) the inability of diagnosticians to agree among themselves on what constitutes symptoms of "diseases"; (3) the unreliability of diagnosing personality disorders; (4) the fact that treatment does not necessarily require knowledge of the "disease"; and (5) the contention that classification inadequacies account for most of the difficulties in diagnoses (Arthur 1969).

The *behavioral model* is the strongest model opposing traditional or medical diagnostic models. Behaviorists (such as B. F. Skinner of Harvard University) are more concerned with modifying behavior than with diagnosing personality. Sidney Bijou (1966) has argued, for example, that diagnosis fails to treat the problem and therefore dissipates the clinician's efforts to change the individual's behavior. If diagnosis occurs at all, it will merely be a determination of what aspects of the environment are reinforcing undesirable behavior (Ferster 1965). The treatment will consist of the elimination of these undesirable behaviors and the reinforcement of desirable behaviors.

Program Evaluation

Personality inventories are sometimes used as the criterion for evaluating the effectiveness of new programs in schools, industry, and the psychological clinic. In education, for example, an innovation instituted with slow learners may be evaluated by the extent to which it modifies personality as well as by achievement measures. Or a school psychologist might want to evaluate his effectiveness by administering personality measures before and after treatment.

From the earlier discussion of the use of personality measures for other purposes, it can be anticipated that these inventories and scales are likely to have only limited value for program evaluation. The possible presence of response biases, inadequate and unreliable criteria, questions or tasks that are specific to a given situation and do not generalize, and a host of other conditions make the use of such measures hazardous.

Many government agencies now require that questionnaires for all research involving human subjects be cleared in advance. Clearance can usually be obtained by assuring a group of institutional associates that the rights of individuals are being protected, that informed consent has been obtained from project participants, and that the participants have been fully informed of any risks they might incur. Participation must be voluntary, and deliberate deception is permitted only when the danger to the individual is minimal and the values to society clear. Parental permission is usually required when minors are involved. The same set of guidelines might well be recommended for all forms of testing.

Using Personality Measures for
Theory Development

Although current measures of personality tend to be crude in comparison with measurement of cognitive skills, their use and development have contributed to a growing body of information about personality and its measurement. Hypotheses about the nature of personality traits, how they are organized, and how they may be used and misused for various purposes have been investigated. Beliefs at one time accepted on the basis of common sense tend to be modified or eliminated as research data are accumulated. Unfortunately many ideas die hard despite the evidence.

New personality theories will probably require new measurement approaches. The use of the electronic computer to simulate human personality is a new development which may yield some interesting hypotheses. Instead of testing humans, it may be possible to "test" the computer to determine areas of similarity and differences. This should contribute to a better understanding of the nature of personality.

In addition, the relationships among such constructs as personality, interest, attitude, intelligence, and achievement need clarification. Factor analyses and prediction studies using reliable criteria could be instrumental in clarifying the meanings of these terms and in using these measurements effectively.

The formal measurement of personality is a relative newcomer to psychometrics. Intelligence testing has had a twenty-year head start and very rapid development. Practical advances in therapy and demands for new personality scales may well provide the impetus to personality assessment that World War I gave to the measurement of intelligence.

Summary

1. Personality inventories are usually constructed to measure theoretical beliefs such as those proposed by psychoanalytically oriented test constructors, typologists, perception theorists, and factor analysts.

2. "Theories" of personality began with pseudoscientific and quasi-pseudoscientific approaches to personality measurement:

   a. Physiognomy was advocated by Aristotle, who believed that personality traits could be determined by examining physical characteristics. Although there is some evidence that a few personality traits can be estimated from physical characteristics, most claims for physiognomy have no empirical support.

   b. Phrenology argues that specific portions of the brain expand when they are overdeveloped by a corresponding personality trait. Although portions of the brain do serve different functions, there is no evidence to support the claims of phrenologists.

   c. Other pseudoscientific approaches to personality measurement include palmistry, astrology, and numerology, none of which enjoys scientific support.

3. Three types of response biases are:

   a. *Acquiescence*. Acquiescence is the tendency to respond to the "agree" or "true" items on cognitive tests and the tendency to be a "yea-sayer" on personality scales. The extent to which acquiescence occurs is debatable.

   b. *Social desirability*. Social desirability, seemingly a pervasive problem in personality measurement, occurs when individuals respond to items in such a way as to make themselves appear more acceptable. The use of forced-choice items reduces this tendency.

c. *Deviant responses.* The deviant response hypothesis argues that atypical individuals can be identified on personality inventories by examining those choices rarely selected by anyone. This hypothesis states that item content is unimportant in identifying atypical persons.

4. In "controlled observation"—such as the interview and the situational test —the examinee is placed in a situation devised to elicit particular kinds of responses.

a. The interview may be structured or unstructured, depending on the degree of freedom given the interviewee to respond. Four types of errors that lower the reliability and validity of the interview are: errors in asking questions, probing errors, errors in motivating, and recording errors. Interviewer bias is the tendency of interviewers and interviewees to respond to irrelevant characteristics. The reliability of the interview can be increased by using additional interviewers or raters to cancel out idiosyncratic ratings. In general, the more structured, factual, and clear the questions are, the higher the reliability and validity will be.

b. Situational tests place the individual in a contrived but lifelike situation which does not appear to be a test. Generally these tests are expensive to arrange, are difficult and time-consuming to prepare, and are task-specific. Ethics must be considered when situational tests are used. In some types of experiments participants will need to be screened and followed up; in others, the risks to the subject may outweigh potential advantages.

5. Self-report inventories can be constructed by rational, empirical, or factor analysis methods. The Woodworth Personal Data Sheet and the Mooney Problem Check List are inventories constructed by the rational approach. Empirically derived inventories are designed to discriminate between groups such as psychiatric patients and "normals." The Minnesota Multiphasic Personality Inventory is an empirically keyed inventory. Some personality inventories have been constructed using the principles of factor analysis. A study by Hase and Goldberg compared the validities of personality inventories constructed by different techniques. In general, the method of construction did not affect the validities. All validity coefficients tended to be low, but it is difficult to find reliable criteria for personality measurement.

6. Five types of projective techniques are:

a. *Association techniques.* Association techniques require the individual to respond as rapidly as he can to a stimulus or group of stimuli. Word-association tests and the Rorschach Inkblot test are examples.

b. *Construction techniques.* Construction techniques require the individual to construct a story. An example is the Thematic Apperception Test.

c. *Completion techniques.* Completion techniques allow the individual to complete a story, add words to a cartoon, and so on. The Rotter Incomplete Sentences Blank, the Madeleine Thomas Completion Stories Test, and the Rosenzweig Picture-Frustration Study are examples.

d. *Ordering techniques.* Choice or ordering techniques require stimuli to be placed in sequence.

e. *Expressive techniques.* Expressive techniques allow the individual to draw, paint, or act out a role to express his personality. Doll play, the Toy World Test, psychodrama, and the Machover Draw-A-Person Test are examples.

7. The advantages of projective techniques over nondisguised approaches to personality assessment are the examinee's greater freedom to respond, the difficulty in faking, and the ease with which they can be used with young children and illiterates. However, they tend to be expensive to administer, score, and interpret; sound evidence to support their use is lacking; and reliability and validity data often do not exist.

8. When personality tests or interviews are used for selection, their predictive validities tend to be low. There is some evidence that credential data and personality inventories are not improved much by adding information from interviews. Most situational tests yield low predictive validities since they are "task-specific." Because of their low validity and high costs, situational tests are not often used for selection decisions. Projective techniques have not proved to be useful in selection either since they yield low validity coefficients and have relatively high costs.

9. Distinctions between the use of personality tests for diagnosis and their use for placement are unclear. The question is whether traits are symptoms of underlying pathology or whether these traits *are* the problem. The former position is based on a medical model; the latter is based on a behavioral model.

10. Many personality tests and inventories are used to understand the meaning and nature of personality. In addition to providing hypotheses about the personality of individuals, they can also be used to study the relationships of personality to other variables such as intelligence and interest.

Suggested Readings

Edwards, Allen L. *The Measurement of Personality Traits by Scales and Inventories*. New York: Holt, Rinehart and Winston, 1970, 306 pp. This book describes how personality is measured by scales and inventories. The section on factor analysis is highly recommended for the student who is interested in the procedures used to extract factors.

Holt, Robert R. *Assessing Personality*. New York: Harcourt Brace Jovanovich, 1971, 245 pp. A paperback that describes the major types of assessment techniques; an illustrative case study is also provided.

Kleinmuntz, Benjamin. *Personality Measurement: An Introduction*. Homewood, Ill.: Dorsey Press, 1967, 463 pp. A more descriptive and less mathematical approach to personality measurement than the Edwards text. It includes chapters on the interview, projective techniques, and situational tests.

Lanyon, Richard, and Goodstein, Leonard D. *Personality Assessment*. New York: John Wiley & Sons, 1971, 267 pp. A general, brief account of various approaches used to measure personality; it provides an excellent overview of personality assessment.

16 The measurement of
personality by controlled observations, self-reports, and projective techniques
was discussed in the preceding chapter. These methods emphasize the individual's responses to questions or tasks designed to learn more about him and
his self-perceptions. This chapter is concerned with the behavior of individuals
as they react with one another in naturalistic or uncontrived situations. The
first part of this chapter describes the nature of observations and methods used
to improve their reliability and validity. The second part discusses group behavior, including sociometry and the guess-who technique.

The Nature of Observation

Chapter 1 defined measurement as the assigning of numbers to attributes
according to rules. Measurement may involve written responses (as in essays),
responses to true-false or multiple-choice items, or oral responses. Sometimes
students may report what they would do in a given circumstance, as in self-reports, or teachers might arrange conditions to evoke particular types of responses, as in situational testing.

Observations may be controlled or naturalistic. *Controlled observations,*
such as situational tests, force the examinee to respond to specific tasks he
perceives as realistic but which are actually staged by the examiner. In *naturalistic observation* an unobtrusive observer records uncontrived, typical behavior.

Counting the number of hostile acts committed by a child on the playfield is an example of naturalistic observation.

Sources of Observational Error*

It is a well-recognized phenomenon that two individuals can observe the same event and still report quite different perceptions. Lawyers are well aware of the tendency for witnesses to disagree about how an accident or crime occurred. Scientists labor to develop instruments for reducing observational error and the "human factor." In the classroom recognition of sources of observational error such as the teacher's personal values, biases, and expectations can help reduce their undesirable effects.

Personal values   Personal values may influence what a person sees or reports. Prohibitionists tend to overestimate the per capita consumption of alcohol; highly religious individuals are more likely to perceive and accept supernatural signs than are skeptics; and communists attach more significance to evidence of capitalistic decadence than do capitalists. Psychologists have studied these personal values and their effects on observation in some detail. In one experiment, for example, college students were able to recognize more tachistoscopically presented words if the words were related to their own values (Postman, Bruner, and McGinnies 1948). Students with strong economic values recognized more words related to economics than words related to politics, religion, or aesthetics, even though all words were equated for length and familiarity.

Another interesting account of the role of personal values in determining "set," or readiness to respond, was reported by Stuart Rice (1929) during the Depression. In this study interviewers questioned indigent men to discover reasons for their destitution. One observer consistently reported that the men blamed alcohol; another was equally certain that poor industrial conditions in the United States were responsible. Rice was unable to resolve this apparent contradiction until he discovered that the first interviewer was a prohibitionist and the other a socialist!

Bias   Any strong belief unsupported by evidence is *bias*. Bias may be either in favor of or against some individual, group, activity, or institution. Because biases are highly emotional, they tend to distort observation.

Numerous experimental studies show the deleterious effects of bias on

---

* Adapted from Gilbert Sax, *Empirical Foundations of Educational Research* (Englewood Cliffs, N. J.: Prentice-Hall, Inc., 1968), chap. 8, by permission of the publisher.

perception. In one, subjects were shown pictures and were asked to communicate the content from memory to another person, who was to report to a third, and so on (Allport and Postman 1947). One picture depicted individuals riding in a trolley car with a white man holding a razor. By the time the story was repeated a few times, the razor was in the hands of a black passenger. Racial stereotypes and bias produced changes in perception.

Group expectations   Groups exert pressures on members to conform to social mores. This effect is particularly strong in formal, organized groups (such as fraternities and clubs), but it is also apparent in less structured groups. A new teacher in a school quickly learns what behavior will be condoned and what will not be tolerated. She or he also learns to accept—or at least to go along with—group expectations and beliefs.

The effect of group pressure on individuals has been experimentally studied by Solomon Asch (1956), who asked subjects to estimate which of several lines was the longest. All persons but one in the group were confederates coached to give the same obviously incorrect answer. Asch discovered that the dependent persons changed their answers to conform to group norms.

Reducing Observational Error

Observational error can be reduced by (1) preparing to observe; (2) using mechanical or electrical recording apparatus; and (3) preparing unambiguous recording forms.

Preparing to observe   Prior to observation the observer should determine what data he will consider relevant and what method he will use to record that behavior. If a teacher wants to evaluate a child's oral report, he should decide whether content, diction, or delivery is important. If content is relevant, a written copy of the speech could be requested; a tape recorder might be used if diction is to be measured. Delivery might include gestures, voice pitch and emphasis, appropriate emotionality, and speed. Specifying what behaviors are to be observed will prevent teachers from being distracted by irrelevant cues and behaviors.

Using mechanical or electronic recording apparatus   Observational apparatus varies from relatively inexpensive, simple devices (tape recorders, stop watches) to expensive, complex electronic instruments. Equipment can be used to present stimuli, to record behavior, or both. Commercial supply houses provide equipment that is useful for measuring perceptual and motor reactions.

Film   Unless a permanent record of behavior is required, film is not usually recommended. It is expensive and wasteful, particularly if relevant behavior is expected to occur only sporadically. Film also necessitates special lighting conditions unless extremely fast or infrared film is used. Moreover, the presence of the camera and its accessories may affect the behavior of students. Videotape has become popular because it can be reused, but cameras and accessories are still expensive and intrusive.

Tape recorders   Tape recorders are simple to use and inexpensive to operate but of course are limited to recording auditory responses. Classroom use of a tape recorder presents difficulties, for sounds from various parts of the room will not be produced equally unless multiple microphones are used. Loud students seated close to a microphone are likely to drown out those who speak more softly or are farther away. Another disadvantage of tape recorders is the difficulty of identifying individuals who have spoken.

Counters and timers   Mechanical or electronic counters and timers are important observational aids. Counters may be used whenever the number of responses emitted is considered relevant. For example, the number of times a child gets out of his seat during a class period can be recorded unobtrusively with a manual counter. The simplest of these devices is activated by pressing a lever that adds one more digit to the accumulated total. If behavior occurs rapidly, an electronic counter may be needed, but of course these are larger and more expensive.

Timers may be used alone or in conjunction with counters. For example, it is possible to plot the number of times a child engages in some activity over a fixed period of time. The amount of time a child spends working on an activity can indicate his attention span or interest.

Preparing unambiguous recording forms   All forms used to record observations should contain the following identification information:

1. The observer's name.
2. The names of all persons being observed. If names are not used (to protect confidentiality), individuals should be identified by code numbers. If anonymity is important, neither names nor any other identifying labels or marks should be used.
3. The date and time of observation.
4. The form number or date of form preparation. This is important since forms are often revised.
5. The name of the teacher, classroom, and school. This information will more completely identify the observed group regardless of the location of the observations.

6. A title for the observation record. This will distinguish one form from another.

Methods of preparing observational recording forms for ratings, checklists, and anecdotal reports will be discussed later in this chapter. However, one point should be clarified here. Although an observation recording form may *appear* to be unambiguous, its reliability and validity must be determined. Unless forms permit the observation of consistent individual differences (reliability) and are relevant (valid) to a specified purpose, they serve little value.

Ratings

Ratings are observations that have been categorized or organized to provide summary information about the behavior of individuals or groups. At least three types of rating forms can be prepared: unstructured, numerical, and graphic.

Unstructured Ratings

Unstructured ratings appear in essay form with various degrees of explicitness. Perhaps the least structured rating form is the *letter of recommendation,* in which the rater is allowed to express his attitudes, beliefs, and knowledge in any way he sees fit. Directions to raters vary from such statements as "The following student has listed you as someone knowledgeable about his background, personality, and work habits. A statement from you with regard to these traits will be appreciated and kept in confidence" to statements asking for specific examples of behavior.

Although they are widely used in education, letters of recommendation are usually not satisfactory. Virtually all ratings are favorable since raters are usually selected for their willingness to cooperate. Furthermore, raters are unwilling to make negative comments in writing. In one investigation, for example, sixty-seven letters of recommendation for thirty-three prospective psychological interns were collected from nineteen universities, resulting in a total of 958 statements (Siskind 1966). Four pairs of raters divided the statements into four categories: positive statements, statements indicating lack of knowledge about an applicant's characteristics, statements referring to a shortcoming resulting from inexperience or age, and statements referring to a shortcoming not the result of inexperience or age. Siskind found that 838 statements, or 87 percent were positive, and only 6 percent were from the fourth category. Interestingly, one letter accounted for about half the negative comments.

Letters of recommendation tend to be highly favorable and are thus of limited value for *selection* since they contribute little or nothing to incremental validity. However, if the purpose of the letter of recommendation is for *placement* (usually made for the benefit of both the individual and the organization), it is to the advantage of the ratee to secure evaluations from judges who are competent to rate both strengths and weaknesses.

Anyone who has read many unstructured ratings soon discovers that more is learned from what is *not* said than from what is said. Many recommendations, for example, contain such commonly used approbations that they resemble the Boy Scout Law (trustworthy, loyal, helpful, friendly, courteous, and so forth). Unless the letter of recommendation is extremely laudatory, it is likely to be interpreted negatively.

Unstructured ratings and letters of recommendation can be improved in the following ways:

1. The student should submit a comprehensive list of persons familiar with his work and personal characteristics. This list should include a wide sampling of persons having *relevant* information about him.

2. Raters should be asked to indicate the student's weaknesses as well as his strengths.

3. Raters should be asked to report examples of behaviors that justify evaluative statements. Rather than simply stating that a student is trustworthy, evidence of trustworthiness should be provided.

4. Raters should be told the specific reasons for requesting the recommendations so that irrelevant and possibly damaging reports are not written. It is one thing to do poorly in an advanced mathematics course if one is applying for a position as kindergarten teacher; it is quite another matter if the ratee wants to teach mathematics.

5. All ratings, whether unstructured or structured, should be treated confidentially, or both the rater and the student should be aware that information will be circulated. Sometimes university policies state that students may have access to their personal files to protect themselves against unwarranted, malicious, or damaging statements. If this policy is followed, raters should be so informed.

6. Letters of recommendation should be followed up by letters of appreciation. This is both a simple act of courtesy and a means of ensuring that letters have not been fabricated. A "thank you" card written to each person from whom a recommendation has been received will discourage students from submitting their own recommendations (Weigel and Boulger 1970).

Anecdotal records   *Anecdotal records* are continuous, objective descriptions of behavior as it occurs at a given time, place, and circumstance. They are *continuous* in the sense that sequential records are kept of a child's behavior over relatively long periods of time, such as a semester or school year. They are *objective* insofar as they describe what the child has done or accomplished; interpretation and evaluation are kept separate from descriptions of the behavior.

Anectodal observations can later form the basis for evaluation (decision making) by aiding human memory, which is both fallible and selective. Also, these records can be reexamined for evidence of improvement, to describe typical student behavior, or for indications of emotional or social problems. They can be used in parent and staff conferences and are of great value in discussing a child's behavior with school psychologists, social workers, or other specialists.

Episode sampling   Anecdotal reports may be used to record specific behavior episodes of concern to parents, teachers, or other professional workers. For example, teachers may keep records of specific acts of aggression, withdrawal, crying, negativism, or dependence or more positive episodes such as contributing to class discussions, helping others, cooperating with adults or peers, or working on one's own. Which episodes will be recorded depend on the purposes observations are designed to serve. If the purpose is to help a child overcome temper tantrums, anecdotes should consist of descriptions of the factors that instigated, reinforced, and eventually terminated those behaviors. The duration of each tantrum observed, who or what it was directed against, and the reactions of those around the child should also be recorded.

Data obtained from episode sampling can be used to diagnose problems. They can also be used to develop behavioral norms. In one study, for example, Helen Dawe (1934) recorded two hundred quarrels that occurred among preschool children to determine the average rate of quarreling per hour, the average duration of the quarrels, factors that led to and terminated quarrels, and sex differences in quarreling behavior. Knowledge of these norms could be used to evaluate the classroom social climate, the ability to control undesirable behavior, and the effects of innovations designed to improve intersex and intrasex relationships.

Time sampling   Time sampling can help teachers obtain a record of *typical* behavior at different time periods. It provides information on many aspects of behavior rather than on a selected episode.

Behavior is not entirely consistent. Environmental conditions that appear to be similar may prove to be quite different upon closer examination. How a person acts in the morning may differ considerably from his performance later in the day. Mondays are traumatic for some children; days after or before vacations produce anxiety for others. If typical behavior is to be described, sampling of behavior at various prescheduled time periods is necessary.

Time sampling involves preparing an observation schedule that permits each child to be seen at comparable time periods. These time periods differ, depending on the type of behavior to be observed. For example, time samples may be extended throughout the entire day or be restricted to recesses, lunch periods, or any other time period of particular interest to the observer.

Whatever the length of the time period, it should be subdivided into manageable observation intervals. For example, a fifteen-minute recess period could be divided into three five-minute segments, one fifteen-minute period, or five three-minute periods. Observation times should be short enough to permit teachers to record behaviors but long enough to obtain meaningful information. Some trial and error may be necessary to decide upon these optimal periods.

The observation schedule is so arranged that each child is seen under similar circumstances. The names of students being observed should be drawn at random to determine without bias who will be observed first, second, third, and so on. During recess on Monday, for example, student A might be observed for two minutes at the beginning of the period, followed by observations of the other students in random order. On the next day the order of observation is again randomized, and the process is repeated until patterns of behavior are evident.

Because time samples are used to describe typical behaviors, it is necessary to observe the same individual at different times. The more time samples taken, the better picture the teacher will have of students, because any single observation may not be representative of the child's typical behavior. In general, the reliability of observations can be improved by taking as many samples of behavior as possible.

Writing the anecdotal report　　Because anecdotal reports are samples of behavior, they should separate *descriptions* from *interpretations* of behavior. In episode sampling the anecdote should describe the events leading to the episode, the episode itself, and the factors that terminated it. In time sampling the child's behavior within the allotted time period is described. Time samples are usually not interpreted until all samples of behavior have been collected.

To reduce memory errors anecdotal reports should be written immediately following each observation. Brief notes taken during the observation may be helpful in reconstructing observations. In time sampling a portable cassette tape recorder can facilitate the objective recording of behavior. Episode sampling often does not allow sufficient time to use tape recorders, but note taking can increase objectivity.

Anecdotes may be written on 8½ × 11 inch paper in chronological sequence. In the elementary grades it may be feasible for the teacher to obtain time and/or episode samples for each child. If teacher aides or helpers are not available, the teacher may have to be satisfied with recording only the most important episodes. Fights, quarrels, crying, the failure to attempt or complete assignments, refusals to participate in games or other activities, truancy, cheating, shyness, fearfulness, suspiciousness, withdrawal, and other signs of emotional problems should be recorded when they occur. At the secondary level class loads make time sampling almost impossible, and anecdotes are usually written only for serious episodes.

Measurements—whether test scores or anecdotes—are useful to the extent that they aid in evaluation or decision making. The teacher who collects anecdotes and files them away has accomplished little unless he can use them to help the children in his room.

Figure 16.1 shows an anecdotal recording form. Since the section on interpretation is filled out, this particular form describes an episode rather than a time sample. Time samples are usually too brief to allow observers to interpret behavior until many samples are collected. Note that the recorded information includes the identities of the person observed and the observer, the child's sex; the day, date, and duration of the episode of time sampled; the child's age and grade at the time of observation; and the location of the episode at the time sampled.

ANECDOTAL RECORDING FORM

Sunnyside Jr. High School
Form B
1-5-71

Jones   Jim   M   Wed.   9-22-71   3:45-4:15
Last name, First name   Sex   Day   Date   Time

13-6   8th   Baseball field   Mr. Smith
CA   Grade   Location   Observer

Description: Today Jim was not elected to be third baseman as he had hoped to be but was put on the second string team. As the votes came in, tears welled up in his eyes as he ran from the field to the locker room, the teacher said, "Just as your parents go out of their way for you, you'll have to do what's best for the team." Jim's response was that his parents had done nothing for him and he planned on doing nothing for the team. He ran away from the teacher and left the school grounds. None of the other students seemed to notice Jim's reactions.

Interpretation: Jim seemed to take disappointments personally and rather hard, preferring to avoid cooperation and to literally escape from the disappointing situation.

Figure 16.1. An Anecdotal Recording Form for Episode Sampling

The "Description" section clearly describes behavior. It informs the reader what led to Jim's reactions, how he reacted, and how the episode terminated. The episode was important enough to record since crying, running away, and Jim's comments about his parents could be indicative of more serious psychological problems. The "Interpretation" section analyzes and gives meaning to Jim's behavior, but it should always be considered tentative and subject to reinterpretation as additional samples of behavior are obtained.

An example of a well-written time sample is given in figure 16.2. The context of the observation is given ("This is the first day of school" and ". . . was not sobbing as much as she was before the other children arrived and after her mother left her"); clarifiers are placed in parentheses to facilitate

---

ANECDOTAL RECORDING FORM

Sunnydate Elementary School (Form A: 2-5-72)

Olson Alice ____ F __ Mon __ 9-13-72 __ 9:04-9:06 __ 5-4
Last name, First name   Sex   Day   Date   Time   CA

Kindergarten ____ Classroom ____ Mrs Brown ____
Grade   Location   Observer

Description: (This is the first day of school.) Alice sat at her seat when asked to do so by the student teacher, Miss Evans. Alice had tears in her eyes (but was not sobbing as much as she was before the other children arrived and after her mother left her). She kept wiping her eyes with a handkerchief. Miss Evans asked the children to form game lines: those wanting to do individual projects (looking at pictures, listening to records), play in small groups (hop scotch, play house), or group activities (drop the handkerchief, musical chairs). Alice was next to the last one to select an activity (listen to records). She spoke to no one during the observation period.

Figure 16.2. An Anecdotal Recording Form for a Time Sample

later interpretation. All behavior during the observation period is described, but interpretations are omitted since no single observation period will yield reliable (consistent) measures of typical behavior. Some children are fearful on the first day of school but quickly adjust. Indeed, a time sampling of Alice's behavior later in that day might demonstrate a dramatic change. Any single time sample is like a single-item test score. By itself it has little meaning, but as more and more observations are obtained, significant trends in behavior may appear. For example, Alice may cry only after her mother leaves her at school, or she may prefer solitary activities until she knows her classmates more intimately. Obviously it will take additional observations before trends become apparent.

There is little purpose to becoming overly molecular or molar in describing behavior. *Molecular descriptions* are minute and detailed; *molar* or *global* descriptions involve larger and more encompassing behaviors. For example, in describing a child's response to an assignment, it is possible to state that he opened his mouth and inhaled air at the rate of X number of cubic centimeters per second, that he yawned, or that he was bored. The inhalation of X cubic centimeters of air is highly molecular and may be useful if the purpose were to study physiological reactions, but it is unnecessarily specific for an anecdotal report. *Boredom* is an *intepretation* of behavior, not a description. *Yawn,* however, seems to be a reasonable choice of words since it adequately describes behavior without offering a subjective interpretation.

Numerical Rating Scales

Numerical rating scales assign numbers to descriptively ranked categories. Likert and Thurstone scales are numerical scales. A Likert-type scale used to measure the degree of student activity could consist of the following categories:

5	Extremely active						
4	Somewhat active		4	Extremely active			
3	Average activity	OR	3	Somewhat active	OR	2	Active
2	Somewhat inactive		2	Somewhat inactive		1	Inactive
1	Extremely inactive		1	Extremely inactive			

Guilford (1954, pp. 263–64) has developed an eleven-point numerical scale to rate values of colors and odors:

10	Most pleasant imaginable			
9	Most pleasant		4	Mildly unpleasant
8	Extremely pleasant		3	Moderately unpleasant
7	Moderately pleasant		2	Extremely unpleasant
6	Mildly pleasant		1	Most unpleasant
5	Indifferent		0	Most unpleasant imaginable

He has argued that the two extreme positions (0 and 10) should be included on the scale even though they are rarely selected because they spread the ratings out between categories 1 and 9. Since raters tend to avoid extremes, they are more likely to utilize rankings 1 and 9 if the categories 0 and 10 are present.

The reliability of measurements is always a function of group variability. Rating scales, like test scores, tend to increase in reliability as the number of ratable categories and items increases. Other conditions being equal, an eleven-category scale will be more reliable than a five- or four-category scale, provided that raters are capable of making that many discriminations.

The numbers assigned to descriptions are less important than the descriptions themselves. Evaluative terms such as *somewhat active* or *moderately pleasant* are likely to be rated less reliably than specific terms or statements that can be quantified. Dorothy Adkins (1947, p. 240) has provided three examples of vocational items with quantitative or behavioral descriptors that are likely to be measured reliably:

1. How many passes did he require to complete the (machine shop) operation?

Number of Passes	Score
2	3
3	2
4	1
5 or more	0

2. Which tool did he select to turn the square fitting?

Tool	Score
Monkey wrench	3
Off-size end wrench	2
Pipe wrench	1
Pliers	0

3. How many nuts did he try on before he found one to fit?

Number of Tries	Score
1	4
2	3
3	2
4 or 5	1
6 or more	0

By translating descriptive categories into specific behaviors, abstract categories can be made numerical, and rating scales can be improved considerably. For example, a description of specific behaviors can help clarify the meaning of terms such as *extremely active* and *somewhat inactive:*

Extremely active (5 points)

Almost always out of his seat
Rarely sits without squirming
Makes noise, yells a good deal of the time

Somewhat inactive (2 points)

Sits in seat quietly most of the time
Makes few excessive unnecessary movements
Responds to questions but does not initiate conversation

Checklists   *Checklists* usually contain lists of behaviors, traits, or characteristics that are either present or absent. An applicant for a driver's license either makes a complete stop at a signal or fails to do so; turns are signaled or not; speed limits are adhered to or violated. In each instance the observer can simply check off desirable or undesirable behaviors as they occur. One point is usually given for each desirable behavior and zero points for each that is undesirable. The score is simply the sum of the accumulated points.

Checklists have their greatest utility in measuring complex behavior that can be subdivided into more specific behavioral segments. Driving a car, for example, requires many segments of behavior, such as using seat belts, using the rearview mirror, looking out the side window to see whether it is safe to pull out from a parking spot, giving correct arm signals, and so forth.

Constructing checklists involves a thorough analysis of the behaviors required to perform a task satisfactorily. Only someone who is knowledgeable about driving laws, automobile safety regulations, and good driving techniques could develop a complete checklist of automobile driving habits, for instance.

A checklist developed to measure skill in the use of a microscope is shown in figure 16.3 (Tyler 1930). Students are provided with all the materials needed, such as glass slides, lens paper, and culture material. The sequence of student actions is recorded by the teacher, including errors, which have also been incorporated into the checklist (e.g., "wipes slide with finger"). Also included are directions to the student (see category *az,* "told to start new mount"). In addition, this particular checklist allows the teacher to check the skills in which the student needs further training, characteristics of the student's behavior, and characterizations of the student's mount.

A modification of the checklist allows the observer to indicate that he has not had the opportunity to observe or evaluate an item. Responses checked in that category would not be scored. If the "no opportunity to observe" option is included on a checklist, it may be easier to score each positive behavior as $+1$, each negative behavior as -1, and "no opportunity to observe" as 0. The sum of the positive and negative values is the individual's total score.

Graphic Rating Scales

Graphic rating scales consist of either a horizontal or a vertical line representing descriptions or characteristics of behavior along a continuum. The format is often an unbroken line such as the following:

Almost always on time	Usually on time	Usually not on time	Almost never on time

The rater simply places a checkmark on the segment of the line that best represents his impression of the individual. The supposed advantage of this procedure

STUDENT'S ACTIONS	Sequence of Actions	STUDENT'S ACTIONS (Continued)	Sequence of Actions
a. Takes slide	1	ag. With eye away from eyepiece turns down fine adjustment a great distance	15
b. Wipes slide with lens paper	2	ah. Turns up fine adjustment screw a great distance	
c. Wipes slide with cloth		ai. Turns fine adjustment screw a few turns	
d. Wipes slide with finger		aj. Removes slide from stage	16
e. Moves bottle of culture along the table		ak. Wipes objective with lens paper	
f. Places drop or two of culture on slide	3	al. Wipes objective with cloth	
g. Adds more culture		am. Wipes objective with finger	17
h. Adds few drops of water		an. Wipes eyepiece with lens paper	
i. Hunts for cover glasses	4	ao. Wipes eyepiece with cloth	
j. Wipes cover glass with lens paper	5	ap. Wipes eyepiece with finger	18
k. Wipes cover with cloth		aq. Makes another mount	
l. Wipes cover with finger		ar. Takes another microscope	
m. Adjusts cover with finger		as. Finds object	
n. Wipes off surplus fluid		at. Pauses for an interval	
o. Places slide on stage	6	au. Asks, "What do you want me to do?"	
p. Looks through eyepiece with right eye	7	av. Asks whether to use high power	
q. Looks through eyepiece with left eye	9	aw. Says, "I'm satisfied"	
r. Turns to objective of lowest power		ax. Says that the mount is all right for his eye	
s. Turns to low-power objective	21	ay. Says he cannot do it	19,24
t. Turns to high-power objective		az. Told to start new mount	
u. Holds one eye closed	8	aaa. Directed to find object under low power	20
v. Looks for light		aab. Directed to find object under high power,	
w. Adjusts concave mirror			
x. Adjusts plane mirror		NOTICEABLE CHARACTERISTICS OF STUDENT'S BEHAVIOR	
y. Adjusts diaphragm			
z. Does not touch diaphragm	10		
aa. With eye at eyepiece turns down coarse adjustment	11	a. Awkward in movements	
ab. Breaks cover glass	12	b. Obviously dexterous in movements	
ac. Breaks slide		c. Slow and deliberate	✓
ad. With eye away from eyepiece turns down coarse adjustment		d. Very rapid	
		e. Fingers tremble	
ae. Turns up coarse adjustment a great distance	13,22	f. Obviously perturbed	
		g. Obviously angry	
af. With eye at eyepiece turns down fine adjustment a great distance	14,23	h. Does not take work seriously	
		i. Unable to work without specific directions	✓
		j. Obviously satisfied with his unsuccessful efforts	✓

SKILLS IN WHICH STUDENT NEEDS FURTHER TRAINING	Sequence of Actions	CHARACTERIZATION OF THE STUDENT'S MOUNT	Sequence of Actions
a. In cleaning objective	✓	a. Poor light	✓
b. In cleaning eyepiece	✓	b. Poor focus	
c. In focusing low power	✓	c. Excellent mount	
d. In focusing high power	✓	d. Good mount	
e. In adjusting mirror	✓	e. Fair mount	
f. In using diaphragm	✓	f. Poor mount	
g. In keeping both eyes open	✓	g. Very poor mount	
h. In protecting slide and objective from breaking by careless focusing	✓	h. Nothing in view but a thread in his eyepiece	
		i. Something on objective	
		j. Smeared lens	✓
		k. Unable to find object	✓

From Ralph W. Tyler, *Educational Research Bulletin*, 9, 17 (November 19, 1930), p. 494.

Figure 16.3. Checklist for Recording Skills in Using a Microscope

is that it reminds the rater that the trait he is evaluating is continuous and that intermediate points can be selected. A disadvantage is scoring these intermediate points.

Another format also uses a continuous line but separates each category to facilitate scoring (unfortunately raters still put checkmarks on the divisions even when specifically told not to do so):

:	:	:
Almost always on time	Usually on time	Usually not on time	Almost never on time

A third mode of presentation can further reduce this possibility:

Almost always on time	Usually on time	Usually not on time	Almost never on time

Since little evidence is available that reliability or validity is affected by any of these three formats, the decision will have to be made on simplicity and convenience. If only one item will be used to evaluate some aspect of behavior, a continuous one allows raters to select intermediate values and therefore might be a more discriminating procedure. But if a number of related scales have to be summed, the third option will be easiest to score.

There is some evidence that the reliability of graphic scales can be increased by using a vertical format where scales are anchored by examples (Taylor 1968). *Anchoring* is the procedure followed to define categories. Sometimes categories are defined by numbers, as on numerical scales; sometimes bipolar adjectives are used, such as *prompt* versus *late;* and other scales may use examples of behavior. A social support scale in a vertical format using examples of behavior as anchors to define various positions on the scale is shown in figure 16.4 (Taylor et al. 1970).

James Taylor and his associates (1970) have shown that the correlation among raters using the vertical format with examples was .76, compared to numerical scales, which yielded a correlation of only .43. The internal consistency of the Taylor scales ranged from .67 to .89; for numerical scales, the values ranged from .10 to .63. Evidently the case history vignettes or examples aided raters in locating individuals accurately along the thermometerlike scale.

Improving Ratings

One way to improve ratings is to recognize the factors that are responsible for their typically low reliability. Sometimes these factors are related to the characteristics of the rater (lack of training, the halo effect, the generosity error, the error of central tendency); at other times the problem is ambiguity in interpretation of the trait being measured or in the rating instruments themselves.

Characteristics of the Rater

Lack of training   The lack of training in rating and observational skills is often responsible for low reliabilities. A teacher who is required to rate Johnny on "citizenship" by indicating whether he is "satisfactory" or "unsatisfactory" is presumed—often erroneously—to understand how the ratings are to be made and what the criteria for "satisfactory" are.

STRONG SOCIAL SUPPORT

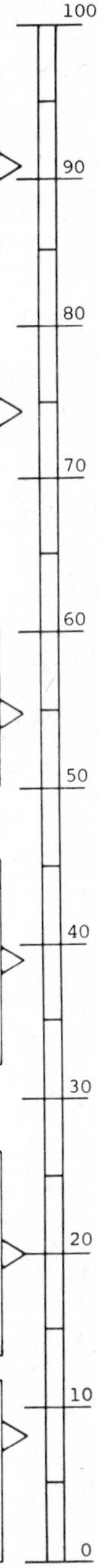

— 100

A 68 year-old man who is married, still employed full-time and in good health. He goes to the office each day and enjoys his work and his business associates. At home he enjoys spending quiet evenings with his wife. They do not go out much, but content themselves with playing cards, watching TV and reading the paper. Two daughters still live at home. He feels close to his family and considers that they are all he needs, together with some close friends he likes to talk with.

— 90

— 80

A 70 year-old man who is married. He is semi-retired, occasionally picking up bookkeeping jobs. He still has a number of business friends and members of his family whom he enjoys visiting. He gets together with friends at least once a week for cards or checkers. He and his wife seem to have a warm relationship and like spending some evenings at home together watching TV.

— 70

— 60

A widower in his early 70's who lives with an unmarried daughter in the family home. Although they live in the same house, they are usually at odds and go their separate ways. She does fix his supper. He enjoys going out to social functions for older people, much more so than when his wife was alive. He has three sons who live in town with their families and he visits with them from time to time.

— 50

A 75 year-old widow who lives alone in a dilapidated apartment. She seemed hungry for visitors and insisted upon showing pictures of herself when she was a young girl. She seemed ashamed of being old and said she hates to go out and face people. She wants to keep up old ties, but waits for her friends to call her, because she is unable to entertain them. She spoke bitterly of a sister-in-law who is resentful of the fact that her brother helped her financially. She has not visited his home for several years because she felt that his wife made it clear that she was not welcome. He comes alone to visit her.

— 40

— 30

A 69 year-old man who has been retired for many years because of a severe arthritic condition. Most of his life since his retirement has been spent at home. He has been dependent upon his wife to take care of him and demanding on her time and attention. She has recently had a severe stroke and has had to be placed in a nursing home. Since he has played the role of the invalid for so long and has made no effort to establish or continue social relationships, he is alone, although he is able to get out. He visits her at the nursing home but resents the effort it takes to go. They have no close relatives.

— 20

— 10

Mrs. N. Lives in a nursing home, one of the poorer ones in town. She is 87 and has survived all the members of her family. She has no children and most of her friends are deceased. The only contact she has with other people is the other elderly people in the home, but there is little stimulation or social interaction between them. Her life is filled with hours of sitting alone in "her spot" and occasionally looking through pictures of people who were important to her in the past.

— 0

From James B. Taylor et al., *Educational and Psychological Measurement*, 30, No. 2 (Summer 1970), p. 304.

Figure 16.4

Another reason why ratings tend to be unreliable is the observer's lack of training in recording information. Teachers need supervised practice in learning these skills. Those who trust their memory to provide them with accurate descriptions of behaviors that occurred sometime in the past are likely to recall selected and perhaps atypical events. Stanley Payne (1949) found that recording errors were 25 percent higher among persons who depended on memory than among those who recorded their observations at the time the behavior occurred.

Halo effect   The *halo effect* is a potential source of invalidity that occurs when a teacher's overall attitude toward a student influences ratings on a specific trait. This subtle form of bias may either spuriously lower or raise current ratings based on the teacher's prior impressions or knowledge of the student in a different situation.

Suppose that it is generally conceded that Johnny is an extremely intelligent child and a teacher is given the task of rating him on a trait such as persistence or drive. In this case the halo effect would probably work to Johnny's advantage since the teacher is likely to believe that intelligence and persistence go together or correlate with one another. But the halo effect may also work against the student. For example, a tenth-grade student who was caught shoplifting might be rated low on some other but irrelevant trait such as loyalty or deportment in school.

The halo effect has a number of interesting psychometric properties. It may tend to increase interrater agreement if raters share the same general impressions of the persons being rated. However, the validity of ratings will decrease because judgments are made on irrelevant characteristics of the person being rated.

One method of avoiding the halo effect is to recognize its pervasiveness and to deliberately try to avoid it. Another possibility is to require raters to judge the same trait for each person before rating a second or third trait. This would reduce the effects of the first rating on the ratings for subsequent traits. Another method of avoiding or reducing the halo effect is to use a forced-choice format. Since options are about equal in social desirability, the rater is forced to make a judgment that is less likely to be influenced by general impressions of the individual and will thus be more valid.

The generosity or leniency error   The tendency of judges to avoid using the lowest possible category on a rating scale is known as the *generosity* or *leniency error*. Although the reason for this phenomenon is not entirely understood, it seems to be consistent. Evidently raters feel some degree of discomfort in stating that someone is extremely weak, and they therefore avoid extremely negative judgments.

The effects of the generosity or leniency error can be noted on many report cards. One might expect that on a five-point rating scale the mean rating for the group as a whole would be close to the center, but the average rating tends to be considerably higher since many teachers avoid low ratings. Of course, when individuals know each other well they have a tendency to boost ratings that is not involved when strangers are rated.

Because some individuals are more susceptible than others, the leniency error varies from rater to rater and is thus a source of unreliability or disagreement among raters. Validity, too, will suffer because ratings are influenced by a factor irrelevant to the trait being measured. If every rater had the same degree of generosity, this error in rating would not be serious since it would then be possible to use more positive synonyms to describe the most negative choices. For example, a scale used to measure "knowledge" could be converted from one that employed such options as the following:

Stupid	Below average	Average	Above average	Brilliant

to one that is likely to be more functional:

Low	Low average	Average	Above average	Brilliant

Since there are systematic differences in raters' tendencies toward leniency, these can be controlled to some extent by adding more positive choices. The generosity error can also be reduced by forcing raters to rank each person being rated. In that way someone must be rated "lowest." The difficulty is that ranked data are relative. The lowest rated student within a given group could be average or above average in another.

Error of central tendency   The *error of central tendency* occurs whenever raters avoid extreme responses and gravitate to the central ones. The leniency or generosity error accounts for the unwillingness of raters to avoid the extremely negative categories, but the error of central tendency indicates that raters also avoid the highly favorable categories, particularly if the person rated is relatively unknown. Evidently familiarity tends to increase ratings—peer ratings in particular tend to be high—but when raters are required to evaluate relatively unknown persons, they tend to be more cautious.

The error of central tendency reduces both reliability and validity because it tends to reduce the variability of ratings. If everyone were rated about "average," there would be little variability, and it would be difficult to measure consistent individual differences (reliability) or to correlate those ratings with some criterion (validity). The techniques used to reduce leniency errors can also be used to reduce the error of central tendency.

Ambiguity in the Trait Being Measured

Some traits are particularly difficult to measure because they cannot be observed directly but must be inferred from behavior. The more explicit the trait, the more difficult it will be to measure. Traits such as *honesty, punctuality,* and *loyalty* will have different meanings for different raters, and since they cannot be observed directly, each trait presents a different set of connotations to the evaluator. One person might equate *honesty* with obeying the law, but another person might interpret it as telling the truth. Although there is no necessary contradiction in these two meanings, it is possible to obey the law but not always tell the truth. Depending on how one interprets *honesty,* it is possible for two raters to come to opposite conclusions that are both "correct."

Any trait can, of course, be made more explicit. Instead of forcing raters to judge internal and unobservable states such as *social adjustment, thoughtfulness,* or *motivation,* these terms should be defined as specifically as possible. Specificity can be obtained in a number of ways. The simplest is to define each term so that raters use the same frame of reference. For example, social adjustment could be defined as "the ability to get along with others"; thoughtfulness as "being considerate of the feelings of others"; motivation as "ability to stay with a task until it is completed." Instead of asking raters to evaluate persons on the abstract value *honesty,* as in the first example below, rating scales could be made more specific, as in the second and third examples.

1. *Honesty*

| Rarely | Sometimes | Generally | Often | Almost always |

2. *Honesty* (the degree to which a person is truthful and open)

| Rarely | Sometimes | Generally | Often | Almost always |

3. *Honesty* (degree to which a person is truthful in dealing with customers)
   a. Rarely truthful about quality of merchandise; will exaggerate value and usefulness of goods to customers; will deceive customers about warranties to make sales.
   b. Sometimes will distort the quality of merchandise; on occasion (but not generally) will exaggerate value and usefulness of goods to customers; is known to have deceived some customers about warranties to make sales.
   c. Rarely untruthful about quality of merchandise; usually will not

exaggerate value and usefulness of goods to customers; has deceived few customers about warranties to make sales.

d. Never untruthful about quality of merchandise; never exaggerates value or usefulness of goods to customers; always describes warranty provisions accurately.

In the first example honesty is undefined, and each rater will interpret it within his own frame of reference. Terms such as *rarely, sometimes, generally, often,* and *almost always* are ambiguous. The second example is more specific—at least honesty is more clearly defined—but the response categories are still vague. The third example defines the trait to be evaluated *and* provides behavior

SCALE B: CLASSROOM OBSERVATION—HIGH SCHOOL
Teacher Characteristics Study

Teacher_____ No._____ Sex_____ Subject_____

School_____ City_____ Date_____ Time_____

Observer_____

Pupil Behavior   Remarks

1. Apathetic	1	2	3	4	N	Alert
2. Obstructive	1	2	3	4	N	Responsible
3. Uncertain	1	2	3	4	N	Confident
4. Dependent	1	2	3	4	N	Initiating

Teacher Behavior

5. Partial	1	2	3	4	N	Fair
6. Autocratic	1	2	3	4	N	Democratic
7. Aloof (G)	1	2	3	4	N	Responsive
8. Aloof (I)	1	2	3	4	N	Responsive
9. Restricted	1	2	3	4	N	Understanding
10. Harsh	1	2	3	4	N	Kindly
11. Dull	1	2	3	4	N	Stimulating
12. Stereotyped	1	2	3	4	N	Original
13. Apathetic	1	2	3	4	N	Alert
14. Unimpressive	1	2	3	4	N	Attractive
15. Inarticulate	1	2	3	4	N	Articulate
16. Monotonous (V)	1	2	3	4	N	Pleasant
17. Evading	1	2	3	4	N	Responsible
18. Erratic	1	2	3	4	N	Steady
19. Excitable	1	2	3	4	N	Poised
20. Uncertain	1	2	3	4	N	Confident
21. Disorganized	1	2	3	4	N	Systematic
22. Inflexible	1	2	3	4	N	Adaptable
23. Pessimistic	1	2	3	4	N	Optimistic
24. Immature	1	2	3	4	N	Integrated
25. Narrow	1	2	3	4	N	Broad

Key: (G) Group, (I) Individual (V) Voice or speech

1, 4 Markedly present
2, 3 Present
N No opportunity for observation

SCORES: TOTAL_____

A_____ D_____

B_____ E_____

C_____ F_____

From D. G. Ryans and E. Wandt, *Educational and Psychological Measurement*, 12 (1952) p. 577.

Figure 16.5

descriptions to clarify ratings. Such terms as *rarely* and *sometimes* are still used but are clarified to some extent by the descriptions of behavior.

In the study of teacher characteristics, D. G. Ryans and E. Wandt (1952) developed a classroom observation record consisting of four pupil behaviors and twenty-one teacher behaviors (figure 16.5). Without clarification and definition the traits would have been difficult to rate. For example, what is meant by obstructive versus responsible pupil behavior or immature versus integrated teacher behavior? To help observers understand the meanings of these traits, Ryans and Wandt provided a glossary for each of the twenty-one characteristics. Some examples are shown in figure 16.6. A glossary of terms is of great value

GLOSSARY B

**To be used with Scale B: Classroom Observation—High School
Teacher Characteristics Study**

Pupil Behavior

Uncertain—Confident

a. Uncertain:
—afraid to try
—unsure
—hesitant
—restrained
—tense
—shy, timid
—easily embarrassed

b. Confident:
—willing to try
—undisturbed by mistakes
—volunteering to recite
—entering freely into activities
—relaxed

Teacher Behavior

Harsh—Kindly

a. Harsh:
—fault finding
—cross
—curt
—sarcastic
—scolding, reprimanding
—resorts to frequent threats and punishment

b. Kindly:
—sympathetic
—considerate
—gracious
—friendly
—appreciative
—disengages effectively
—courteous

Disorganized—Systematic

a. Disorganized:
—unprepared
—no plan in evidence
—expects pupils to know what to do
—wastes time
—undecided
—slip shod
—easily distracted from subject

b. Systematic:
—well prepared
—evidence planned though flexible procedure
—is careful in planning with pupils
—needs are anticipated
—works toward objectives
—holds discussion together
—systematic in routine

From D. G. Ryans and E. Wandt, *Educational and Psychological Measurement,* 12 (1952) p. 578.

Figure 16.6. Excerpts from Glossary of Classroom Observation Scale

to raters because it gives them a common frame of reference. When a glossary is used in conjunction with observer training, high agreement among raters can be obtained.

Analyzing Group Behavior

Individuals exist as members of groups. A child is concommitantly part of a family, a classroom, a neighborhood, and possibly clubs. Adults play the roles of spouse, parent, worker, and friend. The ability to understand an individual often requires an understanding of how he functions within the context of his membership in various groups.

Similarly, it may be important to assess the climate of a group by understanding how members relate to one another. Teachers may be equally concerned with individuals and friendship patterns and peer relations in the class.

Sociometric Ratings

Sociometry is a method developed by Jacob Moreno (1953) to investigate interaction patterns in peer groups. Peer ratings allow group members who know each other well to nominate each other for different activities. Peer ratings also reduce the influence that an external evaluator might have on the group. Furthermore, because teachers cannot be fully aware of how students perceive each other, peer ratings can help clarify the structure of interpersonal relationships within the classroom.

Sociometry requires each person within a group to nominate one or more of its members for a specific activity. The activity chosen depends on the purpose for obtaining these peer ratings. If the purpose were to form compatible play or work groups, the teacher could ask each student to select one or more members of the class with whom he would like to play or work.

Three factors determine the number of nominations that should be requested. First is the maturity of the students. In general, only a first or second choice should be requested from kindergarten or first-grade children; five choices are probably optimal for older children and adults (Gronlund and Barnes 1956).

Second, the number of persons in the group limits the number of choices. In a small group of ten or twelve persons, each member should probably be allowed no more than one choice. In groups of thirty or forty, three to five choices are possible.

A third factor that influences the number of choices is the purpose for obtaining sociometric nominations. If the purpose is to measure the degree of interaction among all members of the group, an unlimited number of choices might be necessary to avoid overlooking a person. But if the purpose is to form work or play groups based on student preferences, the number of choices should be limited.

Preparing the sociometric matrix   Once choices have been obtained, a *sociometric matrix* is prepared. Such a matrix is simply a table listing the names of all members of the group along the side and across the top (see table 16.1). By convention, the names of the individuals chosen are placed at the top of the matrix. If members are allowed more than one choice, the choice number is placed in the row corresponding to the person who is selecting and in the column representing the name of the person selected.

Table 16.1. A Sociometric Matrix

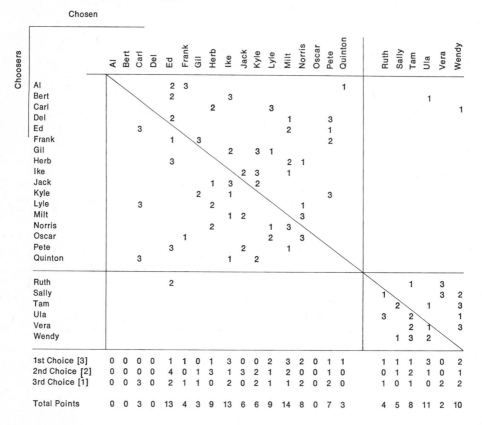

Choosers	Al	Bert	Carl	Del	Ed	Frank	Gil	Herb	Ike	Jack	Kyle	Lyle	Milt	Norris	Oscar	Pete	Quinton	Ruth	Sally	Tam	Ula	Vera	Wendy
Al					2	3											1						
Bert					2			3												1			
Carl							2					3											1
Del					2								1			3							
Ed			3										2			1							
Frank					1		3									2							
Gil								2		3	1												
Herb					3									2	1								
Ike										2	3		1										
Jack								1	3		2												
Kyle							2	1								3							
Lyle			3					2						1									
Milt								1	2					3									
Norris								2				1	3										
Oscar						1						2	3										
Pete								3			2	1											
Quinton								3		1	2												
Ruth					2															1	3		
Sally																		1			3		2
Tam																			2		1		3
Ula																		3	2			1	
Vera																			2	1			3
Wendy																		1	3	2			
1st Choice [3]	0	0	0	0	1	1	0	1	3	0	0	2	3	2	0	1	1	1	1	1	3	0	2
2nd Choice [2]	0	0	0	0	4	0	1	3	1	3	2	1	2	0	0	1	0	0	1	2	1	0	1
3rd Choice [1]	0	0	3	0	2	1	1	0	2	0	2	1	1	2	0	2	0	1	0	1	0	2	2
Total Points	0	0	3	0	13	4	3	9	13	6	6	9	14	8	0	7	3	4	5	8	11	2	10

Table 16.1 is a three-choice sociometric matrix prepared for a third-grade class in response to the question "With whom would you like to work?" The diagonal line is placed at the intersection of the columns and rows where an individual might select himself. The vertical and horizontal lines separate males from females although any criterion other than sex might be used.

At the bottom of the matrix is a summary of the number of persons who were selected as a first, second, or third choice. Al and Bert were not selected by anyone in the class. Milt received three first choices, two second choices, and one third choice. If first, second, and third choices are weighted 3, 2, and 1, respectively, the total number of points can be determined by multiplying the frequency of choices by the weights and summing the products. Ed's total points, for example, are determined using the following type of work table:

Choices	Weights	Frequency of Choices for Ed	Weight Times Frequency
First	3	1	3
Second	2	4	8
Third	1	2	2
		Total points	13

Ed's total points are 13. Milt is the most popular person in the group, with a total of 14 points; the least popular are Al, Bert, Del, and Oscar, who were un-selected. The most highly selected girl is Tam, and the least selected, Vera.

The matrix also points out the number of males who select females, and vice versa. Bert, for example, selected Ula as his first choice, and Carl picked Wendy. Among the girls, Ruth selected Ed as a second choice.

Developing the sociogram   After preparing the matrix, the next step is to develop a *sociogram* (see figure 16.7), which graphically depicts the choice patterns of the group. Numerous techniques for drawing sociograms have been proposed, but since they can provide no more information than what is presented in the matrix table, their main advantage is that they display group relationships as simply and clearly as possible.

The sociogram is plotted directly from the matrix table by developing a frequency distribution of total points. For the present data, the highest number of points is 14 (Milt), and the lowest, 0.

Total Points	Frequency	
14	1	
13	2	Group I
12	0	
11	1	
10	1	
9	2	Group II
8	2	
7	1	
6	2	Group III
5	1	
4	2	
3	3	Group IV
2	1	
1	0	Group V
0	4	

23

Each individual is placed within one of the five concentric circles by dividing the frequency distribution into groups having approximately the same number in each. Those in group I are the most highly selected and are placed in the center circle. Students receiving the fewest number of total points are placed in the outer circle.

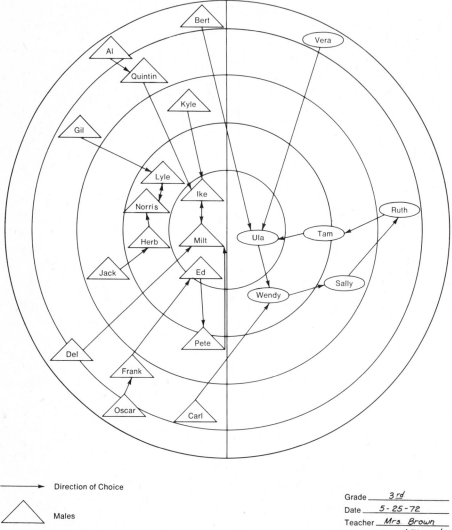

Figure 16.7. Sociogram for a Third-grade Class using "Work" as a Criterion

The number of circles is arbitrary, but four to five are probably optimal for most classroom purposes. Although the numbers of students in the groups will not necessarily be equal, this is of little consequence since the only purpose of the sociogram is to depict graphically the data in the matrix.

The direction of choice on a sociogram is shown by an arrow drawn from one person to another. The sociogram in figure 16.7 represents only the first choice of each member of the class; plotting two or more choices is possible but may produce a crowded and confusing sociogram.

The simpler the sociogram is, the better. Choice lines that cross each other should be avoided when possible since that complicates interpretation. If second or third choices are plotted, using different colors for each choice will be of some help, but some rearrangement of individuals on the sociogram may be necessary to maintain simplicity.

Interpreting sociograms   The relationships among members of the group can be described by examining choice patterns. The most common patterns of choices are cleavages, cliques, stars, mutual choices, isolates, and rejectees.

Cleavages   A *cleavage* is formed when two or more segments of a class fail to nominate each other. In the elementary grades a sex cleavage is a common occurrence, with few choices that cross from one sex to the other. In some groups cleavages may be formed on the basis of race, religion, or socioeconomic status.

Cliques   *Cliques* consist of individuals who select each other and tend to avoid other members of the group. Oscar, Frank, Ed, and Pete, for example, form a clique, as do Jack, Herb, Norris, Lyle, and Gil. The girls in the class form a clique of their own. Note that a *cleavage* is based on group differences but that the individuals *within* cleavages may form *cliques* when they select each other.

Although sociometric methods do not by themselves indicate the bases or reasons for the forming of cliques, they can help to identify tightly knit subgroups. When cliques are formed for socially undesirable purposes, the teacher may find it valuable to identify the leader of the clique to help change group structure and attitudes.

Stars   *Stars* are the most highly selected members of the group, and they often wield a great deal of power. The sociogram in figure 16.7 suggests that Milt, with a total of 14 points, is the most highly selected member of the group.

Mutual Choices   A *mutual choice* is, as the name implies, a selection of two individuals by each other. Lyle and Norris, for example, are mutual choices. Essentially mutual choices are reciprocated friendships based on the same criterion, such as work, play, or seating arrangements.

Mutual choices often represent strong loyalties, especially among adolescents. As long as the relationship is based on socially desirable aims, it serves the important purpose of helping the individual learn about himself. But when mutual choices serve less beneficial purposes, other members of the group can be introduced into the relationship or members may have to be separated.

Isolates   *Isolates* are persons not selected by any other member of the group. Although they may be unpopular, sometimes they are new to the group and have not had a chance to become known. Whether or not a person is classified as an isolate depends, in part, on the number of choices permitted. Probably a student should not be considered an isolate if only one choice was permitted among members of a relatively large group. But as the number of choices is increased, the failure to be selected by anyone could help identify children who need help in becoming more accepted members of the group. Al, Bert, Del, and Oscar were not selected among the first three choices and are therefore classified as isolates.

Rejectees   Although isolates are not selected, they are not necessarily rejected. A *rejectee* is someone identified by the group as undesirable in some way. To identify a rejectee, members of the group must nominate persons whom they actively reject. Asking students to identify classmates they dislike can create problems for some pupils, particularly those who are young, immature, or highly sensitive.

Some limitations of sociometry   Sociometric choices point out patterns of peer group selection. They indicate persons who are most and least chosen for certain kinds of activities. But sociometry has limitations, and it can be misinterpreted:

1. Sociometry does not indicate the reasons for acceptance, non-acceptance, or rejection; it simply identifies the current group choice structure.
2. Sociometric interpretation is hazardous unless the interpreter knows other information about members of the group. Sociometric data may indicate, for example, that Harry and Mary are mutual choices, but further information is needed to understand this relationship. The fact that they are both new to the school or are brother and sister might account for their selections.
3. It is too often assumed that "isolates" must be withdrawn and introverted. Isolates can be quite well adjusted, but they might simply prefer their privacy. Similarly, many unhappy individuals can be extremely popular in some situations.

4. Popularity in one situation does not necessarily imply equal popularity in another. The "star" in a physical education class might be less highly selected in social studies or mathematics. A clique that disrupts one class might not exist in another.
5. Sociometric choices depend highly on the nature of the questions posed. It is one thing to be asked to name your best friend and quite another to be asked to name the person you would want to work with on a class assignment. Questions such as "With whom would you most like to work on an algebra assignment?" might yield a different response if the assignment were changed to social studies.

The reliability of sociometric data   The most common method of determining the reliability of sociometric data is to correlate the number of nominations received by each individual at two different times to yield a coefficient of stability. The factors that affect these coefficients have been summarized by Gronlund (1959):

1. The stability of sociometric results tends to decline as the time span between tests is increased.
2. There is a tendency for the stability of sociometric results to increase as the age of the group members increases.
3. Sociometric status scores based on general criteria (such as work or play) tend to be more stable and more consistent over various situations than those based on specific criteria (such as working on arithmetic or playing football).
4. Composite sociometric status scores based on several sociometric criteria tend to be more stable than sociometric status scores based on a single sociometric criterion.
5. An unlimited number of sociometric choices, five positive choices, and three positive and three negative choices tend to provide similar sociometric results. The use of fewer choices provides less reliable sociometric results.
6. The social structure of a group tends to be less stable than the sociometric status of the individual group members.
7. The sociometric positions of leadership and isolation tend to be more stable and more consistent over various situations than those in the average sociometric categories.

The validity of sociometric data   As might be anticipated, the validity of sociometric data is more difficult to assess than reliability. If the concern is with obtaining a measure of *expressed* choice or preference, sociometry appears to measure that objective directly. If Albert states that he would rather sit next to Harry than to anyone else, it is hard to imagine another method that could provide a more valid measure. Sociometry is inherently valid as a measure of expressed choice.

Nonetheless, it is important to know what these choices mean by relating them to various educational or psychological traits or attributes. It is important to know whether "stars" tend to be well adjusted or whether "isolates" are unhappy. Answers to these questions require the *concurrent validation* of sociometric choices.

According to Gronlund (1959, p. 183), sociometric status is more sensitive to social adjustment than to personal or emotional problems. Generally isolates do seem to be socially ineffective, whereas those who are more highly selected tend to experience fewer social problems. But it would be a mistake to believe that these general trends are true for everyone. Sociometric data should be clarified through interviews with members of the group to better understand the meaning of and reasons for class nominations.

Guess-Who Technique

Another peer nomination procedure has been called the *guess-who* or *casting-characters technique*. It is generally used as a method of measuring reputation or character.

When used with young children, the procedure begins by asking each child to pretend that a class play is going to be presented. The play requires the participation of perhaps ten or more characters. Role descriptions may be both positive and negative, depending on whether the teacher anticipates that any student is likely to be singled out or teased by the others. Examples of positive and negative descriptions are:

1. This person is always happy and smiling with a good word for everyone and everything.
2. This person is almost never happy or smiling but is almost always angry at someone or something.

Students are instructed to write the names of all persons in the class who fit each description. Each student nominated for a positive role receives 1.0 point; negative nominations receive a −1.0. The sum of positive and negative nominations is the student's score.

A variation of this technique is simply to ask students to guess who the description refers to, without referring to a class play. This is a less contrived task for older children or adults.

The guess-who technique is not as widely used as sociometry for at least three reasons. First, it is difficult to create descriptions of different characters. Second, the halo effect has to be guarded against. Students who are generally disliked may have specific traits attributed to them that are based on these generalized impressions. Third, no one might be nominated for some roles, whereas others may fit just about everyone.

The advantage of the guess-who method is that it provides more specific data about a given child than does sociometry. A child who is nominated as the class tattletale, apple-polisher, or troublemaker can be helped to overcome these deficiencies once they are recognized by the teacher. Even if the child has been unfairly categorized into a particular role, the nomination could still accurately reflect the impressions of the peer group. Still, the very process of asking children to label each other may lead to personal difficulties for some of the children. The use of positive role descriptions can avoid this problem.

Summary

1. This chapter describes how behavior can be measured in naturalistic or uncontrived situations.

2. Observational error can result from a number of sources:
   a. Personal values of the observer can affect observations.
   b. Biases and prejudices distort objective observations by forcing them to agree with one's belief systems.
   c. Group expectations also determine what individuals see, or at least what they are willing to report.

3. Observational error can be reduced by following these suggestions:
   a. Be prepared to observe a specific aspect of behavior and to disregard irrelevant cues and behaviors.
   b. Where applicable, use mechanical or electronic recording apparatus to facilitate observation and to reduce observational error. Film is expensive, but tape recorders, counters, and timers can be used to good advantage.
   c. Prepare unambiguous recording forms and pretest them to make sure they are clear.

4. The letter of recommendation is an unstructured rating. Such letters are often unsatisfactory because (1) raters are usually selected or at least nominated by the persons being rated, and (2) because most raters are reluctant to evaluate others negatively. The following suggestions can improve the quality of letters of recommendation:
   a. Letters should be obtained from a wide sampling of persons who know the ratee.

    b. Deficiencies as well as strengths should be requested.

    c. Examples of specific behaviors should be requested.

    d. The purpose of the ratings should be made clear to raters.

    e. Raters should be told who will be allowed to examine their ratings.

    f. A follow-up phone call or letter thanking those who have submitted letters of recommendation can be used to discourage individuals from submitting fabricated letters.

5. Anecdotal records provide the teacher with continuous, objective descriptions of behavior. Anecdotal records can be obtained by episode or time sampling.

    a. In episode sampling the teacher describes the events that created, continued, and terminated a given aspect of behavior, such as crying or hitting another child. In writing anecdotal reports of episodes, descriptions of behavior are kept separate from interpretations. The observation is described as objectively as possible without becoming so detailed that meaning is lost. Interpretations are tentative.

    b. In time sampling the teacher records the behavior at different times of the day and on different days of the week for each child observed. The purpose of time sampling is to describe typical patterns of behavior of the children rather than to single out one type of behavior, as in episode sampling. In writing time samples, the use of a portable cassette tape recorder can facilitate observations. The observed events are described in context but without interpretations.

6. Numerical rating scales contain ranked descriptions of traits or behaviors, each of which has a numerical value. There are advantages to having a large number of categories. Quantifiable responses can be rated more reliably than broad descriptions of behavior.

7. Checklist items describe behaviors that are marked as present or absent. Desirable behaviors can be given $+1$ point; undesirable behaviors can be rated -1. An individual's score is the sum of these values.

8. Graphic rating scales describe behavior along a continuum. Points along this continuum are described to aid in rating. Sometimes only the ends of the continuum are identified or "anchored," but there is some evidence that interrater reliability can be improved by using a vertical format with examples of behaviors to define scale positions.

9. Ratings can be improved by recognizing and eliminating the sources of unreliability, including characteristics of the rater and ambiguity in defining and measuring the trait being rated. Errors to which raters are subject include:

a. Lack of training. Observers must be thoroughly familiar with the scale items and the methods used to record observations.

b. The halo effect, or the tendency to rate a specific trait on the basis of general impressions. If raters share the same impressions of an individual, their interrater agreement is likely to be increased but at the expense of validity since judgments are made on an irrelevant characteristic. Using the forced-choice format or having each rater judge the same trait for all individuals before rating other traits can help reduce the halo effect.

c. The generosity or leniency error, which is the tendency of raters to avoid using the most negative ends of a rating scale. Because this tendency varies among raters, it is a source of unreliability and invalidity. The generosity error can be reduced by placing positively stated categories on rating scales or by forcing raters to rank the persons being rated.

d. The error of central tendency, which occurs when raters avoid both the high and low extremes of a rating scale. It occurs especially when individuals are asked to rate persons whom they do not know well. Both reliability and validity are affected by the error of central tendency.

10. Ambiguity in defining the trait to be rated is also responsible for low reliability and validity coefficients derived from rating scales. By defining each choice point on the scale, ambiguity can be reduced.

11. Classes exist as social groups having characteristics of their own. These characteristics can be assessed by asking members of the group to rate or nominate one another for various activities or roles.

12. Sociometry is a procedure that uses peer ratings to discover classroom structure and interpersonal relations. Students are asked to select one or more members of the group with whom they would like to sit, work, or play.

13. A sociometric matrix is prepared from the choices of students. The matrix contains the number of times each person is selected as a first, second, or third choice for the activity. By weighting these choices, a total score can be obtained for each person.

14. In preparing a sociogram or graphic display of the choices, students are divided into groups based on their weighted score. Each student is placed into one of four or five concentric circles, with the most selected persons in the center and the least selected students in the outer circles. An attempt is made to place individuals so that arrows drawn from one person to another (to indicate direction of choice) do not cross other choice lines.

15. Sociograms are interpreted according to patterns of choices:

a. Cleavages are formed when one section of the group fails to select members from another section. Sex cleavages are common in elementary schools.

b. Cliques are based on individuals who select each other. Cliques may be formed as a part of a cleavage and may be formed for desirable or undesirable purposes.

c. The star is the individual receiving the greatest number of choices.

d. A mutual choice is formed when two individuals select each other. Adolescents in particular form strong attachments to their friends, and same-sex mutual choices are common.

e. An isolate is an individual who has not been selected by any member of the group. In a large group where only a first choice is permitted, the evidence that an individual is an isolate is less than in a smaller group where more choices are allowed.

f. A rejectee is a person who has been rejected by someone in the group. To identify rejectees, the students are asked to indicate those persons with whom they would prefer *not* to sit, work, or play. Whether rejection should be measured depends on the maturity of the group and the need for such information.

16. Sociometry suffers from a number of limitations:

a. The reasons for selections or rejections cannot be known from the sociometric choices but have to be obtained from other sources, such as interviews with students.

b. The interpretation of sociometric choice patterns must be based on other kinds of information about group members.

c. The isolate is not necessarily a withdrawn and unhappy child, although that is a possibility. Similarly, the star may not always be well adjusted and happy.

d. The isolates and stars in one group may not be rated as low or as high in another. The nature of the group is an important determinant of sociometric choice.

e. The nature of the questions asked of students is another determinant of choice.

17. The reliability of sociometric choices is affected by many of the same factors that affect other measurements (time between repeated measurements, the maturity of the group, and so forth). A unique characteristic of sociometric choices is that they are more reliable for individuals than for the group as a whole.

18. Sociometric selections are inherently valid as *expressed* choices. Isolates often (but not always) have problems adjusting to the group; similarly, stars tend to have fewer social problems than others in the group. The concurrent

validity of the choices can be determined by interviewing or testing students to determine the reasons behind choices.

19. The guess-who technique is another peer nomination procedure. A series of character descriptions are prepared by the teacher (e.g., ostensibly for a class play), and students are asked to nominate one or more class members for each role. In comparison to sociometry, the guess-who technique is more difficult to prepare, is more subject to the halo effect, and may create roles that all or no students may fit. The advantage of the guess-who technique is that it measures a more specific trait of an individual than does sociometry. Even if children are unfairly nominated for certain roles, knowledge of stereotyped responses can help the teacher to improve relationships of students with each other.

Suggested Readings

Gronlund, Norman E. *Sociometry in the Classroom.* New York: Harper & Brothers, 1959, 340 pp. An excellent account of the use of sociometry in the classroom.

Horowitz, Herbert. "Prediction of Adolescent Popularity and Rejection from Achievement and Interest Tests." *Journal of Educational Psychology* 58, no. 3 (June 1967): 170–74. In this study sociometric ratings were used as the criterion, and achievement and interest inventories and tests were the predictors. Although athletes tended to be popular, the "athlete-scholars" were most popular among high school students.

Lindzey, Gardner, and Borgatta, Edgar F. "Sociometric Measurement." In Lindzey, ed., *Handbook of Social Psychology,* vol. 1, *Theory and Method,* pp. 405–48. Cambridge, Mass.: Addison-Wesley Publishing Co., 1954. A thorough account of different indices used to describe the structure of groups.

Moreno, J. L. *Who Shall Survive? Foundations of Sociometry, Group Psychotherapy, and Sociodrama.* Rev. ed. New York: Beacon House, 1953. This is a work that describes sociometry and its relations to counseling and therapy.

17

Most school districts devote considerable time, funds, and effort to purchasing, administering, and scoring standardized tests and recording their results. In addition, teachers also develop their own tests to measure specific course objectives. Because of the widespread use of tests in education, efficient methods of disseminating and reporting test results must be developed.

Importance of Disseminating Test Results

Disseminating test results is important for a number of reasons:

1. Decision making is often a cooperative endeavor involving teachers, parents, students, and administrators as well as experts in curricula, psychology, social work, and counseling. If members of these groups lack valid information, decision making will be ineffective. A child who is unable to read or who has difficulty adjusting to a classroom needs the support and understanding of persons who are in a position to modify his behavior, but without valid information, even the most competent individuals may be unable to intervene effectively in the child's behalf.

2. In order for tests to provide valid information about pupils, the students must consider tests as important, relevant, and beneficial, and they must perform as well as they can. Telling students their test scores will keep them informed of

their progress and help them improve areas that are weak. This can motivate students to do their best on future tests.

3. Taxpayers, who face many conflicting pressures for funds, are increasingly demanding that the schools hold themselves accountable for the progress and achievement of their pupils. Competition for public tax funds makes informing the public about educational needs and student progress mandatory.

4. Both students and parents need specific information to plan effectively for the future. What are the chances that a student will be successful in a four-year college? Should Johnny pursue an academic or a vocational curriculum? What courses will help him overcome a specific problem? What specific problems does he have? Answers to these and similar questions require valid information.

5. Teachers and administrators need to plan educational experiences realistically. Should one curriculum innovation be substituted for another? How effective is a particular textbook in teaching social studies? Is one method of teaching slow learners more effective than another? Should classes be organized by ability, sex, age, or interest? Again, valid information must be provided to those who are in a position to modify educational practices.

Factors Preventing the Optimal Use of Measurements

Because it is so important that test information is made available to those in decision-making roles, it might appear strange that teachers make relatively little use of test results. The following conditions most often account for the failure of teachers to use test results:

1. Teachers may not be consulted about the selection of tests. The failure to include teachers on test selection committees probably stems from a number of factors. Teachers who are not well versed in principles of measurement and evaluation often feel unqualified to help select tests. This objection has some validity, but nothing prevents committees from employing the technical services of counselors or school psychologists. Teachers can examine some of the practical considerations of test selection discussed in chapter 10.

New developments in educational and psychological measurement call for periodic retraining of teachers. Colleges and universities can offer refresher courses in measurement and evaluation, or districts can schedule in-service training programs. Teachers who understand basic principles of tests and measurements will want the opportunity to select tests for their classes.

2. Reasons for testing may not be specified. The purposes of testing programs should be made clear to teachers. Administrators may develop a test program to show taxpayers that students are learning academic fundamentals;

teachers, in contrast, may want to know specific deficiencies; parents, too, are interested in knowing how their children compare with national norms. The philosophy behind the testing program should be clarified and provisions should be made for employing tests that serve these different needs.

3. Testing programs often fail to provide a uniform picture of the child's progress. Because norms and the subtest content vary for different tests, making it difficult to judge student progress, it is advantageous to use the same test battery from grade to grade if possible. Test programs should provide information that will be of value in decision making throughout the child's years in school.

4. Teachers and administrators often lack experience in interpreting test results to others. No matter how well conceived a testing program may be, it will probably not be effective if results cannot be communicated to those it was designed to help. Here again some form of in-service training can be beneficial.

5. Test results may be inaccessible or inconvenient to use—for example, if records are kept in a central file. Junior and senior high school teachers do not have the time to copy test results of each of their students, and some school districts are unwilling to allow elementary school teachers to retain student files for fear that information may be lost. These problems can be resolved at least partially by using scoring systems that provide multiple copies of gummed labels.

6. The failure of school personnel to specify objectives has led many teachers and parents to become disillusioned with invalid test results. Too often tests are selected for their practicality (ease of administration and scoring and low costs) rather than on the basis of their validity and reliability.

Criteria for Developing a School or District Testing Program

Although no testing program is "ideal" for all purposes and for all districts, the following criteria should be considered in developing and evaluating district or school testing programs:

1. Testing programs should be developed cooperatively with teachers, administrators, parents, and specialists in measurement and evaluation. The testing committee should be district-wide, if possible, and should represent teachers at all grade levels as well as supervisors of special subjects and areas, such as reading, arithmetic, and counseling.

2. The test program should consist of a *minimum program,* required of all students, and a *supplemental program* to meet the needs of limited numbers of students and teachers. The minimum program should be designed to meet a wide variety of purposes, such as placement, remediation, feedback to parents, and curriculum evaluation. The supplemental program should enrich the minimum testing program in specific fields not commonly taken by all students

(algebra, chemistry, and so forth); it could be used by teachers who require or request special test services for remedial or advanced students.

3. Tests selected for the minimum testing program should employ norms that are commonly understood by teachers and that can easily be communicated to parents. Percentile bands (see pp. 191-193) are particularly desirable for this purpose. Other norms, such as standard scores, might be difficult to interpret to parents.

4. A test analysis form such as the one on page 271 should be used for selecting tests. Although both practical and technical considerations need to be evaluated, problems of validity and reliability should be given highest priority. The test committee should utilize published evaluations of all tests and should examine both the test booklet and the manual thoroughly before making final decisions.

5. Wherever possible, the same series of examinations in the minimum testing program should be used throughout the grade levels to ensure comparability of norms and subtests. In general, test interpretation will be facilitated if forms of the same test are given throughout the grades rather than if tests with different norms are used indiscriminately.

6. Testing costs can be reduced substantially by using separate answer sheets rather than allowing students to mark their answers on the test booklet. However, consumable test booklets are advisable at the primary grades.

7. Tests should measure wide ranges of abilities. Tests that are too restricted in range will necessitate additional testing with either higher-level or lower-level forms, requiring additional testing time and adding to the cost of the testing program.

8. Tests should be administered no more often than is necessary to provide reliable data on student progress. To administer intelligence tests every year, for example, is probably unnecessary since IQs are relatively stable measurements, particularly at the upper elementary levels and above.

9. The emphasis should be on achievement. If interest inventories are used, some measure of aptitude should also be administered since the correlation between them is low to moderate. Other noncognitive tests, such as attitude and personality measures, should probably be reserved for the supplemental testing program.

10. Because of the importance of reading in all phases of the curriculum, it may be desirable to administer alternate forms of reading tests annually at the elementary grades. This is particularly important in schools where student performance in reading is low.

11. Tests administered at the beginning of the school year are especially useful for the diagnosis of learning difficulties. Furthermore, fall testing allows the teacher to assess achievement after the typical drop in retention over the summer vacation. Tests administered at the end of a school year provide information about the effectiveness of the current year's program. When students are about to graduate to junior or senior high schools, it may be desirable to test late in the year to evaluate the cumulative effects of the school program.

12. Testing programs should be evaluated periodically and revised if

necessary to meet new demands or major changes in school philosophy. The minimum testing program, however, should be revised only after considerable deliberation because comparability of norms and subtests will be forfeited when a school switches from one battery of tests to another.

An Example of a Testing Program

This is a case history of the development of a testing program. Teachers, administrators, parents, and students had complained that testing was excessive and that relatively little use was made of test results. To remedy this situation, a test committee consisting of teachers from each grade level, administrators, counselors, parents, and a specialist in measurement from a nearby university was formed.

At one of the committee's early meetings the members agreed to develop a sequence of activities that would eventually lead to a defensible and useful testing program. The steps to be followed were:

1. Interview faculty, parents, and administrators on the type of information the testing program should provide.
2. Write a statement of district objectives for the testing program which would include priorities.
3. Develop criteria for the testing program.
4. Select tests that meet district objectives and criteria for the testing program.
5. Meet with the faculty to discuss the proposed program.
6. Establish in-service training programs for teachers.
7. Request the administration to appoint a director of testing to order tests, to determine testing dates, to deliver tests to schools and to teachers, to arrange for scoring services, to disseminate test results, and to act as chairman of the test committee.

Objectives and Priorities of the Testing Program

After meeting with the faculty, administration, and parents, the committee decided that the primary purpose of testing at the elementary grades should be to help diagnose pupil strengths and weaknesses; at the secondary grade levels it established the highest priorities as placement in order to help students make important curriculum decisions to prepare for appropriate careers. The administrators, however, were particularly anxious to have evidence about the adequacy of the school's curriculum.

Test Selection

Recommending tests to the faculty and administration occupied most of the committee's time. Representatives of test publishers discussed their services and allowed members of the committee to examine tests, manuals, and technical data. Cost and time factors were deemed important, but technical considerations relating to reliability and validity received the most careful attention. The program recommended by the test committee is summarized in table 17.1. *Remember that tests suitable for one district might not be acceptable in another.*

Table 17.1. Minimum Testing Program Recommended for the _____ School District

	Grade	Test	Testing Time	Major Purpose of Test*
Elementary	2	Lorge-Thorndike Intelligence Test	35 min.	Selecting atypical children for special guidance and placement
	2	Metropolitan Reading Test (word knowledge, word discrimination)	90 min. in 3 sessions	Initial diagnosis of reading problems; placement
	3	Metropolitan Achievement Test Battery (same as grade 2 plus reading, spelling, language, arithmetic)	3 hrs. in 5 sessions	General survey; initial diagnosis of achievement; curriculum evaluation
	4	Metropolitan Reading Test (word knowledge, reading: main thought, details, inferences, context)	45 min.	Measurement of reading improvement; diagnosis; curriculum evaluation
	5	Lorge-Thorndike Intelligence Test	50 min. (verbal) 42 min. (nonverbal)	Diagnosis, guidance; recheck on second-grade results
	6	Metropolitan Achievement Test (word knowledge, reading, spelling, language, language study skills, arithmetic, social studies study skills, social studies information, science)	4½ hrs. in 5 sessions	Curriculum evaluation
Junior High	9	Differential Aptitude Test	2 hrs.	Career and educational guidance
	9	Kuder Interest: Vocational	30 min.	Career and educational guidance
Senior High	10	Metropolitan Achievement Test (reading, spelling, language, language study skills, social studies, mathematics, science)	5½ hrs.	Survey; diagnosis; placement; career and educational guidance
	12	Metropolitan Achievement Test (same as grade 10)**	5½ hrs.	Curriculum evaluation
	12	Lorge-Thorndike Intelligence Test**	35 min. (verbal) 27 min. (nonverbal)	Curriculum evaluation

* It was assumed that all standardized tests in the minimum testing program would be used for feedback.
** To be administered approximately once every three years.

A group intelligence test was included in the minimum program in grades two and five. The second-grade teachers wanted an initial measure of scholastic aptitude that would help them to identify atypical children and to interpret the meaning of reading test scores. Students reading at levels far below their general aptitude level might require remedial services. Note that it was necessary to select an intelligence test that provided a nonverbal score; otherwise, a child who was unable to read might do poorly on the intelligence test when his problem was reading rather than low scholastic aptitude.

The same intelligence battery (but designed for grades 4–6) was recommended in grade 5 because the committee realized that test scores tend to be relatively unstable for younger children. Since children would be taking reading tests in each of the preceding three grades, it would be useful to relate their reading scores to scholastic aptitude. At the junior and senior high school levels no intelligence tests were recommended for annual use because they tend to correlate highly with achievement measures and because the verbal ability and numerical ability subtests of the Differential Aptitude Tests (administered in grade 9) also correlate highly with measures of intelligence. An intelligence test was recommended for periodic administration to high school seniors as an aid in interpreting the scholastic ability of the district's graduates.

The full battery of the Metropolitan Achievement Tests was recommended for grades 3, 6, 10, and periodically grade 12. At the third-grade level it provides initial feedback to parents about achievement in subjects deemed important by committee members. It also helps teachers to identify students in need of remediation in subjects other than reading. At the sixth-grade level the administrators wanted a thorough analysis of the cumulative effects of the elementary school curriculum. High school teachers also wanted to use the Metropolitan Achievement Test battery early enough to help students explore career potentials, to identify students with serious academic problems, and to help evaluate the school curriculum.

Although many schools might prefer to give no tests at the twelfth-grade level except perhaps those from "external" sources (college entrance examinations, special scholarship tests, and so forth), this committee believed that sufficient funds were available to justify a repeat of the Metropolitan Achievement Test battery to evaluate periodically the achievement of the district's graduates.

The only other tests recommended for inclusion in the minimum testing program were the Differential Aptitude Tests and the Kuder Vocational Interest Inventory. The committee asked that these tests be administered as early in the ninth grade as possible to help entering high school students decide their major course of study. Since the Kuder can be scored by the students themselves, the committee felt that teachers would have the time to help students interpret these data before program choices had to be made. Because of the low correlations between aptitude and interest test scores, the committee recommended that students take both of these tests.

No personality or attitude tests were included in the minimum test program. Most of the committee members preferred to have these tests administered only with the permission of the parent, but some took the position that the school's responsibilities toward attitude and personality development were as important as that for cognitive goals.

Supplementary testing at the kindergarten and first-grade levels might—at the request of individual teachers—include a reading readiness test to be used for diagnosis and for placement of pupils into differential reading groups. Provision was also made for individually administered intelligence tests for students who might need placement into special classes for slow learners. Because a thorough physical examination was provided by the district as a matter of policy for entering kindergarten students, the committee left this to the nursing staff and medical consultants.

Methods of Reporting Group Data

School districts have an obligation to inform parents and other citizens about student progress. Although parents have the right to know how well their own children are doing, they can also benefit from learning information about the average progress of students as a group.

Reports of pupil progress may be recorded in expository, tabular, graphic, or pictorial form. Many school administrators have discovered that recipients of written expositions about student progress often do not spend the necessary time to understand the communication. However, tabular and graphic information often requires at least a brief statement to help parents interpret data meaningfully and accurately.

Tables

Tables present data in columns and rows and may consist of frequencies (the number of persons obtaining various score values), percentages, proportions, or other statistical data such as means, standard deviations, or correlation coefficients.

The following suggestions will help teachers prepare tables that are simple, clear, and complete:

1. Tables should be numbered consecutively. If a report contains chapters, tables could be identified by chapter and then sequenced, such as table 4.2, which refers to the second table in chapter 4.

2. Every table should have a title describing the main information. The title is usually located above the table.

3. All columns and rows should be titled.

4. All relevant information needed to interpret the table should either be incorporated into the table itself or included as footnotes on the same page.

5. Long columns of numbers should be separated into groups of five to ten each to avoid overcrowding and to help in reading across rows.

6. Tables are usually located immediately after their introduction in the text. However, if a report consists of a large number of tables, it might be more convenient to group them together in an appendix.

7. Avoid vertical lines within the table or as borders. These lines often complicate the table and make it difficult to read.

8. Horizontal lines may be used to separate the title of the table from entries. Column totals may also be separated by horizontal lines.

9. Tables should not extend over more than one page, if possible. Several short tables may appear on the same page.

10. Because tables require time to read and understand, it is better to duplicate them and allow each person to have his own copy than to project a table on a slide or overhead projector in front of a group of parents.

Graphs

A graph is a drawing or figure used to convey statistical information. Graphs greatly simplify communication because figures have easily visualized shapes. Unfortunately graphs can also grossly misrepresent data.

Some general rules for constructing graphs are:

1. Graphs should be numbered consecutively as figure 1, figure 2, and so forth. In long reports divided into chapters, figure 1 in chapter 1 may be described as figure 1.1 or figure 1-1. By convention, the first numeral refers to the chapter and the second to the sequence within the chapter.

2. Every graph should have a title. This is usually located next to the figure number and may be placed above or below the graph. The common method is to place the title of a graph beneath the figure.

3. All symbols used on the graph should be clearly identified.

4. Feel free to use more than one type of graph if different kinds of information are to be communicated.

5. All graphs, with the exception of *pie graphs* (which are circular) are plotted on a horizontal axis (called the X axis or *abscissa*) and a vertical axis (called the Y axis or *ordinate*). The horizontal axis usually represents dates, number of trials, scores, or other fixed values, whereas the vertical axis represents the corresponding frequencies or percentages. Since frequencies and percentages vary or depend on certain fixed values, they are called *dependent variables* and are plotted on the vertical axis. The fixed or known values are called *independent variables* and are plotted on the horizontal axis. By convention, the value to be predicted (i.e., the dependent variables) is located on the vertical axis, and the value from which the prediction is made (the independent

variable) is plotted on the horizontal axis. Some examples may help clarify these relationships:

a. Number of new cars purchased in relation to average income. In this example the number of cars purchased is the dependent variable since it depends on the average income. The vertical and horizontal axes should be labeled as in figure 17.1.

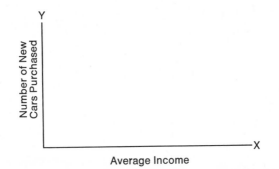

Figure 17.1. Example Showing the Labelling of X and Y Axes

b. Achievement test scores related to the annual number of dollars spent per child on education. In this example one has to decide if the graph is to show that achievement scores depend on the number of dollars spent for education or if the number of dollars spent depends on how well children perform on achievement tests. If the second interpretation is correct, plot different dollar amounts on the Y axis and the score values on the X axis.

c. Amount of vitamin C taken and number of colds per year. Because the number of colds is the dependent variable, it is placed on the ordinate; the amount of vitamin C is located on the abscissa, or horizontal axis.

6. The horizontal axis should be about one-fourth to one-third longer than the vertical axis. This will reduce optical distortions and improve the aesthetics of the graph.

Line graphs   The *line graph* consists of a series of straight lines connecting the points that correspond to the values on the X and Y axes. For example, to depict the mean achievement level in grade equivalent units from 1959 to 1971 in a hypothetical school district, the graph could be prepared as in figure 17.2. This graph indicates that students made rather consistent increases in reading comprehension mean scores from 1959 to 1971, with only a slight decrease in arithmetic reasoning from 1966 to 1967. Assuming that the students' *actual grade level* was 3.5, they attained this level in arithmetic reasoning by 1970 and were considerably below national averages prior to that time. In contrast, the students made more rapid progress in reading comprehension

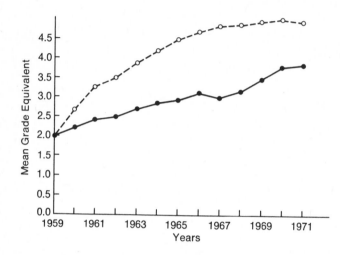

Figure 17.2. Hypothetical Line Graph Showing Mean Grade Equivalents for Third Graders at Mallard Elementary School in Arithmetic Reasoning (_____) and Reading Comprehension (_ _ _ _ _) from 1959 to 1971

and are considerably above national norms. The graphs cannot, of course, indicate the reasons for the increase in mean performance. This will have to be assessed from other factors, such as changes in the school curriculum, lower teacher-pupil ratios, practice effects (if students take the same test over and over again), or changes in housing patterns.

The histogram   A *histogram* (see figure 17.3) consists of a number of columns where the height of each column represents a corresponding frequency on the vertical axis. The higher the column, the greater the frequency is. One disadvantage of the histogram is the necessity of beginning the vertical scale with 0. If this is not done, the relationships between the heights of each column may present a distorted impression. For example, if the Y axis in figure 17.3 began at some value other than 0, the differences in frequencies could appear to be out of proportion. If the smallest frequency was a 5, a 6 could be drawn halfway up the page. Although the figures along the side make it clear that no such gain

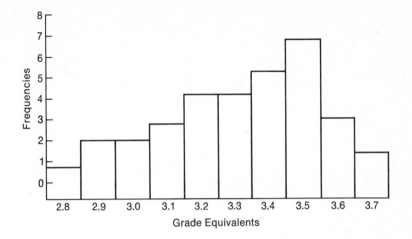

Figure 17.3. Hypothetical Frequencies of Grade Equivalents on Arithmetic Reasoning for a Third-Grade Class at Mallard High School (N = 31)

was realized, the *apparent* column heights give a vastly different impression. Beginning with 0 along the vertical axis avoids this misimpression.

The bar graph   The *bar graph* is essentially the same as a histogram except that (1) horizontal bars replace columns, and (2) the categories are separate rather than continuous (see p. 135). However, these are minor differences which many statisticians are willing to overlook since no more information is conveyed by a histogram than by a bar graph. Nonetheless, statistical purists may still insist that bar graphs be used only with discrete variables.

An example of a bar graph is given in figure 17.4. Again, it is necessary to begin with 0 and to make the length of each line proportional to the others. Bar graphs typically report the exact frequencies for each category. Data may be further analyzed by sex by using two bars for each category or by using two colors for each bar—one color for males and a different color for females.

The pie chart   The *pie chart* is a circular figure that is especially useful for demonstrating how various proportions of a total are related to one another, such as for showing the proportion of males and females in a class or the proportion of a total budget spent on various items. The number of persons voting along political party lines (as shown in the bar graph of figure 17.4) may be converted to percentages of the total number of students and displayed as a pie chart, as in figure 17.5.

Each segment of a pie chart should be proportional to the total area. This can be accomplished most easily by using a compass and a protractor, but those who are inexperienced in using these instruments may find it simpler to

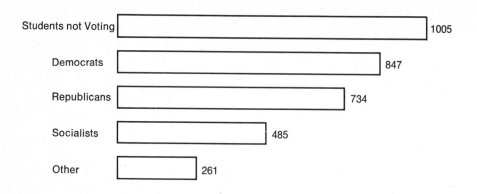

Figure 17.4. Number of Students at Bear University Expressing Voting Preferences for Presidential Candidates as of October, 1972

divide the circle into halves, quarters, eighths, sixteenths and thirty-seconds. These values correspond to 50 percent, 25 percent, 12.5 percent, 6.25 percent, and 3⅛ percent, respectively. Sixty percent can be estimated, for example, by using half of the pie plus three segments of $\frac{1}{32}$. If the pie is to be divided into a large number of very small segments, it is wise to consider some other method of visual presentation, such as a bar chart.

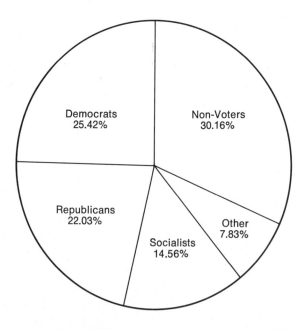

Figure 17.5. Example of a Pie Chart Showing the Percentage of Students at Bear University (N = 3332) Expressing Voting Preferences for Presidential Candidates as of November 1972

Pictographs   A *pictograph* is a series of pictures, each representing a given frequency or percentage of occurrence, such as that shown by the expectancy table in figure 17.6 which depicts the percentage of successful and unsuccessful freshman students at the University of Hawaii as predicted by the verbal reasoning subtest of the Differential Aptitude Tests administered in the eleventh grade (see figure 17.6). In this example N = 109; r = .52.

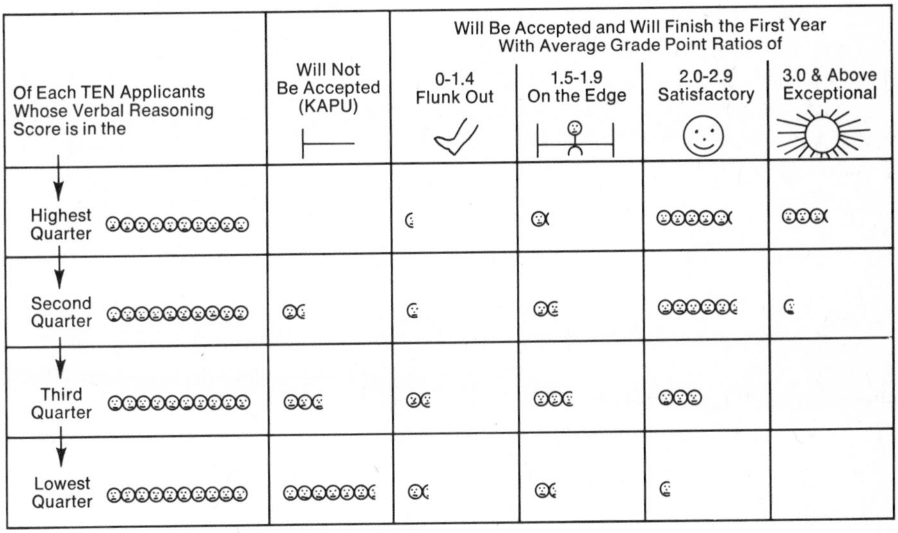

Of Each TEN Applicants Whose Verbal Reasoning Score is in the	Will Not Be Accepted (KAPU)	Will Be Accepted and Will Finish the First Year With Average Grade Point Ratios of			
		0-1.4 Flunk Out	1.5-1.9 On the Edge	2.0-2.9 Satisfactory	3.0 & Above Exceptional
Highest Quarter		(	(	(((((	(((
Second Quarter	(	(	((	(((((	(
Third Quarter	((	((	(((	(((	
Lowest Quarter	((((((	(	((	(	

Figure 17.6. A Pictograph Showing the Relationship Between the Verbal Reasoning Test of the Different Aptitude Tests and Freshman Academic Success at the University of Hawaii (1956)

Symbols used on pictographs should be simple but symbolic. Stick figures or faces are easily identified as people, greenbacks can represent expenditures, and so forth. No more than fifteen or so symbols should be used in any row to avoid confusion.

Reporting Standardized Test Scores

Reporting IQ Scores

In general, IQ scores should *not* be reported without interpretation to either parents or students because they are easily misinterpreted as "capacities for learning." Parents often fail to consider that such factors as motivation, personality, and interest also help determine school success. Perhaps worse, parents too often react punitively when their children fail to achieve what is expected of them.

Today the tendency is to replace the term *intelligence* with a less loaded term such as *academic aptitude*. Rather than saying that Johnny has an IQ of 115, the teacher can tell his parents that he is performing as well as or better than about 85 percent of other students his age who have taken this examination. Parents who think of an IQ as an unalterable state can be told that Johnny is in the upper quarter of students on a test designed to predict how well he will do in school.

Expectancy tables relating performance on intelligence tests to such criteria as school or college marks, on-the-job success, or other standardized achievement test scores may also make test interpretation more meaningful.

Reporting Grade Equivalent Scores

Grade equivalent norms are too easily misinterpreted to be given to parents indiscriminately. These norms are often extrapolated, making extreme scores difficult to explain and interpret properly. The amount of error in any grade equivalent norm may be anywhere from half a year to a year and a half—a fact not easily appreciated by most parents. Differences of four or five months between scores on different subtests may reflect random error rather than differences in achievement level.

Grade norms should not be used in counseling with parents. A parent of a tenth-grade student who is told that his son is functioning at the seventh-grade level is likely to greet this disclosure with hostility; furthermore, the student will not appreciate being compared with those in a lower grade level. For counseling purposes, the student should be compared with his peers.

Reporting Percentile Scores

Percentiles are probably the simplest and the norm that is least likely to be misinterpreted to or by parents. The teacher should, however, clarify the group with which the child is being compared and remind parents that differences in percentiles at the extremes of a distribution have greater significance than differences of equal numerical value near the center of the distribution. Parents should also be cautioned to avoid confusing percentiles with the percentage of items answered correctly. It might be better to state: "In comparison with other fifth-grade children throughout the United States, Billy is in the upper 10 or 15 percent as measured by the reading vocabulary subtest of the California Tests of Basic Skills when these were taken last October." A statement such as this reminds the parents that test scores are fallible.

Reporting Noncognitive Scores

Noncognitive test scores (such as interest, personality, and attitude) are the most difficult to interpret properly. These scores tend to be less reliable than cognitive measures, and they require more caution in interpretation. Furthermore, subtest titles do not always mean what parents assume they mean. For example, a masculinity-femininity scale could be grossly misunderstood unless parents and students are told exactly what that subscale measures.

In reporting the results of noncognitive tests, teachers should be aware of the limited item sampling that such tests typically provide. Telling a parent that her son has trouble getting along with adults because he has a high score on dominance is asking for trouble. A more reasonable statement might be something like, "The scores seem to suggest that Al may have some difficulty in getting along with adults. What is your impression of this?" Keep in mind that in interviews with parents, the teacher can learn as much as the parent.

Interest measures should be interpreted as *inventoried interests*. They do not indicate what the student *ought* to do but only how he rates one activity over another in relationship to some specific norm group. Interest inventory results should be discussed by area (i.e, medicine) as well as by level (orderly, nurse, physician). The teacher should also keep in mind and remind parents that an individual may be interested in auto racing but might not wish to pursue this as a vocation.

Criteria for Reporting Pupil Progress

Methods of reporting pupil progress should be objective, continuous, reliable, and valid. They should be simple for parents and students to understand and not too time-consuming for teachers to prepare. Furthermore, they should provide enough information to help students, teachers, and parents make important educational decisions.

Suffice it to say no one technique will accomplish all these objectives, and school districts will find it necessary to establish priorities and to develop reporting systems that best meet their own purposes. Although this may mean sacrificing ease of preparation for reliability, for example, there is no justification in sacrificing validity for convenience.

Reporting systems should be adapted to meet parental or community demands. A community that insists on the use of letter grades (A for excellent, B for good, and so forth) may not be willing to accept a simple pass-fail system, parent conferences, or any other method of reporting pupil progress.

Because reporting systems are (or at least should be) designed to help make important educational decisions that often require the cooperation of parents, children, and teachers, they should be developed by school committees composed of interested citizens and professional workers.

Objectivity

An objective reporting system means that observers agree on evaluations of students. A statement on a report card that Johnny seems "well adjusted" or that his deportment is "adequate" fails to clarify the meaning of these terms. Observations can be made more objective by defining vague terms, providing examples of "adequate" deportment, and keeping accurate records of student behavior (see pp. 474-476).

Continuity

Reporting systems should provide continuous information about student progress. Parents and students should be informed of progress regularly, preferably in time to be of value in modifying pupil behavior. Districts that report grades only at the end of a quarter or semester do not give parents adequate time to help children improve.

Continuity implies that record systems should not be modified except for good reason. There is not much difference between a five-point recording system (A, B, C, D, and E or F) and one that uses plus, check, and minus to represent good, average, and below average progress, respectively. Even minor changes in the system can make it difficult for parents to get a clear picture of the student's progress since it is difficult to equate one system with another. It is therefore recommended that much consideration be given before changing a recording system, especially if it has been in use for a long time. This is not a plea to maintain the status quo, but it is an admonition to avoid ill-conceived modifications that are likely to be changed again soon.

Reliability

The factors (discussed in chap. 7) that affect reliability of measurements also affect the reliability of marks and reporting systems. Subjectivity in observing and recording student behavior is likely to lead to low reliability. Factors that increase reliability are group heterogeneity, increasing the number of categories on the reporting form, and basing marks on as many observations as possible.

Validity

Marking systems should measure reliably what they were designed to measure. A number of suggestions can be made to improve the validity of marks:

1. Reliability is necessary (but not sufficient) for validity.

2. Do not allow irrelevant factors to influence marking practices. For example, marks are sometimes based on effort and sometimes on achievement, but the marking system should clearly indicate which criterion is being used. The presence of irrelevant factors can also reduce validity, such as when marks are used punitively or as rewards for class behavior.

3. The final marks received by students in a course are usually obtained by averaging projects, papers, tests, and ratings, with each yielding different units of measurement. Teachers often erroneously believe that each activity contributes equally to the composite or that a final examination, for example, can be given twice the weight of a less important activity simply by adding its scores into the composite twice before averaging. The actual weight or contribution of each activity to the final course mark, however, depends entirely on the standard deviation of each component and not its mean or necessarily the number of times it is added to form the composite. *The contribution of each activity to the composite is directly proportional to its standard deviation.*

To demonstrate this principle, observe what happens if the composite scores of two students, Alice and Betty, are compared by simply adding together their individual component scores, as shown in table 17.2. It appears from that table that Alice and Betty did equally well in the class since their total points (181) are the same. However, scores should not be compared with one another if they are based on different means or different standard deviations (see chap. 6). In addition to providing the raw scores for Alice and Betty on the five components, table 17.2 provides information about the means, the ranges and standard deviations of scores, the students' z scores on each component, and the teacher's desired weights for each component. On quiz 1, for example, Alice

Table 17.2. Raw and z Scores for Two Students on Five Components Having Different Means and Standard Deviations

	Quiz 1	Quiz 2	Class Participation	Term Paper	Final Exam
Means	26.36	27.53	2.36	86.77	38.96
SDs	2.05	4.14	1.08	2.93	3.26
Ranges	21–30	20–32	0–4	81–92	31–45
Weights	1	1	1	2	3
Alice's raw scores	29	28	4	81	39 = 181 (total)
Betty's raw scores	24	32	0	89	36 = 181 (total)
Alice's z scores	1.29	.11	1.52	−1.97	.012
Betty's z scores	−1.15	1.08	−2.19	.76	−.91

is 1.29 standard deviations above the mean, but this is only given a weight of 1; on the same quiz Betty is 1.15 standard deviations below the mean.* If no attention were paid to the standard deviations, the students' marks in class participation would not make much difference in the total grade since the range is only four points, but in z scores Alice is above the mean, whereas Betty is far below. Converting each of the scores to z scores in effect gives each of the five components equal weight. If this were not done, the components with the largest standard deviations would contribute more weight than those with smaller standard deviations. The extreme case would be a component where all students performed equally well, yielding a standard deviation of 0. No matter how many points each person received, that component would add nothing to the composite or total grade. Conversely, some minor assignment could be given more weight than a final examination if its standard deviation were larger.

The z scores in table 17.2 allow the teacher to compare the performance of Alice and Betty on each of the five components. A simple average of these z scores for each of the students would provide a total or composite value in which each component would be weighted equally. If the z scores are multiplied by the desired weights and then divided by the sum of the weights, the original distribution of scores will have been converted to properly weighted composites, as in the following example:

	ALICE			BETTY		
	z	Desired Weight	z Times Desired Weights	z	Desired Weight	z Times Desired Weights
Quiz 1	1.29	1	1.29	−1.15	1	−1.15
Quiz 2	.11	1	.11	1.08	1	1.08
Class participation	1.52	1	1.52	−2.19	1	−2.19
Term paper	−1.97	2	−3.94	.76	2	1.52
Final exam	.012	3	.036	− .91	3	−2.73
			Sum = −.984			Sum = −3.37

$$\text{Composite} = \frac{-.984}{8} = -.123 \qquad \text{Composite} = \frac{-3.47}{8} = -.43$$

Although Alice and Betty *appeared* to be performing equally well when the raw scores on each of the five components were averaged, Alice is about one-eighth of a standard deviation below the class mean, whereas Betty is almost one-half of a standard deviation below the mean.

---

*Recall that

$$z = \frac{\text{score} - \text{mean}}{SD}$$

In the examples these are

$$\frac{29 - 26.36}{2.05} = 1.29 \text{ and } \frac{24 - 26.36}{2.05} = -1.15$$

for Alice and Betty, respectively, on quiz 1.

Converting to z scores is particularly important if differences in variability occur because the standard deviations of each component are artifacts of units of measurement. For example, if letter grades are given on some assignments, they usually vary from 0 (F or fail) to 4.0 (A or excellent); a less important assignment, however, might be marked using percentages, which potentially range from 0 to 100. These differences in variability are artifacts of the units of measurement that have been selected by the teacher, and such distributions should be converted to z scores to make them comparable in weight.

Methods Used to Report Pupil Progress

Various methods have been devised to report pupil progress, including conferences, written evaluations, letter grades, percentages checklists, and rating scales. Each method has advantages and limitations that sometimes make it advantageous to combine methods into a comprehensive reporting system. Many schools, for example, use parent conferences and letter grades; other schools prefer that written evaluations on each child be sent to parents.

Conferences

The parent-teacher conference has been widely used to communicate with parents, especially at the elementary grades, where one or two 20- to 30-minute conferences per year are common. Junior and senior high school teachers usually plan individual conferences with parents only when requested by the parents or when students are experiencing difficulties requiring the help of parents. Nothing about the conference precludes its general use with parents of older children except the high teacher-pupil ratios commonly found in secondary schools.

The teacher-parent conference is used to greatest advantage when a two-way flow of information results. Teachers can learn much about a child and how best to help him if they know his family and their expectations, values, interests, and problems. In turn, the parent wants to know how well his child is doing in school. Because the conference permits face-to-face interaction, it is especially useful in helping to clarify and resolve misunderstandings, especially when teachers meet with individual parents before serious difficulties arise.

Parent conferences require thorough planning. Before the conference the teacher should read the pupil's permanent record and summarize data on a sheet of paper or two for easy reference, although many schools allow teachers to use the permanent records during conferences. Some school districts have prepared parent-teacher conference report forms (see figure 17.7), which teachers are to complete prior to meeting with parents. Often a carbon copy of the report form is given to parents to help them recall details of the conference.

If information such as that presented in figure 17.7 is not available in the school records, the parent-teacher conference report form provides a basis for the teacher to better understand the child and his home environment. In addition, it gives the teacher a list of possible topics to discuss with parents. Information provided in confidence by the parent should *not* be included in the child's permanent record.

Some suggestions for the parent-teacher conference follow:

1. Put the parent at ease. Welcome him and see that he has a comfortable seat and good lighting and that there is privacy.

2. Before presenting information to a parent, find out what information the parent has already received from other teachers, counselors, or administrators. Failure to do so may put you in the uncomfortable position of contradicting a colleague, having to change your position, or reporting information with which the parent is well acquainted.

3. Before presenting information, determine what kind of information the parent wants. Little learning occurs when all conference time is spent discussing academic achievement when the parent is most interested in his child's social adjustment.

4. Asking questions that can be answered by a simple yes or no is not likely to motivate parents to speak openly. Also how one makes a statement may be as important as its content. Telling parents to "keep to the topic" will probably render the parent defensive and the conference ineffective. A better question might be "What was it you said earlier about . . . ?"

5. Try to determine the parent's reactions to the child's progress in school. This gives you an opportunity to describe test and other evaluation results as they relate to the parent's attitudes and beliefs. Failure to be cognizant of the parent's attitudes may force the parent to contradict your position or it may— if the parent is made to feel inferior—motivate him to take an even more passive role in the conference.

6. If information is inadequate or contradictory, the teacher should be willing to admit the weaknesses of evaluations based on these data.

7. As in any learning situation, there should be a clear understanding of what the conference goals are. The teacher may want to report the child's progress, reinforce parental beliefs, gather needed information, or change parental attitudes. The purpose of the conference should be stated or agreed upon and sufficient time taken to resolve as many of the parent's questions as possible.

8. Before terminating the conference, summarize or have the parent summarize topics discussed to reduce misunderstandings. Such quesitons as "How do things seem now?" or "Have we done all we can for John?" may be useful.

9. Immediately following the conference, summarize in writing all nonconfidential information provided by the parent that may be of value to other

Unless the conference is called for a specific purpose, the following checklist may be used to help the teacher plan the conference more effectively:

1. Parent or guardian's last name (if different from child's)
2. Child's age
3. Age, sex, and number of siblings or other children in household
4. Other adults living in household with child
5. Father and mother's occupation and education
6. Number and location of schools child has attended
7. Reasons for changing location
8. Health factors

   a. vision
   b. hearing
   c. weight
   d. height
   e. allergies
   f. medications
   g. innoculations
   h. physical abnormalities
   i. handedness

   j. speech difficulties
   k. nutritional difficulties
   l. posture
   m. cleanliness
   n. coordination
   o. nervousness or tics
   p. energy and vitality
   q. condition of teeth & gums
   r. sleep habits

9. Attendance records including tardiness
10. Anecdotal reports
11. Standardized Test results

    a. group
    b. individual

12. Teacher-made test results
13. Sociometric data
14. Previous parent-teacher report forms
15. Court records
16. Counseling and social work reports
17. Psychologist or psychiatrist reports
18. Previous evaluations by other teachers
19. Interests

    a. Expressed
    b. Manifest
    c. Inventoried

20. Deportment

    a. Number of disciplinary transfers
    b. Number of times sent to principal or counselor
    c. Number of suspensions
    d. Specific anecdotes regarding deportment

21. Work habits

    a. Number of times work is turned in late or not at all
    b. Neatness
    c. Amount of time required to begin work on his own
    d. Degree of dependence on teacher or peers

22. After school activities

    a. At-home chores
    b. Jobs for pay
    c. Amount of television watched

23. Fears, anxieties, phobias
24. Personal habits

    a. Ability to dress self
    b. Ability to use bathroom himself

Figure 17.7. An Example of a Parent-Teacher Conference Report Form

teachers who will have contact with the child. This might mean adding information to the permanent record to keep it current.

Regularly scheduled parent conferences are time-consuming but valuable because they can promote greater understanding between parent and teacher. Unfortunately many parents cannot attend these sessions because of other obligations or will not because of disinterest. Some other form of reporting pupil progress might be needed for these parents.

Written Communications

In some school districts teachers send progress or report letters to parents who are unable to attend conferences. The parents can read these at their leisure, discuss the contents with each other and with the child, have a record of the child's behavior as described by the teacher, and respond in writing should there be reasons for doing so. Written communications can also further good public relations if they are carefully thought out.

But written communications have a number of problems. First, they are extremely time-consuming to write, particularly if other means of communicating with parents (such as conferences) have not been planned for. At the secondary level it would be impractical to have the teacher write more than a sentence or two about each student on a report form.

A second problem is that written communications become stereotyped and vague:

> Albert has made some progress in social and academic skills this year. He behaves quite well in class and is dependable and liked by the other members of the class. He particularly seems to enjoy reading and has met the objectives of the class very well.

This letter provides little information. For example, what is meant by "some progress"? Progress in comparison with what and in what specific areas? Dependable in which areas? What were the objectives of the course that Albert met? Such "communications" raise more questions than they resolve.

Also, written communications may be misunderstood or comments may be taken out of context.

Fourth, while a grammatical error may be excused by a parent during a conference, it is not likely to be overlooked in a letter, particularly a letter reporting poor pupil progress. Spelling, handwriting, and punctuation errors become matters of permanent record, and teachers must be both tactful and grammatical. Even typing errors can cause embarrassment.

The following suggestions should prove helpful in writing communications to parents:

1. Begin and end each written communication with optimism and encouragement.
2. Indicate specific strengths and weaknesses, but state what steps are being taken or will be taken to help the child overcome the weaknesses.
3. Improvement of student deficiencies should be considered a joint responsibility of home and school. Little is gained by blaming either the student or his parents for those deficiencies.
4. Give parents specific suggestions. Telling a parent that John's work in arithmetic is unsatisfactory only indicates the teacher's dissatisfaction with John's progress; it provides little help for the student.
5. Encourage parents to communicate directly with the teacher either by telephone or in a conference for clarification. Pointing out the difficulty in expressing progress in a letter can help parents understand the teacher's desire to be more complete than the letter allows.
6. Avoid technical terms, jargon, and trite expressions. The purpose of the letter is communication, not displaying one's knowledge or intelligence.
7. There is a difference between tact and rudeness or honesty and evasiveness. The purpose in writing to parents is to communicate with them, not create anxiety or defensiveness. One school district prepared the following list of negative expressions and their more positive counterparts (Federal Way Public Schools):

Negative Expressions	More Positive Expressions
Must	Should
Is lazy	Can do more when he tries
Is a troublemaker	Disturbs the class
Is uncooperative	Should learn to work with others
Cheats	Depends on others to do his work
Is stupid	Can do better work with help
Below average	Working at his own level
Steals	Without permission
Disinterested	Complacent, not challenged
Is insolent	Insists on having his own way
Lies	Tends to exaggerate
Wastes time	Could make better use of his time
Is sloppy	Could do neater work
Is a failure	Has not met requirements
Time and time again	Usually
Poor quality of work	Below his usual standard
Swears	Uses unbecoming language
Shows off	Tries to gain attention
Will fail	Has a chance of passing if . . .

8. Teachers should be given sufficient time to write letters. Some districts allow teachers to send letters to parents at various times to avoid the necessity of writing thirty or forty letters at the same time. Other districts release students from class or provide substitute teachers to enable regular teachers to compose meaningful letters.

Letter Grades

Because conferences and letters to parents are so time-consuming, many school districts find it simpler to summarize student progress by using letter grades, as on the traditional *report card*. Its major advantage is simplicity—it is easy for the teacher to fill out and for the parent to understand. Its main disadvantages include the fact that each mark is often a composite of different skills (a C in arithmetic, for example, could mean average performance on all tests or that the student excelled in one area but failed another) and the problems of deciding on what basis the marks will be given and how to assign these marks to students (see figure 17.8).

1. Using intraclass comparisons based on relative achievement   Letter marks are often used to distinguish among the relative amounts of knowledge the members of a class possess. When teachers use this basis for marking, students who have the most knowledge receive marks of A, those with less knowledge receive Bs, and so forth. The percentage of students receiving each mark may be fixed in advance by the teacher or by the school district's policy, but the most common approach is to let the class average be a C (or some other value) and then to let gaps in the distribution separate one category from another.

If classes were composed of students at the same grade level and same level of ability who differed greatly in degree of achievement, the assignment of marks by comparing students with each other within the class would not be an unreasonable way of marking. Marks would represent relative performance within the group independent of ability level. But many elementary and secondary school classes are grouped homogeneously to facilitate instruction. This presents two difficulties. First, it is more difficult to reliably divide a homogeneous class than a heterogeneous group. If there is little spread in achievement, differences between students are small and differences between letter marks will be based on these small differences. A more variable group is easier to subdivide into different achievement levels.

Second, marks for a class composed of honor students probably should not have C as the average since many universities admit students at least partially on the basis of grade point averages. For these students, it may be desirable to set B+ or A− as the class average, with very few, if any, C grades given. If students are graded from A through E or F in every class, the nature of the groups being compared should be made clear because an A obtained by a student in a gifted group would not have the same meaning as an A given in a class of slow learners.

2. Using intraindividual comparisons based on ability level   Sometimes marks depend on the difference between the student's level of performance in

Figure 17.8

class and some estimate of his ability. Students with low ability (usually measured by an intelligence test or by the teacher's subjective estimate) but high achievement obtain higher grades than those who have the same level of achievement but higher levels of ability. A mark of A would have no absolute value but rather, would represent high achievement relative to ability.

The theoretical advantage of this system of marking is that higher achievement will be expected of high-ability students and lower levels of achievement for those with less ability. The system rewards those who work hard and in effect punishes bright students who have learned that they do not have to study very hard for high marks.

However, this method suffers from a number of serious deficiencies. First, what should the teacher use to measure ability? The discussion of overachievement and underachievement on pages 381-382 indicates that there is some question whether any test can measure potential for learning.

Second, if teachers select students who are high on some measure of "ability," the achievement test scores for these persons will probably be lower because of the *regression effect*. The regression effect was first described by Sir Francis Galton, who believed that successive generations have a tendency to regress toward the average—a condition he accepted as hereditary. But as used here, the regression effect is a statistical artifact that is expected to occur whenever individuals who are at the extremes of a distribution are selected. Persons classified as gifted were selected because they obtained unusually high scores on some intelligence or other "ability" test, at least partially due to the favorable operation of chance. When these persons then take any other test, including one of achievement, those favorable chance factors are no longer present, and scores on the second test tend to be lower, although they may still be far above the average on both measures.

At the other end of the distribution, the regression effect operates in the reverse way. When students are selected on the basis of low intelligence or "ability" measures, they have been selected—at least in part—on the basis of unfavorable chance factors. When they then take an achievement test, these unfavorable events are no longer present, and they obtain scores that are above their intelligence level but still below the average level of achievement for the population.

The implication of the regression effect for intraindividual comparisons based on "ability" is clear: high-ability students are almost always going to be "underachievers" and low-ability students, "overachievers." At least for those at the extremes of the distribution, marks based on ability will penalize the brighter student, who is not "working up to capacity," and will reward the child of lower ability, who will appear to be working "beyond expectancy."

3. Assigning marks based on effort   Some pupils try very hard to do well in class but for a variety of reasons do not succeed (see figure 17.9); others may work less, but because they are bright or have had some previous experience

© 1968 Washington Star Syndicate, Inc.

Figure 17.9

with the subject matter, they perform at a high level. Recognizing these differences, teachers often base grades on a combination of effort and achievement. A student who has tried may be given a "courtesy" passing mark although his level of achievement may be poor; his brighter counterpart may get a grade of B or C even though his level of achievement may be quite high.

The most serious disadvantage of this system of marking is that validity is reduced since identical marks might represent different levels of achievement and effort. It also raises some other important questions: Should a child who already understands the material be penalized for not working harder than other members of the class? How will effort be measured and how will achievement and effort be weighted relative to each other?

Figure 17.10 shows a report card—used in a conference with parents—on which effort and achievement are reported separately for each subject. This type of reporting system provides more information to parents and students than a system based solely on achievement *or* effort. It also avoids the problem of combining achievement and effort into a single mark that is difficult to interpret. Because the report card is used in a parent-teacher conference, the teacher can explain the basis of the achievement and effort marks.

Measuring degrees of effort can be difficult. Anecdotal reports may be helpful if teachers keep records of the number of times the student asks for help, the amount of time spent in doing extra assignments, hours spent in after-class supervised study, and so forth.

4. Basing marks on improvement   The degree of student improvement from the beginning of the school year can also be used as a basis for assigning marks. The students who improve the most receive the highest marks, and those who show the least amount of improvement, the lower marks. This system has the advantage of rewarding gains regardless of the initial level of achievement.

But what should teachers do about the student who has gained little

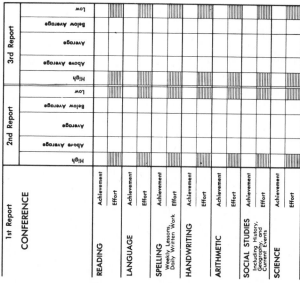

Used by permission of Bellingham Public Schools, District 501, Bellingham, Washington.

Figure 17.10. Report Card Showing Separate Effort and Achievement Evaluation

because he is at the top of his class or the student who has gained much but is still far below the rest of the class? This is another example of how the regression effect can penalize bright students while rewarding those who are less capable. It is not reasonable to expect a child who is already performing at a high level to continue to make even greater gains than his less able classmates.

Basing marks on improvement also involves the use of difference scores, which, as already indicated, tend to have low reliability. Furthermore, gains of the same number of points at different levels of the distribution are not necessarily equal. Many examinations are arranged so that the easiest items precede the more difficult ones. If student A originally received a score of 3 and later raised his score to 10, he has improved 7 points; if student B initially received a score of 10 and later obtained a score of 17, he too has improved 7 points. But if the second student's 7 points were derived from more difficult questions than the first student's, the gains do not represent equal amounts of improvement.

Another difficulty with using improvement as a basis for marking is that it may encourage students to do poorly at the beginning of the year in order to show greater improvement later. The student who does well at the beginning will be forced to improve even more if he wants a high grade. For all of these reasons, using improvement as a basis for marking is not recommended.

5. Basing marks on predetermined levels of achievement   Sometimes marks are assigned on the basis of predetermined levels of achievement, such as the following:

90–100 percent = A
80–89 percent = B
70–79 percent = C
60–69 percent = D
 0–59 percent = E

With this system, students receive a mark depending on the percentage of items answered correctly. On any given assignment or test it is possible for all to fail or to receive any other mark. The advantage of this system is that the basis for assigning marks appears to be clear and unambiguous: no one will fail simply because he is at the bottom of the class distribution. Another advantage is that anxiety may be reduced since no one must fail.

However, there are some serious disadvantages. First, the difficulty level and variability of a test will determine the percentage of students who receive each letter mark. On an easy test or assignment, almost all students will receive high marks; more difficult tasks will result in more low grades. The extreme case is an examination composed of a single item. If it is easy, everyone will respond correctly and will receive an A; those who respond incorrectly will fail.

Tests with small standard deviations will restrict the variability of marks given.

Second, if teachers prepare overly difficult examinations, they may have to fail a large proportion of the class, in which case public relations suffers along with class morale. If examinations are too easy, fixed standards will require that the teacher give everyone high marks. Some parents may then believe that their children are doing extremely well, although the implication is only that the test was too easy to measure individual differences in achievement or knowledge.

6. Basing marks on the normal distribution   Distributions that approximate bell-shaped curves are often found when testing large numbers of persons, a fact which has led some teachers to assign marks based on characteristics of the normal curve. Stanine norms (described on pp. 157-158) divide the normal distribution into nine parts, each of which is one-half a standard deviation in value. Should teachers prefer a five-point system of marking, the normal curve could be divided into units that are one standard deviation apart, as in figure 17.11. Using this system, 38 percent of the students would receive Cs, 24 percent would receive Bs and 24 percent Ds, 7 percent would receive As, and 7 percent would fail.

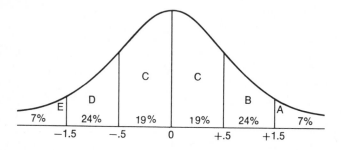

Figure 17.11. A Normal Distribution of Letter Grades Showing the Percentage Within Each Category

Nothing requires teachers to base marks on a normal curve or to use units of equal length. Most classes are not composed of large numbers of randomly selected persons, and not all traits are normally distributed. Nor is there any necessary reason for automatically failing students because they happen to be in the lowest 7 percent of a group. Most teachers prefer to have more As and Bs than Ds and Es. Furthermore, there may be some advantage in having negatively or positively skewed distributions if the purpose is to identify slow and gifted pupils, respectively (see pp. 243-247). While the difference between marks of A and B may not be crucial, there is a great difference between getting a D and having to repeat an entire course. To best discriminate between D and E students, negatively skewed distributions would be desirable.

Most teachers will not want an inflexible system of marking. If classes have been highly selected, it may be desirable to set the mean at B or B+ or even higher. In small seminars or in groups where marks are rather subjectively determined, the instructor may prefer a simple pass-fail system. If marks are to be assigned to slow students, one must consider that continually receiving low marks may have detrimental effects. And perhaps most important, it must be admitted that no entirely satisfactory procedures have been devised to separate students into categories.

Orville Palmer (1962) has suggested seven ways of grading students dishonestly:

1. Grading by abdication   Teachers may abdicate their responsibility to mark students by claiming they are too busy to construct meaningful examinations or by constructing unreliable and invalid tests. Sometimes teachers avoid this responsibility altogether by allowing students to vote on their own marks, claiming that the only "real" evaluation is self-evaluation. But unless the student is capable of judging the reliability and validity of tests he has taken and unless he is able to observe himself objectively in comparison with other members of the group, in comparison with himself, or with some given standard, the teacher has abdicated his responsibility to help the student evaluate his progress.

2. Grading by the "carrots and clubs" system   In this system the teacher excessively rewards irrelevant behaviors and drastically punishes trivial errors. The "carrots and clubs" system, for example, rewards students with high marks for performing extra work even when their required performance is low. A student who fails to learn how to use commas may still get a high grade if he performs some irrelevant task. What the student needs is not work of a different kind but a higher level of performance on assigned tasks.

3. Grading by default   The instructor grades by default when he devotes as little time to testing as possible. A final examination or a single term paper may constitute the entire basis for marking. Many rationalizations defend this method, but tests, papers, quizzes, and other assignments are only samples of the student's knowledge, and fairness dictates that as many samples as possible of this knowledge be obtained if grades are to represent a reliable level of performance.

4. Grading by overgrading   The opposite of grading by default is grading by overgrading. Using this system, the teacher checks on every aspect of student behavior by assigning a grade to everything. The classroom becomes a place whose only function is grading, checking, and policing student behavior.

Overzealousness in grading can detract from instruction as much as grading by default.

5. Grading by rule changing   The rule-changer is extremely "flexible." He tells students how they will be graded and then changes the system without good reason. He announces that spelling errors will not count but counts them anyway. He fails large number of students at the beginning of the year to show them who is boss and to maintain "high academic standards" but gives everyone A s at the end of the year as a gesture of friendship. The student is never given a consistent philosophy of why and how marks are assigned.

6. Grading by psychic subjectivity   Some teachers have the unique ability to evaluate students merely by looking at them. Clearly the student with the long forehead and thick horn-rimmed glasses should get an A. To the psychic grader the halo effect is the most important method he can depend on. Anything so coarse as a test might interfere with his prejudgments and biases.

7. Grading by impossible standards   The person who uses impossible standards informs his students that no one in the group is bright enough or mature enough to deserve an A and that only a few will be fortunate enough to get a B. To him, high standards mean that many students must fail the course. Instead of doing his best to provide excellence in instruction, impossible standards are set for students. The fact that students cannot meet these standards is taken as evidence that even higher admissions standards are necessary.

Behavioral Mastery Reports

Dissatisfaction with the traditional reporting system has led to the development of *behavioral mastery reports*. These usually consist of a number of objectives stated in behavioral terms and some indication of the extent to which the student has met or mastered each objective. The advantages of a behavioral report over the letter grade system are:

1. They tell the parents about the school program in specific terms. Instead of reporting that Albert is average in arithmetic, a behavioral mastery reporting system would state that Albert was able to perform some specific task such as add a list of up to six single-digit whole numbers without error.

2. They force the teacher to specify objectives behaviorally. Many traditional report cards contain vague terms, such as *cooperation, work habits, habits of thrift,* and the like. A mastery approach to reporting defines each of these terms behaviorally since it is necessary to determine the extent to which mastery

has taken place. In developing a mastery reporting system, the teacher must ask himself what a person who is cooperative, shows good work habits, or demonstrates habits of thrift *does*.

3. They are diagnostic. That is, they tell parents and other teachers about specific student strengths and weaknesses. This is accomplished in two ways: (1) by defining objectives behaviorally, and (2) by substituting corrective suggestions for the traditional letter grade. Knowing that a child received a C in arithmetic will be of little value to either his next year's teacher or to the parent who wants to help him, but knowing that the teacher is recommending remedial services to help a child learn some specific task can be useful to the parent, to the child, and to his other teachers.

4. They are nonpunitive. A mastery reporting system places less of a value judgment on student behavior than does the traditional marking system. The student is not punished for failing to master some concept but is given the help needed to learn the task. No matter how one looks at it, a D grade indicates a relatively low level of teacher satisfaction with the student's progress, and at least to the student, it is a punishment for not performing at a higher level. With mastery reporting, the intent is to indicate specific activities in which the child needs help or has met minimum levels of acceptable performance.

5. Competition for grades is reduced. Letter grade report cards are traumatic for many youngsters who are unable to compete academically. Students compare their grades with one another's, forcing those with low marks to defend their egos as best they can—sometimes by withdrawing and sometimes by clowning or other forms of negative behavior. The mastery reporting system reduces the competition for grades by substituting decisions for vague value judgments. It is one thing to tell a child he needs remedial help, but quite another to tell him he has failed.

6. The student is not compared with other members of the class but against a minimum level of acceptable performance. When students are compared with one another, the less able or less competitive students suffer. A behavioral mastery system avoids this by establishing realistic levels of minimum performance for each student.

7. Reporting does not become a goal in and of itself but is a decision-making function. A behavioral mastery system of reporting specifies that the child needs help in some specific area. This makes it possible for parents and school principals to hold teachers accountable for modifying their educational practices to reduce the number of students who are having difficulty in some curriculum area.

8. They encourage schools to experiment with new approaches to individualize instruction. This is done by listing objectives in sequence and allowing the student to skip those objectives he has mastered and to devote additional time to enriched or advanced activities.

However, there are a number of limitations and disadvantages to developing and using behavioral mastery systems:

1. They are difficult to prepare. An objective such as "is able to count"

is too broad since it fails to inform the parent of the limits of the child's ability to count and whether the counting is by rote or if the child is able to count actual objects. But in their desire to be explicit about the nature of the curriculum, teachers may try to include unnecessary detail into the reporting system. Instead of stating that Johnny can count by rote through nine, some behavioral reports break that objective into nine separate objectives such as "counts by rote to 1, counts by rote to 2," and so forth. An excessive amount of detail fails to give the parent a reasonable idea of the child's overall progress and is time-consuming for the teacher. Objectives should be as inclusive as possible (see chapter 3).

2. Some subjectivity enters into the categories used to evaluate how well the child has mastered each objective. On one day a child may be able to perform at a relatively high level; on another day objectives mastered at an easier level may be completely forgotten. Whether mastery should consist of perfect performance on a few samples of behavior or "reasonably accurate" performance on a large number of occasions is a point of disagreement.

3. Some areas of the curriculum are not well suited to a mastery approach. Some courses are offered as exploratory experiences; for example, the student needs only to experiment with different art forms and is not expected to reach any particular level of accomplishment. Mastery approaches are best suited to areas of the curriculum that are agreed upon as basic and necessary, such as reading and arithmetic, and are less suited to more complex objectives, particularly in noncognitive areas and in elective subjects.

4. Behavioral reporting presumes that teachers will have the materials and help necessary to provide remediation or to allow students to work on more advanced topics if they have already met course objectives. Schools that attempt to individualize instruction by developing sequential objectives to be mastered at the child's own rate of progress have found it possible to do so only if the teacher is provided with materials at different levels of complexity. Furthermore, each objective requires that the teacher develop a number of different tests to measure whether or not the objective has been mastered. For example, an objective might state that the child will "identify examples of squares, circles, triangles, and rectangles." If only one example of each concept is provided, the student may soon learn that a particular object is a square but might not be able to form the concept of a square by differentiating between squares of different sizes and objects that are not squares. To avoid this difficulty, teachers must construct a variety of criterion tests.

5. Objectives sometimes use technical terminology that may be confusing to parents. For example, the objective "adds from 1 through 9 using the commutative law" may be perfectly clear to teachers and perhaps to students, but few parents are familiar with the technical terms.

Some examples of behavioral reporting systems are offered in tables 17.3 and 17.4 for mathematics and reading, respectively, designed for an ungraded elementary school system in the state of Washington. Although it is not possible to reproduce the entire set of objectives, examples are provided to clarify some of their essential characteristics.

First, note that each objective is first measured by a pretest to avoid having the child spend instructional time working on skills in which he can demonstrate competence or mastery. This test should be given as early in the school year as possible. The teacher may prefer to indicate the percentage of items responded to correctly on the pretest rather than the R, P, M coding system identified at the top of tables 17.3 and 17.4.

Second, the level of mastery required may differ for each objective. While all students must learn to count by rote through 9 (table 17.3, level 1), it may

Table 17.3. A Behavioral Reporting System for Elementary Mathematics

Code: X = Not yet presented by teacher
R = Remedial help recommended
P = Making reasonable progress toward objectives; recommend additional practice
M = Mastered

	Pretest	Progress	Posttest
Level 1			
Counts by rote through 9			
Identifies orally numerals through 9			
Writes numerals through 5			
Recognizes the number for groups contained through 5 by counting members in corresponding sets			
Identifies and describes a set by using many collections of objects			
Arranges members of sets in order as to height and length by using objects and pictures			
Predicts the next object in a sequence, such as ○ □ ○ □ _ _ _			
Level 2			
Identifies and describes equivalent and nonequivalent sets by using collections of various objects in comparing two sets			
Identifies and describes equal sets arranged in different patterns			
Identifies and describes subsets, recognizing smaller groups within a larger group, excluding the empty set			
Matches the numeral with the number of members in sets up to 5			
Identifies the printed word with the number of members in a set through 5			
Identifies orally the penny, nickel, and ¢ sign, using coins and associating symbol 1¢ with 1 penny, 5¢ with a nickel			
Identifies orally the numbers for groups contained through 9 by counting the numbers in corresponding sets			
·			
·			
·			
Level 30			
Uses proportions to find a number when the percent is known			
Computes percent of error in measurement problems			
Computes the volume of polygons using the metric system			
Identifies complimentary and supplementary angles by drawing and labeling each			
Computes the angles of polygons and intersecting lines			
Computes the arithmetic mean of a series of numerals			
Adds and subtracts positive and negative integers			
Multiplies and divides positive and negative integers			
Uses tables to determine solution for an equation in two variables			
Identifies the median in a series of numerals			

Table 17.4. A Behavioral Reporting System in Elementary Reading

Code: X = Not yet presented by teacher
R = Remedial help recommended
P = Making reasonable progress towards objective; recommend additional practice
M = Mastered

	Pretest	Progress	Posttest
Reading Readiness: Visual Discrimination			
Level A			
Selects similar and different pictures			
Selects similar and different objects other than pictures			
Selects relative sizes, lengths, heights			
Identifies capital and small letters asked orally			
Orally names each letter presented visually			
Identifies groups of letters as words			
Circles each word in a sentence			
Matches letters to sample			
Identifies colors of objects by pointing			
Names colors that are visually presented			
Matches color name to color word			
Orally identifies printed name of color			
Evaluative Comprehension			
Level A			
Supplies parts of an incomplete picture			
Marks portions of picture that are absurd			
Level B			
Selects picture that belongs to a different concept			
Marks picture that does not belong in a story sequence			
Marks sentence that does not belong to a paragraph			
Level C			
Selects sentence that is a consequent of a story			
Answers questions (1–2 words) about a picture			
Draws a picture illustrating a story read			
Selects author's purpose			
Level K			
Justifies in writing why a conclusion is valid or invalid			
Identifies statements as facts or inferences			
Compares or contrasts two editorials on same topic			
Identifies form of propaganda used in advertisement			
Identifies author's bias or prejudice			
Identifies implied main idea			
Library Skills			
Level A			
Points to the title of a book or story			
Tells a story from a book of pictures			
Level B			
Points to the author and title of a book			
Moves finger from left to right and top to bottom of page			
Level C			
Locates page number of story from table of contents			
Indicates whether a book contains a specific story			
States whether a book is fiction or not fiction			

Level J

Locates specific information in *World Almanac* _____

Synthesizes information found in *World Almanac* and encyclopedia_____

not be as important for students to identify the median (level 30) or to predict the next object in a sequence. But it is important to specify what constitutes mastery on each objective, perhaps by indicating these criteria next to the objective itself or on the reverse side of the reporting form.

Third, when pretest results indicate that the students have not mastered a particular objective or skill, instructional strategies need to be selected to help them reach learning criteria. These criteria should be set at reasonable levels. Different objectives and different levels of expectancy might be prepared for different students.

Fourth, it may be necessary to rearrange objectives within and between levels, depending on school organization and the amount of time needed to reach certain objectives. In schools emphasizing continuous progress (each child works at his own rate of speed independent of his grade level), students might be required to master a certain number of levels over a period of several years before transferring to a junior or senior high school. But in schools in which students are promoted annually by grade level, successful completion of a year's course of study might mean mastering some minimum number of levels each year.

Generally a student is allowed to take an examination when he believes he is capable of mastering an objective. For example, at level 30 in table 17.3, a student may have taken a pretest on "computing an arithmetic mean" and not have any items correct. His pretest score would then be 0. After studying how means are computed he may feel prepared to take his first test. If ten items are given, the criterion for mastery may consist of any number correct up to ten. Should he have five out of ten correct, for example, the teacher would place 50 percent under the column titled "Progress" and in the row that corresponds to the appropriate objective. If he obtains mastery on the third test, an M could be placed in the "Posttest" column. If at any point the student seemed to be making little or no progress, his score on the test along with an R would indicate the teacher's belief that remedial help was required.

The symbol P is reserved for the column marked "Posttest," which is a summary of the child's progress in meeting each objective throughout the school year. A P signifies that although the child has not yet mastered the objective, he is making reasonable progress and that remedial services are not indicated. An M means that the child has mastered a course objective; an R informs the parent and his next year's teacher that the level of attainment was not sufficient for mastery and that some form of remedial intervention is recommended. Any objective not taught (because of lack of time) would contain an X in the "Posttest" column.

Using Reporting Systems for Various Purposes

Selection and Placement

Marking systems have been widely used to select individuals into institutions or organizations and to place them in curricula in which they are most likely to be successful. Many universities, for example, require some minimum high school grade point average to admit a student; sometimes employers are interested in grades as predictors of probable success within the organization.*

Most studies concur that previous marks, despite their limitations, tend to be one of the best predictors of future academic success. One reason marks predict subsequent achievement is that both earlier and later instructors often include the same type of information in determining a student's mark. A student who is in constant trouble may end up with a low mark even though his test scores may be quite high. The same factors that led him into trouble at an earlier time may well get him into the same difficulties with his subsequent teachers, and the mark would reliably measure teacher dissatisfaction, although it might not be a valid measure of the student's accomplishments. Furthermore, a student's grade point average is determined by many marks, and idiosyncratic ratings cancel each other out.

In general, the extent to which marks are useful predictors of "success" depends on the nature of the criterion. If the criterion is also based on academics, such as in predicting college freshman grades from high school grade point averages, predictive validity coefficients generally vary between .50 and .65; when criteria are more remote (such as in predicting long-term success), correlations drop considerably.

When marks are used for selection, their comparability is important. One school district may have a policy of assigning mostly high marks, whereas another may fail many students. Selecting students on the basis of marks assumes that the distributions of marks are equal from all schools or that they will be transformed into standard scores to make them more comparable (Davis 1964).

Even within the same school teachers may have the problem of making marks comparable. One teacher may tend to be a "hard grader," whereas another may be easier. A student who received a grade of C in one class might possess the same amount of knowledge as a student with an A in another class. Here again it is necessary to transform scores to z scores or other types of standard scores if comparability is to be maintained.

The most commonly used criterion for academic success is the student's grade or mark. The student's marks, academic aptitude, and class standing are

---

* In Griggs v. Duke Power Company, Mr. Chief Justice Burger of the U. S. Supreme Court delivered the opinion of the Court that the high school completion requirement is discriminatory (and illegal) unless it can be demonstrated that graduation is specifically related to job success.

most often used as predictors, not only because they correlate well with subsequent marks but also because they are easier criteria to justify to those who are not selected. For example, there is some evidence that social class, the mother's educational level, the father's income, the geographical region of the family home, and the high school principal's estimates of success can improve predictions of academic marks, but the serious social and ethical consequences that may result persuade most admissions officers to disregard such personal data (Mayhew 1965).

Remediation

Diagnosing student learning difficulties involves two levels of evaluation. First, students who need some form of remediation must be *identified*. Consistently low test scores and low marks imply the need to intervene and modify student behavior. Second, the *specific areas of weakness* must be determined. It is one thing to realize that a child is having trouble with reading but quite another to discover what type of trouble he is having. Unfortunately the traditional report card provides an average or composite rating that conceals specific strengths and weakness.

When teachers examine previous report cards of students and find that some students are consistently receiving low marks, they should recommend diagnostic testing to pinpoint the types of difficulty. If students are weak in curriculum areas in which no published diagnostic tests are available, teachers will have to construct their own diagnostic tests. The teacher will also have to decide the seriousness of the student's deficiency before embarking on the arduous task of constructing diagnostic instruments. It is relatively simple to find or construct diagnostic tests in reading and mathematics, but it is much more difficult—and perhaps not as crucial—to do so in science, social studies, or art. Reading and mathematics are basic to most other areas of the curriculum, and a child who is having trouble with either will be penalized in most of his courses until remediation is provided. This is not necessarily true of other subjects.

Behavioral mastery systems are particularly valuable in diagnosing and evaluating specific aspects of the curriculum. Each of the teacher's objectives is stated, and the student's progress toward that objective is delineated. However, if a student is weak in different subjects, the teacher may have some difficulty in deciding which objective should be met first. If objectives are placed in ascending order of difficulty, the teacher can begin with the simplest task and progress to the more complex.

Feedback

Certainly the most important purpose of any reporting system is to communicate the child's progress, strengths, and deficiencies. Any system that fails to inform parents accurately and meaningfully may confuse, frustrate, and anger them. Unless parents understand and agree with the philosophy and procedures underlying a district's reporting system, it can widen the gap instead of improving relations between the school and the home. Sometimes, of course, understanding is not always appreciated by the student (see figure 17.12).

Parents are not the only ones who are interested in student achievement. Many segments of business, labor, and the professions are also concerned with student performance. Many school districts attempt to maintain good public relations by preparing information sheets that inform interested groups about the nature of the curriculum, the average levels of student performance on standardized tests, and how many students continue their education beyond high school.

Feedback is also important to the students themselves. It gives them an idea of their achievement level and can help them make more realistic decisions.

© 1969, Washington Star Syndicate, Inc.

Figure 17.12

They need to know not only how well they are meeting teacher or school objectives but also how well they are doing in comparison to individuals with whom they are most likely to compete. The student who contemplates entering a four-year college should know how he stands in relation to others who are contemplating the same decision. Standardized tests can often provide this information.

Motivation

The use of marks to motivate students has been investigated in a number of studies. In extensive research on the effects of teacher comments on subsequent student grades, Ellis Page (1958) asked teachers to rank students in their classes on the basis of the first regularly scheduled examination and to divide them into triads, with the highest three students forming the first triad, the next three students in the second triad, and so forth. Each teacher was given a specially constructed die marked *N* for no comment, *F* for free comment, and *S* for specified comment. Within each triad students were assigned to the *N, F,* or *S* groups by a toss of the die.

Examination papers were returned to students with both numerical and letter grades on them. Students in the no comment group received only the teacher's marks; students in the free comment group received marks and any type of comment the teacher wanted to make about the student's progress; those in the specified comment group received marks and a predetermined comment, depending on how well the student had done. For example, students who received high letter grades received the comment "Excellent, keep it up," whereas students who failed the test were told, "Let's raise this grade!"

Page found that on the final examination the students from both the free comment and specified comment groups did much better than those who received no comments from the teacher. Interestingly, the greatest gains were made by the failing students who were encouraged by teacher comments to raise their grades.

In another study Lewis Goldberg (1965) tested the hypothesis that the grading policy of the instructor affects student achievement. In his study college students were graded by several methods: *strict* (no As, with a mode of D), *lenient* (no Fs, with a mode of B), *bimodal* (no Cs, with modes of B and D), *normal* (mostly Cs), and *rectangular,* where an equal number of students were given each grade. Goldberg found that students performed equally well in all five groups. At least for college students, then, it appears that the distribution of grades has little, if any, effect on students' achievement levels.

Goldberg's study does not determine whether students would achieve equally well if no grades were assigned. Unfortunately there is no conclusive answer to this question because no long-term studies on the effects of different kinds of grading systems have been compared. There is evidence that incentives *can* improve learning and that students who have been given specific feedback perform better than those who are given no knowledge of how well they performed. However, the type of incentive that is most effective for different kinds of students is still being debated. Until these issues have been resolved, perhaps the best teachers can do is to emphasize the use of reporting systems as feedback mechanisms rather than as incentives.

Summary

1. Test results should be reported if proper decisions are to be made, if students are to receive feedback on their progress, if members of the com-

munity are to be effective in supporting the schools, if parents are to help students plan for the future, and if school administrators are to evaluate the effectiveness of programs and curricula. Methods that teachers can use to disseminate and report test data are discussed in this chapter.

2. Barriers to the effective use of tests include the failure to place teachers on test selection committees, the failure to define the purposes of testing, the failure of some testing programs to provide useful and uniform norms and information about students, teachers' lack of experience in interpreting tests to students and parents, the inconvenient locations of test files, and the failure to specify the objectives of education.

3. Twelve criteria for an adequate testing program are:
   a. Schools should develop testing committees whose membership is broadly represented.
   b. Test programs should consist of both minimum and supplemental testing programs.
   c. Norms on the minimal testing program should be easily interpretable to parents.
   d. When selecting tests, a test analysis form such as the one on page 271 should be completed, with highest priority given to validity.
   e. Multilevel examinations should be used whenever possible in the minimum testing program to ensure comparability of norms.
   f. The use of separate answer sheets is advisable at the upper elementary level and beyond.
   g. Variability in the range of abilities tested is an important characteristic for tests in the minimum program.
   h. In particular, the reliability (stability) of measurements should determine the frequency of testing.
   i. The minimum testing program should emphasize achievement, with non-cognitive measures reserved for the supplemental testing program.
   j. Of all the skills taught, reading is probably most crucial; for that reason, reading tests should be administered annually if the reading achievement of students is low.
   k. For diagnostic purposes most tests should be administered early in the school year; testing late in the year can provide information on the effectiveness of school programs.
   l. The minimum testing program should be changed only for good reason.

4. An example of how one testing program was developed emphasized that the tests selected in one district might not be appropriate in another.

5. Tables and graphs can be used to present data. The horizontal axis of a graph is called the X axis or abscissa; the vertical axis is the Y axis or

ordinate. The known or independent variables are plotted on the abscissa; the predicted values or dependent variables are plotted on the ordinate.

a. Line graphs can be used to compare changes in means at different times by connecting points corresponding to values listed on the X and Y axes.

b. Histograms consist of columns having heights that correspond to frequencies; on histograms the Y axis should start at 0 to avoid incorrect impressions.

c. The bar graph consists of horizontal bars having lengths that correspond to frequencies. Usually the bars are separated from one another to indicate that each represents some discrete category. The X axis should begin with 0 to avoid misconceptions.

d. Pie charts are used to show how a total value is divided into proportions. A circle could be divided in half, for example, to show that half the students are male.

e. Pictographs can show frequencies by using pictures to represent numbers.

6. Suggestions for reporting standardized test results include:

a. IQ scores should probably not be reported directly to parents because they are often misunderstood as measures of capacity. As academic or scholastic aptitudes expressed in percentiles, however, they are less likely to be misinterpreted. Relating these scores to criteria on expectancy tables can be meaningful to parents and students.

b. Because grade equivalents on achievement tests are both interpolated and extrapolated, they are difficult to explain to parents. Parents too often believe that these scores are standards that all children are expected to reach.

c. Percentiles are probably most easily interpreted to parents. The teacher should remember that these percentiles yield ordinal measurements. The characteristics of the norm group are also important.

d. Scores from noncognitive tests are the most difficult to report, but they can be used to encourage parents to discuss their children's problems.

7. Four criteria for reporting pupil progress are:

a. Objectivity or agreement among individuals on the meaning of terms used on report cards is important.

b. Reporting to parents should occur before the end of the quarter or semester to allow parents an opportunity to help their children.

c. Student reporting systems should be reliable. Reliability can be increased by using specific terms on report cards rather than vague generalizations. Basing marks on more than a single observation can also improve reliability.

d. Reporting systems should be valid; they should not be influenced by extraneous or irrelevant characteristics of the student's behavior.

8. When marks are combined from different assignments, quizzes, and examinations to form a composite or total mark, the weight of each component in this total is a function of the standard deviation of the assignment, quiz, or exam. To ensure that all variables are given equal weight, each person's score on each project should be converted to a z score. If one assignment is to receive twice the weight of another, the z scores on that assignment can be doubled and a mean of the weighted z scores can be obtained.

9. Pupil progress can be reported by various methods:

   a. *Conferences.* Conferences between parents and teachers can help resolve misunderstandings and improve communication. Some suggestions for conducting the conference are:

      i. Put the parent at ease.

      ii. Ask the parents' beliefs or attitudes before unnecessarily contradicting them.

      iii. Find out what parents would like to discuss.

      iv. Ask questions that encourage parents to discuss problems.

      v. Try to get the parents' reactions to the child's progress.

      vi. Admit errors or lack of information.

      vii. Establish goals for the conference.

      viii. Summarize what has been discussed in the conference.

      ix. Write a summary of the nonconfidential aspects of the conference that can help other teachers.

   b. *Written communications.* These may be used to inform parents about the child's progress in school and allow parents time to think about these problems. But they are (1) time-consuming to write; (2) often written vaguely; do not come to terms with the child's problems; (3) often misunderstood by parents; and (4) require care in spelling, grammar, and penmanship. Suggestions were made for improving the quality of written communications.

   c. *Letter grades.* These grades can be assigned on the following criteria:

      i. *Intraclass comparisons based on relative achievement.* Marks can be assigned by letting the average level of performance equal some grade, such as C. (If students are homogeneously grouped, the mean can be set at some other level.) Differences in marks can be determined by school policy or by gaps in the distribution.

      ii. *Intraindividual comparisons based on ability level.* Marks may be assigned by comparing the student's level of performance with some estimate of his ability. These estimates are often subjective but can be improved by having knowledge of the student's past performance and measures of scholastic aptitude. Ideally this approach could benefit the less able student who is working as hard as he can. In practice, however, "ability" may be very difficult to measure and the "regression effect" may work against students with higher aptitude scores.

iii. *Effort.* Assigning marks on the basis of effort is often used to encourage students who have tried to succeed, but it penalizes the more able student, who may not need to try so hard. By using effort as the criterion, higher grades may be received by students who perform at a lower level than others in the class. One way to avoid this problem is to have separate marks for effort and achievement.

iv. *Improvement.* The amount of student gain in knowledge can also be used to report achievement, but difference or gain scores tend to be unreliable. Also, students who do well in class initially will have a harder time showing improvement.

v. *Predetermined levels of achievement.* Sometimes teachers assign marks that are based on fixed values, such as 90–100 percent = A, 80–89 percent = B, and so on. These marks appear to allow all students to pass or fail, depending on the percentage of items answered correctly. But the difficulty level of each item will affect the number of students who will fall into each percentage category. Large discrimination indices will also spread students out and include more of them in lower and higher categories.

vi. *The normal distribution.* "Curve grading" occurs when teachers assign the same percentage of As as Es (failures), and the same percentage of Bs and Ds, with most students receiving average or C marks. But there is no good reason to require that a fixed percentage of students fail. Furthermore, the normal curve is a theoretical curve that one would not find in any classroom.

No entirely satisfactory system has been developed for reporting student achievement. Some degree of flexibility and judgment will enter into any decision the teacher makes. Palmer offers seven ways in which teachers grade students dishonestly.

10. *Behavioral mastery reports* are one method that can be used to report student progress. They have the following advantages:

a. Parents are informed about school objectives in clearly defined terms.

b. They are diagnostic.

c. They are nonpunitive if plans for remediation are included on the report.

d. Competition for grades is reduced.

e. The student is not compared with others but with some minimum standard of accomplishment.

f. Reporting student progress includes a decision-making procedure regarding how that student can be helped.

g. Instruction can be individualized since students need not be working on the same materials.

The disadvantages of behavioral reporting systems include:

a. They are difficult to prepare.

b. Subjectivity enters into the establishment of "mastery" criteria.

c. Not all areas of the curriculum lend themselves to the "mastery" approach.

d. They assume that teachers will have the materials and assistance needed to help children who are not mastering course content.

e. Some objectives may be stated too technically for parents to readily understand.

Behavioral mastery reports consist of a series of "terminal behaviors" organized sequentially. A pretest indicates whether or not the child has mastered an objective. Each student is allowed to work at his own rate of speed. After studying to master an objective, the student takes a criterion-referenced test. For each area in which the student experiences difficulties in learning, remedial help should be provided; as each objective is mastered, the student can proceed to the next most complex objective.

11. Marks can be used for various purposes:

a. *Selection.* High school marks, despite their many limitations, are one of the best predictors of college success. If marking practices vary greatly among high schools, marks can be converted to standard scores. Marks are also used as criteria of student achievement or knowledge. Although other variables may also correlate highly with marks (socioeconomic status, for example), most college admission officers prefer not to use such data because of social and ethical consequences.

b. *Remediation.* Marks can be used to identify students who are having trouble in areas of the curriculum such as reading and mathematics. Consistently low marks in areas of the curriculum that require much reading indicate that the student needs further diagnostic testing to determine the specific types of reading errors he is making. Behavioral mastery systems are useful in pointing out objectives on which students need help.

c. *Feedback.* The purpose of most reporting systems is to provide feedback to the parent, the child, and other teachers. If students are to improve, they need specific knowledge of their strengths and weaknesses.

d. *Motivation.* Comments by teachers on examination papers increase student motivation. One study compared different grading policies—strict, lenient, bimodal, normal, and rectangular—but students performed equally well in all five groups. Because there are virtually no long-term studies of the effects of different kinds of marking systems on student achievement, the effects of marks in motivating students is unknown.

Suggested Readings

Davis, J. A. "Use of Measurement in Student Planning and Guidance." In Robert L. Thorndike, ed., *Educational Measurement,* 2d ed., pp. 671–79. Washington, D.C.: American Council on Education, 1971. A general account of how tests can be used in counseling with students.

Ricks, James H., Jr. "On Telling Parents about Test Results." *Test Service Bulletin of the Psychological Corporation,* no. 54 (December 1959): 1–4. A brief but clearly written report on how test results should be reported to parents.

Terwillinger, James S. "Individual Differences in the Marking Practices of Secondary School Teachers." *Journal of Educational Measurement* 5, no. 1 (Spring 1968): 9–15. The marking practices of thirty-nine teachers were studied. The author shows the relationships of marks assigned by teachers to various characteristics of students.

18

The preceding chapter described the various characteristics and techniques of disseminating measurement in education. Evaluation was characterized as a decision-making process that depends on reliable and valid observations about pupil progress, but it is necessary to describe the specific steps involved in the evaluation process itself. This chapter summarizes different strategies used to evaluate pupils and programs.

The Meaning of *Evaluation Strategies*

An *evaluation strategy* is a plan for describing the procedures used to arrive at a decision about a student or program. An evaluation strategy that specifies the use of tests to measure stated objectives will reduce the probability that unnecessary testing will occur and will increase the probability that students will learn as effectively as possible.

Although it is not absolutely necessary, strategies are often presented in the form of flowcharts that map out the steps for reaching an educational decision. The flowchart serves many of the same purposes as a road map except that alternative procedures are planned for different contingencies.

In general, strategies should be simple but help to clarify what the teacher should do under different circumstances. Because no one strategy contains all elements necessary for decision making, this chapter will describe a number of different strategies.

The IPI Strategy for the Evaluation of Individualized Instruction

IPI, or Individually Prescribed Instruction, is a project being developed and implemented at the University of Pittsburgh. IPI presumes that instruction is most effective when it is highly organized and sequenced to ensure student mastery of concepts, particularly those in mathematics, reading, and science. The purpose of IPI is to allow each student to progress at his own rate by ensuring that prerequisite skills are mastered before more complex skills are introduced.

The strategy underlying IPI has been described by C. M. Lindvall and Richard Cox (1969) in the form of a flowchart that depicts the steps used to evaluate and monitor student progress (see figure 18.1). This evaluation strategy requires that a *placement test,* constructed to broadly sample each area of the curriculum, be administered early in the year. The placement test has the following characteristics:

1. Its purpose is to place individuals differentially in various units of instruction.
2. It is designed to yield a maximum of information in the least amount of time.
3. It helps determine what general skills the child has.
4. It is *criterion-referenced;* that is, its purpose is not to measure individual differences so much as it is to determine whether specific areas of the curriculum have been learned to mastery.

Figure 18.2 shows how each level of attainment is described on a profile sheet. Level A, for example, contains the simplest content, and unit I, the most complex. Within each of these nine areas, a checkmark means that the content has been mastered at that level. The highest level mastered describes the performance of a student. The hypothetical student whose progress is shown in figure 18.2 would be described as being at level C in numeration, place value, and fractions; at level D in addition, subtraction, multiplication, division, and combination of processes; and at level E in systems of measurement, time, money, and geometry.

The placement test determines into which specific unit of instruction the student is placed. Different placement tests are designed for each grade level, but since each grade contains an achievement span of several years, the teacher's responsibility is to determine which level is most suitable for each pupil. Students may take placement tests at different levels to establish optimal levels of assignments.

The selection of an instructional unit for a child requires the use of a

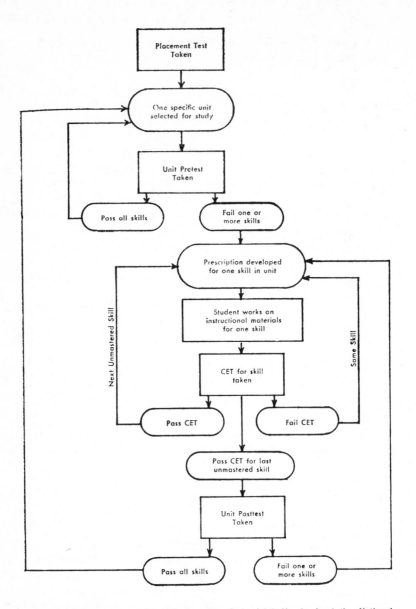

From C. M. Lindvall and Richard C. Cox, *The Sixty-eighth Yearbook of the National Society for the Study of Education* (1969), Part II, p. 174, Ralph W. Tyler, ed., by permission of NSSE.

Figure 18.1. Flow-chart of Steps in the Cycle of Evaluating and Monitoring of Pupil Progress in the IPI Procedure

Student A

	A	B	C	D	E	F	G	H
Numeration............	√	√	√					
Place Value...........	√	√	√					
Addition..............	√	√	√	√				
Subtraction...........	√	√	√	√				
Multiplication.........	√	√	√	√				
Division..............	√	√	√	√				
Combination of Processes	√	√	√	√				
Fractions.............	√	√	√					
Money...............	√	√	√	√	√			
Time.................	√	√	√	√	√			
Systems of Measurement.	√	√	√	√	√			
Geometry............	√	√	√	√	√			

Lindvall and Cox, 1969, p. 174.

Figure 18.2. Example of a Performance Profile Indicated by Mathematics Placement Tests

diagnostic pretest to discover specific strengths and weaknesses (see table 18.1). An instructional unit, for example, might encompass a number of different objectives, and the purpose of the pretest is to discover in which specific areas the child is having problems. Thus the placement test determines what unit the child will take, and the pretest indicates in what specific aspects of the unit the child needs help.

But suppose that the child does not fail any items on the pretest. According to the strategy (figure 18.1), another unit is selected, and the child takes that pretest. This process is continued until a pretest indicates that the child has failed to master at least one of the skills presented at that level.

The student's progress is monitored to the point where all skills have been passed. *Curriculum-embedded tests* (CETs) are provided as checks to make sure that the student has mastered each particular objective in the sequence. If any of these CETs are failed, the child is "recycled" and the same skill is re-taught; if CETs are passed, the child is allowed to work on the next unmastered skill.

A reevaluation of the child's progress utilizes unit posttests to make certain that he has learned all the skills required in the unit. If the posttest is passed successfully, he is ready to proceed to the next unit; if he fails the posttest, the procedure is repeated for the unmastered skill.

In summary, Individually Prescribed Instruction (IPI) is a method that depends largely on data obtained from placement, diagnostic, and mastery examinations. The placement tests indicate on which units the child will work; diagnostic tests help determine those specific areas within a unit of instruction in which the child needs help; and mastery tests inform the teacher whether or not the child has met minimum unit objectives. After completing each test, the

Table 18.1. Description of Selected Mathematics Curriculum Units

Unit No.	Level	Unit Label	Short Description	Approximate Conventional Grade Level
23	D	Numeration	Counting and skip counting to 1,000	3–4
24	D	Place value	Makes place value charts to thousands	
25	D	Addition	Begins addition with carrying	
26	D	Subtraction	Begins subtraction with borrowing	
27	D	Multiplication	Begins multiplication as repeated addition with factors to 5	
28	D	Division	Begins division as partition with divisors to 5	
29	D	COP (combination of processes)	Problems requiring many processes	
.				
.				
.				
37	E	Numeration	Identifies odd and even numbers; converts mixed decimal fractions	4–5
38	E	Place value	Place value to millions; begins exponents	
39	E	Addition	Addition with carrying to 4 digits	
40	E	Subtraction	Subtraction with borrowing to 3 digits	
41	E	Multiplication	Uses associative and distributive principles and does simple multiplication with carrying	
42	E	Division	Uses ladder algorithm for divsion; solves problems using n as variable	
43	E	COP (combination of processes)		

child is either allowed to progress through the sequence or he is returned to the point where he has experienced some learning problem.

Not all teachers, of course, will be able (or will want) to have programs as highly structured as IPI. But all good teaching involves many of the same principles. That is, placement, diagnosis, and mastery decisions are needed for each child.

In most schools children are placed in classes according to chronological age, but the range of abilities within each class can easily span five or more grade levels. Using mental or educational age grade equivalents for placement can reduce some of this spread in ability, but it will not eliminate individual differences, which will tax the abilities of even the most creative teachers.

The procedures used to diagnose reasons for student failure are complex but necessary if the child is not to repeat assignments already mastered or if he is not to be given instruction at too advanced a level. Diagnosis is particularly important in reading and mathematics because so many other subjects depend on strong backgrounds in both.

Finally, the decision of whether or not a child should be permitted to advance in a sequence of instruction or be given remediation is a crucial one no matter how structured the curriculum is. The failure to utilize measurement optimally does not avoid decision making; it simply increases the difficulty of making reasonable decisions.

The CIPP Strategy for the Evaluation of Student Programs

One of the most interesting strategies used to evaluate school programs has been offered by Daniel Stufflebeam (1967) at Ohio State University. Stufflebeam was particularly concerned about the generally low quality of evaluation in Title III projects approved under the provisions of the Elementary and Secondary Education Act, passed by Congress in 1965. The purpose of Title III was to encourage school districts to implement "innovative and exemplary" programs in various aspects of the curriculum. But one of the requirements of Title III was that recipients of federal funds hold themselves accountable to the public by evaluating the impact and effectiveness of these programs.

As Stufflebeam noted, the results of these evaluations were not particularly satisfying. One reason was that evaluation strategies were crude and generally not well understood by Title III project directors and staff. Although powerful experimental techniques were available for research, many of the questions posed by Title III teachers were not amenable to experimentation.

It is important to remember that although Stufflebeam's evaluation strategy was initially designed for Title III, the types of projects funded under that act varied considerably in scope, and his strategy has wide applicability to other than federally funded projects. Teachers were encouraged to develop innovative and exemplary teaching practices and to submit them for review. Virtually all areas of the curriculum received funding through Title III or other similar acts passed by Congress, and many teachers have participated in these programs. The position taken here is that all teachers are obligated to evaluate the effectiveness of their teaching and to modify, improve upon, or eliminate phases of a curriculum that require such action.

Four major educational decisions that require evaluation have been identified by Stufflebeam: context, input, process, and product. The strategy is called the CIPP Evaluation Model (the four letters are the initial letters of each type of decision). Figure 18.3 summarizes the meaning of these four stages of evaluation.

The Strategies

	Context Evaluation	Input Evaluation	Process Evaluation	Product Evaluation
OBJECTIVE	To define the operation context, to identify and assess needs in the context, and to identify and delineate problems underlying the needs.	To identify and assess system capabilities, available input strategies, and designs for implementing the strategies.	To identify or predict, in process, defects in the procedural design or its implementation, and to maintain a record of procedural events and activities.	To relate outcome information to objectives and to context, input, and process information.
METHOD	By describing individually and in relevant perspectives the major subsystems of the context: by comparing actual and intended inputs and outputs of the subsystems; and by analyzing possible causes of discrepancies between actualities and intentions.	By describing and analyzing available human and material resources, solution strategies, and procedural designs for relevance, feasibility, and economy in the course of action to be taken.	By monitoring the activity's potential procedural barriers and remaining alert to unanticipated ones.	By defining operational and measuring criteria associated with the objectives, by comparing these measurements with predetermined standards or comparative bases, and by interpreting the outcome in terms of recorded input and process information.
RELATION TO DECISION-MAKING IN THE CHANGE PROCESS	For deciding upon the setting to be served, the goals associated with meeting needs and the objectives associated with solving problems, i.e., for planning needed changes.	For selecting sources of support, solution strategies, and procedural designs, i.e., for programing change activities.	For implementing and refining the problem design and procedure, i.e., for effecting process control.	For deciding to continue, terminate, modify, or refocus a change activity and for linking the activity to other major phases of the change process, i.e., for evolving change activities.

From Daniel L. Stufflebeam, *Theory Into Practice*, 6, No. 3 (June 1967), p. 130.

Figure 18.3. The CIPP Evaluation Model: A Classification Scheme of Strategies for Evaluating Educational Change

Context Evaluation

Context evaluation is the delineation and specification of the project's environment, its unmet needs, the population and sample of individuals to be served, and the project objectives. Context evaluation provides a rationale for justifying a particular type of program intervention.

As an example, consider a particular rural community where library and cultural resources are meager or unavailable. The closest cultural center may be too far for many of the students to reach easily, especially if they have to depend on public transportation. The school library has some reference books but is staffed only on a parttime basis during the school day. One movie theater is nearby, but it is open only on weekends. Few students have seen plays, musicals, art exhibits, scientific displays, a zoo, or other benefits available to students in urban communities.

Context evaluation involves taking stock of the situation and determining priorities among needs. At least four major questions can be posed at this initial state of evaluation (Stufflebeam 1971):

1. What unmet needs exist in the context served by a particular institution?
2. What improvement-oriented objectives should be pursued in order to meet identified needs?
3. What improvement-oriented objectives will receive the endorsement and support of the community?
4. Which set of objectives is most feasible to achieve?

Stufflebeam (1971, p. 269) has suggested some examples of the information required to answer these four questions. For example, unmet needs can be determined by examining the goals of the school and the performance of its students, and then comparing the two. If the school expects a stated minimum level of achievement, student learning can be measured to determine whether objectives have been met.

Which objectives should be pursued depends on the conditions that account for differences in goals and student attainment. For example, if some students fail to reach criterion levels established for the district as a whole, their cases can be examined in greater detail to find the reason. Stufflebeam (1971) also suggests that examining the literature published by other evaluators who have experienced similar problems may help explain why student performance is low.

Whether or not a community will endorse a suggested improvement can be determined through polling or interviewing individuals and community groups. These techniques were described in chapters 15 and 16.

Determining which set of objectives is most feasible depends on estimates of costs and resources available to the community and school district. School principals, budget officers, the superintendent, and (ultimately) the board of education will have to decide which objectives are likely to have the greatest value to students and the community.

Input Evaluation

The second stage of the CIPP strategy is *input evaluation.* The purpose of input is to list the potentials of the school. For example, teachers may find that the school is able to provide resource personnel in curriculum, testing, counseling, administration, social work, and health services.

In addition to gaining the cooperation of personnel, input evaluation should help list potential "solutions" to the problem. Stufflebeam (1971, p. 270) has raised five questions that input evaluation should be capable of answering:

1. Does a given project strategy provide a logical response to a set of specified objectives?
2. Is a given strategy legal?
3. What strategies already exist with potential relevance for meeting previously established objectives?
4. What specific procedures and time schedules will be needed to implement a given strategy?
5. What are the operating characteristics and effects of competing strategies under pilot conditions?

Whether or not a proposed project will resolve the problems specified by its objectives is primarily a logical decision. Suppose, for example, that the rural district referred to earlier decided to "enrich" the lives of its students by contracting for an educational television cable. Is that likely to increase the enrichment of students? Although it is tempting to argue affirmatively, other questions need to be asked: How many students now watch television after school hours? What will educational TV replace that is currently being shown or other channels? Are parents willing to forego their regular programs to watch educational TV? Answers to these questions may require expert opinion, or it may be necessary to conduct community-wide polls.

The legality of a strategy can best be answered by school attorneys. For example, is it legal for teachers to require students to watch programs on television? Would this requirement discriminate against children whose families cannot afford television sets? What penalities, if any, can or should be levied against a child whose family believes that television is immoral or corrupting?

Examining similar programs in other communities or conducting library research of the pertinent literature can help determine what strategies or programs that can help meet objectives are available. An examination of indexes to documents listed by various Educational Resource Information Centers (ERIC) can help locate what other districts and projects have tried in similar situations. Many university libraries are able to provide computer-assisted document searches for published studies.

The procedures and time schedules to be followed in implementing a strategy can be worked out with a simple time line that also specifies which individuals will be responsible for each activity. Who, for example, is going to go through the ERIC document search? When must this be completed if the project is to be on schedule? Should legal counsel be obtained before or after the ERIC search, before or after a community-wide poll is taken?

The effectiveness of programs can also be estimated from literature searches such as that provided by ERIC. Sometimes small pilot studies may be undertaken in a district to discover whether or not some proposal has merit and what some of the potential problems might be. Some schools have found it useful to allow teachers to visit neighboring schools or districts to observe how a particular program operates before such a program is recommended.

Process Evaluation

Chapter 3 defined *process objective* as one that describes *who* will be responsible for a given activity, *what* the activity is, and *when* it will be completed. Within the CIPP framework, *process evaluation* helps provide feedback to the teacher (or project director) on how the project is progressing. Its purpose is to help monitor the various aspects of the project so that potential problems can be identified and remedied.

Stufflebeam (1971, p. 271) has raised four questions about process evaluation that help define its role:

1. Is the project on schedule?
2. Should the staff be retrained or reoriented prior to completion of the present project cycle?
3. Are the facilities and materials being used adequately and appropriately?
4. What major procedural barriers need to be overcome during the present project cycle?

Whether or not the project is on schedule is easily determined if specific time lines have been prepared. In some federally sponsored projects an external auditor is required to ensure that the schedule is being followed. But even in smaller projects initiated by teachers, some concern for scheduling is important if the project is to get underway properly.

Staff retraining is necessary in many projects. New equipment and procedures call for training sessions in which staff members can use materials and ask questions about them. In large projects staff training can require a full-time position; in smaller programs teachers may need help from supervisors or from the manufacturers or publishers of instructional materials. Even the decision to adopt a new textbook may require extensive retraining of teachers, particularly if the approach is new or complex.

No matter how extensive the training is, process evaluation should indicate how the materials and facilities are being used. This can be determined by observing teachers while they use these materials. These observations can be improved by following the suggestions offered in chapter 16.

Informal reports from teachers participating in projects can help determine barriers to effective instruction. Stufflebeam (1971) suggests the use of forums to discuss these problems and recommends that a suggestion box be made available for teachers. In smaller projects initiated by individual teachers, instructional barriers will be easier to detect since the projects can be monitored more easily.

Product Evaluation

Chapter 3 defined *product objectives* as statements that indicate what the student must *do* or *know* as a result of instruction. *Product evaluation* is the final stage in the Stufflebeam CIPP strategy. Its function is to allow the project director (or teacher) to make a decision regarding the continuance, termination, or modification of the program.

Product evaluation requires a comparison of the outcomes of a project with its stated objectives. These outcomes may consist of test scores, observations, ratings, interviews, sociometric data, and so forth, which are then compared with specific objectives. Stufflebeam (1971, p. 272), suggests four kinds of illustrative questions that can be asked about product evaluation:

1. Are objectives being achieved?
2. What probabilistic statements can be made about the relationship between procedural specifications and actual project attainment?
3. To what extent were the varied needs of individual students met as a result of the project?
4. What is the long-range worth of the actual achievements in relation to the mission of the host institution?

Whether or not objectives have been achieved depends on the extent to which measurements correspond to criteria. For example, a criterion could call for at least 80 percent of students to watch a minimum of one "enrichment" TV program per month. A student poll could then be taken to determine whether or not this objective had been reached.

Experiments can also compare the effectiveness of two or more programs. Ideally students should be assigned randomly to each of the programs to eliminate or reduce the probability that initial differences among students will account for differences on a criterion task. An experimental treatment is accorded one group and withheld from the control group. Differences between experimental and control groups at the end of the project will either be attributable to chance (if differences between groups are small) or "statistically significant" (if differences are greater than what would be expected on the basis of chance). (The details of experimental strategies are beyond the scope of this text but the interested student should see Campbell and Stanley (1963) or Sax (1968).

The effectiveness of one experimental treatment or program over another is usually evaluated by comparing the *means* of the various groups. In practice, any number of means can be compared simultaneously. The comparison involves the determination of the likelihood that the differences among the two or more means are due to chance. For example, if the posttest scores of an experimental and control group are both exactly 25.0, it would be concluded that no differences were found and that the measured effectiveness of the two approaches was equal. But suppose that the experimental group mean is 26.0 and that of the control is 25.0. Would it be best to argue that the difference is due to chance or that the difference is *significant* (i.e., reliable)? The decision to be made is similar to deciding whether there is a "true" difference between two coins each flipped 100 times. On the basis of chance alone, the most likely expected value would be 50 heads and 50 tails for each coin, or a mean of .50 on each. In practice, however, even the same coin will not always yield exactly 50 heads and 50 tails. That is, each coin displays some *variability*. When means are compared, differences between them should be attributed to chance if those differences are small, particularly if each mean is based on a small number of cases and a large standard deviation of scores. Means based on small Ns and large standard deviations tend to be unreliable. (A large standard deviation indicates that scores are inconsistent and tend to vary.) *Experimental evidence required by an evaluation strategy should be planned with expert help.* This help can often be obtained from district research staff members or from evaluation specialists in colleges and universities.

The extent to which individual differences have been met as a result of the project is best evaluated by examining the case histories of students who failed to reach criterion. In experimental comparisons students who were in the least successful group could be interviewed, or item analyses of their errors could be obtained (see chap. 9 about diagnostic uses of item analysis data).

Although experiments can point out the differences in attainment between two or more groups, the decision to continue a project or to modify or terminate it depends on other factors as well. The long-range worth of the program, for example, could be analyzed by comparing project costs with benefits to students and society. If costs tend to be low relative to benefits, the teacher will probably want to recommend the adoption of the program; if benefits are low relative to costs, the project will probably be discontinued or modifications will be recommended.

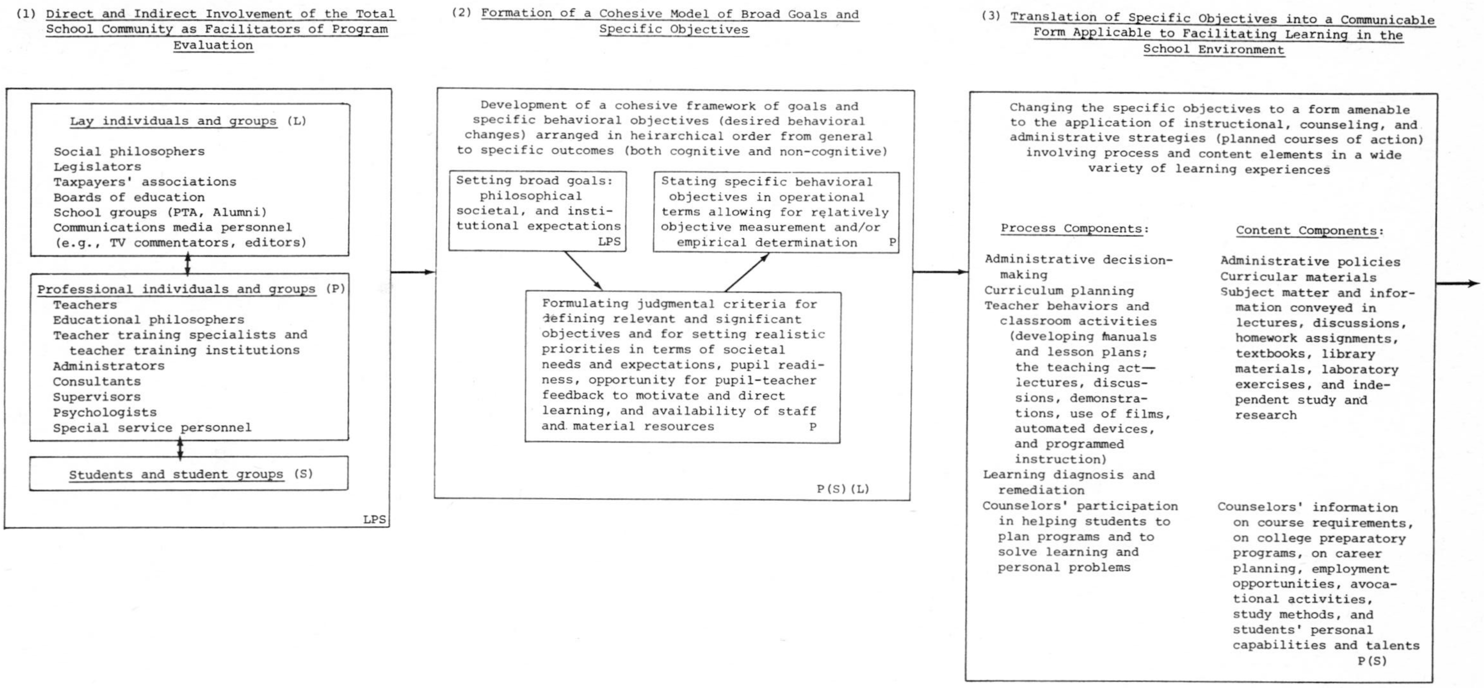

(1) Direct and Indirect Involvement of the Total School Community as Facilitators of Program Evaluation

Lay individuals and groups (L)

Social philosophers
Legislators
Taxpayers' associations
Boards of education
School groups (PTA, Alumni)
Communications media personnel
(e.g., TV commentators, editors)

Professional individuals and groups (P)

Teachers
Educational philosophers
Teacher training specialists and
  teacher training institutions
Administrators
Consultants
Supervisors
Psychologists
Special service personnel

Students and student groups (S)

LPS

(2) Formation of a Cohesive Model of Broad Goals and Specific Objectives

Development of a cohesive framework of goals and specific behavioral objectives (desired behavioral changes) arranged in heirarchical order from general to specific outcomes (both cognitive and non-cognitive)

Setting broad goals: philosophical societal, and institutional expectations
LPS

Stating specific behavioral objectives in operational terms allowing for relatively objective measurement and/or empirical determination P

Formulating judgmental criteria for defining relevant and significant objectives and for setting realistic priorities in terms of societal needs and expectations, pupil readiness, opportunity for pupil-teacher feedback to motivate and direct learning, and availability of staff and material resources P

P(S)(L)

(3) Translation of Specific Objectives into a Communicable Form Applicable to Facilitating Learning in the School Environment

Changing the specific objectives to a form amenable to the application of instructional, counseling, and administrative strategies (planned courses of action) involving process and content elements in a wide variety of learning experiences

Process Components:

Administrative decision-making
Curriculum planning
Teacher behaviors and classroom activities (developing manuals and lesson plans; the teaching activities, discussions, demonstrations, use of films, automated devices, and programmed instruction)
Learning diagnosis and remediation
Counselors' participation in helping students to plan programs and to solve learning and personal problems

Content Components:

Administrative policies
Curricular materials
Subject matter and information conveyed in lectures, discussions, homework assignments, textbooks, library materials, laboratory exercises, and independent study and research

Counselors' information on course requirements, on college preparatory programs, on career planning, employment opportunities, avocational activities, study methods, and students' personal capabilities and talents
P(S)

Figure 18.4. The Metfessel and Michael Strategy of Evaluation

(4) Instrumentation Necessary for Furnishing Measures Allowing Inferences about Program Effectiveness

Selection and/or construction of a variety of relatively objective tests, scales, and indices furnishing measures from which inferences can be drawn concerning the degree to which cognitive and non-cognitive objectives have been attained

Standardized aptitude, ability, and achievement tests

Standardized self-inventories concerned with adjustment, appreciations, attitudes, interests, and temperament

Standardized observational devices such as rating scales and check lists concerned with achievement, affectivity, and products

Informal teacher-made tests and scales concerned with knowledge, skills, problem solving, attitudes, and appreciations

Interviews and questionnaires

Miscellaneous indicators of the behaviors of students, school personnel, or community members such as GPA or numbers of awards, absences, days in attendance, withdrawals, transfers, referrals, telephone calls, books and magazines read, peer nominations, elective offices held, service points earned, frequency and types of disciplinary actions, requests for information, articles published, conferences held, concerts attended, memberships in professional or social organizations, time spent in community activities, and many others

P(S)

(5) Periodic Observations of Behaviors

Periodic administration of tests and scales and use of other indicators over sufficient period of time to furnish reliable and valid indices of the status at a given moment and of changes in behaviors sampled relative to specific objectives

P

(6) Analysis of Data Given by Status and Change Measures

Data analysis preparatory to drawing conclusions about the effectiveness of the school program

Typical statistical methods

1. Comparing obtained measures (corresponding to objectives) with those of norm groups

2. Significance of differences between means and proportions

3. Intercorrelations of measures including multiple regression and factor analysis

P

(7) Interpretation of Data Relative to Specific Objectives and Broad Goals

Setting judgmental standards and values concerning what are considered desirable levels of performance on the totality of measures collated and summarized through comprehensive measurement, observation, and other samplings of behaviors--standards that permit interpretations concerning how adequately (meaningfully and significantly) measures of a performance, standing, or change on each of several outcomes (objectives) considered to be important approximate the minimal acceptable levels within the expectations of the evaluation model; a basis for drawing conclusions about the direction of growth, the progress of students, and the effectiveness of the total school program and for validating hypotheses which both lay and professional individuals have had concerning the relative effectiveness of various administrative, counseling, and instructional strategies

P(S)

(8) Recommendations Culminating in Further Implementation, Modifications, and in Revisions of Broad Goals and Specific Objectives

On the basis of the inferences and interpretations made concerning the nature and degree of the relationship of program outcomes to antecedent instructional, counseling, and administrative strategies, suggestions are made concerning either how certain specific as well as broad objectives which are unrealistic or unattainable in present form can be modified or new changes can be made in the strategies employed. Feedback in the form of information communicated to all individuals involved in the school program is essential if the evaluation efforts are to result in substantial improvements in the school program. Once the outcomes are made known to all individuals concerned, the cycle of the evaluation process starts once again

P(S) (L)

From Newton S. Metfessel and William B. Michael, *Educational and Psychological Measurement*, 27, No. 4 (Winter 1967), pp. 934-935.

Other Evaluation Strategies

The fact that the IPI and CIPP evaluation strategies were discussed does not mean that other strategies are of less value. For example, Newton Metfessel and William Michael (1967), have presented a strategy that should also be of interest to teachers and program evaluators. Their model or strategy consists of eight steps:

1. Direct and indirect involvement of various members of the community, including laymen, professional school personnel, and students
2. Construction of a set of educational objectives and priorities
3. Development of a set of behavioral objectives useful for instruction
4. Development of criterion measures needed to evaluate school programs
5. Administration of tests and other instruments considered valid for specific purposes
6. Analysis of data, such as the comparison of mean test performance
7. Interpretation of data using various judgmental standards and values
8. Formulation of recommendations needed to improve the project or program being evaluated

The Metfessel and Michael strategy can be shown diagrammatically (see figure 18.4). Although it is not quite as simple as the CIPP, it has the advantage of specifying which individuals (laymen, professionals, and students) have primary and secondary responsibilities for each of the eight steps. Seven pages of criteria that can be used to evaluate projects have also been provided, including standardized measures and scales, teacher-made instruments and techniques, demographic data for students (absenteeism, anecdotal records, assignments, and so forth), demographic data related to teachers (advanced courses, publications, dismissals, transfers), and data related to community behaviors (attendance, alumni participation, mail and telephone calls received, and so forth).

Perhaps one other strategy should be noted in this chapter—that of Robert Glaser (1970). Glaser has been particularly effective in specifying the conditions necessary for the evaluation of instruction, although there are similarities between his strategy and those discussed by Stufflebeam and Metfessel and Michael. Six steps are required by Glaser for the evaluation of instruction:

1. Outcomes of learning are specified. Glaser argues that objectives should be stated behaviorally because these objectives indicate what skills the student must attain. He particularly warns against accepting vague (implicit) goals simply because they are easier to state. Glaser also emphasizes the need for criterion-referenced measurements since these are specifically related to curriculum re-

quirements. Norm-referenced testing is seen as ineffective because a learner is compared with others, not with a degree of competence required to meet some objective.

2. A detailed diagnosis is made of the learner's *entry behavior*—the student's repertoire of learned skills and the prerequisite background necessary for learning. Entry behavior differs from aptitude in that the former is related to a specific task (e.g., learning the alphabet), whereas aptitudes tend to be more general.

3. Instructional alternatives are provided to the student. These alternatives can be based on differences in learning rate, amount of previous accomplishment, the amount of practice the student will need, and the extent to which the student can learn on his own. Student failure on any selected instructional alternative can—at least theoretically— be followed by another alternative on which the student has a higher probability of being successful.

4. The student's performance is observed and monitored. At first this monitoring is continuous, but as the student develops his learning styles, less observation by the teacher should be necessary. This monitoring of behavior helps provide selective feedback to students and teachers.

5. The reassessment of behavior leads to an optimal instructional alternative. This reassessment is based on the available instructional alternatives as well as on the monitoring of the student's behavior. Glaser brings out a crucial point that is not thoroughly discussed by other strategies—the nature of the criterion task. Should it be acquisition time (the time required to learn a task), the ability to retain information once it has been learned, the degree to which the student is able to generalize or transfer his knowledge, differences between pretest and posttest scores, or the ability to learn skills on his own? The point is that the optimum instructional alternative depends on what the teacher wishes to accomplish.

6. Methods for evaluating and improving upon instruction are needed. Here Glaser refers to the need for "formative evaluation," or ongoing feedback designed to improve each aspect of the program. Unfortunately a theoretical model of instruction that can accept input, evaluate it, and then revise or modify the system has not been developed.

Concluding Remarks

The purpose of this chapter has been to introduce the student to various strategies for evaluation in education and to help place many of the details described throughout this text into a perspective that is useful to both practicing and prospective teachers.

Many of the concepts discussed in this chapter have been referred to in detail in previous chapters. Now, after having completed the text, the student may want to review the topics described previously. The previous chapter, "Disseminating and Reporting Test Information and Data," also contains strategies for evaluating and reporting pupil and class progress. The use of mastery reporting systems, for example, is a part of the strategy of most programs that stress individualized instruction. Certainly this is a crucial part of IPI and Glaser models.

In comparison with the rich sources of information about educational evaluation that are currently available, this text can do no more than introduce the student to those concepts and procedures necessary to *begin* a teaching career. No one is capable of assimilating all the information about evaluation— nor, fortunately, is this necessary. The student should understand the nature of measurement and how tests can be used most effectively by teachers. Instead of being the end of a book, hopefully this will be the beginning of a rewarding and productive career based on a science and technology of education.

Summary

1. This chapter introduces the student to various evaluation strategies or decision-making plans.

2. One plan for individualizing instruction is called IPI, or Individually Prescribed Instruction. By using placement, diagnostic, and mastery examinations, students are allowed to progress at their own rate, particularly in reading, mathematics, and science. The steps followed by this plan include:

   a. Placement examinations are used to select the units of instruction in which the child needs help. The placement examinations are criterion-referenced to indicate which general skills have not been mastered.

   b. A unit of instruction which contains a number of pretests used for specific diagnosis is selected for each child. If all skills on the pretest are passed, the student is given another unit of instruction with additional pretests. For each skill not passed on the pretest, a prescription or assignment is given to the child to provide him with the background necessary to learn that skill.

   c. When the child reaches the point where he has learned the skills in a unit, he takes criterion-referenced or mastery tests to demonstrate that he has the competence to begin a new unit. A posttest on all skills in the unit is given to make sure that each skill learned separately is being retained by the student when the unit has been completed.

3. Although not all teachers will have the facilities, time, or desire to institute

a program that is as highly structured as IPI, all good teaching involves the ability to place the child at an appropriate level, to diagnose his learning difficulties, and to demonstrate his mastery of essential skills.

4. The CIPP (context, input, process, and product) evaluation strategy is a plan for evaluating the effectiveness of school programs (curricula, courses of study, materials, and so forth). Teachers have the obligation to evaluate their courses of study and to modify them when evidence so warrants.

   a. *Context evaluation.* The context of a program is an assessment of needs, the objectives that are derived from these needs, and the characteristics of the individuals to be served by the program. The evaluator must be able to determine priorities among needs and to select objectives that have the greatest probability of being carried out successfully.

   b. *Input evaluation.* The purpose of input evaluation is to determine which particular strategy is most likely to resolve the problem identified in the context phase. Generally input evaluation is a logical procedure that estimates the extent to which a given strategy is likely to be successful. This means that alternative procedures have to be weighed and a choice made among them. The choice can be made on the basis of legal requirements, evaluating how similar programs have worked in other school districts, and trying out the strategy under limited, experimental conditions.

   c. *Process evaluation.* Process evaluation monitors the operations of a project to make sure that it is functioning efficiently. The efficiency of a project or program can be measured by finding out whether it is on schedule, whether each person in the program is doing the job described for him, and whether facilities and materials are being used properly, and by trying to discover the conditions that are responsible for barriers that impede the operation of the project.

   d. *Product evaluation.* Product evaluation indicates whether or not objectives specified for the program are being met. Some objectives state what the minimum level of student performance must be for the project to be judged successful. In other instances an experiment can be conducted to compare the performance of students in an experimental program with the performance of a control group. By relating differences between the mean scores of these groups to chance expectations, it is possible to determine whether differences are "statistically significant" or probably due to chance. Cost/benefit ratios can also be prepared to help determine whether costs are worth the expenditures to continue a project.

5. Metfessel and Michael have suggested an eight-step strategy to evaluate programs. Their strategy indicates which individuals have primary and secondary responsibilities for each phase of the evaluation.

6. Another useful strategy has been provided by Glaser. His six steps include (1) specifying the outcome of learning; (2) diagnosing the student's *entry behavior* or repertoire of learned skills needed for a given task; (3) providing

instructional alternatives; (4) monitoring the student's behavior throughout the learning sequence; (5) reassessing behavior to select an optimal instructional alternative; and (6) providing ongoing feedback on each phase of the program to make it as effective as possible.

7. Many of the basic concepts developed in this chapter have been referred to elsewhere in the text. The strategies that teachers can use in marking or grading students are a case in point. The purpose of most criterion-referenced tests is to indicate how well students have learned essential skills, concepts, and knowledge. It is expected that the principles of educational measurement and evaluation form the basis of a science and technology of education that can help teachers and students make effective decisions.

Suggested Readings

Atkinson, R. C., and Paulson, J. A. "An Approach to the Psychology of Instruction." *Psychological Bulletin* 78, no. 1 (July 1972): 49–61. The authors describe the steps required to evaluate instructional strategies and show how measurements are related to these strategies.

Block, James H., ed. *Mastery Learning: Theory and Practice.* New York: Holt, Rinehart and Winston, 1971, 152 pp. A paperback containing six chapters plus annotated readings on the theory, practice, and research findings related to mastery learning.

Emrick, John A. "An Evaluation Model for Mastery Testing." *Journal of Educational Measurement* 8, no. 4 (Winter 1971): 321–26. Some of the assumptions underlying mastery are presented.

Sanders, James R., and Cunningham, Donald J. "A Structure for Formative Evaluation in Product Development," *Review of Educational Research* 43, no. 2 (Spring 1973): 217–236. An excellent summary of various descriptions and procedures relating to formative evaluation.

Welch, Wayne W., and Walberg, Herbert J. "A National Experiment in Curriculum Evaluation." *American Educational Research Journal* 9, no. 3 (Summer 1972): 373–83. This study describes a national evaluation of Project Physics.

Wittrock, M. C., and Wiley, David E., eds. *The Evaluation of Instruction: Issues and Problems.* New York: Holt, Rinehart and Winston, 494 pp. This is the result of a symposium on educational measurement and its relationship to instruction. Each presentation is followed by interesting discussions.

Glossary

Accomplishment quotient:	The ratio of educational age to mental age multiplied by 100, or

$$AQ = \frac{EA}{MA} \times 100$$

Incorrectly used to compare achievement with "ability."

Achievement test:	A test designed to measure formal or "school-taught" learning.
Acquiescence:	A response bias that refers to the subconscious tendency to overrespond to the "agree" items in a true-false test or to the middle alternatives in a multiple-choice examination. See *Response biases.*
Age equivalent norms:	The chronological age level at which students perform (usually on standardized achievement tests). See *Educational age.*
Age of arrest:	The "plateau" region on a mental age curve where group performance fails to increase. Typically the age of arrest occurs in the middle to late teens and results from the inability of items to discriminate among individuals of differing chronological age.
Alternative:	A choice or option in multiple-choice tests.
Ambiguity:	The extent to which (1) experts or (2) the most knowledgeable persons in a class disagree with a keyed response.
Anchoring:	The procedure used to establish the extreme response positions on attitude scales.
Anecdotal report:	An objective, written description of a child's behavior obtained through direct observation; a report of an incident obtained through *time* or *episode sampling.*
Anticipated achievement:	Predicted grade or standard score equivalents on achievement tests.
Aptitude test:	A cognitive test designed to predict achievement prior to instruction or selection.
Assembly test:	A mechanical *performance test* that requires the examinee to assemble or construct different objects.

Attenuation, correction for:	Formulas used to estimate the maximum validity when predictors, criteria, or both are made perfectly reliable.
Attitude test:	An examination that measures the tendency to respond favorably or unfavorably toward specific groups, institutions, or objects.
Bar graph:	A series of parallel lines, usually horizontal, used to compare the frequencies of discrete variables.
Basal age:	The lowest age level on an intelligence test at which the individual responds correctly to all items.
Battery:	Two or more tests standardized on the same persons and designed to measure different aspects of achievement or aptitude.
Behavioral objective:	An objective that describes what the student must *do* to demonstrate the attainment of the goal.
Ceiling age:	The age level on an intelligence test at which the individual misses or fails all items.
Central tendency:	A measure of the "average" performance of individuals. See *Mean, Median,* and *Mode.*
Central tendency, error of:	The tendency of raters to avoid making extreme judgments on rating scales.
Chance score:	The most likely score individuals will attain by randomly responding to all items; computed by multiplying the number of items by the probability of responding correctly on each item by chance (e.g., on a 100-item true-false test, the chance score is $100 \times \frac{1}{2}$, or 50).
Checklist:	A type of rating scale containing items that are checked or left blank depending on whether some aspect of behavior has been observed or not.
Chronological age:	Age computed from one's date of birth; used as the denominator in many *quotient norms.*
Cleavage, sociometric:	Divisions within a group characterized by the failure to select members of the group who differ in sex, race, and the like as measured by *peer rating.*
Clique, sociometric:	Individuals who select one another and exclude others as determined by *peer rating.*

Completion test: A test in which items are presented in the form of an incomplete sentence to be completed by examinees.

Composite method: The combining of scores from different predictor tests to maximize validity. A low score on one test may be compensated for by a high score on another.

Confidence weighting: A procedure used to score true-false and multiple-choice items by giving different amounts of credit depending on whether or not responses are correct and the degree of student certainty.

Continuous variable: A value that may be subdivided into a smaller unit, particularly as the accuracy of measurement is increased.

Controlled observation: A highly structured and planned observational task that appears to the examinee to be uncontrived.

Correlation, coefficient of: A measure of the extent to which two variables are related; an average product of z scores that is positive if paired z scores have the same sign or negative if signs are opposite. The lowest correlation is 0 and the highest is ± 1.0. The symbol for correlation is r. See *Regression line.*

Cost/benefit ratio: An estimate of the costs and benefits to be derived from new program. Used as a criterion or standard for evaluating programs.

Covariance: Technically the *correlation coefficient* between two variables multiplied by their respective *standard deviations.* The covariance is similar to the correlation among items; the greater the covariance among items, the more they correlate with one another and thus measure the same ability or trait. The covariances are contained in the numerator of the *Kuder-Richardson formula 20* reliability.

Creativity test: A measure of novel or divergent thinking.

Criterion: A measure considered to be a standard of excellence.

Criterion contamination: The unacceptable procedure of allowing criterion ratings to be influenced by or "contaminated" with prior knowledge obtained from the measure to be validated.

Criterion-referenced test: A test designed to measure content as specified by *behavioral objectives;* generally any test having a specified minimal level of attainment and not designed to measure individual differences.

Cross-validation: The process of readministering a set of items originally given to one sample of individuals to determine the extent to which item characteristics (e.g., *discrimination, difficulty*) are retained with another group. Cross-validation is particularly necessary if items were selected originally from a small sample, where chance factors could have determined item characteristics.

Culture-fair test: A test that does not overselect or underselect members of various groups when they would have performed equally well on a *criterion*.

Cutoff method: A selection strategy where the failing of any test in a *battery* eliminates the applicant. The cutoff method does not allow individuals to compensate for low scores on one test by a high score on another.

Cutting score: A test score used to separate persons selected from those rejected. High cutting scores help select more highly qualified persons but reduce the number of persons given a chance to succeed.

Decile: A point that divides a distribution into equal tenths. Thus the first decile refers to a point below which 10 percent of the scores fall; the second decile corresponds to the 20th percentile; the third decile, the 30th percentile, and so on.

Determination, coefficient of: The square of the correlation coefficient, r^2, times 100. The coefficient of determination indicates the percentage of factors held in common between or associated with two correlated variables; i.e., if the correlation between two variables is .80, then the two variables overlap by $100(.80^2)$, or 64 percent.

Deviant response hypothesis: The theoretical position (Berg) that argues that atypical responses are indicative of abnormality no matter what the test content is.

Deviation IQ: A *standard score* used to express intelligence test performance usually with a mean of 100 and a standard deviation of 16 points. Computed by converting all scores to z *scores,* multiplying by 16, and adding 100.

Diagnostic test: A test used to point out specific strengths and weaknesses of individuals. Standardized diagnostic tests are available in mathematics and reading.

Difference score: A value obtained by subtracting an individual's score on one test from his score on another test. Generally these difference or gain scores tend to be unreliable, particularly when the separate reliabilities of the two measures are low and when there is a high correlation between them.

Difficulty level: Usually the proportion of individuals responding correctly to an item. Thus the larger the proportion, the easier the item is. The symbol for item difficulty is p. The difficulty level of a test is the sum of the item difficulties (Σp) divided by the number of items. However, because Σp equals the mean, test difficulty may be defined as the mean divided by the number of items; the higher this value is, the easier the test is.

Discrete variable: A value that exists as an amount not divisible into more exact parts—the number of students in a room, for example.

Discrimination index: A measure of the extent to which an item is capable of separating the most from the least knowledgeable students using either *external* or *internal criteria.* As described in this text, the discrimination index, D, is obtained by subtracting the proportion of students responding correctly on an item in upper and lower criterion groups. The maximum positive value of D is 1.0, and the minimum, 0. Negative discrimination indices usually suggest some deficiency in an item.

Distracter: An incorrect *alternative* on a multiple-choice item.

Educational age: The *chronological age* level at which an individual is functioning on an *achievement test;* abbreviated EA. An EA of 12-6 in reading means that a student is doing as well as the average twelve-and-one-half-year-old on a reading achievement test.

Empirical keying: The development and selection of test items based on their ability to discriminate between or among various groups, such as "successful" men in different occupations.

Episode sampling: A method of obtaining *anecdotal reports* by systematically recording specific types of episodes, such as crying, aggression, and so forth.

Equivalence: See *Reliability.*

Error of estimate: The difference between a predicted and an *obtained score.* See *Standard error of estimate.*

Error of measurement:	The difference between an *obtained* and a hypothetical *true score*. See *Standard error of measurement*.
Error variance:	That portion of variance responsible for unreliability.
Essay test:	A test containing questions requiring the student to respond in writing. Essay tests emphasize recall rather than recognition of the correct *alternative*. Essay tests may require relatively brief responses or extensive responses.
Evaluation:	The process of making decisions based on the results of measurements or observations. Evaluation *strategies* describe the elements that compose this decision-making process.
Expectancy table:	A table used to estimate or predict the probability of obtaining *criterion* scores from different values on a predictor test.
Expressed interests:	Interests measured by asking individuals to describe activities they enjoy or for which they have a preference.
External criterion:	A standard of excellence used to validate test scores; also, a criterion used to select items that discriminate among those persons judged or rated high and low on the job.
Extrapolation:	The process of extending measurements above and below those grade levels actually measured by a test. Used particularly on *grade equivalent norms* to estimate performance outside of the range of grade levels covered by the test.
Factor:	A trait, ability, attribute, or construct derived from *factor analysis* procedures. Factors consist of items that tend to correlate with each other but are independent of other factors.
Factor analysis:	A mathematical procedure used to extract or identify those factors that account for the correlations among items or test scores. The purpose of factor analysis is to simplify complex interrelationships among different tests on observations.
Factor loading:	The correlation of items or tests with each of the *factors* extracted in a *factor analysis*. For example, if an item correlates .80 with factor A, .03 with factor B, and −.02 with factor C, the loadings are .80, .03, and −.02 with

the three *factors,* respectively. The item is therefore a good measure only of factor A.

Feedback: The use of test results to inform students and parents about student progress. Feedback may compare students with others, as in *norm-referenced tests,* or students may be compared with some level of performance, as on *criterion-referenced tests.*

Forced-choice item: A test item consisting of two or more statements (often matched on *social desirability* but differing in validity); the individual is to select the statement most descriptive of himself. To the extent that *social desirability* is controlled, differences in endorsement represent differences in the trait being measured.

Formative evaluation: The use of tests to obtain *feedback* during the course of a program rather than at its termination point (see *Summative evaluation*). Formative evaluation allows projects to be modified and improved upon while they are in progress.

Frequency distribution: A tabular and sequential arrangement of scores showing the frequencies or numbers of persons obtaining different score values; used to summarize large numbers of scores.

g: Spearman's general factor of intelligence which was presumed to be present on all measures of intelligence.

Gambling: A *response set* produced by the use of correction for guessing formulas (see *Guessing, correction for*). When faced with a penalty for responding incorrectly, some persons are more willing than others to gamble or attempt items, although they may have equal amounts of knowledge. This tendency for some persons to gamble reduces validity since the test measures a personality trait rather than the degree of knowledge.

Generosity error: Sometimes called the *leniency error;* the tendency of raters to avoid the most negative categories on rating scales.

Grade equivalent norms: The grade level at which a student performs on a standardized achievement test; abbreviated GE. A GE of 6.5 means the student is doing as well as the average child in the fifth month of the sixth grade.

Graphic rating scale: A line containing different response positions and *anchored* at least on extreme ends. By checking some point on the line, the rater indicates his evaluation of a trait along a continuum.

Group factor: A factor that correlates with some but not all variables in a set.

Group test: A test designed to be administered to more than one person at a time.

Guessing, correction for: A penalty for responding incorrectly on true-false or multiple-choice items. The most often used formula is

$$\text{rights} - \frac{\text{wrongs}}{\text{no. of alternatives minus 1}}$$

This simplifies to rights minus wrongs on true-false tests. Items omitted are counted as being neither right nor wrong.

Guess-who technique: A *peer rating* procedure in which individuals nominate members of their group who best appear to fit certain roles or character descriptions. After a role description is read by the teacher, students "guess who" is being described. The more nominations a person receives, the greater the agreement among members of the group.

Halo effect: The tendency of raters to judge specific traits or behaviors on the basis of previously obtained over-all knowledge about the individual being rated. The halo effect is a source of invalidity since ratings are influenced by a general impression of an individual and not necessarily by knowledge of the specific trait being evaluated.

Histogram: A graph consisting of vertical bars of different lengths. The base of each bar on the horizontal axis corresponds to the midpoint of each score interval; the height of each bar corresponds to the score frequency.

Homogeneity: See *Reliability*.

Immediate objective: An objective over which the school has direct control. Usually refers to goals involving training rather than to long-term objectives that can be realized only after a formal training program has been completed.

Implicit objective: An objective that specifies what students must know, realize, or appreciate. Implicit objectives are not directly observable but must be inferred from student behavior.

Inclusive objective: A broadly stated objective that subsumes more *restricted objectives*. Inclusive objectives summarize and comprise subsets of objectives. For example, five separate objectives could be written or the teacher could write one inclusive objective indicating that students will "print the first five letters of the alphabet."

Incremental validity: See *Validity*.

Individual test: A test designed to be administered to one person at a time. Such a test is usually given to observe how the individual responds. Many oral tests and tests designed for young children are also individually administered.

Intellectual status index: *Mental age* divided by the average *chronological age* of students in a given grade level. Used by California Test Bureau to predict *anticipated achievement* norms.

Intelligence: A theoretical construct usually equated with scholastic aptitude; measured by cognitive tests that contain items designed to be culture-free.

Intelligence quotient: Abbreviated IQ; originally the ratio of *mental age* to *chronological age* times 100 (to eliminate decimals). Currently, however, IQ refers to a *standard score* norm. See *Deviation IQ*.

Interest: A preference for one activity over another.

Internal consistency: See *Reliability*.

Internal criterion: Scores on a test used to separate individuals into upper and lower groups for *item analysis* purposes. Usually the total score is used to separate groups.

Interpolation: The process of estimating intermediate values in a series of measurements. On *grade equivalent norms,* for example, values between grade levels are estimated and not obtained from direct measurements.

Interval scale: A scale yielding equal differences in the attribute being measured in much the same way that the difference between 80° and 90° is the same as the difference between 120° and 130°.

Interview: As used in measurement, a planned procedure for the obtaining of oral information in a face-to-face situation. Respondents may be given freedom to respond in any way

they prefer, or questions may be structured so that responses may be categorized easily.

Interviewer bias: The personal characteristics (such as age, sex, race) of
interviewers that affect the responses given them by interviewees.

Inventoried interest: Interests as measured by tests or inventories. Because
each inventory measures different types of preferences,
each can be expected to yield different inventoried interests.

Inventory: Usually a series of items having no "correct" answer but
which measure individual differences in affect (e.g., personality, interests, attitudes).

Ipsative scale: A scale in which the mean scores on different subtests are
the same for all individuals. These scales are used for
intraindividual comparisons because if an individual is
high on some subtests, he must be low on others; it is not
possible to be high or low on all subtests.

**Isolate,
sociometric:** An individual who is unselected on any activity as determined by sociometric choices.

Item analysis: The procedure used to determine item characteristics,
such as *ambiguity, difficulty level,* and *discrimination.* Item
analysis is used both to select items having specified characteristics and to diagnose class errors.

Key: A list or form that contains the differential weights to be
given each response on a test or inventory. For most tests,
the key contains the correct answer, which is usually accorded one point. Wrong answers receive no credit.

**Kuder-Richardson
formula 20:** A mathematical formula used to estimate internal-consistency *reliability.* It has a maximum value of 1.0 and a
minimum of zero. High Kuder-Richardson 20 reliabilities
mean that all items are highly correlated with one another
and therefore measure the same trait or ability. The formula for the Kuder-Richardson formula 20 is

$$\frac{n}{n-1}\left(\frac{SD^2 - \Sigma pq}{SD^2}\right)$$

where n = the number of items, SD^2 = the test *variance*
and Σpq = the item variance. See *Covariance.*

Line graph: Chart or graph showing means, frequencies, or changes
over time prepared by connecting lines between various

points that correspond to given values on the X and Y *Axes.*

Local norms: *Norms* derived entirely from data obtained in a given school or district. Local norms are particularly useful in atypical schools to avoid having many scores that are high or low.

Mastery test: See *Criterion-referenced test.*

Matching item: A test format that requires the student to match a series of responses with corresponding terms in a stimulus list.

Mean: A measure of central tendency sometimes referred to as the "arithmetic average." It is found by summing all values and dividing by the number of cases.

Measurement: The assignment of numbers to attributes or characteristics of persons, events, or objects according to explicit formulations or "rules."

Median: The middle point in a series of measurements after all values have been placed in sequence.

Mental age: The age level at which an individual performs on an intelligence test. For example, a mental age (MA) of 8–0 means that the individual obtained the same score as an average group of eight-year-olds.

Mental age grade placement: The grade level at which an individual performs on an intelligence test. If a child has a MAGP of 3.5, he obtained the same score as an average group of children in the fifth month of the third grade.

Mode: The most frequently occurring score in a distribution.

Multpile-choice item: An item containing a "stem" (either a question or incomplete sentence) and a number of *alternatives* from which the student is to select the correct one.

Multiple-factor theory of intelligence: Thurstone's theory of intelligence, which states that intelligence may be divided into a number of "primary mental abilities." Considered more broadly, a multiple-factor theory may also refer to any position that argues for there being different kinds of "intelligences." In this latter sense, the theories of Thorndike and Guilford may also be considered "multiple-factor theories."

Multiple-level examination: A standardized test designed to cover a wide range of grade levels.

Mutual choice, sociometric:	In *sociometry,* the mutual selection of two individuals.
N:	Abbreviation for the number of persons composing a sample.
Nominal scale:	A qualitative scale that is derived from mutually exclusive categories without regard to order.
Nonlanguage test:	A test that is administered in pantomime and that requires no language skills to respond; used primarily for deaf children. Often used as a synonym for *nonverbal test.*
Nonverbal test:	A test that de-emphasizes the role of reading, speaking, and writing; often used for aptitude and intelligence tests to predict achievement, particularly for persons who might have reading problems. See *nonlanguage test.*
Normal curve:	A mathematically defined curve that is bell-shaped in appearance. Many distributions in education approximate normal distributions with most of the scores in the center and fewer scores at the extremes. The normal curve is never found in practice since it extends infinitely above and below the mean. In a normal distribution, about 68 percent of the cases fall between z scores of $+1.0$ and -1.0.
Norm group:	Sometimes called a *standardization group;* it consists of those persons selected to be representative of specified *populations,* such as third-graders in the United States or applicants for specified types of jobs.
Norm-referenced test:	A test designed to measure individual differences on some trait or ability. See *Criterion-referenced test.*
Norms:	Distributions of scores obtained from *norm groups.* These distributions may include *percentiles, age* and *grade equivalents,* and *standard scores* (*z scores, T scores, ETS scores, stanines, deviation IQs*).
Objective test:	Any test having clear and unambiguous scoring criteria. Because multiple-choice and true-false tests can usually be scored objectively, they are sometimes referred to as objective tests.
Obtained score:	The number of points an individual receives on a test; a *raw score.* In theory, obtained scores consist of *true scores* plus *errors of measurement.*

Obtained variance: The variance of obtained scores; the square of the standard deviation of obtained scores.

Option: See *Alternative*.

Ordinal scale: A scale described as having unequal differences between successive categories of the trait being measured. Letter grades, for example, are ordinal since differences between them do not represent equal amounts of attainment or knowledge.

Overachiever: A term generally taken to refer to those students who have achievement test scores that are higher than what would have been predicted by intelligence test scores. Rather than referring to students as being overachievers, it is more accurate to refer to achievement scores as being higher than predicted by intelligence test scores. The emphasis is removed from a characterization of the student to the failure of a test to predict accurately.

p: The proportion of individuals responding correctly to an item; a measure of item *difficulty*.

Peer rating: A generic term that refers to any of a number of methods used to allow members of a group to rate one another. *Sociometry* and the *guess-who* technique are often used to obtain peer ratings.

Pegboard: A measure of hand and finger dexterity. Pegboards have rows of holes into which pegs can be placed. On some tests washers and nuts can be screwed onto pegs, and the amount of time required to complete the task constitutes the "score."

Pencil-and-paper test: Generally, a *group test* consisting of a test booklet and answer sheet on which individuals are to mark their answers; usually contrasted with *performance test*.

Percentile: That point on a distribution below which a given percentage of individuals fall. The 50th percentile, for example, is that score that divides the distribution in half. Percentiles are *ordinal* measurements.

Percentile band: A percentile band is determined by calculating the percentile that corresponds to each person's raw score and then extending that value by one *standard error of measurement* above and below that point. The larger the percentile band, the greater the amount of error and the less certain the location of an individual's *true score*.

Performance test: A test that requires examinees to perform a task rather than to answer questions. The performance subtests of the Wechsler Intelligence Scale for Children include such tasks as rearranging pictures in correct sequence, pointing to parts of a missing puzzle, assembling objects in puzzle form, and so forth.

Pictograph: A graph consisting of pictorial objects used to represent frequencies.

Pie chart: A circular chart subdivided into proportional amounts to show how each segment is related to the total.

Placement test: A test designed to predict the optimal program or course of study for an individual. For example, a placement test might be used to help a student determine which curriculum is best suited for him.

Population: Also a *universe*. The total number of individuals, items, objects, etc. Populations may be infinite (all possible items that could measure intelligence) or finite (the total number of students attending a given school). A test may be thought of as a *sample* of items selected from a population or universe of such items.

Power test: A test consisting of relatively difficult items and having generous time limits.

Practice effect: An increase in test scores resulting from having prior experience with a test.

Predictive validity: See *Validity*.

Process objective: An objective that indicates whether a particular goal has completing a task by a given date or time. Process objectives are used to monitor the progress of a program. Unlike *product objectives,* process objectives do not indicate the quality of the project or program.

Product objective: An objective that indicates whether a particular goal has been reached. The product is usually student behavior or achievement.

Product scale: An achievement measure consisting of graded samples of performance against which student behavior is compared.

Profile: A graphic presentation of an individual's pattern of scores on various subtests of an examination. Sometimes scores from different tests are compared on a profile after they have been converted to *standard scores* or *percentiles*.

Projective technique: Any of a number of relatively unstructured tasks used to measure the projections of one's personality. The classes of projective techniques described in this text include measures of association; construction, choice, expression, and completion tasks.

q: The proportion of individuals responding incorrectly to an item.

Q: See *Semi-interquartile range*.

Quartile: One of the three points that divides a serially arranged distribution into four groups having equal frequencies. The first quartile (symbolized as Q_1) corresponds to the 25th percentile. Q_2 corresponds to the 50th percentile, and Q_3 corresponds to the 75th percentile.

Quotient norms: *Norms* based on ratios, usually with *chronological age* as the denominator. Examples are:

$$IQ = \frac{MA}{CA} \times 100$$

$$\text{educational quotient (EQ)} = \frac{EA}{CA} \times 100$$

r: Symbol for a *correlation coefficient*.

Random sample: A *sample* selected from a *population* by chance; also a *sample* selected from a *population* so that everyone has an equal probability of being selected.

Range: The difference between the highest and lowest scores in a distribution used as a measure of *variability* or spread of scores. Although easy to compute, the range tends to be unreliable since its value depends only on the two extreme scores.

Rating scale: Any of a number of structured techniques used to record observations systematically.

Ratio scale: A scale having equal intervals and an absolute zero.

Raw score: See *Obtained score*.

Readiness test: A test designed to predict performance, especially in reading or arithmetic; any aptitude measure designed for primary and elementary school children.

Rectangular distribution: A distribution of scores having equal frequencies at all levels.

Regression effect: The tendency for a predicted value to be closer to its mean than a predictor is to its own mean. The regression effect occurs because extreme scores tend to be unreliable. An individual who obtains a particularly low score is unlikely to be equally low should he be retested. Similarly, a person who achieves a high score is likely to regress or rank closer to the mean on a repeated testing.

Regression equation: A mathematical formula used to predict scores on one variable from knowledge of scores on one or more other variables.

Regression line: A line drawn to minimize the sum of squared differences of scores around a predicted value.

Rejectee, sociometric: An individual who has been actively rejected by members of the peer group.

Reliability: The extent to which individual differences are measured consistently as determined by coefficients of stability, equivalence, stability and equivalence, and internal consistency or homogeneity:

1. Stability: The correlation of a set of measurements with themselves over a specified time period.
2. Equivalence: The correlation between scores on two or more forms of a test with no time interval between testings.
3. Stability and equivalence: The correlation obtained from testing individuals on two or more forms of a test over specified periods of time.
4. Internal consistency or homogeneity: The extent to which items correlate among themselves using either the *Kuder-Richardson formula 20* or *split-halves*.

Technically, reliability is the ratio of *true variance* divided by *obtained variance*. When this ratio is 1.0, there is no *error variance,* and reliability is perfect.

Response bias: A tendency on the part of examinees that invalidates test scores. In this text, the response biases of *acquiescence, social desirability,* and *deviance* were discussed.

Restricted objective: One of the elements composing an *inclusive objective;* an objective that approximates an individual item rather than a class of items.

S: A term used by Spearman to refer to *specific factors* or factors that do not correlate with other tests.

Sample: Any subset of persons, items, or the like selected from a *population*.

Sample test: As opposed to *sign test,* an examination consisting of items sampled from some *population* of items.

Scorer reliability: The extent to which two or more raters or scorers agree on the number of points to be accorded responses.

SD: The symbol for the *standard deviation*.

Selection: The process of using tests to admit individuals into institutions or to deny them admission.

Selection ratio: A ratio formed by dividing the number of individuals selected into an institution by the total number of individuals available for *selection*.

Self-report inventory: An inventory used to measure an individual's personality by asking questions about one's feelings, beliefs, opinions, and so forth.

Semi-interquartile range: Half the difference in score values between the 75th percentile and the 25th percentile; used as a measure of *variability*.

Sensory test: A test of hearing, vision, and the like.

Sigma: A general term for the *standard deviation;* the capital Greek sigma, Σ, is the mathematical symbol meaning to add whatever follows it. Thus ΣX means to add all values of the variable X.

Sign test: An examination designed to empirically distinguish between two or more groups without regard to item content; often contrasted with *sample test*.

Situational test: A contrived but lifelike task designed to measure how an individual will behave in a given situation without realizing he is being tested.

Skew: The degree of symmetry in a distribution. Distributions are "negatively skewed" when the "tail" of the distribution is to the left; they are "positively skewed" when the "tail" is to the right, with scores piling up at the left end of the distribution.

Social desirability:　A *response bias* in which individuals respond to *self-report inventories* by trying to make themselves appear favorably to others.

Sociogram:　A graphic representation showing the pattern of choices (and sometimes rejections) among members of a group.

Sociometric matrix:　A chart showing the number of times each member of a group is selected for a particular activity.

Sociometry:　A method of describing and analyzing *peer ratings,* as developed by Moreno.

Spearman-Brown formula:　A formula used to estimate the reliability of measurements when the test is increased or decreased in length. The formula is

$$\frac{kr}{1 + [k - 1]r}$$

where k = the number of times a test is increased or decreased in length, and where r is the reliability coefficient. If a test is doubled in length, the formula is

$$\frac{2r}{1 + r}$$

This formula must be used to estimate the reliability of a total number of items when *split-half reliabilities* are computed.

Specific aptitude test:　A test used to predict learning in specific subjects or occupations, such as welding, clerical work, and so forth.

Speed test:　A test containing items that are so simple that virtually no one will be expected to miss any except for carelessness. The score is determined by counting the number of items marked correctly within restricted time limitations.

Specific determiner:　Any clue in an item that suggests that a particular alternative is either correct or incorrect.

Spiral-omnibus format:　The arrangement of different types of items in ascending order of difficulty within a single test.

Split-half reliability:　See *Reliability*.

Stability and equivalence, coefficient of:	See *Reliability*.
Stability, coefficient of:	See *Reliability*.
Standard deviation:	A measure of the *variability* or dispersion of scores around the *mean*. The formula for the standard deviation is

$$\sqrt{\frac{\Sigma(X - M)^2}{N}}$$

The larger the standard deviation, the greater the spread of scores around the *mean*.

Standard error of estimate:	The estimated *standard deviation* of scores around a predicted value. Abbreviated SE_{est} and computed by the following formula:

$$SE_{\text{est}} = SD_c\sqrt{1 - r^2}$$

SD_c is the standard deviation of criterion scores and when r^2 is the square of the *reliability* coefficient. When scores are perfectly reliable, SE_{est} is zero.

Standard error of measurement:	The *standard deviation* of *obtained scores* around a theoretical *true score*. Abbreviated SE_{meas} and computed by the following formula:

$$SD\sqrt{1 - r}$$

where r is the *reliability* coefficient. If *reliability* is perfect, there are no errors of measurement, and each person received an *obtained score* equal to his *true score*.

Standardization group:	See *norm group*.
Standardized test:	As opposed to a *teacher-made test,* a standardized test is designed to be administered and scored under uniform testing conditions. *Norms* are also usually provided.
Standard scores:	A score based on the number of *standard deviations* a person is from the mean. Standard scores include *z scores, T scores, stanines,* and *deviation IQs.*
Stanine:	A *standard score* obtained by dividing the *normal curve* into nine segments for the purpose of expressing scores in a single-digit whole number from one to nine. Stanines of 1 and 9 contain the lowest scoring and highest scoring 4

percent of individuals, respectively; stanines of 2 and 8, the next lowest and highest 7 percent; stanines of 3 and 7, the next 12 percent; stanines of 4 and 6, the next 17 percent; and a stanine of 5, the middle 20 percent. When scores are converted to stanines, the shape of the original distribution is changed into a *normal curve*.

Star, sociometric: In *sociometry*, the most highly selected member of a group.

Stem: The question or open-ended statement in a *multiple-choice item* that contains the problem or task.

Success ratio: A ratio found by dividing the number of individuals judged successful by the total number of individuals admitted into a program or institution.

Summative evaluation: A decision reached near the end of a project that determines whether it has been successful or not; contrasted with *formative evaluation*.

Supplementary testing program: The discretionary part of a *standardized* testing program. Teachers are allowed to select whatever tests are needed for special purposes in a supplementary testing program. Tests required of all students are part of a district's "minimum testing program."

T score: A *standard score* having a *mean* of 50 and a *standard deviation* of 10 points. Found by multiplying the *z score* by 10 and adding 50 points to the product.

Taxonomy: A classification plan or scheme consisting of hierarchically arranged elements.

Test: Any planned, intrusive procedure or series of tasks used to obtain observations.

Teacher-made test: A test prepared by the teacher for intragroup comparison. If *norm-referenced*, the test is designed to measure differences among individuals composing the class or group. A *criterion-referenced test* is a teacher-made test that specifies minimum levels of acceptable performance.

Time sampling: A method of obtaining and recording *samples* of behavior at various time periods; used to obtain general patterns of pupil behavior at different times.

True score: A score containing no *errors of measurement;* a perfectly reliable score, sometimes defined as the *mean* of an infinite set of repeated testings with the same instrument when *practice effects* and memory are disregarded.

True variance: That part of *obtained variance* that is attributable to perfectly reliable measurements. When true variance and *obtained variance* are equal, reliability is perfect.

Two-way grid: A test "blueprint" that specifies the number of items to be included on a test according to their content and level of complexity.

Ultimate objective: A long-range goal usually not directly taught in school; contrasted with *immediate objective* over which the school has control.

Underachiever: As contrasted with overachiever, the underachiever is an individual who has *achievement test* scores that are lower than those predicted by an *intelligence* test.

Universe: See *Population*.

Validity: The extent to which *measurements* correspond with criteria.

Concurrent: The extent to which measurements correlate with a criterion when both are obtained at approximately the same time.

Construct: The extent to which measurements support the existence of an hypothesized trait or ability.

Content: The extent to which item content corresponds with objectives.

Convergent: The extent to which two or more sets of *measurements* are highly correlated and thus measure the same trait; used to obtain evidence regarding construct validity.

Criterion-related: The general term for concurrent and predictive validity.

Discriminant: The extent to which an hypothesized trait does not measure (or is uncorrelated with) variables judged to be irrelevant; used to obtain evidence regarding construct validity.

Face: The degree to which items appear to be relevant and important to examinees.

Incremental: The increase in knowledge obtained from using test scores over what would be known without their use.

Predictive: The correlation between test scores and performance on a criterion where there is a time lapse between the two.

Variability: The extent to which scores differ, spread out, or vary.

Variance: The *standard deviation* squared.

Verbal test: A test emphasizing skills in reading, writing, and oral communication.

X: The symbol for an *obtained* or *raw score.*

X axis: The horizontal axis of a graph; sometimes called the "abscissa."

Y axis: The vertical axis of a graph; sometimes called the "ordinate."

z score: A *standard score* having a *mean* of 0 and a *standard deviation* of 1.0. The z score indicates the number of *standard deviations* an individual's score is from the *mean* of the distribution. The formula for a z score is:

$$\frac{X - M}{SD}$$

where X is the *raw score,* M is the *mean,* and SD is the *standard deviation.*

Appendix 1
How to Extract a Square Root

Procedures	**Example I**	**Example II**
1. Locate the decimal point. Place it above the square root sign or radical.	$\sqrt{2467.}$	$\sqrt{123.45}$
2. Estimate the square root. This can be any approximate value.	50 [50 × 50 = 2500]	11 [11 × 11 = 121]
3. Divide the number under the radical by the estimate of its square root.	2467 ÷ 50 = 49.34	123.45 ÷ 11 = 11.22
4. Add the quotient found in step 3 to the estimate in step 2. Divide that sum by 2. This is the new estimate.	$\dfrac{49.34 + 50 = 49.67}{2}$	$\dfrac{11.22 + 11 = 11.11}{2}$
5. For most purposes, the answer found in step 4 will be adequate. Square the answer from step 4 to see how close it is to the number under the radical.	$49.67^2 = 2467.1089$	$11.11^2 = 123.432$
6. If greater accuracy is required, divide the number under the radical by the new estimate; add the new estimate to the previous estimate and divide by 2.	2467 ÷ 49.67 = 49.6678 $\dfrac{49.6678 + 49.67 = 49.6689}{2}$	123.45 ÷ 11.11 = 11.1116 $\dfrac{11.1116 + 11.11 = 11.1108}{2}$

Additional Examples

Step 1: $\sqrt{.70400}$
Step 2: .80 [.80 × .80 = .6400]
Step 3: .70400 ÷ .80 = .8800
Step 4: $\dfrac{.8800 + .80 = .8400}{2}$
Step 5: $.8400^2 = .70560000$
Step 6: .704000 ÷ .8400 = .83809523
$\dfrac{.83809523 + .8400 = .83904}{2}$

1. $\sqrt{1.15}$
2. 1 [1 × 1 = 1]
3. 1.15 ÷ 1 = 1.15
4. $\dfrac{1.15 + 1 = 1.075}{2}$
5. $1.075^2 = 1.15562$
6. 1.15 ÷ 1.075 = 1.06976744
$\dfrac{1.06976744 + 1.075 = 1.07238}{2}$

1. $\sqrt{.00751}$
2. .08 [.08 × .08 = .0064]
3. .00751 ÷ .08 = .093875
4. $\dfrac{.093875 + .08 = .0869375}{2}$
5. $.0869375^2 = .00755812$
6. .00751 ÷ .0869375 = .08638389
$\dfrac{.08638389 + .0869375 = .08666}{2}$

Appendix 2
Computation of a Mean from a Frequency Distribution

Two methods may be used to compute a mean from a frequency distribution: the *midpoint* method and the *assumed mean* method.

(1) The Midpoint Method

Scores	f	mp Interval Midpoint	f(mp)
95–99	1	97	97
90–94	2	92	184
85–89	4	87	348
80–84	2	82	164
75–79	4	77	308
70–74	4	72	288
65–69	5	67	335
60–64	5	62	310
55–59	4	57	228
50–54	10	52	520
45–49	7	47	329
40–44	3	42	126
35–39	2	37	74
30–34	3	32	96
25–29	2	27	54
20–24	2	22	44
	$N = 60$		$\Sigma f(mp) =$ 3505

Using this method, allow the midpoint of each interval to represent all the scores within that interval. In the interval 75-79, for example, a score of 77 represents all 4 of the scores in that interval. The validity of this method depends on how well the midpoint actually represents all scores in the interval. Under most circumstances an error of overrepresentation in one interval will be balanced by an error of underrepresentation in another. If the midpoint represents the scores within an interval, there will be one score of 97, two scores of 92, four scores of 87, and so forth. One score of 97 = 97, two scores of 92 = 184, four scores of 87 = 348, and so on (see column f(mp)). By multiplying f by its midpoint and by summing these products, a fairly close equivalent to the Σx in the raw score formula is found. The mean is computed by dividing the sum of the products of f(mp) by N.

$$\text{Mean} = \frac{\Sigma f(mp)}{N} = \frac{3505}{60} = 58.42$$

Summary of Procedures

1. Locate the midpoint of each interval.
2. Multiply the midpoint of each interval by its frequency to yield the column headed $f(mp)$.
3. Sum $f(mp)$.
4. Divide by N or the number of cases.
   By formula, the midpoint method is represented by

$$M = \frac{\Sigma f(mp)}{N}$$

where mp is the midpoint of each interval.
Substituting for the above formula,

$$M = \frac{3505}{60} = 58.42$$

(2) The Assumed Mean Method

Another method for computing a mean when data are arranged in a frequency distribution is the *assumed-mean method*. Although this method may appear complex at first, it saves time and requires less computational effort than does the midpoint method. It is especially recommended if standard deviations need to be computed also.

Remember that in the midpoint method, the midpoint of each interval is assumed to represent all scores within the interval. In the assumed-mean method, substitue for the midpoint of each interval a number that is as small as possible to reduce computational work. Generally it is best to assign a zero to the interval containing the largest number of scores or to the interval nearest the center of the distribution to facilitate computations. In the example below, assume that the mean is somewhere near the interval 50–54, but it makes no difference where the mean is assumed to be as far as the answer is concerned. Assign a zero to the interval 50–54 to indicate that the mean lies within that interval.

Scores	f	d	fd
95–99	1	+9	+ 9
90–94	2	+8	+16
85–89	4	+7	+28
80–84	2	+6	+12
75–79	4	+5	+20
70–74	4	+4	+16
65–69	5	+3	+15
60–64	5	+2	+10
55–59	4	+1	+ 4
50–54	10	0	0
45–49	7	−1	− 7
40–44	3	−2	− 6
35–39	2	−3	− 6
30–34	3	−4	−12
25–29	2	−5	−10
20–24	2	−6	−12
	N = 60		Σfd = +77

The interval 55–59 is then assigned +1 to indicate that it is one deviation or interval *above* the assumed mean. The interval 45–49 is assigned a −1 to indicate that it is one interval *below* the assumed mean. These values are placed in the column headed d (deviations above and below the assumed mean). The 0 then represents the scores between 50 and 54, and a +4 represents the scores between 70 and 74. Just as in the midpoint method, it is necessary to know how many scores are at each interval. There is one score of +9, two scores of +8, four scores of +7, etc. These are multiplied to obtain the column marked fd (f times d). This column is summed to give the Σfd and divided by N to yield a mean of the substituted scores. In the above example the Σfd = +77, N = 60, and Σfd/N = +1.283. This +1.283 indicates the mean of the scores in the distribution is actually 1.283 intervals above the assumed mean. Notice also that each deviation above or below the assumed mean is equivalent to five units of scores (the size of each interval). Five times +1.283 = +6.42. The +6.42 refers to the fact that the mean is 6.42 points above the assumed mean. The assumed mean is between 50 and 54; let the midpoint of that interval (52) represent all scores within that interval. The mean in score units is therefore 52 + 6.42, or 58.42. A convenient formula for the computation of a mean by the assumed-mean method is

$$M = AM + \left(\frac{\Sigma fd}{N}\right) i$$

where AM = midpoint of the interval containing the assumed mean
i = size of each interval
f = frequency of each interval
d = deviations above or below an assumed mean
N = number of scores

Summary of Procedures

1. Estimate the interval that contains the mean and assign a 0 to it in the column marked d.
2. Number each interval consecutively above and below the interval assumed to contain the mean (all values above that interval are positive; all values below are negative).

3. Multiply the frequency of each interval by its corresponding *d* value to obtain a column headed *fd*.
4. Sum the *fd* column (be sure to add the negative and positive values algebraically).
5. Divide the sum of *fd* by *N*, the number of cases.
6. Multiply the quotient by the size of each interval.
7. Add the product to the midpoint of the interval assumed to contain the mean.

Appendix 3
Computation of a Median from a
Frequency Distribution

When scores are arranged in a frequency distribution, the procedure for computing a median is as follows: the definition of a median requires finding the middle score which is $N/2$. Because there are 60 scores in the distribution below, find the 30th score. Counting the frequencies from the bottom of the distribution, there are 29 scores up to and including the interval 50–54. Only one of the 4 scores in the interval 55–59 is needed to reach the 30th score. It is assumed that the frequencies are divided equally throughout each interval and that each interval is an interval of five points. One-fourth of the interval 55–59 is ¼ times 5, which equals 1.25. Keep in mind that a score of 54.5 represents the lower limit of the interval containing the median, since scores are continuous variables. Add 1.25 to 54.5; the median is 55.75.

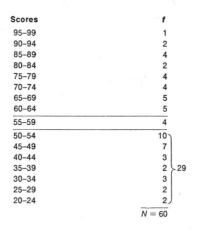

Scores	f
95–99	1
90–94	2
85–89	4
80–84	2
75–79	4
70–74	4
65–69	5
60–64	5
55–59	4
50–54	10 ⎫
45–49	7 ⎪
40–44	3 ⎪
35–39	2 ⎬ 29
30–34	3 ⎪
25–29	2 ⎪
20–24	2 ⎭
	$N = 60$

By formula, the median for grouped data is

$$\text{median} = L + \left(\frac{N/2 - \Sigma fb}{f_m}\right) i$$

where L = lower limit of interval containing median
  Σfb = sum of frequencies below interval containing the median
  f_m = frequency of the interval containing the median

For the above data,

$$\text{median} = 54.5 + \left(\frac{30 - 29}{4}\right) 5$$

Summary of Procedures

1. Divide the number of cases by 2 to find the median score.
2. From the lowest interval, sum the frequencies until the interval is found that contains the median score.
3. Subtract the sum of the frequencies below the interval containing the median score from $N/2$.
4. Divide the difference by the frequency of scores in the interval that contains the median score.
5. Multiply the quotient by the size of each interval.
6. Add the product to the lower limit of the interval containing the median score.

Appendix 4
Converting Raw Scores to Percentiles

Teachers often find it desirable to convert raw scores to percentile equivalents. If the need for extreme accuracy is not great, graphic methods can be used effectively. The simplest procedure is to develop a frequency distribution such as the one below. In the interval 30–32 there are 2 scores considered to be *at* or *below* the upper limits of the interval. In the interval 33–35 there are 4 scores, and so on. Six scores are at or below the interval 33–35; 8 scores are at or below the interval 36–38. All the scores (40) are either at or below the highest interval, 57–59. The percentiles are found by dividing the number of scores at or below each interval by the number of scores (40) and multiplying by 100. These values have been rounded to the nearest integer.

Scores	f	Number of Scores at or below Each Interval	Percentage of Scores at or below Each Interval (Percentiles)
57–59	3	40	100
54–56	1	37	93
51–53	2	36	90
48–50	7	34	85
45–47	8	27	68
42–44	8	19	48
39–41	3	11	28
36–38	2	8	20
33–35	4	6	15
30–32	2	2	5
	40		

Plot the percentile graph by listing percentiles along the vertical axis and the upper limits of each score interval on the horizontal axis. The upper limits are used because percentiles indicate the percentage of scores that are below each interval. Because 5 percent of the scores are at or below a score value of 32.5 (the upper limit of the interval 30–32), a dot placed above the 32.5 on the horizontal axis and across from a percentile of 5 on the vertical axis. Follow the same procedure for the remaining values.

According to the graph, a score of 51 corresponds to the 85th percentile. Also, a score of 45 (approximately) equals the 50th percentile or median.

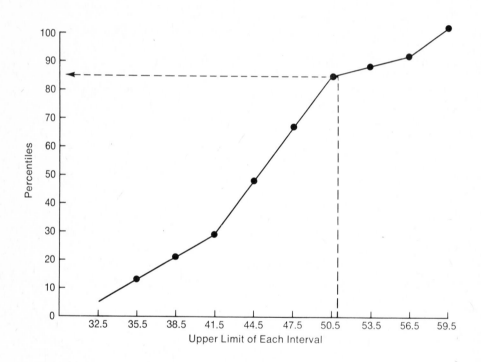

Summary of Procedures

1. Count the number of scores within and below each interval.
2. Divide each of those values by the number of cases.
3. Multiply the quotient by 100.
4. List the percentiles from 0 to 100 on the Y axis; list the upper limits of each interval on the X axis.
5. Plot the percentage of scores at or below each interval against the upper limits of each interval.

Appendix 5
Computation of a Standard Deviation from a
Frequency Distribution

When scores are arranged in a frequency distribution, a convenient method may be used to compute a standard deviation. This particular method requires only a few additional steps beyond what is needed for computing a mean by the assumed-mean method. Columns marked f, d, and fd are found in the same manner as was

Scores	f	d	fd	d times fd, or fd^2
95–99	1	+9	+ 9	81
90–94	2	+8	+16	128
85–89	4	+7	+28	196
80–84	2	+6	+12	72
75–79	4	+5	+20	100
70–74	4	+4	+16	64
65–69	5	+3	+15	45
60–64	5	+2	+10	20
55–59	4	+1	+ 4	4
50–54	10	0	− 0	0
45–49	7	−1	− 7	7
40–44	3	−2	− 6	12
35–39	2	−3	− 6	18
30–34	3	−4	−12	48
25–29	2	−5	−10	50
20–24	2	−6	−12	72
	$N = 60$		$\Sigma fd = +77$	$\Sigma fd^2 = 917$
			$(\Sigma fd)^2 = 5929$	

found in the computation of a mean by the assumed-mean method. The only additional steps are to multiply the d column by the fd column to get fd^2. The fd^2 column is summed to yield the Σfd^2, and the Σfd is squared to yield the $(\Sigma fd)^2$. These values are then substituted in the formula

$$SD = \frac{i\sqrt{N \Sigma fd^2 - (\Sigma fd)^2}}{N} = \frac{5\sqrt{60 \times 917 - (77)^2}}{60} =$$

$$\frac{5\sqrt{55020 - 5929}}{60} = \frac{5\sqrt{49091}}{60} = \frac{5 \times 221.56}{60} =$$

$$\frac{1107.80}{60} = 18.46$$

Appendix 6
A Raw Score Formula for Computing
Correlations

Rather than having to convert all scores to z scores, the following formula may be used:

$$r = \frac{N\Sigma XY - (\Sigma X)(\Sigma Y)}{\sqrt{[N\Sigma X^2 - (\Sigma X)^2][N\Sigma Y^2 - (\Sigma Y)^2]}}$$

For illustrative purposes, only five scores are used.

Student	X Height	Y Weight	XY	X²	Y²
Charles	71"	195	13845	$71^2 =$ 5041	$195^2 =$ 38025
Bernie	73"	235	17155	$73^2 =$ 5329	$235^2 =$ 55225
Belle	63"	115	7245	$63^2 =$ 3969	$115^2 =$ 13225
Joe	70"	160	11200	$70^2 =$ 4900	$160^2 =$ 25600
Eve	64"	122	7808	$64^2 =$ 4096	$122^2 =$ 14884

$\Sigma X = 341$ $\Sigma Y = 827$ $\Sigma XY = 57253$ $\Sigma X^2 = 23335$ $\Sigma Y^2 = 146959$

$(\Sigma X)(\Sigma Y) = (341)(827) = 282007;\ N\Sigma XY = 5(57253) = 286265$

$(\Sigma X)^2 = (341)^2 = 116281$ $N\Sigma X^2 =$ $N\Sigma Y^2 =$

$(\Sigma Y)^2 = (827)^2 = 683929$ $5(23335) = 116675$ $5(146959) = 734795$

Using these values in the formula yields

$$r = \frac{286265 - 282007}{\sqrt{[116675 - 116281][734795 - 683929]}} = \frac{4258}{\sqrt{[394][50866]}} =$$

$$\frac{4258}{\sqrt{20041204}} = \frac{4258}{4476.7} = .95$$

Appendix 7
Computation of Rank-Order Correlations
(RHO or ρ)

Instead of correlating raw scores, it is sometimes simpler to rank the individuals from highest (given a rank of 1) to lowest and then correlate the ranks.

Suppose that a teacher is interested in the degree of relationship between grades in English (A, B, C, D, or E) and the amount of time the student spends studying for English. Consider the data below:

Student	Grade	Time Spent	Rank on Grade	Rank on Time	D (Difference)	D²
John	A	30 min./day	1.5	5	3.5	12.25
Bill	A	45 min./day	1.5	2.5	1.0	1.00
Mary	C	45 min./day	3	2.5	.5	.25
Alice	D	37 min./day	4	4	0.0	0.00
Paul	E	55 min./day	5	1	4.0	16.00

$\Sigma D^2 = 29.50$

John and Bill both received A s in English and shoud therefore have received ranks of 1. However, this would have given Mary a rank of 2, Alice a 3, and Paul a 4. The last rank should have been a 5 since five individuals were being ranked. By giving John and Bill the average of ranks 1 and 2, or 1.5, and by giving Mary a rank of 3 (ranks 1 and 2 were already used for John and Bill), the last rank (Paul) is 5. The same procedure is applied to time spent in studying, except that now ranks 2 and 3 are tied, giving Bill and Mary average ranks of 2.5. Because the first three ranks have been assigned, rank 4 is given to Alice, and 5 to John. The differences between the ranks are found and placed in column D. These differences are squared to yield D^2, and the squares are summed to yield ΣD^2. The formula for the rank-order correlation (sometimes referred to as *rho* or symbolized by the figure ρ) is

$$rho = 1 - \frac{6\ \Sigma D^2}{N(N^2 - 1)} \quad \text{or} \quad 1 - \frac{6 \times 29.50}{5(5^2 - 1)} = 1 - \frac{177}{120} = 1 - 1.48 = -.48$$

Summary of Procedures

1. Rank-order each of the two variables.
2. Find the difference between corresponding ranks.
3. Square the differences.
4. Sum the squared differences.
5. Multiply the sum of the squared differences by 6 (a 6 is a constant value).
6. Divide by the number of cases multiplied by the number minus 1.
7. Subtract the quotient from 1.0.

Appendix 8
Instrumentation of the Taxonomy of Educational Objectives:*

Cognitive Domain

| | | Key Words | |
| | Examples of | | Examples of |
Taxonomy Classification	Infinitives		Direct Objects
1.00 Knowledge			
1.10 Knowledge of Specifics			
1.11 Knowledge of Terminology	to define, to distinguish to acquire, to identify, to recall, to recognize		vocabulary, terms, terminology, meaning(s), definitions, referents, elements
1.12 Knowledge of Specific Facts	to recall, to recognize, to acquire, to identify		facts, factual information, (sources), (names), (dates), (events), (persons), (places), (time periods), properties, examples, phenomena
1.20 Knowledge of Ways and Means of Dealing with Specifics			

*Metfessel, Michael, and Kirsner 1969.

Cognitive Domain (continued)

Taxonomy Classification	Key Words	
	Examples of Infinitives	Examples of Direct Objects
1.21 Knowledge of Conventions	to recall, to identify to recognize, to acquire	form(s), conventions, uses, usage, rules, ways, devices, symbols, representations, style(s), format(s)
1.22 Knowledge of Trends, Sequences	to recall, to recognize, to acquire, to identify	action(s), processes, movement(s), continuity, development(s), trend(s), sequence(s), causes, relationship(s), forces, influences
1.23 Knowledge of Classifications and Categories	to recall, to recognize, to acquire, to identify	area(s), type(s), feature(s), class(es), set(s), division(s), arrangement(s), classification(s), category/categories
1.24 Knowledge of Criteria	to recall, to recognize, to acquire, to identify	criteria, basics, elements
1.25 Knowledge of Methodology	to recall, to recognize, to acquire, to identify	methods, techniques, approaches, uses, procedures, treatments
1.30 Knowledge of the Universals and Abstractions in a Field		
1.31 Knowledge of Principles, Generalizations	to recall, to recognize, to acquire, to identify	principle(s), generalization(s), proposition(s), fundamentals, laws, principal elements, implication(s)
1.32 Knowledge of Theories and Structures	to recall, to recognize, to acquire, to identify	theories, bases, interrelations, structure(s), organization(s), formulation(s)
2.00 Comprehension		
2.10 Translation	to translate, to transform, to give in own words, to illustrate, to prepare, to read, to represent, to change, to rephrase, to restate	meaning(s), sample(s), definitions, abstractions, representations, words, phrases
2.20 Interpretation	to interpret, to reorder, to rearrange, to differentiate, to distinguish, to make, to draw, to explain, to demonstrate	relevancies, relationships, essentials, aspects, new view(s), qualifications, conclusions, methods, theories, abstractions
2.30 Extrapolation	to estimate, to infer, to conclude, to predict, to differentiate, to determine, to extend, to interpolate, to extrapolate, to fill in, to draw	consequences, implications, conclusions, factors, ramifications, meanings, corollaries, effects, probabilities
3.00 Application	to apply, to generalize, to relate, to choose, to develop, to organize, to use, to employ, to transfer, to restructure, to classify	principles, laws, conclusions, effects, methods, theories, abstractions, situations, generalizations, processes, phenomena, procedures
4.00 Analysis		
4.10 Analysis of Elements	to distinguish, to detect, to identify, to classify, to discriminate, to recognize, to categorize, to deduce	elements, hypothesis/ hypotheses, conclusions, assumptions, statements (of fact), statements (of intent), arguments, particulars

Cognitive Domain (continued)

Taxonomy Classification		Key Words Examples of Infinitives	Examples of Direct Objects
4.20	Analysis of Relationships	to analyze, to contrast, to compare, to distinguish, to deduce	relationships, interrelations, relevance, relevancies, themes, evidence, fallacies, arguments, cause-effect(s), consistency/consistencies, parts, ideas, assumptions
4.30	Analysis of Organizational Principles	to analyze, to distinguish, to detect, to deduce	form(s), pattern(s), purpose(s), point(s) of view(s), techniques, bias(es), structure(s), theme(s), arrangement(s), organization(s)
5.00	Synthesis		
5.10	Production of a Unique Communication	to write, to tell, to relate, to produce, to constitute, to transmit, to originate, to modify, to document	structure(s), pattern(s), product(s), performance(s), design(s), work(s), communications, effort(s), specifics, composition(s)
5.20	Production of a Plan, or Proposed Set of Operations	to propose, to plan, to produce, to design, to modify, to specify	plan(s), objectives, specification(s), schematic(s), operations, way(s), solution(s), means
5.30	Derivation of a Set of Abstract Relations	to produce, to derive, to develop, to combine, to organize, to synthesize, to classify, to deduce, to develop, to formulate, to modify	phenomena, taxonomies, concept(s), scheme(s), theories, relationships, abstractions, generalizations, hypothesis/hypotheses, perceptions, ways, discoveries
6.00	Evaluation		
6.10	Judgments in Terms of Internal Evidence	to judge, to argue, to validate, to assess, to decide	accuracy/accuracies, consistency/consistencies, fallacies, reliability, flaws, errors, precision, exactness
6.20	Judgments in Terms of External Criteria	to judge, to argue, to consider, to compare, to contrast, to standardize, to appraise	ends, means, efficiency, economy/economies, utility, alternatives, courses of action, standards, theories, generalizations

Affective Domain

Taxonomy Classification		Key Words Examples of Infinitives	Examples of Direct Objects
1.0	Receiving		
1.1	Awareness	to differentiate, to separate, to set apart, to share	sights, sounds, events, designs, arrangements
1.2	Willingness to Receive	to accumulate, to select, to combine, to accept	models, examples, shapes, sizes, meters, cadences
1.3	Controlled or Selected Attention	to select, to posturally respond to, to listen (for), to control	alternatives, answers, rhythms, nuances
2.0	Responding		
2.1	Acquiescence in Responding	to comply (with), to follow, to commend, to approve	directions, instructions, laws, policies, demonstrations

Affective Domain (continued)

Taxonomy Classification	Key Words	
	Examples of Infinitives	Examples of Direct Objects
2.2 Willingness to Respond	to volunteer, to discuss, to practice, to play	instruments, games, dramatic works, charades, burlesques
2.3 Satisfaction in Response	to applaud, to acclaim, to spend leisure time in, to augment	speeches, plays, presentations, writings
3.0 Valuing		
3.1 Acceptance of a Value	to increase measured proficiency in, to increase numbers of, to relinquish, to specify	group membership(s), artistic production(s), musical productions, personal friendships
3.2 Preference for a Value	to assist, to subsidize, to help, to support	artists, projects, viewpoints, arguments
3.3 Commitment	to deny, to protest, to debate, to argue	deceptions, irrelevancies, abdications, irrationalities
4.0 Organization		
4.1 Conceptualization of a Value	to discuss, to theorize (on), to abstract, to compare	parameters, codes, standards, goals
4.2 Organization of a Value System	to balance, to organize, to define, to formulate	systems, approaches, criteria, limits
5.0 Characterization by Value or Value Complex		
5.1 Generalized Set	to revise, to change, to complete, to require	plans, behavior, methods, effort(s)
5.2 Characterization	to be rated high by peers in, to be rated high by superiors in, to be rated high by subordinates in and	humanitarianism, ethics, integrity, maturity
	to avoid, to manage, to resolve, to resist	extravagance(s), excesses, conflicts, exorbitancy/exorbitancies

Bibliography

Adjutant General's Office, U. S. Army, Personnel Research Section. "The Army General Classification Test." *Psychological Bulletin* 42, no. 10 (December 1945):760–68.

Adkins, Dorothy C. *Construction and Analysis of Achievement Tests: The Development of Written and Performance Tests of Achievement for Predicting Job Performance of Public Personnel.* Washington, D. C.: Superintendent of Documents, U. S. Government Printing Office, 1947.

Allport, Gordon W. "Attitudes." In C. Murchison, ed., *Handbook of Social Psychology.* Worcester, Mass.: Clark University Press, 1935.

Allport, Gordon W., and Allport, Floyd H. *The A-S Reaction Study.* Boston: Houghton Mifflin Co., 1939.

Allport, Gordon W., and Odbert, H. S. "Trait Names: A Psycho-Lexical Study." *Psychological Monographs* 47, no. 1 (1936), whole no. 211:1–171.

Allport, Gordon W., and Postman, Leo. *The Psychology of Rumor.* New York: Henry Holt and Co., 1947.

Allport, Gordon W., and Vernon, P. E. *Studies in Expressive Movement.* New York: Macmillan Co., 1933.

Allport, Gordon W.; Vernon, P. E.; and Lindzey, Gardner. *Study of Values: A Scale for Measuring the Dominant Interests in Personality.* 3d ed. Boston: Houghton Mifflin Co., 1960.

American Psychological Association. "Ethical Standards of Psychologists." *American Psychologist* 18, no. 1 (January 1963):59–60.

———. "Ethical Standards of Psychologists." *American Psychologist* 23, no. 5 (May 1968):357–61.

———. "Pickets at APA Headquarters Protest Psychological Tests." *American Psychologist* 20, no. 11 (November 1965):871–72.

———. *Standards for Educational and Psychological Tests and Manuals.* Washington, D. C.: American Psychological Association, 1966.

American Psychological Association, American Education Research Association, and National Council on Measurements Used in Education. "Technical Recommendations for Psychological Tests and Diagnostic Techniques." Supplement to *Psychological Bulletin* 51, no. 2, part 2 (March 1954).

Anastasi, Anne. *Psychological Testing.* 3d ed. New York: Macmillan Co., 1968.

Arthur, A. Z. "Diagnostic Testing and the New Alternatives." *Psychological Bulletin* 72, no. 3 (September 1969):183–92.

Asch, Solomon E. "Studies of Independence and Conformity: A Minority of One against an Unanimous Majority." *Psychological Monographs* 70, no. 9 (1956):1–70.

Ashburn, Robert R. "An Experiment in the Essay-Type Question." *The Journal of Experimental Education* 7 (September 1938):1–3.

Baker, Frank B. "Automation of Test Scoring, Reporting, and Analysis." In Robert L. Thorndike, ed., *Educational Measurement,* 2d ed., pp. 202–34. Washington, D. C.: American Council on Education, 1971.

Baker, Robert L., and Doyle, Roy P. "Teacher Knowledge of Pupil Data and Marking Practices at the Elementary School Level." *The Personnel and Guidance Journal* 37 (May 1959):644–47.

Bayley, Nancy. "Consistency and Variability in the Growth of Intelligence from Birth to Eighteen Years." *The Pedagogical Seminary and Journal of Genetic Psychology* 75 (1949):165–96.

Bennett, George K.; Seashore, Harold G.; and Wesman, Alexander G. *Fourth Edition for the Differential Aptitude Tests, Forms L and M.* New York: The Psychological Corporation, 1966.

Berg, I. A. "Response Bias and Personality: The Deviation Hypothesis." *Journal of Psychology* 40, no. 1 (July 1955):61–72.

Bijou, Sidney W. "Implications of Behavioral Science for Counseling and Guidance." In J. D. Krumboltz, ed., *Revolution in Counseling,* pp. 27–48. Boston: Houghton Mifflin Co., 1966.

Birdwhistell, Ray L. *Introduction to Kinesics.* Louisville, Ky.: University of Louisville Press, 1952.

Block, James H., ed. *Mastery Learning: Theory and Practice.* New York: Holt, Rinehart and Winston, 1971.

Bloom, Benjamin S., ed. *Taxonomy of Educational Objectives: The Classification of Educational Goals, Handkbook I: Cognitive Domain.* New York: Longmans, Green and Co., 1956.

Boehm, Ann E., *Boehm Test of Basic Concepts.* New York: The Psychological Corporation, 1967.

Bogardus, Emory S. "Measuring Social Distances." *Journal of Applied Sociology* 9 no. 4 (March 1925):299–308.

Borstelmann, L. J., and Klopfer, W. G. "The Szondi Test: A Review and Critical Evaluation." *Psychological Bulletin* 50, no. 2 (March 1953):116.

Brigham, John C., and Cook, Stuart W. "The Influence of Attitude on Judgments of Plausibility: A Replication and Extension." *Educational and Psychological Measurement* 30, no. 2 (Summer 1970):283–92.

Broudy, Harry S. *Building a Philosophy of Education.* 2d ed. Englewood Cliffs, N. J.: Prentice-Hall, 1961.

Brown, W. F., and Holtzman, W. H. *The Survey of Study Habits and Attitudes.* New York: The Psychological Corporation, 1965.

Buros, Oscar Krisen. "Educational, Psychological, and Personality Tests of 1933, 1934, and 1935." *Rutgers University Bulletin* 13, no. 1, New Brunswick, N. J.: Rutgers University, 1936.

_____. "Educational, Psychological, and Personality Tests of 1936." *Rutgers University Bulletin* 14, no. 2A, Studies in Education, no. 11. New Brunswick, N. J.: School of Education, Rutgers University, 1937.

_____, ed. *The 1938 Mental Measurements Yearbook.* New Brunswick, N. J.: Rutgers University Press, 1938.

_____, ed. *The 1940 Mental Measurements Yearbook.* New Brunswick, N. J.: Rutgers University Press, 1941.

_____, ed. *The Third Mental Measurements Yearbook.* New Brunswick, N. J.: Rutgers University Press, 1949.

_____, ed. *The Fourth Mental Measurements Yearbook.* Highland Park, N. J.: Gryphon Press, 1953.

_____, ed. *The Fifth Mental Measurements Yearbook.* Highland Park, N. J.: Gryphon Press, 1959.

_____, ed. *Tests in Print.* Highland Park, N. J.: Gryphon Press, 1961.

_____, ed. *The Sixth Mental Measurements Yearbook.* Highland Park, N. J.: Gryphon Press, 1965.

_____, ed. *Reading Tests and Reviews.* Highland Park, N. J.: Gryphon Press, 1968.

_____, ed. *Personality Tests and Reviews.* Highland Park, N. J.: Gryphon Press, 1970.

_____, ed. *The Seventh Mental Measurements Yearbook.* Highland Park, N. J.: Gryphon Press, 1972.

Calandra, Alexander. "Angels on a Pin." *Saturday Review of Literature,* December 21, 1968, p. 60.

Campbell, David P. *Handbook for the Strong Vocational Interest Blank.* Stanford, Calif.: Stanford University Press, 1971.

Campbell, Donald T. "The Indirect Assessment of Social Attitudes." *Psychological Bulletin* 47, no. 1 (January 1950):15–38.

————. "A Typology of Tests, Projective and Otherwise." *Journal of Consulting Psychology* 21, no. 3 (June 1957):207–10.

Campbell, Donald T., and Fiske, Donald W. "Convergent and Discriminant Validation by the Multitrait-Multimethod Matrix." *Psychological Bulletin* 56 (1959):81–105.

Campbell, Donald T., and Stanley, Julian C. "Experimental and Quasi-Experimental Designs for Research on Teaching." In N. L. Gage, ed., *Handbook of Research on Teaching,* pp. 171–246. Chicago: Rand McNally, 1963.

Carr, William G., ed., for the Educational Policies Commission. *Book III: The Purposes of Education in American Democracy.* Washington, D. C.: National Education Association of the United States and the American Association of School Administrators, 1946.

Cattell, Raymond Bernard. *Description and Measurement of Personality.* Yonkers, N. Y.: World Book, 1964.

Clark, Kenneth E., and Campbell, David P. *Navy Vocational Interest Inventory Manual.* New York: The Psychological Corporation, 1965.

Cleary, T. Anne. "Test Bias: Prediction of Grades of Negro and White Students in Integrated Colleges." *Journal of Educational Measurement* 5, no. 2 (Summer 1968):115–24.

Clymer, Theodore. "What is 'Reading'? Some Current Concepts." In Helen B. Robinson, ed., *Innovation and Change in Reading Instruction: The Sixty-seventh Yearbook of the National Society for the Study of Education: Part II,* pp. 19–23. Chicago: University of Chicago Press, 1968. The Barrett taxonomy used by permission.

Coffman, William E. "On the Reliability of Ratings of Essay Examinations." *NCME Reports on Measurement in Education* 3, no. 3 (March 1972):7.

Collet, LeVerne S. "Elimination Scoring: An Empirical Evaluation." *Journal of Educational Measurement* 8, no. 3 (Fall 1971):209–14.

Commission on the Reorganization of Secondary Education (appointed by the National Education Association, Department of the Interior, Bureau of Education). *Cardinal Principles of Secondary Education: A Report of the Commission on the Reorganization of Secondary Education,* Bulletin 1918, no. 35. Washington, D. C.: U. S. Government Printing Office, 1918.

Coupeville Consolidated School District 204. *Individualized Learning Program for a Small School District.* Coupeville, Wash.: Coupeville Consolidated School District 204, 1968–69.

Coupeville Consolidated School District 204. *Skill Development in Reading: An Experimental Program of Instruction to Facilitate the Continuous Progress of Pupils in a Nongraded Elementary School.* Coupeville, Wash.: Coupeville Consolidated School District 204, 1968–69.

Cronbach, Lee J. *Essentials of Psychological Testing, Third Edition.* p. 447. New York: Harper & Row Publishers, 1970.

_____. "Test Validation." In Robert C. Thorndike, ed., *Educational Measurement,* 2d ed., 443–507. Washington, D. C.: American Council on Education, 1971.

Davis, Frederick B. *Educational Measurements and Their Interpretation.* Belmont, Calif.: Wadsworth Publishing Co., 1964.

Dawe, Helen C. "An Analysis of Two Hundred Quarrels of Preschool Children." *Child Development* 5, no. 2 (June 1934): 139–57.

Dickens, Charles F. "Simulated Patterns on the Edwards Personal Preference Schedule." *Journal of Applied Psychology* 43 (December 1959):372–78.

Dohrenwend, Barbara Snell, and Richardson, Stephen A. "Directiveness and Nondirectiveness in Research Interviewing: A Reformulation of the Problem." *Psychological Bulletin* 60, no. 5 (September 1963):475–85.

Doob, Leonard W. "The Behavior of Attitudes." *Psychological Review* 54, no. 3 (May 1947):135–56.

Ebel, Robert L. *Measuring Educational Achievement.* Englewood Cliffs, N. J.: Prentice-Hall, 1965.

_____. "Why Is a Longer Test Usually a More Reliable Test?" *Educational and Psychological Measurement* 32, no. 2 (Summer 1972):249–53.

Educational Testing Service. *SCAT Student Profile.* Princeton, N. J.: Educational Testing Service, 1957.

Edwards, Allen L. *Edwards Personal Preference Schedule.* New York: The Psychological Corporation, 1953.

————. *The Measurement of Personality Traits by Scales and Inventories.* New York: Holt, Rinehart and Winston, 1970.

————. "The Relationship between the Judged Desirability of a Trait and the Probability that the Trait Will Be Endorsed." *Journal of Applied Psychology* 37, no. 2 (April 1953):90–93.

Edwards, Allen L., and Kenney, Kathryn Claire. "A Comparison of the Thurstone and Likert Techniques of Attitude Scale Construction." *Journal of Applied Psychology* 30, no. 1 (February 1946): 72–83.

Eels, Kenneth; Davis, Allison; Havighurst, Robert J.; Herrick, Virgil E.; and Tyler, Ralph W. *Intelligence and Cultural Differences.* Chicago: University of Chicago Press, 1951.

Elliott, James M., and Osburn, H. G. "The Effects of Partial-Pacing on Test Parameters." *Educational and Psychological Measurement* 25, no. 2 (Summer 1965):347–53.

Ellis, Albert, and Conrad, Herbert S. "The Validity of Personality Inventories in Military Practice." *Psychological Bulletin* 45, no. 5 (September 1948): 385–426.

Engelhart, Max D. "A Comparison of Several Discrimination Indexes." *Journal of Educational Measurement* 2 no. 1 (June 1965):69–76.

Fargo, George; Crowell, Doris C.; Noyes, Mary; Fuchigami, Robert; Gordon, John M.; and Dunn-Rankin, Peter. "Comparability of Group Television and Individual Administration of the Peabody Picture Vocabulary Test: Implications for Screening." *Journal of Educational Psychology* 58, no. 3 (June 1967):137–40.

Fast, Julius. *Body Language.* New York: Pocket Books, 1971.

Federal Way School District. "Watch Your Language." *Reporting to Parents.* Federal Way, Wash.: Federal Way School District.

Feldhusen, John F. "Student Perceptions of Frequent Quizzes and Post-Mortem Discussions of Tests." *Journal of Educational Measurement* 1, no. 1 (June 1964):51–54.

Ferguson, George A. *Statistical Analysis in Psychology and Education.* 3d ed. New York: McGraw-Hill Book Co., 1971.

Ferris, Manford J., and Nichols, Daryl G. "The Effects of Four Methods of Administration on Test Achievement." *Journal of Educational Measurement* 6, no. 2 (Summer 1969):85–91.

Ferster, C. B. "Classification of Behavior Pathology." In L. Krasner and L. P. Ullman, eds., *Research in Behavior Modification,* pp. 6–26. New York: Holt, Rinehart and Winston, 1965.

Fishman, Joshua; Deutsch, Martin; Rogan, Leonard; North, Robert; and Whiteman, Martin. "Guidelines for Testing Minority Group Children." Supplement to the *Journal of Social Issues* 20, no. 2 (1964):137.

Fiske, Donald W. "The Subject Reacts to Tests." *American Psychologist* 22, no. 4 (April 1967):287–96.

Flanagan, John C., ed. *The Aviation Psychology Program in the Army Air Forces,* No. 1, Report No. 1, Army Air Force Aviation Psychology Program Research Reports. Washington, D. C.: Superintendent of Documents, U. S. Government Printing Office, 1948.

Flavell, John H. *The Developmental Psychology of Jean Piaget.* Princeton, N. J.: Van Nostrand Co., 1963.

Forer, Bertram R. "The Fallacy of Personal Validations: A Classroom Demonstration of Gullibility." *Journal of Abnormal and Social Psychology* 44, no. 1 (January 1949):118–23.

Franzen, Raymond. "The Accomplishment Quotient." *Teachers College Record* 21 (November 1920):432–40.

French, Bryan. "Out of the Mouths of Babes." *Phi Delta Kappan* 43, no. 6 (March 1962): inside back cover.

Gaffney, Richard F., and Maguire, Thomas O. "Use of Optically Scored Test Answer Sheets with Young Children." *Journal of Educational Measurement* 8, no. 2 (Summer 1971):103–6.

Galton, Francis. *Heredity Genius: An Inquiry into Its Laws and Consequences.* London: Macmillan and Co., 1925.

Garber, Herbert. "The Digital Computer Simulates Human Rating Behavior." In John T. Flynn and Herbert Garber, eds., *Assessing Behavior: Readings in Educational and Psychological Measurement,* pp. 367–73. Reading, Mass.: Addison-Wesley Publishing Co., 1967.

Gardner, Eric F.; Merwin, Jack C.; Callis, Robert; and Madden, Richard. *Stanford Achievement Test High School Battery Manual.* New York: Harcourt Brace Jovanovich, 1965.

Glaser, Robert. "Adapting the Elementary School Curriculum to Individual Performance." In *Proceedings of the 1967 Invitational Conference on Testing Problems,* pp. 8–9. Princeton. N. J.: Educational Testing Service, 1968.

————. "Evaluation of Instruction and Changing Educational Models." In M. C. Whittrock and David E. Wiley, eds., *The Evaluation of Instruction: Issues and Problems,* pp. 70–86. New York: Holt, Rinehart and Winston, 1970.

Goldberg, Lewis R. "Grades and Motivants." *Psychology in the Schools* 2, no. 1 (January 1965):17–23.

Gordon, H. *Mental and Scholastic Tests among Retarded Children.* Educational Pamphlet no. 44. London: Board of Education, 1923.

Green, Russel F. "Does a Selection Situation Induce Testees to Bias Their Answers on Interest and Temperament Tests?" *Educational and Psychological Measurement* 11, no. 3 (Autumn 1951):503–15.

Gronlund, Norman E., and Barnes, Fred P. "The Reliability of Social-Acceptability Scores Using Various Sociometric-Choice Limits." *Elementary School Journal* 57, no. 3 (December 1956):153–57.

Gronlund, Norman E. *Sociometry in the Classroom.* New York: Harper & Brothers, 1959.

Guilford, J. P. *Fundamental Statistics in Psychology and Education.* 4th ed. New York: McGraw-Hill Book Co., 1965.

————. *The Nature of Human Intelligence.* New York: McGraw-Hill Book Co., 1967.

————. *Psychometric Methods.* New York: McGraw-Hill Book Co., 1954.

————. "Three Faces of Intellect." *American Psychologist* 14, no. 8 (August 1959):469–79.

Gulliksen, Harold. *Theory of Mental Tests.* New York: John Wiley, 1950.

Hamilton, David L. "Personality Attributes Associated with Extreme Response Style." *Psychological Bulletin* 69, no. 3 (March 1968):192–203.

Harrell, T. W., and Harrell, M. S. "Army General Classification Test Scores for Civilian Occupations." *Educational and Psychological Measurement* 5 (Autumn 1945):229–39.

Hartshorne, Hugh, and May, Mark W. *Studies in Deceit.* New York: Macmillan Co., 1928.

Hase, Harold D., and Goldberg, Lewis R. "Comparative Validity of Different Strategies of Constructing Personality Inventory Scales." *Psychological Bulletin* 67, no. 4 (April 1967):231–48.

Hathaway, Starke Rosecrans, and Meehl, P. E. *An Atlas for the Clinical Use of the MMPI.* Minneapolis: University of Minnesota Press, 1951.

Havighurst, Robert J. *Development Tasks and Education.* 2d ed. New York: Longmans, Green and Co., 1952.

Hoffmann, Banesh. *The Tyranny of Testing.* New York: Crowell-Collier Press, 1962.

Holland, John L., and Astin, Alexander W. "The Prediction of the Academic, Artistic, Scientific, and Social Achievement of Undergraduates of Superior Scholastic Aptitude." *Journal of Educational Psychology* 53, no. 3 (June 1962):136.

Holly, Keith A., and Michael, William B. "The Relationship of Structure-of-Intellect Factor Abilities to Performance in High School Modern Algebra." *Educational and Psychological Measurement* 32, no. 2 (Summer 1972):447–50.

Hovland, Carl I., and Sherif, Muzafer. "Judgmental Phenomena and Scales of Attitude Measurement: Item Displacement in Thurstone Scales." *Journal of Abnormal and Social Psychology* 47, no. 4 (October 1952):822–32.

Hoyt, K. B. "A Study of the Effects of Teacher Knowledge of Pupil Characteristics on Pupil Achievement and Attitudes Towards Classwork." *Journal of Educational Psychology* 46, no. 5 (May 1955):302–10.

Hsü, E. H. "An Experimental Study of Rationalization." *Journal of Abnormal and Social Psychology* 44, no. 2 (April 1949):277–78.

Husen, Torsten. "The Influence of Schooling Upon IQ." *Theoria* 17, no. 1–3 in one issue (1951):61–88.

Jacobs, Paul I., and Vandeventer, Mary. "Evaluating the Teaching of Intelligence." *Educational and Psychological Measurement* 32, no. 2 (Summer 1972):235–48.

Jensen, Arthur R. "How Much Can We Boost IQ and Scholastic Achievement?" *Harvard Educational Review* 39, no. 1 (Winter 1969):1–123.

Kahn, Robert L., and Cannell, Charles F. *The Dynamics of Interviewing.* New York: John Wiley, 1957.

Kalish, Richard A. "An Experimental Evaluation of the Open Book Examination." *Journal of Educational Psychology* 49, no. 4 (August 1958):200–204.

Kaufman, Bel. *Up the Down Staircase.* New York: Avon Books, 1964.

Kelley, Truman Lee. *Interpretation of Educational Measurements.* Yonkers-on-Hudson, N. Y.: World Book Co., 1927.

———. "The Selection of Upper and Lower Groups for the Validation of Test Items." *Journal of Educational Psychology* 30, no. 1 (January 1939):17–24.

————; Madden, Richard; Gardner, Eric F.; and Rudman, Herbert C. *Stanford Achievement Test Primary II Battery Manual,* p. 26. New York: Harcourt, Brace & World, 1964.

Keys, Noel. "The Influence on Learning and Retention of Weekly as Opposed to Monthly Tests." *Journal of Educational Psychology* 25, no. 6 (1934):427–36.

Kilman, Herbert C. "Human Use of Human Subjects: The Problem of Deception in Social Psychological Experiments." *Psychological Bulletin* 67, no. 1 (January 1967):1–11.

Kirk, Samuel A. *Educating Exceptional Children.* 2d ed. Boston: Houghton Mifflin Co., 1972.

Kirkland, Marjorie C. "The Effect of Tests on Students and Schools." *Review of Educational Research* 41, no. 4 (October 1971):303–50.

Krathwohl, David R.; Bloom, Benjamin S.; and Masia, Bertram B. *Taxonomy of Educational Objectives: The Classification of Educational Goals: Handbook II: Affective Domain.* New York: David McKay Co., 1964.

Kuder, G. Frederic. "Expected Developments in Interest and Personality Inventories." *Educational and Psychological Measurement* 14, no. 2 (Summer 1954):265–71.

————. *Occupational Interest Survey General Manual.* Chicago: Science Research Associates, 1966, p. 6.

————. "Suggested Occupations for High Computational and Artistic Interests on the Kuder Preference Record." *Examiner Manual: Vocational Form C.* Chicago: Science Research Associates, 1970.

Kuder, G. Frederic, and Richardson, M. W. "The Theory of the Estimation of Test Reliability." *Psychometrika* 2 (September 1937):151–60.

Lange, Allan; Lehmann, Irvin J.; and Mehrens, William A. "Using Item Analysis to Improve Tests." *Journal of Educational Measurement* 4, no. 2 (Summer 1967):65–68.

LaPiere, Richard T. "Attitudes Versus Actions." *Social Forces* 13, no. 2 (December 1934):230–37.

Leacock, Stephen. *College Days.* New York: Dodd, Mead & Co., 1923.

————. *Funny Pieces.* New York: Dodd, Mead & Co., 1936.

Likert, Rensis. "A Technique for the Measurement of Attitudes." *Archives of Psychology,* no. 140 (1932):52.

Lindquist, E. L. "The Iowa Electronic Test Processing Equipment." *Testing Today*. Boston: Houghton Mifflin Co., n.d.

Lindvall, C. M., and Cox, Richard C. "The Role of Evaluation for Individualized Instruction." In Ralph W. Tyler, ed., *Educational Evaluation: New Roles, New Means: The Sixty-eighth Yearbook of the National Society for the Study of Education, Part II*. Chicago: University of Chicago Press, 1969.

Lindzey, Gardner. "On the Classification of Projective Techniques." *Psychological Bulletin* 56, no. 2 (March 1959):158–68.

Littell, William M. "The Wechsler Intelligence Scale for Children: Review of a Decade of Research." *Psychological Bulletin* 57, no. 2 (March 1960):136.

Livingston, Samuel A. "Reply to Shavelson, Block, and Ravitch's 'Criterion-Referenced Testing: Comments on Reliability.'" *Journal of Educational Measurement* 9, no. 2 (Summer 1972):139–40.

Lord, Frederic M. "Further Problems in the Measurement of Growth." *Educational and Psychological Measurement* 18, no. 3 (Autumn 1958):446.

————. "The Relationship of the Reliability of Multiple-Choice Tests to the Distribution of Item Difficulties." *Psychometrika* 17, no. 2 (June 1952):181–94.

Lorge, Irving; Thorndike, Robert L.; and Hagen, Elizabeth. *Lorge-Thorndike Intelligence Tests: Manual for Administration, Multi-Level Edition*. Boston: Houghton Mifflin Co., 1964.

Mager, Robert F. *Preparing Objectives for Programmed Instruction*. San Francisco, Calif.: Fearon Publishers, 1962, 66 pages.

Marshall, Jon C. "Composition Errors and Essay Examination Grades Re-Examined." *American Educational Research Journal* 4, no. 4 (November 1967):375–85.

Maslow, Abraham H. *Toward a Psychology of Being*. 2d ed. Princeton, N. J.: Van Nostrand, 1968.

Maslow, Abraham H.; Honigmann, I.; McGrath, F.; Plason, A.; and Stein, M. *The S. I. Inventory*. Palo Alto, Calif.: Consulting Psychologists Press, 1952.

Mayhew, Lewis B. "Non-test Predictors of Academic Achievement." *Educational and Psychological Measurement* 25 no. 1 (Spring 1965):39–46.

McNemar, Quinn. *Revision of the Stanford-Binet Scale*. Boston: Houghton Mifflin Co., 1942.

Meeker, Mary Nacol. *The Structure of Intellect: Its Interpretation and Uses*. Columbus, Ohio: Charles E. Merrill Publishing Co., 1969.

Merritt, Ray. "The Predictive Validity of the American College Test for Students from Low Socioeconomic Levels." *Educational and Psychological Measurement* 32, no. 2 (Summer 1972):444.

Metfessel, Newton S., and Michael, William B. "A Paradigm Involving Multiple Criterion Measures for the Evaluation of the Effectiveness of School Programs." *Educational and Psychological Measurement* 27, no. 4 (Winter 1967):931–43.

Metfessel, Newton S.; Michael, William B.; and Kirsner, Donald A. "Instrumentation of Bloom's and Krathwohl's Taxonomies for the Writing of Educational Objectives." *Psychology in the Schools* 6, no. 3 (July 1969):227–31.

Milgram, Stanley. "Behavioral Study of Obedience." *Journal of Abnormal and Social Psychology* 67, no. 4 (October 1963):371–78.

Miller, Delbert C. *Handbook of Research Design and Social Measurement.* 2d ed. New York: David McKay Co., 1970.

Mills, Eugene S. "The Madeline Thomas Completion Stories Test." *Journal of Consulting Psychology* 17, no. 2 (April 1953):139–41.

Moreno, Jacob L. *Who Shall Survive? Foundations of Sociometry, Group Psychotherapy, and Sociodrama.* New York: Beacon House, 1953.

National Education Association. *NEA Handbook 1969–70.* Washington, D. C.: National Education Association.

Nettler, Gwynn. "Test Burning in Texas." *American Psychologist* 14, no. 11 (November 1959):682–88.

Newman, Horatio H.; Freeman, Frank N.; and Holzinger, Karl J. *Twins: A Study of Heredity and Environment.* Chicago: University of Chicago Press, 1937.

Nolan, James S., and Jacobson, James. "The California Comprehensive Test of Basic Skills: A Predictor of Success for High School Freshmen." *Educational and Psychological Measurement* 32, no. 2 (Summer 1972):452.

Noll, Victor H. "The Effect of Written Tests Upon Achievement in College Classes: An Experiment and a Summary of Evidence." *Journal of Educational Research* 32, no. 5 (January 1939):345–58.

Norman, Warren T. "On Estimating Psychological Relationships: Social Desirability and Self-Report." *Psychological Bulletin* 67, no. 4 (April 1967): 273–93.

Nunnally, Jum C. *Psychometric Theory.* New York: McGraw-Hill Book Co., 1967.

Olson, Carl J. "Review of Borman-Sanders Elementary Science Test." In Oscar Krison Buros, ed., *The Seventh Mental Measurements Yearbook,* p. 1217. Highland Park, N.J.: Gryphon Press, 1972.

Oosterhof, Albert C., and Glasnapp, Douglas R. "Comparative Reliabilities of the Multiple Choice and True-False Formats." Paper presented at the meeting of the American Educational Research Association, Chicago, April 3–7, 1972.

Page, Ellis Batten. "Imminence of Grading Essays by Computers." *Phi Delta Kappan* 47, no. 5 (January 1966):238–43.

————. "Teacher Comments and Student Performance: A Seventy-four Classroom Experiment in Social Motivation." *Journal of Educational Psychology* 49, no. 4 (August 1958):173–81.

Palmer, Orville. "Seven Classic Ways of Grading Dishonestly." *The English Journal* 51, no. 7 (October 1962):464–67.

Parry, Hugh J., and Crossley, Helen M. "Validity of Responses to Survey Questions." *Public Opinion Quarterly* 14, no. 1 (Spring 1950):61–80.

Payne, Stanley L. "Interviewer Memory Faults." *Public Opinion Quarterly* 13 no. 4 (Winter 1949):684–85.

Phillips, Beenam N., and Weathers, Garrett R. "Analysis of Errors Made in Scoring Standardized Tests." *Educational and Psychological Measurement* 18, no. 3 (Autumn 1958):563–67.

Popham, W. James, and Husek, T. R. "Implications of Criterion-Referenced Measurement." *Journal of Educational Measurement* 6, no. 1 (Spring 1969):1–9.

Postman, Leo; Bruner, Jerome S.; and McGinnies, Elliott. "Personal Values as Selective Factors in Perception." *Journal of Abnormal and Social Psychology* 43, no. 2 (April 1948):142–54.

Progressive Educational Association. "Interpretation of Data" Test 2.2. University of Chicago: Chicago, Ill., 1938.

————. "Social Problems" Test 1.42. University of Chicago: Chicago, Ill., 1940.

Psychological Corporation. *The Psychological Corporation Test Catalog 1972.* New York: The Psychological Corporation, 1972.

Ramul, Konstantin. "Some Early Measurements and Ratings in Psychology." *American Psychologist* 18, no. 10 (October 1963):653–59.

Rice, J. M. "The Futility of the Spelling Grind." *The Forum* 23 (April 1897): 163–72.

Rice, Stuart A. "Contagious Bias in the Interview: A Methodological Note." *American Journal of Sociology* 35, no. 3 (November 1929):420–23.

Rosenzweig, Saul. *Rosenzweig Picture-Frustration Study.* St. Louis, Mo.: published privately, 1949.

Ross, C. C., and Henry, Lyle K. "The Relationship Between Frequency of Testing and Learning in Psychology." *Journal of Educational Research* 30, no. 8 (November 1939):604–11.

Rubin, Zick. "Jokers Wild in the Lab." *Psychology Today* 4, no. 7 (December 1970):18, 20, 22–24.

Ryans, D. G., and Wandt, E. "A Factor Analysis of Observed Teacher Behavior in the Secondary School: A Study of Criterion Data." *Educational and Psychological Measurement* 12 (1952):574–86.

Sax, Gilbert. *Empirical Foundations of Educational Research.* Englewood Cliffs, N. J.: Prentice-Hall, 1968.

Sax, Gilbert, and Carr, Albert. "An Investigation of Response Sets on Altered Parallel Forms." *Educational and Psychological Measurement* 22, no. 2 (1962):371–76.

Sax, Gilbert, and Collet, LeVerne S. "An Empirical Comparison of the Effects of Recall and Multiple-Choice Tests on Student Achievement." *Journal of Educational Measurement* 5, no. 2 (Summer 1968):169–73.

————. "The Effects of Differing Instructions and Guessing Formulas on Reliability and Validity." *Educational and Psychological Measurement* 28, no. 4 (Winter 1968):1127–36.

Sax, Gilbert, and Cromack, Theodore R. "The Effects of Various Forms of Item Arrangements on Test Performance." *Journal of Educational Measurement* 3, no. 4 (1966):309–11.

Sax, Gilbert, and Greenberg, William. "An Empirical Evaluation of Some Banesh Hoffman Allegations." Unpublished. Seattle: University of Washington, 1969.

Sax, Gilbert, and Reade, Marybell. "Achievement as a Function of Test Difficulty Level." *American Educational Research Journal* 1, no. 1 (February 1964):22–25.

Sax, Gilbert; Eilenberg, Enid G.; and Klockars, Alan J. "Achievement as a Function of Test Item Complexity and Difficulty." *Journal of Experimental Education* 40, no. 4 (Summer 1972):90–93.

Schram, Hugh. "Think English Is Easy Here?" *Michigan Educational Journal* (February 1, 1957):520.

Schwarz, J. Conrad. "A New Procedure for Administering Objective Tests to Large Classes." *Journal of Educational Measurement* 4, no. 3 (Fall 1967): 167–68.

Sechrest, Lee, and Jackson, Douglas N. "Deviant Response Tendencies: Their Measurement and Interpretation." *Educational and Psychological Measurement* 23, no. 1 (Spring 1963): 33–53.

Shaw, Marvin E., and Wright, Jack M. *Scales for the Measurement of Attitudes.* New York: McGraw-Hill Book Co., 1967.

Singh, J. A. L., and Zing, Robert M. *Wolf-Children and Feral Man.* Hamden, Conn.: Archon Books, 1966.

Siskind, George. "Mine Eyes Have Seen a Host of Angels." *American Psychologist* 21, no. 8 (August 1966):804–06.

Spearman, Charles. *The Abilities of Man: Their Nature and Measurement.* New York: The Macmillan Co., 1927.

———. " 'General Intelligence': Objectively Determined and Measured." *American Journal of Psychology* 15, no. 2 (April 1904):201–93.

Stake, Robert E., and Gooler, Dennis. "Measuring Educational Priorities." Revision of paper presented at the meeting of the American Educational Research Association, Minneapolis, March 1970.

Stanley, Julian C. "Reliability." In Robert Thorndike, ed., *Educational Measurements,* 2d. ed., pp. 356–442. Washington, D. C.: American Council on Education, 1971.

Starch, Daniel, and Elliott, Edward C. "Reliability of Grading Work in History." *School Review* 21 (1913):676–81.

———. "Reliability of Grading Work in Mathematics." *School Review* 21 (1913):254–95.

———. "Reliability of the Grading of High School Work in English." *School Review* 20 (1912):442–57.

Strong, Edward Kellogg, Jr. *Vocational Interests 18 Years After College.* Minneapolis: University of Minnesota Press, 1955.

———. *Vocational Interests of Men and Women.* Stanford, Calif.: Stanford University Press, 1943.

Stufflebeam, Daniel L. "The Use and Abuse of Evaluation in Title III." *Theory into Practice* 6, no. 3 (June 1967):126–33.

———. "The Use of Experimental Design in Education." *Journal of Educational Measurement* 8, no. 4 (Winter 1971): 267–74.

Super, Donald E., and Crites, John O. *Appraising Vocational Fitness by Means of Psychological Tests.* New York: Harper & Brothers, 1962.

Swensen, Clifford H. "Empirical Evaluations of Human Figure Drawings: 1957–1966." *Psychological Bulletin* 70, no. 1 (July 1968):20–44.

Taylor, H. C., and Russell, J. T. "The Relationship of Validity Coefficients to the Practical Effectiveness of Tests in Selection: Discussion and Tables." *Journal of Applied Psychology* 23 (October 1939):565–78.

Taylor, James Bentley. "Rating Scales as Measures of Clinical Judgment: A Method for Increasing Scale Reliability and Sensitivity." *Educational and Psychological Measurement* 28, no. 3 (Autumn 1968):747–66.

Taylor, James Bentley; Haefele, Ethel; Thompson, Prescott; and O'Donoghue, Cathleen. "Rating Scales as Measures of Clinical Judgment II: The Reliability of Example-Anchored Scales under conditions of Rater Heterogeneity and Divergent Behavior Sampling." *Educational and Psychological Measurement* 30, no. 2 (Summer 1970):301–10.

Terman, Lewis M., ed. *Genetic Studies of Genius.* Vol. 1–4. Stanford, Calif.: Stanford University Press, 1929–1959.

Terman, Lewis M., and Merrill, Maud A. *Stanford-Binet Intelligence Scale: Manual for the Third Revision: Form L-M.* Boston: Houghton Mifflin Co., 1960.

Terwillinger, J. S. "Representation of Vocational Interests on an Absolute Scale." Master's thesis, University of Illinois, 1960. In Lee J. Cronach, *Essentials of Psychological Testing,* 3d ed., pp. 486–87. New York: Harper & Row, 1970.

Thompson, Anton. "Tentative Guidelines for Proper and Improper Practice with Standardized Achievement Tests." *California Test Bureau Bulletin* no. 1360.

Thorndike, Robert L. "Reliability." In E. F. Lindquist, ed., *Educational Measurement,* pp. 593–94. Washington, D. C.: American Council on Education, 1951.

_____. *The Concepts of Over- and Underachievement.* New York: Teachers College, Columbia University, 1963.

Thorndike, Robert L., and Hagen. Elizabeth. *Measurement and Evaluation in Psychology and Education.* 3d ed. New York: John Wiley, 1969.

Thurstone, Louis Leon. "Attitudes Can Be Measured." *American Journal of Sociology* 33, no. 4 (January 1928):529–54.

_____. *Primary Mental Abilities.* Psychometric Monograph, no. 1. Chicago: University of Chicago Press, 1938.

Thurstone, Louis Leon, and Chave, E. J. *The Measurement of Attitude.* Chicago: University of Chicago Press, 1929.

Travers, R. M. W. "Significant Research on the Prediction of Academic Success." In Wilma T. Donahue, C. H. Coomb, R. W. Travers, eds., *The Measurement of Student Adjustment and Achievement,* pp. 147–90. Ann Arbor: University of Michigan Press, 1949.

Triandis, Harry C., and Triandis, Leigh M. "Race, Social Class, Religion, and Nationality as Determinants of Social Distance." *Journal of Abnormal and Social Psychology* 61, no. 1 (July 1960):110–18.

Tyler, F. T., and Chalmers, T. M. "The Effect on Scores of Warning Junior High School Pupils of Coming Tests." *Journal of Educational Research* 37, no. 4 (December 1943):290–96.

Tyler, Ralph W. "A Test of Skill in Using a Microscope." *Educational Research Bulletin* 9, no. 17 (November 19, 1930):493–96.

Ulrich, Lynn, and Trumbo, Don. "The Selection Interview Since 1949." *Psychological Bulletin* 63, no. 2 (February 1965):100–16.

U. S. Department of Commerce, Bureau of the Census. *Current Population Reports: Current Income,* Series P-60, no. 77 (May 7, 1971):1.

U. S. Office of Strategic Services. *Assessment of Men.* New York: Rinehart, 1948.

Watson, Goodwin Barbour. *The Measurement of Fair-Mindedness.* Columbia University Contributions to Education, no. 176. New York: Teachers College, Columbia University, 1925.

Wechsler, David. *The Measurement and Appraisal of Adult Intelligence.* 4th ed., Baltimore: Williams and Wilkins, 1958.

_____. *WAIS Manual.* New York: Psychological Corporation, 1955.

Weiden, Sister Robertine. "The Effect of Checked and Directed Study upon Achievement in Ninth Grade Algebra." In Florence E. Bamberger, ed., *The Johns Hopkins University Studies in Education,* no. 34. Baltimore: Johns Hopkins Press, 1945.

Weigel, Richard G., and Boulger, John R. "Tarnished Angel?" *American Psychologist* 25, no. 4 (April 1970):365.

Wheeler, Lester R. "The Intelligence of East Tennessee Mountain Children." *Journal of Educational Psychology* 23, no. 5 (May 1932):351–70.

Wiseman, Stephen, and Wrigley, Jack. "Essay Reliability: The Effect of Choice of Essay Title." *Educational and Psychological Measurement* 18, no. 1 (Spring 1958):129–38.

Wissler, Clark. "The Correlation of Mental and Physical Tests." *The Psychological Review Monograph Supplement* 3, no. 6 (1901):62.

Woodworth, R. S. Personal Data Sheet. Chicago: C. H. Stoelting, 1918.

Yamamoto, Kaoru, and Dizney, Henry F. "Effects of Three Sets of Test Instructions on Scores on an Intelligence Test." *Educational and Psychological Measurement* 25, no. 1 (Spring 1965):87–94.

Index